Silhouettes

1. MOURNING DOVE
2. HOUSE SPARROW
3. BLUEBIRD
4. STARLING
5. COWBIRD
6. BLACKBIRD
7. KINGFISHER
8. SCRUB JAY
9. MOCKINGBIRD
10. LARK SPARROW
11. SHRIKE
12. FLICKER
13. MAGPIE
14. NIGHTHAWK
15. ROBIN
16. BURROWING OWL
17. PHEASANT
18. CALIFORNIA QUAIL
19. PURPLE MARTIN
20. BARN SWALLOW
21. CLIFF SWALLOW
22. SPARROW HAWK
23. SWIFT
    (VAUX'S OR CHIMNEY)
24. SCISSOR-TAILED
    FLYCATCHER
25. MEADOWLARK
26. KINGBIRD
27. HORNED LARK
28. PHOEBE
29. KILLDEER
30. CROW

A Field Guide
to Western Birds

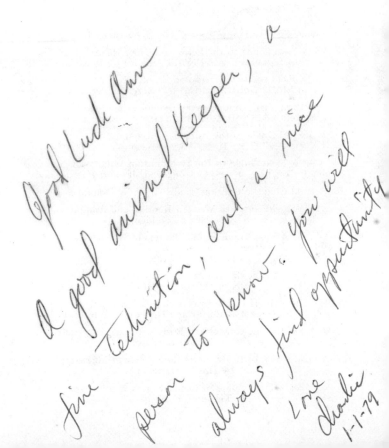

Good Luck Ann —
A good animal Keeper, a
fine Technician, and a nice
person to know. you will
always find opportunity

Love
Charlie
1-1-79

THE PETERSON FIELD GUIDE SERIES

EDITED BY ROGER TORY PETERSON

1. A Field Guide to the Birds by Roger Tory Peterson

2. A Field Guide to Western Birds by Roger Tory Peterson

3. A Field Guide to Shells of the Atlantic and Gulf Coasts and the West Indies by Percy A. Morris

4. A Field Guide to the Butterflies by Alexander B. Klots

5. A Field Guide to the Mammals by William H. Burt and Richard P. Grossenheider

6. A Field Guide to Pacific Coast Shells (including shells of Hawaii and the Gulf of California) by Percy A. Morris

7. A Field Guide to Rocks and Minerals by Frederick H. Pough

8. A Field Guide to the Birds of Britain and Europe by Roger Tory Peterson, Guy Mountfort, and P. A. D. Hollom

9. A Field Guide to Animal Tracks by Olaus J. Murie

10. A Field Guide to the Ferns and Their Related Families of Northeastern and Central North America by Boughton Cobb

11. A Field Guide to Trees and Shrubs (Northeastern and Central North America) by George A. Petrides

12. A Field Guide to Reptiles and Amphibians of Eastern and Central North America by Roger Conant

13. A Field Guide to the Birds of Texas and Adjacent States by Roger Tory Peterson

14. A Field Guide to Rocky Mountain Wildflowers by John J. Craighead, Frank C. Craighead, Jr., and Ray J. Davis

15. A Field Guide to the Stars and Planets by Donald H. Menzel

16. A Field Guide to Western Reptiles and Amphibians by Robert C. Stebbins

17. A Field Guide to Wildflowers of Northeastern and North-central North America by Roger Tory Peterson and Margaret McKenny

18. A Field Guide to the Mammals of Britain and Europe by F. H. van den Brink

19. A Field Guide to the Insects of America North of Mexico by Donald J. Borror and Richard E. White

20. A Field Guide to Mexican Birds by Roger Tory Peterson and Edward L. Chalif

21. A Field Guide to Birds' Nests (found east of Mississippi River) by Hal H. Harrison

22. A Field Guide to Pacific States Wildflowers by Theodore F. Niehaus

THE PETERSON FIELD GUIDE SERIES

A Field Guide to Western Birds

Field marks of all species found in
North America west of the 100th meridian,
with a section on the birds of
the Hawaiian Islands

Text and Illustrations by

ROGER TORY PETERSON

Second Edition

Sponsored by the National Audubon Society
and National Wildlife Federation

HOUGHTON MIFFLIN COMPANY BOSTON

Preface

In 1934 my first *Field Guide* was published, covering the birds east of the 100th meridian in North America. This book was designed so that live birds could be run down by their field marks without resorting to the anatomical differences and measurements that the old-time collector used. The "Peterson System," as it is now called, is based on patternistic drawings that indicate the key field marks with arrows. These and the comparisons between similar species are the core of the system. This practical method has enjoyed universal acceptance not only in this country but also in Europe, where Field Guides now exist in eight languages.

Years ago, Clinton G. Abbott, then director of the Natural History Museum at San Diego, asked why I didn't do a Field Guide for the West. I dismissed the idea at first, thinking that although the plan worked out well for eastern North America, it would be almost impossible to do the same thing for the West, where the situation was, it seemed to me, much more complicated. However, after constant prompting by Guy Emerson, then president of the National Audubon Society, I decided to give it a try. After tussling with a few of the problems, I came to the conclusion that field identification was no more difficult in the West than in the East, and that most publications made things look more involved than they were. There was already one excellent handbook in use — Hoffmann's *Birds of the Pacific States* — but this covered only the states of Washington, Oregon, and California, whereas there was hardly a thing that was adequate for most other parts of the West.

The entire manuscript of my first edition was critically read by Guy Emerson, Frank Watson, and Laidlaw Williams. Ludlow Griscom of Harvard University, who was regarded as the dean of field ornithologists and who brought the science of field identification to its greatest perfection, also examined the complete manuscript. Mr. Francis H. Allen, veteran editor of many widely known ornithological works, gave the text a complete editorial polishing. Portions of the manuscript were also sent to the following experts: L. Irby Davis (Texan and Mexican species), Charles W. Lockerbie (Rocky Mountain birds), Dr. Alden Miller (owls, flycatchers, thrashers, juncos, etc.), James Moffitt (ducks and geese), Dr. Robert Cushman Murphy (oceanic birds), Robert J. Niedrach (Rocky Mountain and Great Plains species), Dr. Robert T. Orr (shorebirds), and Dr. George Miksch Sutton (Mexican and southwestern birds).

During my field work I received constant cooperation from

numerous well-known bird students. Among those who unselfishly put their time and knowledge at my disposal were Amelia Allen, Edward Chalif, H. M. Dubois, Garrett Eddy, Frank Gander, Harold S. Gilbert, W. Hagenstein, C. A. Harwell, H. W. Higman, L. M. Huey, Randolph Jenks, Junea Kelly, Mr. and Mrs. Charles Lockerbie, Charles Michael, Vincent Mowbray, James Murdock, Commander H. E. Parmenter, Helen Pratt, Dorothy Dean Sheldon, Dr. James Stevenson, Dr. Charles Vorhies, Thomas Waddell, Lewis Wayne Walker, Frank Watson, Laidlaw Williams, and Dr. A. M. Woodbury.

Dr. Arthur A. Allen and Charles Brand of Cornell University spent days with me in their sound laboratory playing off all the recordings they had made on their trips west. In this way I was able to make a final check on some of the more puzzling bird voices and compare closely related species that could not always be compared conveniently in the field.

In addition to the foregoing, I was also indebted to the following for notes, suggestions, and other aid in the preparation of the first edition: R. P. Allen, H. H. Axtell, J. H. Baker, H. C. Blanchard, Margaret Brooks, Paul Brooks, Brighton Cain, Dr. Clarence Cottam, David Lloyd Garrison, Dr. W. T. Helmuth, J. J. Hickey, Richard Johnson, J. O. Larson, Sigrid Lee, D. Lehrmann, J. N. McDonald, L. N. Nichols, Dr. H. C. Oberholser, Charles O'Brien, R. H. Pough, Dr. William Sargent, Charles Shell, Alexander Sprunt, Jr., Mrs. A. H. Stephens, Wendell Taber, Lovell Thompson, Mrs. Whiting Washington, Dr. Alexander Wetmore, Dr. J. T. Zimmer, and especially Mildred Busse, who assisted me with much of the research and detail work on the manuscript.

With the advent of this greatly enlarged edition (1961) I believe this book has come of age. The changes are extensive. *All the illustrations are new.* There is 6 times as much color; black and white is used mostly when it is of more aid in identification than color would be. The cross references between plates and text will make the book easier to use, as will the capsule field marks for each species on the key pages opposite the illustrations. The sections entitled *Similar species* will be particularly useful to the observer who invariably asks "What else could it be?" Accidentals (birds recorded less than 20 times in western North America west of the 100th meridian) are relegated to an appendix. Subspecies are omitted; exceptions are those few easily identified in the field. Family statements have been expanded to include notes on *Food, Range* (world), and *Number of species.* The section on range (*Where found*) is extended to include *general range, western range, habitat,* and *nest.* Whereas the earlier edition covered only the western U.S. and stopped precisely at the Canadian border, this revision includes not only western Canada and Alaska but also salutes the 50th state of the U.S. with a section on Hawaiian birds.

This new book has had the advantage of experience gained in the preparation of 3 other Field Guides: the 2nd revised edition of

A Field Guide to the Birds (1947); its European counterpart, *A Field Guide to the Birds of Britain and Europe* (1954; with Guy Mountfort and P. A. D. Hollom); and *A Field Guide to the Birds of Texas* (published in 1960 for the Texas Game and Fish Commission by Houghton Mifflin Company).

I shall not list again the mass of ornithological literature digested in the preparation of the 1st edition of this guide, nor the regional works, checklists, papers, and periodicals that went into the compilation of this revision. Assiduously I consulted them all and intentionally ignored none. Nor shall I list again the 200 collaborators who contributed to the Eastern guide and its revisions, nor the 60 who made the Texas *Field Guide* possible. However, much of that material (particularly in the Texas adaptation) has been applicable to this book as well.

Duplicating his feat with the Texas manuscript, in fact, out-doing his previous efforts, Edgar Kincaid gave this revision as scholarly a combing as ever a manuscript has had. His forte is detecting the flaws in the sweeping statement. However, if any "unsanitary" statements still remain, the responsibility is mine. Dr. Howard Cogswell, whose field skill is second to none, gave his critical attention to such difficult groups as the gulls, shearwaters, hummingbirds, flycatchers, and sparrows. Dr. Arnold Small, whose fine field work is legendary in California, gave the pelagic birds his editorial penciling. The improved analysis of adult gulls owes much to the suggestions of Dudley Ross

My first redraft of the ranges (*Where found*) was based on the A.O.U. *Check-list of North American Birds* (5th ed., 1957) and was altered after consulting all regional publications (including the useful *Audubon Field Notes*). Over 30 sets of rough drafts were then circulated to key people for their scrutiny. To these ornithologists who materially modified the original statements the book owes one of its most important contributions: Dr. Clifford Carl and C. J. Guiguet (British Columbia); Dr. W. Ray Salt (Alberta); Dr. Robert Nero and Dr. C. Stuart Houston (Saskatchewan); Dr. Gordon Alcorn, Garrett Eddy, Lynn LaFave, W. A. Hall, Harry Higman, and Dr. Thomas Rogers (Washington); Dr. Thomas D. Burleigh, Dr. Malcolm Jollie, and Dr. Earl Larrison (Idaho); Dr. Clifford Davis (Montana); David Marshall (Oregon); Dr. William Behle and Charles Lockerbie (Utah); Dr. Oliver Scott (Wyoming); Dr. Howard Cogswell, Dr. Thomas R. Howell, and Dr. Arnold Small (California); Dr. Ned Johnson and Dr. Frank Richardson (Nevada); Dr. Alfred Bailey, Dennis Carter, Margaret and John Douglass, Robert Niedrach, Dr. Ronald A. Ryder, Don Thatcher, and Dr. Terry Vaughan (Colorado); Dr. Gale Monson and Mrs. Florence Thornberg (Arizona); Dr. Stokely Ligon and Dr. Dale Zimmerman (New Mexico); Edgar Kincaid, and others (Texas); Guy Emerson, Dr. Herbert Friedmann, and Dudley Ross (general).

In addition to the range material, anywhere from one or two

suggestions to 100 or more were offered by the following people: Dr. Gordon Alcorn, Dr. Dean Amadon, A. V. Arlton, Don Bleitz, D. H. Braithewaite, Shirley Briggs, J. Calunby, G. Carlton, Dr. Howard Cogswell, A. L. Curl, L. Irby Davis, Mrs. Paul DeDecker, Margaret Douglass, Merritt Dunlap, Whitney and Karen Eastman, Garrett Eddy, Eugene Eisenmann, J. R. M. Fadyen, Earle R. Greene, G. W. Gullion, Dr. J. J. Hickey, Mrs. A. W. Hood, V. H. Housholder, Dr. Stuart Houston, Dr. Phillip Humphrey, Junea Kelly, Karl Kenyon, O. A. Knorr, Levon Lee, D. T. Lees-Smith, Seymour Levy, Stokely Ligon, Charles Lockerbie, Dr. R. M. Lockwood, Donald McHenry, Dr. Locke Mackenzie, Thompson Marsh, David B. Marshall, James A. Murdock, Dr. Robert Nero, Ralph O'Reilly, Fred Packard, George Perry, Dr. A. Phillips, G. H. Potts, R. H. Pough, Dr. I. W. Preston, Dudley Ross, J. R. Sams, Zella Schultz, Dr. Oliver Scott, Dr. Arnold Small, Lieut. Col. C. H. Snyder, Mildred O. Snyder, Murray Spiers, Dr. Walter Spofford, Alexander Sprunt III, Kenn Stott, Dr. George Sutton, Wendell Taber, Don Thatcher, Mrs. R. J. Thornburg, Oakleigh Thorne II, Dr. Harrison Tordoff, Isabel Wasson, Dr. George Williams, Laidlaw Williams, Dr. Leonard Wing, Bryce Wood, Mr. and Mrs. K. J. Wright, and Dr. Dale Zimmerman.

Edgar Kincaid with his usual persuasiveness convinced me that Hawaii should be included in this new edition and he generously gave me full use of his Hawaiian files. In addition to Mr. Kincaid, Dr. Dean Amadon, Dr. Paul Baldwin, Mr. and Mrs. Robert Baldwin, Paul Breese, Dr. E. H. Bryan, Dr. Howard Cogswell, William Dunmire, Eugene Eisenmann, Dr. H. Johnson, Joseph E. King, Robert Pyle, Dr. Frank Richardson, Chandler Robbins, Dr. M. D. F. Udvardy, Ron Walker, William V. Ward, and David Woodside all went over my first draft and bolstered my own limited knowledge of Hawaiian birds.

Before completing the manuscript I had another session with the tape recordings of western birds at Cornell's Laboratory of Ornithology. To those pioneers of sound recording, Dr. Peter Paul Kellogg and Dr. Arthur A. Allen, I am much in debt.

For specimen material I made use of the extensive collections at the American Museum of Natural History in New York, the Peabody Museum of Natural History in New Haven, and the Smithsonian Institution in Washington. The staffs of these fine old institutions have been most kind and helpful during my many visits.

I would like to express my gratitude to Dorothy E. Umberger for her secretarial labors, to G. W. Cottrell, Jr., for assistance during my absence from the country, and to my wife, Barbara, who took care of a mountain of correspondence and typed and retyped the manuscript several times. Those of the staff of Houghton Mifflin Company who wrestled with the involved problems of actual publication were Morton Baker, Katharine Bernard, Paul Brooks, Lovell Thompson, Benjamin Tilghman, and especially Helen Phillips, who is a marvel of editorial thoroughness.

An Appreciation

It can be truly said that this manual is written not only for the bird watchers of America but by them. The number of people who contributed in some tangible way runs into the hundreds, many of whom I have acknowledged in the previous pages.

Four in particular I would like to name, for without them this book would not know its present form.

Ludlow Griscom, "the virtuoso of field identification," who taught me the fundamentals of field recognition.

Guy Emerson, my constant spur and friendly critic, who urged me to apply my Field Guide *system to the West.*

Edgar Kincaid, who sharpened my critical approach and also insisted that I include the Hawaiian Islands.

Barbara, my wife, who, doubling as secretary, virtually became an ornithological widow when I was in the field. She took in stride the months of pressure when her husband found it expedient to work around the clock. To her, more than to any other, I owe the completion of this book.

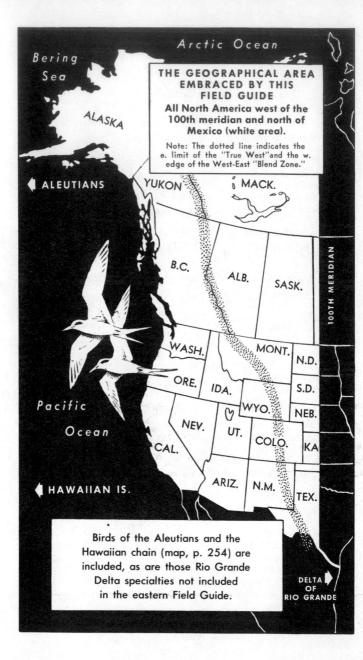

Arctic Ocean

Bering
Sea

ALASKA

◀ ALEUTIANS

**THE GEOGRAPHICAL AREA
EMBRACED BY THIS
FIELD GUIDE**
**All North America west of the
100th meridian and north of
Mexico (white area).**

Note: The dotted line indicates the
e. limit of the "True West" and the w.
edge of the West-East "Blend Zone."

YUKON   MACK.

B.C.   ALB.   SASK.

WASH.   MONT.   N.D.

ORE.   IDA.   S.D.

WYO.   NEB.

NEV.   UT.

CAL.   COLO.   KA

ARIZ.   N.M.

HAWAIIAN IS.   TEX.

Pacific

Ocean

100TH MERIDIAN

Birds of the Aleutians and the
Hawaiian chain (map, p. 254) are
included, as are those Rio Grande
Delta specialties not included
in the eastern Field Guide.

DELTA ▶
OF
RIO GRANDE

Contents

Illustrations

Endpapers: Roadside Silhouettes, front; Shore Silhouettes, back

How to Use This Book

VETERANS who have watched birds for years will know how to use this book. Beginners, however, should spend a few moments becoming familiar, in a general way, with the illustrations: ducks, it will be seen, do not resemble loons; gulls are readily distinguishable from terns. The needlelike bills of the warblers immediately differentiate them from the seed-cracking bills of the sparrows. Birds that could be confused are here grouped together when easy comparison is possible. Thus, when a bird has been seen the observer can turn to the picture most resembling it and feel confident that he has reduced the possibilities to the few species in its own group.

In most instances the pictures and their legend pages tell the story without help from the main text. The arrows point to outstanding field marks, briefly explained on the page opposite. In every case it is well to check identifications by referring to the text. The plates give visual field marks; the text gives aids such as manner of flight, range, season, habitat, etc., not visually portrayable, and under a separate heading discusses the species that might be confused.

One need only take a trip with an expert to realize the possibility of identifying almost any bird, with amazing certainty virtually at the snap of a finger. Most of the "rare finds" are made by people who are alive to the possibilities and know just what field marks to look for. It is the discovery of rarities that gives birding all the elements of a sport. When we become more proficient we may attempt to list as many birds as we can in a day, totting them up on the widely used small white checklists. The "big day" or "century run," taken at the peak of the spring migration, is the apogee of this sort of thing.

In the basic part of this book 583 species are treated. An additional 104 species have been noted fewer than 20 times west of the 100th meridian in North America or are "marginal," flirting with the 100th meridian. These are described briefly in an appendix, page 277. Hawaii (p. 255) adds at least another 60 species, making a grand total of 747 on the western list. This does not include subspecies.

Subspecies: Subspecies have no definite entity, but merely represent subdivisions within the geographic range of a species. They are races, usually determined by morphological characteristics such as slight differences in measurements, shades of color, etc. These subdivisions, generally discernible only by comparison of museum series, are seldom apparent in the field and should not concern the field observer. To illustrate: the Mockingbirds of the West (*Mimus polyglottos leucopterus*) differ very slightly from those in the East (*M. p. polyglottos*) and are given a different subspecific name. No one but an expert comparing specimens would detect the difference.

So forget about subspecies. It is a challenge, however, to be able to identify some of the more well-marked races. In this book subspecies are ignored unless field distinctions are fairly obvious. There are not many such inclusions. Advanced students, using skins in a good museum, might work out ways of telling others, but a too thorough treatment in these pages would lead to many errors in the field.

Make This Guide a Personal Thing: It is gratifying to see a *Field Guide* marked on every page, for I know it has been well used. Although the covers are waterproofed, I have seen copies with homemade oilcloth jackets; others are jacketed in plastic envelopes, obtainable in bookstores. I have seen copies reorganized and rebound to suit the owner's taste; local checklists, and even illustrations from other books, have been bound in. Many have been tabbed with index tabs on the margins, or fitted with flaps or envelopes to hold daily checklists. In this book I have included a checklist, to be used in making up a "life list," so that the owner need not mark up the index.

The Illustrations: The plates and line cuts throughout the text are intended as diagrams, arranged for quick comparison of the species most resembling each other. As they are not intended to be pictures or portraits, modeling of form and feathering is often subordinated to simple contour and pattern. Some birds are better adapted than others to this simplified handling, hence the variation in treatment. In many of the water birds pattern is more important than color; therefore many of the diagrams are in black and white.

Range: The area covered by this book is North America west of the 100th meridian. Nevertheless, in order that the user may have an over-all concept of each bird's distribution, I have under the heading *Where found* first given a capsule statement of the bird's general range (if widespread) and then, under *West*, described how it fits into the western picture. *Note:* General statements in the descriptions and habitats apply only to the area covered by this book.

For convenience, biologists usually separate East and West along the 100th meridian. This slices through the Edwards Plateau in Texas and follows precisely the eastern edge of the Texas panhandle. To the north it severs the panhandle of Oklahoma and the western part of Kansas; it divides the state of Nebraska, and also the Dakotas. The invisible line continues just east of the Saskatchewan border and cuts through the Northwest

Territories to the Arctic Ocean just east of Victoria Island.

The *True West* actually starts at the eastern edge of the Rockies. The broad belt between 100° and the mountains is a blend zone, or twilight zone, where many eastern forms overlap those of the West. In a general way, the eastern birds penetrate westward along the river valleys, while western species pioneer the arid outcroppings on the Plains. Although the Rockies define the "True West" there are outlying ranges and foothills farther east that are basically western in their avifauna. Notable outliers are the Cypress Hills (se. Alberta, sw. Saskatchewan), the Black Hills (w. South Dakota), and the Edwards Plateau (c. Texas).

The *Great Plains* (or Plains) occupy most of the wide twilight belt east of the Rockies. They form a great ecological barrier.

The *Great Basin,* lying between the Rockies and the Cascade Sierra ranges, is another great highway for some of the waterfowl and shorebirds that also use the Great Plains or Pacific routes. The Lower Colorado River is part of this flyway.

The *Central Valley,* or *Great Valley,* of California, which includes the Sacramento and San Joaquin Valleys, is also a major highway and wintering ground for water birds. It frequently acts as a barrier, marking the limits of certain upland species.

The *Northwest coast belt,* frequently referred to in this book, is roughly the humid belt from San Francisco bay to se. coastal Alaska, west of the Sacramento Valley and the Cascades.

The *Cascade-Sierra divide* is one of the major divisions affecting the avifauna of the West. Basically dry to the eastward, wet on the seaward slope, it sharply limits many species.

The *boreal forest of Canada* swings west past the northern end of the Plains and through it many "eastern" woodland species extend almost to 120° W. at the approaches of the Rockies.

The *Arctic,* roughly speaking, is the far North *beyond tree limit* where the subsoil is *permanently frozen.* However, many areas along the Alaskan coast have an arctic bird life and are treeless, but might be called *Subarctic* because the subsoil is not permanently frozen. Arctic conditions also extend far southward along the mountain tops (usually referred to as *alpine*).

Definitions of Terms and Symbols: ♂ is the symbol for male; ♀ means female.

Accidentals, on the continental level, are defined as species that have been recorded less than 20 times west of the 100th meridian in North America (including Aleutians, but not Hawaii). These are relegated to an appendix (p. 277). On the state or provincial level an *accidental* is a bird that has appeared but once, or perhaps more than once, but is so far out of its normal range that it might not be reasonably expected again.

Casual means from one to several records in a decade in a state or province — a bird to be looked for again. It implies greater rarity than *rare* (rare means seldom seen but of regular occurrence).

I have also used the term *casual* for those species recorded but once or twice in states immediately adjacent to their normal range.

Question mark: A question mark (?) after a locality means "probable, not certain; needs confirmation."

Resident means the same as *permanent resident;* the bird is found throughout the year.

Migrant means a bird of passage, a bird whose stay is brief while en route between its summer and winter homes. *Breeds* and *winters* are self-evident terms, but some of the birds recorded within the areas thus outlined may actually be birds in passage, not yet on their summering or wintering grounds.

Anatomical and plumage terms: See the diagram on page 2.

Names of Birds: The names of all birds are those officially designated by the A.O.U. *Check-list of North American Birds,* 5th edition. When the names differ from those in earlier editions of the Field Guides, I have also given the previous official name in parentheses. If a name within the parentheses appears in quotes, it has never been official (sanctioned by the A.O.U.) but has attained wide popular use because of its adoption in Richard Pough's Audubon Bird Guides. I have seldom listed other unofficial vernacular names; their perpetuation in most instances would serve no useful purpose.

Number of Birds: The comparative numbers of species in families will interest students. The world numbers follow the appraisal of Ernst Mayr and Dean Amadon (*American Museum Novitates* for Apr. 2, 1951). When Josselyn Van Tyne and Andrew J. Berger (*Fundamentals of Ornithology,* 1959) differ notably, I have usually given both figures. The North American figures are based on the A.O.U. *Check-list of North American Birds,* 5th edition.

Habitat: One looks for meadowlarks in meadows, thrushes in woods. Therefore, those of the field-glass fraternity out to run up a list do not work only one environment. The experienced birder can look at a woodland, a piece of brush, a prairie, or a marsh and predict almost exactly what he will find there.

Each bird's preferred environment is indicated briefly under *Habitat,* but do not be surprised if your bird is not always where it is supposed to be, particularly in migration. At coastal points, islands, city parks, and desert oases, birds in passage will often be found in an untypical environment.

Nest: Nest location and nest form are noted very briefly (but only if the species breeds within the area covered by the book). Only the merest mention of egg numbers and appearance is given. The more usual clutch sizes are given, with exceptional clutches indicated thus: 3–5; 9. When eggs are spotted, ground color is mentioned only when it is obvious, not whitish or near-white. To go into the more subtle distinctions between nests and eggs of various species would require a book in itself. The main reason for including these data at all is not to aid the observer in recognizing an unattended nest, but to alert him as to where he might look for a suspected nest.

Voice: We make our first identification of a species as a rule by sight. Then we become familiar with its voice. A "sizzling trill" or a "bubbling warble" conveys but a wretched idea of the voice of a bird. Though inadequate descriptions, they do help to fix a note or song in our minds. Word syllabifications in most books vary; ears differ. There are some species whose voices we may know long before we ever see the bird in life. Who has known the Poor-will or the Pauraque before hearing their cries at night? And there are those few — such as the small flycatchers — far more readily recognized by voice than by appearance.

In learning bird voices (and some experts do 90 percent of their fieldwork by ear), there is no substitute for actual sounds. Authors often attempt to fit songs into syllables, words, and phrases. Musical notations, comparative descriptions, and ingenious systems of symbols have been employed. But with the advent of tape recording these techniques have been eclipsed.

A Field Guide to Western Bird Songs: This album contains the most comprehensive collection of sound recordings yet attempted of western species. Three 12-inch LP records, prepared by Peter Paul Kellogg, Arthur A. Allen, William W. H. Gunn, and others of the Laboratory of Ornithology, Cornell University, and published by Houghton Mifflin Company, are arranged to accompany, page by page, this revised and enlarged edition of *A Field Guide to Western Birds. A Field Guide to Bird Songs* (Eastern), also published by Houghton Mifflin Company, is available, and, of the 304 land and water birds covered, actually includes 260 species that occur in the West.

Play the records repeatedly and compare similar songs. Repetition is the key to learning bird voices. Remember that there are "song dialects"; birds in your locality may not always sing precisely as those on the record do. However, the quality will be the same and the effect will be recognizable.

A Guide to Bird Finding: I urge the birder who has an itching foot to obtain a copy of *A Guide to Bird Finding West of the Mississippi* (1953) by Dr. Olin Sewall Pettingill. In this Baedeker of bird localities Dr. Pettingill devotes hundreds of pages to the theme of where to go, what to look for. In a very thorough manner he covers every portion of each state west of the great river except Alaska and Hawaii; he names outstanding places, gives explicit directions for getting to them, and lists the special birds to be looked for. When struggling to learn my birds I would have given my whole reference library for such a guide book as Pettingill's and such an album of recordings as Kellogg and Allen's. They are as essential as the binocular.

Checklists and Regional Works: Many bird clubs have published their own checklists. Some are mimeographed, others are printed on cards small enough to be slipped into the pocket or into the *Field Guide*. These cards are available in quantity and are used for keeping the daily tally. Some give abbreviated information on local status. Of necessity, a field guide covering a great area can outline ranges only in general terms. A regional publication can be more precise. There is not room here to list all the publications and checklists dealing with limited areas; they are constantly appearing and are very useful.

The most comprehensive works (published since 1940) dealing with entire states and provinces are: (1) *Birds of Alaska* by I. Gabrielson and F. Lincoln (Wildlife Management Institute, 1959); (2) *Arctic Birds of Canada* by L. L. Snyder (U. of Toronto Press, 1957); (3) *The Bird Fauna of British Columbia* by J. A. Munro and I. McT. Cowan (British Columbia Provincial Museum, 1947); (4) *The Birds of Alberta* by W. R. Salt and A. L. Wilk (Edmonton, Hamly Press, 1958); (5) *Birds of Washington State* by S. G. Jewett, W. P. Taylor, W. T. Shaw, and J. W. Aldrich (U. of Washington Press, 1953); (6) *Birds of Oregon* by I. Gabrielson and S. G. Jewett (Oregon State College, 1940); (7) *Distribution of the Birds of California* by J. Grinnell and A. Miller (Cooper Ornithological Club, 1944); (8) *A Field Guide to the Birds of Texas* by R. T. Peterson (Texas Game and Fish Commission, 1960); (9) *Birds of Hawaii* by George C. Munro (Honolulu, Tongg Publishing Company, 1944). Other state volumes soon to be published include Arizona (A. Phillips), New Mexico (S. Ligon), and Colorado (A. Bailey and R. Niedrach). Manuscripts dealing with most of the remaining states and provinces have been or are being prepared.

Ralph Hoffmann's *Birds of the Pacific States* (Houghton Mifflin, 1927) is still one of the most useful publications on western birds and is a must for anyone working in California, Oregon, or Washington. So is Richard Pough's excellent *Audubon Western Bird Guide* (Doubleday, 1957), which illustrates many of the stragglers as well as typical western specialties. His three volumes cover all the birds of North America.

Caution in Sight Records: One should always use caution in making identification, especially of rarities. A generation ago ornithologists would not accept sight records unless they were made along the barrel of a shotgun. Today it is difficult for the average person to secure collecting privileges; moreover, rarities may show up in parks, sanctuaries, or on municipal property, where collecting is out of the question. There is no reason why we should not trust our eyes — at least after we have a good basic knowledge of the commoner species. In the case of a very rare bird, the rule is that at least two very competent observers should see it to make the record valid. Photography, especially color photography, is becoming increasingly useful in substantiating records. "First records" for a number of states have been authenticated in this way.

Checklist

Keep a "Life List." Check the birds you have seen.
This list does not include the Hawaiian species.

.... COMMON LOON
.... YELLOW-BILLED LOON
.... ARCTIC LOON
.... RED-THROATED LOON
.... RED-NECKED GREBE
.... HORNED GREBE
.... EARED GREBE
.... LEAST GREBE
.... WESTERN GREBE
.... PIED-BILLED GREBE
.... BLACK-FOOTED ALBATROSS
.... LAYSAN ALBATROSS
.... FULMAR
.... PINK-FOOTED SHEARWATER
.... PALE-FOOTED SHEARWATER
.... NEW ZEALAND
    SHEARWATER
.... SOOTY SHEARWATER
.... SLENDER-B. SHEARWATER
.... MANX SHEARWATER
.... FORK-TAILED PETREL
.... LEACH'S PETREL
.... ASHY PETREL
.... BLACK PETREL
.... LEAST PETREL
.... RED-BILLED TROPICBIRD
.... WHITE PELICAN
.... BROWN PELICAN
.... BLUE-FOOTED BOOBY
.... D.-CRESTED CORMORANT
.... BRANDT'S CORMORANT
.... PELAGIC CORMORANT
.... RED-FACED CORMORANT
.... MAG. FRIGATEBIRD
.... GREAT BLUE HERON
.... GREEN HERON
.... LITTLE BLUE HERON
.... COMMON EGRET
.... SNOWY EGRET
.... LOUISIANA HERON
.... BLACK-CR. NIGHT HERON
.... LEAST BITTERN
.... AMERICAN BITTERN
.... WOOD IBIS
.... WHITE-FACED IBIS
.... WHISTLING SWAN
.... TRUMPETER SWAN
.... CANADA GOOSE
.... BRANT

.... BLACK BRANT
.... EMPEROR GOOSE
.... WHITE-FRONTED GOOSE
.... SNOW GOOSE
.... BLUE GOOSE
.... ROSS' GOOSE
.... BLACK-BELLIED TREE DUCK
.... FULVOUS TREE DUCK
.... MALLARD
.... MEXICAN DUCK
.... BLACK DUCK
.... GADWALL
.... PINTAIL
.... COMMON (EUROPEAN) TEAL
.... GREEN-WINGED TEAL
.... BLUE-WINGED TEAL
.... CINNAMON TEAL
.... EUROPEAN WIDGEON
.... AMERICAN WIDGEON
.... SHOVELER
.... WOOD DUCK
.... REDHEAD
.... RING-NECKED DUCK
.... CANVASBACK
.... GREATER SCAUP
.... LESSER SCAUP
.... COMMON GOLDENEYE
.... BARROW'S GOLDENEYE
.... BUFFLEHEAD
.... OLDSQUAW
.... HARLEQUIN DUCK
.... STELLER'S EIDER
.... COMMON EIDER
.... KING EIDER
.... SPECTACLED EIDER
.... WHITE-WINGED SCOTER
.... SURF SCOTER
.... COMMON SCOTER
.... RUDDY DUCK
.... MASKED DUCK
.... HOODED MERGANSER
.... COMMON MERGANSER
.... R.-BREASTED MERGANSER
.... TURKEY VULTURE
.... BLACK VULTURE
.... CALIFORNIA CONDOR
.... WHITE-TAILED KITE
.... MISSISSIPPI KITE
.... GOSHAWK

.... SHARP-SHINNED HAWK
.... COOPER'S HAWK
.... RED-TAILED HAWK
.... HARLAN'S HAWK
.... RED-SHOULDERED HAWK
.... BROAD-WINGED HAWK
.... SWAINSON'S HAWK
.... ZONE-TAILED HAWK
.... WHITE-TAILED HAWK
.... ROUGH-LEGGED HAWK
.... FERRUGINOUS HAWK
.... GRAY HAWK
.... HARRIS' HAWK
.... BLACK HAWK
.... GOLDEN EAGLE
.... BALD EAGLE
.... MARSH HAWK
.... OSPREY
.... CARACARA
.... GYRFALCON
.... PRAIRIE FALCON
.... PEREGRINE FALCON
.... APLOMADO FALCON
.... PIGEON HAWK
.... SPARROW HAWK
.... CHACHALACA
.... BLUE GROUSE
.... SPRUCE GROUSE
.... RUFFED GROUSE
.... WILLOW PTARMIGAN
.... ROCK PTARMIGAN
.... WHITE-TAILED PTARMIGAN
.... GR. PRAIRIE CHICKEN
.... LESSER PRAIRIE CHICKEN
.... SHARP-TAILED GROUSE
.... SAGE GROUSE
.... BOBWHITE
.... SCALED QUAIL
.... CALIFORNIA QUAIL
.... GAMBEL'S QUAIL
.... MOUNTAIN QUAIL
.... HARLEQUIN QUAIL
.... RING-NECKED PHEASANT
.... CHUKAR
.... GRAY PARTRIDGE
.... TURKEY
.... WHOOPING CRANE
.... SANDHILL CRANE
.... CLAPPER RAIL
.... VIRGINIA RAIL
.... SORA
.... YELLOW RAIL
.... BLACK RAIL
.... COMMON GALLINULE
.... AMERICAN COOT
.... JAÇANA
.... BLACK OYSTERCATCHER
.... SEMIPALMATED PLOVER
.... PIPING PLOVER
.... SNOWY PLOVER
.... KILLDEER
.... MOUNTAIN PLOVER

.... AMERICAN GOLDEN PLOVER
.... BLACK-BELLIED PLOVER
.... SURFBIRD
.... RUDDY TURNSTONE
.... BLACK TURNSTONE
.... COMMON SNIPE
.... LONG-BILLED CURLEW
.... WHIMBREL
.... BRISTLE-THIGHED CURLEW
.... UPLAND PLOVER
.... SPOTTED SANDPIPER
.... SOLITARY SANDPIPER
.... WANDERING TATTLER
.... WILLET
.... GREATER YELLOWLEGS
.... LESSER YELLOWLEGS
.... KNOT
.... ROCK SANDPIPER
.... SHARP-TAILED SANDPIPER
.... PECTORAL SANDPIPER
.... WHITE-RUMPED SANDPIPER
.... BAIRD'S SANDPIPER
.... LEAST SANDPIPER
.... RUFOUS-NECKED
    SANDPIPER
.... DUNLIN
.... SHORT-BILLED DOWITCHER
.... LONG-BILLED DOWITCHER
.... STILT SANDPIPER
.... SEMIPALMATED SANDPIPER
.... WESTERN SANDPIPER
.... BUFF-BREASTED SANDPIPER
.... MARBLED GODWIT
.... BAR-TAILED GODWIT
.... HUDSONIAN GODWIT
.... SANDERLING
.... AMERICAN AVOCET
.... BLACK-NECKED STILT
.... RED PHALAROPE
.... WILSON'S PHALAROPE
.... NORTHERN PHALAROPE
.... POMARINE JAEGER
.... PARASITIC JAEGER
.... LONG-TAILED JAEGER
.... SKUA
.... GLAUCOUS GULL
.... GLAUCOUS-WINGED GULL
.... SLATY-BACKED GULL
.... WESTERN GULL
.... HERRING GULL
.... CALIFORNIA GULL
.... RING-BILLED GULL
.... MEW GULL
.... LAUGHING GULL
.... FRANKLIN'S GULL
.... BONAPARTE'S GULL
.... HEERMANN'S GULL
.... IVORY GULL
.... BLACK-LEGGED KITTIWAKE
.... RED-LEGGED KITTIWAKE
.... ROSS' GULL
.... SABINE'S GULL

.... GULL-BILLED TERN
.... FORSTER'S TERN
.... COMMON TERN
.... ARCTIC TERN
.... ALEUTIAN TERN
.... LEAST TERN
.... ROYAL TERN
.... ELEGANT TERN
.... CASPIAN TERN
.... BLACK TERN
.... COMMON MURRE
.... THICK-BILLED MURRE
.... BLACK GUILLEMOT
.... PIGEON GUILLEMOT
.... MARBLED MURRELET
.... KITTLITZ'S MURRELET
.... XANTUS' MURRELET
.... ANCIENT MURRELET
.... CASSIN'S AUKLET
.... PARAKEET AUKLET
.... CRESTED AUKLET
.... LEAST AUKLET
.... WHISKERED AUKLET
.... RHINOCEROS AUKLET
.... HORNED PUFFIN
.... TUFTED PUFFIN
.... BAND-TAILED PIGEON
.... RED-BILLED PIGEON
.... ROCK DOVE
.... WHITE-WINGED DOVE
.... MOURNING DOVE
.... SPOTTED DOVE
.... RINGED TURTLE DOVE
.... GROUND DOVE
.... INCA DOVE
.... WHITE-FRONTED DOVE
.... YELLOW-BILLED CUCKOO
.... BLACK-BILLED CUCKOO
.... ROADRUNNER
.... GROOVE-BILLED ANI
.... BARN OWL
.... SCREECH OWL
.... WHISKERED OWL
.... FLAMMULATED OWL
.... GREAT HORNED OWL
.... SNOWY OWL
.... HAWK OWL
.... PYGMY OWL
.... FERRUGINOUS OWL
.... ELF OWL
.... BURROWING OWL
.... BARRED OWL
.... SPOTTED OWL
.... GREAT GRAY OWL
.... LONG-EARED OWL
.... SHORT-EARED OWL
.... BOREAL OWL
.... SAW-WHET OWL
.... RIDGWAY'S
     WHIP-POOR-WILL
.... WHIP-POOR-WILL
.... POOR-WILL

.... PAURAQUE
.... COMMON NIGHTHAWK
.... LESSER NIGHTHAWK
.... BLACK SWIFT
.... CHIMNEY SWIFT
.... VAUX'S SWIFT
.... WHITE-THROATED SWIFT
.... LUCIFER HUMMINGBIRD
.... RUBY-THR. HUMMINGBIRD
.... BLACK-CH. HUMMINGBIRD
.... COSTA'S HUMMINGBIRD
.... ANNA'S HUMMINGBIRD
.... BROAD-T. HUMMINGBIRD
.... RUFOUS HUMMINGBIRD
.... ALLEN'S HUMMINGBIRD
.... CALLIOPE HUMMINGBIRD
.... RIVOLI'S HUMMINGBIRD
.... BLUE-THROATED
     HUMMINGBIRD
.... BUFF-B. HUMMINGBIRD
.... VIOLET-CR. HUMMINGBIRD
.... WH.-EARED HUMMINGBIRD
.... BROAD-B. HUMMINGBIRD
.... COPPERY-TAILED TROGON
.... BELTED KINGFISHER
.... GREEN KINGFISHER
.... YELLOW-SHAFTED FLICKER
.... RED-SHAFTED FLICKER
.... GILDED FLICKER
.... PILEATED WOODPECKER
.... RED-BELLIED WOODPECKER
.... GOLDEN-FR. WOODPECKER
.... GILA WOODPECKER
.... RED-HEADED WOODPECKER
.... ACORN WOODPECKER
.... LEWIS' WOODPECKER
.... YELLOW-B. SAPSUCKER
.... "RED-BR." SAPSUCKER
.... WILLIAMSON'S SAPSUCKER
.... HAIRY WOODPECKER
.... DOWNY WOODPECKER
.... LADDER-B. WOODPECKER
.... NUTTALL'S WOODPECKER
.... ARIZONA WOODPECKER
.... WHITE-HEADED WOOD-
     PECKER
.... BLACK-B. THREE-TOED
     WOODPECKER
.... N. THREE-T. WOODPECKER
.... ROSE-THROATED BECARD
.... EASTERN KINGBIRD
.... THICK-BILLED KINGBIRD
.... TROPICAL KINGBIRD
.... WESTERN KINGBIRD
.... CASSIN'S KINGBIRD
.... SCISSOR-T. FLYCATCHER
.... KISKADEE FLYCATCHER
.... SULPHUR-B. FLYCATCHER
.... GREAT CRESTED FLYC.
.... WIED'S CRESTED FLYC.
.... ASH-THROATED FLYC.
.... OLIVACEOUS FLYCATCHER

.... EASTERN PHOEBE
.... BLACK PHOEBE
.... SAY'S PHOEBE
.... YELLOW-BELLIED FLYC.
.... TRAILL'S FLYCATCHER
.... LEAST FLYCATCHER
.... HAMMOND'S FLYCATCHER
.... DUSKY FLYCATCHER
.... GRAY FLYCATCHER
.... WESTERN FLYCATCHER
.... BUFF-BREASTED FLYC.
.... COUES' FLYCATCHER
.... EASTERN WOOD PEWEE
.... WESTERN WOOD PEWEE
.... OLIVE-SIDED FLYCATCHER
.... VERMILION FLYCATCHER
.... BEARDLESS FLYCATCHER
.... SKYLARK
.... HORNED LARK
.... VIOLET-GREEN SWALLOW
.... TREE SWALLOW
.... BANK SWALLOW
.... ROUGH-WINGED SWALLOW
.... BARN SWALLOW
.... CLIFF SWALLOW
.... CAVE SWALLOW
.... PURPLE MARTIN
.... GRAY JAY
.... BLUE JAY
.... STELLER'S JAY
.... SCRUB JAY
.... MEXICAN JAY
.... GREEN JAY
.... BLACK-BILLED MAGPIE
.... YELLOW-BILLED MAGPIE
.... COMMON RAVEN
.... WHITE-NECKED RAVEN
.... COMMON CROW
.... NORTHWESTERN CROW
.... PIÑON JAY
.... CLARK'S NUTCRACKER
.... BLACK-CAPPED CHICKADEE
.... MEXICAN CHICKADEE
.... MOUNTAIN CHICKADEE
.... GRAY-HEADED CHICKADEE
.... BOREAL CHICKADEE
.... CHESTNUT-B. CHICKADEE
.... BLACK-CRESTED TITMOUSE
.... PLAIN TITMOUSE
.... BRIDLED TITMOUSE
.... VERDIN
.... COMMON BUSHTIT
.... BLACK-EARED BUSHTIT
.... WHITE-BR. NUTHATCH
.... RED-BR. NUTHATCH
.... PYGMY NUTHATCH
.... BROWN CREEPER
.... WRENTIT
.... DIPPER
.... HOUSE WREN
.... BROWN-THROATED WREN
.... WINTER WREN

.... BEWICK'S WREN
.... CAROLINA WREN
.... CACTUS WREN
.... LONG-BILLED MARSH WREN
.... SHORT-B. MARSH WREN
.... CAÑON WREN
.... ROCK WREN
.... MOCKINGBIRD
.... CATBIRD
.... BROWN THRASHER
.... LONG-BILLED THRASHER
.... BENDIRE'S THRASHER
.... CURVE-BILLED THRASHER
.... CALIFORNIA THRASHER
.... LE CONTE'S THRASHER
.... CRISSAL THRASHER
.... SAGE THRASHER
.... ROBIN
.... VARIED THRUSH
.... HERMIT THRUSH
.... SWAINSON'S THRUSH
.... GRAY-CHEEKED THRUSH
.... VEERY
.... EASTERN BLUEBIRD
.... WESTERN BLUEBIRD
.... MOUNTAIN BLUEBIRD
.... WHEATEAR
.... BLUETHROAT
.... TOWNSEND'S SOLITAIRE
.... ARCTIC WARBLER
.... BLUE-GRAY GNATCATCHER
.... BLACK-T. GNATCATCHER
.... GOLDEN-CR. KINGLET
.... RUBY-CROWNED KINGLET
.... YELLOW WAGTAIL
.... WATER PIPIT
.... SPRAGUE'S PIPIT
.... BOHEMIAN WAXWING
.... CEDAR WAXWING
.... PHAINOPEPLA
.... NORTHERN SHRIKE
.... LOGGERHEAD SHRIKE
.... STARLING
.... CRESTED MYNA
.... BLACK-CAPPED VIREO
.... HUTTON'S VIREO
.... BELL'S VIREO
.... GRAY VIREO
.... SOLITARY VIREO
.... YELLOW-GREEN VIREO
.... RED-EYED VIREO
.... PHILADELPHIA VIREO
.... WARBLING VIREO
.... BLACK-AND-WH. WARBLER
.... TENNESSEE WARBLER
.... ORANGE-CROWNED
    WARBLER
.... NASHVILLE WARBLER
.... VIRGINIA'S WARBLER
.... COLIMA WARBLER
.... LUCY'S WARBLER
.... OLIVE-BACKED WARBLER

Checklist of Accidentals

(also marginal species as defined on page 277)

.... SHORT-TAIL. ALBATROSS
.... WHITE-CAPPED ALBATROSS
.... CAPE PETREL
.... BLACK-T. SHEARWATER
.... SCALED PETREL
.... COOK'S PETREL
.... WHITE-WINGED PETREL
.... WILSON'S PETREL
.... BLUE-FOOTED BOOBY
.... BROWN BOOBY
.... OLIVACEOUS CORMORANT
.... ANHINGA
.... REDDISH EGRET
.... YELLOW-CR. NIGHT HERON
.... WHITE IBIS
.... ROSEATE SPOONBILL
.... WHOOPER SWAN
.... BEAN GOOSE
.... MOTTLED DUCK
.... FALCATED TEAL
.... BAIKAL TEAL
.... COMMON POCHARD
.... BAER'S POCHARD
.... TUFTED DUCK
.... SWALLOW-TAILED KITE
.... GRAY SEA EAGLE
.... STELLER'S SEA EAGLE
.... EUROPEAN CRANE
.... KING RAIL
.... PURPLE GALLINULE
.... AM. OYSTERCATCHER
.... MONGOLIAN PLOVER
.... WILSON'S PLOVER
.... DOTTEREL
.... AMERICAN WOODCOCK
.... EUROPEAN JACKSNIPE
.... ESKIMO CURLEW
.... WOOD SANDPIPER
.... POLYNESIAN TATTLER
.... GREAT KNOT
.... PURPLE SANDPIPER
.... LONG-TOED STINT
.... CURLEW SANDPIPER
.... RUFF
.... SPOON-BILL SANDPIPER
.... ICELAND GULL
.... GREAT BLACK-B. GULL
.... BLACK-TAILED GULL
.... BLACK-HEADED GULL
.... LITTLE GULL
.... DOVEKIE
.... CRAVERI'S MURRELET
.... COMMON PUFFIN

.... RUDDY GROUND DOVE
.... THICK-BILLED PARROT
.... ORIENTAL CUCKOO
.... CHUCK-WILL'S-WIDOW
.... WHITE-RUMPED SWIFT
.... COMMON SWIFT
.... HELOISE'S HUMMINGBIRD
.... RIEFFER'S HUMMINGBIRD
.... RINGED KINGFISHER
.... WRYNECK
.... GRAY KINGBIRD
.... NUTTING'S FLYCATCHER
.... ACADIAN FLYCATCHER
.... GRAY-BREASTED MARTIN
.... SAN BLAS JAY
.... CAROLINA CHICKADEE
.... EYE-BROWED THRUSH
.... CLAY-COLORED ROBIN
.... WOOD THRUSH
.... RUBYTHROAT
.... MID. GRASSHOP. WARBLER
.... GRAY-SPOTTED FLY-
    CATCHER
.... MOUNTAIN ACCENTOR
.... WHITE WAGTAIL
.... PECHORA PIPIT
.... RED-THROATED PIPIT
.... WHITE-EYED VIREO
.... YELLOW-THROATED VIREO
.... PROTHONOTARY WARBLER
.... SWAINSON'S WARBLER
.... WORM-EATING WARBLER
.... GOLDEN-WINGED WARBLER
.... BLUE-WINGED WARBLER
.... PARULA WARBLER
.... BL.-THR. BLUE WARBLER
.... CERULEAN WARBLER
.... YELLOW-THR. WARBLER
.... PINE WARBLER
.... PRAIRIE WARBLER
.... LOUISIANA WATERTHRUSH
.... KENTUCKY WARBLER
.... GROUND-CHAT
.... GOLDEN-CR. WARBLER
.... HOODED WARBLER
.... SCARLET-HEADED ORIOLE
.... BRAMBLING
.... HAWFINCH
.... BULLFINCH
.... FIVE-STRIPED SPARROW
.... WORTHEN'S SPARROW
.... RUSTIC BUNTING

Part I

North America West of the 100th Meridian

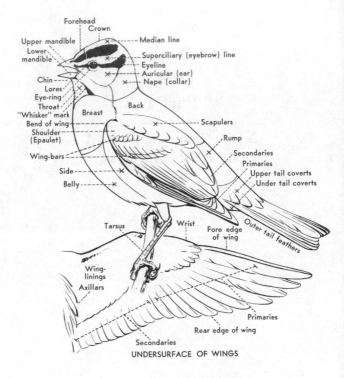

Forehead

Crown

Upper mandible

Lower mandible

Median line

Superciliary (eyebrow) line

Eyeline

Auricular (ear)

Nape (collar)

Chin

Lores

Eye-ring

Throat

"Whisker" mark

Bend of wing

Shoulder (Epaulet)

Wing-bars

Side

Belly

Breast

Back

Scapulars

Rump

Secondaries

Primaries

Upper tail coverts

Under tail coverts

Tarsus

Wrist

Fore edge of wing

Outer tail feathers

Wing-linings

Axillars

Primaries

Rear edge of wing

Secondaries

UNDERSURFACE OF WINGS

TOPOGRAPHY OF A BIRD

Showing the terms used in this book

Loons: Gaviidae

OPEN-WATER swimming birds with daggerlike bills. Larger than most ducks; longer-bodied, thicker-necked than grebes. Can dive to 200 ft.; may dive or merely submerge; sometimes swim with only head above water. Usually thrash along surface on take off. In flight, outline is hunchbacked, with a slight droop to neck; broad webbed feet project rudderlike beyond stubby tail. Seldom on land except at nest. Sexes alike. *Note:* Immature cormorants have thinner necks, longer tails. They swim with hook-tipped bill angled upward and fly with neck above horizontal. **Food:** Small fish, other aquatic animals. **Range:** Northern parts of N. Hemisphere. **No. of species:** World, 4; West, 4.

COMMON LOON *Gavia immer* 28–36   **p. 4, Pl. 1**
   Field marks: A large long-bodied, low-swimming bird with a dagger-shaped bill. In flight, downward droop of neck and feet gives a sagging look. Wingbeats slower than most ducks'. *Breeding plumage:* Head and neck glossy black with broken white collar; *back checkered with black and white;* underparts white. *Winter:* Top of head, back of neck, and back dark gray; cheek, throat, and underparts white.
   Similar species: (1) See other loons. (2) Cormorants may be confused with loons (see family discussion).
   Voice: On breeding waters, a long falsetto wail, weird yodeling, maniacal laughter; at night, a ringing *ha-oo-oo.* Flight call a short, barking *kwuk.* Usually silent in winter.
   Where found: Alaska, Canada, n. U.S., Greenland, Iceland. Winters chiefly along coasts to n. Mexico, w. Mediterranean. **West:** *Breeds* from Aleutians (Kiska), nw. Alaska, n. Yukon, Mackenzie south to Washington (probably Oregon, ne. California), nw. Wyoming, N. Dakota. *Migrates* throughout West. *Winters* mainly along coast from e. Aleutians to Sonora. **Habitat:** Coniferous lakes (summer); open lakes, bays, sea. **Nest:** A mass of debris on islet, muskrat house, or grassy edge of fresh lake or pond. Eggs (2) brown, spotted.

YELLOW-BILLED LOON *Gavia adamsii* 33–38   **p. 4**
   Field marks: Note the stout, pale, upturned bill (straight above, angled below). Similar to Common Loon, but averages larger; bill *yellowish* or *ivory-white,* not dark. However, winter bills of many Common Loons are bluish white toward the base. Bills of young Yellow-billed Loons have less upturn.

3

Voice: Similar to Common Loon's. Said to be less vocal.
Where found: Arctic, north of tree limit, from n. U.S.S.R. to nw. Canada; winters n. Eurasia, se. Alaska. **West:** *Summers* in n. Alaska, nw. Canada (south to Great Slave Lake). *Winters* south along coast to se. Alaska (Alexander Archipelago), rarely Vancouver I. *Accidental,* Colorado. **Habitat:** Tundra lakes (summer), bays, ocean. **Nest:** Similar to Common Loon's.

ARCTIC LOON *Gavia arctica* 23–29 **below, Pl. 1**
(Pacific Loon)
Field marks: Note the straight thin bill. Near size of Red-throated Loon; bill quite as slender as that of Red-throat, but *straight,* the lower mandible never angling up; depth at base much less than that of Common Loon. *Breeding plumage:* Resembles Common Loon, but crown and hind neck *pale smoke-gray.* Squarish white spots on back arranged in *4 patches,* 2 on each side. *Winter adult:* Like Common Loon, but head and hind neck often lighter than blackish back; note the size and slender bill. *Young:* Distinguishable only by size and bill shape.
Similar species: In winter, Red-throated Loons are brownish gray above (with a profusion of white specks), whereas the feathers of Arctic Loons have *pale edgings,* giving a scaly effect. (Young Common Loons may have obscurely barred backs.)
Voice: A deep, barking *kwow.* Falsetto wails, rising in pitch, often followed by a honk.

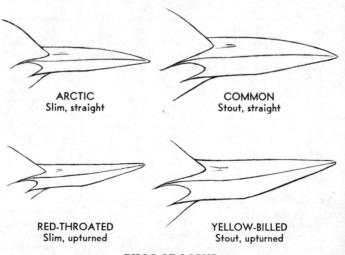

ARCTIC
Slim, straight

COMMON
Stout, straight

RED-THROATED
Slim, upturned

YELLOW-BILLED
Stout, upturned

BILLS OF LOONS

Where found: N. Eurasia, nw. N. America. Winters along coasts to Mediterranean, India, nw. Mexico. **West:** *Breeds* from Arctic coast south to Kodiak, s. Mackenzie. *Winters* along coast from se. Alaska to nw. Mexico. *Accidental,* e. Washington, Nevada, Utah, Colorado, Arizona, New Mexico. **Habitat:** Cold lakes (summer), ocean. **Nest:** A platform on islet or margin of lake. Eggs (2) brown, spotted.

RED-THROATED LOON *Gavia stellata* 24–27 **p. 4, Pl. 1**
  Field marks: The sharp thin bill, *distinctly upturned,* is the key mark. Near size of Arctic Loon. *Breeding plumage:* Gray head, unpatterned back and *rufous throat patch. Winter:* Grayish above, white beneath; similar to Arctic Loon, but back spotted with white, creating a paler appearance. Head paler, with less contrast than Common Loon's; profile more snaky.
  Similar species: (1) Arctic Loon has slender *straight* bill. (2) Common Loon is larger with more robust, *straight* bill. See also (3) Western Grebe (p. 7) and (4) Red-necked Grebe (below).
  Voice: Usually silent. In Arctic, falsetto wails, falling in pitch, followed by ducklike quacks. Also a repeated *kwuk.*
  Where found: Arctic; circumpolar. Winters south along coasts to Mediterranean, China, nw. Mexico. **West:** *Breeds* from Arctic coast south to Aleutians, n. Vancouver I., s. Mackenzie. *Winters* along coast from Aleutians to Sonora. *Casual,* Colorado, New Mexico. **Habitat:** Tundra lakes (summer), bays, estuaries, ocean. **Nest:** A muddy platform on islet or margin of lake or tundra pool. Eggs (2) brownish, spotted.

Grebes: Podicipedidae

HIGHLY aquatic; expert divers but labored fliers (with drooping neck). Distinguished from ducks by thin neck, tailless look, pointed bill (except in Pied-bill). Feet *lobed* (flaps along toes). Sometimes submerge instead of diving. Skitter on water when taking wing. Most young grebes (except Western) have striped heads. Sexes alike. All N. American species except Pied-bill have white wing patches (seldom visible except in flight). **Food:** Small fish, crustaceans, tadpoles, aquatic insects; they also eat their own *feathers* (reason unknown). **Range:** Nearly worldwide. **No. of species:** World, 20; West, 6.

RED-NECKED GREBE *Podiceps grisegena* 18–22½ **Pl. 1**
(Holboell's Grebe)
  Field marks: Note the dull yellow bill. Much larger than other grebes, except Western. *Breeding plumage:* Body gray; neck rufous; *cheeks whitish;* crown black (slightly tufted); bill *yel-*

lowish. Winter: Grayish; crown dark; *vertical white crescent* on side of gray head (often absent in young birds).

Similar species: In winter plumage, separated from (1) Horned and (2) Eared Grebes by larger size, heavier head and neck, large dull yellow bill, more uniform gray color; from (3) winter loons by grayer face and neck, dull yellow bill, shorter body, white wing patches. (4) See Western Grebe.

Voice: Usually silent. On nesting grounds, a high *keck;* also a long, wailing, neighing song; trills.

Where found: N. Eurasia, n. N. America. Winters along coasts to s. U.S., n. Africa, Japan. **West:** *Breeds* from Arctic coast to e. Oregon, Idaho, Montana, N. Dakota. *Winters* on coast from Alaska (Pribilofs) to s. California (rare). Rare migrant inland.

Habitat: Coastal waters; lakes (summer). **Nest:** A raft of reeds in reedy lake. Eggs (3–5; 8) whitish, stained.

HORNED GREBE *Podiceps auritus* 12–15¼ **Pl. 1**
Field marks: A small compact ducklike bird with a small pointed bill. *Breeding plumage:* Note the combination of conspicuous *golden ear tufts* and *rufous foreneck.* Head black. *Winter:* Note the clear white cheeks. Contrastingly patterned; top of head, line down back of neck, and back dark gray; underparts, neck, cheeks, white. Cap ends at *eye level.*

Similar species: See Eared Grebe.

Voice: When nesting, a squealing trill; harsh *kerra's.*

Where found: N. Eurasia, n. N. America. Winters to s. U.S., s. Eurasia. **West:** *Breeds* from c. Alaska, n. Yukon, n. Mackenzie to Oregon, n. Montana, n. S. Dakota. *Winters* on coast from e. Aleutians to n. Baja California. Mainly a migrant in interior.

Habitat: Lakes, ponds; in winter, bays, ocean. **Nest:** Floating, anchored to reeds of fresh pond. Eggs (4–5; 10) whitish.

EARED GREBE *Podiceps caspicus* 12–14 **Pl. 1**
Field marks: A small thin-necked, dark-backed diving bird. *Breeding plumage:* Note the *crested* black head with its golden ear tufts, and the *black neck* (Horned Grebe has a *chestnut* neck). *Winter:* Very similar to Horned Grebe. Forehead more abruptly vertical; dark cap extending slightly below eye level and *less clearly defined,* giving a "dirtier" look; almost invariably a whitish patch on side of head just behind ear. Neck more slender; bill *slimmer, appears slightly upturned.* On water, stern seems to ride higher.

Voice: On nesting ponds a mellow *poo-eep;* froglike peeping.

Where found: Eurasia, Africa, w. N. America. **West:** *Breeds* from c. B.C., n. Alberta, c. Saskatchewan south (mainly east of Cascades, Sierra) to n. Baja California, c. Arizona, n. New Mexico, c. Texas. *Winters* from Vancouver I. through Pacific states to Mexico; locally in Great Basin, sw. U.S. **Habitat:**

Lakes, bays, ocean. **Nest:** A floating mass anchored to reeds in fresh lake, in loose colony. Eggs (4–5; 9) white, stained.

LEAST GREBE *Podiceps dominicus* 8–10 **Pl. 1**
(Mexican Grebe)
    Field marks: A very small *slaty grebe,* smaller than Pied-billed; distinguished from it by *white wing patches* (often concealed), dark under tail coverts, a slender *black* pointed bill, and *golden eyes* (red during mating). In winter, throat is white.
    Similar species: See (1) Pied-billed Grebe, (2) Eared Grebe.
    Voice: A ringing *beep* or *pete;* a trill or chatter (P. James). A sharp reedy *queek;* a roll, *ker-r-r-r-r-r-r-r-r* (I. Davis).
    Where found: Tropical America. **West:** *Resident* in s. Texas north to Eagle Pass, San Antonio, Rockport. Has bred se. California (Imperial Dam). *Casual,* s. Arizona. **Habitat:** Freshwater ponds, resacas. **Nest:** A semifloating raft in shallow water or anchored to marsh vegetation. Eggs (4–6) buffy.

WESTERN GREBE **Pl. 1**
Aechmophorus occidentalis 22–29
    Field marks: A large grebe with an extremely long swanlike neck. In any plumage, blackish above, white below. Bill *light yellow,* straight or slightly upturned. Top of head, back of neck, and back dark; cheeks, neck, and underparts white. Downy young (gray) are only young American grebes without stripes.
    Similar species: (1) Winter Red-necked Grebe is dingy, gray-looking. (2) Loons are shorter-necked, have solid dark wings.
    Voice: A shrill whistle suggesting Osprey. A rolling croak.
    Where found: W. N. America (east to Manitoba, Minnesota). Winters to w. Mexico. **West:** *Breeds* from s.-c. B.C., n.-c. Alberta, c. Saskatchewan south (east of Cascades) to s. California, c. Nevada, n. Utah, sw. Colorado, w. Nebraska. *Winters* along coast from se. Alaska to Mexico, locally inland (Pacific states, Great Basin, Colorado River). **Habitat:** Rushy lakes (nesting), sloughs, bays, ocean. **Nest:** Usually floating among reeds; in colony. Eggs (3–6; 11) bluish white, stained.

PIED-BILLED GREBE *Podilymbus podiceps* 12–15 **Pl. 1**
    Field marks: Note the ungrebelike "chicken bill." A small, brown diver of ponds and fresh marshes. May ride with stern high, showing conspicuous white under tail coverts. Like other grebes, dives with a forward leap or may slowly submerge. *Breeding plumage:* Gray-brown, darkest on crown and back. Note the *black throat patch* and *black ring* around *thick* whitish bill. *Winter:* Browner, *without* throat patch and bill mark.
    Similar species: (1) Horned, (2) Eared, and (3) Least Grebes have slender bills. Pied-bill has no white wing patches as have the others.
    Voice: A cuckoo-like *cow-cow-cow-cow-cow-cow-cowm-cowm,* etc.

Where found: Most of N., Cent., and S. America. Migrates from colder areas. **West:** *Breeds* from Vancouver I., c. B.C., s. Mackenzie south throughout w. U.S. *Winters* from s. B.C. through Pacific states and from n. Utah, Colorado south. *Casual,* se. Alaska. **Habitat:** Fresh ponds, lakes, streams, marshes; in winter, also salt bays. **Nest:** A semifloating raft among reeds. Eggs (5–7; 10) whitish, stained.

Albatrosses: Diomedeidae

GLIDING birds of the open ocean. "Tube-nosed" (nostrils in 2 tubes). Bill large, hooked, covered with horny plates. Much larger than gulls; wings proportionately far longer (Wandering Albatross reaches greatest wing span of any modern bird — up to 11½ ft.). Rigid gliding and banking flight. Sexes alike. **Food:** Cuttlefish, fish, small marine animals; some feeding at night. **Range:** Mainly cold oceans of S. Hemisphere; 3 species nesting north of equator in Pacific. **No. of species:** World, 13 (Mayr-Amadon), 14 (Van Tyne-Berger); West, 2 (+2 accidentals).

BLACK-FOOTED ALBATROSS   **p. 14**
Diomedea nigripes   28–36
   Field marks: Spread 7 ft. The great size, *dusky color,* tremendously long saber-like wings and rigid shearwater-like gliding identify this species, the only albatross now found regularly off our continental Pacific Coast. Seldom seen from shore except near colonies. At close range shows whitish face and pale areas toward tips of wings. Bill and feet dark. Some birds, presumably adults, show white patches at base of tail.
   Similar species: (1) See Magnificent Frigatebird (p. 19). (2) Immature Short-tailed Albatross has *pinkish bill and feet.*
   Voice: When quarreling over food, loud screeches, groans. On nesting grounds whistles, quacks, groans, bill clapping.
   Where found: Breeds on islands in c. and w. Pacific (chiefly nw. chain of Hawaiian Is.). Ranges from Bering Sea, Aleutians to Baja California. **Habitat:** Open ocean. **Nest:** On sand of sea island; in colony. Eggs (1) white; sometimes blotched.

LAYSAN ALBATROSS *Diomedea immutabilis* 32   **p. 14**
   Field marks: Spread 6½ ft. A white-bodied albatross with *dark back and wings.* Bill and feet dull flesh or pale flesh-gray. Immature similar.
   Similar species: Adult Short-tailed Albatross (extremely rare) has a *white back,* pink bill, bluish-white feet (see p. 277).
   Voice: On nesting grounds, shrill neighing whistles, bill clapping, growls, groans, and puppylike sounds. Notes of Black-footed coarser.

Where found: Breeds in nw. islands of Hawaiian chain. Ranges from Hawaii to Aleutians, Gulf of Alaska. A straggler (perhaps regular) far off coast of Oregon, California. **Nest:** A depression or rimmed saucer on sand of sea island; in colony. Eggs (1) white or buff, with or without spots.

Shearwaters, Fulmars, Large Petrels: Procellariidae

GULL-SIZED birds of open oca. Bills thin (except Fulmar's) with tubelike external nostrils, fused together (Fulmar) or separate (shearwaters). Wings narrower than a gull's, tail smaller, not as fanlike. Fulmar is more robust than a shearwater. Sexes alike. The flight, several flaps and a glide, banking and skimming on stiff wings low over the waves, is distinctive. In calm weather, patter on surface when taking flight. On their distant nesting islands, shearwaters are noisy at night; at sea they are usually silent but may occasionally utter croaking, grunting, or gull-like notes when feeding. Comparative voice descriptions and habitats (open ocean, sometimes open-mouthed bays) are omitted in the following accounts. **Food:** Fish, squid, crustaceans; fat, refuse thrown from ships. **Range:** Oceans of world. **No. of species:** World, 33 (Mayr-Amadon), 56 (Van Tyne-Berger); West, 7 (+4 accidentals; +6 in Hawaii).

FULMAR *Fulmarus glacialis* 17-20   **Pl. 2**
   Field marks: Note the stubby yellow bill (with tubed nostrils). Oceanic; stubbier and slightly larger than Kittiwake. Glides and banks on stiff wings in style of shearwaters; swims buoyantly. Head and underparts white; back, wings, *and tail* pale gray; wings darker toward tips and with pale patch at base of primaries. Legs bluish. *Dark phase:* Smoky gray; wing-tips darker, bill yellowish. Intermediates may be noted.
   Similar species: (1) Resembles a gull, but thick bull-neck, stubby tubed bill, and stiff-winged flight are distinctive. Fulmar has dusky primaries, lacks sharply patterned wing-tips of most gulls. (2) Dark Fulmar may be mistaken for Sooty or Slender-billed Shearwaters, but is paler, with stubby yellowish bill.
   Voice: A hoarse grunting *ag-ag-ag-arrr* or *ek-ek-ek-ek-ek*.
   Where found: Northern oceans of N. Hemisphere. Winters to Japan, Baja California, Newfoundland, n. France. **West:** *Breeds* on islands of Bering Sea, Aleutians, Alaska Peninsula. *Winters* offshore, Bering Sea to c. California; irregularly to Baja California. **Nest:** On sea cliff, in colony. Eggs (1) white.

PINK-FOOTED SHEARWATER   Pl. 2
Puffinus creatopus   19–20
  Field marks: Two common white-bellied shearwaters, the Pink-
  footed and Manx, are frequently associated with the abundant
  Sooty Shearwaters. The Pink-foot is *larger* than the Sooty and
  has slower wingbeats, whereas the Manx is smaller.
  Similar species: Manx Shearwater (smaller) is blacker above,
  whiter on underwing, and has more rapid wingbeats.
  Where found: Breeds on islands off coast of Chile. Wanders
  widely. **West:** Ranges in spring, summer, fall off California,
  Oregon; rarely to B.C., se. Alaska.

PALE-FOOTED SHEARWATER   Pl. 2
Puffinus carneipes   19½
  Field marks: A very rare dark-bodied shearwater, *larger* than
  the abundant Sooty Shearwater; distinguished by its *pale
  flesh or whitish bill* (with dark tip), *flesh-colored feet,* and lack of
  pale wing-linings. Flight more sluggish than Sooty's.
  Similar species: See Slender-billed Shearwater (dark bill and
  feet).
  Where found: Breeds on islands off Australia, New Zealand.
  West: Rare visitor. Recorded off B.C., Washington, California.

NEW ZEALAND SHEARWATER   Pl. 2
Puffinus bulleri   16½
  Field marks: Note the broad M or W formed by the dark flight
  pattern. A rather rare white-bellied shearwater; separated from
  the 2 other white-bellied species by the pale gray areas of the
  back, tail coverts, and wings. At close range, the feet are
  yellowish instead of flesh-colored. Tail, wedge-shaped.
  Where found: Breeds in New Zealand (North I.). **West:**
  Regular fall visitant in small numbers off California (mainly off
  Monterey in Oct.). *Casual,* Oregon, Washington.

SOOTY SHEARWATER   *Puffinus griseus*   16–18   Pl. 2
  Field marks: A gull-like sea bird (smaller than California Gull)
  that looks all dark at a distance; glides and tilts over the waves
  on narrow rigid wings. Undersurface of wings show pale or
  whitish linings. Thin black bill. The commonest shearwater,
  frequently in very large flocks (sometimes numbering millions).
  Usually patters on surface when taking flight.
  Similar species: (1) Dark jaegers show white at base of primaries, have angled wings, fly with hawklike wingbeats. See (2)
  Slender-billed Shearwater and (3) Pale-footed Shearwater.
  (4) Near Hawaii see other dark shearwaters (pp. 255–56).
  Where found: Breeds on islands off New Zealand, s. S. America;
  ranges to N. Atlantic, N. Pacific. **West:** Ranges throughout
  year off coast from s. California to Puget Sound, se. Alaska,
  Aleutians. Most abundant spring and fall.

SLENDER-BILLED SHEARWATER   Pl. 2
Puffinus tenuirostris 13–14
  Field marks: A dark shearwater; distinguished from Sooty
  Shearwater by somewhat smaller size, shorter tail, and *dark
  wing-linings* (Sooty has pale *whitish* linings). In most Slender-
  bills the wing-linings are smoky (in a few individuals whitish,
  and therefore not to be distinguished). Be sure underwing is
  well seen when bird tilts. May have some white on throat.
  Wingbeat more rapid than Sooty's. Best looked for in late fall
  and early winter after Sooty has decreased.
  Where found: Breeds on islands off s. Australia. **West:** Ranges
  north to Aleutians (some through Bering Sea to Arctic Ocean)
  and thence south off coast to Baja California.

MANX SHEARWATER *Puffinus puffinus* 12½–15   Pl. 2
(Black-vented Shearwater, "Common Shearwater")
  Field marks: A white-breasted shearwater similar in appearance
  to Pink-footed Shearwater; much smaller, blacker above
  (showing more contrast), and with a more rapid wing motion.
  Note also the *white wing-linings* and *blackish bill* (Pink-foot has
  grayer wing-linings and pale flesh-colored bill).
  Where found: Breeds on islands in N. Atlantic; also off Baja
  California and w. Mexico. **West:** Ranges (often close to shore)
  north to Monterey, California. *Casual,* San Francisco and
  Vancouver I. A race is resident in Hawaii.

Storm Petrels: Hydrobatidae

LITTLE dark birds that flit erratically over the *open sea,* at times
"running" or "dancing" briefly on the surface with slender legs,
dangling webbed feet. Some species habitually follow boats and
may be "chummed" in by tossing out bait of ground fish, fish oil,
puffed wheat, suet, etc. Like shearwaters, they nest on sea islands,
returning to their burrows at night. Nostrils in tube on bill; closely
fused. Sexes alike. **Food:** Plankton, crustaceans, small fish.
Range: Oceans of world (except Arctic). **No. of species:** World,
33 (Mayr-Amadon), 18 (Van Tyne-Berger); West, 5 (+1 accidental; +2 in Hawaii).

FORK-TAILED PETREL *Oceanodroma furcata* 8–9   Pl. 2
  Field marks: A *pearly-gray* petrel, almost white below; unlike
  all other w. storm petrels, which are blackish.
  Voice: A high-pitched twitter.
  Where found: N. Pacific. Ranges from Bering Sea to s. Cali-
  fornia. *Breeds* from Kuriles east through Aleutians to Sanak,
  and from Alexander Archipelago (Alaska) to n. California.
  Nest: In burrow on sea island. Eggs (1) white.

LEACH'S PETREL   *Oceanodroma leucorhoa*   7½–9   **Pl. 2**
(Beal's Petrel; including Socorro Petrel)
   Field marks: Note the *conspicuous white rump.* The other
common w. black petrels have dark rumps. In flight it bounds
about erratically, constantly changing speed and direction
(suggesting Nighthawk).
   Similar species: (1) Wilson's Petrel (accidental) also has white
rump, but is smaller, has square-cut, not notched tail and longer
legs with yellow webbed feet extending beyond tail-tip. (2) A
dark-rumped race of Leach's Petrel (*O. l. willetti*) breeds in
company with the Black Petrel on the Coronados near San
Diego. When compared, it is smaller, with a grayer rump. It
may have a touch of white on the sides of the rump. Black
Petrel has a much lazier, less erratic flight.
   Voice: At night, in flight on breeding grounds, rhythmic falsetto
hooting notes, *WER-kutawuka, ik-ik-ikoo* (M. North and E.
Simms). From burrows, long crooning trills.
   Where found: N. Atlantic, N. Pacific. **West:** *Breeds* in Aleutians
and locally off coast from se. Alaska to c. California (Farallons),
w. Mexico (Coronado, San Benito, and Guadalupe Is.). **Nest:** In
burrow; in colony on sea island. Eggs (1) white.

ASHY PETREL   *Oceanodroma homochroa*   7½   **Pl. 2**
   Field marks: The smallest of our fork-tailed, all-black petrels.
When seen with the Black Petrel it can be separated by its
decidedly smaller size, shorter wings, more fluttery flight. At
very close range it shows a mottling of white under the wings
and an ash-gray suffusion on head and neck.
   Voice: Twittering notes. Vocal at night on breeding islands.
   Where found: Ranges at sea from n. California (Point Reyes)
to c. Baja California. *Breeds* on Farallon and Channel Is.,
California, also a few on Coronados. **Nest:** Under rocks, in
colony. Eggs (1) white.

BLACK PETREL   *Loomelania melania*   9   **Pl. 2**
   Field marks: The most common of the various all-black petrels
found off California. It can be told from the others by its larger
size, longer wings, *more languid flight.*
   Similar species: See (1) Leach's Petrel, (2) Ashy Petrel. (3) In
Hawaii see Sooty Storm and Bulwer's Petrels (p. 258).
   Voice: At night, in nesting colony, a ventriloquial *puck-apoo —
puck-puck-a-poo* (J. Fisher).
   Where found: *Breeds* on Coronados and other islands off n.
Baja California and in Gulf of California. Ranges north along
California coast to Point Reyes (above San Francisco).

LEAST PETREL   *Halocyptena microsoma*   5½–6   **Pl. 2**
   Field marks: A very small black petrel with a rounded or

wedge-shaped tail (all other w. storm petrels have forked tails). Flight swift and erratic, close to water.
Where found: Pacific. *Breeds* on islands off both coasts of Baja California. A few range north in late summer, early fall to San Diego and south to Ecuador.

Tropicbirds: Phaethontidae

ALTHOUGH related to pelicans and cormorants, tropicbirds resemble large terns with greatly elongated central tail feathers and stouter, slightly decurved bills. Ternlike, they dive headfirst. Sexes alike. **Food:** Squids, crustaceans. **Range:** Tropical seas. **No. of species:** World, 3; West, 1 (+2 in Hawaii).

RED-BILLED TROPICBIRD   p. 14
Phaethon aethereus   24–40
    Field marks: Note the 2 *extremely long central tail feathers* (1–2 ft.). A slender white sea bird, near size of California Gull, with *heavy red bill,* black patch through cheek; black primaries; finely barred back. Strong flight and white tail streamers are distinctive. Swims with tail cocked clear of water. Young lack long tail, have orange-yellow bill.
    Similar species: (1) See Royal Tern (p. 106). In Hawaii see (2) Red-tailed Tropicbird (p. 260) and (3) White-tailed Tropicbird (p. 258).
    Voice: Gull-like notes; also a chattering rattle.
    Where found: Tropical Atlantic and Pacific. **West:** Ranges, perhaps regularly, to offshore waters of s. California. Has been observed in small numbers off s. Channel Is. *Accidental,* Washington, Arizona. **Habitat:** Open ocean.

Pelicans: Pelecanidae

HUGE water birds with long flat bills and great throat pouches (flat when deflated). Neck long, body robust. Sexes alike. They swim buoyantly and fly with head hunched back on shoulders and long flat bill resting on breast. Flocks fly in orderly lines, and alternate several flaps with a glide, each bird taking the rhythm from the bird ahead. **Food:** Mainly fish, crustaceans. **Range:** N. and S. America, Africa, se. Europe, s. Asia, E. Indies, Australia. **No. of species:** World, 6; West, 2

WHITE PELICAN   *Pelecanus erythrorhynchos*   54–70   **p. 14**
    Field marks: Huge; spread 8–9½ ft. White with black primaries

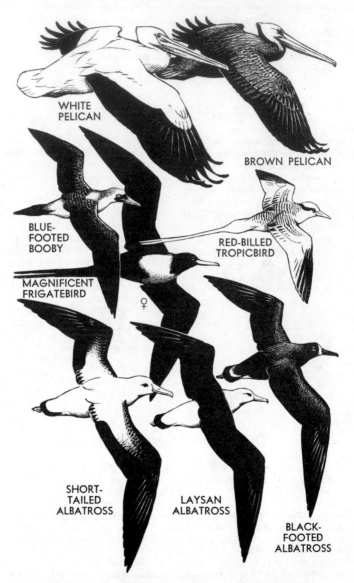

WHITE
PELICAN

BROWN PELICAN

BLUE-
FOOTED
BOOBY

RED-BILLED
TROPICBIRD

MAGNIFICENT
FRIGATEBIRD

♀

SHORT-
TAILED
ALBATROSS

LAYSAN
ALBATROSS

BLACK-
FOOTED
ALBATROSS

PELICANS AND ALLIES; ALBATROSSES

and a great yellow bill. When breeding, has projection or "centerboard" on ridge of bill. Swims buoyantly. Scoops up fish while swimming; does not plunge from air like Brown Pelican. Flocks fly in lines, often circle high in sky.

Similar species: (1) Swans have no black in wings. (2) Wood Ibis and (3) extremely rare Whooping Crane have much black in wings but fly with necks extended and long legs trailing. (4) Snow Goose is much smaller, with a small bill; noisy.

Voice: Adults virtually silent (in colony, a low groan). Young birds utter whining grunts.

Where found: W. and c. N. America. Winters from s. U.S. to Guatemala. **West:** *Breeds* locally from B.C., s. Mackenzie south (east of Cascades, Sierra) to w. Nevada, n. Utah, nw. Wyoming, N. Dakota; also California (San Joaquin Valley and Salton Sea). Nonbreeding birds widespread in summer. *Migrates* through interior. *Winters* from n.-c. and coastal California, s. Arizona south, occasionally in Great Basin. **Habitat:** Lakes, marshes, salt bays, beaches. **Nest:** On ground or bulrushes of lake island; in colony. Eggs (2–3) whitish, stained.

BROWN PELICAN *Pelecanus occidentalis* 45–54 **p. 14**
Field marks: Spread 6½ ft. A ponderous dark water bird; adult with much white about head and neck; immature differs in having a dark head, whitish underparts. Often perches on posts, rocks, boats. Bulk, great bill, and flight (a few flaps and a sail) indicate a pelican; dusky color and habit of *plunging* bill-first from the air proclaim it this species. Lines of pelicans scale close to water, almost touching it with wing-tips.

Voice: Adults silent (rarely a low croak). Nestlings squeal.

Where found: Coasts of s. U.S. to S. America. **West:** *Breeds* locally and sporadically along California coast north to Pt. Lobos, Monterey Co. Wanders to coastal B.C.; a few to Lower Colorado River, Arizona. *Accidental* inland in California, Nevada, Utah, Colorado. **Habitat:** Salt bays, ocean. **Nests:** On ground on island; in colony. Eggs (2–3) whitish.

Boobies and Gannets: Sulidae

LARGE sea birds with large, pointed bills, pointed tails; shaped somewhat like fat cigars. Larger than most gulls, with a "pointed at both ends" look; neck longer. Sexes alike. They fish by spectacular plunges from the air. **Food:** Fish, squids. **Range:** Gannets are birds of cold seas (N. Atlantic, S. Africa, Australia); boobies inhabit tropical seas. **No. of species:** World, 9; West, 2 (casual or accidental); +2 in Hawaii.

BLUE-FOOTED BOOBY *Sula nebouxii* 32–34 **p. 14**
Field marks: Larger than any gull, with a longer neck, larger pointed bill, and *pointed* tail. White body, whitish head, mottled dark back and wings and big blue feet. Face and bill dark. Sits on buoys. Dives Brown-Pelican-like. In distance suggests young Brown Pelican. Young birds have brownish head.
Similar species: Adult Brown Booby (p. 260) has clean-cut contrast between blackish chest, white underparts. Young Brown Booby is brown throughout (young Blue-footed is whitish below).
Where found: W. Mexico to Ecuador. West: The 14–15 records for the U.S. are concentrated at Salton Sea and the Lower Colorado River in se. California, sw. Arizona, suggesting more than merely casual status. *Accidental,* Washington.

Cormorants: Phalacrocoracidae

LARGE, blackish, slender-billed water birds; often perch *upright* on rocks or posts with neck in an S; sometimes strike a "spread eagle" pose. Adults often have colorful face skin, gular pouch, eyes (usually green). Sexes alike. Often confused with loons; tail longer, bill hook-tipped. In flight, axis of body and neck is tilted upward slightly (loon's neck droops). Young birds are browner, with pale breasts. Swimming, they lie low like loons, but with necks more erect and snakelike, bills tilted slightly upward. Flocks fly in line or wedge formation much like geese but are *silent.* **Food:** Fish, crustaceans. **Range:** Nearly cosmopolitan. **No. of species:** World, 30; West, 4 (+1 marginal).

DOUBLE-CRESTED CORMORANT **p. 17**
Phalacrocorax auritus 30–36
Field marks: See family discussion. Any cormorant found well inland in w. U.S. can quite safely be called this species. Along the West coast it may be told from other cormorants by its *orange-yellow* throat pouch. Crest is seldom evident.
Similar species: (1) See Brandt's Cormorant. (2) See Pelagic Cormorant (often shows distinct double crest). (3) The very similar Olivaceous Cormorant (p. 278) sometimes occurs west to 100° in s. Texas. (4) See also loons (p. 3).
Voice: Silent, except for low grunts in nesting colony.
Where found: Most of N. America. Winters south to B. Honduras. **West:** *Breeds* from e. Aleutians, Kodiak south along coast to Baja California; inland from c. Alberta, c. Saskatchewan to w. Arizona, New Mexico, Texas. *Winters* along coast from s. Alaska south; also inland in California, s. Arizona. **Habitat:** Coast, bays, lakes, rivers. **Nest:** A mass of sticks in tree, bush,

PELAGIC
(Dull red face,
black forehead)

Adult

DOUBLE-
CRESTED
(Yellow pouch)

RED-FACED
(Bright red face,
red forehead)

BRANDT'S
(Blue pouch)
buff patch)

Adult

Adult

Adult

Adult

PELAGIC
and
RED-FACED
have white
flank patches
in breeding
plumage

DOUBLE-
CRESTED

Adult

Note: Brandt's
Cormorant has
similar build.

Immature

Cormorants stand erect (lower right), often hold a
"spread eagle" pose (lower left). They swim low in the
water with the bill pointed slightly upward.

CORMORANTS

or marsh on lake margin, or of sticks or seaweed on island or sea cliff; in colony. Eggs (3–4) pale blue, chalky.

BRANDT'S CORMORANT   p. 17
Phalacrocorax penicillatus   33–35

Field marks: Size of Double-crested Cormorant but has a dark throat pouch (*blue* in breeding season, but hard to see). Has a *buffy-brown band across throat* behind pouch. Young birds are brownish, with paler underparts.

Similar species: Young Double-crested Cormorants are usually *whiter* on underparts, and show a *yellow* pouch. On the Pacific, if a young cormorant has a decidedly whitish breast it is a Double-crest; if the breast is buffy or pale brown, it might be a Double-crest but more likely a Brandt's. If underparts are deep rich brown, the bird is a Brandt's.

Voice: Occasional low grunts.

Where found: *Resident* along coast from Vancouver I. to Baja California. *Casual,* se. Alaska. **Habitat:** Ocean, coast, littoral.

Nest: Of seaweed and sticks on rocky island or coastal cliff; in colony. Eggs (3–6) pale blue, chalky.

PELAGIC CORMORANT   *Phalacrocorax pelagicus*   25½–30
(Baird's Cormorant)   **p. 17**

Field marks: Noticeably smaller than the preceding two. Much more iridescent at close range. Has a more slender neck, small head, much *thinner bill.* In breeding season (Feb.–June) has double crest and *white patch* (conspicuous in flight) on each flank. Throat pouch and part of face dull red (seen at very close range). Young deep brown, darkest on back.

Similar species: In Alaska see Red-faced Cormorant.

Voice: A low croak.

Where found: *Breeds* from Bering Sea to Japan and south along our coast to Coronados, near San Diego. *Winters* in Aleutians and from B.C. to Baja California. **Habitat:** Coast, bays, sounds.

Nest: A mass of seaweed, grass on narrow ledge of sea cliff; in colony. Eggs (3–5) pale blue, chalky, stained.

RED-FACED CORMORANT   p. 17
Phalacrocorax urile   28–30

Field marks: Note the *bright red* of adult's face (extending to forehead and behind eye). Throat pouch *bright blue.* Otherwise, similar to Pelagic Cormorant (conspicuous double crest; white patches on flanks in breeding plumage).

Similar species: Pelagic Cormorant has dull red pouch, restricted dull red on face. Immature has darker bill.

Voice: A low *korr;* hoarse croaks.

Where found: Bering Sea, ne. Asia. **West:** *Resident* from Pribilofs to Aleutians (east to Semidi Is.). **Nest:** Of seaweed, grass, on rocky sea island; single or in scattered colony. Eggs (3–4) pale blue, chalky.

Frigatebirds: Fregatidae

TROPICAL sea birds with a greater plane area in proportion to weight than any other birds. Bill long, strongly hooked. Tail deeply forked. Sexes unlike. Although sea birds, they normally cannot swim. Food is snatched from water in flight. They also scavenge and rob other sea birds. **Food:** Fish, jellyfish, crustaceans, squids, young birds. **Range:** Pan-tropical oceans. **No. of species:** World, 5; West, 1 (+1 in Hawaii).

MAGNIFICENT FRIGATEBIRD *Fregata magnificens* 37½–41
(Man-o'-War Bird)   **p. 14**
  Field marks: Spread 7–8 ft. "Man-o'-Wars," long-winged black birds, with scissorlike tails (usually folded in a point), soar with an ease that gulls cannot match. Their extremely long, angled wings seem to have a hump in middle. Bill long, hooked. They do not swim but often perch. *Male:* Black, with red throat pouch (inflatable in breeding season). *Female:* White breast, dark head. *Immature:* Head and underparts white.
  Similar species: (1) See Black-footed Albatross (p. 8). (2) In Hawaii see also Great Frigatebird (p. 261).
  Voice: Voiceless at sea. A gurgling note during courtship.
  Where found: Gulf of Mexico, tropical Atlantic, e. Pacific oceans. **West:** Wanders irregularly along coast north to n. California. *Casual,* Oregon. *Accidental,* Arizona, New Mexico, Nevada. **Habitat:** Oceanic coasts.

Herons and Bitterns: Ardeidae

LARGE wading birds with long necks, long legs, spearlike bills. In sustained flight, heads are tucked back in an S; legs trail; wingbeats slow and "bowed." At rest, neck may be erect or "pulled in." May have plumes when breeding. Sexes similar. Subject to post-breeding wanderings. **Food:** Fish, frogs, crayfish, other aquatic life; sometimes mice, insects. **Range:** Nearly worldwide except n. N. America, n. Asia, some islands. **No. of species:** World, 59; West, 10 (+2 accidentals).

GREAT BLUE HERON *Ardea herodias* 42–52   **Pl. 4**
  Field marks: This lean bird, often miscalled "crane," stands 4 ft. tall, and is, next to the Sandhill Crane, the largest long-legged bird widely found in the West. Its long legs, long neck, dagger bill, and, in sustained flight, folded neck and trailing legs mark it as a heron. Great size (wingspread 6 ft.) and blue-gray

color, whiter about head (in adults), identify it as this species. Stands motionless with neck erect, or head between shoulders. **Similar species:** See Sandhill Crane (p. 71). **Voice:** Deep, harsh croaks: *frahnk, frahnk, frawnk*. **Where found:** Most of N. America. Winters to n. S. America. **West:** *Breeds* from se. Alaska, n. Alberta, c. Saskatchewan, south locally to Mexico. *Winters* from B.C., n. Idaho, Montana (rarely) south. **Habitat:** Marshes, swamps, streams, shores, tideflats, kelp beds, irrigation ditches. **Nest:** A platform of sticks in tree in swamp or on rocky island; sometimes in marsh; rarely on cliff; in colony. Eggs (3–6) bluish.

GREEN HERON *Butorides virescens* 16–22   **Pl. 4**
Field marks: A small heron that in distant flight looks quite dark and crowlike (but flies with more arched wingbeats). Stretches neck, elevates shaggy crest, and jerks tail when alarmed. The comparatively short legs are orange (breeding) or greenish yellow. Black bluish, neck deep chestnut. Young birds have streaked necks. **Voice:** A series of *kuck*'s or a loud *skyow* or *skewk*. **Where found:** Nw. U.S., e. Canada to n. S. America. **West:** *Breeds* from w. Washington, w. Nevada, sw. Utah, c. Arizona, s. New Mexico south. *Straggles* to s. B.C., n. Utah, Wyoming. *Winters* in c. and s. California, s. Arizona, s. New Mexico, w. Texas (El Paso). **Habitat:** Lakes, fresh marshes, slow streams. **Nest:** A flimsy stick platform in tree or willow thicket; usually solitary. Eggs (3–6; 9) bluish green.

LITTLE BLUE HERON *Florida caerulea* 20–29   **Pl. 4**
Field marks: A medium-sized, slender heron. *Adult:* Slaty blue with dark maroon neck; legs dark. *Immature:* Snowy white; legs dull *greenish;* bill *bluish* tipped with black. White birds changing to adulthood are boldly pied with dark. **Similar species:** (1) Green Heron is smaller, with shorter yellow or orange legs. (2) Young Snowy Egrets may be misidentified as young Little Blues because of a stripe of yellowish up rear leg. Note the Snowy's all-black bill. **Where found:** E. U.S. south to Peru, Argentina. Migratory in U.S. **West:** A casual straggler to s. California (sight records), s. Nevada, Utah, Colorado, Arizona, New Mexico, w. Texas (frequent at El Paso), Saskatchewan.

CATTLE EGRET *Bubulcus ibis* 20   **Pl. 4**
Note: This small white heron that associates with grazing cattle will, I predict, invade the sw. U.S. At this writing (1960) there are no records west of 100°. A colonizer of Old World origin (via S. America), it was first reported in U.S. in 1952, reached Texas by 1955. It has recently been introduced into the

Hawaiian Is. It is slightly smaller, stockier, thicker-necked than the Snowy Egret. When breeding, shows *buff* on crown, breast, and back (looks quite white at a distance); little or no buff in winter. Bill yellow (orange-pink at nesting). Legs coral-pink (nesting), yellow, greenish, or blackish (immature). Compare with Snowy Egret (black bill, black legs, yellow feet) and Common Egret (large, long-necked).

COMMON EGRET *Casmerodius albus* 37–41   **Pl. 4**
(American Egret)
  Field marks: A large, slender white heron with a *yellow bill* (orange when breeding). Legs and feet black. *Straight* plumes on back during breeding. Posture when feeding: neck extended in an eager, leaning-forward look, unlike Snowy.
  Similar species: Snowy Egret has *black* bill, yellow feet.
  Voice: A low, hoarse croak. Also *cuk, cuk, cuk.*
  Where found: N. U.S. to Strait of Magellan; warmer parts of Old World. **West:** *Breeds* locally in se. Oregon, w. Nevada, California, w. Arizona, s. New Mexico. Has bred casually in s. Idaho, Montana. Wanders widely, casually north to Washington, Alberta, s. Saskatchewan. *Winters* from se. Oregon, c. Nevada, c. Arizona, c. New Mexico (rarely) south. **Habitat:** Marshes, irrigated lands, ponds, shores, mudflats. **Nest:** A platform of sticks in large trees, dead brush over water, or in tule marsh; in colony. Eggs (3–5) pale bluish.

SNOWY EGRET *Leucophoyx thula* 20–27   **Pl. 4**
  Field marks: Note the "golden slippers." A rather small white heron with a *slender black bill,* black legs, and *yellow feet. Recurved* plumes on back during breeding. Area before eye (lores) yellow or red (breeding). Often shuffles feet so as to stir up food; rushes about actively.
  Similar species: (1) Common Egret is much larger, has a *yellow* bill, *black* feet. (2) Young Snowies have a yellowish stripe up back of leg and may appear yellow-legged when walking away; thus easily confused with white young of the Little Blue Heron (rare or local in West).
  Voice: A low croak; in colony, a bubbling *wulla-wulla-wulla.*
  Where found: N. U.S. to Argentina. **West:** *Breeds* locally in California, se. Oregon, Nevada, n. Utah, Colorado, w. Arizona, New Mexico, w. Texas (El Paso). Wanders widely; casual northward to Washington, Alberta, s. Saskatchewan. *Accidental,* se. Alaska. *Winters* from n. California, s. Arizona, w. Texas south. **Habitat:** Marshes, ponds, irrigated land, tideflats, shores. **Nest:** A platform of sticks in tules or bushes in marsh; in colony. Eggs (3–6) pale greenish blue.

LOUISIANA HERON *Hydranassa tricolor* 24–28 **Pl. 4**
("Tricolored Heron")
> **Field marks:** Note the contrasting *white belly* — in any plumage this is the key mark of this rather small *dark* heron. Rump white. A very slender, snaky species.
> **Where found:** New Jersey south to Brazil. **West:** Rare visitor to San Diego area in California. *Casual* straggler to Oregon, Nevada, Colorado, Arizona, New Mexico, w. Texas.

BLACK-CROWNED NIGHT HERON **Pl. 4**
Nycticorax nycticorax 23–28
> **Field marks:** A stocky, short-billed, short-legged heron. Usually sits hunched and inactive by day; flies to feed at dusk. *Adult:* Note the *black* back. Pale gray or white below; gray wings, black cap, red eyes, yellowish legs. When breeding, acquires 2 long white head plumes, pink legs. *Immature:* Brown, spotted, and streaked with white.
> **Similar species:** See immature American Bittern.
> **Voice:** A flat *quok!* or *quark!,* most often heard in evening.
> **Where found:** Eurasia, Africa, N. and S. America, Pacific islands. **West:** *Breeds* locally from e. Washington, Idaho, c. Alberta, s.-c. Saskatchewan to Mexico. *Casual,* B.C. *Winters* from Oregon, Nevada, Utah, Colorado south. Also *resident* in Hawaii. **Habitat:** Marshes, lake margins, shores. **Nest:** A loose platform of sticks or stalks in tules or willow thickets in marsh, or in trees; in colony. Eggs (3–6) blue-green.

LEAST BITTERN *Ixobrychus exilis* 11–14 **Pl. 4**
> **Field marks:** The tiniest, most furtive heron; near size of meadowlark, but body much thinner. Usually straddles reed stems; flushes close at hand, flies a short distance and drops in again. Note the *large buff wing patches,* black back, small size. Females and young have streaked necks.
> **Similar species:** (1) Rails lack buff wing patches, lack strong pattern. (2) Beginners sometimes mistake the Green Heron (dark wings) for Least Bittern. Green Heron often perches in trees. (3) See American Bittern (very much larger).
> **Voice:** "Song," a low muted *coo-coo-coo* heard in the marsh (cuckoo-like, but not in long series).
> **Where found:** Oregon, Wyoming, se. Canada to S. America. Winters from s. U.S. south. **West:** *Breeds* in se. Oregon, California, and along Lower Colorado River; locally on Rio Grande; also east of Rockies from Wyoming (?) to Texas. *Winters* (sparsely) from n. California, s. Arizona, w. Texas (El Paso) south. *Casual,* B.C., Montana, Saskatchewan. **Habitat:** Fresh marshes, reedy ponds, tules. **Nest:** A flimsy platform among tules, reeds; not in colony. Eggs (4–6) bluish white.

AMERICAN BITTERN *Botaurus lentiginosus* 23–34 **Pl. 4**
Field marks: In crossing a marsh we flush this large, stocky, brown bird. In flight the blackish outer wing contrasts with the streaked buffy brown of the bird. Discovered, it often stands rigid, pointing bill skyward; shows a black stripe on side of neck (sometimes concealed). Rarely ever sits in trees.
Similar species: (1) Young Black-crowned Night Heron is not as rich a brown, lacks blackish outer wing. Silhouetted in flight, the faster wingbeats and less curved wings are the Bittern's marks; its bill is held more horizontal. (2) Least Bittern is tiny, contrastingly patterned with buff and black.
Voice: The "pumping," or spring song is a slow, deep *oong-ka-choonk-oong-ka choonk-oong-ka-choonk,* etc. Distorted by distance, only the *ka* may be audible and sounds like a mallet driving a stake. Flushing note, *kok-kok-kok.*
Where found: Canada to Gulf states. Winters to Panama.
West: *Breeds* from c. B.C., s. Mackenzie south to c. California, c. Arizona, s. New Mexico. *Casual,* se. Alaska. *Winters* from sw. B.C., Utah, c. New Mexico south. **Habitat:** Marshes, tules, reedy lakes. **Nest:** A platform of dead stalks among marsh plants; not in colony. Eggs (3–7) olive.

Storks and Wood Ibises: Ciconiidae

LARGE, long-legged, heron-like birds with long bills (straight, recurved, or decurved). Some species with naked heads. Sexes alike. Flight deliberate; neck and legs extended and slightly drooped. Gait a sedate walk. **Food:** Frogs, crustaceans, lizards, rodents. **Range:** S. U.S., Cent. and S. America, Africa, Eurasia, E. Indies, Australia. **No. of species:** World, 17; West, 1.

WOOD IBIS or WOOD STORK
p. 71, Pl. 4
Mycteria americana 34–47
Field marks: Spread 5½ ft. A very large white stork with a *dark, naked head* and extensive *black wing areas* and black tail. Bill long, thick at base, and *decurved.* Young birds are dingier, with a lighter head and neck. When feeding, keeps head down and walks thus. Flies by alternate flapping and sailing. Often soars in flocks at a great height, then resembling White Pelican (which also soars) except for shape, black tail, and more extensive black in wing (including entire rear edge).
Similar species: (1) White Pelican, see *Field marks* above. (2) White herons in flight retract necks, have no black in wings. (3) See Whooping Crane (p. 70).
Voice: A hoarse croak; usually silent.

Where found: S. U.S. to Argentina. **West:** Regular visitor, especially in late summer and fall, to s. California (often common at Salton Sea), sw. and c. Arizona, s. Nevada; casually to ne. California, Utah, s. Idaho, s. Montana, Wyoming, Colorado, New Mexico, w. Texas. **Habitat:** Marshes, ponds, lagoons.

Ibises and Spoonbills: Threskiornithidae

IBISES are long-legged marsh birds with long, decurved bills similar to those of curlews. Their name describes the spoonbills. They travel in lines or bunched formations; unlike herons, they fly with necks outstretched, alternately flapping and sailing. **Food:** Crustaceans, insects, leeches, small fish. **Range:** Tropical and warm-temperate regions of world. **No. of species:** World, 28; West, 1 (+2 accidentals).

WHITE-FACED IBIS *Plegadis chihi* 19–26   **Pl. 4**
(White-faced Glossy Ibis)
    Field marks: A medium-sized marsh wader with a *long, decurved bill;* deep purplish chestnut; at a distance looks like a large black curlew. In breeding plumage shows a *white border* of feathers at base of bill. Flies in lines with neck outstretched, with quicker wingbeats than herons, alternately flapping and gliding. Immature and also adult in nonbreeding plumage lack white face. *Caution:* These are often reported as Glossy Ibis! Winter adults have some white speckling about head.
    Voice: A piglike *ka-onk,* repeated; a low *kruk, kruk.*
    Where found: W. U.S., Louisiana to Argentina, Chile. **West:** *Breeds* very locally in se. Oregon, c. California, Nevada, n. Utah. Occurs in summer north to s. Idaho, Wyoming. *Casual,* Washington, Montana. *Winters* from s. California, sw. Arizona, s. Texas south. **Habitat:** Fresh marshes, irrigated land, tules. **Nest:** A cupped platform of reeds in marsh, or of sticks in bushes; in colony. Eggs (3–5) pale blue.

Swans, Geese, and Ducks: Anatidae

THE BEST-KNOWN family of water birds, divided into several subfamilies (discussed separately). It might be pointed out here that ducks and geese of many species may summer well south of their breeding range. **Range:** Almost worldwide. **No. of species:** World, 145; West, 47 (+8 accidentals; +3 in Hawaii).

Swans: Cygninae

HUGE, all-white swimming birds, larger and with much longer necks than geese. Young are brownish white. Sexes alike. More aquatic than most geese, and like some geese they migrate in lines or V-formation. They feed by immersing the head and neck, sometimes "tipping up." **Food:** Chiefly aquatic plants, seeds.

WHISTLING SWAN *Olor columbianus* 47–58 **Pls. 5, 6**
Field marks: Spread 6–7 ft. The common wild swan of the West. Often heard long before the ribbonlike flock can be detected in the sky. Their completely white wings and long necks stretched full length mark them as swans. A small yellow spot at the base of the black bill can sometimes be seen at close range. Feeds by "tipping up," also dabbles. Young birds are quite dingy, with dull pinkish bills.
Similar species: (1) Snow Goose has black primaries, much shorter neck. (2) White Pelican has black in wings, big bill. (3) Mute Swan (park variety) has *orange bill* with black knob at base; swims with neck in S. (4) See also Trumpeter Swan.
Voice: High-pitched cooing notes, less harsh than honking of geese; "a musical *woo-ho, woo-woo, woo-ho*" (J. Moffitt).
Where found: Arctic America, e. Siberia. Winters in U.S. **West:** *Breeds* from Arctic coast south to Alaska Peninsula and Barren Grounds of Canada. *Winters* from s. Alaska through Pacific states to s. California; also in Great Basin, Lower Colorado River, and New Mexico. *Migrant* on large bodies of water in interior. **Habitat:** Tundra (summer), lakes, large rivers, bays, estuaries, fields. **Nest:** A bulky mound on island or margin of tundra pool. Eggs (4–5; 7) white, stained.

TRUMPETER SWAN *Olor buccinator* 58½–72 **Pl. 5**
Field marks: Larger than Whistling Swan. Adults can be distinguished at close range by heavier *all-black* bill without yellow basal spot; this is not infallible, since some Whistlers lack this spot. Where it is resident it may be distinguished from transient Whistlers by its deeper voice.
Voice: Much louder, lower-pitched, and more bugle-like than that of Whistling Swan. In flight, wings make rasping sound.
Where found: *Breeds* locally in s. and se. Alaska, w. and se. Alberta (Grande Prairie, Cypress Hills), sw. Saskatchewan (Cypress Hills), e. Idaho (Island Park), sw. Montana (Red Rock Lakes), Wyoming (Yellowstone). Reintroduced locally elsewhere in e. Oregon, Nevada, nw. Wyoming. Formerly more widespread. *Winters* in so. Alaska, B.C., nw. Washington (?), e. Idaho, Montana, nw. Wyoming. **Habitat:** Lakes, ponds, large rivers; in winter, also bays. **Nest:** A large mound on beaver house, island, or margin of lake. Eggs (4–6; 10) whitish.

Geese: Anserinae

LARGE waterfowl; larger, heavier-bodied, longer-necked than ducks; bills thick at base. Noisy in flight; some fly in line or V-formation. *Sexes are colored alike* at all seasons. More terrestrial than ducks, grazing on land (except Brant and Emperor Goose); may be looked for in grassy marshes; grain or stubble fields; sometimes upend in water. Gregarious most of year. **Food:** Mainly grasses, seeds, aquatic plants. Brants prefer eelgrass. Emperor Goose eats shellfish.

CANADA GOOSE *Branta canadensis* 22–36   **Pls. 5, 6**
   Field marks: Note the "chin strap." The most widespread goose; gray-brown with *black head and neck,* or "stocking," and light-colored breast. The most characteristic mark is the *white patch* running onto each side of the head. Bill and legs black. When traveling, long strings of these geese pass high overhead in V-formation. Canada Geese vary greatly in size from the largest w. form, *B. c. moffitti* (32–36), to the Mallard-sized *B. c. minima* (22–27). Ten races are recognized by the A.O.U. *Check-list* (1957), at least 6 of which winter in the West. Although there is variation and a clinal blend, it is possible to compare and separate certain races where they mingle in winter.
   B. c. moffitti (Western or Moffitt's Canada Goose). The large form (32–36) that nests in nw. U.S. and Prairie Provinces of Canada and winters from the Canadian border to California. **Voice:** A deep double-syllabled honking or barking *ka-ronk* or *ha-lunk, ha, lunk* (slurred up).
   B. c. parvipes (Lesser Canada Goose). Medium-sized (26–31), about size of Snow Goose. Breeds in e. and c. Alaska, nw. Canada. Abundant in winter, interior valleys of California. **Voice:** Higher-pitched than Western Canada's; lower than that of Cackling; *lo-ank, lo-ank, a-lank, a-lank* (J. Moffitt).
   B. c. fulva (Vancouver Canada Goose). A fairly large bird (31–35) with dark underparts; resident along coast from Glacier Bay, Alaska, to Vancouver I. Winters to nw. California.
   B. c. occidentalis (Dusky Canada Goose), 27–32. Even darker, chocolate-colored beneath. Resident Prince William Sound, Alaska. Some winter to coastal Oregon.
   B. c. minima (Cackling Canada Goose). Hardly larger (22–27) than a Mallard; small bill, stubby neck; dark underparts. In some Cackling Geese there is a partial white collar near the base of the black neck (other races sometimes show this). **Voice:** A high-pitched yelping *yelk, yelk, a-lick, a-lick,* or *lick, lick, lick* (J. Moffitt). Breeds in Alaska and Yukon; winters mainly in Central Valley of California. Another small race — *B. c. leucopareia* (Aleutian Canada Goose) — with a wider white neck collar, breeds in the Aleutians (quite rare).

Where found: Arctic America to n. U.S.; winters to Mexico and Gulf states. Introduced in Iceland, Britain, New Zealand. **West:** *Breeds* from Arctic slope south (mainly east of Cascades, Sierra) to ne. California, w. Nevada, n. Utah, Wyoming, S. Dakota. *Winters* from s. Alaska, s. Canada (a few) to Mexico. *Migrant* throughout. **Habitat:** Lakes, bays, marshes, prairies, grainfields; in summer also tundra. **Nest:** On muskrat house or islet or in marsh; occasionally in old tree nest of large bird of prey, tree platform, or cliff. Eggs (4–6; 10) white.

BRANT (AMERICAN BRANT) Pl. 6
Branta bernicla   22–26
Field marks: When flying, the Brant is mainly distinguished from the Black Brant by the *light belly* contrasting sharply with the black breast. However, sides of Black Brant are quite light; the two probably cannot be separated when swimming.
Where found: Breeds on Arctic coasts across n. Eurasia and in N. America from about 100° E. **West:** A few examples of this form winter along the Pacific Coast from Vancouver I. to California. Recorded also in Alaska, Idaho.

BLACK BRANT *Branta nigricans* 23–26 Pls. 5, 6
Field marks: A small black-necked goose not much larger than a Mallard. Has a white stern, conspicuous when it upends; and a fleck of white on side of neck (absent in immature). Travels in large, irregular flocks.
Similar species: Canada Goose's breast shows light above water. (Foreparts of Brant are black *to the waterline*.) Canada Goose has a large "chin strap" of white. *Caution:* Hunters often use the term "brant" for various other geese.
Voice: A throaty *cr-r-r-ruk* or *krr-onk, krrr-onk.*
Where found: Arctic coasts of Siberia, Alaska, nw. Canada. **West:** *Breeds* on coasts of arctic Alaska south to Nelson I.; east to 110° in arctic Canada. *Winters* along coast and bays from sw. B.C. to Baja California; locally or rarely inland (Washington, Oregon, s. Idaho, Utah, ne. California, Nevada). *Accidental,* Saskatchewan, Wyoming, Texas. **Habitat:** Mainly salt bays, ocean, mudflats; tundra (summer). **Nest:** A thick bed of down in depression by tundra pool. Eggs (4–8) buff.

EMPEROR GOOSE *Philacte canagica* 26–28 Pls. 5, 6
Field marks: Alaskan. *Adult:* A small blue-gray goose *handsomely scaled* with black and white; identified by its *white head and hind neck.* Immature birds are not so distinctly marked and have the head and neck dusky, speckled with white.
Similar species: The Blue Goose (a straggler) also has a white head, but lacks the black throat. It has pink legs (Emperor, *yellow or orange*). Immature Blue (6–10 months) may have whitish face, dark throat (ill defined). Note leg color.

Voice: A hoarse *kla-ha, kla-ha.*
Where found: Ne. Siberia, w. Alaska. **West:** *Breeds* along coast of nw. Alaska (Kotzebue Sound to mouth of Kuskokwim River). *Winters* in Aleutians and east to Sanak I., Bristol Bay; strays south to Oregon, c. California (casual). **Habitat:** Tundra (summer), marshes, coastal littoral. **Nest:** A down-lined hollow by tundra pool, islet. Eggs (3–8) whitish.

WHITE-FRONTED GOOSE   Pls. 5, 6
Anser albifrons   26–34
Field marks: No other American goose except Emperor has *yellow or orange feet. Adult:* Gray-brown with a pink bill, white patch *on front of face,* and irregular *black bars* on belly (variable); white crescent on rump. *Immature:* Dusky with pale bill, *yellow or orange* feet; lacks distinctive marks of adult. A large dark race, *A. a. gambelli* (Tule Goose), is said to have a longer neck, slower wingbeats, deeper voice. (Winters chiefly in Sutter and Solano Cos., California.)
Similar species: Canada Goose, on water or overhead, shows contrast of black neck "stocking," light chest.
Voice: *Kah-lah-a-luck,* high-pitched "tootling," uttered from 1–3 times (J. Moffitt). *Kow-lyow* or *lyo-lyok.*
Where found: Arctic; circumpolar, except ne. Canada. Winters to Mexico, Gulf states, n. Africa, India. **West:** *Breeds* in w. and n. Alaska (south to Bristol Bay), arctic nw. Canada. *Winters* mainly from s. B.C. south through Pacific states. *Migrant* through Great Basin, Great Plains. **Habitat:** Marshes, prairies, fields, lakes, bays, tundra (summer). **Nest:** A down-lined depression in tundra. Eggs (4–7) creamy.

SNOW GOOSE   *Chen hyperborea*   25–31   Pls. 5, 6
Field marks: A *white* goose, smaller than the large Canada, with *black primaries.* Often rust-stained on head. Bill and feet pink. Young duskier, with dark bill, but recognizable.
Similar species: (1) Swans have *no black* in wings, have longer necks, more elegant shape. (2) At a great distance Snow Goose and White Pelican might be confused. (3) See Ross' Goose.
Voice: Loud, nasal, resonant *whouk* or *houck* uttered 1–2 (rarely 3) times (J. Moffitt). A conversational *zung-ung-ung.*
Where found: Ne. Siberia, arctic America. Winters to Japan, n. Mexico, Gulf Coast. **West:** *Breeds* from n. Alaska (Pt. Barrow) east into arctic Canada. *Migrates* throughout West. *Winters* in Central and Imperial Valleys of California; locally in Puget Sound, Lower Colorado River. **Habitat:** Tundra (summer); marshes, grainfields, prairies, ponds, bays. **Nest:** A down-lined hollow in tundra. Eggs (4–8) whitish.

BLUE GOOSE   *Chen caerulescens*   25–30   Pls. 5, 6
Field marks: A dark goose, size of the Snow, with a *white head*

and neck. Face often stained with rusty. Normally associates with Snow Goose and believed by most authorities to be a color phase of that bird. Intermediates with white breasts; dark backs occur. *Immature:* Dusky, similar to immature White-front, but bill and feet *dark;* wings paler, bluish.
Similar species: (1) Adult Emperor Goose (mainly Alaska) has black *on front of neck to chin.* (2) Immature White-front has light bill, yellow legs.
Voice: Exactly like Snow Goose's.
Where found: Islands near mouth of Hudson Bay; migrates via Manitoba, Mississippi Valley to Louisiana. **West:** Sometimes locally abundant in Saskatchewan. Scattered birds occur among flocks of Snows west to w. edge of Great Plains. Strays reach California. *Casual,* Oregon, Utah, Arizona, New Mexico.

ROSS' GOOSE   *Chen rossii*   21–25½   **Pl. 5**
Field marks: Ross' Goose is usually a bit *smaller* than the Snow (but size is a poor criterion — the two may overlap). The Ross may be known by its *small bill,* which shows no black "lips." Its neck is shorter, head rounder, less elongated (D. B. Marshall). Young bird is paler than young Snow.
Voice: No loud notes like Snow Goose's; a gruntlike *kug,* or weak *kek, kek* or *ke-gak, ke-gak;* suggests Cackling Goose.
Where found: Arctic Canada. *Breeds* on Perry River (ne. Mackenzie) and Southampton I. *Migrant* through Alberta, sw. Saskatchewan, w. Montana, Idaho (probably), se. Oregon, ne. California. *Winters* in California (Sacramento, San Joaquin and Imperial Valleys). *Casual,* se. Alaska, B.C., Utah, Nevada, Colorado, Arizona, Texas. **Habitat:** That of Snow Goose.
Nest: Down-lined; on tundra; in loose colony. Eggs (3–6) white.

Tree Ducks: Dendrocygninae

GOOSELIKE ducks with long legs, erect necks. Mainly found in warm-temperate and tropical regions. Called "Whistling Ducks." Sexes similar in color, as in geese, swans. **Food:** Grass, seeds.

BLACK-BELLIED TREE DUCK   **Pls. 8, 13**
Dendrocygna autumnalis   20–22
   Field marks: A gooselike duck with long pink legs. Rusty with *black belly,* bright *coral-pink* bill. Very broad *white patch* along forewing. Immature has gray bill and legs. Thrusts head and feet down when landing. Frequently perches in trees.
   Similar species: Muscovy Duck (Mexico) is larger, blacker, short-legged, with *squarish* white wing patch; does not whistle. Feral Muscovies (black or white) may be seen in U.S.
   Voice: A squealing whistle, *pe-che-che-ne.*

Where found: S. Texas to n. Argentina. Winters from s. Mexico, south. *Summers* in Rio Grande Delta; upriver to Rio Grande City; north locally to Corpus Christi. *Casual,* se. California, s. Arizona (has bred), s. New Mexico, w. Texas. **Habitat:** Ponds, resacas, fresh marshes. **Nest:** In tree cavity or in marsh. Eggs (12–16) whitish.

FULVOUS TREE DUCK

Pls. 8, 13

Dendrocygna bicolor   18–21

Field marks: Note the *tawny* body, dark back, and broad *creamy stripe* on the side. This long-legged, gangly gooselike duck does not ordinarily perch in trees. Flying, it looks dark, with blackish underwings and a *white crescent* at the tail base. Flies with slightly drooped neck, long legs extending beyond the tail, and slow wingbeats (for a duck). When alighting, the long "landing gear" and the head are thrust downward.

Similar species: (1) Cinnamon Teal is smaller, not gooselike; it is of a deeper color. (2) See Black-bellied Tree Duck.

Voice: In flight, a squealing slurred whistle, *ka-whee-oo* (R. M. Lockwood); a weak, whistled *kill-dee* (E. Kincaid).

Where found: California, Texas coast to Cent. America; also S. America, s. Asia, e. Africa. **West:** *Breeds* in c. and s. California, s. Nevada. *Winters* rarely. *Casual,* B.C., Washington, ne. California, Utah, s. Arizona, s. New Mexico, w. Texas. **Habitat:** Fresh marshes, irrigated land. **Nest:** In grass or marsh; rarely in tree cavity. Eggs (12–17; 32+) whitish.

Surface-feeding Ducks: Anatinae

"PUDDLE DUCKS" are characteristic of shallow waters, creeks, ponds, and marshes. They feed by dabbling and upending (they can dive, but seldom do); sometimes feed on land. They swim as a rule with the tail held off the water. When frightened, they spring directly into the air instead of taxiing along the water. Most species have a speculum, an iridescent patch on the trailing edge of the wing. This may be concealed when swimming. Sexes unlike in breeding plumage, but in summer most male ducks molt into a drab plumage known as the "eclipse." The phase is not covered in this book — first, because most ducks are not much in evidence during this period, and second, because they look enough like the females as to be readily identifiable. Before summer is out most species commence their second molt, in which they regain their bright pattern. See Francis H. Kortright's *The Ducks, Geese and Swans of North America* (1953) for pictures and descriptions of eclipse plumages and hybrids. **Food:** Aquatic plants, seeds, grass, small aquatic animals, insects.

MALLARD *Anas platyrhynchos* 20½–28 **Pls. 7, 9, 14**
Field marks: *Male:* Known by the uncrested *glossy green head, narrow white collar.* Grayish, with chestnut breast; white tail with upcurled black central feathers ("duck-tail"), yellowish bill, orange feet, purple-blue speculum. *Female:* Mottled; brown with a *whitish tail.* Bill dark, patched with orange, feet orange. Note in flight the conspicuous white borders *on each side* of the violet blue speculum.
Similar species: (1) Several other ducks have green-glossed heads, but white neck-ring and ruddy breast mark male Mallard (see Red-breasted Merganser). (2) Female Pintails are more streamlined and have a conspicuous white border only on rear edge of dull speculum. Bill of Pintail is gray; that of Mallard usually orange and black. In flight Mallard's wing-linings are whiter. (3) Along Rio Grande see Mexican Duck.
Voice: Female, a boisterous *quack, quack-quack, quack, quack-quack,* descending. Male, a quiet *yeeb;* a low *kwek.*
Where found: Northern parts of N. Hemisphere. Winters to Mexico, n. Africa, India. **West:** *Breeds* from Aleutians, Pribilofs, n.-c. Alaska, c. Mackenzie south to c. California, Arizona, s. New Mexico. *Winters* from s. Alaska, s. Canada south to Mexico.
Habitat: Fresh marshes, irrigated land, grainfields, ponds, rivers, lakes, bays. **Nest:** A down-lined hollow among reeds or grass; rarely in tree crotch or nest of Crow, hawk, magpie. Eggs (8–10; 15) greenish buff.

MEXICAN DUCK *Anas diazi* 20–22 **Pls. 7, 14**
(New Mexican Duck)
Field marks: Both sexes very similar to female Mallard but with a plain *grayish brown* instead of whitish tail. Bill of male like male Mallard's (unmarked yellowish green). Yellow-orange bill of female has a dark ridge rather than usual mottling of female Mallard. Frequently hybridizes with Mallard.
Similar species: Not as dark as Black Duck; more like Mottled Duck of Gulf of Mexico but usually with a white border *on each side* of metallic wing patch as in female Mallard. Black and Mottled Ducks do not normally occur in New Mexico or w. Texas.
Voice: Similar to Mallard's.
Where found: Rare *summer resident* from n. New Mexico south locally in Rio Grande Valley to w. Texas (El Paso; rarely to Big Bend); very locally in sw. New Mexico; south to highlands of c. Mexico. *Winters* mainly south of border. *Accidental,* Colorado, Nebraska. **Habitat:** Similar to Mallard's.

BLACK DUCK *Anas rubripes* 21–25½ **Pls. 7, 9, 14**
Field marks: The Black Duck in flight is *very dark,* with flashing *white wing-linings.* It is sooty brown with a lighter gray-brown

head and a metallic violet wing patch. Feet may be red or brown; bill yellowish or greenish. Sexes similar.

Similar species: (1) Mottled Duck (Texas coast) has identical wing pattern (white border on *rear edge* of speculum only), but is browner, approaching color of female Mallard. (2) Mexican Duck (Rio Grande) and (3) female Mallard are less dark, with a white border on *both edges* of speculum.

Voice: Similar to Mallard's.

Where found: Ne. N. America. Winters south to Gulf Coast. **West:** Mainly a straggler west of 100°. Rare but regular in Saskatchewan. Recorded casually in Mackenzie, Alberta, and in most w. states. **Habitat:** Similar to Mallard's.

GADWALL *Anas strepera* 18½–23   **Pls. 7, 9, 14**
Field marks: *Male:* A slender gray duck with a *black rump,* a *white patch* on the *hind* edge of the wing, and a dull reddish patch on the forewing. When bird swims, the side feathers usually conceal the wing patches; then note the jet-black stern, which contrasts sharply with the gray plumage. Belly white, feet yellow. Male has a more abrupt forehead than similar ducks, darker crown. *Female:* Brown, mottled; *white speculum,* yellow feet, yellow on bill.

Similar species: (1) Female Pintail has obscure speculum, gray feet (not seen when swimming); at close range shows solid gray bill. (2) Female American Widgeon has ruddy sides, gray head, light bluish bill. White wing patch is on *fore edge* of spread wing. Some young Widgeons show so little white on wing that they might be confused with Gadwall, but they swim with stern high in Widgeon fashion. (3) See female Mallard.

Voice: Female quacks loudly, in falling diminuendo, *kaaak-kaaak-kak-kak-kak.* Male has a low *bek;* also a whistled call.

Where found: S. Alaska, Canada, n. U.S., n. Eurasia. Winters south to Mexico, Africa, India. **West:** *Breeds* from se. Alaska, s. B.C., c. Alberta, c. Saskatchewan south to c. California, sw. Arizona, nw. New Mexico, nw. Texas (rarely). *Winters* from s. Alaska (Kodiak), s. B.C., Utah, Colorado south. **Habitat:** Lakes, ponds, rivers, fresh marshes. **Nest:** A down-lined hollow in thick grass or under bush. Eggs (7–13) whitish.

PINTAIL *Anas acuta* ♂ 25–29, ♀ 20½–22½   **Pls. 7, 9, 14**
Field marks: Male Pintails are slender white-breasted ducks with slim necks, quite different in cut from other ducks of ponds and marshes. They have long, *needle-pointed* tails. A conspicuous *white point* runs from the neck onto the side of the brown head. A white patch near the black stern. *Female:* Note the somewhat pointed tail. Mottled brown with a slender neck. In flight shows 1 *light border* on rear of speculum.

Similar species: (1) Oldsquaw, only other duck with a needle-

pointed tail, is not a marsh duck. See (2) female Mallard, (3) female American Widgeon, (4) female Gadwall.
Voice: Seldom vocal. Male utters a double-toned whistle, also wheezy teal-like notes. Female has a low *quack*.
Where found: Northern parts of N. Hemisphere. Winters south to n. S. America, Africa, India. **West:** *Breeds* from arctic Alaska, n. Mackenzie south locally to c. California, n. Arizona, Colorado, n. Texas (rarely). *Winters* mainly in Pacific states north to s. Alaska; in interior north to Utah, Colorado; also Hawaii. **Habitat:** Marshes, prairies, grainfields, fresh ponds, lakes, salt bays. **Nest:** A down-lined hollow; in marsh or on prairie. Eggs (6–12) olive-buff.

COMMON TEAL *Anas crecca* 13–15½   **Pl. 14**
(European Teal)
  Field marks: *Male:* Note the *horizontal white stripe* on scapulars, above wing. Otherwise very similar to male Green-winged Teal, but lacks vertical white mark on side in front of wing. Female indistinguishable from Female Green-wing.
  Where found: Iceland, n. Europe, Asia. **West:** *Resident* in Aleutians from Akutan westward. *Casual,* Pribilofs. *Accidental,* B.C., Oregon, Arizona. **Habitat:** Similar to Green-wing's.

GREEN-WINGED TEAL   **Pls. 7, 9, 14**
Anas carolinensis 12½–15½
  Field marks: When ducks fly from the marsh, teal are conspicuous by their small size. If they show no large light wing patches, they are this species. *Male:* A small compact gray duck with brown head, *vertical white mark* on side in front of wing, and cream-colored patch near tail. In sunlight, shows an iridescent *green speculum* and green patch on side of head. *Female:* A diminutive speckled duck with a green speculum.
  Similar species: (1) Blue-winged and (2) Cinnamon Teal (both sexes) have light blue wing patches. In flight, from below, males show dark bellies; Green-wings, white bellies. Female Green-wings, though smaller, shorter-necked, and shorter-billed, are difficult to distinguish unless absence of blue wing patch is seen. (3) In w. Aleutians see Common Teal.
  Voice: Male utters a short whistle, sometimes repeated; also froglike peeping notes. Female has a crisp *quack*.
  Where found: Northern parts of N. America. Winters to Cent. America, W. Indies. **West:** *Breeds* from Pribilofs, e. Aleutians, c. Alaska, Great Slave Lake south to n. California, e. Arizona, n. New Mexico, n. Nebraska. *Winters* from se. Alaska, Utah, Montana to Mexico. **Habitat:** Marshes, lakes, ponds, rivers, bays. **Nest:** A down-lined hollow in grass or marsh. Eggs (10–12; 18) whitish, buff.

BLUE-WINGED TEAL *Anas discors* 14½–16 **Pls. 7, 9, 14**
Field marks: *Male:* A little half-sized marsh duck; small, dull-colored, with large *white crescent in front of eye,* and large *chalky-blue* patch *on forewing.* The blue at a distance may look whitish. White patch on flank near black tail. Males hold eclipse plumage longer than most ducks (often through end of year) and most birds seen in fall lack the white face crescent or show it poorly. They resemble females. *Female:* Brown, mottled, with large blue patch on forewing.
Similar species: (1) Male Cinnamon Teal (blue wing patches) can be told by deep mahogany color. (In poor light, that species and autumn male Blue-wing without face crescent both may look dark-bodied with pale wing patches.) (2) Shoveler (big bill) also has pale blue wing patches. (3) Female Scaup also has white patch before eye. (4) See Green-winged Teal.
Voice: Males utter peeping notes; females, a light quack.
Where found: Canada to s. U.S. Winters to S. America. **West:** *Breeds* from s.-c. Alaska, Great Slave Lake south (mainly east of Cascades) to n.-c. California, Utah, s. New Mexico, c. Texas. *Winters* from c. California, s. Texas south. **Habitat:** Fresh ponds, marshes. **Nest:** A down-lined hollow among grass near water. Eggs (6–12; 15) whitish.

CINNAMON TEAL *Anas cyanoptera* 14½–17 **Pls. 7, 9, 14**
Field marks: *Male:* A small, dark cinnamon-red duck with a large chalky-blue patch on fore edge of wing. *Female:* A small mottled brown duck with pale blue wing patch.
Similar species: (1) On wing resembles Blue-winged Teal (females cannot be separated except by their associates). (2) Only other small rufous duck is male Ruddy (white cheeks).
Voice: Seldom vocal; male, a low chattering; female, a *quack.*
Where found: Sw. Canada to Mexico; S. America. *Breeds* from s.-c. B.C., s. Alberta south to s. California, Mexico; east to w. Saskatchewan, e. Montana, e. Wyoming, e. Colorado, e. New Mexico, w. Texas. Nearly absent west of Cascades. *Winters* from c. California, c. Nevada, s. Arizona, s. New Mexico south. **Habitat:** Fresh ponds, rivers, marshes. **Nest:** A down-lined hollow in reeds or grass. Eggs (6–12; 14) whitish, buff.

EUROPEAN WIDGEON *Mareca penelope* 16½–20 **Pl. 14**
Field marks: *Male:* Note the *red-brown* head, *buff* crown. A gray widgeon with a pinkish breast. *Female:* Very similar to female American Widgeon, but head is tinged with *reddish* (gray in American). The surest point in the hand is the dusky axillars (in "wingpits"). These are dusky (white in American).
Similar species: (1) Suggests Redhead duck (which has black chest). (2) Male American Widgeon (Baldpate) is *brown,* with a gray head, *white* crown. Female, see above.

Voice: Male, a whistle, *whee-oo.* Female, a purr; a *quack.*
Where found: Iceland, Eurasia. Regular winter visitor to N. America. **West:** Most records near coast (Alaska to interior c. California); scattered records in Great Basin and east of Rockies. **Habitat:** Similar to American Widgeon's.

AMERICAN WIDGEON *Mareca americana* 18-23
(Baldpate) **Pls. 7, 9, 14**
Field marks: Note the shining white crown of the male. In flight, widgeons are recognized by the large white patch on the inner forewing; in other marsh ducks possessing white patches they are on the hind edge. (Similarly placed blue patches of Blue-winged Teal, Cinnamon Teal, and Shoveler may appear whitish.) On water, rides high, picking about surface like a Coot. Often grazes on land. *Male:* Brownish, with gray head, white crown; patch on head deep glossy green; large white patch on forewing and white patch on flank near tail; bill pale blue with black tip. *Female:* Ruddy brown, with gray head and neck; belly and forewing whitish. *Immature:* Brownish, with paler gray head and neck; white belly contrasts with brown breast. **Similar species:** Female is easily confused with (1) female Gadwall and (2) female Pintail. Gray head contrasting with brown breast is best mark; bill paler, bluish. Has whitish wing patches similar to male's. (3) See European Widgeon.
Voice: A whistled *whee whee whew* (male). *Qua-ack* (female).
Where found: Alaska, w. Canada, n. U.S. Winters to Cent. America, W. Indies. **West:** *Breeds* from n.-c. Alaska, nw. Mackenzie south (east of Cascades) to ne. California, n. Nevada, n. New Mexico, nw. Nebraska. *Winters* from s. Alaska, s. B.C., Utah, Colorado south. Also Hawaii. **Habitat:** Fresh marshes, irrigated land, ponds, lakes, bays. **Nest:** A down-lined hollow in grass, often away from water. Eggs (6-12) cream-white.

SHOVELER *Spatula clypeata* 17-20 **Pls. 7, 9, 14**
Field marks: Note the spoon-shaped bill. A small duck; in flight the big bill makes the wings seem set well back. Swimming, the bird sits low, the bill pointed toward the water. *Male:* Largely black and white; belly and *sides rufous;* head blackish glossed with green; breast white; pale blue patch on forewing. Orange legs. On water or overhead the pattern is unique, with alternating contrast: dark, white, dark, white, dark. *Female:* Mottled brownish; big bill, pale blue wing patches, orange legs.
Similar species: Wing pattern suggests Blue-winged Teal.
Voice: Female, a light quack; male a low *took, took, took.*
Where found: Widespread in N. Hemisphere. Winters to Cent. America, Africa. **West:** *Breeds* from w. Alaska, Mackenzie Bay,

Great Slave Lake south to s. California (rarely), s.-c. New Mexico, Nebraska. *Winters* from coast of s. B.C., se. Washington, Utah, Colorado south; also Hawaii. **Habitat:** Fresh marshes, ponds, sloughs; also salt bays (winter). **Nest:** A down-lined hollow in grass or sedge. Eggs (6–14) pale olive.

WOOD DUCK *Aix sponsa* 17–20½ **Pls. 7, 9, 13**
Field marks: The most highly colored duck. Often perches in trees. On the wing, the white belly contrasts strikingly with the dark breast and wings. The long square dark tail, short neck, and angle at which the bill points downward are also good points. *Male:* Note the bizarre face pattern, crest, rainbow iridescence. *Female:* Dark brown with lighter flanks, white belly, dark crested head, *white patch surrounding eye.*
Similar species: In flight, female and young American Widgeon suggest female Wood Duck but have pointed tails.
Voice: A loud distressed *whoo-eek;* a finchlike *jeee,* with rising inflection (male); *crrek, crrek* (female).
Where found: S. Canada, nw. and e. U.S., Cuba. Winters to Mexico, Cuba. **West:** *Breeds* in sw. B.C., s. Alberta (rarely), e. Saskatchewan (rarely), Washington, n. Idaho, nw. Montana, w. and c. Oregon, c. California; rarely Arizona, New Mexico. Occasional transient elsewhere in w. U.S. *Winters* from sw. B.C. (rarely) through Pacific states to s. California; a few from Colorado south. **Habitat:** Wooded swamps and rivers, ponds. **Nest:** A bed of down in tree cavity. Eggs (10–15; 31) whitish.

Diving Ducks: Aythyinae

"SEA DUCKS" or "bay ducks" they are also called, but many are found commonly on lakes and rivers, and breed in marshes. All dive, whereas surface-feeding ducks rarely dive. The hind toe has a paddle-like flap (lacking in surface-feeders). In taking wing they patter along surface while getting under way (legs are placed closer to tail). Sexes unlike. **Food:** Small aquatic animals and plants. Sea ducks eat mollusks and crustaceans.

REDHEAD *Aythya americana* 18–22 **Pls. 8, 10, 11**
Field marks: *Male:* Gray with a black chest and *round red-brown head;* bill blue with black tip. *Female:* Brownish with a *suffused light patch* about base of bill. Both sexes have broad gray wing-stripes.
Similar species: (1) Male Canvasback is much whiter, with long sloping forehead and black bill (Redhead has abrupt forehead, blue bill). Redhead is chunkier, more like Greater Scaup in contour. (2) Male Scaup on wing has a black and white pattern (Redhead is gray with gray wing-stripe). (3) Female Scaup has

a *white* wing-stripe, a *sharply defined* white patch near bill, and a *yellow* eye (female Redhead has dark eye). (4) Other female ducks showing broad *gray* wing-stripes are Canvasback (larger, paler, with long profile); and Ring-neck (smaller, darker, with whiter ring on bill, whiter eye-ring, darker crown).
Voice: Male, a catlike *meow;* a deep purr. Female, a *squak.*
Where found: W. Canada, w. and n.-c. U.S. Winters to Mexico, W. Indies. **West:** *Breeds* from c. B.C., n. Alberta, c. Saskatchewan south locally to c. and sw. California, c. Nevada, Arizona, nw. New Mexico, s. Colorado, w. Nebraska. *Winters* from s. B.C., Utah, ne. Colorado south. *Casual,* Alaska. **Habitat:** Fresh marshes (summer), lakes, estuaries. **Nest:** A down-lined basket in tules, reeds. Eggs (10–15) buff.

RING-NECKED DUCK   Pls. 8, 10, 11
Aythya collaris   14½–18
Field marks: *Male:* Like a *black-backed* Lesser Scaup. Head, chest, and back black; sides light gray with *conspicuous vertical white mark in front of wing;* bill crossed by a white ring. In flight, our only black-backed duck with a broad *gray* wing-stripe. The dull chestnut neck-ring is seldom visible. *Female:* Brown, darkest on crown and back; wing-stripe *grayish;* indistinct whitish area about base of bill; *white eye-ring and ring on bill;* eye dark. Note the rather triangular head shape.
Similar species: (1) Female Scaup has a well-defined white face "mask," *yellow* eye, and, in flight, a *white* wing-stripe; lacks white eye-ring and ring on bill. (2) Female Redhead is larger, paler, with *less* contrast; rings about eye and on bill less conspicuous or lacking.
Voice: ♀, similar to Lesser Scaup's. ♂, a low hissing whistle.
Where found: Canada, n. U.S. Winters to Panama, W. Indies. **West:** *Breeds* from c. B.C. across Alberta, Saskatchewan. "Colonies" in ne. Washington, s. Oregon, w. Montana, ne. Nevada, nw. Wyoming, sw. Colorado; rarely elsewhere. *Winters* mainly from s. B.C. through Pacific states; sparingly in w. Nevada, Colorado, New Mexico, w. Texas. *Casual,* Alaska. **Habitat:** Coniferous lakes, wooded ponds; in winter also marsh ponds, rivers, bays. **Nest:** A down-lined grass cup in marsh. Eggs (6–12; 14) olive-buff.

CANVASBACK   *Aythya valisineria*   19½–24   Pls. 8, 10, 11
Field marks: Note the *long sloping head profile* (both sexes). *Male:* A very white-looking duck with a *rusty-red head and neck,* black breast, long *blackish* bill. *Female:* Grayish, with a suggestion of pale red on head and neck. Travels in lines or V-formation. The long head and neck give a front-heavy look.
Similar species: (1) See Redhead. (2) Female mergansers (redheaded) have crests and whitish chests. (3) See scaups.

Voice: Male, a low croak; growling notes. Female, a *quack*.
Where found: Alaska, w. Canada, nw. U.S. Winters to Mexico,
Atlantic and Gulf Coasts. **West:** *Breeds* in c. Alaska (upper
Yukon), n. Mackenzie; and from Great Slave Lake south (east
of Cascades) to ne. California, n. Nevada, n. Utah, n. Colorado,
w. Nebraska. *Winters* from s. B.C. through Pacific states;
locally in Great Basin and Rocky Mt. states. **Habitat:** Fresh
marshes (summer), lakes, salt bays, estuaries. **Nest:** A down-
lined basket among reeds. Eggs (7–9) gray-green.

GREATER SCAUP   below, Pls. 10, 11
Aythya marila   15½–20

Field marks: Similar to the Lesser Scaup, but averages larger;
male whiter on flanks; head rounder, glossed mainly with *green*
(Lesser has a higher crown and is glossed with dull purple).
These points are evident only nearby in good light. The length
of the wing-stripe in flight is the surest way to separate typical
birds (both sexes). The white in the Lesser extends only halfway
along the rear edge of the wing; in the Greater it extends onto
the primaries. There are occasional intermediates.
Voice: Similar to Lesser Scaup's.
Where found: Alaska, Canada, n. Eurasia. Winters to Mexico,
W. Indies, Mediterranean, India. **West:** *Breeds* from n. Alaska,
n. Mackenzie to Great Slave Lake; rarely to nw. B.C. *Winters*
mainly from se. Alaska south along coast to s. California (rarely).
Much scarcer inland than Lesser Scaup. **Habitat:** Lakes, rivers,

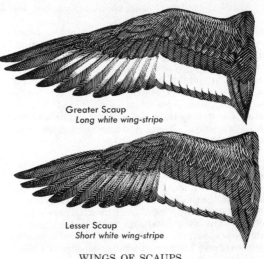

Greater Scaup
Long white wing-stripe

Lesser Scaup
Short white wing-stripe

WINGS OF SCAUPS

tundra ponds (summer), salt bays, estuaries. **Nest:** A down-lined depression on ground. Eggs (7–10; 22) olive-buff.

LESSER SCAUP *Aythya affinis* 15–18½   **p. 38, Pls. 8, 11**
Field marks: *Male:* Scaups on the water appear "black at both ends and white in the middle." The flanks and back are finely barred, but at any distance those parts appear whitish. The bill is blue; head glossed with dull purple. *Female:* Dark brown, with a clean-cut white "mask" at base of bill. In flight scaups (both sexes) are our only ducks possessing a broad white stripe on trailing edge of wing.
Similar species: See Greater Scaup.
Voice: A loud *scaup;* purring notes; a low whistle (♂).
Where found: Alaska, w. Canada. Winters to n. S. America. **West:** *Breeds* in interior from c. Alaska, Mackenzie south locally to Oregon, ne. California, s. Idaho; east of Rockies to ne. Colorado, Nebraska; locally also in c. New Mexico. *Winters* from s. B.C., Utah, Colorado south. **Habitat:** Fresh marshes, ponds (summer); lakes, salt bays, estuaries. **Nest:** A down-lined hollow in grass. Eggs (9–12; 15) olive-buff.

COMMON GOLDENEYE *Bucephala clangula* 16–20
(American Goldeneye)   **Pls. 8, 10, 11**
Field marks: *Male:* Note the large *round white spot* before the eye. A white-looking duck with a black back and puffy green-glossed head (black at a distance). In flight, short-necked; wings show large white patches. Legs orange. *Female:* Gray with a white collar and dark-brown head; wings with large square white patches (showing also on closed wing). The "singing" of the Goldeneye's wings has earned it the nickname "Whistler."
Similar species: (1) See Barrow's Goldeneye. (2) Scaup at a distance bears a slight resemblance but has a black chest. (3) Male Common Merganser (white-chested) is long-lined, low, with an attenuated profile; lacks face spot.
Voice: Courting males have a harsh nasal double note, suggesting *pee-ik* of Nighthawk. Female, a harsh *quack.*
Where found: Northern parts of N. Hemisphere. Winters to Gulf Coast, s. Eurasia. **West:** *Breeds* from c. Alaska, n. Mackenzie, Great Slave Lake south to s. B.C., nw. Montana, c. Alberta, s. Saskatchewan. *Winters* from Aleutians, se. Alaska, s. Alberta south to s. California, Arizona, New Mexico, Texas. **Habitat:** Lakes, rivers; in winter also salt bays, ocean. **Nest:** In cavity in tree near lake or river. Eggs (5–12; 19) pale green.

BARROW'S GOLDENEYE   **Pl. 11**
Bucephala islandica 16½–20
Field marks: *Male:* Note the white *crescent* in front of the eye. (Common Goldeneye has a *round* white spot.) The Barrow's shows more black on its upper parts. The head is glossed with *purple* (not green); the crown is lower, nape more puffy. *Female:*

Very similar to Goldeneye; bill shorter and deeper, forehead more abrupt. As spring approaches the bill may become *all yellow* (said to be a good mark).
Voice: A hoarse croak. Also a mewing cry (courting males).
Where found: Alaska, Canada, nw. U.S., sw. Greenland, Iceland.
West: *Breeds* from s.-c. Alaska, n. Mackenzie south in mts. locally to e. California (Sierra), nw. Wyoming. *Winters* mainly on coast from s. Alaska to c. California (rarely); some in n. Rocky Mt. region. **Habitat:** Wooded lakes, beaver ponds; in winter, coastal waters, a few on inland rivers. **Nest:** In cavity in tree (sometimes in cliff). Eggs (6–12; 15) greenish.

BUFFLEHEAD *Bucephala albeola* 13–15½   **Pls. 8, 10, 13**
Field marks: One of the smallest ducks. *Male:* Mostly white, with black back; puffy head with *great white patch* from eye around back of head; large white wing patches in flight. Suggests small Goldeneye. *Female:* Note the *white* cheek spot. Dark and compact, with large head, small bill, white wing patch.
Similar species: (1) See Hooded Merganser. The dark female Bufflehead can be mistaken for a male Hooded Merganser with its crest laid back. The Merganser has a spikelike bill. (2) See also winter Ruddy Duck.
Voice: A hoarse rolling note; also a squeaky call (male). A hoarse *quack* (female).
Where found: Alaska, Canada. Winters to Mexico, Gulf Coast.
West: *Breeds* from coast of s. Alaska, upper Yukon Valley, Great Slave Lake south to s. B.C., nw. Wyoming, s. Saskatchewan. Also rarely in Oregon, ne. California. *Winters* from Aleutians, s. B.C., s. Alberta south. **Habitat:** Lakes, ponds, rivers; in winter, also salt bays. **Nest:** In tree cavity near water. Eggs (6–12; 16) pale buff.

OLDSQUAW   **Pls. 8, 10, 12**
Clangula hyemalis ♂ 19–22½, ♀ 15–17
Field marks: Oldsquaws are the only sea ducks combining *much white on the body and unpatterned dark wings*. They bunch in irregular flocks. *Male in winter:* Note the *long needle-pointed* tail. Boldly patterned; head, neck, belly, and scapulars white; breast, back, and wings dusky brown; dark patch on cheek; short bill banded with black and pink. *Male in summer:* Dark with white flanks and belly; white patch surrounding eye. *Female in summer:* Similar but darker.
Similar species: See Pintail (a marsh duck).
Voice: Talkative; a musical *ow-owdle-ow,* or *owl-omelet.*
Where found: Arctic; circumpolar. Winters to s. U.S., c. Europe, c. Asia. **West:** *Breeds* from Arctic coasts to Aleutians and s. limits of Barren Grounds. *Winters* mainly along coast from Aleutians to Washington; a few to s. California. Migrates

through n. Alberta, Saskatchewan; sparse inland in w. U.S.
Habitat: Ocean, large lakes; tundra pools (summer). **Nest:** A
down-lined hollow near tundra pool. Eggs (5–7; 17) olive-buff.

HARLEQUIN DUCK   Pls. 10, 12
Histrionicus histrionicus   14½–21
   Field marks: Dark and bizarre. *Male:* A smallish blue-gray
duck (blackish at a distance) with chestnut sides and odd white
patches and spots, best explained by the plate. In flight it has
the stubby shape of a goldeneye, but appears uniformly dark.
Sometimes cocks its tail. *Female:* Dusky with 3 round white
spots on side of head; no wing patch.
   Similar species: (1) Female Bufflehead has *1* elongated spot
behind eye and a white patch on wing. Female scoters are larger
with larger bills (female Harlequin suggests pattern of female
Surf Scoter, shape of Bufflehead).
   Voice: A squeak. Also *gua gua gua* (♂); *ek-ek-ek-ek* (♀).
   Where found: Ne. Asia, Alaska, Canada, w. U.S., Greenland,
Iceland. **West:** *Breeds* from Aleutians and c.-w. Alaska south
locally in mts. to c. California (Sierra) and Wyoming. *Winters*
along coast from Bering Sea to c. (rarely s.) California. *Casual,*
Nevada, Saskatchewan. **Habitat:** Turbulent mt. streams; in
winter, rough coastal water. **Nest:** On ground near mt. stream
or in hole in tree or cliff. Eggs (5–10) pale buff.

STELLER'S EIDER *Polysticta stelleri* 17–18½   Pl. 12
   Field marks: *Male:* Black and white, with *rufous-buff underparts; white head,* black throat and green bump on back of
head. Note the *round black spot* on side of breast. As in other
eiders, white forewing conspicuous in flight. *Female:* Dark
brown, mottled; white wing-bar and purple speculum visible at
short range. Distinguished from other eiders by much smaller
size and *shape of small head and bill* (see diagram opp. Plate
12).
   Voice: Male's crooning note resembles Common Eider's, but
quieter. Female has low growl.
   Where found: Coasts of arctic Siberia, n. Alaska. **West:** *Breeds*
from Arctic coast of Alaska (and probably nw. Mackenzie) south
to mouth of Kuskokwim. *Winters* in Pribilofs and Aleutians;
east to Kodiak. *Casual,* B.C. **Habitat:** Coasts, ocean. **Nest:** A
down-lined hollow on coastal tundra. Eggs (6–10) olive-buff.

COMMON EIDER *Somateria mollissima* 23–27   Pls. 8, 12
   Field marks: Eiders are oceanic, living about n. shoals. They
are bulky and thick-necked; their flight is sluggish and low, usually in a line, often alternately flapping and sailing; the head is
rather low-hung. *Male:* This species and the Spectacled Eider are
the only ducks combining *black bellies* and *entirely white backs.*
Breast and forepart of inner wing white. Head white, with black

crown and pale green nape. The Alaskan birds have a black line along each side of throat, joining in front to form a V. *Female:* A large brown duck with a long flat profile; body heavily *barred* (among female ducks only eiders are so completely *barred*). Immature males are at first grayish brown, later dusky with a white collar; still later may have chocolate heads or breasts, the white areas coming in irregularly.

Similar species: (1) Male Spectacled Eider has large white "goggles." Female also has a suggestion of goggles. (2) Male King Eider has a *black* lower back. Females of King and Common Eiders are difficult to tell apart: Common Eider has a more sloping Canvasback-like profile (see diagram opp. Plate 12). (3) Female scoters are duskier, without the heavy barrings.

Voice: Male has a loud moaning *coo-roo-uh,* 2nd syllable rising and emphasized. Female, a grating *kor-r-r.*

Where found: Northern parts of N. Hemisphere. **West:** *Breeds* from Arctic coast south to Aleutians, s. coast of Alaska; east to Glacier Bay. *Winters* from Aleutians, Alaska Peninsula south casually to Washington. *Casual* inland in n. Canada. *Accidental,* Colorado. **Habitat:** Salt water, rocky coasts, islands. **Nest:** A down-lined hollow on coastal tundra or on island; often in loose colony. Eggs (4–7; 10) olive-buff.

KING EIDER *Somateria spectabilis* 18½–25 **Pls. 8, 12**
Field marks: *Male:* A large, stocky duck. At a distance the foreparts appear white, rear parts mainly black; the only duck with this effect. Wings with large white patches; top of head pearl-gray; cheeks greenish; bill and large knob on forehead orange. *Female:* Stocky, warm brown, heavily barred with black. *Immature male:* Dusky, with light breast, dark brown head. The amount of white varies in birds changing to adult.

Similar species: (1) Male Common and Spectacled Eiders have *entirely white backs.* (2) Female Common Eider's bill extends to a long point before the eye; King Eider has shorter, more rounded lobes (see diagram opp. Plate 12). (3) Female Goldeneye might be confused with immature male King Eider.

Voice: Male has crooning notes, accent on final syllable.

Where found: Arctic regions of N. Hemisphere. **West:** *Breeds* on islands in n. Bering Sea and along Arctic coast north of Bering Strait. *Winters* from Bering Sea south to Aleutians, Kodiak. *Casual,* B.C., Washington, c. California. *Accidental,* Alberta. **Habitat:** Coasts, ocean. **Nest:** A down-lined hollow in tundra. Eggs (4–7) olive-buff.

SPECTACLED EIDER **Pl. 12**
Lampronetta fischeri 20½–22½
Field marks: Note the "spectacles." *Male:* Grotesque; black below, white above, suggesting male Common Eider, but head largely pale green, with large *white "goggles"* narrowly rimmed

with black. *Female:* Brown and barred like other eiders but with a pale *ghost image of the goggles.* Feathering at base of bill extends past nostril.

Where found: Ne. Siberia, n. Alaska. **West:** *Breeds* on Arctic coasts of nw. Alaska from Pt. Barrow south to Baird Inlet. *Winters* in Pribilofs and in Aleutians; east to Sanak, Kodiak. *Accidental,* B.C., California. **Habitat:** Arctic coasts. **Nest:** A down-lined hollow in tundra. Eggs (5–9) olive-buff.

WHITE-WINGED SCOTER   Pls. 8, 10, 12
Melanitta deglandi   19–23½

Field marks: The scoters are the heavy blackish ducks seen coastwise, flying in stringy formation low over the waves. The White-wing is the largest of the 3 species. When it swims the wing patch is often concealed by the side and flank feathers (wait for it to flap its wings). *Male:* Black with squarish *white patch* on rear edge of spread wing and tick of white just below the eye; bill orange with black knob. *Female:* Sooty brown with *white wing patch* and 2 light patches on side of head (sometimes obscure; more pronounced in young birds).

Similar species: See Surf and Common Scoters.

Voice: In flight, "a bell-like low whistle in a series of 6–8 notes" (F. H. Kortright). Said to be produced by wings.

Where found: Alaska, n. Canada; winters to s. U.S. (both coasts). **West:** *Breeds* from n.-c. Alaska (Ft. Yukon), Mackenzie Delta south to s.-c. B.C., s. Alberta, c. N. Dakota. Many non-breeders summer along coast. *Winters* mainly along coast from Aleutians to Baja California. A few migrate inland in w. U.S. **Habitat:** Salt bays; oceans; when nesting, large lakes. **Nest:** A down-lined hollow often under bush. Eggs (9–14) pinkish.

SURF SCOTER *Melanitta perspicillata* 17–21 **Pls. 8, 10, 12**

Field marks: The "Skunk-Duck." *Male:* Black, with 1 or 2 *white patches* on crown and nape. Bill patterned with orange, black, white. *Female:* Dusky brown; 2 light spots on side of head (sometimes obscured; more evident on young birds).

Similar species: (1) Female White-wing is similarly marked around head, but has white wing patches (which often do not show until bird flaps). (2) See Common Scoter.

Voice: Usually silent. A low croak; grunting notes.

Where found: Alaska, nw. Canada. Winters to s. U.S. (both coasts). **West:** *Breeds* from w. and n. Alaska, Mackenzie Delta south to Great Slave Lake. Large nonbreeding flocks summer from s. Alaska to Oregon. *Winters* on coast from Aleutians to Baja California. Migrates inland in B.C., Alberta. *Casual* inland in w. U.S. **Habitat:** Ocean surf, salt bays; in summer, fresh lakes, tundra. **Nest:** A down-lined hollow under bush or in marsh. Eggs (5–9) pale buff.

COMMON SCOTER *Oidemia nigra* 17–20½ **Pls. 8, 10, 12**
(American Scoter, "Black Scoter")
  Field marks: *Male:* The only adult American duck with *entirely* black plumage. This, and the bright yellow-orange knob on the bill ("butter-nose") are diagnostic. In flight, from below has a 2-toned wing effect, more pronounced than in other scoters. *Female:* Sooty; *light cheeks* contrasting with *dark cap.*
  Similar species: (1) Coot is blackish, but has white bill, white patch under tail. Gunners often call scoters "coots." (2) Some young male Surf Scoters may lack head patches and appear all black. Look for round black spot at base of bill of Surf Scoter. (3) Females of the other scoters have 2 light spots on each side of head. (4) Female Common Scoter suggests winter Ruddy Duck (which is smaller, paler; has light chest).
  Voice: Melodious cooing notes (male); growls (female).
  Where found: Alaska, Iceland, n. Eurasia. Winters to s. U.S., Mediterranean. **West:** *Breeds* from Arctic coast of Alaska south to Bristol Bay; rarely, Mt. McKinley National Park, Kodiak. *Winters* along coast from Aleutians to s. California (rarely). *Accidental* inland (e. Oregon, Wyoming, Colorado). **Habitat:** Coast; coastal tundra (summer). **Nest:** A down-lined hollow near water; well hidden. Eggs (6–10) buff.

Stiff-tailed Ducks: Oxyurinae

SMALL, chunky ducks that are nearly helpless on land. The spiky tail has 18 or 20 feathers. Sexes unlike. **Food:** Small aquatic life, insects, water plants.

RUDDY DUCK *Oxyura jamaicensis* 14½–16 **Pls. 8, 10, 13**
  Field marks: A small, chubby duck, unpatterned except for *conspicuous white cheeks,* dark cap. The short wing stroke gives it a "buzzy" flight. Often cocks its tail vertically. It cannot walk on land. *Male in breeding plumage:* Rusty red with *white cheeks,* black cap, large blue bill. *Male in winter:* Gray with *white cheeks,* dark cap, dull blue bill. *Female:* Similar to winter male, but light cheeks crossed by *dark line.*
  Similar species: See (1) Cinnamon Teal, (2) female Common Scoter, (3) Masked Duck. (4) Female Bufflehead has a smaller white patch behind eye only; white patch on spread wing.
  Voice: Usually silent. Displaying males, a low chuckling *chuck-uck-uck-uck-ur-r-r.*
  Where found: Canada south locally to n. S. America. **West:** *Breeds* from c. B.C., n. Alberta, c. Saskatchewan south to Mexico. *Winters* from s. B.C. south through Pacific states and from n. Nevada, n. Utah, Colorado south. *Casual,* se. Alaska. **Habitat:**

Fresh marshes, ponds, lakes; in winter also salt bays. **Nest:** A woven basket attached to reeds above water. Eggs (6–10; 20) whitish, very large.

MASKED DUCK *Oxyura dominica* 12–14 **Pls. 8, 13**
  Field marks: Similar to Ruddy Duck; smaller. *Male:* Rusty, with black marks on back; *black face. Female:* Suggests a small female Ruddy, but with 2 black stripes crossing each cheek instead of 1. Both sexes have *white wing patches* (often concealed when swimming). Ruddy has solid dark wings.
  Voice: A hornlike note; also a henlike clucking.
  Where found: Tropical America. Occasional visitor to s. Texas (mainly Rio Grande Delta). **Habitat:** Resacas, ponds.

Mergansers: Merginae

FISH-DUCKS with spikelike bills and saw-edged mandibles. Most species have crests and are long-lined, slender-bodied. They patter when taking off; flight is swift, direct. In flight, the bill, head, neck, and body are held horizontal, quite unlike those of other ducks. Sexes unlike. **Food:** Chiefly fish.

HOODED MERGANSER **Pls. 7, 9, 13**
Lophodytes cucullatus 16–19
  Field marks: *Male:* Note the vertical *fan-shaped white crest* which it habitually raises. Breast white with 2 vertical black bars on side in front of wing; wing with white patch; back black, flanks brownish. *Female:* Recognized as a merganser by the narrow, spikelike bill; in flight by its long-drawn horizontal lines. Known as this species by its small size, dark coloration, *dark head, bill, and chest,* loose tawny crest.
  Similar species: (1) Male Bufflehead is smaller, chubbier, with *white* (not dark) sides. White crest of Hooded Merganser is *margined* with black (see female Bufflehead). (2) Other female mergansers are larger, *grayer,* with rufous heads, red bills. (3) Female Wood Duck is also dark, with a crest, but square white wing patch, spikelike bill, and flight silhouette identify the merganser. Both frequent wooded pools.
  Voice: Low grunting or croaking notes.
  Where found: Se. Alaska, Canada, n. U.S. Winters to n. Mexico, Gulf Coast. **West:** *Breeds* from se. Alaska, n. B.C., Great Slave Lake south, rarely or locally to w. Oregon, c. Idaho, Wyoming, n. Nebraska. *Winters* mainly from s. B.C. south in Pacific states to c. California. Sparse *migrant* elsewhere in w. U.S. **Habitat:** Wooded lakes, ponds, rivers. **Nest:** In cavity in tree, stump. Eggs (6–12; 18) white.

COMMON MERGANSER *Mergus merganser* 22–27
(American Merganser) **Pls. 7, 9, 13**
Field marks: In line formation, low over the water, these long-bodied ducks follow the winding course of streams. *Male:* Long white body with black back and green-black head; bill and feet red; breast tinged with delicate peach-colored bloom. In flight, the whiteness and the merganser shape (with bill, head, neck, and body all horizontal) identify this species. *Female:* Gray, with *crested* rufous head, clean white underparts, large square white wing patch. Bill and feet red.
Similar species: (1) Male Goldeneye resembles Merganser at a distance, but has a white eye spot, is chubbier, shorter-necked, puffy-headed. (2) Rusty-headed female Merganser suggests Canvasback or Redhead, but those two birds have black chests, no crests. (3) Males may be mistaken for Mallards (because of green head). (4) See Red-breasted Merganser (females similar).
Voice: Low staccato croaks (male); a guttural *karrr* (female).
Where found: Cooler parts of N. Hemisphere. Winters to Mexico, Gulf Coast, s. Eurasia. **West:** *Breeds* from s. Alaska, s. Yukon, Great Slave Lake to s. Canada; in mts. to c. California, Nevada, c. Arizona, nw. New Mexico. *Winters* from s. B.C., s. Alberta south. **Habitat:** Wooded lakes, rivers (summer); in winter also open lakes, ponds, rarely bays. **Nest:** A down-lined hollow on ground or in tree cavity. Eggs (6–12; 17) pale buff.

RED-BREASTED MERGANSER **Pls. 7, 9, 13**
Mergus serrator 19½–26
Field marks: *Male:* Rakish; head black glossed with green and *conspicuously crested;* breast at waterline dark rusty, separated from head by *wide white collar;* bill and feet red. *Female:* Gray, with crested dull rufous head and large square white patch on wing; bill and feet reddish.
Similar species: Male Common Merganser is whiter, without collar and breastband effect; lacks crest. In female Common, the white chin, white chest are sharply defined (in Red-breast rufous of head is paler, *blending* into throat and neck).
Voice: Usually silent. A hoarse croak; *karrr* (female).
Where found: Northern parts of N. Hemisphere. Winters to Mexico, Gulf of Mexico, n. Africa, s. China. **West:** *Breeds* from Arctic coast south to Aleutians, se. Alaska, n. B.C., c. Alberta, c. Saskatchewan. *Winters* mainly along coast from se. Alaska to Mexico. *Migrant* on Plains and in Great Basin. **Habitat:** Lakes; in winter, bays, sea. **Nest:** A down-lined hollow under bush, spruce, roots. Eggs (8–10; 16) olive-buff.

American Vultures: Cathartidae

BLACKISH eagle-like birds, often seen soaring high in wide circles. Their naked heads are relatively small (hawks, eagles have larger heads). Often incorrectly called "buzzards." Sexes alike. **Food:** Carrion. **Range:** S. Canada to Strait of Magellan. **No. of species:** World, 6; West, 3.

TURKEY VULTURE *Cathartes aura* 26–32 **Pl. 18**
Field marks: Note the great 2-toned blackish wings (flight feathers lighter than wing-linings). Nearly eagle size (spread 6 ft). Soars with wings slightly above horizontal (forming dihedral); rocks and tilts unsteadily. At close range *red head* of adult can be seen; young birds have blackish heads.
Similar species: (1) See Black Vulture. (2) Diminutive head and slimmer tail distinguish Turkey Vulture from eagles. Soars with wings above horizontal (eagles with flat plane).
Voice: Usually silent. A hiss when cornered; a low grunt.
Where found: S. Canada to Strait of Magellan. Migratory in north. **West:** *Breeds* from s. B.C., c. Alberta, s. Saskatchewan to Mexico. *Winters* mainly from c. California, sw. Arizona, s. Texas south. **Habitat:** Usually seen in sky or perched on dead trees, posts, carrion, or on ground. **Nest:** In log, rocks, cliff hole, or on ground. Eggs (1–3) blotched.

BLACK VULTURE *Coragyps atratus* 23–27 **Pl. 18**
Field marks: Spread under 5 ft. This big black bird is quickly identified by the short square tail that barely projects beyond the wings and by a whitish patch on spread wing toward tip. Head black. Legs longer and whiter than Turkey Vulture's.
Similar species: Tail of Turkey Vulture is longer and slimmer. Black Vulture is blacker, has much less "sail area"; tail is stubby, wings shorter and wider. It can be spotted at a great distance by its quick, labored flapping — several rapid flaps and a short glide. The Turkey flaps more deliberately, soars more. *Caution:* Young Turkey Vultures have black heads.
Voice: Usually silent. Hissing and low grunting sounds.
Where found: Ohio, Maryland to Chile, Argentina. **West:** *Resident* locally in s. Arizona, w. Texas (s. Big Bend). **Habitat:** Similar to Turkey Vulture's but more restricted to lower altitudes. **Nest:** In ledge, cave, log, tree hollow, or on ground in thicket. Eggs (1–3) blotched. (*Note:* Downy nestlings are dark buff; Turkey Vultures, white.)

CALIFORNIA CONDOR **Pl. 18**
Gymnogyps californianus 45–55
Field marks: Spread 8½–9½ ft. Much larger than Turkey Vulture; adults with extensive *white under wing-linings* toward

fore edge of wings. Head yellow or orange. Young birds are
dusky-headed, lack white linings, but are twice size of Turkey
Vulture and have much broader proportions. Condor has a
flatter wing plane when soaring; does not rock or tilt.
Similar species: (1) See Turkey Vulture. (2) Many Golden
Eagles have some white under the wing, but it is placed differently (see Plate 18); shape of bird is different.
Where found: California. *Resident* mainly in s. Coast Range
from se. Monterey Co. to n. Los Angeles Co.; also mts. at s. end
of San Joaquin Valley. Occasional in w. foothills of Sierra.
Some 40–60 survive. **Habitat:** Mainly mts. and adjacent open
country. **Nest:** In hole or cave in cliff. Eggs (1) white.

Hawks, Kites, Harriers, Eagles: Accipitridae

DIURNAL birds of prey, with hooked beaks, strong hooked claws;
divided into several subfamilies, which will be treated separately.
Persecuted and misunderstood; in need of greater protection.
Predation studies prove they are an important cog in the natural
balance. **Range:** Almost cosmopolitan. **No. of species:** World,
205; West, 28 (+3 accidentals; +1 in Hawaii).

Kites: Elaninae and Milvinae

GRACEFUL hawks of s. distribution; resemble falcons in shape
(pointed wings); becoming scarce. **Food:** Chiefly large insects,
reptiles, small mammals; entirely beneficial.

WHITE-TAILED KITE *Elanus leucurus* 15–17   **Pl. 17**
   Field marks: Spread 3⅓ ft. This whitish kite is falcon-shaped,
   with long, pointed wings and a long tail. Soars and glides like
   a small gull; often hovers like a Sparrow Hawk. *Adult:* Pale
   gray with white head, *tail,* and underparts. Perched or flying,
   shows a *large black patch* toward fore edge of upper wing. No
   other falcon-like bird in California has a white tail. *Immature:*
   Recognizable, but has rusty breast, brown back, and narrow
   band near tip of pale tail.
   Similar species: See White-tailed Hawk.
   Voice: A whistled *kee kee kee,* abrupt or drawn out.
   Where found: California, s. Texas to Chile, Argentina. **West:**
   Resident in California, west of Sierra and deserts; from coastal
   Humboldt Co. and upper Sacramento Valley to San Diego.
   Casual, Oregon. **Habitat:** Open foothills, river valleys, marshes.

Nest: A platform of twigs in tree adjacent to open country. Eggs (3–5) blotched.

MISSISSIPPI KITE *Ictinia misisippiensis* 14   **Pl. 17**
  Field marks: Spread 3 ft. Falcon-shaped; graceful and gray. Dark above, lighter below; head *very pale, almost white;* tail *black.* No other falcon-like hawk has a black unbarred tail. In flight shows from above a broad pale patch on rear of wing. Immature has heavy brown streakings below but has falcon-like shape and the dark tail (somewhat banded below).
  Voice: *Phee-phew* (G. M. Sutton); a clear *kee-ee.*
  Where found: Mainly s.-c. U.S.; winters Cent. and S. America. **West:** *Breeds* locally in Texas panhandle, Oklahoma panhandle, and e. New Mexico; occasionally in vicinity of El Paso. *Casual* in California, Colorado.

Accipiters, or Bird Hawks: Accipitrinae

LONG-TAILED hawks with short, rounded wings; chiefly woodland birds that do not soar as much as do the Buteos. They hunt among trees and thickets, using a hedge-hopping technique. The typical flight is several short quick beats and a glide. Sexes alike, female larger. **Food:** Chiefly birds, some small mammals.

GOSHAWK *Accipiter gentilis* 20–26   **Pls. 16, 17**
  Field marks: Spread 3½–4 ft. *Adult:* A large, robust hawk, with a long tail and rounded wings. Crown and patch behind eye slaty, *stripe over eye whitish.* Underparts whitish, finely barred with gray; back blue-gray, paler than back of Cooper's or Sharp-shin. *Immature:* Very much like immature Cooper's; usually larger, distinguished by light stripe over eye. Size not always reliable (Cooper's may be almost as large).
  Similar species: Cooper's Hawk is Crow-sized or smaller (Goshawk is usually larger than Crow). The gray-backed adult is *reddish* below (Goshawk is whitish or *pale gray* below). Flight is much alike — alternate flapping and gliding. Both hunt with agility among trees. Goshawk is more boreal.
  Voice: *Kak, kak, kak,* or *kuk, kuk, kuk;* heavier than Cooper's.
  Where found: Eurasia, n. N. America. **West:** *Resident* from w. and c. Alaska, nw. Mackenzie, n. Alberta, n. Saskatchewan south in mts. to c. California (Sierra), w. New Mexico. *Winters* to lowlands and south rarely to s. California, n. Mexico. **Habitat:** N. forests, mt. woodlands. **Nest:** A platform of sticks in tree. Eggs (3–5) whitish.

SHARP-SHINNED HAWK   **Pls. 16, 17**
Accipiter striatus   10–14
  Field marks: Spread 2 ft±. A small woodland hawk with a long tail and *short, rounded* wings. Tail *notched or square.* Flies with

several quick beats and a glide. Adult has blue-gray back, rusty-barred breast. Immature is brown, streaked.

Similar species: Two other small hawks, (1) Sparrow and (2) Pigeon Hawks, are *falcons* and have long, pointed (not short, rounded) wings. (3) Small male Cooper's is often nearly identical in size and pattern with large female Sharp-shin, but generally Cooper's has *rounded* tail (Sharp-shin *square-tipped* tail, slightly notched when folded). However, Sharp-shin's square-tipped tail can look slightly rounded when spread.

Voice: Like Cooper's Hawk's but shriller, a high *kik, kik, kik.*

Where found: Most of N. America. **West:** *Breeds* from n. Alaska, Yukon, Great Bear Lake south locally to c. California, Arizona, New Mexico, n. Texas. *Winters* from B.C., w. Montana to Mexico. **Habitat:** Forests, thickets. **Nest:** A platform of twigs in woodland tree, usually conifer. Eggs (3–5; 8) spotted.

COOPER'S HAWK *Accipiter cooperii* 14–20 **Pls. 16, 17**
Field marks: Spread 2¼–3 ft. A short-winged, long-tailed hawk; averaging not quite so large as a Crow. Adults have blue-gray backs, rusty breasts. Immatures are brown; streaked below. Tail *rounded,* even when folded.

Similar species: (1) The smaller Sharp-shin has a *notched* or *square tail* (when folded). Immature Cooper's is more narrowly streaked below than young Sharp-shin. (2) See also Goshawk.

Voice: About nest, a rapid *kek, kek, kek;* suggests Flicker.

Where found: S. Canada to n. Mexico. **West:** *Breeds* from c. B.C., c. Alberta, c. Saskatchewan south to Mexico. *Winters* from w. B.C., Montana south. **Habitat:** Broken woodlands, canyons, river groves. **Nest:** A platform of sticks in tree. Eggs (3–5) white, rarely spotted.

Buteos, or Buzzard Hawks: Buteoninae (in part)

LARGE thick-set hawks with broad wings and broad, relatively short rounded tails. They habitually soar in wide circles. Considerable variation; those illustrated are the most typical. Sexes alike, female larger. Young birds in most species are *streaked lengthwise* below. Black or melanistic phases often occur (Red-tail, Rough-leg, Ferruginous, Swainson's), and one must indeed be an expert to tell some of them apart. Even the seasoned expert gives up on some of the birds he sees. **Food:** Rats, mice, rabbits; occasionally small birds, reptiles. Swainson's Hawk eats many grasshoppers.

RED-TAILED HAWK **Pls. 15, 19, 20**
Buteo jamaicensis 19–25
Field marks: Spread 4–4½ ft. When this large broad-winged,

round-tailed hawk veers in its soaring, the *rufous* of the upper side of the tail can be seen (if adult). From beneath, adults have whitish tails which in strong light might transmit a hint of red. Young birds have dark gray tails, which may or may not show banding. Underparts of typical Red-tails are "zoned" (light breast, broad band of streakings across belly). There is much variation, particularly on the Plains, where more than one race occurs. Individuals vary from the whitish, white-tailed *kriderii* race (Great Plains) and the pale-breasted race *fuertesi* (Big Bend and s. Texas) to reddish birds of the typical western race *calurus,* and even dusky melanistic birds. *Black adults usually show red tails* (unlike other black Buteos). Immatures are often light at base of tail, leading to confusion with Rough-leg and Swainson's.

Similar species: (1) See Swainson's Hawk. (2) Red-shouldered Hawk has a banded tail and is more uniformly patterned below (rufous in adult; striped on both breast and belly in young); Red-tail is "zoned" (light breast, streaked belly); is chunkier, with wider wings, shorter tail. (3) See Harlan's Hawk.

Voice: An asthmatic squeal, *keeer-r-r* (slurring downward).

Where found: Alaska, Canada, to Panama. *West: Breeds* from c. Alaska, Yukon, c. Mackenzie to Mexico. *Winters* from sw. B.C., s. Montana south. **Habitat:** Open country, woodlands, mts., deserts. **Nest:** A platform of sticks in forest tree, isolated low tree, saguaro, cliff, etc. Eggs (2–4) spotted.

HARLAN'S HAWK *Buteo harlani* 21–22½ **Pls. 15, 19**
Field marks: Spread 4-4½ ft. Until recently this prairie *Buteo* was rated as a race of the Red-tail. Typical birds are black-breasted with whitish or pale rusty tails, but light-breasted birds occur. The pale upperside of tail with *black mottling* blending into a broad terminal band is the diagnostic feature. Young birds are probably not separable from young Red-tails.

Similar species: (1) Melanistic Red-tails (adults) show red on tail (topside). (2) *Kriderii* form of Red-tail might be confused with light-colored Harlan's, but is paler above; its white or pale rufous tail has a tendency toward light *barring* near tip (Harlan's is usually *finely mottled*). (3) Black Rough-leg has a somewhat banded (not mottled) tail, is cleaner white on flight feathers below (see plate), and has longer wings and tail. (4) Black Swainson's has less contrast on its dark underwing; it shows a tendency toward dark bands on gray tail.

Voice: Similar to Red-tail's.

Where found: E. Alaska, nw. Canada. Winters to s. U.S. *West: Breeds* from e. Alaska (Yukon Valley) to n. B.C. (east of Coast Mts.), nw. Alberta (probably). *Winters* on Plains from Kansas to Texas. *Casual,* Idaho, Colorado, Arizona, California. **Habitat, etc.:** Similar to Red-tail's.

RED-SHOULDERED HAWK *Buteo lineatus* 17–24
(Red-bellied Hawk)   **Pls. 15, 20**
  Field marks: Spread 3–4 ft. Recognized as a *Buteo* by the
  broad tail, broad wings; as this species, by heavy dark bands
  across both sides of tail. Adults have *rufous shoulders* (not
  always visible) and pale robin-red underparts. Another mark,
  sometimes shared by other Buteos, is a translucent "window"
  toward wing-tip at base of primaries. Immatures are streaked
  below, as are most other young hawks. They can be identified
  by proportions, tailbanding, and, in flight overhead, by the
  "wing windows," a helpful (but not infallible) mark.
  Similar species: (1) Adult Cooper's Hawk (rusty underparts)
  has *Accipiter* shape (shorter wings, longer tail). (2) See Red-
  tailed Hawk. (3) East of Rockies see Broad-winged Hawk.
  Voice: A 2-syllabled scream, *kee-yar* (dropping inflection).
  Where found: Se. Canada, e. U.S., California, Mexico. **West:**
  Resident in California, west of Sierra; chiefly San Joaquin and
  Sacramento Valleys and s. coastal lowlands. *Casual,* Utah,
  Arizona, Colorado, New Mexico, Texas panhandle. **Habitat:**
  Broken woodlands, primarily of lowland rivers. **Nest:** A plat-
  form of sticks in tall woodland tree. Eggs (2–4) blotched.

BROAD-WINGED HAWK   **Pl. 20**
Buteo platypterus 13½–19
  Field marks: Spread 3 ft±. A small chunky *Buteo,* size of a
  Crow. Note the tailbanding of the adult — the white bands are
  about as wide as the black. Occasional melanistic (black-bodied)
  birds occur in w. part of range. The broad tailbanding holds.
  Immature: Tailbands more numerous, crowding out the white.
  This species often migrates in soaring flocks.
  Similar species: (1) See immature Gray Hawk (sw. border of
  U.S.). (2) Young Red-shouldered Hawk is similar to immature
  Broad-wing, but latter bird is chunkier, with stubbier tail,
  shorter wings; underwing usually whiter.
  Voice: A high-pitched shrill *pweeeeeee;* diminishing.
  Where found: S. Canada, e. U.S. to Gulf states. Migrates
  mainly e. of Great Plains. Winters in Cent. and S. America.
  West: *Breeds* across Alberta, Saskatchewan. *Casual* migrant
  west to Colorado, New Mexico, Texas panhandle. *Accidental,*
  se. Arizona. **Habitat:** Mixed woodlands, groves. **Nest:** Of sticks
  in tree. Eggs (2–4) blotched.

SWAINSON'S HAWK   **Pls. 15, 19, 20**
Buteo swainsoni 19–22
  Field marks: Spread 4–4¾ ft. A *Buteo* of the plains; pro-
  portioned like a Red-tail but wings slightly more pointed. When
  gliding, the wings are somewhat above horizontal (slightly
  Marsh-Hawk-like). In typical adults note the *dark breastband.*
  Overhead, the unmarked buffy wing-linings contrast with the

dark flight feathers. Tail gray above, often shading to white at base. There are confusing individuals with light breasts and blackish birds, hard to tell from other melanistic Buteos, but the underwing, with its dusky flight feathers, is usually a good mark. Often migrates in large flocks.

Similar species: (1) Red-tail usually has a light chest (Swainson's, dark chest) and a belt of streaks on belly. (2) Black Red-tail has rusty tail (above). (3) Black Rough-leg has clear white on flight feathers of underwing.

Voice: A shrill plaintive whistle, *kreeeeeeer.*

Where found: Nw. N. America to n. Mexico; winters chiefly in Argentina. **West:** *Breeds* from ne. Alaska, nw. Mackenzie, s.-c. Saskatchewan south throughout most of w. U.S. (casual in humid nw. coast belt). Occasional in winter in w. U.S. **Habitat:** Dry plains, open foothills, alpine meadows, rangeland, open forest, sparse trees. **Nest:** Of sticks in tree (often isolated), bush, yucca, cliff. Eggs (2–4) usually spotted.

ZONE-TAILED HAWK   Pl. 19
Buteo albonotatus 18½–21½

Field marks: Spread 4 ft. A dull *black* hawk with somewhat more slender wings than other Buteos. Might be mistaken for soaring Turkey Vulture because of proportions and *2-toned wing effect.* Hawk head and *white tailbands* (pale gray on topside) identify the adult. Immature has narrower tailbanding and a scattering of *small white spots* on its black underparts.

Similar species: Black Hawk is much chunkier, with longer chicken-like legs. In flight it has much broader, more evenly colored wings below (a white spot sometimes shows at base of primaries). Usually 1 very broad white band (white on both sides) across tail. Zone-tail has 2–3 smaller bands but often only the wide one shows in the field, causing confusion. Young Black Hawk has striped *buffy* head and underparts. Black Hawk prefers sluggish rivers; Zone-tail is often seen in mts.

Voice: A squealing whistle, suggesting Red-tail's.

Where found: *Breeds* from c. Arizona, s. and ne. New Mexico (local), w. Texas (Trans-Pecos) to n. S. America. In U.S., *winters* (rarely) in sw. Arizona. *Accidental* in s. California. **Habitat:** Arid country, rivers, desert mts. **Nest:** A platform of sticks in tall tree or cliff. Eggs (2–3) white.

WHITE-TAILED HAWK   *Buteo albicaudatus* 23–24
(Sennett's White-tailed Hawk)   **Pls. 19, 20**

Field marks: Spread 4–4½ ft. Note the *white tail* with a narrow *black band* near its tip. A long-winged, short-tailed *Buteo* with *clear white underparts.* Upper parts dark gray, shoulders rusty-red. Immature may be quite blackish below, or may have some white on chest and belly. Overhead, it shows a whitish tail and blackish wing-linings that contrast with lighter primaries. The tail may be pale gray, thickly marked with narrow bands.

Similar species: (1) Ferruginous Hawk also has a whitish tail, but it lacks the sharp black band. (2) Rare black Ferruginous may be confused with young White-tail but has undersurface of flight feathers clear white (not clouded). (3) Black Swainson's has a barred grayish tail and is more evenly dusky on underwing (immature White-tail is usually spotted with white on breast). (4) Black Harlan's has black mottling on tail.

Voice: A repeated *ke-ke-ke-ke-ke-ke;* also *cut-a, cut-a,* etc.

Where found: S. Texas to Patagonia. *Resident* of coastal prairie of Texas. *Accidental,* s. Arizona (nested 1897). **Habitat:** Brushy prairie. **Nest:** A bulky platform of sticks in top of yucca, scrub tree. Eggs (2–3) unmarked or faintly spotted.

ROUGH-LEGGED HAWK *Buteo lagopus* 19–24
(American Rough-legged Hawk) **Pls. 15, 19, 20**

Field marks: Spread 4–4½ ft. This big hawk of the open country habitually hovers with beating wings (Sparrow-Hawk-like) in one spot. A *Buteo* by shape; larger, with longer wings and tail than most of the others. Normal phase, viewed from below, usually has a *black belly* and a conspicuous *black patch at "wrist"* of spread wing. Tail *white with a broad black band toward tip.* Black Rough-legs lack extensive white on upper tail, but from below usually show much white at base of flight feathers.

Similar species: (1) Marsh Hawk (white rump patch) is slender, with slim wings, slim tail. (2) Adult black Red-tail has rusty on top of tail, different overhead pattern. See also (3) Golden Eagle, (4) Ferruginous Hawk, (5) Swainson's Hawk.

Voice: Squealing or mewing whistles.

Where found: Arctic; circumpolar. Winters to s. U.S., c. Eurasia. **West:** *Breeds* from n. Alaska, Yukon, n. Mackenzie south to Aleutians, s. Alaska, Great Slave Lake. *Winters* from s. Canada south to s. California (rarely), s. Arizona, s. New Mexico, Texas. **Habitat:** Tundra escarpments, Arctic coasts; in winter, open plains, marshes. **Nest:** Of twigs, moss; on cliff, ravine, or tree top. Eggs (2–6) blotched.

FERRUGINOUS HAWK *Buteo regalis* 22½–25
(Ferruginous Rough-legged Hawk) **Pls. 15, 19, 20**

Field marks: Spread 4⅔ ft. A large *Buteo* of the plains, *rufous above* and whitish below, with a *whitish tail.* Head often quite white. A good mark in typical adults overhead is a dark V formed by the dark rusty feathers on the legs. In flight, shows a light patch on upper wing near tip. (Rough-leg also shows this.) Immatures are dark above and white below without the rufous and without the dark V formed by the legs.

Similar species: (1) White form of Red-tail (*B. j. kriderii*) also

has whitish tail but lacks reddish back and dark V formed by legs. (2) Rough-legged Hawk is darker, with broad black tail-band. Scarce dark phase of Ferruginous is rustier than black Rough-leg; tail is pale, often whitish, without band.
Voice: A loud *kree-a;* a harsh *kaah* (A. C. Bent).
Where found: *Breeds* from e. Washington (rare), s. Alberta, sw. Saskatchewan south to e. Oregon, Nevada, Arizona, New Mexico, nw. Texas (Staked Plain). *Winters* mainly in sw. U.S., n. Mexico; rarely north to e. Oregon, n. Utah, Montana. **Habitat:** Arid plains, open rangeland. **Nest:** Of sticks, on cliff or tree. Eggs (3–5) blotched.

GRAY HAWK *Buteo nitidus* 16–18 **Pl. 20**
(Mexican Goshawk)
    Field marks: Spread 3 ft. A small *Buteo*, not a Goshawk. Adults are distinguished by their *Buteo* proportions, gray back, *gray and white barred* underparts, white rump, and *widely banded* tail (similar to Broad-winged Hawk's). Immature has narrowly barred tail, striped buffy underparts. Note short wing, barred thighs, much yellow at base of bill.
    Similar species: (1) Young Swainson's is larger, has longer wing (reaching nearly to end of tail), has dusky flight feathers below. (2) Young Broad-wing is darker on back, less rusty on breast, has longer wing, and black tips on underwing.
    Voice: A loud plaintive *cree-eer.*
    Where found: U.S.–Mexican border to Brazil. **West:** *Breeds* very locally in se. Arizona. **Habitat:** Wooded lowland streams. **Nest:** Of sticks in mesquite, cottonwood. Eggs (2–3) white.

HARRIS' HAWK *Parabuteo unicinctus* 17½–29 **Pls. 15, 19**
    Field marks: Spread 3½–3¾ ft. A black hawk of the *Buteo* type with a flashy *white rump* and a *white band* at tip of tail. In good light shows *chestnut-colored areas* on thighs and shoulders — a mark of distinction from other black or melanistic Buteos. Immature has light, streaked underparts and *rusty shoulders;* might be confused with Red-shouldered Hawk except for conspicuous white at base of tail.
    Similar species: (1) Male in poor light is frequently confounded with the much chunkier Black Hawk. (2) Immature might also be mistaken for Red-shouldered Hawk or (3) female or young Marsh Hawk (white rumps), but latter are more slender, do not perch conspicuously, and hunt in more open terrain.
    Voice: A harsh *karrr.*
    Where found: Sw. U.S. south locally to Chile, Argentina. **West:** *Resident* from se. California (formerly), Arizona, se. New Mexico, c.-w. Texas south into Mexico. *Casual,* s. California, s. Nevada. **Habitat:** River woodlands, mesquite, brush. **Nest:** A platform of sticks in yucca, mesquite, low tree. Eggs (3–5) whitish.

BLACK HAWK *Buteogallus anthracinus* 20–23   **Pl. 19**
(Mexican Black Hawk)
   Field marks: Spread 4 ft. A black Buteonine Hawk with exceptional width of wing, *long* chicken-like yellow legs. Identified
by chunky shape and broad white *band* crossing middle of tail.
In flight, a whitish spot near tip of wing at base of primaries
can be seen under favorable circumstances. Young bird is dark-
backed with streaked *rich buffy* head and underparts; tail
narrowly banded with black and white (5–6 bands of each).
   Similar species: (1) Zone-tailed Hawk bears a superficial resemblance to Turkey Vulture; Black Hawk to Black Vulture.
See discussion under Zone-tailed Hawk. (2) See also Harris'
Hawk and (3) melanistic Buteos (Swainson's, Red-tail, Harlan's).
   Voice: A weak, high-pitched *quee-quee quee* (I. Davis).
   Where found: U.S.–Mexican border to Ecuador. **West:** *Breeds*
locally in c. and s. Arizona. Has bred in s. New Mexico, s. Texas
(lower Rio Grande). *Casual,* w. Texas (Trans-Pecos). **Habitat:**
Wooded streambottoms. **Nest:** A mass of sticks in tree. Eggs
(1–3) usually spotted.

Eagles: Buteoninae (in part)

EAGLES are distinguished from "buzzard hawks," or Buteos, by
greater size, proportionately longer wings. Bill powerful, nearly
as long as head. **Food:** Golden Eagle eats chiefly rabbits, large
rodents; Bald Eagle, chiefly dead or dying fish.

GOLDEN EAGLE *Aquila chrysaetos* 30–41   **Pl. 18**
   Field marks: Spread 6⅓–7⅔ ft. Majestic, flat-winged gliding
and soaring with occasional wingbeats characterizes the eagle;
its greater size, longer wings set it apart from other large hawks.
Adult: Evenly dark below, or with a slight lightening at base of
tail. When the bird wheels, a wash of gold on the hind neck
may be noticed. *Immature:* From above and below in flight,
shows a *white flash in wing* at base of primaries, and a white
tail with *broad dark terminal band.* All manner of variation
exists between this easy-to-identify "ring-tailed" plumage and
the less distinctive plumage of the adult.
   Similar species: (1) Immature Bald Eagle usually has some
white in wing-linings (not at base of primaries) and often some
on body. It may have tail mottled with white at base (young
Golden has sharply banded tail). Bald Eagle has bare tarsi
(Golden is feathered to toes), a taxonomic character sometimes
useful. Head and massive bill of Bald Eagle project more; wings
are not quite as wide, nor is tail as full. (2) Black Rough-legged
Hawk is smaller, has more white under wing.
   Voice: Seldom heard; a yelping bark, *kya;* whistled notes.
   Where found: Mt. regions of N. Hemisphere. **West:** *Resident*

from n. Alaska, Mackenzie south locally through mts. and badlands of w. N. America to Mexico. Some migration from n. parts. **Habitat:** Open mts., foothills, canyons, plains. **Nest:** A mass of sticks on cliff or tree. Eggs (1–3) blotched.

BALD EAGLE *Haliaeetus leucocephalus* 30–43 **Pl. 18**
Field marks: Spread 6½–8 ft. The national bird of the U.S., with its *white head* and *white tail,* is "all field mark." Bill of adult yellow. Immature has dusky head and tail, dark bill. It shows whitish in the wing-linings and often on the breast.
Similar species: (1) Golden Eagle (which see) is frequently confused with immature Bald Eagle. (2) Black Buteos (Rough-leg, etc.) are much smaller, with smaller bills.
Voice: A harsh, creaking cackle, *kleek-kik-ik-ik-ik-ik,* or a lower *kak-kak-kak.*
Where found: Alaska, Canada, to s. U.S. **West:** *Breeds* from Aleutians, nw. Alaska, Mackenzie south locally to n. Baja California, c. Arizona, w. New Mexico; most numerous in coastal Alaska, B.C. Some withdrawal in winter from colder n. areas. **Habitat:** Coast, lakes, rivers. **Nest:** A bulky platform of sticks in tall tree, cliff. Eggs (2–3) white.

Harriers: Circinae

SLIM hawks with slim, slightly angled wings, long tails, long bodies. Flight low, languid, and gliding; wings in a shallow V. Sexes unlike. Hunt for rodents, small birds, in open country.

MARSH HAWK or HARRIER **Pls. 16, 17**
Circus cyaneus 17½–24
Field marks: Spread 3½–4½ ft. Note the *white rump patch.* A slim hawk. *Males* are pale gray; *females,* streaked brown; *young birds,* rich russet on underparts. Glides buoyantly and unsteadily low over the fields and marshes with wings held slightly above horizontal, suggesting the Turkey Vulture's dihedral. The white rump is always conspicuous. Overhead, the wing-tips of the whitish male have a "dipped in ink" pattern.
Similar species: (1) Rough-leg has white at base of tail, but is much more heavily built. (2) Accipiters (which sometimes appear white-rumped from side) have much shorter wings.
Voice: A weak nasal whistle, *pee, pee, pee.* A lower-pitched *chu-chu-chu;* also *kek* notes about nest.
Where found: Alaska, Canada to s. U.S.; n. Eurasia. Winters to n. S. America, n. Africa. **West:** *Breeds* from n. Alaska, nw. Mackenzie locally to n. Baja California, New Mexico, n. Texas. *Winters* from s. B.C., s. Alberta south. **Habitat:** Marshes, fields, prairies. **Nest:** Of stalks, grass, on ground in sparsely shrubby open land or marsh. Eggs (4–6; 9) white.

Ospreys: Pandionidae

A LARGE fish-eating hawk; resembles a small white-breasted eagle. Plunges feet-first for fish. Sexes alike. **Range:** Nearly cosmopolitan. **No. of species:** World, 1; West, 1.

OSPREY *Pandion haliaetus* 21–24½ **Pl. 20**
 Field marks: Spread 4½–6 ft. Our only hawk that dives into the water. Large; blackish above, *clear white* below. Head largely white, suggestive of Bald Eagle, but *broad black patch through cheeks.* Flies with a crook in its wings, showing black carpal patches on whitish undersides. Hovers on beating wings, and plunges feet-first for fish.
 Voice: A series of sharp, annoyed whistles, *cheep, cheep,* or *yewk, yewk,* etc. Near nest, a frenzied *cheereek!*
 Where found: Almost cosmopolitan. **West:** *Breeds* from nw. Alaska, c. Yukon, Great Slave Lake south locally along coast to Mexico; in interior, locally to n. New Mexico. *Winters* from s. California, Nevada, s. Arizona, s. Texas south. **Habitat:** Rivers, lakes, coast. **Nest:** A bulky mass of sticks in dead tree, rock pinnacle, or on ground. Eggs (2–4) blotched.

Caracaras and Falcons: Falconidae

BECAUSE of dissimilarity, caracaras and falcons are discussed separately. **No. of species:** World, 58; West, 7.

Caracaras: Caracarinae

LARGE, long-legged birds of prey with naked faces. They often associate with vultures. Sexes alike. **Food:** Our species eats chiefly carrion. **Range:** S. U.S. to s. S. America.

CARACARA *Caracara cheriway* 20–25 **Pl. 19**
(Audubon's Caracara)
 Field marks: Spread 4 ft. The "Mexican Eagle" may be seen on fence posts or feeding with vultures, where its *black crest* and red face are its outstanding features. It is a large, long-legged, long-necked, dark hawk. In flight, its underbody presents alternating areas of light and dark — whitish throat and breast, black belly, and white, dark-tipped tail. *Whitish patches* near tips of dark wings are conspicuous. These are determinative when seen in conjunction with the white chest. Young birds are browner, streaked on breast, not barred.

Similar species: Black Vulture (all-black body) also has white patches near wing-tips.
Voice: A hoarse rattling cackle (head thrown back).
Where found: Sw. U.S. and Florida to Peru. **West:** *Resident* in s. Arizona, s. Texas. *Casual,* c. New Mexico (has bred), w. Texas. *Accidental,* w. Washington, Colorado. **Habitat:** Prairies, rangeland. **Nest:** A bulky bowl in top of yucca, saguaro, or tree. Eggs (2–3) blotched.

Falcons: Falconinae

FALCONS, like kites, are streamlined birds of prey, characterized by long, *pointed* wings, longish tails. The wing strokes are rapid; the pointed wings are built for speed, not sustained soaring. Sexes alike in some species; female larger. **Food:** Chiefly birds, rodents, insects. **Range:** Almost cosmopolitan.

GYRFALCON *Falco rusticolus* 20–25   **Pl. 17**
   Field marks: Spread 4 ft. A very large arctic falcon, much larger than the Peregrine; slightly longer-tailed and more uniformly colored. Wingbeats of the "Gyr" are deceptively slower. In the American Arctic there are black, gray, and white types; these are color phases, not subspecies. In w. North America only the gray and white phases normally occur.
   Similar species: Typical gray Gyrfalcons are paler-headed and more uniformly colored than Peregrine, without such marked contrast between dark upper parts, light underparts. They lack dark hood and broad clean-cut "mustaches" of Peregrine.
   Where found: Arctic regions; circumpolar. **West:** *Breeds* in Aleutians, c. and n. Alaska, arctic Canada. *Winters* casually to Oregon, Montana, Wyoming. *Accidental,* ne. California. **Habitat:** Arctic barrens, seacoasts, open mts. **Nest:** Of sticks on ledge of cliff. Eggs (3–4) cinnamon, spotted.

PRAIRIE FALCON *Falco mexicanus* 17–20   **Pl. 17**
   Field marks: Spread 3½ ft. Pointed-winged; very much like Peregrine in size and cut of jib, but of a paler, sandy color ("like a faded young Peregrine"). Overhead, shows *blackish patches* (formed by dark sides and axillars) in "wingpits."
   Similar species: (1) Peregrine has stronger face pattern (wide black "mustaches"), darker back (slaty in adult, brown in immature). (2) Female Sparrow Hawk is smaller, redder.
   Voice: A yelping *kik-kik-kik,* etc.; a repeated *kee, kee, kee.*
   Where found. *Resident* from c. B.C., s. Alberta, s. Saskatchewan to s. Mexico. Scarce in humid coast belt. **Habitat:** Canyons, open mts., plains, prairies, deserts; wide-ranging. **Nest:** On bare niche of cliff. Eggs (3–6) reddish, spotted.

PEREGRINE FALCON *Falco peregrinus* 15-21 **Pls. 16, 17**
(Duck Hawk)

Field marks: Spread 3¼-3¾ ft. Note the heavy black "mustaches." Recognized as a falcon by its pointed wings, narrow tail, and quick wingbeats not unlike a pigeon's. Its size, near that of a Crow, and heavy mustaches identify it. Adults are slaty-backed; pale below, with bars and spots. Young birds are dark brown above, heavily striped below. A very dark race, *F. p. pealei* (Peale's Peregrine), breeds in the Aleutians and s. coastal Alaska and winters to coastal California.

Similar species: (1) Sparrow Hawk and (2) Pigeon Hawk are hardly larger than Robin. (3) Prairie Falcon is pale, sandy.

Voice: Usually silent. Around eyrie a repeated *we' chew;* a rapid rasping *kek kek kek ke-ek,* etc. Also a wailing note.

Where found: Nearly worldwide. **West:** *Breeds* from n. Alaska, n. Mackenzie south locally to Baja California, Arizona, New Mexico, w. Texas. *Winters* from s. B.C. south through Pacific states; inland mainly from Arizona, Colorado south. **Habitat:** Mainly open country (mts. to coast). **Nest:** In scrape on ledge high on cliff. Eggs (2-4; 7) reddish, spotted.

APLOMADO FALCON *Falco femoralis* 15-18 **Pl. 17**
Field marks: Spread 3⅓ ft. Note the *dark wing-linings* and *black belly* contrasting with the white or pale cinnamon breast. A handsome medium-sized falcon, a little smaller than Peregrine. Now very rare in U.S. Thighs and under tail coverts orange-brown.

Where found: U.S.-Mexican border to Patagonia. **West:** Very rare local *summer resident* in s. Arizona, sw. New Mexico (?), w. Texas (Big Bend). *Casual* in Rio Grande Delta. **Habitat:** Arid brushy prairie, yucca flats. **Nest:** A platform of sticks in top of yucca or low tree. Eggs (3-4) speckled.

PIGEON HAWK or MERLIN **Pls. 16, 17**
Falco columbarius 10-13½

Field marks: Spread 2 ft. A small compact falcon, the length of a jay. Male, bluish gray above, with broad black bands on a gray tail. Female and young, dusky brown with banded tails. Both adults and young are boldly streaked below. There is a dark race, *F. c. suckleyi* (Black Pigeon Hawk), in w. British Columbia which winters south along the coast. It may be recognized by its darkness, darker cheeks, more heavily marked underparts. On the Great Plains there is a race, *F. c. richardsonii* (Richardson's Pigeon Hawk), with a pale crown and tail.

Similar species: Suggests a miniature Peregrine. (1) Pointed wings, falcon wing action separate it from Sharp-shinned Hawk (short rounded wings). (2) Lack of rufous on tail or back and

lack of strong "mustaches" distinguish it from the other small falcon, the Sparrow Hawk. Sails less, tail shorter.
Voice: Usually silent. At nest a shrill chatter, *ki-ki-ki-ki.*
Where found: Northern parts of N. Hemisphere. Winters to n. S. America, n. Africa. **West:** *Breeds* from nw. Alaska, n. Yukon, n. Mackenzie south to Oregon, n. Idaho, n. Montana, n. N. Dakota. *Winters* from s. B.C., c. Alberta, s.-c. Saskatchewan south. **Habitat:** Open woodland; in migration also foothills, marshes, open country. **Nest:** On cliff, in tree, tree hollow, magpie nest, on ground. Eggs (3–6) rusty, spotted.

SPARROW HAWK *Falco sparverius* 9–12   **Pls. 16, 17**
("American Kestrel")
Field marks: Spread 1¾–2 ft. A small swallow-like falcon, size of a jay. No other *small* hawk has a *rufous back or tail.* Males have blue-gray wings. Both sexes have a handsome black and white face pattern. Habitually *hovers* on rapidly beating wings, kingfisher-like. Sits fairly erect, with an occasional lift or jerk of tail; perches on poles, posts, wires.
Similar species: (1) Sharp-shinned Hawk has rounded wings. Sharp-shin and (2) Pigeon Hawk have gray or brown backs, tails.
Voice: A rapid, high *klee klee klee* or *killy killy killy.*
Where found: Most of N. and S. America. **West:** *Breeds* from c. Alaska, nw. Mackenzie south throughout West. *Winters* from s. B.C., Idaho, Montana, Nebraska south. **Habitat:** Open country, prairies, deserts, wooded streams, farmland, cities. **Nest:** In cavity in isolated tree, saguaro, cliff, building, magpie nest. Eggs (3–5; 7) whitish, spotted.

Guans and Chachalacas: Cracidae

CHICKEN-LIKE birds of woodlands; long-tailed, strong-legged. **Food:** Fruits, seeds, leaves, buds, insects. **Range:** S. Texas to S. America. **No. of species:** World, 38; West, 1.

CHACHALACA *Ortalis vetula* 20–24   **p. 62**
Field marks: A large gray-brown bird shaped like a half-grown Turkey, with a small head and a long rounded, white-tipped tail. Difficult to observe; a secretive denizen of dense thickets; best found in morning when it calls raucously from treetops.
Similar species: See Roadrunner (p. 117).
Voice: Alarm, a harsh chicken-like cackle. Also a purring note. Spring "song," a raucous *cha' ca-lac,* repeated in chorus from treetops in morning and evening. Dr. A. A. Allen described a chorus as *keep'-it-up, keep'-it-up, keep'-it-up,* etc., answered by a lower *cut'-it-out, cut'-it-out,* etc.

CHACHALACA

Where found: Southern tip of Texas to Nicaragua. *Resident* locally in lower Rio Grande Valley; from near Falcon Dam to Brownsville; north to Raymondville. **Habitat:** Woodlands, tall brush. **Nest:** Frail; of sticks, leaves, in bush or tree. Eggs (3) whitish.

Grouse and Ptarmigans: Tetraonidae

GROUND-DWELLING, chicken-like birds; larger than quail, and without the long tails of pheasants. Sexes alike or unlike. **Food:** Insects, seeds, buds, berries, etc. **Range:** N. America, Europe, Asia. **No. of species:** World, 18; West, 10.

BLUE GROUSE *Dendragapus obscurus* 15½–21　　　**Pl. 21**
(including Dusky Grouse and Sooty Grouse)
　　Field marks: A dusky gray or blackish grouse with a light band at tip of black tail. (Birds of n. Rockies, *D. o. richardsonii,* lack this band.) Males at close range show a yellow or orange "comb" above the eye. Females are gray-brown, barred with black; have blackish tails suggestive of males'.
　　Similar species: (1) Ruffed Grouse may be confused with female Blue Grouse but has lighter tail with sharp *black band* near tip. (2) See Spruce Grouse.
　　Voice: Male in courtship gives a series of 5–7 low, muffled,

booming or hooting notes about one octave lower than notes of
Great Horned Owl; ventriloquial.
Where found: *Resident* from se. Alaska, s. Yukon, sw. Mackenzie
south along coast to n. California and south in mts. of w. U.S.
to s. California (Mt. Pinos), e.-c. Arizona, w.-c. New Mexico.
Habitat: Coniferous forests, open slash, burns. **Nest:** A depression on ground in woods. Eggs (5–10; 16) buff, dotted.

SPRUCE GROUSE *Canachites canadensis* 15–17 **Pl. 21**
(including Franklin's Grouse)
Field marks: The deep wet coniferous forests of the North are
the home of this tame dusky-colored grouse. The male has a
sharply defined black breast and some white spotting on the
sides. At close range, male shows a comb of bare red skin above
eye, and a chestnut band on tip of tail. In *franklinii* race (se.
Alaska to nw. U.S.), male has a row of conspicuous *white spots*
at base of black tail (no chestnut band). Female rusty brown,
thickly barred; has blackish tail with basic pattern of male's.
Similar species: (1) Male Blue Grouse is grayer, less patterned
below; tail larger. (2) Female Blue Grouse is grayer, less rusty;
has basic tail pattern of male. (3) Ruffed Grouse is much paler,
has a large fantail with black band near tip.
Where found: Alaska, Canada, n. U.S. **West:** *Resident* from w.
and n. Alaska, n. Yukon, n. Mackenzie south in mts. to ne.
Oregon, c. Idaho, nw. Wyoming, and in boreal forests to c.
Alberta, c. Saskatchewan. **Habitat:** Spruce forests; jack pines,
lodgepole pines. **Nest:** On ground under conifer. Eggs (8–12;
16) buff, spotted.

RUFFED GROUSE *Bonasa umbellus* 16–19 **Pl. 21**
Field marks: Note the fan-shaped tail with a broad *black band*
near its tip. A large, *red-brown* or *gray-brown* chicken-like bird
of brushy woodlands, usually not seen until it springs into the
air with a startling whir. Two color types occur: "red" birds
with rufous on tail and "gray" birds with gray tails. Red birds
are typical of Pacific states, gray of Rockies.
Similar species: (1) Female pheasants have long *pointed* tails.
See (2) Sharp-tailed and (3) Blue Grouse.
Voice: The male's drumming suggests a distant motor starting
up. The muffled thumping starts slowly, accelerating into a
whir: *Bup . . . bup . . . bup . . . bup . . bup . bup . up. r-rrr.*
Where found: Alaska, Canada, n. U.S.; in East, south to n.
Georgia. **West:** *Resident* from w. Alaska (Yukon River), c.
Yukon, Great Slave Lake south: (1) in coast belt to n. California;
(2) in mts. to ne. Oregon, c. Utah, Wyoming, w. S. Dakota;
(3) on wooded plains to c. Alberta, s. Saskatchewan. **Habitat:**
Mixed or deciduous woodland. **Nest:** A sheltered depression on
forest floor. Eggs (8–14; 23) buff, spotted or not.

WILLOW PTARMIGAN *Lagopus lagopus* 15-17 **Pl. 21**
Field marks: Ptarmigans are small arctic grouse that change their brown summer plumage for white when winter sets in. They frequent bleak tundra and alpine slopes where few other birds would long survive. The 2 widespread arctic species (Willow and Rock) are much alike: in the breeding plumage, brown with white wings, and in winter, white with black tails. **Similar species:** (1) There is no easy way to separate Willow and Rock Ptarmigans in the brown plumage but the Willow is usually more deeply chestnut on head and breast. Some races of the Rock are decidedly gray, finely barred. In winter the Rock Ptarmigan has a *black mark* extending from bill through eye. It has a smaller, more slender bill. There is a difference in habitat: the Willow resorts to willows and sheltered valleys in winter, open tundra and slopes in summer; the Rock Ptarmigan prefers the highest, most barren hills. (2) White-tailed Ptarmigan has white tail.
Voice: Deep raucous calls, *go-out, go-out.* A stuttering crow (male); *kwow, kwow, tobacco, tobacco,* etc., or *go-back, go-back.*
Where found: Arctic regions of N. Hemisphere. **West:** *Resident* from Aleutians, n. Alaska, n. Yukon, nw. Mackenzie south in mts. to c. B.C. Spreads south in winter to c. Alberta, c. Saskatchewan. *Casual,* nw. Montana. **Habitat:** Tundra, willow scrub, muskeg. **Nest:** A hollow lined with grass, feathers; on tundra. Eggs (5-10; 17) red-blotched.

ROCK PTARMIGAN *Lagopus mutus* 13 **Pl. 21**
Field marks: See Willow Ptarmigan.
Voice: Male, a harsh ticking croak, *karr-ke-karr kikikikik* (M. North and E. Simms).
Where found: Arctic and alpine regions of N. Hemisphere. **West:** *Resident* from Aleutians, n. Alaska, n. Yukon, n. Mackenzie south to n. B.C., Great Slave Lake. **Habitat:** Above timberline in mts. (to lower levels in winter); also bleak tundra of n. coasts, Aleutians. **Nest:** A poorly lined hollow on tundra. Eggs (8-12) blotched with dark red.

WHITE-TAILED PTARMIGAN **Pl. 21**
Lagopus leucurus 12-13
Field marks: Note the *white tail.* The only ptarmigan in w. U.S. In summer, brown with a white belly and white wings and tail. In winter, pure white except for black eyes and bill.
Similar species: Other ptarmigans are larger, have *black* tails.
Voice: Cackling notes; clucks, soft hoots.
Where found: *Resident* from s.-c. Alaska, n. Yukon, sw. Mackenzie south to Vancouver I., Cascade Mts. of n. Washington, and in Rockies locally to n. New Mexico (Costilla Peak). **Habitat:** Alpine summits. Lower levels in winter. **Nest:** A depression on open ground. Eggs (4-10; 16) buff, spotted.

GREATER PRAIRIE CHICKEN
Tympanuchus cupido 16¾–18

Field marks: Note the *short rounded dark tail* (black in males, barred in females). A brown henlike bird of prairies; heavily *barred.* "Dancing" male inflates orange air sacs on side of neck; erects blackish neck feathers (pinnae) hornlike.

Similar species: (1) Female Pheasant has long pointed tail. (2) Sharp-tailed Grouse (often called "Prairie Chicken") has pointed whitish tail. (3) Ruffed Grouse lives in woods, has a large fan-shaped tail. (4) See Lesser Prairie Chicken.

Voice: Males in spring make a hollow booming, *oo-loo-woo,* suggesting sound made by blowing across opening of bottle.

Where found: Canadian prairies to coastal Texas. **West:** *Resident* from s. Saskatchewan (very rare) through Dakotas, to e. Colorado, Kansas. Formerly c. Alberta. *Accidental,* Montana, Wyoming. **Habitat:** Tall grass prairie. **Nest:** A grass-lined hollow among grass. Eggs (7–17; 21) olive, spotted.

LESSER PRAIRIE CHICKEN   Pl. 21
Tympanuchus pallidicinctus 16

Field marks: A small, pale prairie chicken; best known by range (below). Gular sacs of male dull red (not orange).

Voice: Not as rolling or loud as booming of Greater Prairie Chicken. Various clucking, cackling, or gobbling notes.

Where found: *Resident* locally in se. Colorado (rare), w. Kansas (rare), w. Oklahoma, e. New Mexico, nw. Texas (Panhandle). Said to be established on Nihoa (Hawaiian Is.). **Habitat:** Sandhill country (sage and blue-stem grass, oak shinnery). **Nest:** A grass-lined hollow in grass or under bush. Eggs (11–13) buff, dotted.

SHARP-TAILED GROUSE   Pl. 21
Pedioecetes phasianellus 15–20

Field marks: Note the *short pointed tail,* which in flight shows white. A pale, speckled brown grouse of prairie brush.

Similar species: (1) Female Pheasant has a *long* pointed tail; (2) Prairie Chicken, short, *rounded, dark* tail; (3) Ruffed Grouse, *fan-shaped* tail.

Voice: Courting note a single low *coot* or *coo-oo,* accompanied by quill-rattling. Also a cackling *cac-cac-cac,* etc.

Where found: Alaska, Canada (east to c. Quebec), n. U.S. (east to n. Michigan). **West:** *Resident* from n.-c. Alaska, Yukon, n. Mackenzie south locally (east of Cascades) to e. Oregon, n. Nevada (rare), Utah, ne. New Mexico, Nebraska. **Habitat:** Prairie, brushy parklands, open thickets, forest edges, clearings. **Nest:** A grass-lined depression in grass or brush. Eggs (7–13; 15) olive-brown, dotted.

SAGE GROUSE *Centrocercus urophasianus* ♂26–30, ♀22–23
(Sage Hen) **Pl. 21**
  Field marks: A large grayish grouse of open country, as
  large as a small Turkey; identified by contrasting *black belly*
  patch and spikelike tail feathers. Male is considerably larger
  than female, has black throat, and in dancing display puffs out
  white chest, exposes yellow air sacs on neck, and erects and
  spreads its pointed tail feathers.
  Voice: Flushing note, *kuk kuk kuk*. In courtship display male
  makes popping sound.
  Where found: *Resident* locally, from s. B.C., e. Washington, s.
  Idaho, se. Alberta, sw. Saskatchewan, w. N. Dakota south (east
  of Cascades, Sierra) to e.-c. California, Nevada, Utah, nw. New
  Mexico, nw. Nebraska. **Habitat:** Sagebrush plains. **Nest:** Under
  sagebrush. Eggs (7–13; 17) olive-buff, spotted.

Quails, Partridges, and Pheasants: Phasianidae

QUAILS and Old World partridges are scratching, chicken-like
birds, usually smaller than grouse. Pheasants are chicken-sized,
with long sweeping tails. Sexes usually unlike. **Food:** Insects,
seeds, buds, berries. **Range:** Nearly cosmopolitan. **No. of species:**
World, 165; West, 9 (+3 or 4 introduced in Hawaii).

BOBWHITE *Colinus virginianus* 8½–10½ **Pl. 22**
  Field marks: A small, brown, chicken-like bird, near size of
  Meadowlark. The male shows a conspicuous white throat and
  eye-stripe (in female, buffy). Tail short, dark.
  Similar species: (1) Distinguished from other quail by browner
  color; (2) from grouse by small size; (3) from meadowlark in
  flight by lack of white outer tail feathers.
  Voice: A clearly whistled *Bob-white!* or *Poor Bob-whoit!*
  "Covey call, *ka-loi-kee?* answered by *whoil-kee*" (T. Roberts).
  Where found: C. and e. U.S. to Guatemala. **West:** *Resident*
  east of Rockies from s. Wyoming through e. Colorado, e. New
  Mexico. *Introduced* in Hawaii, s. B.C., Washington, Oregon,
  Idaho, w. Texas (El Paso). Black-throated *ridgwayi* race
  (Masked Bobwhite) of se. Arizona now extirpated. **Habitat:**
  Farmlands, brushy open country, roadsides. **Nest:** A grass-lined
  hollow in grass or among brush. Eggs (10–20; 37) white.

SCALED QUAIL *Callipepla squamata* 10–12 **Pl. 22**
  Field marks: Note the *bushy white crest* or "cotton top." A
  pale grayish quail ("Blue Quail") of arid country, with scaly

markings on breast and back. Runs; often reluctant to fly. **Voice:** A guinea-hen-like *chekar'* (also interpreted *pay-cos*). **Where found:** Resident from e. Arizona, c. Colorado south to c. Mexico; east to sw. Kansas, w. Oklahoma, w. Texas (to w. parts of Edwards Plateau and se. to lower Rio Grande Valley). *Introduced,* e. Washington. **Habitat:** Grassland, brush, arid country. **Nest:** A hollow under bush. Eggs (9–16) speckled.

CALIFORNIA QUAIL *Lophortyx californicus* 9½–11 **Pl. 22**
Field marks: A small, plump, grayish chicken-like bird with a *short black plume curving* forward from crown. Males have a black and white face and throat pattern. Females are duller.
Similar species: See Gambel's Quail.
Voice: A 3-syllabled call, *qua-quer' go,* variously interpreted as *Where are' you? You go way, Chi-ca' go,* etc. Also light clucking notes. Note of male on territory, a loud *kurr* or *twerk.*
Where found: Resident in s. Oregon, n. Nevada, California, Baja California. In California widespread but replaced in e. parts of Mojave and Colorado Deserts by Gambel's Quail. (On w. edge of these deserts both are found, hybrids occur.) *Introduced* widely elsewhere (Hawaii, s. B.C., Washington, n. Oregon, Idaho, Colorado, Utah, etc.). **Habitat:** Broken chaparral, woodland edges, coastal scrub, parks, estates, farms. **Nest:** A grass-lined hollow on ground. Eggs (10–17; 28) buff, spotted.

GAMBEL'S QUAIL *Lophortyx gambelii* 10–11½ **Pl. 22**
Field marks: Replaces California Quail in deserts. Similar, but male with a *black patch* on a light, unscaled belly; flanks and crown more russet (a local name is "Redhead"). Female *lacks* scaly pattern on belly of California Quail.
Voice: A loud *kway-er* and a querulous 3- or 4-noted call, *yuk-kwair' ga-o.* Similar to California Quail's call.
Where found: Sw. U.S., nw. Mexico. **West:** Resident in s. Nevada, s. Utah, se. Colorado, se. California (deserts), Arizona, New Mexico (east to Rio Grande); w. Texas (El Paso, sparingly to Big Bend). Said to be established Kahoolawe (Hawaiian Is.). **Habitat:** Desert thickets, usually near water. **Nest:** On ground. Eggs (10–16; 20) blotched.

MOUNTAIN QUAIL *Oreortyx pictus* 10½–11½ **Pl. 22**
Field marks: A gray and brown quail of the mts. Distinguished from California Quail by long *straight* head plume, *chestnut* (not black) throat. Note the chestnut and white side pattern. Female similar but duller, with shorter plume.
Voice: A loud mellow cry, *wook?* or *to-wook?* repeated at infrequent intervals by male in breeding season. Both sexes utter rapid, tremulous whistling sounds when alarmed.
Where found: Resident from n. Washington, n. Idaho south

locally through Oregon, nw. Nevada, California to n. Baja
California. *Introduced,* Vancouver I. **Habitat:** Brushy mt.
slopes, brushy forest. **Nest:** A leaf-lined hollow on ground
among brush. Eggs (5–15; 22) pale reddish.

HARLEQUIN QUAIL   *Cyrtonyx montezumae*   8–9½   **Pl. 22**
(Mearns' Quail)
  Field marks: A rotund quail of Mexican mts. Note the oddly
  striped clown's face, pale bushy crest (not always erected), and
  speckled body of the male. Females are brown, with less obvious
  facial stripings. Tame (called "Fool's Quail").
  Voice: A soft whinnying or quavering cry; ventriloquial (vaguely
  suggests Screech Owl).
  Where found: *Resident* locally from s. and e.-c. Arizona, c. New
  Mexico, w. Texas (Trans-Pecos) to s. Mexico. **Habitat:** Grassy
  oak canyons, wooded mt. slopes with bunch grass. **Nest:** A
  grass-lined hollow, arched; among grass. Eggs (8–14) white.

RING-NECKED PHEASANT   **Pl. 22**
Phasianus colchicus   ♂ 30–36, ♀ 21–25
  Field marks: Note the *long, sweeping, pointed* tail. A large
  chicken-like or gamecock-like bird. Male is highly colored and
  iridescent, with scarlet wattles on face and white neck-ring (not
  always present). Female is mottled brown, with a moderately
  long pointed tail. Runs swiftly; flight strong (take-off noisy).
  Similar species: Brown female could be confused with various
  grouse, but *long pointed tail* is characteristic (Sharp-tailed Grouse
  has short whitish tail).
  Voice: Crowing male has a loud double squawk, *kork-kok,*
  followed by brief whir of wing-flapping. When flushed, harsh
  croaks. Roosting call, a 2-syllabled *kutuk — kutuk,* etc.
  Where found: Asia. Introduced widely in N. America, Hawaii,
  and elsewhere. **West:** *Resident* from Queen Charlotte Is., s. B.C.,
  c. Alberta, c. Saskatchewan south to s. California, Nevada,
  Utah, New Mexico, nw. Panhandle of Texas. **Habitat:** Irrigated
  land, farmland. **Nest:** A grass-lined hollow among grass. Eggs
  (6–14) olive-buff.

CHUKAR   *Alectoris graeca*   13   **Pl. 22**
  Field marks: Like a large sandy-colored quail; gray-brown with
  bright red legs and bill; light throat bordered by clean-cut black
  "necklace." Sides boldly barred. Tail rufous.
  Similar species: (1) Gray Partridge lacks the black necklace, has
  dark gray bill and feet. (2) Mountain Quail is dark, has long
  head plume, lacks red tail. (3) *Note:* The related Red-legged
  Partridge, *A. rufa,* introduced into ne. Colorado, is darker, and
  its necklace breaks into short streaks.
  Voice: A series of *chuck*'s; a sharp *wheet-u.*

Where found: Asia, e. Europe. **West:** *Introduced* and established locally in s. B.C., se. Alberta, Hawaii, and most w. states. **Habitat:** Rocky, grassy or brushy slopes; arid mts., canyons. **Nest:** A hollow under bush. Eggs (8–15) buffy, spotted.

GRAY PARTRIDGE *Perdix perdix* 12–14   **Pl. 22**
(Hungarian or European Partridge)
   Field marks: Note the short rufous tail (in flight). A rotund grayish partridge, larger than a quail; has a dark U-shaped splotch on belly, rusty face, chestnut bars on sides.
   Similar species: Chukar (which also has rufous tail) has red bill and feet, black "necklace."
   Voice: A loud hoarse *kar-wit, kar-wit.*
   Where found: Eurasia. Introduced in N. America. **West:** *Resident* from s. B.C., c. Alberta, s. c. Saskatchewan south to ne. California, c. Nevada, n. Utah, c. Wyoming. **Habitat:** Open farmland, grainfields. **Nest:** A grass-lined hollow in grass or under bush. Eggs (10–22) olive.

TURKEY

Turkeys: Meleagrididae

VERY LARGE fowl-like birds; highly iridescent, naked-headed. Males with large tails erected fanwise in display. Females smaller, duller. **Food:** Berries, acorns, nuts, other seeds, insects. **Range:**

E. and s. U.S. to Cent. America. Domestic Turkey introduced by man throughout much of world. **No. of species:** World, 2; West, 1.

TURKEY *Meleagris gallopavo* ♂ 48, ♀ 36   **p. 69**
Field marks: A streamlined version of the barnyard Turkey. Head naked; bluish with red wattles, intensified in male's display. Tail erected fanwise in display by male; bronzy with buff or whitish tip. Bronzy, iridescent body; pale wings (primaries, secondaries). "Beard" on breast. Female is smaller, less iridescent; has smaller head, is less likely to have beard.
Voice: "Gobbling" of male like domestic Turkey's. Alarm, *pit!* or *put-put!* Flock call, *keow-keow.* Hen clucks to brood.
Where found: Colorado, Pennsylvania to s. Mexico. **West:** *Resident* from c. Colorado south locally through e. Arizona (west to San Francisco Peaks and Santa Catalina Mts.), New Mexico, w. Texas. *Introduced* locally with varying success in Hawaii, se. Washington, c. California, s. Utah, Montana, Wyoming, n. Colorado, Black Hills, etc. **Habitat:** In West, mainly mt. forests, broken woodlands. **Nest:** A leaf-lined depression on ground in woods or thicket. Eggs (8–15; 20) buff, dotted.

Cranes: Gruidae

LONG-LEGGED, long-necked stately birds, superficially like large herons; more robust, with shorter bills, bare red skin about face (in some species), and elongated inner secondary feathers that curl down over the ends of the wings, giving a tufted appearance. Sexes alike. Migrate in V or line formation. Neck extended in flight. Blaring trumpet-like calls. **Food:** Omnivorous. **Range:** Nearly worldwide except Cent. and S. America and Oceania. **No. of species:** World, 14; West, 2 (+1 accidental).

WHOOPING CRANE *Grus americana* 49–56   **p. 71**
Field marks: Spread 7–7½ ft. The tallest N. American bird and one of the rarest. A large *white* crane with a red face. Neck outstretched in flight; primary wing feathers *black* (often concealed by curved white secondaries when bird walks). Young are washed with rusty, especially about head and neck.
Similar species: (1) Wood Ibis has dark head, decurved bill, more black in wing (entire rear edge). At a distance (2) White Pelican and (3) Snow Goose could be confused with Whooping Crane because of pattern. (4) Egrets have no black in wings.
Voice: A shrill bugle-like trumpeting, *ker-loo! ker-lee-oo!*
Where found: The remaining flock *breeds* in n. Alberta (Wood Buffalo Park); *migrates* via Great Plains; *winters* in coastal *Texas*

on the Aransas National Wildlife Refuge. **Habitat:** Muskeg (breeding); prairie pools, marshes. **Nest:** A flat mound in marsh or muskeg. Eggs (2) buff, blotched.

WOOD IBIS

WHOOPING CRANE

Note the greater extent of black in Wood Ibis

SANDHILL CRANE *Grus canadensis* 34–48 **Pl. 4**
Field marks: Spread 6–7 ft. A long-legged, long-necked, gray bird with a *bald red crown.* Some birds are stained with rusty. Young birds are brownish; lack red crown. The tufted appearance over the tail marks it as a crane. In flight neck fully *extended;* wing motion distinctive, a smart flick or flap above body level (herons have a bowed downstroke). Often assemble in large flocks. In spring, groups hop, jump, flap.
Similar species: Great Blue Heron is often called "crane" but is less robust. In sustained flight it carries its neck in a loop with the head drawn back to the shoulders.
Voice: A shrill rolling *garooo-a-a-a,* repeated. Also *tuk-tuk — tuk-tuk — tuk-tuk;* a gooselike *onk* (L. Walkinshaw).
Where found: Ne. Siberia, Alaska, n. and c. Canada, nw., n.-c. and se. U.S.; Cuba. Winters s. U.S. to c. Mexico. **West:** *Breeds* from Arctic coast south locally (mainly east of Cascades) to ne. California, n. Nevada, nw. Utah, Colorado. *Winters* in California, s. Arizona, New Mexico, Texas. **Habitat:** Prairies, grainfields, marshes; in summer, also mt. meadows, tundra. **Nest:** A haylike mound in marsh. Eggs (2) olive, spotted.

Rails, Gallinules, and Coots: Rallidae

RAILS are compact, rather hen-shaped marsh birds of secretive habits and mysterious voices; more often heard than seen. Wings short, rounded; tails short, often cocked. Flight brief and reluctant; legs dangle. Gallinules and coots swim (often "pumping" head); resemble ducks except for smaller heads, forehead shields, and rather chicken-like bills. Sexes alike. **Food:** Aquatic plants, insects, frogs, crustaceans, mollusks, seeds, buds. **Range:** Widespread through nonpolar regions. **No. of species:** World, 132; West, 7 (+2 accidentals).

CLAPPER RAIL   *Rallus longirostris*   14–16½   **Pl. 24**
(California Clapper Rail)
   Field marks: The large gray-brown, tawny-breasted "Marsh Hen" of California's coastal marshes. Note the henlike appearance, strong legs, long, slightly decurved bill, heavily barred flanks, and white patch under short tail. Sometimes swims.
   Similar species: The Virginia Rail is the only other thin-billed rail found in California. It is half the size, rusty brown with gray cheeks, blacker flank-barring.
   Voice: A clattering *kek-kek-kek-kek,* or *cha-cha-cha,* etc.
   Where found: Coasts of California and e. U.S. to S. America. **West:** *Resident* locally along coast from Tomales, Suisun, and San Francisco Bays to San Diego; also along Lower Colorado River from Parker Dam to the delta; also se. end of Salton Sea. **Habitat:** Salt marshes, salicornia (Pacific Coast); fresh or brackish marshes (Colorado River). **Nest:** A bowl of grass, arched over, in marsh. Eggs (5–14) buff, spotted.

VIRGINIA RAIL   *Rallus limicola*   8½–10½   **Pl. 24**
   Field marks: A small *rusty* rail with gray cheeks; black bars on flanks, and a long, slightly decurved reddish bill. The only small rail, near size of meadowlark, with a *long slender* bill. Full-grown young in late summer are quite black.
   Similar species: Sora has short bill.
   Voice: *Wak-wak-wak,* etc., descending; also *kidick, kidick,* besides various "kicking" and grunting sounds.
   Where found: S. Canada to Strait of Magellan. Winters mainly from s. U.S. south. **West:** *Breeds* from w. Washington, s.-c. B.C., c. Alberta, c. Saskatchewan to s. California, s.-c. Arizona, New Mexico, w. Oklahoma. *Winters* from s. B.C. through Pacific states; sparsely from Utah, Colorado south. **Habitat:** Fresh marshes, tules; in winter also salt marshes. **Nest:** A loose saucer in marsh. Eggs (5–12) buff, spotted.

SORA   *Porzana carolina*   8–9¾   **Pl. 24**
   Field marks: Note the *short yellow* bill. The adult is a small plump gray-brown rail with a *black patch* on face and throat.

The short cocked tail reveals white under coverts. Immature lacks black throat patch, is buffy brown.

Similar species: (1) The only similarly sized freshwater rail, the Virginia Rail, has a long, slender bill. (2) Immature Sora can be confused with the smaller and rarer Yellow Rail.

Voice: A descending whinny. In spring a plaintive whistled *ker-wee?* When stone is tossed into marsh, a sharp *keek*.

Where found: Canada; w., n.-c., ne. U.S. Winters s. U.S. to Peru. **West:** *Breeds* from B.C., s. Mackenzie south locally to s. California, Nevada, n. Arizona, s. New Mexico, Colorado. *Winters* mainly from c. California, c. Arizona, s. New Mexico, s. Texas south. *Casual,* se. Alaska. **Habitat:** Fresh marshes, wet meadows; in winter also salt marshes. **Nest:** A loose grass cup in fresh marsh. Eggs (6–15; 18) buff, spotted.

YELLOW RAIL *Coturnicops noveboracensis* 6–7½ **Pl. 24**
Field marks: Rare. Note the *white wing patch* (in flight). A small yellowish rail, suggesting a week-old chicken; our only rail with a white wing patch. Very short yellow bill. Yellow Rails are mouselike; to flush them requires a bird dog.

Similar species: Immature Sora might be taken for Yellow Rail but is larger, not so yellow; lacks white wing patch. Notice back pattern in the plate. Sora prefers wetter marshes.

Voice: Ticking notes, often in long series: *tic-tic, tic-tic-tic; tic-tic, tic-tic-tic,* etc. (groups of 2 and 3).

Where found: Mainly Canada, n. U.S. Winters s. U.S. **West:** *Breeds* locally from Great Slave Lake to c. Alberta, N. Dakota; has bred in California (Mono Co.). *Winters* in California (mainly c. coast). *Casual,* Washington, Oregon, Montana, Nevada, Colorado, Arizona, New Mexico. **Habitat:** Grassy fresh marshes, meadows; rarely salt marshes (winter). **Nest:** A cup of grass in marsh. Eggs (7–10) buff, spotted.

BLACK RAIL *Laterallus jamaicensis* 5–6 **Pl. 24**
Field marks: A tiny blackish rail with a small *black* bill; about the size of a young sparrow. Back speckled with white. Nape deep chestnut. Very difficult to glimpse or flush.

Similar species: *Caution:* All downy young rails are glossy black (but when small lack the barring on flanks).

Voice: *Kik* notes; lighter than those of other rails.

Where found: California; c. and ne. U.S. south locally to W. Indies; Peru, Chile. Migrant in n. parts. **West:** *Breeds* locally near San Diego. Occurs north along coast to San Francisco and Tomales Bays. *Accidental* inland (California, Colorado). **Habitat:** Chiefly tidal marshes, salicornia. **Nest:** Hidden under mats of salicornia. Eggs (4–8) dotted.

COMMON GALLINULE *Gallinula chloropus* 12–14½
(Florida Gallinule) **Pl. 24**
Field marks: Note the rather chicken-like *red bill,* red frontal

shield. White feathers under the tail show prominently as does a *band of white feathers* on the sides. This dark cootlike marsh-lover is equally at home wading among reeds or swimming. When swimming, pumps head and neck (so does Coot).
Similar species: American Coot is stockier, shorter-necked; has a gray back, *white bill.*
Voice: A croaking *kr-r-ruk,* repeated; a froglike *kup;* also *kek, kek, kek* and henlike notes, loud, complaining.
Where found: S. Canada to Argentina; Eurasia, Africa. **West:** *Breeds* from n. California, w. and c. Arizona, c. New Mexico, w. Texas (El Paso) south. *Winters* from n.-c. California, s. Arizona south. *Casual,* Utah, Colorado. *Resident,* Hawaiian Is.
Habitat: Fresh marshes, reedy ponds. **Nest:** A shallow saucer of reeds, semifloating or anchored in marsh. Eggs (6–14; 17) buff, spotted.

AMERICAN COOT *Fulica americana* 13–16 **Pl. 24**
Field marks: The only slate-gray ducklike bird with a *white bill.* Head and neck blacker than body; divided white patch under tail. When swimming, pumps neck and small head back and forth (like gallinules). Gregarious much of year. Dabbles but also dives. Taking off, it skitters its big lobed feet ("scallops" on toes). In labored flight, white border shows on rear edge of wing; feet extend beyond tail. Immature is paler, with a duller bill. Downy young has a hairy *orange-red* head.
Similar species: Gallinules are smaller, have smaller heads, red bills (with yellow tips). Coots are more ducklike, resort more to open water and flock more (sometimes large concentrations). Immature Gallinule has a white stripe on side.
Voice: A grating *kuk-kuk-kuk-kuk; kakakakakaka,* etc.; various cackles, croaks. A measured *ka-ha, ka-ha.*
Where found: Canada to Ecuador. **West:** *Breeds* from B.C., s. Mackenzie throughout West. *Winters* mainly from B.C. through Pacific states; also from Utah, Colorado south. *Casual,* se. Alaska, Aleutians. *Resident,* Hawaiian Is. **Habitat:** Ponds, lakes, marshes; in winter also fields, salt bays. **Nest:** A shallow reed basket among reeds or on raft of vegetation. Eggs (8–12; 22) buff, dotted.

Jaçanas: Jacanidae

SLENDER, long-necked marsh birds with extremely long toes and toenails for walking on floating plants. Called "lily-trotters." Sexes alike; female larger. **Food:** Vegetable matter, invertebrates. **Range:** Tropical regions of world. **No. of species:** World, 7; West, 1.

JAÇANA *Jaçana spinosa* 8–9 **Pl. 24**
Field marks: Note the *extremely long toes*. *Adult:* Head and neck blackish, rest of body deep rusty. The best field marks are the conspicuous *yellow forehead shield* and *large pale greenish-yellow wing patches* (flight feathers). *Immature:* Gray-brown above, with whitish underparts and broad white stripe over eye. Slightly suggests Wilson's Phalarope. Extremely long toes, great yellow wing patches, and rail-like flight, notes, and habitat distinguish it from any shorebird.
Voice: A squeaky, reedy *quee quee quee quee* (I. Davis).
Where found: Mexico to Argentina. Rare visitor to Rio Grande Delta (has bred). *Casual* elsewhere in s. Texas. **Habitat:** Resacas, ponds, marshes. **Nest:** Eggs (4) brown, scrawled; laid on floating vegetation.

Oystercatchers: Haematopodidae

LARGE shorebirds with long, laterally flattened, chisel-tipped red bills. Sexes alike. **Food:** Bivalves, oysters, crabs, marine worms. **Range:** Widespread on coasts of world. **No. of Species:** World, 6; West, 1 (+1 accidental).

BLACK OYSTERCATCHER **Pls. 26, 27**
Haematopus bachmani 17–17½
Field marks: A large heavily built, all-black shorebird with a heavy straight *red bill*, pale legs. Unique.
Voice: A piercing, sharply repeated whistled note.
Where found: *Resident* from w. Aleutians (Attu), east and south along coast to Morro Bay, California; on offshore islands to Baja California. *Casual*, Pribilofs. *Accidental*, Utah (sight). **Habitat:** Rocky coasts, sea islets. **Nest:** A pebble-lined hollow on rock or gravel. Eggs (2–3; 4) buff, spotted.

Plovers, Turnstones, and Surfbirds: Charadriidae

WADING BIRDS, more compactly built, thicker-necked than most sandpipers, with shorter, pigeon-like bills and larger eyes. Call notes assist identification. Unlike most sandpipers, plovers run in short starts and stops. Sexes alike. *Note:* Nonbreeders often summer along coast. **Food:** Small marine life, insects, some vegetable matter. **Range:** Worldwide. **No. of species:** World, 63; West, 10 (+3 accidentals).

SEMIPALMATED PLOVER *Charadrius semipalmatus* 6½–8
("Ringed Plover")   **Pls. 25, 28**
   Field marks: Note the *dark breastband* (sometimes incomplete
   in front). A small plump shorebird, *dark* brown above; half the
   size of Killdeer. Has plover habit of running a few steps and
   stopping quite still. Bill may be orange with black tip, or (in
   winter) all-black. Legs orange or yellow.
   Similar species: (1) Killdeer is twice as large and it has 2 black
   rings across its chest. (2) Snowy Plover has *blackish* legs.
   (3) East of Rockies see Piping Plover.
   Voice: A plaintive slurred *chi-we,* or *too-li,* 2nd note higher.
   Where found: Arctic America. Winters to S. America. **West:**
   Breeds from n. Alaska, n. Mackenzie south to s. Alaska, Queen
   Charlotte Is., Great Slave Lake. *Migrant* on coast; less frequent
   in Great Basin, w. Great Plains. *Winters* chiefly on coast from
   San Francisco Bay south. **Habitat:** Shores, tideflats. **Nest:** A
   depression on beach or dune. Eggs (3–4) buff, spotted.

PIPING PLOVER *Charadrius melodus* 6–7½   **Pls. 25, 28**
   Field marks: Nearly as pale as Snowy Plover, but legs *yellow.*
   Bill yellow with black tip. A dark ring about neck.
   Similar species: (1) Semipalmated Plover's back is color of mud
   (Piping Plover's is like dry sand). (2) Snowy Plover has *blackish
   legs,* darker ear patch, *black bill.* See range.
   Voice: A plaintive whistle; *peep-lo* (1st note higher).
   Where found: S. Canada to Nebraska, Great Lakes, Virginia.
   Winters on coasts of s. U.S. **West:** *Breeds* locally in c. Alberta,
   s. Saskatchewan, sw. N. Dakota. *Casual,* se. Wyoming, ne.
   Colorado (has bred). **Habitat:** Sand beaches, lakeshores. **Nest:**
   In scrape on beach. Eggs (3–4) buff, spotted.

SNOWY PLOVER   **Pls. 25, 28**
Charadrius alexandrinus 6–7
   Field marks: A pale ghost-bird of the beaches. Smaller than
   Semipalmated Plover, much paler, with a *slim, black bill, blackish
   legs,* and black mark behind eye. The "ring" is reduced to a
   black mark on each side of the breast.
   Similar species: (1) Semipalmated Plover is much darker, with
   yellowish legs, heavier breastband. In winter the stubby bills of
   most Semipalmateds are also *all-black;* use then the leg color.
   (2) In n. Great Plains see Piping Plover.
   Voice: A musical whistle, *pe-wee-ah* or *o-wee-ah.*
   Where found: Widespread in s. U.S., Cent. and S. America,
   Eurasia, Africa, Australia, etc. **West:** *Breeds* on coast from s.
   Washington to Baja California; locally inland in e. Oregon, s.-c.
   and se. California, w. Nevada, Utah, Colorado, c. New Mexico,
   w. Texas. *Winters* mainly on coasts of Oregon, California.
   Migrant in Arizona. *Casual,* Montana, Wyoming. **Habitat:**
   Beaches, alkali flats, sand flats. **Nest:** A shell-lined scrape on
   beach, alkali flat, dike. Eggs (2–3) buff, speckled.

KILLDEER   *Charadrius vociferus*   9–11   **Pls. 25, 28**
Field marks: The common noisy breeding plover of the farm
country. Note the 2 black breastbands. Other "ringed" plovers
are smaller, have only 1 band. In flight, displays a *golden-red
rump*, longish tail, white wing-stripe.
Voice: Noisy; a loud insistent *kill-deeah,* repeated; a plaintive
dee-ee (rising); *dee-dee-dee,* etc. Also a low trill.
Where found: Canada to c. Mexico, W. Indies; also Peru.
Migrant in North. **West:** *Breeds* from n. B.C., s. Mackenzie
south. Winters from s. B.C., Idaho, w. Montana, se. Wyoming
south. *Casual,* se. Alaska. **Habitat:** Fields, airports, lawns,
riverbanks, irrigated land, shores. **Nest:** A scrape on bare
ground in field, bald spot in pasture, gravel shore, roadway, etc.
Eggs (4) buff, spotted.

MOUNTAIN PLOVER   *Eupoda montana*   8–9½   **Pls. 25, 28**
Field marks: Like a small Killdeer, but with *no breast-rings.* In
breeding season, *white forehead and line over eye,* contrasting with
black crown. In nondescript winter plumage, may be told from
winter Golden Plover by grayer back (devoid of mottling), *pale
legs,* light wing-stripe, dark tailband.
Similar species: American Golden Plover (and see above).
Voice: A low whistle; variable.
Where found: *Breeds* from n. Montana, N. Dakota through
Wyoming, w. Nebraska, w. Kansas, Colorado, New Mexico to
w. Texas. *Winters* from c. California, s. Arizona, s. Texas to c.
Mexico. *Casual,* nw. California, Nevada, Utah, se. Alberta, s.
Saskatchewan. **Habitat:** Semiarid grassland, plains, plateaus.
Nest: In scrape on ground. Eggs (3) olive, spotted.

AMERICAN GOLDEN PLOVER   **Pls. 25, 28**
Pluvialis dominica   9½–11
Field marks: Size of Killdeer. Breeding adults are dark shore-
birds, richly spangled with golden spots above; underparts black.
A broad white stripe extends over eye down side of neck. Young
and winter adults are brown, darker above than below; recog-
nized in flight from other plovers by lack of pattern.
Similar species: Black-bellied Plover is larger, pale gray above,
and has *white rump and upper tail.* Black-belly shows white in
wings and a black axillar patch (beneath wings, in "wingpits").
Golden Plovers are smaller, darker, without pattern.
Voice: A whistled *queedle* or *que-e-a* (dropping at end).
Where found: Siberia, arctic America. Winters, s. Asia, Hawaii
to Australia; s. S. America. **West:** *Breeds* from Arctic coasts to
c. Alaska (Nunivak, upper Yukon), n. B.C. (Spatzizi Plateau),
c. Mackenzie. *Migrant* through Alaska and Great Plains;
sparsely in Pacific states and in Great Basin. *Winters* in
Hawaiian Is. **Habitat:** Prairies, mudflats, shores; tundra (sum-

mer). **Nest:** A moss-lined hollow on tundra or beach. Eggs (3–4) buff, spotted.

BLACK-BELLIED PLOVER   **Pls. 25, 28**
Squatarola squatarola   10½–13½
   Field marks: This large plover, with its black breast and almost whitish back, resembles only the Golden Plover, which is brown-backed. Winter birds and immatures are gray-looking and are recognized as plovers by their stocky proportions and short pigeon-like bills. They have a dejected, hunched posture. In any plumage the *black axillars* ("wingpits") and the whitish rump and tail are determinative.
   Similar species: See American Golden Plover.
   Voice: A plaintive slurred whistle, *tlee-oo-eee* or *whee-er-ee* (middle note lower).
   Where found: Arctic; circumpolar. Winters coastal U.S., s. Eurasia to S. Hemisphere. *Breeds* from Arctic coast south to Hooper Bay, Alaska. *Winters* along coast from sw. B.C. south; also in large valleys of California, Hawaiian Is. Migrant in Great Basin, Great Plains. **Habitat:** Mudflats, open marshes, shores. **Nest:** A moss-lined hollow in tundra. Eggs (4) spotted.

SURFBIRD   *Aphriza virgata*   10   **Pls. 30, 32**
   Field marks: Note the conspicuous *white tail tipped with a broad black band.* A stocky dark gray sandpiper-like bird that inhabits wave-washed rocks where Black Turnstones are also found. In breeding plumage, heavily streaked and spotted with blackish above and below.
   Similar species: (1) Black Turnstone is blacker, has blackish legs, bolder "harlequin" flight pattern. (2) Wandering Tattler is slimmer, lacks any pattern in wings and tail.
   Voice: A sharp *pee-weet* or *key-a-weet.*
   Where found: *Breeds* in s.-c. Alaska (Mt. McKinley area). Ranges widely in w. Alaska. *Winters* from se. Alaska along coast to s. S. America. **Habitat:** Most of year, rocky coasts. **Nest:** On rocky ground of high mts. Eggs (4) buff, spotted.

RUDDY TURNSTONE   **Pls. 25, 28**
Arenaria interpres   8–10
   Field marks: Note the "harlequin" pattern. A squat, robust, orange-legged shorebird. In breeding plumage, with its russet-red back and curious black face- and breast-markings, the bird is very handsome, but when it flies it is even more striking (see Plate 28). Young birds and winter adults are duller, but retain enough breast pattern to be recognizable.
   Similar species: See Black Turnstone.
   Voice: A staccato *tuk-a-tuk* or *kut-a-kut;* also a single *kewk.*
   Where found: Arctic, Subarctic; circumpolar. Winters, s. U.S., Hawaii, s. Eurasia, to S. Hemisphere. **West:** *Breeds* from Arctic

coast south to Yukon Delta. *Migrant* mainly on coast, sparse inland. *Winters* from San Francisco Bay south; also Hawaii. **Habitat:** Surf-swept rocks, beaches, mudflats, jetties. **Nest:** A hollow in tundra or dune. Eggs (4) olive, spotted.

BLACK TURNSTONE *Arenaria melanocephala* 9 **Pl. 25**
Field marks: A squat blackish shorebird with blackish chest and white lower breast and belly. In spring has a round white spot before eye, and some white speckling. Its bold flight pattern is similar to Ruddy Turnstone's.
Voice: A rattling note higher than note of Ruddy Turnstone.
Where found: *Breeds* along coast of w. and s. Alaska (Seward Peninsula to Sitka). *Winters* along coast from se. Alaska to Baja California. *Casual* inland (Yukon, B.C., Montana, Pacific states, w. Arizona). **Habitat:** Rocky shores, breakwaters, bay shores, surf-pounded islets. **Nest:** A depression in coastal tundra. Eggs (4) olive, spotted.

Snipe, Sandpipers, etc.: Scolopacidae

A VARIED family of small or medium-sized wading birds. Most species frequent shores, marshes. Legs slender, long; bills more slender than those of plovers. Wing-stripes, rump and tail patterns are important diagnostically. Chiefly gregarious. Sexes alike in most species. *Note:* Nonbreeders often summer along coast. **Food:** Insects, small crustaceans, mollusks, worms, other invertebrates; sometimes seeds, berries. **Range:** Almost cosmopolitan. **No. of species:** World, 77 (Mayr-Amadon), 82 (Van Tyne-Berger); West, 30 (+11 accidentals).

COMMON SNIPE *Capella gallinago* 10½–11½ **Pls. 29, 31**
(Wilson's Snipe)
Field marks: Note the *extremely long, slender bill.* A tight-sitting bog wader, larger than a Spotted Sandpiper; brown with a *buff-striped back, striped head.* When flushed, it flies off in a *zigzag,* showing a *short orange tail* and uttering a nasal rasping note. Bill pointed somewhat downward in flight.
Similar species: See (1) Woodcock and (2) dowitchers.
Voice: A rasping note. Song, a measured *chip-a, chip-a, chip-a.* In high flight display, a hollow winnowing *huhuhuhuhuhu.*
Where found: N. Eurasia, n. N. America. Winters to c. Africa, Brazil. **West:** *Breeds* from nw. Alaska, n. Yukon, n. Mackenzie south to e. California, c.-e. Arizona, s.-c. Colorado, w. Nebraska. *Winters* from s. B.C., Idaho, Montana, Nebraska south. **Habitat:** Fresh marshes, irrigation ditches, streamsides, bogs, wet meadows. **Nest:** A grass-lined hollow in wet meadow, marsh, muskeg. Eggs (4) olive-brown, spotted.

LONG-BILLED CURLEW   **Pl. 26**
Numenius americanus   20–26
   Field marks: Note the very long sickle-bill (4–8½ in.). Much
   larger than the Whimbrel, more buffy; lacks bold stripes on
   crown. Overhead, shows *bright cinnamon wing-linings*. In many
   adults the bill is twice the length of the Whimbrel's; in young
   birds bill length may approach that of a Whimbrel.
   Similar species: (1) Whimbrel, see above. (2) Marbled Godwit
   has a straight or upturned bill.
   Voice: A loud *cur-lee!* (rising inflection). Also a rapid, whistled
   kli-li-li-li. "Song," a trilled, liquid *curleeeeeeeeuuu.*
   Where found: Sw. Canada, w. U.S. Winters s. U.S. to Guatemala. **West:** *Breeds* from s. B.C., s. Alberta, s. Saskatchewan
   south (east of Cascades) to ne. California, Nevada, c. Utah, ne.
   New Mexico, nw. Texas (Staked Plain). *Winters* from n. California, s. Arizona, se. New Mexico, Texas panhandle south.
   Habitat: High plains, rangeland. In winter also cultivated land,
   tideflats, beaches, salt marshes. **Nest:** A grass-lined hollow on
   open prairie. Eggs (4) olive, spotted.

WHIMBREL   *Numenius phaeopus*   15–18¾   **Pls. 26, 27**
(Hudsonian Curlew)
   Field marks: Bill 2¾–4. A large brown shorebird with a long
   decurved bill (the bills of godwits slightly turn up). *Grayer* than
   Long-billed Curlew; shorter bill, *striped crown*. Whimbrels
   appear as large as some ducks; often fly in lines.
   Similar species: See Long-billed Curlew (more buffy).
   Voice: 5–7 short rapid whistles: *ti-ti-ti-ti-ti-ti.*
   Where found: Arctic, circumpolar. Winters to s. S. America,
   s. Africa. **West:** *Breeds* from Arctic coasts south to Yukon
   Delta. *Migrates* along coast and in valleys of California; sparse
   on Canadian Plains; casual elsewhere inland. *Winters* from c.
   California coast south; a few on s. end of Vancouver I. **Habitat:**
   Shores, tideflats, open marshes, prairies. **Nest:** A grass-lined
   hollow on tundra. Eggs (4) olive, spotted.

BRISTLE-THIGHED CURLEW   **Pl. 26**
Numenius tahitiensis   17
   Field marks: Very similar to Whimbrel; tawnier (especially tail);
   tawny unbarred rump. Breast less streaked, bill paler.
   Voice: A slurred *chi-u-it* (Innuit name); suggests call of Black-
   bellied Plover. Also like "wolf whistle," *whee-wheeo* (A. A. Allen).
   Where found: *Breeds* in w. Alaska (near mouth of Yukon).
   Recorded elsewhere in w. Alaska. *Winters* on islands in c. and
   s. Pacific. **Habitat:** Tundra (Alaska); shores (Hawaii). **Nest:** A
   moss-lined hollow in tundra. Eggs (4) greenish, spotted.

UPLAND PLOVER   **Pls. 30, 31**
Bartramia longicauda   11–12½
   Field marks: A "pigeon-headed," streaked, buffy-brown sand-

piper (not a plover), larger than Killdeer. No really distinctive markings, but general brown coloration, rather short bill (shorter than head), comparatively small-headed, thin-necked, long-tailed appearance are helpful points. Has habit shared by some other waders of holding wings elevated upon alighting. Habitually perches on fence posts and poles.

Similar species: Other sandpiper-like birds in the grass country are (1) curlews and (2) godwits, which are much larger. (3) Pectoral and Buff-breasted Sandpipers are smaller.

Voice: A mellow whistled *kip-ip-ip-ip,* often heard at night. "Song," weird, windy whistles: *whoooleeeeee, wheeeloooooooooo* (starts with a rattle, ascends; 2nd part descends).

Where found: Mainly Canada, n. U.S. Winters on pampas of S. America. **West:** *Breeds* sparsely and locally from n. Alaska, sw. Yukon, s. Mackenzie south (east of Cascades) to e. Washington, ne. Oregon, n. Idaho, c. Colorado; rarely e. New Mexico, nw. Texas (n. Panhandle). *Migrates* mostly east of Rockies. *Casual,* ne. California, Arizona. **Habitat:** Grassy prairies, fields. **Nest:** A depression in clump of grass. Eggs (4) buff, spotted.

SPOTTED SANDPIPER *Actitis macularia* 7–8 Pls. 29, 32

Field marks: Note the *round spots* (breeding plumage). The common nesting sandpiper near lakes and streams throughout much of the West. Teeters up and down as if too delicately balanced. Many other sandpipers are streaked or dotted but this is the only one with such round black spots. Birds in fall and winter lack spotting; they are olive-brown above, whitish below, with a white line over eye. A dusky smudge on side of breast near shoulder encloses a white wedge (a good aid). Wing stroke shallow, quivering, maintaining a stiff, bowed appearance, unlike deeper wing strokes of other small shorebirds. Constant teetering while walking is a useful distinction.

Voice: A clear *peet* or *pee-weet!* or *pee-weet-weet-weet-weet.*

Where found: Alaska, Canada to c. U.S. Winters s. U.S. to n. Argentina. **West:** *Breeds* from nw. Alaska, n. Yukon, n. Mackenzie south to s. California (mts.), s. Nevada, c. Arizona, n. New Mexico, nw. Texas. *Winters* from s. B.C. (rarely) through Pacific states and from sw. Arizona, c. New Mexico south. **Habitat:** Pebbly lakeshores, ponds, streamsides; in winter, also seashores. **Nest:** A grass-lined scrape near shore or under bush. Eggs (4) buff, spotted.

SOLITARY SANDPIPER   Pls. 29, 31
Tringa solitaria 7½–9

Field marks: Note the dark wings and conspicuous *white sides of tail* (crossed by bold black bars). A dark-backed sandpiper, whitish below, with a white eye-ring.

Similar species: (1) Resembles a small Lesser Yellowlegs; nods like one, but has dark rump instead of white, and dark legs instead of yellow. (2) Spotted Sandpiper *teeters* more than it nods and has a white wing-stripe, which dark-winged Solitary lacks. Spotted has a narrow wing arc; Solitary, a darting, almost swallow-like wing stroke. Both may frequent similar places, but Solitary seems to avoid salt margins.

Voice: *Peet!* or *peet-weet-weet!* (higher than Spotted).

Where found: Alaska, Canada. Winters, Gulf of Mexico to Argentina. **West:** *Breeds* from c. Alaska, Mackenzie Delta south to n. B.C., c. Alberta, c. Saskatchewan. *Migrant* through w. U.S. **Habitat:** Streamsides, wooded swamps, ponds, fresh marshes. **Nest:** In old nest of Robin or Rusty Blackbird, near stream. Eggs (4) green or buff, blotched.

WANDERING TATTLER   Pls. 29, 31
Heteroscelus incanum   10½–11¼

Field marks: Note the lack of pattern. A medium-sized shorebird of rocky ocean shores. Solid grayish above, with white line over eye; legs yellowish. In breeding plumage, underparts are narrowly *barred* with black. In fall and winter, unbarred. Bobs and teeters like Spotted Sandpiper.

Similar species: Recognized at any time from the 3 shorebirds that inhabit similar rocks (Black Turnstone, Surfbird, Spotted Sandpiper) by *lack of pattern* in flight.

Voice: A clear *whee-we-we-we,* less sharp than Greater Yellowlegs; *tweet-tweet-tweet,* similar to Spotted Sandpiper's.

Where found: *Breeds* from Mt. McKinley, c. Yukon south to nw. B.C. *Migrates* along coast. *Winters* on coast mainly from s. California to Ecuador and on many Pacific islands. *Accidental,* w. Alberta. **Habitat:** Breeds on mt. streams above timberline. Rest of year, rocky coasts, pebbly beaches; in Hawaii, also tideflats. **Nest:** Of twigs on gravel bar of mt. stream. Eggs (4) greenish, spotted.

WILLET   Pls. 27, 30, 31
Catoptrophorus semipalmatus   14–17

Field marks: Note the *flashy black and white wing pattern.* At rest, when banded wings cannot be seen, this large wader is nondescript; gray above, whitish below in fall and winter; somewhat scaled below in summer. Legs bluish gray.

Similar species: Smaller than the brown godwits and curlews; a bit stockier than Greater Yellowlegs, from which it differs by its grayer look, stockier bill, dark legs, flight pattern.

Voice: A musical oft repeated *pill-will-willet* (in breeding season); a loud *kay-ee* (2nd note lower). Also a rapidly repeated *kip-kip-kip,* etc. In flight, *whee-wee-wee.*

Where found: S. Canada to Gulf of Mexico, W. Indies. Winters s. U.S. to Brazil. **West:** *Breeds* from se. Oregon, s. Idaho, c. Alberta, s.-c. Saskatchewan south to ne. California, c. Nevada, n. Utah, c. Colorado (rarely). *Migrates* along coast from Puget

Sound south; also through sw. U.S. *Winters* in California, mainly along coast. **Habitat:** Fresh marshes, wet meadows; in winter, tideflats, salt marshes, beaches. **Nest:** A depression or grassy cup among grass. Eggs (3–4) olive-buff, spotted.

GREATER YELLOWLEGS
Pls. 29, 31
Totanus melanoleucus 12½–15
Field marks: Note the *bright yellow legs* (shared with next species). A rather large slim sandpiper; back checkered with gray and white. Flying, it is dark-winged (no wing-stripes) with *whitish rump and tail.* Bill long, slightly upturned.
Similar species: See Lesser Yellowlegs.
Voice: A 3-note whistle, *whew-whew-whew,* or *dear! dear! dear!*
Where found: Alaska, Canada. Winters from n. U.S. (coasts) to Tierra del Fuego. **West:** *Breeds* from c. Alaska (Yukon River) south to c. B.C., c. Alberta. Migrant throughout. *Winters* from s. coastal B.C., s. Nevada, Utah (rarely), c. New Mexico south.
Habitat: Open marshes, mudflats, streams, ponds; in summer, wooded muskeg, spruce bogs. **Nest:** A depression on ground in timbered muskeg. Eggs (4) buff, blotched.

LESSER YELLOWLEGS *Totanus flavipes* 9½–11 **Pl. 31**
Field marks: Like Greater Yellowlegs but size of Killdeer; Greater is nearer size of Willet. The shorter, slimmer bill of the Lesser is quite straight; that of Greater ofter appears *slightly upturned.* Most easily identified by calls (see below).
Similar species: (1) Stilt Sandpiper and (2) Wilson's Phalarope (fall) have similar flight pattern. (3) See also Solitary Sandpiper.
Voice: *Yew* or *you-you* (1 or 2 notes); less forceful than clear 3-syllabled *whew-whew-whew* of Greater Yellowlegs.
Where found: Alaska, Canada. Winters from Gulf states to Argentina. **West:** *Breeds* from n.-c. Alaska, n. Yukon, nw. Mackenzie south to e.-c. B.C., c. Alberta, c. Saskatchewan. *Migrates* throughout w. U.S.; most numerous on Great Plains.
Habitat: Marshes, mudflats, shores, pond edges; in summer, open boreal woods. **Nest:** A depression on ground in lightly wooded area. Eggs (4) buff, blotched.

KNOT *Calidris canutus* 10–11 **Pls. 29, 31, 32**
Field marks: Stocky, with a rather short bill. Much larger than Spotted Sandpiper. *Spring:* Breast *pale robin-red,* back mottled buff and black. *Fall:* More nondescript, breast whitish or pale gray. A dumpy, light grayish shorebird with a short bill, whitish rump, greenish legs. At close range shows scaly white feather-edgings. Often in densely packed flocks.
Similar species: (1) Spring dowitchers, also red-breasted, have long snipelike bills (Knot's bill is short). In fall Knot, washed-out gray color, size, and shape are best clues; (2) Sanderlings are smaller, whiter; (3) Dunlins are smaller, darker (both have

dark rumps, blackish legs). (4) In flight, Knot's whitish rump does not show so contrastingly as that of yellowlegs, nor does it extend up back as in dowitchers.

Voice: A low *knut;* also a low mellow *tooit-wit* or *wah-quoit.*
Where found: Greenland, Siberia, nw. Alaska, Arctic islands. Winters to S. Hemisphere. **West:** *Breeds* occasionally in nw. Alaska (Pt. Barrow). *Migrates* along coast (seems to skip Oregon); rare inland in w. U.S. Winters in s. California (coast). **Habitat:** Tidal flats, shores. **Nest:** A depression on gravel of high ridge. Eggs (3-4) olive-buff, spotted.

ROCK SANDPIPER *Erolia ptilocnemis* 8-9 **Pls. 25, 30, 32**
(Aleutian Sandpiper)
Field marks: In breeding plumage suggests the Dunlin, with rusty back, black splotch on breast (but Dunlin is redder, with black splotch lower down, blackish legs; see Plate 25). In winter, very similar to Purple Sandpiper of Atlantic. Stocky and slaty, with white belly, white eye-ring, white wing-stripe. Legs dull yellowish or greenish. Its rock-feeding associates, Black Turnstone and Surfbird, both show in flight a broad *white band* across the base of tail, lacking in Rock Sandpiper.
Voice: A flicker-like *clu-clu-clu.* When breeding, a trill.
Where found: Ne. Siberia, w. Alaska. **West:** *Breeds* on islands of Bering Sea, Aleutians, Shumagins, and coast of c.-w. Alaska. *Winters* on coast from Alaska Peninsula south to Oregon. *Casual,* California. **Habitat:** Rocky shores. **Nest:** A depression on mossy tundra. Eggs (4) olive-buff, spotted.

SHARP-TAILED SANDPIPER **Pl. 32**
Erolia acuminata 8½
Field marks: Like Pectoral Sandpiper, but in winter plumage breast rich buffy (immature) or pale gray-buff (adult); spotted lightly on sides of breast only. In no plumage is there a sharp contrast between white belly, dark breast as in Pectoral.
Voice: *Trrit-trrit* (B. W. Tucker).
Where found: Presumably breeds in n. Siberia (nest unknown). Winters in w. Pacific islands. **West:** Fall migrant along coasts of Alaska, B.C.; casually south to Washington, California.
Habitat: Grassy borders of salt marsh.

PECTORAL SANDPIPER **Pls. 30, 32**
Erolia melanotos 8-9½
Field marks: Note the heavy breast-streaking, which *ends abruptly,* like a bib, against the white belly. A medium-sized sandpiper, the rusty-brown back in streaked with black and lined snipelike with white; wing-stripe faint or lacking. Legs and bill yellowish green. The neck is longer than in the "peeps."
Similar species: (1) Least Sandpiper is colored similarly, but is half the size. Small Pectorals might be confused with (2) White-rumped or (3) Baird's Sandpipers.

Voice: A reedy *krrik, krrik* (heavier than Western's note).
Where found: Ne. Siberia, American Arctic. Winters in s. S. America. **West:** *Breeds* from Arctic coast south to Bristol Bay, Alaska, e.-c. Mackenzie. Migrates through Plains and Rocky Mt. states; scarcer on coast (fall). **Habitat:** Prairie pools, marshy shores, tidal marshes; tundra (summer). **Nest:** A grass-lined hollow on dry tundra. Eggs (4) buff, blotched.

WHITE-RUMPED SANDPIPER   Pls. 30, 32
Erolia fuscicollis   7–8
Field marks: Note, when the bird flies, the *completely white rump;* the only "peep" so marked. Larger than Western Sandpiper, smaller than Pectoral. In spring, quite rusty; in fall, grayer than other "peeps."
Similar species: Other small streaked sandpipers have only *sides* of rump white. (1) Similarly sized Baird's Sandpiper does not have the conspicuous back-stripings of this bird in spring plumage. (2) Fall Dunlin is somewhat similar but larger, with a much longer, more decurved bill. If in doubt, make the bird fly and *look for the completely white rump.*
Voice: A thin mouselike *jeet,* of similar quality to *jee-jeet* note of Water Pipit. Like scraping of two flint pebbles.
Where found: Arctic America. Winters in s. S. America. **West:** *Breeds* on Arctic coasts of n. Alaska, nw. Canada. *Migrant* on plains, west sparsely to Alberta, Montana, Wyoming, Colorado, New Mexico. *Casual:* B.C., Idaho. **Habitat:** Pools, mudflats, shores. **Nest:** A depression in tundra. Eggs (4) olive, spotted.

BAIRD'S SANDPIPER   *Erolia bairdii*   7–7½   Pls. 30, 32
Field marks: Note the *buffy head and breast,* scaly back pattern. A "peep" sandpiper, larger than the Western; paler, with a rather short bill, blackish legs.
Similar species: The 3 smaller "peeps," (1) Least, (2) Western, and (3) Semipalmated, the similarly sized (4) White-rump, and larger (5) Pectoral are more or less *striped* on the back; Baird's has a *more scaly* appearance, and is predominately buff-brown. (6) Buff-breasted Sandpiper is buffy from throat to under tail coverts, not on breast alone, and has *yellowish,* not blackish legs. (7) *Caution:* Spring and summer Sanderlings show much orange-buff around head and breast. Note the bold white wing-stripe (Baird's has indistinct stripe).
Voice: Note, *kreep* or *kree.*
Where found: Ne. Siberia, American Arctic. Winters chiefly in Andes. **West:** *Breeds* along Arctic coasts; south to w. Alaska (Cape Romanzof). *Migrates* along coast; also inland on plains and probably in high mts. **Habitat:** Rainpools, pond margins, mudflats, shores. **Nest:** A depression in dry tundra. Eggs (4) buff, spotted.

LEAST SANDPIPER   **p. 88, Pls. 30, 32**
Erolia minutilla   5–6½
  Field marks: Note the *yellowish* or *greenish* legs. Collectively
  the sparrow-sized sandpipers are called "peeps." All have a
  similar streaked pattern. The Least may be known from the
  slightly larger Western Sandpiper by its yellowish (not blackish)
  legs, browner color, *slighter bill,* more streaked breast.
  Similar species: See above. See also Semipalmated Sandpiper.
  Voice: A thin *kree-eet,* more drawn out than note of Western.
  Where found: Alaska, Canada. Winters s. U.S. to Brazil.
  West: *Breeds* mainly in s. Alaska from Aleutians, Bristol Bay,
  south to Yakutat Bay. Presumably also nw. Alaska to Mackenzie. *Migrant* throughout West. *Winters* on coast from
  Washington south; inland from California, s. Nevada, c. New
  Mexico, w. Texas south. **Habitat:** Tideflats, grassy marshes,
  rainpools, shores. **Nest:** A hollow in moss in tundra marsh or
  bog. Eggs (4) buff, spotted.

RUFOUS-NECKED SANDPIPER   **Pl. 32**
Erolia ruficollis   6½
  Field marks: A "peep" easily recognized in summer by tawny-
  red head and upper breast. In winter, probably not safely
  identifiable unless collected. At that season rather like Semi-
  palmated Sandpiper (black legs, clear breast) but bill *slight,* like
  Least Sandpiper's.
  Where found: Mainly ne. Siberia; winters se. Asia. **West:**
  Breeds locally in nw. Alaska (Wales, Nome). *Casual,* Wainwright,
  St. Paul. **Habitat:** Like Least Sandpiper's.

DUNLIN   *Erolia alpina*   8–9   **Pls. 25, 30, 32**
(Red-backed Sandpiper)
  Field marks: Note the *downward droop* at the tip of the rather
  long stout bill. Slightly larger than Spotted Sandpiper or
  Sanderling. *Breeding plumage:* Rusty-red back; *black patch
  across belly. Winter plumage:* Unpatterned mouse-gray above,
  with gray suffusion across breast (not clean white as in Sanderling); note the bill. Feeding posture "hunched up."
  Similar species: (1) Breeding Black-bellied and Golden Plovers
  and Turnstones also have black on underparts. (2) So does
  breeding Rock Sandpiper (Alaska). (3) Sanderling (winter
  plumage) is whiter. (4) See also Western Sandpiper (smaller).
  Voice: A nasal, rasping *cheezp* or *treezp.*
  Where found: Arctic; circumpolar. Winters from coasts of U.S.,
  s. Eurasia to Mexico, n. Africa, India. **West:** *Breeds* from n.
  Alaska (Pt. Barrow) south along coast to Hooper Bay, Nunivak;
  also n. Mackenzie. *Migrates* chiefly along coast; sparsely through
  Great Basin, Great Plains. *Winters* along coast from Puget
  Sound to Baja California; also inland in California, s. Arizona,
  s. New Mexico. **Habitat:** Tidal flats, beaches, muddy pools;

tundra (summer). **Nest:** A depression in grass in wet tundra. Eggs (4) green or brown, spotted.

SHORT-BILLED DOWITCHER   Pls. 29, 31
Limnodromus griseus   10½–12

Field marks: Dowitchers are normally the *only snipelike birds seen on open mudflats.* In any plumage they are recognized by the *very long straight bill* and *white* lower back and rump. (The white extends up the back much farther than in other shorebirds with white rumps.) In spring plumage the breast is washed with cinnamon; in fall, with light gray. Dowitchers feed with sewing-machine motion; rapidly jab long bills perpendicularly into mud.

Similar species: (1) See Long-billed Dowitcher. (2) Common Snipe, only other bird with similar proportions, is rarely found on open beaches and flats. It has *dark* rump and tail.

Voice: A metallic *tu-tu-tu;* lower than Greater Yellowlegs'.

Where found: S. Alaska, Canada. Winters s. U.S. to Brazil. **West:** *Breeds* on coast of s. Alaska and from ne. B.C., Great Slave Lake south to c. Alberta, c. Saskatchewan. *Migrant* mainly along coast. *Winters* mainly from c. California south. **Habitat:** Mudflats, open marshes, ponds. More frequent on salt water than Long-billed Dowitcher. **Nest:** A depression on tussock in wooded muskeg. Eggs (4) greenish, spotted.

LONG-BILLED DOWITCHER   Pls. 29, 31
Limnodromus scolopaceus   11–12½

Field marks: Until recently the 2 dowitchers were regarded as merely races of the same species. Bill measurements overlap, but birds of this species with extremely long bills (3 in.) are easily recognized. The sides of the breast are barred rather than spotted; the back is darker, with buffy feather-edgings more restricted. Note the very different voices (the best clue). This is the species most likely to be found inland.

Voice: A single thin *keek,* occasionally trebled. (Short-billed Dowitcher has a trebled *tu-tu-tu,* lower in pitch.)

Where found: Ne. Siberia, n. Alaska, nw. Canada. Winters s. U.S. to Guatemala. **West:** *Breeds* on coast of nw. Alaska (Pt. Barrow to Hooper Bay); probably n. Mackenzie. *Migrant* throughout West. *Winters* from n. California, w. Nevada, Utah (rarely), s. New Mexico south. **Habitat:** Mudflats, shallow pools, margins. More addicted to fresh water than other dowitcher. **Nest:** On ground in muskeg. Eggs (4) greenish, spotted.

STILT SANDPIPER   Pls. 29, 31
Micropalama himantopus   7½–9

Field marks: In spring, heavily marked beneath with *transverse bars.* Has *rusty cheek patch.* In fall, not so obvious; gray above, white below; dark-winged and white-rumped (see below). Bill long, tapering; slight droop at tip.

Similar species: (1) Suggests dowitchers; often found in their company and feeds like them, often wading belly-deep and submerging head. Its whiter underparts, shorter bill (with slight droop at tip), longer legs distinguish it. (2) Its flight pattern suggests Lesser Yellowlegs (dark wings, white rump), but it is smaller, with a white stripe over eye and *greenish,* not yellow, legs. (3) Spring Wandering Tattler also has bars below, but its rump and tail are dark.

Voice: A single *whu,* like Lesser Yellowlegs'; lower, hoarser.
Where found: American arctic. Winters mainly in S. America.
West: *Breeds* in n. Mackenzie. *Migrates* through Great Plains west to Alberta and Rocky Mt. states. A few stragglers west to Pacific states and in n. Alaska. **Habitat:** Shallow pools, ponds, mudflats, marshes. **Nest:** A depression in tundra. Eggs (4) buff, blotched.

SEMIPALMATED SANDPIPER   below, Pl. 32
Ereunetes pusillus 5½–6¾

Field marks: Compared with Western Sandpiper the shorter, straighter bill is the best distinction. A trifle smaller, grayer in spring. In fall, lacks the rusty on scapulars often shown by the Western. Legs blackish (as in Western).
Similar species: (1) Typical Western Sandpiper has a longer bill, thicker at base, slightly drooped at tip. (2) Least Sandpiper is smaller, browner, thinner-billed; has *yellowish* legs.
Voice: Note, *crip* or *cheh* (lacks *ee* sound of Least, Western).
Where found: American Arctic. Winters se. U.S. to s. Brazil.
West: *Breeds* along Arctic coast south to Yukon Delta. *Migrates* mainly east of Rockies; west to interior B.C., Alberta, Rocky Mt. states; rarely in Great Basin. *Casual* on w. coast. **Habitat:** Beaches, shores, mudflats. **Nest:** A leaf-lined hollow in damp tundra. Eggs (4) olive-buff, spotted.

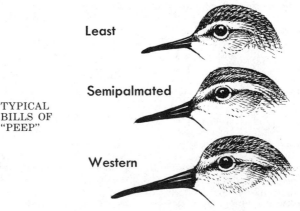

Least

Semipalmated

TYPICAL
BILLS OF
"PEEP"

Western

WESTERN SANDPIPER p. 88, Pls. 30, 32
Ereunetes mauri 6–7
Field marks: This and the Least Sandpiper are the 2 common small "peep" (sparrow-sized streaked sandpipers) west of the Plains. The Western is the larger; its bill is *very noticeably longer, thicker at the base,* and may droop slightly at the tip. In breeding plumage it is rusty on the back, scapulars, and crown. In full fall dress, it lacks the dusky breast of the Least, is grayer above, not so brown. Legs black.
Similar species: (1) Least Sandpiper is smaller, has *yellowish* legs. (2) On Great Plains see also Semipalmated Sandpiper.
Voice: A thin *jeet,* not as drawn out as note of Least.
Where found: Alaska. Winters s. U.S. to Peru. West: *Breeds* on coasts of n. and w. Alaska (south to Nunivak). *Migrates* throughout West. *Winters* on coast, mainly from San Francisco Bay south; (some north to Puget Sound); a few in sw. states. Habitat: Shores, beaches, mudflats, open marshes. Nest: In dry tundra. Eggs (4) spotted.

BUFF-BREASTED SANDPIPER Pls. 30, 32
Tryngites subruficollis 7½–8¾
Field marks: No other small sandpiper is so *evenly buff below* (to under tail coverts). A tame buffy shorebird with short bill, light eye-ring, yellowish legs. Looks long-necked, small-headed like a miniature Upland Plover. In flight, buff body contrasts with underwing (*white* with marbled tip). In spring "display," frequently raises wings, showing white linings.
Similar species: Baird's Sandpiper is buffy only across breast; throat and belly are white; legs are *black.*
Voice: A low, trilled *pr r r reet* (A. Wetmore). A sharp *tik.*
Where found: American Arctic. Winters in Argentina. West: *Breeds* locally on coast of n. Alaska (Pt. Barrow), n. Mackenzie. *Migrates* mainly through Great Plains; concentrations in c. Alberta. *Casual* on Pacific slope. Habitat: Short-grass prairies, fields. Nest: On tundra ridge. Eggs (4) buff, blotched.

MARBLED GODWIT *Limosa fedoa* 16–20 Pls. 26, 27
Field marks: Godwits are large shorebirds with very long, straight or slightly *upturned bills.* The rich mottled *buff-brown* color identifies this species. Wing-linings cinnamon.
Similar species: (1) The bills of curlews turn *down.* See Long-billed Curlew. (2) Other godwits have white in flight pattern.
Voice: An accented *kerwhit'* (or *godwit'*). Also *raddica, raddica.*
Where found: N. Great Plains. Winters s. U.S. to n. S. America. West: *Breeds* from c. Alberta, s.-c. Saskatchewan to c. Montana, w. N. Dakota. *Migrates* along Oregon, California coast, through Great Basin, Great Plains. *Winters* from c. California south. *Casual,* Washington, B.C., s. Alaska. Habitat: Prairies, pools, shores; in winter, beaches, tideflats. Nest: A depression on grassy flat. Eggs (4) olive-buff, spotted.

BAR-TAILED GODWIT   Pls. 26, 27
Limosa lapponica   15–18

Field marks: A small Alaskan godwit, smaller than a Whimbrel. In summer, male looks rich *reddish chestnut,* particularly on head and underparts; female duller. In winter plumage both are grayish above, white below. In any plumage, shows white rump and white tail crossed by narrow dark bars.

Similar species: Hudsonian Godwit has *black tail* with broad white ring at base; also bold white wing-stripe.

Voice: Flight note, a harsh *kirrick;* alarm, a shrill *krick.*

Where found: N. Eurasia, Alaska. Winters c. Eurasia to n. Africa, Australia. **West:** *Breeds* in n. and w. Alaska (Colville Delta to Kuskokwim Delta). *Migrates* in Aleutians. *Accidental,* B.C. **Habitat:** Mudflats, shores, tundra. **Nest:** A moss-lined hollow in tundra. Eggs (4) greenish, spotted.

HUDSONIAN GODWIT   Pls. 26, 27
Limosa haemastica   14–16¾

Field marks: Note the "ringed" tail. The large size (larger than Greater Yellowlegs) and long, straight, or slightly *upturned* bill mark it as a godwit; the black tail, *banded broadly with white* at the base, and a white wing-stripe proclaim it this species (suggests a very long-billed willet). In breeding plumage, dark reddish-breasted; in fall, gray-backed, whitish-breasted. Note the *blackish underwings* (in flight).

Similar species: (1) Marbled Godwit is without contrasting wing or tail pattern. (2) See Bar-tailed Godwit.

Voice: *Tawit'* (or *godwit'*); higher-pitched that Marbled's.

Where found: Arctic Canada. Winters in s. S. America. **West:** *Breeds* in nw. Mackenzie; probably locally in Alaska. *Migrates* through Great Plains. *Casual* west to B.C., Idaho. **Habitat:** Lakeshores, prairie pools. **Nest:** A depression in tundra. Eggs (3–4) olive-buff, spotted.

SANDERLING   *Crocethia alba*   7–8¾   Pls. 29, 32

Field marks: Note the *flashing white wing-stripe.* A plump, active sandpiper of the outer beaches, where it chases the re-treating waves "like a clockwork toy." In no other small sandpiper does the wing-stripe contrast so boldly or extend so far. Bill and legs stout for a sandpiper; black. In breeding plumage, bright rusty gold about head, back, and breast. In winter plumage the *palest sandpiper;* snowy white below, pale gray above; shows a dark *shoulder.*

Voice: A short *twick* or *quit;* distinctive.

Where found: Arctic; circumpolar. Winters from U.S., Britain, China, to S. Hemisphere. **West:** *Breeds* in n. Mackenzie, Arctic islands. *Migrates* mainly along coast; some through Great Basin, Great Plains. *Winters* in Hawaii and on coast from s. B.C. south; rarely Great Salt Lake. **Habitat:** Outer beaches, tideflats, lakeshores. **Nest:** On stony tundra. Eggs (4) buff, spotted.

Avocets and Stilts: Recurvirostridae

SLENDER wading birds with very long legs and very slender bills (bent upward in avocets). Sexes alike. **Food:** Insects, crustaceans, other small aquatic life. **Range:** U.S., Cent. and S. America, Africa, s. Europe, Asia, Australia, Pacific region. **No. of species:** World, 7; West, 2.

AMERICAN AVOCET   Pls. 26, 27
Recurvirostra americana   15½–20
  Field marks: Note the striking white and black pattern. A large shorebird with a slender *upturned* bill. In breeding season the head and neck are pinkish tan; in winter, pale gray. Feeds with scythelike motion of head and bill.
  Voice: A sharp *wheek* or *kleek,* excitedly repeated.
  Where found: Sw. Canada, w. U.S. Winters s. U.S. to Guatemala. **West:** *Breeds* from e. Washington, s. Idaho, c. Alberta, s. Saskatchewan to s. California, s. Nevada, n. Utah, s. New Mexico, w. Texas. Absent on nw. coast. *Winters* in California. *Casual,* B.C. **Habitat:** Marshes, mudflats, alkaline lakes, ponds; coastal bays (winter). **Nest:** A depression on sand or platform of grass on mudflat. Eggs (3–4; 8) olive, blotched.

BLACK-NECKED STILT   Pls. 26, 27
Himantopus mexicanus   13–17
  Field marks: Note the *grotesquely long red legs.* A large, slim wader; black above, white below. In flight it has black *un-patterned* wings, white rump and underparts, pale tail.
  Voice: A sharp yipping, *kyip, kyip, kyip.*
  Where found: W. and se. U.S. to Peru. Winters mainly south of U.S. **West:** *Breeds* locally from s. Oregon, n. Utah, s. Colorado (?) south. A few *winter* north to San Francisco Bay. *Casual,* e. Washington, s. Idaho, Wyoming. A similar species or race is resident in Hawaii. **Habitat:** Grassy marshes, mudflats, pools, shallow lakes (fresh or alkaline). **Nest:** On dry mudflat or on hummock in marsh. Eggs (3–5; 7) buff, spotted.

Phalaropes: Phalaropodidae

SMALL sandpiper-like birds; equally at home wading or swimming. Feet have lobed toes. When feeding they often spin like tops, rapidly dabbing their bills into the disturbed water. Females larger, more colorful than males. **Food:** Plankton, marine invertebrates, brine shrimp, mosquito larvae, insects. **Range:** Arctic (circumpolar) and N. American plains; migrate to S. Hemisphere. Two species, Northern and Red, are oceanic much of year. **No. of species:** World, 3; West, 3.

RED PHALAROPE   Pls. 25, 29, 32
Phalaropus fulicarius 7½–9

Field marks: The seagoing habits (swimming buoyantly like a tiny gull) distinguish it as a phalarope; in breeding plumage, *reddish underparts* and *white face* designate it this species. Male is duller than female. In fall and winter, gray above, white below; resembles Sanderling but has a *phalarope mark* through eye. At close range, note the relatively short thick bill, *yellowish* toward base (young birds may lack yellow).

Similar species: Autumn Northern Phalarope is a bit smaller, darker, with a streaked back. Its white wing-stripe contrasts more; it has a more needlelike black bill.

Voice: Similar to Northern Phalarope's *whit* or *prip*.

Where found: Arctic; circumpolar. Winters at sea mainly in S. Hemisphere. **West:** *Breeds* along Arctic coasts south to Hooper Bay, Alaska. *Migrates* along coast. *Casual* inland. **Habitat:** Open ocean, coastal estuaries, bays; tundra (summer). **Nest:** A depression in marshy tundra. Eggs (4) olive, spotted.

WILSON'S PHALAROPE   Pls. 25, 29, 31
Steganopus tricolor 8½–10

Field marks: This trim phalarope is dark-winged (no wing-stripe), with a white rump. In breeding females the broad face- and neck-stripe of *black blending into cinnamon* is unique. Males are duller, with just a wash of cinnamon on neck and a white spot on hind neck. *Fall plumage,* see below. Swimming and spinning are conclusive, but most often it is seen running nervously along margin.

Similar species: (1) In fall, suggests Lesser Yellowlegs (dark wings, white rump); but is whiter below, with *no breast-streaking;* has *needlelike bill,* and greenish or straw-colored (not canary-yellow) legs. (2) Other phalaropes show wing-stripes in flight.

Voice: A low nasal *wurk*. Also *check, check, check*.

Where found: Sw. Canada, w. U.S. Winters in s. S. America. **West:** *Breeds* from c. B.C., c. Alberta, c. Saskatchewan south through interior to s.-c. California, c. Nevada, Utah, s.-c. Colorado, w. Nebraska. *Migrates* throughout w. U.S. **Habitat:** Shallow lakes, fresh marshes, pools, shores, mudflats; in migration, also salt marshes. **Nest:** A grass-lined hollow in wet or dry meadow. Eggs (4) buff, spotted.

NORTHERN PHALAROPE   Pls. 25, 29, 32
Lobipes lobatus 6½–8

Field marks: Should a "Sanderling" alight on the sea, then it is a phalarope. This is the commoner of the two "sea-snipe" in the West; unlike the Red Phalarope it also migrates inland. Breeding females are gray above, with a patch of *rufous on the neck* and a white throat. Males are browner, similar in pattern.

In winter, both are gray above, white below. Note the dark "phalarope patch" through eye, black needlelike bill.
Similar species: See Red Phalarope.
Voice: A sharp *kit* or *whit*, similar to note of Sanderling.
Where found: Circumboreal. Winters at sea in S. Hemisphere.
West: *Breeds* from Arctic coast to Aleutians, s. Alaska, Great Slave Lake. *Migrates* off coast; also inland throughout West.
Habitat: Ocean, bays, lakes, ponds; tundra (summer). **Nest:** A grass saucer in marshy tundra. Eggs (4) olive, spotted.

Jaegers and Skuas: Stercorariidae

JAEGERS are dark falcon-like sea birds (narrow wings with a pronounced angle, slightly hooked beaks). Piratical, they harass gulls, terns; force them to disgorge. Plumages vary: (1) *light phase*, with black cap, paler back, white underparts; (2) *intermediate phase,* less cleanly marked with barring on sides, dusky breastband; (3) *dark phase* of uniform dark coloration. In all species, note the *flash of white* created by white wing quills. This and the *2 projecting central tail feathers* distinguish these birds as jaegers. Immature birds are square-tailed, lack the tail-points. They are heavily mottled and barred and are nigh hopeless to name in the field. The rare Skua lacks the central tail-points. Sexes alike.
Food: In Arctic, lemmings, eggs, young birds. At sea, food taken from other birds or from the sea. **Range:** Seas of world, breeding near polar regions. **No. of species:** World, 4; West, 4.

POMARINE JAEGER *Stercorarius pomarinus* 20–23 **Pl. 3**
    Field marks: Note the central tail feathers, which are *broad and twisted.* Although sometimes 4 in. long, they are usually stubby, projecting about 1 in. The Pomarine Jaeger is larger and heavier than the other species, usually heavily barred below, with a broad breastband and more white in primaries.
    Similar species: Immatures lacking blunt central tail feathers, when compared with other jaegers, show a much heavier bill and larger size (between that of Ring-billed and Herring Gulls).
    Voice: A harsh, quick *which-you.*
    Where found: Arctic; circumpolar. Winters at sea from latitude of s. U.S. to S. Hemisphere. **West:** *Breeds* along Arctic coasts south to Hooper Bay, Alaska. *Migrates* off coast. *Accidental,* Saskatchewan, Idaho, Colorado, Arizona. **Habitat:** Open sea, sounds, coastal bays; tundra (summer). **Nest:** A grass-lined depression on tundra. Eggs (2) brown, spotted.

PARASITIC JAEGER *Stercorarius parasiticus* 16–21 **Pl. 3**
    Field marks: Note the *pointed* central tail feathers (projecting ½ to 3½ in.). A hawklike sea bird, a bit smaller than a Ring-

billed Gull; chases terns, gulls. Like other jaegers has a flash of white in wings. The most frequently seen jaeger.
Similar species: Even experts let many of them go by as "just jaegers." See under jaegers (p. 93) and the other 2 species.
Voice: A nasal squealing *eee-air;* alarm, *ya-wow.*
Where found: Arctic; circumpolar. Winters at sea from latitude of s. U.S. to S. Hemisphere. **West:** *Breeds* from Arctic Ocean to Aleutians, Kodiak, Great Slave Lake. *Migrates* off and along coast; occasional inland in Great Basin, Great Plains. *Winters* offshore from s. California south. **Habitat:** Open ocean, sounds, coastal bays, large lakes (rarely); tundra (summer). **Nest:** A depression in tundra. Eggs (2) brown, spotted.

LONG-TAILED JAEGER   Pl. 3
Stercorarius longicaudus   20–23
Field marks: Note the long tail-points, sometimes projecting 9–10 in. (usually 3–6 in.). The Long-tail is much less often seen in migration than the other jaegers.
Similar species: As the central tail feathers of the Parasitic Jaeger vary greatly in projection (up to 4 in.), only typical Long-tails with points extending 6–10 in. can be safely identified by this character alone. Long-tails are usually much whiter below than Parasitics, lack the gray breastband, and have a more clean-cut black cap, sharply defined against a broad white collar. The back is paler (in contrast to black cap). Look also for *blue-gray legs* (Parasitic, black), and white on 2–3 outer primary shafts only (Parasitic, 4–5).
Voice: Seldom vocal. At breeding grounds, a shrill *kree.*
Where found: Arctic; circumpolar. Winters at sea, in S. Hemisphere. **West:** *Breeds* on Arctic coast (south to Hooper Bay); also interior Alaska. *Migrates* off coast. *Casual,* Alberta. *Accidental,* Utah, Montana, Colorado, New Mexico. **Habitat:** Open ocean; tundra (summer). **Nest:** A depression in low or hilly tundra. Eggs (2–3) olive, spotted.

SKUA   *Catharacta skua*   20–22   Pl. 3
Field marks: Note the *conspicuous white wing patch.* A rare sea bird, a bit smaller than Western Gull but of stockier appearance. Dark brown, with rusty underparts, short, *square-cut tail.* Suggests a dark *Buteo* more than a gull. Flight surprisingly strong and swift; it easily overtakes other sea birds and forces them to disgorge.
Similar species: Dark jaegers often lack tail-points. Skua's wings are wider and rounded, not long and pointed; white wing patches (as viewed from above) much more striking.
Where found: Wanders widely in oceans of world, breeding locally on islands in colder parts of e. N. Atlantic, s. S. Atlantic, s. S. Pacific. **West:** *Casual* stray off coast. Reported B.C., Washington, California. **Habitat:** Open sea.

Gulls and Terns: Laridae

Gulls: Larinae

LONG-WINGED swimming birds with superb flight. More robust, wider-winged, usually longer-legged than terns. Bills slightly hooked. They usually have square or rounded tails (terns, usually forked). They seldom dive (terns hover, plunge headfirst). **Food:** Omnivorous: Marine life, plant and animal food, refuse, carrion. **Range:** Nearly worldwide, favoring coasts. **No. of species:** World, 43; West, 17 (+5 accidentals).

The 3 gulls most widely seen inland in the w. U.S. and sw. Canada are the California, Ring-billed, and Bonaparte's. The Herring Gull is encountered in lesser numbers and Franklin's Gull is more restricted to the Great Plains and Great Salt Lake.

In gull terminology the word *mantle* means the upper surface of wings and back. In identifying adult gulls (which except for Heermann's have immaculate tails), the most important marks lie in the feet, bills, and wing-tips (see chart, p. 96):

(1) Feet (whether pinkish, yellowish, greenish, red, or black);
(2) Bills (whether yellowish, greenish, red, or black and whether distinctively marked);
(3) Wing-tips (whether solid black, black with white spots or "mirrors," gray, or white; the wing patterns of most species are especially distinctive).

Immature birds are more difficult. They are usually darkest the 1st year, lighter the 2nd, and in the larger species may still not be fully adult the 3rd year. The leg and bill color of most immatures (Glaucous-winged, Western, Herring, California, Ring-bill, and Mew) is not helpful. Most young birds have *pinkish* legs (at least at first). The bills of 1st-year Glaucous-wing, Western, and Herring are usually *blackish;* those of Glaucous, California, Ring-bill, and Mew are more pinkish at base. The bills of 2nd-year birds of all 7 species are basally pinkish or flesh. For the most part, go by plumage pattern and size.

GLAUCOUS GULL *Larus hyperboreus* 26–32 **Pls. 33, 34**
Field marks: Note the *"frosty"* wing-tips. A large chalky-white gull *without dark wing-tips;* usually a little larger than Glaucous-winged Gull. First-winter birds are *pale buffy,* with *light primaries,* which are a shade lighter than the rest of wing. Basal half of bill is often *flesh pink* (mainly dark in 1st-year Glaucous-wing). This is valid in 1st-year birds only. Second-year birds are *white throughout.* Adults have a pale gray mantle but *unmarked white primaries.*
Similar species: Adult Glaucous-winged Gull has gray in primaries. Eye dark (Glaucous, pale). Immature Glaucous-wing

ANALYSIS OF ADULT GULLS

Species	Wing-tips	Bill	Legs
● Ross' 13"–14"	Pale gray, unmarked	Black, small	Red
● Ivory 15"–17"	White, unmarked	Yellowish	Black
○ Glaucous 26"–32"	White primaries, unmarked	Yellow with red spot on lower mandible	Flesh-colored
● Glaucous-winged 24"–27"	Gray spots		
○ Western 24"–27"	Black (with small white tips) blending into dark mantle	Yellow with red spot on lower mandible	Flesh-colored
○ Slaty-backed 27"			
○ Herring 22½"–26" ● (*thayeri*)		Yellow with red spot on lower mandible	Flesh-colored
● California 20"–23"	These 4 species all have contrasty black tips with white spots or "mirrors" within the black	Yellow with red or red and black spot	Greenish
○ Ring-billed 18"–21"		Yellow with complete black ring	Yellowish or yellow-green
● Mew 16"–18"		Greenish yellow, unmarked	Yellow-green
● Laughing* 15½"–17"	Blackish, blending into dark mantle	Dark red or dusky	Dark red or dusky
● Franklin's* 13½"–15½"	Irregular black bar crossing white ground	Dark red	Dark red-brown
● Bonaparte's* 12"–14"	Long white triangle, tipped black	Black	Red
● Sabine's* 13"–14"	Long, clear-cut black triangle	Black, with yellow tip	Black
● Heermann's 18"–21"	Black, unmarked	Red	Black
● Black-legged Kittiwake 16"–18"	Solid black, cut straight across	Yellow, unmarked	Black
● Red-legged Kittiwake 14"–15¾"	Solid black, cut straight across	Yellow, unmarked	Red

○ Yellow eye. ● Dark eye.
* In the breeding season, these 4 species have blackish heads.

is darker. *Caution:* Many a young Glaucous-wing has been transformed into a Glaucous by list-hungry neophytes who view the bird from below, where against the light the primaries look lighter than rest of wing.
Where found: Arctic; circumpolar. Winters to U.S., Britain, n. China. **West:** *Breeds* on Arctic coasts and islands south to Bristol Bay, Alaska. *Winters* along coast from Bering Sea to s. California (sparingly). *Casual* east of Rockies from Alberta to n. Texas; also Utah. **Habitat:** Coastal waters. **Nest:** On sea cliff, in colony. Eggs (3) brown, spotted.

GLAUCOUS-WINGED GULL   Pls. 33, 34
Larus glaucescens   24–27
Field marks: *Adult:* A *pink-footed* gull with a pale gray mantle and *gray* pattern on wing-tips (the black of Herring Gull's wing-tips replaced by gray). *First year:* Gray-brown throughout; similar to 1st-year Western and Herring Gull but lighter and browner; primaries usually *the same gray-brown as rest of bird* (not darker or blackish, as in Western or most other gulls). *Second year:* Paler and grayer; primaries pale gray-brown. *In any plumage, gray or pale gray-brown wing-tips.*
Similar species: See Glaucous Gull.
Voice: A low *kak kak kak* or *klook, klook, klook;* a low *wow;* a high-pitched *keer, keer.*
Where found: *Breeds* from Bering Sea south along coast to nw. Washington. *Winters* along coast and tidal rivers from se. Alaska to Baja California. *Accidental,* w. Arizona, Colorado. **Habitat:** Coast, ocean, bays, beaches, piers, dumps, waterfronts. **Nest:** A mass of seaweed or grass on coastal island or headland; in colony. Eggs (2–3) olive-brown, spotted.

SLATY-BACKED GULL   *Larus schistisagus*   27
Field marks: Any large dark-backed gull in the Bering Sea would most likely be this species. Similar to Great Black-backed Gull of Atlantic but a bit smaller, lighter. Similar also to Western Gull but feet pinker.
Where found: Pacific coast of Asia. **West:** Rare visitor to Alaska. Recorded at a number of points in Pribilofs, Aleutians, and coast of w. Alaska. *Casual,* nw. Mackenzie.

WESTERN GULL   *Larus occidentalis*   24–27   Pls. 33, 34
Field marks: Note the *very dark back and wings* contrasting with the snowy underparts. Feet pinkish. The n. race, *L. o. occidentalis* (c. California to Washington), has a paler mantle, which, however, is still noticeably darker than that of California Gull. The s. race, *L. o. wymani,* is blacker-backed, reminding Easterners of a Great Black-backed Gull. *First year:* A large gray-brown gull, distinguished (a) from 1st-year California Gull

by larger size and much heavier and darker bill; (b) from 1st-year
Glaucous-winged Gull by blackish primaries, and (c) from 1st-
year Herring by greater contrast between light and dark markings. *Second year:* Head and underparts mostly whitish; bird
has "saddle-backed" appearance of adult. Stout bill and black
primaries are aids to identification.
Similar species: In Alaska see Slaty-backed Gull.
Voice: A guttural *kuk kuk kuk.* Also *whee whee whee; ki-aa.*
Where found: *Resident* along coast from nw. Washington south
to Baja California. Some in winter north to sw. B.C. and on
lower reaches of tidal rivers. *Accidental,* w. Arizona. **Habitat:**
Coastal waters, estuaries, beaches, piers, city waterfronts.
Nest: Of grass on offshore islet on mainland sea cliff; in colony.
Eggs (2–4) buff-brown, spotted.

HERRING GULL *Larus argentatus* 22½–26   **Pls. 33, 34**
Field marks: *Adult:* The only large gull with a pearly-gray
mantle that combines *black wing-tips* and *flesh-colored legs.* The
smaller race *thayeri* (wintering mainly from B.C. to San Francisco) has a *light brown eye* (in typical Herring Gull, whitish);
white "mirrors" in black wing-tips larger. *First year:* Dusky
gray-brown throughout (see below). *Second year:* Whiter. Tail
feathers dark, contrasting with white rump.
Similar species: (1) Adult California Gull has greenish legs.
(2) Adult Western Gull has much darker mantle, very dark eye.
(3) First-year Western Gull has shorter bill, with deeper angle
on lower mandible. The brown color is duskier, with more
contrast between dark and light markings. Forehead and front
of face not as pale. (4) Second-year Western Gull has a definitely
"saddle-backed" appearance (more contrast). (5) Young California Gull is almost indistinguishable from young Herring
except by somewhat smaller size, slighter bill.
Voice: A loud *hiyah . . . hiyah . . . hiyah-hyah* or *yuk-yuk-yuk-
yuk-yuckle-yuckle.* Mewing; squeals. Anxiety note,*gah-gah-gah.*
Where found: Northern parts of N. Hemisphere. Winters to
Cent. America, Africa, India. **West:** *Breeds* from c. Alaska,
n. Mackenzie to s. Alaska, c. B.C., ne. Alberta, e. Montana.
Winters from s. Alaska south along coast to Mexico; also
sparsely in interior from e. Washington, Wyoming south. **Habitat:** Ocean, coast, bays, beaches, lakes, piers, farmland, refuse
dumps. **Nest:** A mass of grass, seaweed, usually on ground
or cliff on island; in colony. Eggs (2–3) brown or olive, spotted.

CALIFORNIA GULL *Larus californicus* 20–23 **Pls. 33, 34**
Field marks: *Adult:* Medium-gray mantle, black wing-tips with
white spots, *greenish legs.* Bill with *red, or red and black,* spot
on lower mandible. Several gulls have gray mantles and black
wing-tips. This is one of the commonest. *First year:* Dusky

brown, mottled; bill flesh-colored with black tip. Most 2nd-year gulls have bills like this but in no other brown 1st-year bird is there so much flesh color. *Second year:* Paler; whiter below; more white at base of tail, back medium gray. Sometimes almost a "ringed" bill.
Similar species: (1) Adult Ring-billed Gull is smaller, paler-backed; has a *complete* black ring on bill (no red). Shows less white in wing-tips. (2) Young Ring-billed always has a narrow black tailband. (3) First-year Western Gull is darker than 1st-year California; larger with a larger bill; more contrast between dark and light markings. (4) Second-year Western has a dark-backed ("saddle-backed") look. See also (5) Mew Gull and (6) Herring Gull (young bird very similar).
Voice: A squealing *kiarr;* typical gull vocabulary.
Where found: *Breeds* locally on lakes from n.-c. Mackenzie south through Alberta, Saskatchewan to c.-e. California, w. and c. Nevada, nw. Utah, Wyoming, N. Dakota. *Winters* mainly along coast from s. B.C. to Guatemala; inland locally in Great Basin. *Casual,* se. Alaska, Colorado. **Habitat:** Coast, beaches, lakes, rivers, piers, farmland, cities. **Nest:** On ground, on islet in fresh or alkaline lake; in colony. Eggs (2–3) olive or brown, spotted.

RING-BILLED GULL   Pls. 33, 34
Larus delawarensis   18–21
    Field marks: *Adult:* Very similar to California Gull; distinguished by smaller size, lighter mantle, *complete black ring* encircling bill and more *yellowish*-green legs. *Immature:* Whitish below, gray-brown above; wings brown (mottled); tail with a *narrow black band* (a little over 1 in. wide) near tip.
    Similar species: (1) See California Gull (under *Similar species*). See also (2) Mew Gull and (3) Herring Gull.
    Voice: A shrill *kyow;* squealing cries; anxiety note, *ka-ka-ka.*
    Where found: Canada, n. U.S. Winters n. U.S. to Mexico, Cuba. **West:** *Breeds* from c. Washington, Alberta, n.-c. Saskatchewan to ne. California, s.-c. Idaho, s.-c. Colorado (?). *Migrant* in B.C. and throughout w. U.S. *Winters* from Washington, Wyoming south. **Habitat:** Coast, bays, estuaries, lakes, rivers, piers, refuse dumps, fields, cities. **Nest:** On island in lake; in colony. Eggs (2–4) variable, spotted.

MEW GULL   *Larus canus*   16–18   Pls. 33, 34
(Short-billed Gull)
    Field marks: *Adult:* Has greenish legs; medium-gray mantle. Smaller than Ring-billed Gull, with small, short, *unmarked greenish-yellow bill,* darker back. Shows more white in black wing-tips than either California or Ring-billed Gull. *Immature: 1st year,* uniform grayish brown, like a pint-sized 1st-year Cali-

fornia or Herring Gull with a tiny plover-like bill; *2nd year,* paler; plumage approaching that of adult.
Similar species: Young Ring-billed Gull is larger and has the black on tail confined to a narrow *clean-cut* band.
Voice: A low mewing (which gives the name), *quee'u* or *mee'u.* Also *hiyah-hiyah-hiyah,* etc., higher than other gulls.
Where found: N. Eurasia, w. N. America. Winters to Formosa, California, Mediterranean. **West:** *Breeds* from n. Alaska, w. Mackenzie south on coast to s. B.C.; in interior to s. Yukon, n. Saskatchewan. *Migrant,* n. Alberta. *Winters* from se. Alaska south along coast to s. California. *Accidental,* Wyoming.
Habitat: Coastal waters, tidal rivers (winter); lakes (summer; n. Canada). **Nest:** In marsh, on beach, rocks or tree; usually in colony. Eggs (3) brown, spotted.

LAUGHING GULL *Larus atricilla* 15½–17   **Pl. 33**
Field marks: Note the *dark mantle* that *blends* into black wing-tips and the conspicuous white border along trailing edge of wing. A little smaller than a Ring-billed Gull. In breeding season, head is blackish; in winter, white with dark markings. Bill and legs deep red to blackish. The 1st-year bird is *very dark,* with a *white rump.* The white border on the rear of the wing, the dark breast, blackish legs are also good marks.
Similar species: (1) See Franklin's Gull. (2) Dark young Heermann's Gull lacks white rump of dark young Laughing Gull.
Voice: A strident laugh, *ha-ha-ha-ha-ha-haah-haah-haah,* and *ka-ha, ka-ha.*
Where found: Coast; Nova Scotia to Venezuela, locally in se. California, w. Mexico. Winters from s. U.S. south. **West:** A very few *breed* irregularly at Salton Sea (se. California). *Accidental,* coastal California, Colorado, New Mexico, w. Texas.
Habitat: Salt-water marshes, bays. **Nest:** A platform of grass on marsh island. Eggs (3) buff, spotted.

FRANKLIN'S GULL *Larus pipixcan* 13½–15½ **Pls. 33, 34**
Field marks: The "Prairie Dove." Often fly-catches on wing. Note the *white band* separating the black from the gray on the spread wing. Overhead, this irregular "window" transmits the light. In summer the breast has a faint rosy bloom; the head is black. In fall the head is white, with a dark patch from eye around nape. Young birds are small *dark-mantled* gulls with whitish underparts, *white rump,* dark tailband and dusky smudge on nape.
Similar species: (1) Adult Laughing Gull has dark, *blended* wing-tips; ordinarily, Franklin's and Laughing Gulls do not come in contact in our area. Second-winter Laughing Gulls are so similar to young Franklin's that I do not regard it safe to distinguish them. First-year Laughing Gulls have brown breasts,

brown foreheads and can be recognized. (2) Inland, the only other common black-headed gull is the migrant Bonaparte's. It has a long *wedge of white* on the fore edge of the spread wing. (3) Ring-billed Gull has *white spots* within black wing-tips, and pale legs (Franklin's, dark); it never has a black head.

Voice: A shrill *kuk-kuk-kuk;* also a high nasal *kaar, kaar.*

Where found: *Breeds* from Canadian prairies to Oregon (Malheur Lake), Great Salt Lake, ne. S. Dakota, nw. Iowa. Winters Guatemala to Chile. *Migrates* through Great Plains, sparingly in Great Basin, rarely California. *Casual,* B.C. **Habitat:** Prairies, marshes, lakes; in winter, coast, ocean. **Nest:** Among reeds in prairie marsh; in colony. Eggs (3) brown, spotted.

BONAPARTE'S GULL *Larus philadelphia* 12–14 **Pls. 33, 34**
Field marks: Note the long wedge of white on the fore edge of the spread wing. A very small gull, near size of most terns; often acts like one. In breeding plumage has a blackish head. Legs bright red; bill small, black. In young birds and winter adults, head is white, with a well-defined round black spot behind eye. Immatures have a *narrow* black band on tip of tail.

Voice: A nasal *cheer* or *cherr.* Some notes ternlike.

Where found: Alaska, w. Canada. Winters n. U.S. to Mexico, W. Indies. **West:** *Breeds* from w. and c. Alaska, s. Yukon, n. Mackenzie south to c. B.C., c. Alberta, c. Saskatchewan. *Migrates* coastally and inland throughout West. *Winters* along coast from s. B.C. south; rarely on Lower Colorado River. **Habitat:** Ocean, bays, rivers, lakes; muskeg (summer). **Nest:** In conifer in wooded muskeg. Eggs (2–4) brown, spotted.

HEERMANN'S GULL *Larus heermanni* 18–21 **Pls. 33, 34**
Field marks: The easiest w. gull to identify. *Adult:* Dark gray, with a black tail, *whitish head, red bill. Immature:* All dark; lacks white head; bill brown or partly red.

Voice: A whining *whee-ee;* also a repeated *cow-auk.*

Where found: *Breeds* on islands off coasts of nw. Mexico. Summer and fall visitor along coast north to Puget Sound, s. Vancouver I. Some *winter* along coast of California. *Accidental,* New Mexico. **Habitat:** Coast and nearby open ocean.

IVORY GULL *Pagophila eburnea* 15–17 **Pl. 33**
Field marks: The only *all-white* gull with *black* legs. Pigeon-sized, with a pigeon-like look. The wings are remarkably long and the flight is quite ternlike. Immature birds are similar but have a few dusky spots about head, wings, and tail.

Similar species: (1) The common Alaskan "white-winged" gull, the Glaucous, is much larger, with *flesh-colored* legs. (2) Ross' Gull has pale gray mantle, *red* legs.

Voice: A shrill ternlike *kree-ar* or *keeer.*
Where found: Arctic; local, circumpolar. **West:** *Breeds* on islands of Canadian high Arctic. *Winters* in Arctic Ocean south to coasts of n. Alaska, n. Canada. *Accidental,* B.C., Colorado. **Habitat:** Arctic drift ice. **Nest:** On rocks or sea cliff; in colony. Eggs (1–2) brownish, spotted.

BLACK-LEGGED KITTIWAKE   Pls. 33, 34
Rissa tridactyla 16–18
Field marks: Note the wing-tips, which are solid black and *cut straight across,* as if dipped in ink. An oceanic gull, to be looked for well off shore. Size of Mew Gull. Bill pale yellow, unmarked. Legs black. Immature, see below.
Similar species: (1) Ring-billed and (2) Mew Gulls have white spots within black wing-tips. Subadult birds without white spots could possibly be called Kittiwakes by the inexperienced. Their legs are pale (Kittiwake's black). (3) Young Bonaparte's Gull may be confused with young Kittiwake, but Kittiwake has a *dark bar on nape* and more black in outer primaries and fore border of wing. (4) See Red-legged Kittiwake.
Voice: On nesting grounds, a raucous *kaka-week* or *kitti-waak;* also a mewing moan, *aaaaaaa.*
Where found: Oceans in n. parts of N. Hemisphere. Winters to U.S., Mediterranean, Japan. **West:** *Breeds* on islands from nw. Alaska south to Aleutians, Kodiak. *Winters* off coast from Aleutians to Baja California. *Accidental,* Wyoming, Colorado. **Habitat:** Mainly open ocean, rarely bays. **Nest:** Of seaweed on ledge of sea cliff; in colony. Eggs (2) spotted.

RED-LEGGED KITTIWAKE   Pl. 33
Rissa brevirostris 14–15¾
Field marks: *Adult:* Similar to Black-legged Kittiwake but smaller, legs *bright red* (Bonaparte's Gull also has red legs). Has typical kittiwake wing pattern above, but shows a darkish gray underwing quite unlike whitish underwing of the Black-leg. *Immature:* Similar to young Black-leg, but tail lacks black terminal band; also lacks dark diagonal bar on wing.
Voice: Similar to Black-legged Kittiwake's; a bit higher.
Where found: *Breeds* in Bering Sea (Komandorskies, Pribilofs). Winters in Bering Sea. *Accidental,* Yukon, nw. Oregon. **Nest:** Of grass or seaweed on ledge of sea cliff. Eggs (2) spotted.

ROSS' GULL   *Rhodostethia rosea* 13–14   Pl. 33
Field marks: A little-known gull of the Arctic. Note the *wedge-shaped tail, red feet. Adult:* A small rosy-bodied gull with pearl-gray wings *without* black tips. In summer has a *narrow black collar. Immature:* Rather like young Kittiwake in flight pattern but tail deeply *wedge-shaped.* Lacks bar on nape.

Voice: High-pitched: *a-wō, a-wō, a-wō; cliaw* (S. Buturlin).
Where found: Breeds in n. Siberia. Winters probably in Arctic Ocean. **West:** *Migrant* in late summer to n. Alaska (Pt. Barrow); south casually to Pribilofs, w. Alaska. **Habitat:** Arctic coast, open leads in pack ice.

SABINE'S GULL *Xema sabini* 13–14   **Pls. 33, 34**
    Field marks: Our only gull with a *forked tail* (young Kittiwake's is slightly notched). The jet-black outer primaries and *triangular white patch* behind them create a distinctive flight pattern. Bill black with *yellow tip,* feet black. The head is slate-gray in breeding plumage. The immature is dark grayish brown on the back, with the adult's basic wing pattern.
    Similar species: Immature Kittiwake has similar flight pattern but note the black nape and diagonal band on inner wing.
    Voice: A harsh, grating cry similar to note of Arctic Tern.
    Where found: Arctic; circumpolar. Winters in Pacific to Peru; local in Atlantic. **West:** *Breeds* from Arctic coast south to Bristol Bay, Alaska. *Migrates* mainly off Pacific Coast, but a few (rare rather than casual) pass through Great Plains, Great Basin, and Lower Colorado River. **Habitat:** Mainly oceanic; tundra (summer). **Nest:** A grass-lined depression in low tundra; single or in colony. Eggs (3) olive or brown, spotted.

Terns: Sterninae

GRACEFUL water birds; most species are more streamlined, more maneuverable than gulls. Bill more sharp-pointed, often held pointed toward water. Tail usually forked. Most terns are whitish, with black caps. In winter this cap is imperfect; black of forehead is usually replaced by white. Sexes alike. Terns often hover and plunge headfirst into the water. They do not normally swim (gulls do). **Food:** Small fish, marine life, large insects. **Range:** Almost cosmopolitan. **No. of species:** World, 39; West, 10 (+6 in Hawaii).

GULL-BILLED TERN   **Pls. 36, 37**
Gelochelidon nilotica 13–14½
    Field marks: Note the stout, almost gull-like *black* bill. Stockier than Forster's Tern; tail much less forked; feet black. In winter, the head is nearly white. Young bird looks like a very small gull but has a slightly notched tail. Hawks for insects over land or marshes; seldom plunges into water.
    Voice: A throaty rasping, *za-za-za;* also *kay-weck, kay-weck.*
    Where found: Breeds locally, wanders widely in many parts of world. **West:** *Breeds* on Salton Sea (se. California). *Casual,* sw. Arizona. **Habitat:** In California, lake marshes, fields. **Nest:** On sandy island; in colony. Eggs (2–3) spotted.

FORSTER'S TERN *Sterna forsteri* 14–16¼ **Pls. 36, 37**
Field marks: This is the small black-capped gull-like bird with the orange-red bill so familiar along the coast and on lakes. *Breeding plumage:* White, with pale gray mantle and tail and a *black cap;* bill *red-orange* with black tip; feet orange-red; tail deeply forked. *Fall and winter:* Similar, without black cap; instead, a heavy spot, *like an earcap,* on side of head. Feet yellowish in some birds; bill blackish.
Similar species: In flight (from above), primaries of adult Common Tern are *dusky* (darker than rest of wing); Forster's are *silvery* (lighter than rest of wing). Tail of Common is whiter. Bill of Common is more red (less orange). In fall, Common Tern has a dark patch around back of head. (Forster's has ear patch only.) Young Common Tern has dusky patch on forepart of inner wing (absent in Forster's).
Voice: A harsh, nasal *za-a-ap* and a nasal *kyarr,* not so drawn out as note of Common Tern. Also *kit, kit, kit,* etc.
Where found: W. Canada, c. Atlantic Coast to Tamaulipas. Winters s. U.S. to Guatemala. **West:** *Breeds* from e. Washington, c. Alberta, s. Saskatchewan south locally to s.-c. California, Utah, e. Colorado (?), w. Nebraska. *Migrates* through interior. *Winters* in c. and s. California. **Habitat:** Marshes (fresh and salt), lakes, bays, beaches, ocean. **Nest:** Of marsh vegetation or on muskrat house; in loose colony in fresh or salt marsh. Eggs (3–4) buff or brown, spotted.

COMMON TERN *Sterna hirundo* 13–16 **Pls. 36, 37**
Field marks: *Breeding plumage:* White, with light gray mantle and black cap; bill orange-red with black tip; feet orange-red; tail deeply forked. *Immature and winter adult:* Black cap incomplete; instead, a black patch extending from eye around nape. The red bill becomes mostly blackish.
Similar species: See (1) Forster's Tern and (2) Arctic Tern.
Voice: A drawling *kee-arr* (downward inflection); higher than Forster's hoarse note. Also, *kik-kik-kik;* a quick *kirri-kirri.*
Where found: Temperate zone of N. Hemisphere. Winters to S. Hemisphere. **West:** *Breeds* from c. Mackenzie, n. Saskatchewan to Montana. *Migrant* mainly along coast from B.C. south. **Habitat:** Lakes (summer); ocean, bays, beaches. **Nest:** On lake island; in colony. Eggs (2–4) olive, buff, or brown, spotted.

ARCTIC TERN *Sterna paradisaea* 14–17 **Pls. 36, 37**
Field marks: Note the bill, which usually is *blood-red to the tip.* This species is grayer than Common or Forster's Terns. However, this is not always reliable because of varying effect of light. A fair mark is the *white streak below the black cap.* In the Common the whole face seems whiter.
Similar species: The bills of Common and Forster's are orange-

red, *usually* tipped with black. The tail is more streaming than that of Common Tern, and overhead the wings seem more translucent. Immatures are virtually indistinguishable. Fall adults are not safely told either — bill and feet become quite dusky. *Caution:* Some Common Terns lose the black bill-tip for a while in late summer.

Voice: *Kee-yah* similar to Common Tern's (less slurred, *kee* higher). A high *keer keer* is said to be characteristic.

Where found: Northern parts of N. Hemisphere; circumpolar. Winters in Subantarctic and Antarctic seas. *West: Breeds* from Arctic coasts south to Aleutians, s. Alaska, n. B.C., Great Slave Lake. *Migrates* off coast. *Accidental,* Alberta, e. Washington, Colorado. **Habitat:** Open ocean, coast; tundra lakes (summer). **Nest:** A depression on coastal or lake island, beach or tundra; single or in colony. Eggs (2) olive or brown, spotted.

ALEUTIAN TERN *Sterna aleutica* 15 **Pls. 36, 37**
   Field marks: This lead-colored tern of w. Alaska is seldom found in the Aleutians! In breeding plumage known from Arctic Tern by the much grayer color, largely blackish primaries, *blackish or dark bill and feet,* and *clean-cut white forehead.* Gray body contrasts with white tail and underwing.
   Voice: Has a 3-syllable whistle suggesting a shorebird.
   Where found: *Breeds* on Sakhalin I. and locally in w. Alaska (Norton Sound, Goodnews Bay, Situk, Kodiak). *Winters* in vicinity of Sakhalin and Japan. **Habitat:** Ocean, coastal waters. **Nest:** A depression in moss on island; in colony. Eggs (2) olive or buff, blotched.

LEAST TERN *Sterna albifrons* 8½–9½ **Pls. 36, 37**
   Field marks: A *very small* tern with a *yellow bill. Adult:* White, with pale gray mantle; forehead white, cutting into black cap; feet yellow. *Immature:* Bill darker; dark patch around back of head; dark area on fore edge of wing. In fall adults and young have dark bills but legs show some yellow (quite dull). Has quicker wingbeats than other terns; hovers more.
   Similar species: Fall-plumaged Black Tern is larger, darker above, with dark tail.
   Voice: A sharp repeated *kit;* a harsh squealing *zree-eek* or *zeek;* also a rapid *kitti-kitti-kitti.*
   Where found: Temperate and tropical regions of world; local as a breeder. Winters south of U.S. *West: Breeds* locally along coast from Monterey Co., California, south. Has bred in e. Colorado, se. New Mexico. *Casual,* s. Nevada, sw. Arizona, e. Wyoming, w. Texas. **Habitat:** Mainly beaches, bays, ocean, estuaries. **Nest:** In scrape on sandy beach or gravel bar; in scattered colony. Eggs (2–3) buff, speckled.

ROYAL TERN *Thalasseus maximus* 18–21   **Pls. 36, 37**
   Field marks: A large tern (near size of King-billed Gull) with a
   large orange or yellow-orange bill. Tail deeply forked. Although
   some Royal Terns in spring show a solid cap, they usually have
   much white on the forehead, the black head feathers forming a
   bushy crest — standing out from the back of the head.
   Similar species: See (1) Caspian Tern and (2) Elegant Tern.
   Voice: *Keer,* higher than Caspian's note; also *kaak* or *kak.*
   Where found: Coasts of se. U.S., nw. Mexico, W. Indies, w.
   Africa. Winters s. U.S. to Argentina; w. Africa. **West:** Irregular
   visitor (mainly Sept.–Mar.) along coast from San Francisco Bay
   south. Has bred San Diego. **Habitat:** Coast.

ELEGANT TERN *Thalasseus elegans* 16–17   **Pls. 36, 37**
   Field marks: This Mexican species should be looked for in fall
   along the coast from San Francisco Bay south. In size, it is
   midway between Royal and Forster's Terns. Its bill is deep
   yellow, with no black tip (Forster's has black tip), and is pro-
   portionately much longer and more slender than bill of Royal
   (Royal's is more orange); its black crest is longer.
   Voice: A nasal *karreek,* or *ka-zeek* — "sounds like a low-pitched
   Least Tern" (R. Pyle and A. Small).
   Where found: Breeds on islands off Baja California. *Winters*
   Peru to Chile. **West:** Wanders irregularly (mainly Aug.–Oct.)
   north to San Francisco Bay. Has bred San Diego. **Habitat:** Coast.
   Nest: A scrape on sandy island; in colony. Eggs (1) blotched.

CASPIAN TERN *Hydroprogne caspia* 19–23   **Pls. 36, 37**
   Field marks: About size of California Gull. Distinguished by
   its size, black cap, *large red bill,* moderately forked tail. The
   great size and large bill set the Caspian apart from all other terns
   except the slimmer and rarer Royal.
   Similar species: In the West, the Royal Tern is confined to the
   California coast (Caspian occurs widely). Tail of Royal is forked
   for fully half its length (Caspian for only a quarter). At rest,
   wings of Royal barely reach tail-tip (Caspian's extend beyond
   tail-tip). Bill of Royal is more slender, *orange* (Caspian's is red).
   Royal has a more *crested* look and during most of the year has
   a *clear white* forehead (Caspian when in winter plumage has a
   clouded, streaked forehead). Adult Royals show much less black
   on underside of primaries.
   Voice: A hoarse, low *kraa-uh* or *karr;* also repeated *kak*'s.
   Where found: Breeds locally, wanders widely around world.
   West: *Breeds* at Great Slave Lake, Lake Athabaska; locally in
   Saskatchewan, Washington, Oregon, California, w. Nevada, n.
   Utah, Montana, Wyoming. *Migrates* through Pacific states and
   Lower Colorado River. *Winters* from San Francisco Bay south.
   Habitat: Large lakes, bays, coast. **Nest:** On sandy island or
   dike of lake or coastal bay; in colony. Eggs (2–3) spotted.

BLACK TERN *Chlidonias niger* 9–10¼ **Pls. 36, 37**
Field marks: Our only *black-bodied tern. Breeding plumage:*
Head and underparts black; back and wings gray; under tail
coverts white. *Immature and autumn adults:* Head and underparts white; back and wings gray; dark about eye, ear, and nape;
dark patch on side of breast. Mottled changing birds appear in
midsummer. Short tail and swooping wingbeats are good points.
Similar species: In fall, more graceful flight, grayer look, small
size, and only slightly notched tail distinguish it from the
Forster's-Common-Arctic group. See Least Tern.
Voice: A sharp *kik, keck,* or *klea.*
Where found: Temperate N. America, Eurasia. Winters mainly
in S. America, Africa. **West:** *Breeds* from c. B.C., n. Alberta,
c. Saskatchewan south to s.-c. California, c. Nevada, n. Utah,
e. Colorado. *Migrates* through interior and on coast from San
Francisco Bay south. *Casual,* se. Alaska. **Habitat:** Fresh
marshes, lakes, coast. **Nest:** On floating marsh vegetation,
muskrat house; in loose colony. Eggs (3) brown, spotted.

Auks, etc.: Alcidae

THE AUK family is the northern counterpart of the penguin family. They have short necks and pointed, stubby, or deep, laterally
compressed bills. Flying, beat their small narrow wings in a whir;
are given to veering. They swim and dive expertly. On sea cliffs,
where most species nest in crowded colonies, they stand nearly
erect, penguin-like. Sexes alike. **Food:** Fish, crustaceans, mollusks, algae. **Range:** N. Atlantic, n. Pacific, Arctic oceans. **No. of
species:** World, 22; West, 16 (+3 accidentals).

COMMON MURRE *Uria aalge* 16–17 **p. 108**
(California Murre)
Field marks: Size of a small duck, with a slender pointed bill,
longer than that of any other Alcid. *Breeding plumage:* Head,
neck, back, and wings dark; underparts, wing-linings, and line
on rear edge of wing white. *Winter plumage:* Similar, but throat
and cheeks white. A *black mark extends from eye into white of
cheek.* Murres often raft on water, fly in lines.
Similar species: See Thick-billed Murre.
Voice: Hoarse, deep moans.
Where found: Northern parts of N. Pacific and N. Atlantic.
West: *Breeds* on coasts and islands from nw. Alaska south to
c. California (Monterey Co.). *Winters* in adjacent seas north
to ice limit; a few south to s. California. **Habitat:** Ocean, large
bays. **Nest:** On bare ledge of sea cliff or rocky island; in colony.
Eggs (1) green to buff, blotched.

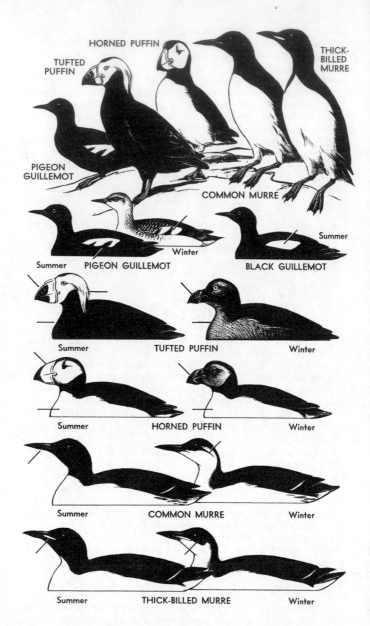

TUFTED PUFFIN
HORNED PUFFIN
THICK-BILLED MURRE
PIGEON GUILLEMOT
COMMON MURRE

Summer PIGEON GUILLEMOT Winter

BLACK GUILLEMOT Summer

Summer TUFTED PUFFIN Winter

Summer HORNED PUFFIN Winter

Summer COMMON MURRE Winter

Summer THICK-BILLED MURRE Winter

THE LARGER AUKS (ALCIDAE)

THICK-BILLED MURRE *Uria lomvia* 17–19 **p. 108**
(Brunnich's Murre)
Field marks: Similar to Common Murre but a bit larger; bill shorter, thicker, with a *whitish line* at base of bill near gape. In winter, black of crown extends *well below eye;* no dark stripe through white ear coverts.
Voice: Very similar to Common Murre's.
Where found: Cold oceans of N. Hemisphere. West: *Breeds* from n. Alaska (Pt. Barrow) south to Pribilofs, Aleutians, Kodiak. Local in n. Mackenzie. *Winters* from Bering Sea to se. Alaska. *Casual,* n. Yukon, B.C. Habitat: Ocean. Nest: On bare rock of sea cliff. Eggs (1) greenish, blotched.

BLACK GUILLEMOT *Cepphus grylle* 12–14 **p. 108**
Field marks: Very similar to Pigeon Guillemot but more northerly. The 2 forms may be conspecific. The chief distinction is a wedge of black in the white wing patch of the Pigeon Guillemot (not always evident when the bird is swimming). This point is especially untrustworthy in winter because immatures of both forms have dark bars across the white patch.
Where found: Northern parts of N. Atlantic; Arctic coast of Eurasia. West: *Breeds* on islands of Canadian Arctic; probably coast of n. Alaska. *Winters* along coast of n. Alaska (Pt. Barrow, Wainwright) and south in Bering Sea to St. Lawrence I.

PIGEON GUILLEMOT *Cepphus columba* 12–14 **p. 108**
Field marks: Size of a small teal. *Breeding plumage:* A small black pigeon-like water bird with large *white shoulder patches, red feet,* and a pointed bill. *Winter plumage:* Pale with white underparts and blackish wings with large white patches as in summer. *No other* Alcid except the very similar Black Guillemot (Arctic Ocean) has large white wing patches, although others have white linings on underwings.
Similar species: (1) White-winged Scoter is much larger, with white patches on *rear edge* of wing (not visible when swimming). (2) In n. Alaska, arctic Canada see Black Guillemot.
Voice: A feeble wheezy or hissing whistle, *peeeeee.*
Where found: Bering Sea to Japan, s. California. West: *Resident* from islands in Bering Sea (not Pribilofs) and Aleutians south to Santa Barbara I., California. Habitat: Rocky coast, ocean. Nest: In crevice, burrow or broken rock in sea cliff. Eggs (1–2) greenish or white, spotted.

MARBLED MURRELET **Pl. 35**
Brachyramphus marmoratum 9½–10
Field marks: Three murrelets (Marbled, Xantus', Ancient) occur commonly in winter along the coast south of Alaska. They are very small, chubby, neckless-looking sea birds, dark above and white below, with white throats. This species may be known

in *nonbreeding* plumage by the *strip of white between back and wing. Breeding plumage: Dark brown* above; *heavily* barred on underparts. The only Alcid south of Alaska so colored.

Similar species: (1) In Alaska, from Glacier Bay north, see Kittlitz's Murrelet. (2) Least Auklet (Aleutians and Bering Sea) is similar in winter but much smaller, with stubbier bill. Ranges do not overlap. (3) See also Cassin's Auklet.

Voice: A sharp *keer, keer* or a lower *kee* (R. Hoffmann).

Where found: Kamchatka to Japan; s. Alaska to California. **West:** *Resident,* bays and ocean from se. Alaska to c. California. *Breeds* (apparently) on mts. near coast. *Winters* in adjacent salt water and south to at least Newport, California. **Habitat:** Coastal waters, tide-rips, bays. **Nest:** First-known nest found "in a rock slide far above timberline at 1900 ft. on Chichagof I., Alaska, on June 13, 1931" (Gabrielson and Lincoln, *Birds of Alaska*). Eggs (1) yellowish, spotted.

KITTLITZ'S MURRELET   Pl. 35
Brachyramphus brevirostre   9

Field marks: Resembles Marbled Murrelet. Ranges barely overlap in se. Alaska. In summer, scaled below (as in Marbled Murrelet) but upper parts freckled with white, giving a distinctly grayer cast. In winter (not likely to be seen in Alaska), more distinctive. Has similar white bar on scapulars, but white on face completely surrounds eye. A narrow dark breastband.

Voice: Said to be a hoarse, long-drawn *squak* quite unlike the high-pitched cry of Marbled Murrelet.

Where found: *Summers* locally along coast of Alaska from Pt. Barrow south at least to Glacier Bay (where common). *Winters* in nw. Pacific (Kamchatka to Japan). **Habitat:** Ocean, glacier waters. **Nest:** Probably on bare rock above timberline in coastal mts. Eggs (1) olive, dotted.

XANTUS' MURRELET   *Endomychura hypoleuca*   9½–10½
(Scripps' Murrelet)   Pl. 35

Field marks: Darker than the other 2 California murrelets; white of underparts does not run so far up on sides of neck (see plate); upper parts without distinctive pattern (other 2 species are distinctively patterned). No seasonal change.

Similar species: (1) Craveri's Murrelet, *E. craveri,* a former straggler from Baja California, has not been recorded in California since 1914. It is separable from Xantus' *in the hand* by its grayish wing-linings (wing-linings of Xantus' are usually immaculate). Thought by some authorities to be merely a race of Xantus'. See also (2) Ancient and (3) Marbled Murrelets.

Voice: Twittering, finchlike whistles heard after dark.

Where found: *Breeds* from s. California (Anacapa and Santa Barbara Is.) to c. Baja California. Some *winter* north to Monterey Bay. *Casual,* Washington. **Habitat:** Ocean. **Nest:** In rock crevice on sea island. Eggs (1–2) variable, spotted.

ANCIENT MURRELET   **Pl. 35**
Synthliboramphus antiquum 9½–10½
    Field marks: *Breeding plumage:* Note the sharply cut *black throat patch and white stripe over eye. Winter plumage:* Similar to Marbled Murrelet's but *without* white stripe on scapulars. *Back paler, contrasting with black cap.* Throat often dusky, but white extending up sides of neck as in Marbled Murrelet.
    Voice: In colony at night, low whistles, chirping calls.
    Where found: Bering Sea and n. parts of N. Pacific (both coasts). **West:** *Breeds* from Aleutians and Kodiak south to Queen Charlotte Is. (B.C.); casually, Washington. *Winters* from Pribilofs south to n. Baja California. *Accidental* inland (B.C., Washington, Oregon, Idaho, Utah, Nevada, Colorado). **Habitat:** Open ocean, sounds, rarely salt bays. **Nest:** In burrow or on bare rocks on island. Eggs (2) spotted.

CASSIN'S AUKLET *Ptychoramphus aleutica* 8–9 **Pl. 35**
    Field marks: A small, stubby sea bird, smaller than any of the murrelets, from which it can be told at any season by its obscure dark color (dusky throat, sides). Belly white.
    Similar species: (1) In winter, all other *small* Alcidae wintering in its range have white on throat or sides of neck. (2) Marbled Murrelet in summer is dusky but bill is more pointed and underparts thickly scaled (Cassin's shows white belly in flight). (3) See immature Rhinoceros Auklet (much larger). (4) In e. Aleutians see young Crested Auklet.
    Voice: In colony at night, an oft-repeated rasping note.
    Where found: *Breeds* from s. Alaska (Shumagin, Kodiak Is.), south locally to Baja California. *Winters* from Vancouver I. south. **Habitat:** Ocean. **Nest:** In crevice in rocks or in burrow on sea island; in colony. Eggs (1) white.

PARAKEET AUKLET *Cyclorrhynchus psittacula* 10 **Pl. 35**
(Paroquet Auklet)
    Field marks: Note the *stubby, upturned red bill,* white underparts. A small black and white Alcid; in summer the whole head is black, with a thin white plume behind the eye.
    Voice: A low, vibrating whistle or trill.
    Where found: *Breeds* in ne. Siberia, islands in Bering Sea and Aleutians. *Winters* from Bering Sea to Japan and on coast of w. N. America to Oregon. *Casual,* c. California. **Habitat:** Ocean. **Nest:** In crevice on sea cliff. Eggs (1) whitish.

CRESTED AUKLET *Aethia cristatella* 9½ **Pl. 35**
    Field marks: A droll, completely slate-gray auklet of the Bering Sea; darker on back; thin white plume behind eye. In summer, with a stubby *bright orange bill* and a curious crest *curled forward* over the bill. In winter, loses orange on bill; crest shorter.
    Similar species: (1) Immature is sooty; perhaps not separable

in field from Cassin's Auklet, but ranges overlap only in e. end of Aleutians (Shumagins). (2) See Whiskered Auklet.
Voice: A loud honking or grunting sound on nesting grounds.
Where found: Ne. Asia, w. Alaska. **West:** *Resident* in Alaska from Pribilofs and Aleutians east to Shumagins. **Habitat:** Ocean. **Nest:** In crevice on sea cliff. Eggs (1) whitish.

LEAST AUKLET *Aethia pusilla* 6   Pl. 35
Field marks: The tiniest auk; chubby, neckless. Black above, white below. In summer, with wide dusky band across upper breast, white throat, and irregularly spotted sides and underparts. At close range, a thin white plume on cheek. In winter, clean white on underparts (so are the murrelets) with white strip on scapulars. Tiny size and extremely stubby bill separate it from any other wintering Alcid of the Aleutians.
Similar species: In winter see Ancient Murrelet.
Voice: In colonies, light chattering, unseabirdlike notes.
Where found: *Breeds* on islands of Bering Sea south to Aleutians and Shumagins. *Winters* from Aleutians to n. Japan. *Accidental,* n. Mackenzie. **Habitat:** Ocean. **Nest:** Under rocks on sea islands; in large colonies. Eggs (1) white.

WHISKERED AUKLET *Aethia pygmaea* 7   Pl. 35
Field marks: Similar to Crested Auklet but curled black plume on forehead more attenuated; *3* wispy white plumes on each side of face; bill much smaller.
Similar species: See Crested Auklet (young birds are probably not safely separable in the field).
Where found: *Resident* in Komandorskie Is., s. Kuriles; locally in c. Aleutians. **Habitat:** Ocean, tide-rips. **Nest:** In crevice in sea cliff; in colony. Eggs (1) white.

RHINOCEROS AUKLET   Pl. 35
Cerorhinca monocerata 14–15½
Field marks: A dark stubby sea bird, larger than murrelets, smaller than murres. *Breeding plumage:* Acquired in late winter; *white "mustaches,"* narrow *white plume* behind eye, *short erect horn* at base of yellowish bill. *Winter:* When bird rests on water, the size, *uniform dark color,* lack of white throat are points to look for. White plumes (in adult) shorter, horn absent.
Similar species: (1) Young bird closely resembles immature Tufted Puffin. Smaller, more slender bill and tendency to occur closer inshore help identify this auklet. (2) Cassin's Auklet is also dusky with dark throat, but is very tiny (9 in.).
Voice: In colony at night, growling and shrieking cries.
Where found: N. N. Pacific (both sides). **West:** *Breeds* from se. Alaska to Washington (Destruction I.). *Winters* along coast from Vancouver I. to Baja California. **Habitat:** Ocean, tide-rips.
Nest: In burrow on sea island; in colony. Eggs (1) often spotted.

HORNED PUFFIN *Fratercula corniculata* 14½ **p. 108**
Field marks: A puffin with *clear white underparts* and a
complete broad black collar. Feet bright orange, *Summer:*
Cheeks *white,* small erectile dark horn above eye. Bill triangular,
laterally flat; yellow with red tip. *Winter:* Cheeks dusky gray;
bill blackish with red tip. Young birds resemble winter adults
with dusky cheeks, but bill is smaller, with no red.
Similar species: Tufted Puffin is never clear white below.
Voice: In nesting burrows, harsh quarreling notes.
Where found: N. Pacific (both sides). West: *Breeds* in Alaska
from Cape Lisburne and islands of Bering Sea to Aleutians; east
and south to Glacier Bay, Forrester I. *Winters* in adjacent seas.
Casual or *sporadic,* Washington, Oregon, California. Habitat:
Ocean. Nest: In burrow or crevice on sea cliff; in colony. Eggs
(1) pale-spotted.

TUFTED PUFFIN *Lunda cirrhata* 14½-15½ **p. 108**
Field marks: A stocky, blackish sea bird with a weird bill.
Breeding plumage: Blackish with *large triangular orange-
red* bill, white face, and *long curved ivory ear tufts.* Feet orange.
Winter adult: White face and ear tufts gone; a blackish bird
with orange-red bill (not as triangular as in summer). *Im-
mature:* Light grayish below, bill smaller; no red.
Similar species: See immature Rhinoceros Auklet.
Voice: Usually silent. In colonies, low growls.
Where found: N. Pacific (both sides). West: *Breeds* from n.
Alaska (Kotzebue Sound) through Bering Sea to Aleutians and
south locally to s. California (San Nicolas I.). *Winters* south of
ice line. Habitat: Ocean. Nest: In burrow in sea island or
headland. Eggs (1) white, often spotted.

Pigeons and Doves: Columbidae

PLUMP, fast-flying birds with small heads and low cooing voices.
Two types occur in N. America: those with fanlike tails (Domestic
Pigeon) and the smaller, brownish type with rounded or pointed
tails (Mourning Dove). Sexes similar. **Food:** Seeds, waste grain,
fruits, insects. **Range:** Nearly worldwide in tropical and temperate
regions. **No. of species:** World, 289; West, 10 (+1 in Hawaii).

BAND-TAILED PIGEON *Columba fasciata* 14-15½ **Pl. 23**
Field marks: Note the *pale broad band* across the end of the
fanlike tail. A heavily built pigeon; might be mistaken for Rock
Dove except for its woodland or mt. habitat and greater tendency
to alight in trees. At close range, shows a white crescent on nape.
Feet *yellow.* Bill *yellow* with *dark tip.*

Similar species: Rock Dove (Domestic Pigeon) has *white rump* and *black band* on tail. Feet *red*. Seldom sits in trees.
Voice: A hollow owl-like *oo-whoo* or *whoo-oo-whoo,* repeated.
Where found: *Breeds* from sw. B.C., Utah, n.-c. Colorado through Pacific states, Rockies to Cent. America. *Winters* from Puget Sound through Pacific states and from c. Arizona, New Mexico south. *Casual,* Idaho, Nevada. **Habitat:** Oak canyons, foothills, chaparral, mt. forests; spreads in winter. **Nest:** A flimsy stick platform on branch. Eggs (1) white.

RED-BILLED PIGEON *Columba flavirostris* 13–14 **Pl. 23**
Field marks: Distinguished from all other pigeons in the lower Rio Grande Valley by its uniform dark appearance. A rather large dark pigeon, with a broad fanlike tail, small red bill. In favorable light shows much deep maroon on foreparts.
Similar species: Some Domestic Pigeons are quite dark, but usually have whitish rumps; seldom sit in trees.
Voice: Cooing more drawn out than White-winged Dove's: *who who woooooo* (long note swelling). "Song" of male, *ooooooo, up-cup-a-coo, up-cup-a-coo, up-cup-a-coo* (G. M. Sutton).
Where found: S. Texas to Costa Rica. *Resident* in lower Rio Grande Valley; upriver to Falcon Dam; north near coast to Norias. **Habitat:** River woodlands, tall brush. **Nest:** A flimsy platform in thicket, low tree. Eggs (1) white.

ROCK DOVE or DOMESTIC PIGEON **Pl. 23**
Columba livia 13
Field marks: Note the *white rump.* Feral; in places self-sustaining. Typical birds are gray, with a *whitish rump, 2 black bars* on secondaries, and broad *black band* on tail. Feet red. Domestic birds exhibit gray, white, tan, blackish varieties.
Voice: Familiar to city dwellers; a soft gurgling *oo-roo-coo.*
Where found: Old World origin; worldwide in domestication.
West: Sustains self in wild about many cities (and in some canyons) in w. U.S., s. Canada, Hawaii. **Habitat:** Cities, farms, cliffs. **Nest:** On building or cliff. Eggs (2) white.

WHITE-WINGED DOVE *Zenaida asiatica* 11–12½ **Pl. 23**
Field marks: The only N. American dove with a large *white patch* on the wing. Similar to Mourning Dove but heavier; tail *rounded,* tipped with broad white corners.
Voice: A harsh cooing, *"who cooks for you?";* also, *ooo-uh-cuck'oo.* Sounds vaguely like crowing of young rooster.
Where found: Sw. U.S. to n. Chile. **West:** *Breeds* (a few winter) from se. California, s. Nevada, c. Arizona, s. New Mexico, w. Texas (Rio Grande) south. *Accidental,* B.C., Washington, Utah, Wyoming, Colorado. **Habitat:** River woods, mesquite, groves, saguaros, desert oases, towns. **Nest:** A flimsy twig platform in tree, thicket. Eggs (2) pale buff.

MOURNING DOVE *Zenaidura macroura* 11–13 **Pl. 23**
Field marks: Note the *pointed tail* bordered with large white spots. The most widespread wild dove in the West. A brown dove, smaller and slimmer than Domestic Pigeon.
Similar species: (1) White-winged Dove has rounded tail and white wing patches. (2) See Band-tailed Pigeon.
Voice: A hollow mournful *ooah, cooo, cooo, coo.* At a distance only the 3 *coo's* are audible.
Where found: Se. Alaska, s. Canada to Panama. Mainly migratory in North. **West:** *Breeds* from se. Alaska (?), c. B.C., c. Alberta, c. Saskatchewan south throughout w. U.S. *Winters* in most of range; mainly from n. California, Arizona, Colorado south. Habitat: Farmlands, towns, open woods, mesquite, coastal scrub, grassland, desert. Nest: A flimsy twig platform in tree, shrub, cactus, or on ground. Eggs (2) white.

SPOTTED DOVE *Streptopelia chinensis* 13 **Pl. 23**
(Chinese Spotted Dove)
Field marks: Note the *broad collar of black and white spots* on the hind neck. A bit larger than Mourning Dove; a rounded or blunt-tipped tail with much white in the corners.
Similar species: Juvenile birds lack the collar but may be told by shape of spread tail (Mourning Dove's is pointed).
Voice: *Coo-who-coo;* resembles cooing of White-winged Dove.
Where found: Asia. **West:** *Introduced* in Los Angeles and strongly established. Has spread radially to Santa Barbara, Bakersfield, Oceanside. *Introduced* also in Hawaii. Habitat: Residential areas, parks, river woods. Nest: A small stick platform in tree. Eggs (2) white.

RINGED TURTLE DOVE *Streptopelia risoria* 12 **Pl. 23**
Field marks: Note *narrow black ring on the hind neck.* Near size of Mourning Dove; much paler. Tail moderately long, *rounded,* with much white in the corners. In flight, the dark primaries contrast boldly with the pale coloration.
Voice: A purring cooing; rising, then dropping in pitch.
Where found: Origin unknown; domesticated widely. **West:** Established very locally in Los Angeles. Habitat: City parks.
Nest: A frail stick platform in tree. Eggs (2) white.

GROUND DOVE *Columbigallina passerina* 6–6¾ **Pl. 23**
Field marks: A very small dove, *not much larger than a sparrow.* Note the *stubby black tail* and rounded wings that flash *rufous* in flight. Nods its head as it walks. Feet yellow.
Similar species: See Inca Dove.
Voice: A soft monotonously repeated *woo-oo, woo-oo.* In distance sounds monosyllabic: *wooo,* with rising inflection.
Where found: S. U.S. to Costa Rica; n. S. America. **West:**

Resident from s. California, c. Arizona, s. New Mexico, w̃. Texas (Trans-Pecos) south. *Casual,* Colorado, c. California. **Habitat:** Riverbottoms, farms, dirt roads, wood edges, brush, orchards. **Nest:** A flimsy saucer in vines, cactus, bush, low tree, on ground. Eggs (2) white.

INCA DOVE *Scardafella inca* 7½–8   **Pl. 23**
  Field marks: A very small dove with a pale, scaly appearance. Differs from Ground Dove by *comparatively long* square-ended tail (looks pointed when folded; shows white sides when spread). Like Ground Dove, Inca shows rufous in wing in flight.
  Similar species: Ground Dove's tail is dark and stubby. Ground Dove has black spots on wings (Inca has scaly wings).
  Voice: Two notes on same pitch, *coo-hoo.* Some interpret it *"no hope."* Also *coo-co-hoo* or *hink-a-doo* (I. Davis).
  Where found: *Resident* locally from s. Arizona, s. New Mexico, w. and s. Texas south to nw. Costa Rica. *Casual,* s. California, s. Nevada. **Accidental,** w. Kansas. **Habitat:** Towns, gardens, chicken pens, parks, farms. **Nest:** A saucer of twigs, straw, in bush, low tree, shed. Eggs (2) white.

WHITE-FRONTED DOVE *Leptotila verreauxi* 11–12 **Pl. 23**
  Field marks: A large dark-backed, ground-inhabiting dove with a rounded, white-cornered tail. Further distinguished from other similarly sized doves by its *pale underparts,* whitish forehead. In flight, shows reddish underwings.
  Similar species: (1) White-winged Dove has white wing patches, more white in tail. (2) See Red-billed Pigeon (all dark).
  Voice: A low, soft, ghostly *oo-whooooooo,* lower in pitch and softer than the notes of any other dove; at a distance, only the hollow long-drawn *whooooooo* is audible.
  Where found: S. Texas to Argentina. *Resident* in lower Rio Grande Valley; upriver to Rio Grande City, Texas. **Habitat:** Shady woodlands, river thickets. **Nest:** A frail platform of twigs in low tree, bush. Eggs (2) pale buff.

Cuckoos, Roadrunners, Anis:
Cuculidae

BIRDS OF this family are slender, long-tailed. Feet zygodactyl (2 toes forward, 2 behind). Sexes usually similar. Our cuckoos are slim, brown above, whitish below. Roadrunners are large streaked cuckoos that travel on the ground. Anis are loose-jointed and slender, coal-black, with deep, high-ridged bills. **Food:** Caterpillars, other insects. Anis may eat seeds, fruits, grasshoppers; roadrunners eat insects, reptiles, etc. **Range:** Nearly all warm and temperate parts of world. **No. of species:** World, 128; West, 4 (+1 accidental).

YELLOW-BILLED CUCKOO   Pl. 38
Coccyzus americanus 11–13½
   Field marks: Note the flash of rufous in the wings. Known as a cuckoo by the slim sinuous look, dull brown back, white breast; as this species, by *rufous* in wings, *large white spots* at tips of black tail feathers (most noticeable below). It has a *yellow* lower mandible on its slightly curved bill.
   Similar species: Black-billed is duller, has small tail spots, no rufous in wings. Lower mandible black, eye-ring red.
   Voice: Song, a rapid throaty *ka ka ka ka ka ka ka ka ka ka ka ka kow kow kowlp kowlp kowlp kowlp* (retarded toward end).
   Where found: S. Canada to Mexico, W. Indies. Winters in S. America. **West:** *Breeds* rarely from Puget Sound, s. Idaho, w. Montana south very locally throughout w. U.S. **Habitat:** River thickets, willows, mesquite. **Nest:** A frail twig saucer in bush, small tree. Eggs (2–4; 8) pale blue-green.

BLACK-BILLED CUCKOO   Pl. 38
Coccyzus erythropthalmus 11–12½
   Field marks: Brown above, white below; bill *black* (may have touch of yellow at base); narrow *red* eye-ring (adults). No rufous in wing; only small tail spots (seen best on underside).
   Similar species: See Yellow-billed Cuckoo.
   Voice: A fast rhythmic *cu cu cu, cucucu, cucucu cucucu cucucu,* etc. The grouped rhythm (3 or 4) is distinctive. Sometimes a series of single *kuk*'s. Frequently sings at night.
   Where found: S. Canada, and mainly c. and ne. U.S. Winters in n. S. America. **West:** *Breeds* west to se. Alberta, Montana, w. Wyoming, n. Colorado. *Migrant* in Texas panhandle. *Casual,* B.C., e. Washington, Idaho. **Habitat:** Wood edges, groves, willow thickets. **Nest:** A shallow twig saucer in bush, low tree. Eggs (2–5; 8) blue-green.

ROADRUNNER *Geococcyx californianus* 20–24   Pl. 38
   Field marks: A cuckoo that runs on the ground (tracks show 2 toes forward, 2 backward). Slender, heavily streaked; long, maneuverable, white-tipped tail, shaggy crest, strong legs. In flight the short rounded wings display a white crescent.
   Voice: Song, 6–8 dovelike *coo*'s descending in pitch (last note about pitch of Mourning Dove). The bird makes a clattering noise by rolling mandibles together.
   Where found: Sw. U.S. (east to e. Oklahoma, nw. Louisiana); south to c. Mexico. **West:** *Resident* from n. California (n. Sacramento Valley), s. Nevada, s. Utah, c. Colorado, sw. Kansas

south. **Habitat:** Open country with scattered cover, stony deserts, dry brush, open piñon-juniper. **Nest:** A shallow saucer in bush, cactus, low tree. Eggs (3–8; 12) white.

GROOVE-BILLED ANI *Crotophaga sulcirostris* 13 **Pl. 38**
  Field marks: Note the deep bill with its *high, curved ridge.* A coal-black cuckoo-like bird, with a loose-jointed tail, short rounded wings (weak flight); alternately flaps and sails. Bill shape creates a puffin-like or parrot-like profile.
  Similar species: Boat-tailed Grackle has slender bill (p. 219).
  Voice: A repeated *whee-o,* or *tee-ho* (1st note slurring up and thin; 2nd lower); also a low chuckling note in flight.
  Where found: S. Texas to Peru. *Resident* (mostly migratory) in Rio Grande Delta. *Casual,* w. Texas (Big Bend), s. Arizona, sw. New Mexico. **Habitat:** Thick brush. **Nest:** A mass of twigs lined with green leaves in thick bush, low tree. Often used by more than one female. Eggs (3–4 each female) pale bluish.

Owls: Tytonidae (Barn Owls) and Strigidae

LARGELY nocturnal birds of prey, with large heads, flattened faces forming "facial disks," and large forward-facing eyes. Hooked bills, hooked claws, and usually feathered feet (outer toe reversible). Flight noiseless, mothlike. Some species have conspicuous feather tufts ("horns" or "ears"). Sexes similar; females larger. **Food:** Rodents, birds, reptiles, fish, large insects. **Range:** Nearly cosmopolitan. **No. of species:** World, 134 (Barn Owls 11; other owls, 123); West, 18.

BARN OWL *Tyto alba* 14–20   **p. 120**
  Field marks: Our only owl with a *white heart-shaped face.* A long-legged, knock-kneed, pale, monkey-faced owl. *Dark eyes,* no ear tufts. Distinguished in flight as an owl by the large head and light, mothlike flight; as this species, by the unstreaked whitish or pale cinnamon underparts (ghostly at night) and golden-buff or rusty upper plumage.
  Similar species: Short-eared Owl (marshes) is streaked, has darker face and underparts, yellow eyes, shorter legs.
  Voice: A shrill rasping hiss or snore: *kschh* or *shiiish.*
  Where found: Nearly worldwide in tropical and temperate regions; in New World from s. Canada to Tierra del Fuego.
  West: *Resident* from sw. B.C. through Pacific states; locally from e. Washington, Idaho, se. Wyoming, Nebraska south. *Casual,* Saskatchewan. **Habitat:** Woodlands, groves, fields,

farms, towns, canyons, cliffs. **Nest:** On litter of fur pellets in barn, belfry, hollow tree, cave, hole in bank. Eggs (5–7; 11) white.

SCREECH OWL   *Otus asio*   7–10   p. 123
Field marks: A common widespread small owl with conspicuous ear tufts. Screech Owls in w. N. America are gray except for the n. Great Basin population (*O. a. macfarlanei*), which has 2 color phases, gray and brown, and the nw. coastal race (*O. a. kennicottii*), which is *usually* dark brown. Young birds lack conspicuous ears.
Similar species: (1) In se. Arizona and sw. New Mexico see Whiskered Owl. (2) See also Flammulated Owl.
Voice: A series of hollow whistles on one pitch, separated at first, but running into a tremulo (rhythm of a small ball bouncing to a standstill); sometimes preceded by 2 prolonged notes. Unlike descending whinny of e. Screech Owls.
Where found: Se. Alaska, s. Canada to c. Mexico. **West:** *Resident* from se. Alaska (Sitka), coastal and s. B.C., Montana, s. Saskatchewan south. *Casual,* Alberta. **Habitat:** Woodlands, farm groves, shade trees, wooded canyons. **Nest:** In tree cavity, woodpecker hole. Eggs (4–5; 7) white.

WHISKERED OWL   *Otus trichopsis*   6½–8
(Spotted Screech Owl)
Field marks: Often lives in same localities as Screech Owl and is virtually identical in appearance. Distinguished only in hand by large white spots on scapulars, coarser black spots on underparts, and longer facial bristles. At night easily identified by voice and attracted by imitation.
Voice: *Boobooboo-boo, booboohoo-hoo,* etc. (3 *boo*'s, a pause, a *boo*); arrangement of this "code" may vary. At times a repeated 4-syllabled *chooyoo-coocooo,* vaguely suggestive of White-winged Dove; also a rapid series on one pitch, *boo boo boo boo boo boo boo boo,* usually slowing toward end.
Where found: *Resident* from mts. of se. Arizona, sw. New Mexico (?) to El Salvador. **Habitat:** Mt. canyons, pine-oak woods, oaks, sycamores. **Nest:** In tree cavity, woodpecker hole. Eggs (3–4) white.

FLAMMULATED OWL   *Otus flammeolus*   6–7   p. 123
(Flammulated Screech Owl)
Field marks: *The only small N. American owl with dark eyes.* A little-known owl, smaller than Screech Owl, largely gray (and a touch of tawny), with inconspicuous ear tufts.
Voice: A mellow *hoot* (or *hoo-hoot*), low in pitch for so small an owl; repeated steadily at intervals of 2–3 seconds.
Where found: *Breeds* from s. B.C. (rare), Idaho, n. Colorado

LONG-EARED

GREAT HORNED

GREAT GRAY

SNOWY

BARRED

SPOTTED

SHORT-EARED

BARN

THE LARGER OWLS

south locally through mts. of w. U.S. and Mexico to Guatemala. *Winters* mainly south of U.S. **Habitat:** Open pine, fir forests in mts. **Nest:** In woodpecker hole. Eggs (3–4) white.

GREAT HORNED OWL *Bubo virginianus* 18–25 **p. 120**
Field marks: The "Cat Owl"; the only *large* N. American owl with ear tufts, or "horns." Heavily barred beneath; conspicuous white throat-collar. In flight, as large as our largest hawks; dark (most races), looks neckless, large-headed. The race *B. v. wapacuthu* (Arctic Horned Owl) of n. Canada is very pale; occasionally wanders to nw. U.S.
Similar species: Long-eared Owl is much smaller (Crow-sized in flight), with lengthwise streakings, rather than crosswise barrings, beneath. "Ears" closer together.
Voice: A resonant hooting of 3–8 hoots; males usually 4–5, in this rhythm: *hoo, hoo-oo, hoo, hoo;* females (lower in pitch) 6–8: *hoo, hoo-hoo-hoo, hoo-oo, hoo-oo.*
Where found: Arctic to Strait of Magellan. **West:** *Resident* from Yukon drainage in Alaska and tree limit in Mackenzie south throughout West. **Habitat:** Forests, woodlands, thickets, chaparral, streamsides, open country, deserts, canyons, cliffs. **Nest:** In old nest of heron or hawk; in tree, pothole, cliff, or river bluff; even on ground. Eggs (2–3) white.

SNOWY OWL *Nyctea scandiaca* 20–27 **p. 120**
Field marks: A large *white* owl; flecked or barred with dusky. Round head, *yellow* eyes. Some birds are much whiter than others. Day-flying. Perches on dunes, posts, haystacks, etc.
Similar species: (1) The subarctic race of the Horned Owl (very pale, almost whitish) has *ear tufts.* (2) Barn Owl is whitish on underparts only; has dark eyes. (3) Young owls of all species are whitish before feathers replace the down.
Voice: Usually silent. Flight note when breeding, a repeated loud *krow-ow* or a repeated *rick.*
Where found: Arctic; circumpolar. Has cyclic migrations southward. **West:** *Breeds* along Arctic coasts south to Hooper Bay, Alaska. *Winters* irregularly from Arctic south to n. U.S.; rarely to c. California, Nevada, Utah, Colorado. **Habitat:** Prairies, fields, marshes, beaches; tundra (summer). **Nest:** A grass-lined hollow on tundra. Eggs (5–8; 13) whitish.

HAWK OWL *Surnia ulula* 14½–17½ **p. 123**
Field marks: A medium-sized, hawklike, day-flying owl (smaller than Crow), with a *long, rounded tail and completely barred underparts.* Does not sit so upright as other owls; often perches at the tip of a tree and jerks its tail like a Sparrow Hawk. Shrikelike, it flies low, rising abruptly to its perch. Note the broad black *"sideburns"* framing its face.

Voice: A chattering *kikikiki,* more like hawk than owl.
Where found: Boreal forests of N. Hemisphere. **West:** *Resident* from n. Alaska, Yukon, nw. Mackenzie south to n. B.C., c. Alberta, c. Saskatchewan. Wanders south casually to Washington, n. Idaho, w. Montana, nw. Wyoming. **Habitat:** Conifer forests, birch scrub. **Nest:** In tree cavity, stub, or Crow's or hawk's nest. Eggs (3–7; 9) white.

PYGMY OWL   *Glaucidium gnoma*   7–7½   **p. 123**
    Field marks: Note the *black patch* on each side of hind neck; suggests "eyes on back of head." A very small "earless" owl; brown with *sharply streaked flanks* and a rather long barred tail. Frequently heard calling or seen flying (shrikelike) in daytime. Head proportionately smaller than that of Saw-whet or Screech Owls. Tail is often held at a perky angle.
    Similar species: (1) In sw. deserts see Ferruginous Owl. (2) Saw-whet Owl (large head, stubby tail, blotchy streaks).
    Voice: A single mellow whistle, *hoo,* repeated every 2 seconds. Also a rolling series, ending with 2–3 deliberate notes: *too-too-too-too-too-too-too-too-took-too-took.*
    Where found: *Resident* from se. Alaska, n. B.C., w. Alberta south through Pacific states (coast and mts.) and wooded mts. of Great Basin ranges and Rockies through w. U.S. and Mexico to Guatemala. *Casual,* w. Texas (El Paso). **Habitat:** Open coniferous or mixed woods, wooded canyons. **Nest:** In woodpecker hole. Eggs (3–4; 6) white.

FERRUGINOUS OWL   *Glaucidium brasilianum*   6½–7
(Ferruginous Pygmy Owl)   **p. 123**
    Field marks: Very similar to the Pygmy Owl; perhaps best recognized by its lowland habitat, within the range outlined below. The breast-streakings are *brownish* rather than black; the crown has fine pale streaks (not dots). Jerks or flips its tail.
    Similar species: See (1) Pygmy Owl (mts.) and (2) Elf Owl.
    Voice: *Chook* or *took;* sometimes repeated monotonously 2–3 times per second. Calls in daytime but more often at night.
    Where found: *Resident* from s. Arizona, lower Rio Grande Valley, Texas, to Strait of Magellan. **Habitat:** Mesquite thickets, desert river woods, saguaros. **Nest:** In woodpecker hole, tree cavity. Eggs (3–4) white.

ELF OWL   *Micrathene whitneyi*   5–6   **p. 123**
    Field marks: A tiny, small-headed earless owl, size of a chunky sparrow. Underparts softly striped with rusty; "eyebrows" white. Hides in hole in cactus or tree by day. Found at night by calls.
    Similar species: Ferruginous and Pygmy Owls have longer tails, extending well beyond wing-tips. Have black "eyes" on hind neck, stripes on flanks.

FERRUGINOUS

ELF

PYGMY

SAW-WHET

FLAMMULATED

BOREAL

SCREECH

BURROWING

HAWK

THE SMALLER OWLS

Voice: A rapid high-pitched *whi-whi-whi-whi-whi-whi,* or *chewk-chewk-chewk-chewk,* etc., often becoming higher, more yipping, "puppy-like," and chattering in middle of series.
Where found: *Breeds* from se. California, s. Arizona, sw. New Mexico, w. Texas (Chisos Mts.) to c. Mexico. *Winters* south of U.S. **Habitat:** Saguaro deserts, wooded canyons. **Nest:** In woodpecker hole in saguaro or tree. Eggs (3–4) white.

BURROWING OWL *Speotyto cunicularia* 9–11 **p. 123**
Field marks: Note the *very long legs* (for an owl). A small brown owl of open country, often seen by day standing on the ground or on fence posts. About size of Screech Owl; round head, long legs, stubby tail. Bobs and bows when agitated.
Voice: A rapid chattering *quick-quick-quick;* at night a mellow *co-hoo,* higher than Mourning Dove's coo.
Where found: Sw. Canada, Florida to Tierra del Fuego. Migratory in North. **West:** *Breeds* from s. B.C., s. Alberta, s.-c. Saskatchewan south locally throughout West (in nw. coast belt mainly in winter). Leaves colder areas in winter. **Habitat:** Open grassland, prairies, dikes, desert, farms. **Nest:** In rodent burrow in open ground. Eggs (5–9; 12) white.

BARRED OWL *Strix varia* 17–24 **p. 120**
Field marks: A large gray-brown, puffy-headed owl of river woodlands. The large moist *brown* eyes and the pattern — barred *crosswise* on puffy chest and streaked *lengthwise* on belly — identify it. Back spotted with white.
Similar species: (1) In Pacific states, s. Rocky Mts. see Spotted Owl (browner; lower breast and belly barred). (2) Great Gray Owl is larger, grayer, has yellow eyes.
Voice: Hooting is more emphatic than Great Horned Owl's; not so deep. May sound like barking of dog. Usually consists of 8 accented hoots, in 2 groups of 4: *hoohoo-hoohoo-hoohoo-hoohoooaw.* The *aw* at close is characteristic.
Where found: Canada (east of Rockies), to Honduras. **West:** *Resident* from n. B.C. (rare), n. Alberta, c. Saskatchewan (rare) south locally through e. Montana, e. Wyoming, ne. Colorado (casual) to Texas panhandle. **Habitat:** River woodlands. **Nest:** In tree cavity or nest of hawk. Eggs (2–3) white.

SPOTTED OWL *Strix occidentalis* 16½–19 **p. 120**
Field marks: A large dark-brown forest owl with a puffy round head. The large *dark* eyes (all other *large* N. American owls except Barn and Barred Owls have yellow eyes) and the heavily barred and spotted underparts identify this rather rare bird.
Similar species: See Barred Owl (note different range).
Voice: A high-pitched hooting, like barking of a small dog. Usually in groups of 3 (*hoo, hoo-hoo*) or 4 (*hoo, who-who-whooo*). Also a longer series of rapid hoots in crescendo.

Where found: *Resident* from sw. B.C. south in humid coastal belt to San Francisco Bay; also in Sierra, coastal slope, and interior ranges of s. California; in s. Rockies from n. Utah, c. Colorado to c. Mexico. *Accidental,* nw. Montana. **Habitat:** Heavy forest, conifers, wooded canyons. **Nest:** In tree cavity, nest of hawk, cave in canyon wall. Eggs (2–3) white.

GREAT GRAY OWL *Strix nebulosa* 24–33   **p. 120**
Field marks: The largest N. American owl; dusky gray, striped lengthwise on underparts. It is round-headed, without ear tufts; the eyes are *yellow,* and it has a noticeable black chin spot; the strongly lined facial disks are very large proportionately. The tail is very long for an owl (about 12 in.).
Similar species: Spotted and Barred Owls are much smaller, browner, have *brown* eyes, smaller face disks, shorter tails.
Voice: A deep booming *whoo-hoo-hoo.* Also deep single *whoo's.*
Where found: Boreal forests of N. Hemisphere. **West:** *Resident* from Yukon Valley, Alaska, n. Yukon, n. Mackenzie south locally to c. California (high Sierra, esp. Yosemite), n. Idaho (?), w. Wyoming; also east across boreal forests of Canada. In nw. U.S., more frequent in winter. **Habitat:** Dense forests, adjacent meadows. **Nest:** In old nest of hawk, Crow. Eggs (2–5) white.

LONG-EARED OWL *Asio otus* 13–16   **p. 120**
Field marks: A slender, medium-sized, grayish owl with long ear tufts; much smaller than Horned Owl, streaked *lengthwise,* rather than barred, beneath. "Ears" closer together, toward center of forehead, giving a different aspect. Face dark rusty. Usually seen "frozen" close to trunk of dense tree.
Similar species: (1) Great Horned Owl is much larger; ear tufts more spread apart; seldom allows a close approach. (2) Screech Owl is smaller, has shorter ears, lacks rusty face. (3) In flight, Long-eared Owl's ear tufts are depressed; then grayer color, habitat distinguish it from Short-eared Owl.
Voice: A low moaning *hooooo.* Also a catlike whine and a slurred whistle, *whee-you* (Ludlow Griscom).
Where found: Canada to nw. Baja California, sw. and s.-c. U.S.; Eurasia, n. Africa. **West:** *Breeds* from c. B.C., s. Mackenzie south locally to s. California, s. Arizona, New Mexico, w. Texas. *Casual,* se. Alaska. Some migration from n. range. **Habitat:** River woods, willow thickets, live oaks, mt. forest, junipers. **Nest:** In old nest of Crow, magpie, hawk. Eggs (3–8) white.

SHORT-EARED OWL *Asio flammeus* 13–17   **p. 120**
Field marks: Nearly Crow-sized; an owl of open country, often abroad by day. The streaked tawny-brown color and irregular flopping flight identify it. Large buffy wing patches show in flight, and on underwing, a black patch at the carpal joint. The dark face disks emphasize the yellow eyes.

Similar species: (1) Barn Owl has pale breast, white face, dark eyes. See also (2) female Marsh Hawk (p. 57) and (3) Rough-legged Hawk (p. 54) — both are tawny marsh hunters.
Voice: An emphatic sneezy bark, *kee-yow!, wow!,* or *waow!*
Where found: Nearly cosmopolitan. In N. America, breeds mainly from Arctic coast to c. U.S.; winters to Mexico, Gulf Coast. **West:** *Breeds* from Arctic coast to s. California (rarely), c. Nevada, Utah, s. Colorado. *Winters* from s. Canada throughout w. U.S. *Resident* in Hawaii. **Habitat:** Prairies, marshes (fresh and salt), irrigated land, dunes, tundra. **Nest:** A grass-lined hollow in meadow, marsh, tundra. Eggs (4–9) white.

BOREAL OWL *Aegolius funereus* 8½–12　　**p. 123**
(Richardson's Owl)
　　Field marks: A large-headed, *earless* small owl. Similar to Saw-whet Owl, but a bit larger; face disks *framed with black;* bill *yellowish;* forehead heavily dotted with white. *Juvenal:* Dark brown with broad white "eyebrows." Very tame.
　　Similar species: (1) Saw-whet Owl is smaller, has black bill, *lacks* black facial "frames." (2) Hawk Owl is larger, grayer, *long-tailed,* and *barred below.* (3) Pygmy Owl is small-headed, longer-tailed, lacks facial frames.
　　Voice: "Song like a soft high-pitched bell or dropping of water" (Bent). Also a harsh grating call.
　　Where found: Boreal forests of N. Hemisphere. **West:** *Resident* from n. Alaska, n. Yukon, Mackenzie south to n. B.C., c. Alberta, c. Saskatchewan. *Winters* irregularly to s. B.C., n. Idaho, n. Montana. *Accidental,* Oregon, Colorado. **Habitat:** Mixed and conifer forests. **Nest:** In tree cavity, woodpecker hole, old tree nest. Eggs (4–7) white.

SAW-WHET OWL *Aegolius acadicus* 7–8½　　**p. 123**
　　Field marks: A tame little owl; smaller than Screech Owl, *without* ear tufts. Underparts with blotchy brown streaks. Juvenal birds in summer are dark chocolate-brown, with conspicuous white "eyebrows" forming a broad V.
　　Similar species: (1) See Boreal Owl. (2) Pygmy Owl has small head, black "eyes" on hind neck, longer tail, sharp flank-stripes.
　　Voice: "Song," a mellow whistled note repeated mechanically in endless succession, often 100–130 times per minute: *too, too, too, too, too, too,* etc.
　　Where found: Se. Alaska, Canada, w. and ne. U.S., mts. of n. and c. Mexico. **West:** *Resident* from se. Alaska, n. B.C., across c. Alberta, c. Saskatchewan, and south in w. U.S. to mts. of s. California, Arizona, New Mexico. *Winters* casually to sw. deserts. **Habitat:** Forests, conifers, groves. **Nest:** In tree cavity, woodpecker hole. Eggs (4–7) white.

Goatsuckers: Caprimulgidae

NOCTURNAL birds with ample tails, large eyes, tiny bills, huge gapes, and very short legs. During the day they rest horizontally on a limb or on the ground, camouflaged by "dead leaf" pattern. Nighthawks are aberrant goatsuckers, often abroad by day. **Food:** Mainly nocturnal insects. **Range:** Nearly worldwide in temperate and tropical land regions. **No. of species:** World, 67; West, 6 (+1 marginal).

RIDGWAY'S WHIP-POOR-WILL or COOKACHEEA
(Buff-collared Nightjar) *Caprimulgus ridgwayi* 8½–9
Field marks: Similar to the Whip-poor-will, but with a buff or tawny collar across the hind neck.
Voice: "Song, a series of almost identical staccato notes terminating with a longer, more strongly accented phrase higher in pitch: *cuk-cuk-cuk-cuk-cuk-cuk-cuk-cukacheea*. May be mistaken for an insect such as a Katydid. Song delivered from a perch and repeated over and over" (I. Davis).
Where found: Mainly Mexico (s. Sonora to Chiapas). **West:** Discovered recently in Guadalupe Canyon, sw. New Mexico and probably breeds. **Habitat:** Rocky juniper-mesquite slopes.

WHIP-POOR-WILL *Caprimulgus vociferus* 9–10   Pl. 38
Field marks: Best known by its vigorous cry heard at night in woodlands. When flushed by day, the bird flits away on rounded wings like a large brown moth. If it is a male, large white tail patches flash; if a female, it appears largely brown.
Similar species: Nighthawks show white wing patches; *pointed* wings at rest extend beyond *notched* tail (Whip-poor-will's *rounded* wings fall far short of *rounded* tail-tip).
Voice: At night, a rolling, oft repeated *prrrip' purr-rill'* or *whip' poor-weel'*, accent on 1st and last syllables.
Where found: Canada (c. and e.) to Honduras. Winters from Gulf states to Honduras. **West:** *Breeds* in c. Saskatchewan; also in mts. of c. and s. Arizona, s. New Mexico, w. Texas. *Casual,* Colorado. **Habitat:** In Saskatchewan, poplar woods; in Southwest, mt. slopes, oak-pine canyons. **Nest:** Eggs (2) unspotted or lightly spotted; laid on dead leaves.

POOR-WILL *Phalaenoptilus nuttallii* 7–8½   Pl. 38
Field marks: Best known by its night cry in arid hills. Flushed, the Poor-will flutters up like a large gray-brown moth. Appears smaller than a nighthawk, has more rounded wings (no white bar). Its short rounded tail has white corners.
Similar species: Nighthawks are larger, have pointed (not rounded) wings with a conspicuous white bar.

Voice: At night a loud, repeated *poor-will* or, more exactly, *poor-jill;* when close, *poor-jill-ip.*
Where found: *Breeds* from se. B.C., se. Alberta (casual) south (east of Cascades) throughout w. U.S. to c. Mexico. Ranges east to se. Montana, nw. S. Dakota, Nebraska, e. Kansas, nw. Oklahoma, c. Texas. *Casual* in nw. coast belt. *Winters* from c. California, s. Arizona, s. Texas south. Recorded in hibernation in California, Arizona. **Habitat:** Stony arid hills, open piñon-juniper, sparse brush. **Nest:** Eggs (2) white; laid on bare ground.

PAURAQUE *Nyctidromus albicollis* 10–12 **Pl. 38**
Field marks: A large goatsucker of s. Texas, best identified at night by voice. Whip-poor-will and Chuck-will's-widow migrate through its range, but it can be told from those similar birds by the *white band* across the wing (reduced in female).
Similar species: Nighthawks also have white in wing, but lack the large white tail patches (note shape of wings and tail).
Voice: At night a hoarse whistle, *pur-we' eeeeer;* sometimes with 1 or more preliminary notes (*pup-pup-pur-we' eeeeer*). At a distance only the breezy *we' eeeeer* is heard.
Where found: S. Texas to s. Brazil. Mainly *resident* in s. Texas; north along lower Rio Grande to Starr Co.; on coastal plain to Rockport, Beeville. Inactive in cold weather (hence thought to be absent). **Habitat:** Woodlands, brush, river thickets, coastal prairie. **Nest:** Eggs (2) pinkish, pale-spotted; laid on bare ground.

COMMON NIGHTHAWK *Chordeiles minor* 8½–10 **Pl. 38**
("Booming Nighthawk")
Field marks: A slim-winged gray or gray-brown bird often seen high in the air; flies with easy strokes, "changing gear" to quicker erratic strokes. An aberrant goatsucker; prefers dusk but also flies abroad during midday. Note the *broad white bar* across the *pointed* wing. Male has white bar across notched tail, white throat. Sits on fence posts, rails.
Similar species: See Lesser Nighthawk.
Voice: A nasal *peent* or *pee-ik.* In aerial display, male dives earthward, then zooms up sharply with a sudden deep whir.
Where found: Canada to s. Mexico. Winters in S. America.
West: *Breeds* from s. Yukon, upper Mackenzie Valley south to mts. of s. California (Sierra, San Bernardinos), s. Arizona, s. New Mexico, w. Texas. Migrant throughout w. U.S. *Casual,* se. Alaska. **Habitat:** Treeless plains to mts., open pine woods; often seen in open air over countryside or towns. **Nest:** Eggs (2) speckled; laid on bare ground, flat city roof.

LESSER NIGHTHAWK *Chordeiles acutipennis* 8–9 **Pl. 38**
(Texas Nighthawk, "Trilling Nighthawk")
Field marks: Smaller than Common Nighthawk, with white bar (buffy in female) *closer to tip of wing.* More readily identified by

its odd calls and manner of flight, *very low,* seldom high. Does not power-dive. A bird of the lowlands (in sw. U.S. the other nighthawk prefers the mts.).

Voice: Does not have characteristic *spee-ik* or *peent* of other nighthawk; instead a low *chuck chuck* and a soft purring or whinnying sound very like trilling of toad.

Where found: *Breeds* from c. California, s. Nevada, sw. Utah, Arizona, s. New Mexico, w. and s. Texas south to n. Chile, Brazil. Winters south of U.S. *Accidental,* Colorado. **Habitat:** Arid open scrub, dry grassland, fields, prairie, gravelly desert, washes. **Nest:** Eggs (2) dotted; laid on open ground.

Swifts: Apodidae

SWALLOW-LIKE in appearance and behavior, but with slimmer, more scythelike wings, short tails. Structurally distinct, with flat skulls, and all 4 toes pointing forward (hallux reversible). Flight very rapid, "twinkling," sailing between spurts; wings often stiffly *bowed.* Sexes similar. **Food:** Flying insects. **Range:** Nearly cosmopolitan. **No. of species:** World, 79; West, 4 (+2 accidentals).

BLACK SWIFT *Cypseloides niger* 7–7½ **p. 130**
Field marks: A large *black* swift with a slightly forked tail (sometimes fanned). At close range, a touch of white on forehead. Flight more leisurely than other U.S. swifts'.
Similar species: (1) Purple Martin has wider, differently shaped wings and swallow flight. (2) Vaux's Swift is much smaller, with paler underparts, rounded tail.
Voice: A sharp *plik-plik-plik-plik-plik,* etc. (H. Cogswell).
Where found: Se. Alaska to Costa Rica; Cuba to B. Guiana. Winters mainly in tropics. **West:** *Breeds* locally from se. Alaska, B.C. to Washington, sw. Alberta, nw. Montana. Also mts. of c. and s. (?) California, coast of c. California, mesa country of w. Colorado. Sparse migrant in Great Basin, sw. states. **Habitat:** Open sky; favors mt. country, coastal cliffs. **Nest:** Of green algae, moss, in crevice of sea cliff or wet mt. cliff, often behind waterfall. Eggs (1) white.

CHIMNEY SWIFT *Chaetura pelagica* 4¾–5½
Field marks: Very similar to Vaux's Swift, but somewhat larger; darker, especially on underparts. Not easily separable in the field, but any small dark swift east of the Rockies would almost certainly be this species.
Voice: Loud, rapid, ticking or chippering notes.
Where found: C. and e. Canada to Gulf states. Winters in upper Amazon basin. **West:** *Breeds* west locally to s.-c. Sas-

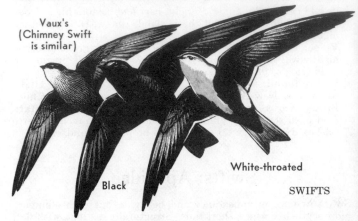

Vaux's (Chimney Swift is similar)

White-throated

Black

SWIFTS

katchewan, n.-c. Colorado (Boulder), w.-c. Texas (San Angelo); spreading. *Casual,* Montana, Utah, Wyoming, New Mexico. **Habitat:** Open sky, especially over towns. **Nest:** A bracket of twigs, usually in chimney. Eggs (4–6) white.

VAUX'S SWIFT *Chaetura vauxi* 4–4½   **above**
  Field marks: A small, dark swallow-like bird with no apparent tail (except when tail is spread). A good metaphor that can be applied to it is "a cigar with wings." The long, slightly curved, stiff wings and twinkling flight mark it as a swift; the small size and dingy underparts, as this species.
  Similar species: East of Rockies see Chimney Swift.
  Voice: A feeble chipping call.
  Where found: Se. Alaska through w. N. America locally to Panama, Venezuela. Winters mainly in tropics. **West:** *Breeds* from se. Alaska, n. B.C. south, mainly in coast belt to c. California; locally inland in e. Washington, ne. Oregon, n. California (Sierra), Idaho, w. Montana. Widespread in migration; east to Idaho, Utah, Arizona. **Habitat:** Open sky, forest burns, openings. Breeds in forests of redwood, douglasfir. **Nest:** A bracket of twigs glued to inside of hollow tree; rarely in chimney. Eggs (3–5) white.

WHITE-THROATED SWIFT   **above**
Aeronautes saxatalis 6–7
  Field marks: Known as a swift by its long, narrow, stiff wings and characteristic twinkling and gliding flight; from other N. American swifts by its contrasting *black and white pattern.* Underparts white, with black side patches.
  Similar species: See Violet-green Swallow (p. 159).

Voice: A shrill, excited *jejejejeje,* in descending scale.
Where found: *Breeds* from s. B.C., Montana, Black Hills south through mt. regions of w. U.S. and Mexico to Guatemala; absent in nw. coast belt and most of Idaho. *Winters* from c. California, s. Arizona, w. Texas south. **Habitat:** Open sky; cruising widely. Breeds mainly in dry mts., canyons, locally sea cliffs (California). **Nest:** A saliva-glued bracket in crevice in cliff; rarely in building. Eggs (3–6) white.

Hummingbirds: Trochilidae

THE SMALLEST of all birds are included in this family. Usually iridescent, with needlelike bills for sipping nectar from flowers The wing motion is so rapid that the wings in most species are blurred. Hover when feeding. Pugnacious. Jewel-like throat feathers, or gorgets, adorn the adult males of most species. (*Note:* The iridescence of back and gorget can vary, depending on age, individual variation, angle of light, etc.) Females lack the gorgets and are mostly greenish above, whitish below. Some females and young are not safely distinguishable in the field even for experts. In late summer and fall the mt. meadows are often full of young hummers, which are just about impossible to identify. It is important to realize this. **Food:** Flower nectar (favoring red flowers), aphids, small insects, spiders. **Range:** W. Hemisphere; majority in tropics. **No. of species:** World, 319; West, 15 (+2 accidentals).

LUCIFER HUMMINGBIRD *Calothorax lucifer* 3¾ **Pl. 39**
  Field marks: Note the *decurved bill.* The male of this hummer (rare in U.S.) has a *purple throat* and *rusty sides.* No purple on crown; tail deeply forked. *Female:* Known from other female hummers by decurved bill, *uniform buff* underparts.
  Similar species: Male Costa's Hummingbird also has purple throat, but in addition has *purple crown;* bill straighter, sides green, tail not deeply forked.
  Where found: W. Texas to s. Mexico (Chiapas). *Summers* in w. Texas (Chisos Mts.). Rare. *Accidental,* s. Arizona. **Habitat:** Arid slopes, agaves. **Nest:** Similar to other hummingbirds'.

RUBY-THROATED HUMMINGBIRD **Pl. 39**
Archilochus colubris 3–3¾
  Field marks: The only hummingbird widespread in the East. Male has fiery *vermilion-red* throat, green back, forked tail. Female indistinguishable from female Black-chin.
  Similar species: Male Broad-tailed Hummingbird has *rose*-red throat, lacks strong fork in tail; trills with wings as it flies. Male Anna's Hummingbird has *red crown.*
  Voice: Male in aerial display swings like pendulum in wide

arc, each swing accompanied by a hum. Notes high, squeaky.
Where found: S. Canada to Gulf states. Winters in Mexico,
Cent. America. **West:** *Breeds* east of Rockies in Alberta, Saskatchewan, ne. Montana; also on Edwards Plateau, Texas (west
to San Angelo). Sparse *migrant* through Great Plains. *Accidental,* Alaska. **Habitat:** Flowering plants, gardens, woods.
Nest: A tiny lichen-covered cup on branch. Eggs (2) white.

BLACK-CHINNED HUMMINGBIRD   Pl. 39
Archilochus alexandri   3⅓–3¾

Field marks: *Male:* Note the *black throat* and conspicuous white
collar below it. The blue-violet band on lower throat shows only
in certain lights (but make certain you see it). *Female:* Greenish
above, whitish below. Cannot safely be told in field from female
of Costa's or Ruby-throat.
Similar species: Throats of other male hummers may look black
until they catch the light. See Costa's Hummingbird.
Voice: Male in display whirs as it swoops back and forth in a
shallow arc. Note, a thin excited chippering.
Where found: *Breeds* from se. B.C. (rare), Idaho, nw. Montana
to n. Mexico; east to w. Colorado, New Mexico, c. and sw. Texas.
Absent in nw. coast belt. *Winters* in Mexico (rarely s. California).
Habitat: Semiarid country near water; semiwooded canyons and
slopes, chaparral, river groves, foothill suburbs. **Nest:** A tiny
feltlike cup in shrub or tree. Eggs (2) white.

COSTA'S HUMMINGBIRD   *Calypte costae*   3–3½   Pl. 39

Field marks: *Male:* Note the *purple* or *amethyst* throat and
crown. Feathers of gorget project greatly at sides. *Female:* Inseparable from female Black-chin but prefers more arid conditions. Often *soars* from one flower clump to another.
Similar species: (1) Male Anna's is larger; has throat and crown
rose-red, not purple. (2) Male Black-chin has restricted blue-
purple on throat; none on crown. (3) Females of Costa's and
Black-chin may differ in nest construction (see below).
Voice: A soft *chik.* In male's aerial display, a high hissing;
ventriloquial, growing louder toward bottom of U-shaped arc.
Where found: *Breeds* in s.-c. and s. California (mainly from
Ventura Co., Mojave and Colorado Deserts south), s. Nevada,
sw. Utah, w. and s. Arizona, sw. New Mexico, nw. Mexico.
Casual north to San Francisco Bay. *Winters* from se. California,
s. Arizona south. **Habitat:** Deserts, washes, mesas, sage scrub,
arid hillsides. **Nest:** A tiny cup in bush or small tree; thatched
with lichens, bits of leaves (Black-chin's is more cocoon-like,
often devoid of decoration). Eggs (2) white.

ANNA'S HUMMINGBIRD   *Calypte anna*   3½–4   Pl. 39

Field marks: *Male:* The only U.S. hummer with a *red crown.*

Throat red. Usually a bit larger than other hummingbirds in its California range. *Female:* Similar to females of other California hummingbirds, but larger and darker green above. Usually grayer below and with a more heavily spotted throat than female Costa's or Black-chin. Often a central patch of red spots on throat. *Caution:* East of California, immature males of other hummingbirds may show similar throat spots. The only hummingbird commonly found in California in midwinter.
Similar species: (1) Adult males of Broad-tail (east of Sierra), (2) Ruby-throat (east of Rockies) lack red crown.
Voice: Feeding note, *chick.* Song, from a perch, a series of squeaking, grating notes. Diving in its aerial "pendulum display" the male makes a *sharp popping sound* at the bottom of arc.
Where found: *Resident* in California west of Sierra from San Francisco and head of Sacramento Valley to nw. Baja California. Post-breeding wanderings to nw. California, s. Arizona, Sonora. *Casual,* s. Vancouver I. (has bred), w. Texas. **Habitat:** Chaparral, broken woodland, gardens. **Nest:** A tiny lichen-covered cup in bush, tree. Eggs (2) white.

BROAD-TAILED HUMMINGBIRD   Pl. 39
Selasphorus platycercus 4–4½
Field marks: The male of this Rocky Mt. species may be known at once by the sound of its wings, a *shrill trilling* as it flies. *Male:* Back green; throat bright *rose-red. Female:* Larger than female Black-chin; sides tinged with buffy; touch of rufous at sides of tail (near base when spread).
Similar species: Other red-throated hummers are: (1) male Rufous and (2) male Allen's (rufous coloration), (3) male Anna's (red crown), (4) male Ruby-throated (orange-red throat; eastern). (5) *Similar* females are Calliope, Rufous, and Allen's.
Voice: Note, a high *chip.* Male trills with wings in flight.
Where found: *Breeds* mainly in mt. regions from e. California (White and Inyo Mts.), n. Nevada, Idaho (local), n. Wyoming through Great Basin and Rocky Mt. ranges to c. Mexico. *Casual,* w. Montana. *Winters* in Mexico, Guatemala. **Habitat:** Mt. glades, high meadows, willow thickets, open undergrowth. **Nest:** A lichen-covered cup in bush, small tree. Eggs (2) white.

RUFOUS HUMMINGBIRD *Selasphorus rufus* 3.3–3.9 Pl. 39
Field marks: *Adult male:* No other N. American hummingbird has a *rufous back.* Upper parts bright non-iridescent red-brown, throat flaming orange-red. *Female:* Green-backed; has dull rufous sides and considerable rufous at base of tail.
Similar species: (1) Male Allen's Hummingbird looks very much like a Rufous Hummingbird. *Be sure to see the middle of the back,* which is green. (2) Female Allen's cannot be told from female Rufous in the field (in the hand, Allen's has narrower outer tail

feathers). (3) Female Broad-tail shows a touch of rufous at base of tail and on sides and therefore may not be safely separable from some female Rufous hummers.
Voice: Note, a sharp, high *bzee;* squeaks, light chips. Sound of wings of adult males of Rufous and Allen's unlike that of other California hummers, a heavy *zz-zzz-zz-zzz* quality. Aerial flight display of Rufous, a closed ellipse with diagonal axis; abrupt slowdown on return climb. Sound on dive, a strident stuttered *v-v-v-v-vvrip* (H. Cogswell).
Where found: *Breeds* from se. Alaska, s. Yukon, sw. Alberta south to nw. California (mts.), Oregon, Idaho, w. Montana. *Migrates* mainly through lowlands of Pacific states in spring and through mts. in late summer (east to e. foothills of Rockies); a few to w. edge of Plains, Gulf Coast. *Winters* in Mexico. **Habitat:** Forest edges, flowering plants. Streamsides, lowlands in spring; mainly mt. meadows, forest openings in fall. **Nest:** A tiny lichen-covered cup in bush, tree. Eggs (2) white.

ALLEN'S HUMMINGBIRD *Selasphorus sasin* 3.3–3.4 **Pl. 39**
Field marks: *Adult male:* Green back, rufous sides, rump, tail, and cheeks; fiery orange-red throat. *Female:* Not distinguishable in field from female Rufous Hummingbird (in hand, Allen's has narrower outer tail feathers).
Similar species: Typical male Rufous has entire back rufous.
Voice: Similar to Rufous Hummingbird's. Full aerial display of male unlike that of Rufous. Starts with "pendulum display" in shallow arc (*bzz, bzz, bzz, bzz, bzz* produced by tail feathers) and after several to many swoops goes into a steep, wavering climb (80–150 ft.) and swoops back, with an air-splitting *vrrrip* at the "focus"; then flies off (H. Cogswell).
Where found: *Breeds* in coastal district of California from Oregon line south to Ventura Co. (?) *Casual,* sw. Oregon, w. Washington. *Migrates* through s. California, Arizona. *Resident* on Channel Is. *Winters* in nw. Mexico. **Habitat:** Wooded or brushy canyons, parks, gardens; mt. meadows (late summer). **Nest:** Similar to other hummingbirds'.

CALLIOPE HUMMINGBIRD *Stellula calliope* 2.8–3.5 **Pl. 39**
Field marks: The smallest hummer normally found in the U.S.; seldom away from high mountains. *Male: Throat with purple-red rays on a white ground* (may be folded like a dark inverted V on a white throat); the only U.S. hummingbird with this effect. *Female:* Very similar to females of Broad-tailed and Rufous Hummingbirds (buffy sides, rufous base of tail) but usually decidedly smaller; rusty on sides paler.
Similar species: (1) Female Broad-tail is decidedly larger (4–4.5 in.); (2) female Rufous (3.3–3.9 in.) may not always be separated unless it shows some rusty on central tail feathers.

Voice: Male in aerial display dives in shallow U-shaped arc, making a brief *pfft* at bottom of dive. Feeding note, *tsip*.
Where found: *Breeds* from c. B.C., sw. Alberta south through Cascades, Sierra, to mts. of s. California, Nevada, n. Baja California; and in Rockies to Utah, Colorado. *Migrates* through mts. of Arizona, New Mexico. *Casual,* Saskatchewan, w. Texas (El Paso). *Winters* in Mexico. **Habitat:** High mts.; canyons, forest glades. **Nest:** Similar to other hummingbirds'.

RIVOLI'S HUMMINGBIRD *Eugenes fulgens* 4½–5 **Pl. 39**
Field marks: *Male:* A very large hummingbird with *blackish belly, bright green throat,* and *purple crown.* Looks all-black at a distance. Wingbeats discernible; sometimes scales on set wings like a swift. *Female:* Large; greenish above, heavily washed with greenish or dusky below. Known from female Blue-throated by more mottled underparts, spotted throat, dark greenish tail, obscure pale-gray tail corners.
Similar species: Female Blue-throated is uniformly gray below with very large white spots on blue-black tail.
Voice: Note, a thin sharp *chip.*
Where found: *Breeds* or summers from mts. of se. Arizona; occasionally in sw. New Mexico, w. Texas (Chisos Mts.) south to n. Nicaragua. *Casual,* Colorado. *Winters* south of U.S. **Habitat:** High mt. glades, pine-oak woods, canyons. **Nest:** A lichen-covered cup in bush. Eggs (2) white.

BLUE-THROATED HUMMINGBIRD **Pl. 39**
Lampornis clemenciae 4½–5¼
Field marks: Note the big tail with its exceptionally *large white patches. Male:* A very large hummingbird with black and white streaks around the eye and a light *blue throat.* Only hummer normally found in U.S. in which *male* has *white tail spots. Female:* Large, with *evenly gray* underparts, white marks on face, and big blue-black tail with *large white corners.*
Similar species: See female Rivoli's Hummingbird.
Voice: Note, a squeaking *seek.*
Where found: *Resident* from mts. of se. Arizona, extreme sw. New Mexico, w. Texas (Chisos Mts.) south to s. Mexico. **Habitat:** Wooded streams in lower canyons of mts. **Nest:** A feltlike cup fastened to slender (vertical) support along stream, under bridge, etc. Old nests built higher each year. Eggs (2) white.

BUFF-BELLIED HUMMINGBIRD **Pl. 39**
Amazilia yucatanensis 4–4½
Field marks: The only *red-billed* hummingbird in the Rio Grande Delta and the only one with a *green throat.* A rather large green hummer with a *rufous* tail, buffy belly. Sexes similar.
Voice: Shrill, squeaky notes.

Where found: S. Texas to Guatemala. *Breeds* in Rio Grande Delta; winters rarely. **Habitat:** Woods, thickets, flowering shrubs, citrus groves. **Nest:** Similar to other hummingbirds'.

VIOLET-CROWNED HUMMINGBIRD   Pl. 39
Amazilia verticalis 3¾–4¼

Field marks: A rather large hummer with *immaculate white underparts, including throat;* bill red, with black tip. Sexes similar, but crown violet-blue in male, dull greenish blue in female and immature. No iridescent gorget on male.

Where found: Mainly Sonora to Chiapas. *Breeds* (perhaps irregularly) in Guadalupe Canyon in extreme se. Arizona, sw. New Mexico. *Occasional* elsewhere in se. Arizona (Huachuca, Chiricahua Mts.). **Habitat:** Riparian groves in canyons; sycamores, agaves. **Nest:** A lichen-thatched cup in sycamore.

WHITE-EARED HUMMINGBIRD   Pl. 39
Hylocharis leucotis 3½

Field marks: *Male:* Bill red with black tip, *broad white stripe behind eye.* Underparts dark greenish, throat blue and green, crown purple. *Female:* Has the red bill, bold white stripe behind eye. Note the small *spots* on throat.

Similar species: Male Broad-billed Hummingbird has a well-forked tail and only a touch of white behind eye. *Caution:* Female Broad-billed is often mistaken for female White-eared (it has a red bill and a pronounced white eye-stripe). If the throat and underparts are evenly gray, it is the Broad-bill.

Voice: "A low, clear *tink, tink, tink,* sounding like a small bell" (A. Skutch). A metallic rattle; various other notes.

Where found: Mts. of Mexican border to Nicaragua. A very rare summer visitor to mts. of se. Arizona. *Accidental,* w. Texas (Chisos Mts.). **Habitat:** Pine-oak woods near streams.

BROAD-BILLED HUMMINGBIRD   Pl. 39
Cynanthus latirostris 3¼–4

Field marks: *Male:* Dark green above and below with a *blue throat* (bird looks all-black in distance). Bill bright *red,* with black tip. *Female:* Identified by combination of red *bill* and *unmarked pearly-gray* throat and underparts. Females of most other hummers have some spots on throat.

Similar species: Female White-eared Hummingbird has a bit more white behind eye, *spotted throat,* mottled sides.

Voice: A chatter. In aerial display arc, hum of male is higher-pitched than in other species; has "*zing* of a rifle bullet" (Willard).

Where found: *Summers* from s. Arizona, sw. New Mexico, w. Texas (sparse; Big Bend to Alpine) to s. Mexico. *Winters* in Mexico. **Habitat:** Desert canyons, mt. slopes, agaves, mesquite. **Nest:** Rough, less cottony than Costa's or Black-chin's.

Trogons: Trogonidae

BRIGHTLY colored solitary forest birds; short neck, stubby bill; tail long and truncate. Quiet, erect, when perched; flutter in air when plucking small fruit. Feet very small, 1st and 2nd toes turned backward. **Food:** Small fruits, insects. **Range:** Mainly tropical parts of world. **No. of species:** World, 34; West, 1.

COPPERY-TAILED TROGON *Trogon elegans* 11–12 **Pl. 38**
   Field marks: Note the erect posture, slightly parrot-like profile and *geranium-red belly. Male:* Head, chest, and upper parts dark glossy green, separated from the red belly by a narrow white band across the breast. Tail square-tipped and moderately long; bill stout and pale. *Female:* Head and upper parts brown; much less red on underparts; *white mark* on cheek.
   Voice: A series of low, coarse notes, suggesting a hen Turkey: *kowm kowm kowm kowm kowm kowm* or *koa koa, koa,* etc.
   Where found: *Breeds* from mts. of s. Arizona (rare or irregular in Santa Ritas, Huachucas, Chiricahuas) to Costa Rica. *Winters* south of U.S. *Casual,* sw. Mexico, lower Rio Grande Valley, Texas. **Habitat:** Mt. forests, pine-oak or sycamore canyons. **Nest:** In tree cavity. Eggs (3–4) white.

Kingfishers: Alcedinidae

SOLITARY birds with large heads, heron-like bills, small weak syndactyl feet (2 toes joined for part of length). American species are fish-eaters, fishing from a perch above water, or they may hover and plunge headlong. **Food:** Mainly fish; some species eat insects, lizards. **Range:** Almost worldwide. **No. of species:** World, 87; West, 2 (+1 accidental).

BELTED KINGFISHER *Megaceryle alcyon* 11–14½ **Pl. 44**
   Field marks: Hovering on rapidly beating wings in readiness for the plunge, or flying with uneven wingbeats ("as if changing gear"), rattling as it goes, the Kingfisher is easily learned. Perched, it is big-headed and big-billed, larger than a Robin, blue-gray above, with a ragged, bushy crest and a broad gray breastband. Female has a 2nd band (rusty).
   Voice: A loud high rattle.
   Where found: Alaska, Canada to s. U.S. Winters to Panama. **West:** *Breeds* from c. Alaska, Yukon, Mackenzie to s. California, New Mexico, c. Texas. *Winters* from se. Alaska, s. B.C., Montana south. **Habitat:** Rivers, ponds, lakes, bays, coast. **Nest:** In burrow in riverbank, sandbank. Eggs (5–8; 14) white.

GREEN KINGFISHER *Chloroceryle americana* 7–8½ **Pl. 44**
(Texas Kingfisher)
> **Field marks:** The kingfisher shape and the small size identify it.
> Flight buzzy, direct. Upper parts deep green with white spots;
> collar and underparts white, sides spotted. The *male* has a *rusty
> breastband;* replaced by 1 or 2 greenish bands in female. (Note
> the switch: In Belted Kingfisher, *female* has rusty.)
> **Voice:** A sharp clicking, *tick tick tick;* also a sharp squeak.
> **Where found:** Texas to Argentina. **West:** *Resident* in s. Texas
> north to Kerrville, San Marcos, and along Rio Grande to Pecos
> River. *Casual,* s. Arizona. **Habitat:** Rivers, streams, resacas.
> **Nest:** In burrow in bank. Eggs (4–6) white.

Woodpeckers: Picidae

CHISEL-BILLED wood-boring birds with powerful zygodactyl feet
(usually 2 toes front, 2 rear), remarkably long tongues and stiff,
spiny tails which act as props when climbing. Flight usually
undulating. Most males have some red on head. **Food:** Mainly
tree-boring insects; some eat ants, flying insects, berries, acorns,
sap. **Range:** Mainly wooded parts of world but absent in Australian region, Madagascar, most oceanic islands. **No. of species**
(including relatives): World, 210; West, 20 (+1 accidental).

YELLOW-SHAFTED FLICKER   **Pl. 40**
Colaptes auratus 12–14
> **Field marks:** Similar to Red-shafted Flicker but with the pinkish
> red of wing- and tail-linings replaced by *golden yellow.* Both
> sexes have a *red crescent* on back of head (lacking in other
> flickers). The male has *black* "mustache" instead of red.
> The basic head colors are reversed, i.e.: gray crown, brown
> throat and cheeks (Yellow-shafted); brown crown, gray throat
> and cheeks (Red-shafted). *Note:* Where the breeding ranges
> overlap (B.C. and w. edge of Great Plains) hybrids are often
> produced with *orange-yellow* wing-linings or with one whisker
> black, one red; also other combinations of characters.
> **Similar species:** See other flickers.
> **Voice:** Similar to Red-shafted Flicker's.
> **Where found:** Tree limit in Alaska, Canada south to Gulf states,
> Cuba. Migrant in n. parts of range. **West:** *Breeds* from tree
> limit south to c. B.C. and thence east of Rockies to n. Texas.
> Some occur in migration or winter throughout w. U.S. but most
> Pacific Coast birds seem to have hybrid blood. **Habitat and
> Nest:** Similar to Red-shafted Flickers'.

WILLIAMSON'S
SAPSUCKER ♂

FLICKER

RED-
HEADED

ACORN

HAIRY

WHITE-
HEADED

PILEATED

LEWIS'

FLIGHT PATTERNS OF WOODPECKERS

RED-SHAFTED FLICKER p. 139, Pl. 40
Colaptes cafer 12½–14
 Field marks: Note the conspicuous *white rump,* visible as the bird flies. This and the brown back mark it as a flicker. The flight is deeply undulating. Overhead this species flashes much *salmon-red* under the wings and tail. Close up, it shows a wide black crescent across the chest, numerous round black spots on underparts. Male has red "mustache"; no red on nape. Often feeds on ground, hops awkwardly.
 Similar species: See Yellow-shafted and Gilded Flickers.
 Voice: Song, a loud *wick wick wick wick wick,* etc. Notes, a loud *klee-yer* and a squeaky *flick-a, flick-a,* etc.
 Where found: Se. Alaska, c. B.C., w.-c. and s. Alberta, sw. Saskatchewan south through w. U.S., Mexico to Guatemala; east to w. parts of Great Plains. Some withdrawal in winter from n. sections and mts. **Habitat:** Groves, river woods, open forest, farms, towns, canyons, semiopen country. **Nest:** In excavation in tree, post, building. Eggs (5–10) white.

GILDED FLICKER *Colaptes chrysoides* 10–12 Pl. 40
(Mearns's Gilded Flicker)
 Field marks: The flicker of the saguaros. Similar to Red-shafted Flicker but usually with wing- and tail-linings *yellow.* (*Note:* Occasional red variants look almost exactly like Red-shafted Flickers.) Differs from Yellow-shafted, which is not a year-round resident in the desert, in lacking the red crescent on nape. Males have a red "mustache." In short, this species has the head of Red-shafted (brown crown, gray cheeks and throat), body of Yellow-shafted.
 Voice: Slightly higher in pitch than other flickers'.
 Where found: *Resident* in se. California (Colorado River), s. Arizona, Baja California, Sonora, n. Sinaloa. **Habitat:** Deserts, saguaros, river groves. **Nest:** In hole in saguaro; sometimes in cottonwood, tree-yucca, etc. Eggs (3–5) white.

PILEATED WOODPECKER p. 139
Dryocopus pileatus 16–19½
 Field marks: A spectacular, black, *Crow-sized* woodpecker with a red *crest.* Female has blackish forehead, lacks red on "whisker" stripe. The great size, sweeping wingbeats, and flashing white underwing areas identify the Pileated in flight. The diggings, large *oval* or *oblong* holes, indicate its presence.
 Voice: Call resembles Flicker's but louder, irregular: *kik — kik — kikkik —— kik-kik,* etc. Also a more ringing, hurried call; often rises or falls slightly in pitch.
 Where found: Canada to California, Gulf states. **West:** *Resident* from n. B.C. through Pacific states to c. California (Sonoma Co. on coast, Greenhorn Mt. in s. Sierra); south in n. Rockies

to Idaho, w. Montana; also east of Rockies across wooded Canada. *Accidental,* Utah, n. Arizona. **Habitat:** Coniferous and mixed forests. **Nest:** In hole in tree. Eggs (3–5) white.

RED-BELLIED WOODPECKER *Centurus carolinus* 9–10½
Field marks: See illustration in Eastern or Texas *Field Guide.* Similar to Golden-fronted Woodpecker but male has entire crown red (all in one piece). Female is *red* on nape, not orange or yellow. In our area, central tail feathers (topside) are *barred* (solid black in Golden-fronted).
Voice: Note, *churr* or *chaw;* also *chiv, chiv.*
Where found: Great Lakes area to Gulf of Mexico. *Resident* locally in Texas panhandle. *Casual,* e. New Mexico, e. Colorado (has bred). *Accidental,* Saskatchewan. **Habitat:** Woodlands, groves, towns. **Nest:** In hole in tree. Eggs (4–5) white.

GOLDEN-FRONTED WOODPECKER Pl. 40
Centurus aurifrons 8½–10½
Field marks: *Male:* Note the separated patches of bright color on the head (yellow near bill, poppy-red on crown, orange nape). A "zebra-backed" woodpecker with light-colored underparts and a white rump. Shows a white wing patch in flight. *Female:* Similar, without red crown patch; has yellow-orange nape patch. Young bird lacks head patches.
Similar species: See Red-bellied Woodpecker.
Voice: A tremulous rolling *churrrr.* A flicker-like *kek-kek-kek-kek,* etc.
Where found: Sw. Oklahoma, middle Texas (east to Austin, c. coast); south to Nicaragua. **West:** *Resident* in middle Texas; west to Panhandle, San Angelo, Big Spring, Big Bend. **Habitat:** Mesquite, stream woodlands, groves. **Nest:** In hole in post, pole, tree. Eggs (4–5) white.

GILA WOODPECKER *Centurus uropygialis* 8–10 **Pl. 40**
Field marks: *Male:* Note the *round red cap.* A "zebra-backed" woodpecker showing, in flight, a white wing patch, head and underparts gray-brown. *Female:* Similar, without red cap.
Similar species: The only other woodpeckers resident in the low desert where this bird is found are: (1) the flickers, which are brown; (2) Ladder-backed Woodpecker, which has a striped face. Neither shows a white wing patch.
Voice: A rolling *churr* and a sharp *pit* or *yip.*
Where found: *Resident* from se. California (Imperial Valley), s. tip of Nevada, s. Arizona, sw. New Mexico to c. Mexico. **Habitat:** Desert washes, saguaros, river groves, cottonwoods, towns. **Nest:** In hole in saguaro, tree. Eggs (3–5) white.

RED-HEADED WOODPECKER   p. 139, Pl. 40
Melanerpes erythrocephalus   8½–9½

Field marks: A black-backed woodpecker with the *entire head red*. White rump and large square white patches on rear edge of wing are conspicuous in flight; when bird is on tree, these patches make lower back look white. Sexes similar. Immature dusky-headed; large white wing patches identify it.

Similar species: Red-breasted Sapsucker also has an entirely red head but a different range (Pacific states).

Voice: A loud *queer* or *queeoh*.

Where found: S. Canada, mainly east of Rockies to Gulf states. **West:** *Breeds* west to sw. Saskatchewan, c. Montana, w. Wyoming, c. Colorado, c. New Mexico, Texas panhandle. *Migrant* in North. *Casual,* Alberta, Idaho, Utah, Arizona. **Habitat:** Groves, farm country, towns, scattered trees. **Nest:** In hole in pole or tree. Eggs (4–6) white.

ACORN WOODPECKER   *Melanerpes formicivorus*   8–9½
(California Woodpecker)   p. 139, Pl. 40

Field marks: Note the clownish black, white, and red head pattern (see plate). A black-backed woodpecker with a large white rump and a white wing patch in flight. Both sexes have whitish eyes, red on crown. Stores acorns in bark of trees.

Voice: *Whack-up, whack-up, whack-up,* or *ja-cob, ja-cob.*

Where found: *Resident* from Oregon (local) south through California (w. of Sierra divide); and from Arizona, New Mexico, w. Texas (Trans-Pecos) to w. Panama. *Casual,* Nevada. **Habitat:** Oak woods, groves, mixed forest, oak-pine canyons, foothills. **Nest:** In hole in tree or pole. Eggs (4–5) white.

LEWIS' WOODPECKER   p. 139, Pl. 40
Asyndesmus lewis   10½–11½

Field marks: A large dark, black-backed woodpecker, with an extensive pinkish-red belly (the only N. American Woodpecker so colored). Has a wide gray collar, dark red face patch. The pink underparts, wide black wings are the best marks. Sexes similar. Has fly-catching habit, crowlike flight.

Voice: Usually silent. Occasionally a harsh *churr* or *chee-ur.*

Where found: *Breeds* from c. B.C., sw. Alberta, Montana, Black Hills south to mts. of s.-c. California (sparse), n. Arizona, s. New Mexico. *Winters* from n. Oregon, n. Utah, Colorado to n. Mexico; a few near coast north to B.C. Wanders to w. parts of Great Plains. **Habitat:** Scattered or logged forest, river groves, burns. **Nest:** In hole in tree, stub. Eggs (6–8) white.

YELLOW-BELLIED SAPSUCKER   Pl. 40
Sphyrapicus varius (in part)   8–9
(Red-naped Sapsucker, "Common Sapsucker")

Field marks: Adults are identified by the combination of *red*

forehead patch and *long white wing patch* (shows well at rest).
Male has a patch of red on both forehead and throat. Female
has white throat (east of Rockies) or partly red throat (Rockies,
west). Young bird is brown but the long white wing patch
identifies it. Sapsuckers drill orderly rows of small holes in trees.
For red-breasted form see next entry.
Voice: A nasal mewing note, or squeal: *cheerrrr,* slurring downward. On nesting grounds, distinctive drumming; several rapid
thumps followed by several slow rhythmic ones.
Where found: Canada to s. Rocky Mts., s. Appalachians.
Winters to Cent. America, W. Indies. **West:** *Breeds* from s.-c.
B.C., c. Mackenzie south through Great Basin ranges and
Rockies to ne. California, n. Nevada, c. Arizona, s. New Mexico;
also east across forests of Canada. *Winters* mainly east of Sierra
from Utah, Colorado south. **Habitat:** Woodlands, aspen groves;
in winter also orchards, other trees. **Nest:** In hole in tree.
Eggs (4–6) white.

"RED-BREASTED" SAPSUCKER   Pl. 40
Sphyrapicus varius (in part)
   Field marks: In the Pacific area, 2 races of the Yellow-bellied
Sapsucker (*S. v. ruber* and *S. v. daggetti*) have the *entire head and
breast bright red* and are popularly known as "Red-breasted"
Sapsuckers. The long white wing patch and other markings are
much like those of other Yellow-bellied Sapsuckers.
   Similar species: Red-headed Woodpecker (east of Rockies).
   Where found: Pacific area. *Breeds* from se. Alaska, w. B.C.,
south in coast belt to n. California and through Cascades, Sierra
to high mts. of s. California. *Winters* in lowlands and along
coast to Baja California. *Casual,* Arizona. **Habitat and Nest:**
Similar to other Yellow-bellied Sapsuckers'.

WILLIAMSON'S SAPSUCKER   p. 139, Pl. 40
Sphyrapicus thyroideus 9½
   Field marks: *Male:* Note the black crown, black back, long
white shoulder patch. The white face-stripes and narrow bright
red throat patch are also distinctive. Flying, looks black, with
white rump and shoulder patches. *Female:* Like a different
species, a brownish *"zebra-backed"* woodpecker with a white
rump, *barred sides, brown head.* Belly yellow in both sexes.
   Similar species: Barred sides, brown head, evergreen habitat
separate female from other zebra-backed woodpeckers.
   Voice: A nasal *cheeer* or *que-yer;* suggests squeal of Red-tailed
Hawk. Drumming distinctive; several rapid thumps followed
by 3–4 slow, accented ones, thus: = = – – – –, -, -, -.
   Where found: *Breeds* in mts. from se. B.C., ne. Washington,
Idaho, w. Montana south through Cascades (e. slope), Sierra to
high mts. of s. California, Nevada; in Rockies to c. Arizona,

sw. New Mexico. *Winters* to adjacent lower elevations in Pacific states and from Arizona, New Mexico, w. Texas south into n. Mexico. **Habitat:** Higher conifer forests, burns. **Nest:** In hole in stub or tree. Eggs (3–7) white.

HAIRY WOODPECKER   p. 139, Pl. 40
Dendrocopos villosus   8½–10½

Field marks: Note the white back, large bill. Other woodpeckers have white rumps or white bars on the back, but the Downy and the Hairy are the only common woodpeckers with clear *white backs.* They are almost identical in pattern, spotted with white on wings; males with a small red patch on back of head; *females,* without. The Hairy is like a magnified Downy; bill is especially large in relation to Downy's little bill. The Hairy and Downy Woodpecker of the Pacific states are noticeably darker, with less white spotting; underparts tinged with brownish. Birds east of Rockies are whitest, with most spotting.

Similar species: (1) Downy at close range shows spots on outer tail feathers. Small bill is best character. (2) Northern Three-toed Woodpecker of boreal forests may have white back.

Voice: A kingfisher-like rattle, run together more than call of Downy. Note, a sharp *peek!*

Where found: Alaska, Canada to Panama. **West:** Largely *resident* from tree limit south throughout w. Canada and much of w. U.S.; mainly in mts. in sw. U.S. Some down-mountain drift in winter. **Habitat:** Mt. forests, woodlands, river groves. **Nest:** In hole in tree stub. Eggs (3–6) white.

DOWNY WOODPECKER   Pl. 40
Dendrocopos pubescens   6–7

Field marks: Note the white back, small bill.

Similar species: See Hairy and Ladder-backed Woodpeckers.

Voice: A rapid whinny of notes, descending in pitch. Note, a flat *pick,* not as sharp as Hairy's note.

Where found: Alaska, Canada, to s. U.S. **West:** *Resident* from Alaska (Yukon Valley), sw. Mackenzie, n. Alberta, n. Saskatchewan south to s. California (San Diego), c. Arizona, c. New Mexico, nw. Texas panhandle. **Habitat:** Broken or mixed forest, woods, willows, poplars, river groves, orchards, shade trees. **Nest:** In hole in tree. Eggs (4–7) white.

LADDER-BACKED WOODPECKER   Pl. 40
Dendrocopos scalaris   6–7½
("Mexican Woodpecker")

Field marks: The only black and white "zebra-backed" woodpecker with a *black and white striped face* in the arid country outlined below. Males have red caps.

Similar species: (1) Nuttall's Woodpecker is found only in California, west of Sierra, not in the desert. There are minor differences in the amount of black on upper back, pattern on face (see plate). (2) Downy Woodpecker has white back.

Voice: A rattling series; *chikikikikikikikikik;* diminishing. Note, a sharp *pick* or *chik.*

Where found: *Resident* from se. California, s. Nevada, sw. Utah, se. Colorado, w. Oklahoma, w. Texas (east to 97°); south to Chiapas, B. Honduras. **Habitat:** Deserts, canyons, cottonwoods, arid brush, prairie groves. **Nest:** In hole in tree, post, yucca, agave. Eggs (4–5) white.

NUTTALL'S WOODPECKER   Pl. 40
Dendrocopos nuttallii   7–7½

Field marks: The only black and white "zebra-backed" woodpecker with a *black and white striped face* found in California west of the Sierra. Males have red caps.

Similar species: (1) Ladder-backed Woodpecker lives in arid country; ranges do not overlap. (2) The Downy, the only similar small woodpecker sharing its range, has a white, unbarred back.

Voice: A high-pitched rattle and a loud *prrit.*

Where found: *Resident* in California, west of the Sierra and deserts, from s. Humboldt Co. and head of Sacramento Valley south to nw. Baja California. *Accidental,* Arizona. **Habitat:** Wooded canyons and foothills, river woods, groves, orchards. **Nest:** In hole in tree. Eggs (4–5) white.

ARIZONA WOODPECKER   Pl. 40
Dendrocopos arizonae   7–8

Field marks: A dark, *brown-backed* woodpecker with a *white striped face,* spotted and barred below. Male has red nape patch. The only U.S. woodpecker with a solid brown back (flickers have *barred* backs, white rumps).

Voice: A sharp *spik* or *tseek,* sharper than notes of Downy and Ladder-backed Woodpeckers. A hoarse whinny.

Where found: *Resident* from mts. of se. Arizona, sw. New Mexico south to s.-c. Mexico. **Habitat:** Oaks in mts., pine-oak canyons. **Nest:** A hole in dead branch. Eggs (3–4) white.

WHITE-HEADED WOODPECKER   p. 139, Pl. 40
Dendrocopos albolarvatus   9

Field marks: No other U.S. woodpecker has a *white head.* Black, with a large white wing patch. Male has a red patch on nape.

Voice: A sharp *chick,* sometimes rapidly repeated, *chick — ik-ik-ik;* also a rattle similar to Downy Woodpecker's.

Where found: *Resident* from n. Washington, n. Idaho south through Oregon (mainly east of Cascade summits) to California (inner Coast Ranges to Colusa Co. and through Sierra, including e. slope in w. Nevada); also higher mts. of s. California. *Casual,* s. B.C. **Habitat:** Mainly pine forest, firs. **Nest:** In hole in stub. Eggs (3–5) white.

Plates

Plate 1

GREBES AND LOONS

HORNED GREBE p. 6
Summer: Buffy "ears"; rufous neck.
Winter: Black and white pattern, thin dark bill.

EARED GREBE p. 6
Summer: Buffy "ears"; black neck.
Winter: Like Horned Grebe; grayer neck, upturned bill, dark cap to below eye.

PIED-BILLED GREBE p. 7
Rounded bill, white under tail coverts.
Summer: Black bill ring, black throat.
Winter (not shown): Lacks black on throat and bill.
Juvenal: Striped face.

LEAST GREBE p. 7
Very small, dark; small dark bill, yellow eye. In winter, throat whitish.

WESTERN GREBE p. 7
Blackish upper parts, long white neck.
Head pattern is of 2 types (black cap above eye or extending below eye).

RED-NECKED GREBE p. 5
Summer: Reddish neck, whitish chin and cheek.
Winter: Grayish neck, yellowish bill.

RED-THROATED LOON p. 5
Summer: Gray head; rufous throat.
Winter: Pale color; slender upturned bill.

ARCTIC LOON p. 4
Summer: Gray crown; back spots in patches.
Winter: Bill slender, but not upturned.

COMMON LOON p. 3
Summer: Black head, all-checkered back.
Winter: Dark back; stout, straight bill.

YELLOW-BILLED LOON (not illustrated) p. 3
Arctic. Similar to Common Loon. See bill diagram, page 4.

Loons in flight are hunchbacked and gangly, with a slight downward sweep to the neck and the feet projecting behind the scanty tail.

HORNED GREBE

Summer   Winter

EARED GREBE

Summer   Winter

PIED-BILLED GREBE

Summer   Juvenal

LEAST GREBE

Summer   Winter

WESTERN GREBE

RED-NECKED GREBE

Summer   Winter

Summer

RED-THROATED LOON

Winter

Summer

ARCTIC LOON

Winter

Summer

COMMON LOON

Winter

Plate 2

SHEARWATERS, FULMAR, AND STORM PETRELS

SOOTY SHEARWATER p. 10
Sooty body, whitish wing-linings.

SLENDER-BILLED SHEARWATER p. 11
Sooty body, sooty wing-linings.

PALE-FOOTED SHEARWATER p. 10
Like Slender-bill, but pale pink bill and feet.

FULMAR p. 9
Bull-necked; stubby yellow bill. Stiff-winged gliding.
Light phase: White head; light patch at base of primaries.
Dark phase: Smoky gray; yellowish bill.

NEW ZEALAND SHEARWATER p. 10
Note black pattern on gray (like wide M or W).

MANX SHEARWATER p. 11
Much smaller than Pink-footed; blackish above, whiter
wing-linings, small blackish bill.

PINK-FOOTED SHEARWATER p. 10
Large; dark gray above, white below; pinkish bill.

FORK-TAILED PETREL p. 11
Our only gray storm petrel.

LEACH'S PETREL p. 12
White rump patch.

BLACK PETREL p. 12
The largest all-dark petrel; flight languid.

ASHY PETREL p. 12
Smaller than Black Petrel; flight fluttery.
At close range, white mottling under wing.

LEAST PETREL p. 12
Very small; tail wedge-shaped.

PALE-
FOOTED
SHEARWATER

SOOTY
SHEARWATER

SLENDER-
BILLED
SHEARWATER

Dark phase

Light phase

FULMAR

EW ZEALAND
HEARWATER

FORK-
TAILED
PETREL

MANX
SHEARWATER

PINK-FOOTED
SHEARWATER

LEACH'S
PETREL

BLACK
PETREL

ASHY
PETREL

LEAST
PETREL

Plate 3

SKUA AND JAEGERS

Hawklike sea birds that pursue gulls, terns in a piratical manner. All show a white flash in the wing. Adult jaegers have falcon-shaped wings and elongated tail feathers and occur in light, intermediate, and dark phases; the tail-points are often broken off. Immatures have stubbier tail-points and are very difficult to separate.

The Skua is blunter winged (more like a Buteo) and has a blunt tail. *Note:* The British also call the three jaegers "Skuas."

SKUA   p. 94
    Dark, heavily-built; white wing patches, blunt tail.
    Wings blunter than those of jaegers.

PARASITIC JAEGER   p. 93
    Pointed central tail feathers (moderate length).

POMARINE JAEGER   p. 93
    Blunt (and partially twisted) central tail feathers.

LONG-TAILED JAEGER   p. 94
    Very long, flexible, pointed central tail feathers.

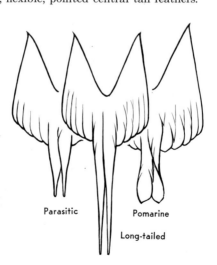

Parasitic   Pomarine

Long-tailed

TAILS OF JAEGERS (ADULTS)

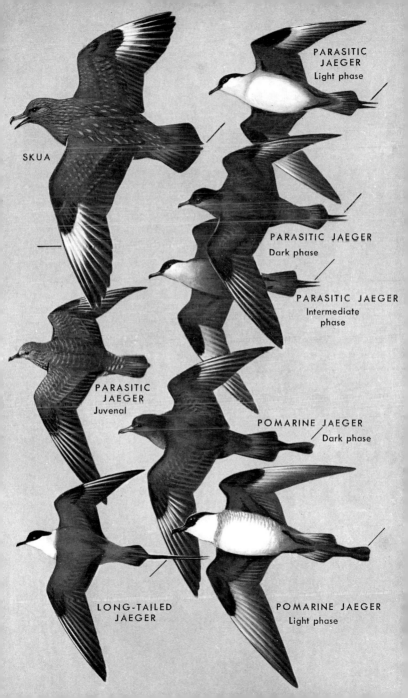

SKUA

PARASITIC
JAEGER
Light phase

PARASITIC JAEGER
Dark phase

PARASITIC JAEGER
Intermediate
phase

PARASITIC
JAEGER
Juvenal

POMARINE JAEGER
Dark phase

LONG-TAILED
JAEGER

POMARINE JAEGER
Light phase

Plate 4

LONG-LEGGED WADING BIRDS

AMERICAN BITTERN p. 23
Tawny; black neck mark; bill pointed up.

BLACK-CROWNED NIGHT HERON p. 22
Adult: White breast, black back, black crown.
Immature: Brown; white spotting on back.

GREEN HERON p. 20
Small dark; short yellowish legs (orange when breeding).
Immature: Neck streaked.

LEAST BITTERN p. 22
Tiny; back and crown black, wings buff.

WHITE-FACED IBIS p. 24
Dark, glossy; decurved bill. White face only in breeding
plumage.

LITTLE BLUE HERON p. 20
Adult: Dark body, slender dark legs, bill bluish at base.
Immature: White body; dark bill and feet (see text).

LOUISIANA HERON p. 22
Dark; white belly.

COMMON EGRET p. 21
Large; yellow bill, dark legs.

CATTLE EGRET p. 20
Small, yellow bill; yellow, greenish, pink, or blackish legs.
Invading East. To be looked for in West. Associates with
cattle.

SNOWY EGRET p. 21
Small, white; black bill, yellow feet.

SANDHILL CRANE p. 71
Gray; red crown, tufted rear.

GREAT BLUE HERON p. 19
Large; blue-gray; yellowish bill.

WOOD IBIS or **WOOD STORK** p. 23
Naked gray head, decurved bill; black in wings in flight.

Herons and egrets fly with necks
folded; cranes and ibises, with necks
extended.

AMERICAN
BITTERN

BLACK-CROWNED
NIGHT HERON

Immature

Adult

GREEN HERON

Immature

Adult

LEAST BITTERN

WHITE-FACED IBIS

LITTLE BLUE
HERON
Adult

LOUISIANA HERON

CATTLE
EGRET

LITTLE BLUE
HERON
Immature

SNOWY
EGRET

COMMON EGRET

SANDHILL
CRANE

GREAT BLUE
HERON

WOOD
IBIS

Plate 5

GEESE AND SWANS

CANADA GOOSE* p. 26

Black "stocking," white cheek patch.
Several races of the Canada Goose, varying in size, occur in the West, but separation in the field is not too safe — there is some intergradation (see text for details). The **Cackling Canada Goose** is the small extreme.

BLACK BRANT p. 27

Black chest and "stocking"; white neck spot.

WHITE-FRONTED GOOSE p. 28

Adult: White at base of bill.
Immature: Dusky, with pale bill.

BLUE GOOSE p. 28

Adult: White head (including throat).
Immature: Dusky, with dark bill, light wing (see text).

EMPEROR GOOSE p. 27

Adult: White head (but black throat).
Immature: Dusky, with dark bill (see text).

SNOW GOOSE p. 28

Adult: White with black wing-tips.
Immature: Similar but duskier, dark bill.

ROSS' GOOSE p. 29

Smaller than Snow Goose; bill smaller, lacking black "lips" or "grinning patch."

WHISTLING SWAN p. 25

Black bill, long straight neck; no black in wings.

TRUMPETER SWAN p. 25

Larger; heavier bill; deeper voice. See text.

---

* The large form of the Canada Goose (upper right) is perhaps more properly known as Moffitt's Canada Goose. It has also been called the Basin Canada Goose. Although this is the most widespread Canada Goose in the West, the Dusky Canada Goose (*B. c. occidentalis*) of Prince William Sound, Alaska, has also been called Western Canada Goose by some writers (see p. 26). When dealing with subspecies it is safer to use the scientific names.

Cackling Canada

Lesser Canada

Western Canada

CANADA GOOSE (3 forms)

BLACK BRANT

Immature

Adult

WHITE-FRONTED GOOSE

Immature

BLUE GOOSE

Adult

Immature

Adult

EMPEROR GOOSE

Immature

Adult

SNOW GOOSE

ROSS' GOOSE

WHISTLING SWAN

TRUMPETER SWAN

Plate 6

GEESE AND SWANS

Many geese and swans fly in line or wedge formation.

CANADA GOOSE p. 26
Black "stocking," light chest, white "chin strap."

BRANT (both species) p. 27
Small; black "stocking," black chest, black head.
Black Brant: Dark underparts.
Brant: Light underparts.

WHITE-FRONTED GOOSE p. 28
Adult: Gray neck, black splotches on belly.
Immature: Dusky; light bill, light feet.

EMPEROR GOOSE p. 27
Adult: Dark body, white head (but throat black).

SNOW GOOSE p. 28
White body, black primaries.

WHISTLING SWAN p. 25
Very long neck; wings with no black.

BLUE GOOSE p. 28
Adult: Dark body, white head (including throat).

CANADA
GOOSE

BLACK
BRANT

BRANT

Adult

WHITE-FRONTED
GOOSE

Immature

EMPEROR
GOOSE

SNOW
GOOSE

BLUE
GOOSE

WHISTLING SWAN

Plate 7

DUCKS IN FLIGHT
(through the binocular)

Note: Males are analyzed below. Some females are similar.

MEXICAN DUCK p. 31
Pattern of female Mallard, but bill unmarked. See text.

BLACK DUCK p. 31
Dark body, paler head (see Plate 14).

MALLARD p. 31
Dark head, 2 white borders on speculum; neck-ring.

GADWALL p. 32
White speculum.

PINTAIL p. 32
Needle tail, 1 white border on speculum, neck-stripe.

AMERICAN WIDGEON p. 35
Large white shoulder patch.

SHOVELER p. 35
Spoon bill, large bluish shoulder patch.

WOOD DUCK p. 36
Stocky; long dark tail, white border on dark wing.

BLUE-WINGED TEAL p. 34
Small; large bluish shoulder patch.
Females of Blue-winged and Cinnamon Teal are nearly identical.

CINNAMON TEAL p. 34
Very dark (mahogany); bluish shoulder patch.

GREEN-WINGED TEAL p. 31
Small, dark-winged; green speculum.

HOODED MERGANSER p. 45
Merganser shape; small wing patch.

COMMON MERGANSER p. 46
Merganser shape; white chest, large wing patch.

RED-BREASTED MERGANSER p. 46
Merganser shape; dark chest, large wing patch.

Mergansers fly with bill, head, neck, and body held in a horizontal line.

BLACK DUCK

Sexes
Similar

Sexes
Similar

MEXICAN
DUCK

MALLARD

♂ GADWALL

PINTAIL

AMERICAN
WIDGEON

SHOVELER

CINNAMON
TEAL

BLUE-WINGED
TEAL

GREEN-WINGED
TEAL

WOOD
DUCK

HOODED MERGANSER

COMMON MERGANSER

RED-BREASTED
MERGANSER

Plate 8

DUCKS IN FLIGHT
(through the binocular)

Note: Males are analyzed below. Some females are similar.

REDHEAD p. 36
Gray back, broad gray wing-stripe.

LESSER SCAUP p. 39
Broad white wing-stripe (see Greater Scaup).

RING-NECKED DUCK p. 37
Black back, broad gray wing-stripe.

CANVASBACK p. 37
White back, long profile.

COMMON GOLDENEYE p. 39
Large white wing-squares, short neck, black head.

BUFFLEHEAD p. 40
Small; large wing patches, white head patch.

RUDDY DUCK p. 44
Small, dark; white cheek.

OLDSQUAW p. 40
Dark wings, white on body.

KING EIDER p. 42
Whitish foreparts, black rear parts.

COMMON EIDER p. 41
White back, white forewings, black belly.

MASKED DUCK p. 45
Resembles Ruddy, but white patch in wing, black face.

BLACK-BELLIED TREE DUCK p. 29
Great white wing patches, dark body.

FULVOUS TREE DUCK p. 30
Dark wings, white rump patch.

WHITE-WINGED SCOTER p. 43
Black; white wing patch.

SURF SCOTER p. 43
Black; white head patches.

COMMON SCOTER p. 44
All-black plumage; orange on bill.

LESSER SCAUP

REDHEAD

RING-NECKED DUCK

CANVASBACK

BUFFLEHEAD

COMMON GOLDENEYE

OLDSQUAW

KING EIDER

COMMON EIDER

RUDDY DUCK

BLACK-BELLIED TREE DUCK
Sexes alike

FULVOUS TREE DUCK
Sexes alike

MASKED DUCK

WHITE-WINGED SCOTER

SURF SCOTER

COMMON SCOTER

Plate 9

DUCKS OVERHEAD
(as the sportsman often sees them)

Note: Only males are analyzed below.

BLACK DUCK   p. 31
Very dark body, white wing-linings.

GADWALL   p. 32
White belly, white rear wing patches.

MEXICAN DUCK (not illustrated)   p. 31
Similar to female Mallard. See text.

MALLARD   p. 31
Dark chest, light belly, white neck-ring.

PINTAIL   p. 32
White breast, thin neck, needle tail.

AMERICAN WIDGEON   p. 35
White belly, dark pointed tail.

SHOVELER   p. 35
Dark belly, white chest; big bill.

WOOD DUCK   p. 36
White belly, dusky wings, long square tail.

BLUE-WINGED TEAL   p. 34
Small; dark belly.
Females of Blue-winged and Cinnamon Teal inseparable.

CINNAMON TEAL   p. 34
Small; very dark below (deep rufous).

GREEN-WINGED TEAL   p. 33
Small; light belly, dark head.

HOODED MERGANSER   p. 45
Merganser shape; dark bar in wing-linings.

COMMON MERGANSER   p. 46
Blackish head, white body, very white wing-linings.

RED-BREASTED MERGANSER   p. 46
Merganser shape; dark breastband.

BLACK DUCK
(Sexes similar)

GADWALL ♂

MALLARD

PINTAIL

AMERICAN
WIDGEON

SHOVELER

CINNAMON
TEAL

BLUE-
WINGED
TEAL

GREEN-WINGED
TEAL

WOOD DUCK

HOODED
MERGANSER

COMMON
MERGANSER

RED-BREASTED
MERGANSER

Plate 10

DUCKS OVERHEAD
(as the sportsman often sees them)

Note: Only males are analyzed below. The first four all have black chests and white wing-linings, and look very much alike.

GREATER SCAUP
Black chest, white stripe showing through wing.

REDHEAD
Black chest, round rufous head.

CANVASBACK
Black chest, long profile.

RING-NECKED DUCK
Not surely distinguished from Scaup overhead (except possibly for lack of white rear wing-stripe).

COMMON GOLDENEYE
Blackish wing-linings, white patches.

BUFFLEHEAD
Resembles small Goldeneye; note head pattern.

OLDSQUAW
Solid dark wings, white belly.

RUDDY DUCK
Stubby; white face, dark chest.

HARLEQUIN DUCK
Solid dark color, white spots, small bill.

WHITE-WINGED SCOTER
Black; white wing patch.

SURF SCOTER
Black; white on head.

COMMON SCOTER
Black; lighter flight feathers.

GREATER SCAUP

REDHEAD

RING-NECKED DUCK

CANVASBACK

COMMON GOLDENEYE

BUFFLEHEAD

OLDSQUAW

RUDDY DUCK   Male

HARLEQUIN DUCK

WHITE-WINGED SCOTER

SURF SCOTER

COMMON SCOTER

Plate 11

BAY DUCKS

Diving Ducks (Bay Ducks and Sea Ducks) run and patter along the water when taking flight. Surface-feeding Ducks (Marsh Ducks, Plate 14) spring directly up.

Note: Males of the first five species share a generic similarity, the black chest.

CANVASBACK   p. 37
Male: White body, rusty head, long sloping profile.
Female: Grayish; dark chest, sloping profile.

REDHEAD   p. 36
Male: Gray; black chest, round rufous head.
Female: Indistinct face patch near bill. See text.

RING-NECKED DUCK   p. 37
Male: Black back, white mark before wing.
Female: Eye-ring and ring on bill. See text.

LESSER SCAUP   p. 39
Male: Black chest, black head (purple gloss), blue bill.
Female: Sharp white patch at base of bill.

GREATER SCAUP   p. 38
Male: Like preceding; head rounder (green gloss).
Female: Similar to preceding. See text.

BARROW'S GOLDENEYE   p. 39
Male: White crescent on face; blacker above than Common Goldeneye.

COMMON GOLDENEYE   p. 39
Male: Round white spot before eye.
Female: Gray body, brown head, light collar.

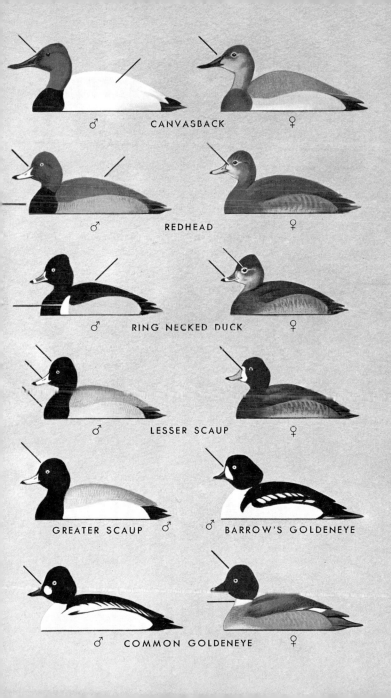

CANVASBACK ♂ ♀

REDHEAD ♂ ♀

RING NECKED DUCK ♂ ♀

LESSER SCAUP ♂ ♀

GREATER SCAUP ♂

BARROW'S GOLDENEYE ♂

COMMON GOLDENEYE ♂ ♀

Plate 12

SEA DUCKS

OLDSQUAW   p. 40
  Male in summer: Needle tail, white face patch.
  Male in winter: Needle tail, pied pattern.
  Female in winter: Dark wings; white face, dark cheek mark.

HARLEQUIN DUCK   p. 41
  Male: Dark; rusty flanks, harlequin pattern.
  Female: Dark; 3 face spots, small bill.

COMMON SCOTER   p. 44
  Male: Plumage all-black, yellow-orange on bill.
  Female: Dark body, light cheek, dark crown.

SURF SCOTER   p. 43
  Male: Black; white head patches.
  Female: Light face spots, no white in wing.

WHITE-WINGED SCOTER   p. 43
  Male: Black; white wing patch.
  Female: Light face spots, white wing patch.

KING EIDER   p. 42
  Male: Whitish foreparts, black back, orange bill shield.
  Female: See bill diagram below.

STELLER'S EIDER   p. 41
  Male: White head, rufous-buff underparts, black spot.
  Female: See bill diagram below.

COMMON EIDER   p. 41
  Male: White above, black below, black crown.
  Female: Brown, heavily barred (see below).

SPECTACLED EIDER   p. 42
  Male: Grotesque "goggles."
  Female: Ghost image of "goggles."

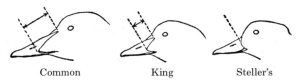

Common   King   Steller's

FEMALE EIDERS can be told by the amount of lobing and
feathering at the base of their bills.

Winter   Winter ♀

♂

Summer

♂ OLDSQUAW

HARLEQUIN DUCK

♀
♂

♂   COMMON SCOTER   ♀

♂   SURF SCOTER   ♀

♂   WHITE-WINGED SCOTER   ♀

♀
♂

KING EIDER

♀
♂

STELLER'S EIDER

♀
♂

COMMON EIDER

♀
♂

SPECTACLED EIDER

Plate 13

MERGANSERS, TREE DUCKS, AND OTHERS

BUFFLEHEAD p. 40
Male: Large white head patch, white sides.
Female: Small, dark; white cheek spot.

WOOD DUCK p. 36
Male: Distinctive face pattern.
Female: White spot around eye.

HOODED MERGANSER p. 45
Male: White crest, dark sides.
Female: Dark head, tawny crest.

RED-BREASTED MERGANSER p. 46
Male: White collar; crest.
Female: Crested rufous head, *blended* throat and neck.

COMMON MERGANSER p. 46
Male: Long whitish body, dark head.
Female: Crested rufous head, *sharply* separated white.

MASKED DUCK p. 45
Male: Similar to Ruddy, but black face, white wing patch.
Female: Two dark lines on face, white wing patch.
Note: Wing patch may be concealed when bird is swimming.

RUDDY DUCK p. 44
Male in spring: Rufous, white cheek.
Male in winter: Gray, white cheek.
Female: Light cheek crossed by dark line.

BLACK-BELLIED TREE DUCK p. 29
Black belly, large white wing patches, pink bill. Sexes similar.

FULVOUS TREE DUCK p. 30
Tawny color, white side-stripe. Sexes similar.

| Marsh and Pond Ducks (Dabblers) | Bay and Sea Ducks (Divers) | Mergansers (Divers) | Stiff-tails (Divers) | Tree Ducks (Dabblers) |

POSTURES OF DUCKS ON LAND

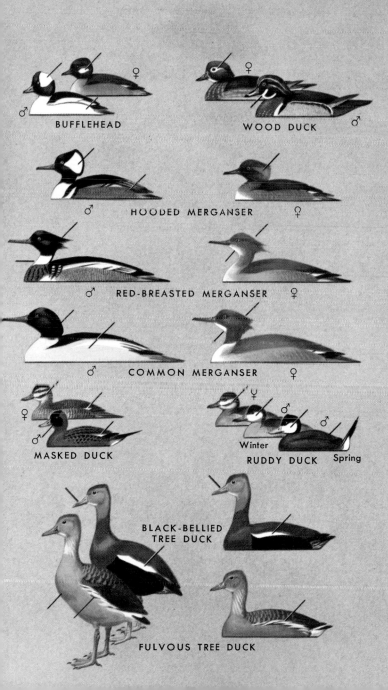

BUFFLEHEAD

WOOD DUCK

HOODED MERGANSER

RED-BREASTED MERGANSER

COMMON MERGANSER

MASKED DUCK

RUDDY DUCK

Winter

Spring

BLACK-BELLIED
TREE DUCK

FULVOUS TREE DUCK

Plate 14

MARSH AND POND DUCKS
(Surface-feeding Ducks)

MEXICAN DUCK   p. 31
  Male: Bill like male Mallard's (yellowish);
  body like female Mallard's (white borders
  on speculum). *Female:* See text.

BLACK DUCK   p. 31
  Dusky body, pale head. Sexes similar.
  No double white border on speculum.

GADWALL   p. 32
  Male: Gray body, black rear.
  Female: White patch (in flight); yellowish bill.

MALLARD   p. 31
  Male: Green head, white neck-ring.
  Female: Orange on bill, whitish tail.

PINTAIL   p. 32
  Male: Needle tail, neck-stripe.
  Female: Gray bill, slim pointed tail.

EUROPEAN WIDGEON   p. 34
  Male: Rufous head, buffy crown.
  Female: See text.

AMERICAN WIDGEON   p. 35
  Male: White crown.
  Female: Gray head, brown body.

SHOVELER   p. 35
  Male: Shovel bill, dark chestnut sides.
  Female: Shovel bill.

BLUE-WINGED TEAL   p. 34
  Male: White face crescent, bluish wing patch.
  Female: Small size, bluish wing patch.

GREEN-WINGED TEAL   p. 33
  Male: Vertical white mark on body.
  Female: Small size, dark wing.

COMMON (EUROPEAN) TEAL   p. 33
  Male: Horizontal white stripe.
  Female: Like female Green-wing.

CINNAMON TEAL   p. 34
  Male: Deep rufous; bluish wing patch.
  Female: Like female Blue-wing.

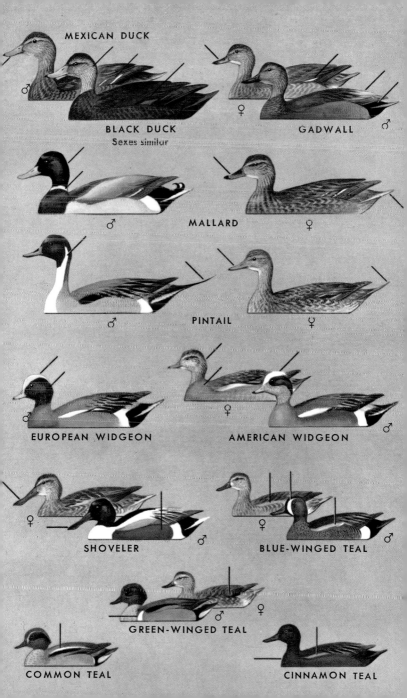

MEXICAN DUCK

♂

BLACK DUCK
Sexes similar

GADWALL
♀   ♂

MALLARD
♂   ♀

PINTAIL
♂   ♀

EUROPEAN WIDGEON
♂

AMERICAN WIDGEON
♀   ♂

SHOVELER
♀   ♂

BLUE-WINGED TEAL
♀   ♂

GREEN-WINGED TEAL
♂   ♀

COMMON TEAL   CINNAMON TEAL

Plate 15

BUTEOS OR BUZZARD HAWKS

BUTEOS have heavy bodies, short wide tails.

SWAINSON'S HAWK p. 52
Typical adult: Heavy dark breastband.
Dark phase: Best identified by flight pattern (Plate 19).
Immature: Buff underparts, streaked throughout.

RED-TAILED HAWK p. 50
Adult: Rufous tail. Dark phase (not shown) also has rufous tail.
Immature (and typical adult): Light upper breast, streaked belly.

RED-SHOULDERED HAWK p. 52
Adult: Rufous shoulders and underparts; narrow white tailbands.
Immature: Streaked on both breast and belly. Strong tailbands.

HARLAN'S HAWK p. 51
Dark body; whitish, mottled tail.

KRIDER'S RED-TAILED HAWK
Pale body; white or pale rufous tail. See under Red-tailed Hawk (pp. 50–51).

FERRUGINOUS HAWK p. 54
Typical adult: Rufous upper parts and "trousers"; white or rusty tail.

HARRIS' HAWK p. 55
Adult: Black; rufous shoulders and "trousers"; white bands at base and tip of tail.
Immature: Long tail, rufous shoulders. See text.

ROUGH-LEGGED HAWK p. 54
Light phase: Dark belly; white tail with broad black band.
Dark phase: Dusky body. See text.

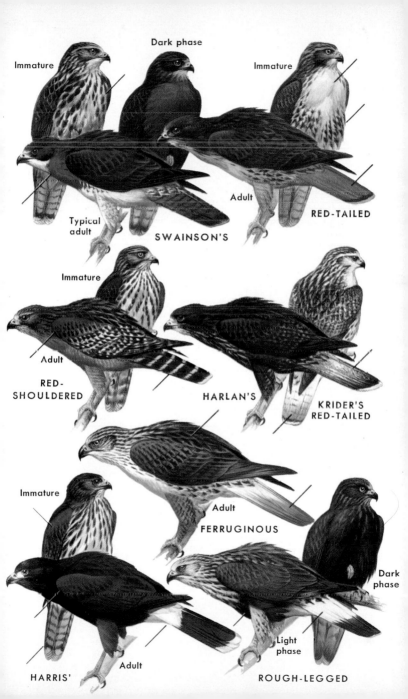

Immature

Dark phase

Immature

Typical
adult

SWAINSON'S

Adult

RED-TAILED

Immature

Adult

RED-
SHOULDERED

HARLAN'S

KRIDER'S
RED-TAILED

Adult

FERRUGINOUS

Immature

Adult

HARRIS'

Dark
phase

Light
phase

ROUGH-LEGGED

Plate 16

HAWKS

ACCIPITERS (True Hawks)
Small head, short wings, long tail.
Adults, barred breasts; immatures streaked.

COOPER'S HAWK   p. 50
  Crow-sized; rounded tail.

GOSHAWK   p. 49
  Adult: Pearly breast, light gray back.
  Immature: Large; pronounced eye-stripe.

SHARP-SHINNED HAWK   p. 49
  Small; notched or square tail.

FALCONS
Large head, broad shoulders.
Long pointed wings, long tail.

SPARROW HAWK or AMERICAN KESTREL   p. 61
  Both sexes: Rufous back, rufous tail.

PIGEON HAWK or MERLIN   p. 60
  Male: Small; slaty back, banded gray tail.
  Female: Dusky back, banded tail.

PEREGRINE FALCON   p. 60
  Adult: Slaty back, light breast, black "mustaches."
  Immature: Brown, streaked; typical "mustaches."

HARRIERS
Small head, long body.
Longish wings, long tail.

MARSH HAWK (HARRIER)   p. 57
  Male: Pale gray back, white rump.
  Female: Brown, with white rump.

COOPER'S HAWK

Adult

Immature

GOSHAWK

Adult

Immature

SHARP-SHINNED HAWK

Immature

Adult

SPARROW HAWK (KESTREL)

♂

♀

PIGEON HAWK (MERLIN)

♂

♀

Adult

Immature

PEREGRINE FALCON

MARSH HAWK (HARRIER)

♂

♀

Plate 17

ACCIPITERS, FALCONS, KITES, HARRIER

ACCIPITERS have short, rounded wings, long tails. They fly with several rapid beats and a short glide.

COOPER'S HAWK p. 50
  Near size of Crow; rounded tail.
GOSHAWK p. 49
  Adult: Very large; pale pearly-gray breast.
  Immature (not shown): See text.
SHARP-SHINNED HAWK p. 49
  Small; tail square or notched.

FALCONS have long, pointed wings, long tails. Their wing strokes are strong, rapid but shallow.

PEREGRINE FALCON p. 60
  Falcon shape; near size of Crow; bold face pattern.
PRAIRIE FALCON p. 59
  Dark axillars (in "wingpits").
APLOMADO FALCON p. 60
  Black belly, light chest.
PIGEON HAWK or MERLIN p. 60
  Banded gray tail.
SPARROW HAWK or AMERICAN KESTREL p. 61
  Banded rufous tail.
GYRFALCON p. 59
  Larger than Peregrine; grayer, without contrasting pattern.
  Arctic. A white phase also occurs in our area.

KITES are falcon-shaped but are buoyant gliders, not power-fliers.

WHITE-TAILED KITE p. 48
  Falcon-shaped, with white tail.
MISSISSIPPI KITE p. 49
  Falcon-shaped, with black tail.
  Immature: See text.

HARRIERS are slim, with somewhat rounded wings, long tails, and long bodies. They fly low with a vulture-like dihedral and languid flight.

MARSH HAWK (HARRIER) p. 57
  Male: Whitish, with black wing-tips.
  Female: Harrier shape; brown, streaked.

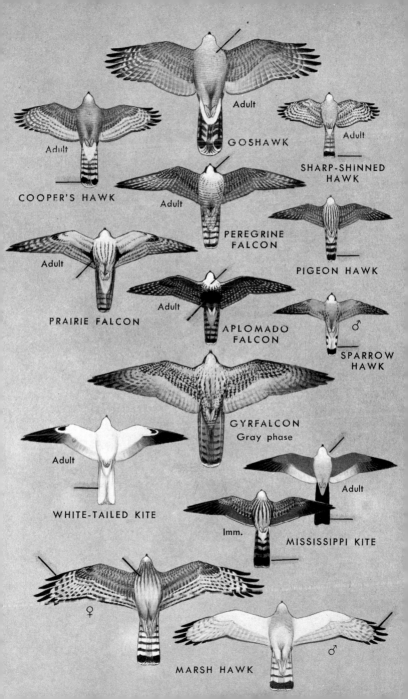

Adult

GOSHAWK

Adult

Adult

SHARP-SHINNED
HAWK

COOPER'S HAWK

Adult

PEREGRINE
FALCON

Adult

PIGEON HAWK

Adult

PRAIRIE FALCON

Adult

APLOMADO
FALCON

♂

SPARROW
HAWK

GYRFALCON
Gray phase

Adult

WHITE-TAILED KITE

Adult

Imm.

MISSISSIPPI KITE

♀

♂

MARSH HAWK

Plate 18

EAGLES AND VULTURES

BALD EAGLE p. 57
Adult: White head and white tail.
Immature: Some white in wing-linings.

GOLDEN EAGLE p. 56
Adult: Almost uniformly dark; wing-linings dark.
Immature: "Ringed" tail; white patch at base of primaries.

BLACK VULTURE p. 47
Stubby tail, whitish wing patch.

TURKEY VULTURE p. 47
Two-toned wings, small head, longish tail.

(Above): Where the Bald Eagle, Turkey Vulture, and Osprey all are found, they can be separated at a great distance by their manner of soaring — the Bald Eagle, with flat wings; the Turkey Vulture, with a dihedral; the Osprey, with a kink or crook in its wings.

CALIFORNIA CONDOR (above) p. 47
Great size, white wing-linings. California only.

BALD EAGLE   Adult

BALD EAGLE   Immature

GOLDEN EAGLE   Adult

GOLDEN EAGLE   Immature

BLACK VULTURE

TURKEY VULTURE

Plate 19

CARACARA AND BLACK BUTEOS

CARACARA p. 58

White chest, dark wings with pale patches toward tips.

ROUGH-LEGGED HAWK (dark form) p. 54

Dark body, whitish flight feathers; tail light from below, dark terminal band.

FERRUGINOUS HAWK (dark form) p. 54

Similar to dark form of Rough-leg but pale tail does not have dark banding.

SWAINSON'S HAWK (dark form) p. 52

Wings usually dark throughout, including flight feathers. Tail narrowly banded.

RED-TAILED HAWK (dark form) p. 50

Chunky; tail reddish above, colorless below; variable.

HARLAN'S HAWK p. 51

Shape of Red-tail; tail whitish above, mottled.
Not safely distinguishable below from dark form of Red-tail.

WHITE-TAILED HAWK (immature) p. 53

Body patched black and white.
Tail white (above and below).

ZONE-TAILED HAWK p. 53

Narrow two-toned wings.
Several white tailbands.

HARRIS' HAWK p. 55

Chestnut wing-linings.
Very broad white band at base of tail.

BLACK HAWK p. 56

Thick-set black wings; small light spots. Broad white band at mid-tail.

CARACARA

ROUGH-LEGGED
HAWK

Dark form

FERRUGINOUS
HAWK

Dark form

SWAINSON'S
HAWK

Dark form

RED-TAILED
HAWK

Dark form

HARLAN'S
HAWK

WHITE-TAILED
HAWK

Immature

ZONE-TAILED
HAWK

Adult

HARRIS' HAWK

Adult

BLACK HAWK   Adult

Plate 20

OSPREY AND BUTEOS

Note: The birds shown opposite are adults.

OSPREY p. 58
Clear white underparts. Black "wrist" marks (carpal patches).

BUTEOS or BUZZARD HAWKS are chunky, with broad wings and broad, rounded tails. They soar and wheel high in the open sky.

ROUGH-LEGGED HAWK p. 54
Dark belly, black "wrist" marks. Whitish tail with broad dark terminal band.

FERRUGINOUS HAWK p. 54
Whitish underparts; dark V formed by legs.

WHITE-TAILED HAWK p. 53
White underparts; white tail, narrow black band.

RED-TAILED HAWK p. 50
Light chest, streaked belly. Tail with little or no banding.

SWAINSON'S HAWK p. 52
Dark breastband, light wing-linings, dark flight feathers.

RED-SHOULDERED HAWK p. 52
Banded tail (white bands narrow); rusty underparts. Translucent wing "windows" (not infallible).

BROAD-WINGED HAWK p. 52
Banded tail (white bands wide); rusty underparts.

GRAY HAWK p. 55
Broadly banded tail; gray-barred underparts.

Both Rough-legged Hawk (left) and Marsh Hawk (right) show some white at the base of the tail when viewed from above. So does Harris' Hawk.

OSPREY

ROUGH-LEGGED HAWK

FERRUGINOUS HAWK

WHITE-TAILED HAWK

RED-TAILED HAWK

SWAINSON'S HAWK

RED-SHOULDERED HAWK

BROAD-WINGED HAWK

GRAY HAWK

Plate 21

PTARMIGANS AND GROUSE

Note: The birds on the page opposite are males. Females are less distinctively patterned and in some species are browner. The key is the tail pattern — always quite similar to the male's.

WILLOW PTARMIGAN p. 64
White wings and black tail in all plumages.
Usually much rufous in summer males.

ROCK PTARMIGAN p. 64
Similar to Willow Ptarmigan, but in summer usually less rufous. Black eye mark in winter.

WHITE-TAILED PTARMIGAN p. 64
White wings, white tail in all plumages.

SPRUCE GROUSE p. 63
Blackish, with short black tail.
(a) *Typical forms:* Rusty band on tip of tail.
(b) *Franklin's form* (n. Rockies, Cascades): White spots at base of tail.

BLUE GROUSE p. 62
Dusky, with large black tail.
(a) *Richardson's form* (n. Rockies): All-dark tail.
(b) *Other forms:* Pale tailband.

RUFFED GROUSE p. 63
Rusty or gray; fantail with black band.

LESSER PRAIRIE CHICKEN p. 65
Heavily barred; short, rounded dark tail.

GREATER PRAIRIE CHICKEN (not illustrated) p. 65
Larger, darker; more northern and eastern in range.

SHARP-TAILED GROUSE p. 65
Spotted; short pointed tail (shows white in flight).

SAGE GROUSE p. 66
Blackish belly, whitish chest; spike-pointed tail.
Female is smaller; lacks black throat, whitish chest.

WILLOW PTARMIGAN

Winter

Summer

Winter

ROCK PTARMIGAN

Summer

WHITE-TAILED PTARMIGAN

Winter

Summer

SPRUCE GROUSE

a

b

Red form

a

b

BLUE GROUSE

Gray form

RUFFED GROUSE

LESSER PRAIRIE CHICKEN

SHARP-TAILED GROUSE

SAGE GROUSE

Plate 22

QUAILS, PARTRIDGES, AND PHEASANT

Note: The birds on the page opposite are males unless otherwise noted. Females are basically similar.

BOBWHITE p. 66
Red-brown; striped head, white throat.
Female has buff throat.

SCALED QUAIL p. 66
Pale gray, scaly; "cotton top."

HARLEQUIN QUAIL p. 68
Gray; spotted; harlequin face.
Female is brown, has white throat.

CALIFORNIA QUAIL p. 67
Curved head plume, scaled belly.
Female has light throat.

GAMBEL'S QUAIL p. 67
Similar, but black patch on unscaled belly.

MOUNTAIN QUAIL p. 67
Long straight head plume; white bars on sides.

GRAY (HUNGARIAN) PARTRIDGE p. 69
Gray; rufous face, splotch on belly, rusty tail, dark legs.

CHUKAR p. 68
Sandy; striped flanks, black "necklace"; rusty tail, red legs.

RING-NECKED PHEASANT p. 68
Male: Highly colored; white neck-ring, long tail.
Female: Brown; long pointed tail.

BOBWHITE

SCALED QUAIL

HARLEQUIN QUAIL

CALIFORNIA QUAIL

GAMBEL'S QUAIL

MOUNTAIN QUAIL

GRAY PARTRIDGE

CHUKAR

♀

♂

RING-NECKED PHEASANT

Plate 23

PIGEONS AND DOVES

The terms "pigeon" and "dove" are loosely used, and often interchangeably, but for the most part "pigeon" refers to the larger species, "dove" to the smaller. Sexes are similar.

MOURNING DOVE p. 115
Pointed tail.

WHITE-WINGED DOVE p. 114
White wing patch.

GROUND DOVE p. 115
Short black tail; reddish wings.

WHITE-FRONTED DOVE p. 116
Light underparts, rounded tail, no wing patches.
Lower Rio Grande.

RED-BILLED PIGEON p. 114
Uniformly dark coloration.
Lower Rio Grande.

INCA DOVE p. 116
Slender tail with white sides; reddish wings.

BAND-TAILED PIGEON p. 113
White crescent on nape; light band at tail-tip.

ROCK DOVE or DOMESTIC PIGEON p. 114
Typical form: White rump; black band at tail-tip; black wing-bars.

SPOTTED DOVE p. 115
Long, rounded tail, white in corners; spotted collar.
S. California; Hawaii.

RINGED TURTLE DOVE p. 115
Pale creamy tan; black ring near nape.
Los Angeles area.

WHITE-WINGED
DOVE

MOURNING
DOVE

GROUND
DOVE

RED-
BILLED
PIGEON

WHITE-FRONTED
DOVE

INCA DOVE

BAND-TAILED
PIGEON

ROCK
DOVE

RINGED
TURTLE
DOVE

SPOTTED
DOVE

Plate 24

RAILS, JAÇANA, GALLINULE, COOT

SORA p. 72
Adult: Gray-brown; short yellow bill, black face.
Immature: Buffy brown; short bill.

VIRGINIA RAIL p. 72
Adult: Small; rusty with gray cheek, long bill.
Immature: Blackish with brown wings.

YELLOW RAIL p. 73
Buffy; striped back, white wing patch (seldom visible except in flight).

BLACK RAIL p. 73
Very small; slaty with black bill.
All young rails are black, so do not call them Black Rails.

CLAPPER RAIL p. 72
Large; gray-brown with tawny breast, long bill. Mainly salt marshes.
Chick: All-black, fuzzy (as are all rail chicks).

JAÇANA p. 75
Adult: Dark; yellow frontal shield.
Extremely long toes; lemon-yellow wing patches in any plumage.

COMMON GALLINULE p. 73
Adult: Red bill, white side-stripe.
Immature: Dark bill, suggestion of side-stripe.
Chick: Glossy black; red on bill.

AMERICAN COOT p. 74
Adult: White bill.
Immature: Dull whitish bill; no side-stripe as in Gallinule.
Chick: Orange-red head.

Coots and gallinules skitter over the water when taking flight.

Adult

Immature

SORA

BLACK RAIL

Immature

Adult

VIRGINIA RAIL

YELLOW RAIL

CLAPPER RAIL

Chick

Adult

Immature

JACANA

COMMON GALLINULE

Immature

Adult

COMMON GALLINULE

Chick

Chick

Immature

Adult

AMERICAN COOT

Plate 25

SHOREBIRDS

SNOWY PLOVER p. 76
Dark legs, dark ear patch, *slender* black bill.

PIPING PLOVER p. 76
"Ringed"; color of *dry* sand (pale).

SEMIPALMATED PLOVER p. 76
"Ringed"; color of *wet* sand (dark).

MOUNTAIN PLOVER p. 77
Near Killdeer size; white eyebrow-stripe, no breast-ring. See text.
Face pattern less distinct in winter.

KILLDEER p. 77
Two breast-rings; long, tawny tail.

BLACK-BELLIED PLOVER p. 78
Breeding: Black below, pale above.
Nonbreeding: Plover shape; large, gray.

AMERICAN GOLDEN PLOVER p. 77
Breeding: Black below, dark above.
Nonbreeding: Plover shape; brown.

DUNLIN (RED-BACKED SANDPIPER) p. 86
Breeding: Rusty back, black belly.

ROCK SANDPIPER p. 84
Breeding: Black splotch higher than on Dunlin; paler legs.

BLACK TURNSTONE p. 79
Nonbreeding: Blackish; black legs. Turnstone shape and flight pattern.

RUDDY TURNSTONE p. 78
Breeding: Rusty back; harlequin face pattern.
Nonbreeding: Dark breast, orange or orangish legs.

WILSON'S PHALAROPE p. 92
Breeding female: Dark neck-stripe.
Breeding male: Paler. Note white nape spot.

NORTHERN PHALAROPE p. 92
Breeding female: Rusty neck, white throat.
Breeding male: Duller; similar pattern.

RED PHALAROPE p. 92
Breeding female: Deep rusty below, white cheek.
Breeding male: Duller; similar pattern.

Breeding

Breeding

SEMIPALMATED
PLOVER

PIPING PLOVER

SNOWY
PLOVER

Breeding

Breeding

MOUNTAIN
PLOVER

KILLDEER

Nonbreeding

Nonbreeding

Breeding

BLACK-BELLIED
PLOVER

AMERICAN
GOLDEN
PLOVER

Breeding

ROCK
SANDPIPER

Breeding

DUNLIN

AMERICAN
GOLDEN
PLOVER

Nonbreeding

BLACK
TURNSTONE

RUDDY
TURNSTONE
Breeding

Nonbreeding

RUDDY
TURNSTONE

♂

♀

WILSON'S
PHALAROPE
Breeding

♂

♀

NORTHERN
PHALAROPE
Breeding

♂

♀

RED
PHALAROPE
Breeding

Plate 26

LARGE SHOREBIRDS

BLACK OYSTERCATCHER p. 75
Large, black; large red bill.

AMERICAN AVOCET p. 91
Upturned bill, black and white back. Pale rusty or pinkish-tan neck (breeding plumage).

BLACK-NECKED STILT p. 91
Black above, white below; very long red legs.

BAR-TAILED GODWIT p. 90
Long, upturned bill, whitish barred tail.
Alaska only.

MARBLED GODWIT p. 89
Tawny brown; long upturned bill.

HUDSONIAN GODWIT p. 90
Breeding: Upturned bill, rusty breast; white ring near tail.
Nonbreeding: Upturned bill, grayish breast; white ring near tail.

WHIMBREL p. 80
Decurved bill; gray-brown, striped head.

LONG-BILLED CURLEW p. 80
Very long bill; buffy, no head-stripes.

BRISTLE-THIGHED CURLEW p. 80
Similar to Whimbrel; tawnier, with pale tawny tail and rump.
Alaska and Hawaii.

BLACK OYSTERCATCHER

Breeding

BLACK-NECKED
STILT

AMERICAN
AVOCET

Breeding

Nonbreeding

Breeding

MARBLED
GODWIT

HUDSONIAN
GODWIT

BAR-TAILED
GODWIT

WHIMBREL

BRISTLE-THIGHED
CURLEW

LONG-BILLED
CURLEW

Plate 27

LARGE SHOREBIRDS

AMERICAN AVOCET   p. 91
Black and white back pattern, thin upturned bill.

BLACK-NECKED STILT   p. 91
White below; black unpatterned wings.

BLACK OYSTERCATCHER   p. 75
All black, heavy red bill, pale legs.

HUDSONIAN GODWIT   p. 90
Upturned bill, ringed tail, white wing-stripe.

BAR-TAILED GODWIT   p. 90
Upturned bill, white rump, barred tail.

MARBLED GODWIT   p. 89
Long upturned bill, buff-brown color.

WHIMBREL   p. 80
Decurved bill, gray-brown color, striped crown.

LONG-BILLED CURLEW (not illustrated)   p. 80
Larger than above; much longer bill.

WILLET (See Plates 30 and 31)

AMERICAN
AVOCET

BLACK-
NECKED
STILT

BLACK
OYSTERCATCHER

HUDSONIAN
GODWIT

BAR-TAILED
GODWIT

MARBLED
GODWIT

WHIMBREL

Plate 28

PLOVERS AND TURNSTONES

SNOWY PLOVER p. 76
  Pale sand color; white sides of tail.

PIPING PLOVER (see head below) p. 76
  Pale sand color; whitish rump and broad dark patch across
  end of tail.

SEMIPALMATED PLOVER p. 76
  Mud-brown; dark tail with white borders.

KILLDEER p. 77
  Tawny-red rump, longish tail.

BLACK-BELLIED PLOVER p. 78
  Spring: Black breast, white lower belly.
  Fall: Black axillars, white in wing and tail.

AMERICAN GOLDEN PLOVER p. 77
  Spring: Black from throat to under tail coverts.
  Fall: Lack of pattern above and below.

RUDDY TURNSTONE p. 78
  Harlequin pattern.

BLACK TURNSTONE (illustrated on Plate 25) p. 79

MOUNTAIN PLOVER p. 77
  Dark tail patch. See text.

Semipalmated   Snowy   Piping

HEADS OF SMALL "RINGED" PLOVERS

SEMIPALMATED PLOVER

SNOWY PLOVER

KILLDEER

Below BLACK-BELLIED PLOVER (Spring)

Below AMERICAN GOLDEN PLOVER (Spring)

Below

Above

BLACK-BELLIED PLOVER (Fall)

Above

Below

AMERICAN GOLDEN PLOVER (Fall)

RUDDY TURNSTONE (Spring)

MOUNTAIN PLOVER

Plate 29

SNIPE, SANDPIPERS, AND PHALAROPES

COMMON (WILSON'S) SNIPE   p. 79
Long bill, pointed wings, orange tail, zigzag flight.

DOWITCHER   p. 87
Snipe bill, white rump and lower back. For identification of the two dowitchers, see text.

WANDERING TATTLER   p. 82
No pattern in wings and tail.

GREATER YELLOWLEGS   p. 83
Dark wings, whitish rump and tail.

STILT SANDPIPER   p. 87
Similar to preceding but legs greenish (see text).

WILSON'S PHALAROPE   p. 92
Nonbreeding: Suggests Yellowlegs; smaller, breast whiter, bill needlelike.

SOLITARY SANDPIPER   p. 81
Dark wings, conspicuous white sides on tail.

SPOTTED SANDPIPER   p. 81
Identify by very short wing stroke (giving a stiff, bowed appearance).

KNOT   p. 83
Nonbreeding: Stocky; grayish with light rump. Compare with Yellowlegs and Dowitcher.

SANDERLING   p. 90
Has most flashing stripe of any small sandpiper. Follows retreating waves like a clockwork toy.

NORTHERN PHALAROPE   p. 92
Nonbreeding: Sanderling-like; wing-stripe shorter, bill more needlelike.

RED PHALAROPE   p. 92
Nonbreeding: Sanderling-like; wing-stripe less contrasting; bill thicker than Northern Phalarope's.

 Phalaropes swim on water; spin and dab.

COMMON SNIPE

DOWITCHER

WANDERING TATTLER

GREATER YELLOWLEGS

STILT SANDPIPER

WILSON'S PHALAROPE
Nonbreeding

SOLITARY SANDPIPER

SPOTTED SANDPIPER

KNOT
Nonbreeding

SANDERLING
Nonbreeding

NORTHERN PHALAROPE
Nonbreeding

RED PHALAROPE
Nonbreeding

Plate 30

SANDPIPERS

LEAST SANDPIPER * p. 86
Very small, brown; faint wing-stripe.

WESTERN SANDPIPER * p. 89
Similar; larger, longer bill (see text).

SEMIPALMATED SANDPIPER * (not illustrated) p. 88
Similar to Western; shorter bill. Identify by notes.

BAIRD'S SANDPIPER * p. 85
Larger than Western, browner; dark rump (see text).

WHITE-RUMPED SANDPIPER * p. 85
White rump (only "peep" so marked).

PECTORAL SANDPIPER p. 84
Like double-sized Least Sandpiper. Wing-stripe faint or lacking.

BUFF-BREASTED SANDPIPER p. 89
Evenly buff below, contrasting with white wing-linings.

SURFBIRD p. 78
Broad white band across rump; wing-stripe.

ROCK SANDPIPER p. 84
Slaty color; rocks by sea.

DUNLIN (RED-BACKED SANDPIPER) p. 86
Nonbreeding: Gray; larger than "peep," darker than Sanderling.

UPLAND PLOVER p. 80
Brown; small head, long tail. Often flies like Spotted Sandpiper.

WILLET p. 82
Large size, flashing wing pattern.

* These 5 sparrow-sized streaked sandpipers are collectively nick-named "peep."

LEAST
SANDPIPER

WESTERN
SANDPIPER

BAIRD'S
SANDPIPER

WHITE-
RUMPED
SANDPIPER

PECTORAL
SANDPIPER

BUFF-
BREASTED
SANDPIPER

Below

SURFBIRD

ROCK
SANDPIPER

DUNLIN

UPLAND
PLOVER

WILLET

Plate 31

SHOREBIRDS

COMMON (WILSON'S) SNIPE p. 79
Long bill, striped crown.

DOWITCHER p. 87
Breeding: Snipe bill, rusty breast.
Nonbreeding: Snipe bill, gray breast.
For distinctions between the two species, **Long-billed Dowitcher** and **Short-billed Dowitcher,** see text.

KNOT p. 83
Breeding: Chunky; short bill, rusty breast.

STILT SANDPIPER p. 87
Breeding: Barred underparts, rusty ear patch, greenish legs.
Nonbreeding: Long greenish legs, white rump, eyeline (see text).

WILSON'S PHALAROPE p. 92
Nonbreeding: Needle bill, white breast, yellowish legs. See text.

UPLAND PLOVER p. 80
Small head, short bill, thin neck, long tail.

WANDERING TATTLER p. 82
Breeding: Barred underparts, yellowish legs.
Nonbreeding: Grayish, lacking pattern; yellowish legs. See text.

SOLITARY SANDPIPER p. 81
Dark back, whitish eye-ring, darkish legs.

LESSER YELLOWLEGS p. 83
Yellow legs, slim bill.
Call, a 1- or 2-syllabled *yew* or *you-you.*

GREATER YELLOWLEGS p. 83
Yellow legs, larger bill (very slightly upturned).
Call, a clear, 3-syllabled *whew-whew-whew.*

WILLET p. 82
Gray color, stocky bill, darkish legs.
Spectacular wing pattern when on wing.

COMMON
SNIPE

DOWITCHER

Nonbreeding

Breeding

KNOT

Nonbreeding

Breeding

Breeding

Nonbreeding

STILT
SANDPIPER

WILSON'S
PHALAROPE

Breeding

UPLAND
PLOVER

Nonbreeding

WANDERING TATTLER

Breeding

SOLITARY
SANDPIPER

WILLET

LESSER
YELLOWLEGS

GREATER
YELLOWLEGS

Plate 32

SHOREBIRDS

Nonbreeding

Breeding

Breeding

SPOTTED S.

Nonbreeding

SURFBIRD

Non-breeding

Non-breeding

DUNLIN

ED HALAROPE

ROCK SANDPIPER

Nonbreeding

Breeding

NORTHERN PHALAROPE

Non-breeding

KNOT

Non-breeding

Nonbreeding

SANDERLING

Non-breeding

BUFF- BREASTED S.

PECTORAL S.

SHARP- TAILED S.

Breeding

BAIRD'S S.

Nonbreeding

LEAST S.

Breeding

RUFOUS- NECKED S.

Breeding

Breeding

Nonbreeding

WHITE-RUMPED S.

Nonbreeding

SEMIPALMATED S.

Nonbreeding

WESTERN S.

Plate 33

GULLS (Adult)

In identifying adult gulls the most important points are: (1) wing pattern, particularly wing-tips, (2) leg color, (3) bill color.

GLAUCOUS GULL   p. 95
Very large; white primaries, flesh legs.

IVORY GULL   p. 101
All white, black legs.

ROSS' GULL   p. 102
Wedge-shaped tail; no markings on pearl-gray wings.

GLAUCOUS-WINGED GULL   p. 97
Gray primaries with white "mirrors."

HERRING GULL   p. 98
Black wing-tips with "mirrors," pink or flesh legs.

CALIFORNIA GULL   p. 98
Gray mantle; red, or red and black, spot on bill; greenish legs.

WESTERN GULL   p. 97
Blackish or slaty mantle, flesh legs.

RING-BILLED GULL   p. 99
Like small Herring Gull. Ring on bill; yellowish legs.

HEERMANN'S GULL   p. 101
Dark, with black tail, whitish head.

FRANKLIN'S GULL*   p. 100
White "windows" separating black from gray.

MEW GULL   p. 99
Short, unmarked yellow or greenish-yellow bill.

LAUGHING GULL*   p. 100
Small size, dark wings with white trailing edge.

BONAPARTE'S GULL*   p. 101
Long wedge of white in primaries.

SABINE'S GULL*   p. 103
Black outer primaries, white triangle, forked tail.

BLACK-LEGGED KITTIWAKE   p. 102
Solid "dipped-in-ink" wing-tips, black legs.

RED-LEGGED KITTIWAKE   p. 102
Similar; red legs; dusky on underwing.

*Adults in winter lose black heads.

GLAUCOUS

IVORY

ROSS'

GLAUCOUS-WINGED

HERRING

CALIFORNIA

WESTERN

RING-BILLED

HEERMANN'S

MEW

FRANKLIN'S

LAUGHING

Below

BLACK-LEGGED
KITTIWAKE

BONAPARTE'S

SABINE'S

Below

RED-LEGGED
KITTIWAKE

Plate 34

GULLS (Immature)

GLAUCOUS GULL p. 95
1st year: Primaries paler than rest of wing. Much pink on bill.

GLAUCOUS-WINGED GULL p. 97
1st year: Wing-tips gray-brown (not blackish).

WESTERN GULL p. 97
1st year: More contrast between dark and light markings than in next two species. Primaries blackish.
2nd year: "Saddle-backed" look.

HERRING GULL p. 98
1st year: Relatively uniform brown.
2nd year: Whiter; tail broadly blackish.

CALIFORNIA GULL p. 98
1st year: Very similar to Herring Gull except for size. Bill slighter and may have considerable pink at base.
2nd year: Whiter; back medium gray. Bill may appear "ringed."

MEW GULL p. 99
Like a pint-sized Herring or California Gull with a small plover-like bill.

RING-BILLED GULL p. 99
Clean-cut narrow tailband (about 1 in. wide).

FRANKLIN'S GULL p. 100
Dark mantle, white base of tail; dark about head.

HEERMANN'S GULL p. 101
Very dark throughout.

BLACK-LEGGED KITTIWAKE p. 102
Dark diagonal band across wing, black nape.

SABINE'S GULL p. 103
Forked tail and Sabine's wing pattern.
(Young Kittiwakes are quite similar.)

BONAPARTE'S GULL p. 101
Black cheek spot, narrow tailband.

GLAUCOUS 1st winter

GLAUCOUS-WINGED 1st winter

WESTERN 1st winter

WESTERN 2nd winter

HERRING 1st winter

HERRING 2nd winter

CALIFORNIA 1st winter

CALIF. 2nd winter

MEW

RING-BILLED

FRANKLIN'S

HEERMANN'S

BLACK-LEGGED KITTIWAKE

SABINE'S

BONAPARTE'S

Plate 35

THE SMALLER AUKS

Auks are rather penguin-like sea birds, most species with stubby necks. They have a whirring flight and a straddle-legged look when about to land. The larger auks are illustrated on page 108.

RHINOCEROS AUKLET p. 112
Size of puffin.
Breeding: White head plumes; horn on yellowish bill.
Winter (not shown): Lacks horn. May or may not have head plumes. Immature has smaller bill.

CASSIN'S AUKLET p. 111
Very small, dark; light spot on bill.
No seasonal change.

CRESTED AUKLET p. 111
Breeding: All dark, recurved crest, orange or red bill.
Winter (not shown): Plume shorter, bill yellowish.
Immature: All dark; stubby bill. See text.

WHISKERED AUKLET p. 112
Breeding: Very wispy crest and head plumes.
Immature (not shown): Dusky; perhaps inseparable from young Crested Auklet.

MARBLED MURRELET p. 109
Breeding: Sooty brown, closely scaled.
Winter: White stripe on scapulars.

KITTLITZ'S MURRELET p. 110
Breeding: Like Marbled but paler back, freckled.
Winter: Like Marbled but white surrounds eye.

ANCIENT MURRELET p. 111
Breeding: White eyebrow-stripe; black throat.
Winter: Contrast of black cap gray back.

PARAKEET AUKLET p. 111
Stubby red bill, white underparts.

XANTUS' MURRELET p. 110
Small, southern; solid black above, white below.
No seasonal change.

LEAST AUKLET p. 112
Very small, stubby bill. Broad neck-ring in summer.

Breeding   Immature

RHINOCEROS AUKLET

CASSIN'S AUKLET

Immature

Breeding

CRESTED AUKLET

Breeding

WHISKERED AUKLET

Winter

Breeding

MARBLED MURRELET

Winter

Breeding

KITTLITZ'S MURRELET

Winter

Breeding

ANCIENT MURRELET

Winter

Breeding

PARAKEET AUKLET

XANTUS' MURRELET

Winter

Breeding

LEAST AUKLET

Plate 36

TERNS

Terns are more slender in build, narrower of wing than gulls. Bills sharply pointed and tails usually forked. Most terns have black caps (white foreheads in fall and winter).

CASPIAN TERN p. 106
Very large; large red bill. Tail only slightly forked.
Much black on under primaries. Forehead streaked in winter, not white.

ROYAL TERN p. 106
Smaller than Caspian; bill more orange. Tail deeply forked.

GULL-BILLED TERN p. 103
Stout gull-like black bill.

ELEGANT TERN p. 106
Smaller than Royal, bill more yellow; bill and crest extremely long.

FORSTER'S TERN p. 104
Breeding: Pale primaries; orange, black-tipped bill.
Immature: Black patch through eye and ear only.

COMMON TERN p. 104
Breeding: Dusky primaries; orange-red bill, black tip.
Immature: Black patch around nape; dusky shoulder.

ARCTIC TERN p. 104
Grayer than Forster's or Common. Bill blood-red to tip.

ALEUTIAN TERN p. 105
Very gray body contrasting with white tail; bill blackish.

BLACK TERN p. 107
Breeding: Black body.
Fall: Pied head, dark back, gray tail.

LEAST TERN p. 105
Breeding: Small size, yellow bill.
Immature: Small size, black fore edge of wing.

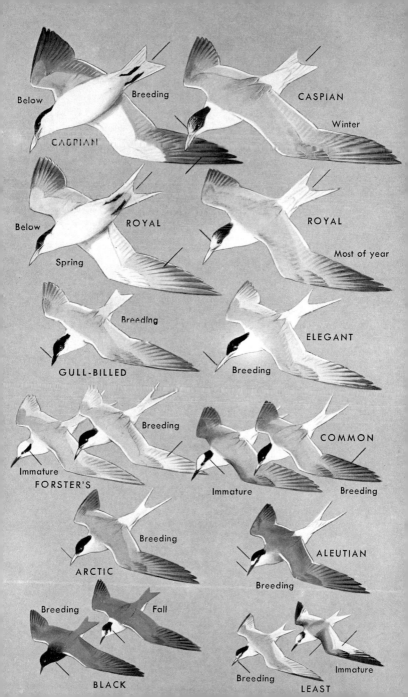

Below   Breeding

CASPIAN

CASPIAN

Winter

Below   ROYAL

Spring

ROYAL

Most of year

Breeding

GULL-BILLED

ELEGANT

Breeding

Immature   Breeding

FORSTER'S

COMMON

Immature

Breeding

Breeding

ARCTIC

ALEUTIAN

Breeding

Breeding   Fall

BLACK

Breeding   Immature

LEAST

Plate 37

HEADS OF TERNS

The bills of terns are the key feature in their recognition. Most terns in breeding season have black caps. By late summer they begin to get the white foreheads typical of winter plumage.

BLACK TERN   p. 107
Breeding: Black head.
Winter: "Pied" head. See text.

LEAST TERN   p. 105
Breeding: Yellow bill, white forehead patch.
Immature: Small size. See text.

FORSTER'S TERN   p. 104
Breeding: Orange bill, black tip. See text.
Winter: Black eye patch; light or gray nape.

COMMON TERN   p. 104
Breeding: Orange-red bill, black tip. See text.
Winter: Black patch from eye *around nape.*

ARCTIC TERN   p. 104
Breeding: Bill blood-red; no black tip.
Caution: Some late-summer Common Terns may lack black tip.

ALEUTIAN TERN   p. 105
Clean-cut white forehead patch, blackish bill.
Alaska only.

GULL-BILLED TERN   p. 103
Breeding: Bill gull-like, stout, and black.
Immature: Very gull-like. See text.
Salton Sea, California.

ELEGANT TERN   p. 106
Slender yellow-orange bill, long crest.
Smaller than Royal Tern, bill much more slender.
Seasonal change similar to Royal's.

ROYAL TERN   p. 106
Spring: Solid black cap, orange bill.
Most of year: Orange bill, white forehead, tufted crest.

CASPIAN TERN   p. 106
Breeding: Large scarlet bill, less crest than Royal.
Winter: Large scarlet bill, streaked forehead.

Winter

Breeding

BLACK TERN

Immature

Breeding

LEAST TERN

Winter

Breeding

FORSTER'S TERN

Winter

Breeding

COMMON TERN

Breeding

ARCTIC TERN

Breeding

ALEUTIAN TERN

Immature

Breeding

GULL-BILLED TERN

Breeding

ELEGANT TERN

Spring

Winter

ROYAL TERN

Breeding

Winter

CASPIAN TERN

Plate 38

CUCKOOS, TROGON, AND GOATSUCKERS

YELLOW-BILLED CUCKOO p. 117
Yellow bill, rufous wings, large tail spots.

BLACK-BILLED CUCKOO p. 117
Black bill, red eye-ring, small tail spots.

COPPERY-TAILED TROGON p. 137
Male: Deep green; geranium-red belly.
Female: Brown; reddish belly, white spot on cheek.

ROADRUNNER p. 117
Long tail; streaked; ragged crest.

GROOVE-BILLED ANI p. 118
Black; high-ridged bill, long loose-jointed tail.

WHIP-POOR-WILL p. 127
"Dead-leaf" pattern; white tail patches.
Female has smaller buffy tail patches. Male has blackish throat.

RIDGWAY'S WHIP-POOR-WILL (not illustrated) p. 127
Guadalupe Canyon (Arizona, N.M.). See text.

POOR-WILL p. 127
Small, gray-brown; small white corners in short tail (male).
See text.

PAURAQUE p. 128
Patches in both wings and tail; rounded wings.

COMMON NIGHTHAWK p. 128
White wing patches, pointed wings.
At rest, wings reach end of tail.

LESSER NIGHTHAWK p. 128
White bar nearer wing-tip.
Flies lower than Common Nighthawk.

BLACK-
BILLED
CUCKOO

YELLOW-BILLED
CUCKOO

GROOVE-
BILLED
ANI

ROADRUNNER

♀

♂

COPPERY-TAILED
TROGON

POOR-WILL

♂

WHIP-POOR-WILL

♂

LESSER
NIGHTHAWK

COMMON
NIGHTHAWK

♂

PAURAQUE

Plate 39

HUMMINGBIRDS

Only males are briefly described below. For the field marks of the confusing females refer to the text. Some females and particularly young birds are not safely distinguishable in the field even for experts. It is important to realize this.

BLACK-CHINNED HUMMINGBIRD   p. 132
Black chin, blue-violet throat.

VIOLET-CROWNED HUMMINGBIRD   p. 136
Clear white underparts, red bill. Sexes similar.

BUFF-BELLIED HUMMINGBIRD   p. 135
Buff belly, green throat, red or pink bill. Sexes similar.

WHITE-EARED HUMMINGBIRD   p. 136
Blue and green throat, white ear-stripe, red bill.

BROAD-BILLED HUMMINGBIRD   p. 136
Blue throat, dark underparts, red bill.

CALLIOPE HUMMINGBIRD   p. 134
Gorget with red rays on white ground.

LUCIFER HUMMINGBIRD   p. 131
Purple throat, green crown, decurved bill.

COSTA'S HUMMINGBIRD   p. 132
Purple throat, purple crown.

RIVOLI'S HUMMINGBIRD   p. 135
Large, black; green throat.

BLUE-THROATED HUMMINGBIRD   p. 135
Large; blue throat, large tail spots.

ANNA'S HUMMINGBIRD   p. 132
Rose-red throat and crown.

BROAD-TAILED HUMMINGBIRD   p. 133
Rose-red throat, green crown and back.
Trills with wings in flight.

RUBY-THROATED HUMMINGBIRD   p. 131
Fire-red throat, green crown and back.
East of Rockies (only eastern hummingbird).

ALLEN'S HUMMINGBIRD   p. 134
Like Rufous Hummingbird but upper back green.

RUFOUS HUMMINGBIRD   p. 133
Fire-red throat, rufous back.

MALES

BLACK-CHINNED

VIOLET-CROWNED

BUFF-BELLIED

WHITE-EARED

BROAD-BILLED

CALLIOPE

LUCIFER

COSTA'S

RIVOLI'S

BLUE-THROATED

ANNA'S

BROAD-TAILED

RUBY-THROATED

ALLEN'S

RUFOUS

FEMALES

BLACK-CHINNED
RUBY-THROATED
COSTA'S (similar)

LUCIFER

BROAD-TAILED

CALLIOPE

RUFOUS

ANNA'S

BROAD-BILLED

RIVOLI'S

BLUE-THROATED

WHITE-EARED

Plate 40

WOODPECKERS

RED-SHAFTED
FLICKER

YELLOW-SHAFTED
FLICKER

GILDED FLICKER

ARIZONA

Juv.

GILA

GOLDEN-
FRONTED

LADDER-
BACKED

NUTTALL'S

BLACK-
BACKED
3-TOED

NORTHERN
3-TOED

HAIRY

DOWNY

WHITE-
HEADED

Imm.

YELLOW-BELLIED
SAPSUCKER

"RED-BREASTED
SAPSUCKER

Imm.

WILLIAMSON'S
SAPSUCKER

LEWIS'

ACORN

RED-HEADED

Plate 41

FLYCATCHERS

Flycatchers perch in an upright atti-
tude and often sit quite motionless.
Sexes are similar.

THICK-BILLED KINGBIRD   p. 147
Whitish underparts (tinged yellow); big bill, bull-headed.
Guadalupe Canyon (se. Arizona, sw. N.M.).

WIED'S CRESTED FLYCATCHER   p. 150
Cinnamon wings and tail, yellowish belly. Local in sw.
states.

GREAT CRESTED FLYCATCHER (not illustrated)   p. 150
Very similar to Wied's. Eastern. See text.

ASH-THROATED FLYCATCHER   p. 151
Smaller, paler; whitish throat. See text.

OLIVACEOUS FLYCATCHER   p. 151
Smaller than Ash-throated; throat grayish.

WESTERN KINGBIRD   p. 148
Yellow belly, black tail with narrow white sides.

CASSIN'S KINGBIRD   p. 148
Whiter chin, darker breast; black tail, no white on sides.

TROPICAL KINGBIRD   p. 148
Tail forked, dusky brown, no white on sides. Upper breast
yellowish, not gray.

EASTERN KINGBIRD   p. 147
Wide white band at tip of tail; white underparts.

KISKADEE FLYCATCHER   p. 149
Rufous wings and tail; striking head pattern.

SULPHUR-BELLIED FLYCATCHER   p. 150
Yellow underparts boldly *streaked;* rufous tail.

WIED'S CRESTED
FLYCATCHER

OLIVACEOUS
FLYCATCHER

THICK-BILLED
KINGBIRD

ASH-THROATED
FLYCATCHER

WESTERN
KINGBIRD

CASSIN'S
KINGBIRD

TROPICAL
KINGBIRD

EASTERN
KINGBIRD

KISKADEE
FLYCATCHER

SULPHUR-BELLIED
FLYCATCHER

Plate 42

BECARD AND FLYCATCHERS

ROSE-THROATED BECARD p. 146
Male: Blackish cap, rose throat.
Female: Dark cap, buffy collar and underparts.

SCISSOR-TAILED FLYCATCHER p. 149
Very long forked tail.

VERMILION FLYCATCHER p. 157
Male: Vermilion underparts, crown; blackish back.
Female: Streaked pinkish or yellowish belly.

OLIVE-SIDED FLYCATCHER p. 156
Dark "vest" unbuttoned down front; white tufts.

COUES' FLYCATCHER p. 155
Similar to Olive-sided; more uniform gray; grayer throat.

SAY'S PHOEBE p. 152
Pale rusty underparts.

EASTERN WOOD PEWEE p. 156
Conspicuous wing-bars, no eye-ring. Song sweet, plaintive.

WESTERN WOOD PEWEE p. 156
Darker on breast and sides than Eastern Wood Pewee.
Song nasal.

EASTERN PHOEBE p. 151
No strong wing-bars (may have dull ones), no eye-ring;
wags tail.

EMPIDONAX FLYCATCHERS
Small; white wing-bars and eye-ring.
Traill's Flycatcher: Whitish underparts. p. 153
Other Empidonax Flycatchers, extremely close to
Traill's Flycatcher in appearance, are not illustrated
(for a full discussion see text, pp. 152–55). These are
Least, Hammond's, Dusky, and **Gray Flycatchers.**
Western Flycatcher: Yellowish underparts. p. 155
Similar is **Yellow-bellied Flycatcher** (Canada, east of
Rockies), not illustrated. See text, page 153.
Buff-breasted Flycatcher (not illustrated) p. 155
Buff underparts.

BEARDLESS FLYCATCHER p. 157
Very small; light brownish wing-bars. See text.

BLACK PHOEBE p. 152
The only black-breasted flycatcher.

SCISSOR-
TAILED
FLYCATCHER

ROSE-
THROATED
BECARD

VERMILION
FLYCATCHER

COUES'
FLYC.

OLIVE-
SIDED
FLYC.

SAY'S
PHOEBE

EASTERN
PHOEBE

EASTERN
WOOD PEWEE

WESTERN
WOOD PEWEE

BLACK
PHOEBE

TRAILL'S
EMPIDONAX FLYCATCHERS

WESTERN

BEARDLESS
FLYCATCHER

Plate 43

SWALLOWS

PURPLE MARTIN   p. 161
   Male: Black breast.
   Female: Grayish breast.

CLIFF SWALLOW   p. 161
   Pale rump, square tail, dark throat.

CAVE SWALLOW   p. 161
   Like Cliff Swallow but throat pale, forehead dark.
   C. Texas, sw. New Mexico.

BARN SWALLOW   p. 160
   Deeply forked tail.

ROUGH-WINGED SWALLOW   p. 160
   Brown back, dingy throat.

BANK SWALLOW   p. 160
   Brown back, dark breastband.

TREE SWALLOW   p. 159
   Back blue-black; breast snow-white.

VIOLET-GREEN SWALLOW   p. 159
   White patches on sides of rump. White around eye.

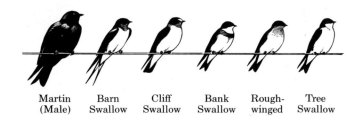

| Martin (Male) | Barn Swallow | Cliff Swallow | Bank Swallow | Rough-winged Swallow | Tree Swallow |

SWALLOWS ON A WIRE

PURPLE MARTIN

♂

♀

CLIFF SWALLOW

CAVE SWALLOW

BARN SWALLOW

ROUGH-WINGED SWALLOW

BANK SWALLOW

TREE SWALLOW

VIOLET-GREEN SWALLOW

Plate 44

JAYS, MAGPIES, AND KINGFISHERS

In the jays and magpies the sexes are alike in appearance. In the kingfishers there are differences in the sexes, usually in the presence or absence of rufous on the underparts, or its extent.

BLUE JAY p. 162
Crested; white spots in wings and tail, black "necklace."

STELLER'S JAY p. 163
Crested; dark; no white spots.

SCRUB JAY p. 163
Crestless; white throat, "necklace."

MEXICAN JAY p. 163
Crestless; gray throat, no "necklace."

PIÑON JAY p. 166
Dull blue throughout; short tail.

GREEN JAY p. 164
Green; black throat patch.

GRAY (CANADA) JAY p. 162
Adult: Gray, dark cap, white forehead.
Juvenal: Dusky; blackish head, light "whisker."

CLARK'S NUTCRACKER p. 167
Gray; white patches in black wings, tail.

GREEN KINGFISHER p. 138
Small, green-backed; rusty breastband (male); 1 or 2 greenish bands (female).

BELTED KINGFISHER p. 137
Bushy crest, gray band across white breast (male). Female has 2 bands (1 rusty).

BLACK-BILLED MAGPIE p. 164
Long wedge-shaped tail; white wing patches, black bill.

YELLOW-BILLED MAGPIE p. 164
Similar; yellow bill.

BLUE JAY

STELLER'S JAY

SCRUB JAY

MEXICAN JAY

PIÑON JAY

GREEN JAY

GRAY JAY Adult

CLARK'S
NUTCRACKER

GREEN
KING-
FISHER

♂

GRAY JAY Juvenal

BELTED
KINGFISHER

♀

BLACK-BILLED MAGPIE

YELLOW-BILLED MAGPIE

Plate 45

TITMICE, WRENTIT, CREEPER, AND NUTHATCHES

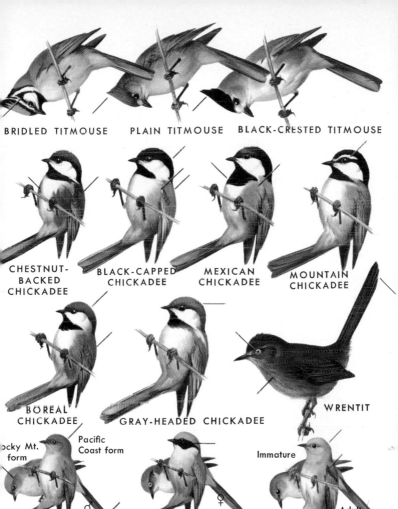

BRIDLED TITMOUSE   PLAIN TITMOUSE   BLACK-CRESTED TITMOUSE

CHESTNUT-
BACKED
CHICKADEE

BLACK-CAPPED
CHICKADEE

MEXICAN
CHICKADEE

MOUNTAIN
CHICKADEE

BOREAL
CHICKADEE

GRAY-HEADED CHICKADEE

WRENTIT

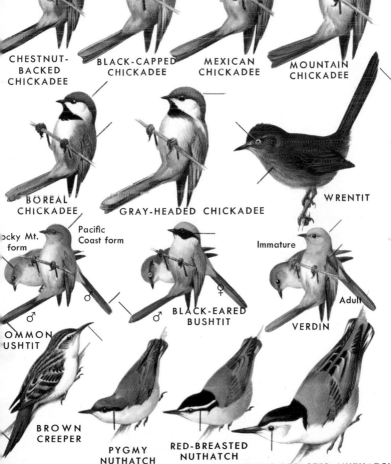

Rocky Mt.
form

Pacific
Coast form

Immature

♂

COMMON
BUSHTIT

BLACK-EARED
BUSHTIT
♀

♂

Adult

VERDIN

BROWN
CREEPER

PYGMY
NUTHATCH

RED-BREASTED
NUTHATCH

WHITE-BREASTED NUTHATCH

Plate 46

WRENS AND GNATCATCHERS

WINTER WREN
Dark; stubby tail, heavily barred flanks.

LONG-BILLED MARSH WREN
Strong eye-stripe; back-stripes.

SHORT-BILLED MARSH WREN
Buffy; streaked crown, streaked back; buffy under tail coverts.

HOUSE WREN
No evident facial striping; gray-brown.

BEWICK'S WREN
Whiter underparts; eye-stripe, white tail corners.

CAROLINA WREN
Rusty coloration; strong eye-stripe.

CAÑON WREN
White throat, dark belly.

ROCK WREN
Grayish; narrowly streaked breast; buffy tail corners.

CACTUS WREN
Large; heavily spotted breast.

BLUE-GRAY GNATCATCHER
Blue-gray, whitish below; long tail, white eye-ring.

BLACK-TAILED GNATCATCHER
Male in spring: Black cap.
Female: Very similar to Blue-gray Gnatcatcher (see text).
Underside of tail largely black (largely white in Blue-gray Gnatcatcher).
Note: Birds of sw. California race are dull gray on underparts.

LONG-BILLED
MARSH WREN

WINTER WREN

SHORT-BILLED
MARSH WREN

HOUSE WREN

BEWICK'S WREN

CAÑON WREN

CAROLINA
WREN

ROCK WREN

CACTUS WREN

♂

♀

♂

Spring

BLUE-GRAY
GNATCATCHER

BLACK-TAILED
GNATCATCHER

Plate 47

SHRIKES AND MIMIC THRUSHES

LOGGERHEAD SHRIKE p. 191
Black mask through eye; black wings and tail, white patches.

NORTHERN SHRIKE p. 191
Black mask does not meet over bill; lower mandible pale; breast faintly barred (more noticeable in brown young).

CATBIRD p. 178
Slaty; black crown, chestnut under tail coverts.

MOCKINGBIRD p. 177
Gray; large white wing and tail patches; no face mask.

BROWN THRASHER p. 178
Rufous; bold stripes, wing-bars.

LONG-BILLED THRASHER p. 179
Less rufous than Brown Thrasher; cheek grayer, stripes blacker. Bill longer, blacker.

BENDIRE'S THRASHER p. 179
Rather straight bill, lightly spotted breast.

SAGE THRASHER p. 181
Striped; bill and tail relatively short; tail shows white corners.

CURVE-BILLED THRASHER p. 179
Gray; curved bill, softly spotted breast.

LE CONTE'S THRASHER p. 180
Very pale, sandy; dark eye.

CALIFORNIA THRASHER p. 180
Dark brown, deeply curved bill; pale cinnamon belly. California.

CRISSAL THRASHER p. 180
Long sickle bill, plain breast, dark chestnut patch under tail (crissum).

NORTHERN SHRIKE

Immature

Adult

LOGGERHEAD SHRIKE

MOCKING-BIRD

CATBIRD

LONG-BILLED THRASHER

BROWN THRASHER

SAGE THRASHER

BENDIRE'S THRASHER

LE CONTE'S THRASHER

CURVE-BILLED THRASHER

CALIFORNIA THRASHER

CRISSAL THRASHER

Plate 48

THRUSHES

MOUNTAIN BLUEBIRD p. 184
Male: Turquoise-blue breast.
Female: No rusty on gray-brown breast.

WESTERN BLUEBIRD p. 184
Male: Rusty patch on back (usually); blue throat.
Female: Duller than male, throat whitish, rusty breast.

EASTERN BLUEBIRD p. 183
Male: Blue back, rusty breast, rusty throat.
Female (not shown): Duller; whitish throat.
Juvenal: Speckled breast, blue in wing and tail.

ROBIN p. 181
Brick-red breast, gray back.
Juvenal: Speckled breast; trace of rusty.

VARIED THRUSH p. 182
Similar to Robin but with black "necklace"; orange eye-stripe and wing-bars.

TOWNSEND'S SOLITAIRE p. 185
Gray; white eye-ring, white tail sides; buffy wing patch.

VEERY p. 183
Tawny from head to tail; relatively little spotting.

HERMIT THRUSH p. 182
Rufous tail.

WOOD THRUSH p. 282
Rufous head; large spots. Accidental in West.

SWAINSON'S THRUSH p. 182
Dull gray-brown above; no strong rusty. Buffy cheek, conspicuous buffy eye-ring.

GRAY-CHEEKED THRUSH p. 183
Dull gray-brown above; no rusty. Grayish cheek, inconspicuous eye-ring.

MOUNTAIN BLUEBIRD

WESTERN BLUEBIRD
♀
♂
♀
♂

EASTERN BLUEBIRD
Juvenal
♂

VARIED THRUSH
♂

TOWNSEND'S SOLITAIRE

ROBIN
Juvenal
♂

VEERY

HERMIT THRUSH

WOOD THRUSH

SWAINSON'S THRUSH

GRAY-CHEEKED THRUSH

Plate 49

VIREOS AND KINGLETS

VIREOS WITHOUT WING-BARS
These have eyebrow-stripes.

RED-EYED VIREO p. 196
Gray crown, black and white eyebrow-stripes.

YELLOW-GREEN VIREO p. 195
Like Red-eyed but yellower; yellow under tail coverts.
Rio Grande Delta.

WARBLING VIREO p. 196
Light eyebrow line, whitish or buffy breast.

PHILADELPHIA VIREO p. 196
Light eyebrow line, yellowish underparts. Note dark lores.

VIREOS WITH ONE FAINT WING-BAR OR NONE

GRAY VIREO p. 195
Very gray; light eye-ring. See text.

VIREOS WITH WING-BARS
These have eye-rings or "spectacles."

BELL'S VIREO p. 194
Eye-ring and wing-bars not too prominent. See text.
Streamsides, willows.

BLACK-CAPPED VIREO p. 194
Black or dark cap, very conspicuous "spectacles."

SOLITARY VIREO p. 195
Blue-gray head, olive back, white throat.
Plumbeous form: No contrast between head and back.

HUTTON'S VIREO p. 194
Incomplete eye-ring; dingy underparts. Lacks strong black
bar of Ruby-crowned Kinglet's wing.

KINGLETS

GOLDEN-CROWNED KINGLET p. 187
Male: Striped head, yellow and orange-red crown.
Female: Striped head, yellow crown.

RUBY-CROWNED KINGLET p. 187
Male: Broken eye-ring, red crown spot.
Female: Broken eye-ring, black wing-bar, stubby tail.
Note: Kinglets nervously twitch or flick wings.

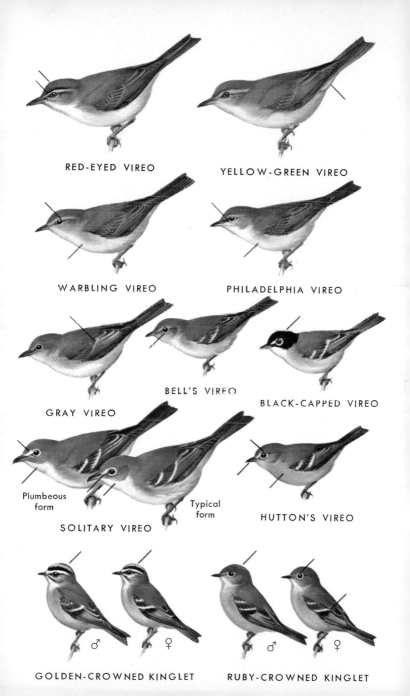

RED-EYED VIREO

YELLOW-GREEN VIREO

WARBLING VIREO

PHILADELPHIA VIREO

GRAY VIREO

BELL'S VIREO

BLACK-CAPPED VIREO

Plumbeous form

Typical form

SOLITARY VIREO

HUTTON'S VIREO

GOLDEN-CROWNED KINGLET

♂ ♀

RUBY-CROWNED KINGLET

♂ ♀

Plate 50

WARBLERS

Most of these have streaked underparts. They
are breeding birds unless otherwise noted.

GRACE'S WARBLER p. 205
Yellow throat and breast, striped sides. Sexes similar.

MYRTLE WARBLER p. 202
Similar to Audubon's but throat whitish.

AUDUBON'S WARBLER p. 203
Yellow rump; yellow throat. White wing patch, black chest
on breeding male.

MAGNOLIA WARBLER p. 201
White tailband; heavy breast-stripes.

BLACK-THROATED GRAY WARBLER p. 203
Male: Black crown, cheek patch, and throat.
Female: Slaty crown and cheek patch.

BLACKPOLL WARBLER p. 206
Male: Black cap, white cheek. *Female and fall:* See text.

BLACK-AND-WHITE WARBLER p. 197
Black and white crown-stripes.

TOWNSEND'S WARBLER p. 203
Pattern of Black-throated Gray, but with yellow.

GOLDEN-CHEEKED WARBLER p. 204
Male: Yellow cheek, black back. Texas. *Female:* See text.

BLACK-THROATED GREEN WARBLER p. 204
Black throat, yellow cheek, green back. *Female:* See text.

HERMIT WARBLER p. 205
Yellow head, black throat, gray back. Female duller.

YELLOW WARBLER p. 201
Yellowish, yellow tail spots. Reddish streaks (male).

PALM WARBLER p. 207
Chestnut cap; wags tail. Fall plumage, see text.

CAPE MAY WARBLER p. 202
Male: Chestnut cheek. *Female:* See text.

CANADA WARBLER p. 211
"Necklace" of streaks; no wing-bars.

OVENBIRD p. 207
Eye-ring; dull orange crown; stripes.

NORTHERN WATERTHRUSH p. 207
Whitish or yellowish eye-stripe; striped buffy underparts.

BLACKBURNIAN WARBLER p. 205
Orange throat. Female paler; note face and back pattern.

CHESTNUT-SIDED WARBLER p. 206
Chestnut sides. Yellow crown.

GRACE'S ♂

MYRTLE
Winter
♂

AUDUBON'S
Winter
♂

MAGNOLIA
♂

BLACK-THROATED GRAY
♀
♂

BLACKPOLL
Fall
♀
♂

BLACK-AND-WHITE
♀
♂

TOWNSEND'S
♀
♂

GOLDEN-CHEEKED
♂

BLACK-THROATED GREEN
♂

HERMIT
♂
♀

YELLOW
(Alaskan)
Imm.
♂

PALM
Fall
♂

CAPE MAY
♂

CANADA
♂

OVENBIRD

NORTHERN WATERTHRUSH

BLACKBURNIAN
Fall
♀
♂

CHESTNUT-SIDED
♂

Plate 51

WARBLERS

Most of these have unstreaked underparts. They
are breeding birds unless otherwise noted.

RED-FACED WARBLER   p. 210
    Bright red face and upper breast. Sexes similar.
PAINTED REDSTART   p. 211
    Bright red breast; white patches. Sexes similar.
AMERICAN REDSTART   p. 211
    Male: Orange tail patches. *Female:* Yellow patches.
BAY-BREASTED WARBLER   p. 206
    Deep chestnut breast, pale neck spot.
OLIVE WARBLER   p. 201
    Male: Tawny head, black ear patch. *Female:* See text.
OLIVE-BACKED WARBLER   p. 200
    Bluish and yellow; wing-bars, black face (male).
YELLOW-BREASTED CHAT   p. 209
    Large; white "spectacles," yellow breast, thick bill.
YELLOWTHROAT   p. 209
    Male: Black mask, yellow throat.
    Female: Yellow throat, brownish sides, whitish belly.
WILSON'S WARBLER   p. 210
    Male: Round black cap. *Female:* See text.
ORANGE-CROWNED WARBLER   p. 198
    Dull greenish, faint streaks; no white in wings, tail.
MOURNING WARBLER   p. 208
    Gray hood, black throat (male). No eye-ring (breeding).
MacGILLIVRAY'S WARBLER   p. 209
    Similar, but with broken eye-ring (breeding).
CONNECTICUT WARBLER   p. 208
    Gray hood, complete eye-ring. No black on throat.
NASHVILLE WARBLER   p. 199
    Yellow throat, white eye-ring.
VIRGINIA'S WARBLER   p. 199
    Gray; yellowish rump, yellowish on breast.
COLIMA WARBLER   p. 199
    Like Virginia's but larger.
    Usually lacks yellow on breast. Chisos Mts., Texas.
LUCY'S WARBLER   p. 200
    Gray above; chestnut rump patch.
TENNESSEE WARBLER   p. 198
    Breeding male: Gray head, white eye-stripe, whitish breast.
    Fall: Olive-yellow. Trace of wing-bar; white under tail.
ARCTIC WARBLER (an Old World warbler)   p. 186
    Alaska only; stripe over eye, pale legs, trace of wing-bar.

RED-FACED

PAINTED REDSTART

AMERICAN REDSTART

♀ ♂

BAY-BREASTED

♀ ♂

OLIVE

♀ ♂

OLIVE-BACKED

♀ ♂

YELLOW-THROAT

Fall

WILSON'S ♂

ORANGE-CROWNED ♂

YELLOW-BREASTED CHAT

NASHVILLE

MOURNING ♂

MacGILLIVRAY'S ♀ ♂

CONNECTICUT ♀

COLIMA ♂

ARCTIC

VIRGINIA'S ♂

LUCY'S ♂

TENNESSEE Fall

TENNESSEE

Plate 52

BLACKBIRDS AND STARLING

BREWER'S BLACKBIRD p. 218
Male in spring: Purplish head, yellow eye, medium tail.
Female in spring: Grayish; dark eye.
Winter: May have slight barring of rusty (usually blacker than shown, with little or no barring). See text.

RUSTY BLACKBIRD p. 218
Male in spring: Differs from Brewer's by lack of iridescence.
Female in spring: Grayish; yellow eye.
Winter: Rusty; barred breast.

BROWN-HEADED COWBIRD p. 219
Male: Brown head, short bill.
Female: Grayish; short bill.

BRONZED COWBIRD p. 220
Male: Blackish throughout; ruff on neck.
Female (not shown): Blackish; smaller ruff.

STARLING p. 192
Spring: Iridescent; sharp yellow bill, short tail. Sexes similar.
Winter: Finely spotted; sharp black bill.
Juvenal: Gray or gray-brown; short tail, sharp bill.

COMMON GRACKLE p. 219
Male: Bronzy back, purple head; creased tail.
Female (not shown): Smaller; less iridescent.

BOAT-TAILED GRACKLE p. 219
Male: Very large; long creased tail.
Female: Smaller; brown.

YELLOW-HEADED BLACKBIRD p. 214
Male: Yellow head.
Female: Yellow throat and breast.

RED-WINGED BLACKBIRD p. 214
Male: Red "epaulets" with yellow edge. Race known as "Bicolored" Red-winged Blackbird (California) lacks yellow edge.
Female: Heavily striped.

TRICOLORED BLACKBIRD (not illustrated) p. 215
Male: Darker red wing patch with white edge.
Female: Duskier than female Red-wing.
Mainly California. Highly colonial.

BREWER'S
BLACKBIRD

Spring ♂
Spring ♀
Winter

RUSTY
BLACKBIRD

Spring ♂
Spring ♀
Winter

BROWN-HEADED
COWBIRD

♂
♀

Adult
Spring
Juvenal
Winter

STARLING

BRONZED
COWBIRD

♂

COMMON
GRACKLE

♂

♂

♀

BOAT-TAILED
GRACKLE

YELLOW-HEADED BLACKBIRD

♂
♀

RED-WINGED BLACKBIRD

♂
♀

Plate 53

ORIOLES AND TANAGERS

Note: Female orioles differ from female tanagers
by their sharper bills, and from all but the female Western
Tanager by their white wing-bars.

SCOTT'S ORIOLE p. 216
Male: Yellow and black; black back.
Female: Greenish yellow; wing-bars. See text.
Immature male: Extensive black on throat. See text.

ORCHARD ORIOLE p. 215
Adult male: Deep chestnut breast and rump.
Female: Yellow-green; wing-bars.
Immature male: Yellow-green; black throat.

BLACK-HEADED ORIOLE p. 215
Dull yellow and black; yellowish black. Female duller.

BULLOCK'S ORIOLE p. 217
Male: Black crown, orange cheek; large wing patch.
Female: Olive-gray back; whitish belly.

BALTIMORE ORIOLE p. 217
Male: Orange below, black head.
Female: Yellow-orange breast.

HOODED ORIOLE p. 216
Male: Orange crown, black throat.
Female: Similar to Bullock's but belly yellowish.
Immature male: Black throat. See text.

LICHTENSTEIN'S ORIOLE p. 216
Much larger than Hooded Oriole; thick bill. Upper wing-bar
yellow or orange (not always visible). Sexes similar.
Rio Grande Delta only.

WESTERN TANAGER p. 220
Male: Red face, black back.
Female: Wing-bars, tanager bill.

SUMMER TANAGER p. 221
Male: Rose-red all over; light bill.
Female: Deeper yellow than Scarlet Tanager; wings not as
dusky.

HEPATIC TANAGER p. 221
Male: Deep dull red; blackish bill.
Female: Resembles female Summer but has blackish bill,
gray cheek.

SCARLET TANAGER p. 221
Male: Scarlet, with black wings and tail.
Female: Yellow-green; dusky wings and tail.
Eastern.

SCOTT'S ORIOLE

♂ Adult
Immature
♀

ORCHARD ORIOLE

♂ Immature
♂ Adult
♀

BLACK-HEADED ORIOLE

♂

BULLOCK'S ORIOLE

♀
♂

BALTIMORE ORIOLE

♂
♀

HOODED ORIOLE

♂ Adult
Immature
♀

LICHTENSTEIN'S ORIOLE

WESTERN TANAGER

♂
♀

SUMMER TANAGER

♂
♀

SCARLET TANAGER

♂
♀

HEPATIC TANAGER

♀
♂

Plate 54

BIRDS OF FIELDS, PRAIRIES, PLAINS

BOBOLINK p. 213
Breeding male: Black below; white patches above.
Female: Striped crown; buffy breast.
Autumn male is similar to female.

DICKCISSEL p. 225
Male: "Like a little meadowlark."
Female: Sparrow-like. See text.

WESTERN MEADOWLARK p. 213
Black V; short tail, white outer feathers.

EASTERN MEADOWLARK (not illustrated) p. 213
Different song. See text.

LARK BUNTING p. 234
Breeding male: Black body, white wing patch.
Female: Streaked; some white in wing.

HORNED LARK p. 158
Adult: "Horns," face patch, breast splotch.
Immature: Suggestion of adult pattern.

WATER PIPIT p. 188

SPRAGUE'S PIPIT p. 189
Both pipits: Thin bill, white outer tail feathers.
Water Pipit: Dark back, dark legs (usually).
Sprague's Pipit: Striped back, pale legs.

LAPLAND LONGSPUR p. 248
Breeding male: Black throat, rusty collar.
Winter: Smudge on breast, rusty nape (male).
Tail pattern below (No. 1).

SMITH'S LONGSPUR p. 249
Breeding male: Buffy; black and white ear patch.
Winter: Buffy; tail pattern No. 2. Adult male may show
white patch near shoulder.

McCOWN'S LONGSPUR p. 248
Breeding male: Black breast splotch, black cap.
Female and winter male: Rusty shoulder; tail pattern No. 4.

CHESTNUT-COLLARED LONGSPUR p. 249
Breeding male: Black breast and belly; chestnut collar.
Female and winter male: Tail pattern below (No. 3).

TAILS OF LONGSPURS

BOBOLINK

♀

♂
Breeding

DICKCISSEL

♂

♀

WESTERN
MEADOWLARK

LARK BUNTING

Breeding

♂

♀

HORNED LARK

Immature

WATER PIPIT

SPRAGUE'S
PIPIT

LAPLAND LONGSPUR

♂
Breeding

♂
Winter

McCOWN'S
LONGSPUR

♂

Breeding

♀

SMITH'S LONGSPUR

♂

♂
Winter

Breeding

CHESTNUT-COLLARED LONGSPUR

♂
Breeding

♀

Plate 55

FINCHES

PURPLE FINCH   p. 226
  Male: Rosy; no stripes on flanks.
  Female: Light eye-stripe, heavy dark jaw-stripe.
CASSIN'S FINCH   p. 227
  Male: Paler rose than Purple Finch; high mts. See text.
  Female: See text.
HOUSE FINCH   p. 227
  Male: Red breast, rump. Striped belly and sides.
  Female: Face without strong pattern; bill stubby.
RED CROSSBILL   p. 231
  Male: Dull red, blackish wings, crossed bill.
  Female: Dull olive-gray, dark wings.
WHITE-WINGED CROSSBILL   p. 232
  Male: Rose-pink; white wing-bars, crossed bill.
  Female: Olive-gray; white wing-bars, streaks.
HOARY REDPOLL   p. 229
  Paler than Common Redpoll; frosty unstreaked rump.
COMMON REDPOLL   p. 229
  Red forehead, black chin (male, pink breast).
GRAY-CROWNED ROSY FINCH   p. 228
  Brown; rosy wings and rump; gray head patch.
BROWN-CAPPED ROSY FINCH   p. 229
  Similar, but lacking distinct head patch.
BLACK ROSY FINCH   p. 229
  Blacker, with gray head patch.
PINE SISKIN   p. 230
  Streaked; touch of yellow in wings and tail.
PINE GROSBEAK   p. 228
  Male: Large, rosy; white wing-bars, stubby bill.
  Female: Gray; wing-bars; dull yellow crown and rump.
EVENING GROSBEAK   p. 226
  Male: Dull yellow; black and white wings, large pale bill.
  Female: Silver-gray and yellow, large pale bill.
CARDINAL   p. 222
  Male: Red; crested, black patch on face.
  Female: Brownish; red bill and crest.
PYRRHULOXIA   p. 223
  Male: Gray; red down front, red crest, yellow bill.
  Female: Gray-brown, yellow bill.
AMERICAN GOLDFINCH   p. 230
  Breeding male: Yellow body, black wings.
  Female and winter birds: Yellow-olive, black wings, whitish rump.
LESSER GOLDFINCH   p. 231
  Male: Black cap, black or greenish back, yellow underparts.
  Female: Greener than American Goldfinch; olive rump.
LAWRENCE'S GOLDFINCH   p. 231
  Male: Black face, gray head; yellow wing-bars.
  Female: Gray head, yellow wing-bars.
WHITE-COLLARED SEEDEATER   p. 227
  Male: Dark cap, incomplete collar and breastband.
  Female: Small, buffy; light wing-bars, stubby bill.

CASSIN'S
FINCH

HOUSE
FINCH

♀

♂

PURPLE
FINCH

♀

♂

♀

HOARY
REDPOLL

♀

♂

♂

RED
CROSSBILL

WHITE-
WINGED
CROSS-
BILL

♂

COMMON
REDPOLL

♂

Hepburn's
form →

BROWN-
CAPPED
↓

GRAY-
CROWNED

ROSY FINCHES   BLACK

♂

♂

PINE   SISKIN

♀

PINE
GROSBEAK

EVENING
GROSBEAK

♀

♂

♂

♀

♂

CARDINAL

♀

PYRRHULOXIA

Black-
backed
form

Green-
backed
form

♂

♂

♂

♂

♀

♀

♀

♂

♀

AMERICAN
GOLDFINCH

LESSER
GOLDFINCH

LAWRENCE'S
GOLDFINCH

WHITE-COLLARED
SEEDEATER

Plate 56

FINCHES

BLUE GROSBEAK   p. 224
Male: Blue; tan wing-bars, large bill.
Female: Brown, tan wing-bars, large bill.

INDIGO BUNTING   p. 224
Male: Blue all over; no wing-bars.
Female: Brown; faint streakings. See text.

LAZULI BUNTING   p. 224
Male: Blue back, reddish breast; white wing-bars.
Female: Brownish; wing-bars but no streaks. See text.

PAINTED BUNTING   p. 225
Male: Red underparts, violet head, green back.
Female: A small all-green finch; no wing-bars.

VARIED BUNTING   p. 225
Male: Dark; red patch on nape. *Female:* See text.

ROSE-BREASTED GROSBEAK   p. 223
Male: Rose breast patch.
Female: Whiter breast than Black-head's; well streaked.

BLACK-HEADED GROSBEAK   p. 223
Male: Black head, rusty breast; white wing spots.
Female: Striped head, large bill. Tan breast; few streaks.

RUFOUS-SIDED TOWHEE   p. 233
Rufous sides, large white tail spots.

GREEN-TAILED TOWHEE   p. 232
Greenish; rufous cap, white throat.

OLIVE SPARROW   p. 232
Olive; striped crown.

BROWN TOWHEE   p. 233
Brown; rusty cap, buff throat with short streaks.

ABERT'S TOWHEE   p. 233
Brown; black patch around base of bill.

SLATE-COLORED JUNCO   p. 240
Gray sides, gray back. White tail sides (all juncos).

WHITE-WINGED JUNCO   p. 239
White wing-bars.

GRAY-HEADED JUNCO   p. 240
Gray sides, rufous back. *Caniceps form:* Entire bill pale.
Dorsalis form: Upper mandible dark.

MEXICAN JUNCO   p. 241
Yellow eyes.

OREGON JUNCO   p. 240
Rusty or buffy sides; brown back; black head (male).
"Pink-sided" form: Clear gray hood (male); dull brown back.

INDIGO BUNTING

♂

♀

LAZULI BUNTING

♂

♀

BLUE GROSBEAK

♂

♀

PAINTED BUNTING

♂

♀

VARIED BUNTING

♂

♀

ROSE-BREASTED GROSBEAK

♂

RUFOUS-SIDED TOWHEE

♀

♂

BLACK-HEADED GROSBEAK

♂

OLIVE SPARROW

GREEN-TAILED TOWHEE

ABERT'S TOWHEE

Rocky Mt. states

BROWN TOWHEE

Pacific states

MEXICAN JUNCO

"Pink-sided" form (*mearnsi*)

♂

WHITE-WINGED JUNCO

SLATE-COLORED JUNCO

caniceps form

GRAY-HEADED JUNCO

dorsalis form

OREGON JUNCO

Plate 57

SPARROWS
(A majority of these have *streaked* breasts.)

FOX SPARROW   p. 246
  Rusty tail, heavily striped breast.
  Three types: (1) Rusty.
               (2) Dusky brown; brown-headed.
               (3) Slaty- or gray-headed.

SONG SPARROW   p. 247
  Streaked breast, with large central spot.
  Much variation, varying from pale desert forms to dark
  races of humid regions. Alaskan races very large.

VESPER SPARROW   p. 236
  White outer tail feathers.

SAVANNAH SPARROW   p. 234
  Like Song Sparrow but striped crown, short notched tail.
  For pale Large-billed and dark Belding's races, see text.

LINCOLN'S SPARROW   p. 247
  Like Song, but buffy breast, fine black streaks.

SHARP-TAILED SPARROW   p. 236
  Ocher face pattern, gray ear patch.

LE CONTE'S SPARROW   p. 235
  Buffy breast, streaked sides, white crown-stripe, pinkish-
  brown nape.

BAIRD'S SPARROW   p. 235
  Ocher crown-stripe, "necklace" of short streaks.

RUFOUS-WINGED SPARROW   p. 237
  Like gray Chipping Sparrow; tail lacks notch. Note
  "whisker," median line, rufous shoulder. Very local; se.
  Arizona.

CASSIN'S SPARROW   p. 238
  Streaked crown with no center stripe; dull unmarked breast;
  "skylarking" song. See text.

BOTTERI'S SPARROW   p. 237
  Very similar to Cassin's but browner, with brown tail.
  See text. Local; s. Texas, se. Arizona.

GRASSHOPPER SPARROW   p. 234
  Clear buffy breast, striped crown.

FOX Rusty form

FOX Dusky-brown form

FOX Slaty form

SONG

SONG (Unalaska)

VESPER

SAVANNAH — Nevada form

SAVANNAH — Belding's form

SAVANNAH — Large-billed form

LINCOLN'S

SHARP-TAILED

LE CONTE'S

BAIRD'S

RUFOUS-WINGED

CASSIN'S

BOTTERI'S

GRASSHOPPER

Plate 58

SPARROWS
(Most of these have unstreaked breasts.)

BLACK-THROATED SPARROW p. 238
  Black throat, white face-stripes.

HARRIS' SPARROW p. 243
  Adult: Black face and crown, black bib.
  Immature: Buffy face, dark breast splotch.

BLACK-CHINNED SPARROW p. 243
  Male: Gray head, black surrounding pink bill.
  Female: Gray head, no black on face.

WHITE-CROWNED SPARROW p. 244
  Adult: Striped crown, grayish throat.
  Immature: Brown and buff head-stripes, pink or yellow bill.

WHITE-THROATED SPARROW p. 246
  Adult: Striped crown, white throat.
  Immature: Striped crown, white throat.

GOLDEN-CROWNED SPARROW p. 245
  Adult: Yellow crown, bordered with black.
  Immature: House-Sparrow-like. See text.

SAGE SPARROW p. 238
  White outlining gray cheek; dark "stickpin."

LARK SPARROW p. 236
  "Quail" head pattern, "stickpin," white in tail.

FIELD SPARROW p. 243
  Rusty cap, pink bill.

TREE SPARROW p. 241
  Rusty cap, dark "stickpin."

RUFOUS-CROWNED SPARROW p. 237
  Rufous cap, black "whisker" mark.

SWAMP SPARROW p. 247
  Adult: Rusty cap, gray breast, white throat.
  Immature: Dull breast-streaking (see text).

CHIPPING SPARROW p. 241
  Adult: Rusty cap, white eyebrow-stripe.
  Immature: Gray rump (see text).

CLAY-COLORED SPARROW p. 242
  Adult: Striped crown, brown ear patch.
  Immature: Buffy rump (see text).

BREWER'S SPARROW p. 242
  Crown solid, finely streaked.

BLACK-
THROATED

Immature

Adult
HARRIS'

♀
♂
BLACK-CHINNED

Immature
WHITE-
CROWNED
Adult

Immature
Adult
WHITE-
THROATED

Immature
Adult
GOLDEN-
CROWNED

SAGE

LARK

FIELD

TREE

RUFOUS-
CROWNED

Immature

Adult
Spring
SWAMP

Immature
Adult
Spring
CHIPPING

Immature
Adult
Spring
CLAY-COLORED

BREWER'S

Plate 59

HAWAIIAN LAND BIRDS (NATIVE)

APAPANE p. 268
Red with black wings, blackish bill, white abdomen.
Immature: Gray-brown above, buff below; black bill.
Kauai, Oahu, Molokai, Maui, Hawaii.

IIWI p. 268
Vermilion with black wings, curved salmon bill.
Immature: Yellowish; black wings, curved pale bill.
Kauai, Oahu, Maui, Hawaii.

AKEPA p. 269
Hawaii form: Male red-orange, wings not black; bill short, pale.
Female greenish; bill short, pale, siskin-like.
Kauai form: Blackish mask, yellow crown, short bluish bill; sexes
similar. Kauai, Maui, Hawaii. Rare.

ANIANIAU (LESSER AMAKIHI) p. 269
Similar to Amakihi; smaller, yellower, straighter bill, no dark
lores; different voice. See text. Kauai.

AMAKIHI p. 268
Olive-green above, yellow below; slightly curved dark bill.
Kauai, Oahu, Molokai, Maui, Hawaii; scarce Lanai.

CREEPER (ALAUWAHIO) p. 269
Similar to Amakihi; straighter bill. See text.
Kauai form is whitish below. Kauai, Oahu, Maui, Hawaii.

MAUI PARROTBILL (PSEUDONESTOR) p. 271
Stubby; parrot bill, yellow eye-stripe. Very rare, Maui.

AKIAPOLAAU p. 270
Upper mandible decurved; lower short, straight. Hawaii.

NUKUPUU p. 271
Like preceding but short lower mandible decurved.
Extremely rare, Kauai.

KAUAI AKIALOA p. 271
Greenish yellow; very long decurved bill. Rare, Kauai.

CRESTED HONEYCREEPER p. 268
Orange-red nape, white tuft on forehead. Very rare, Maui.

OU p. 270
Yellow head (male), green body; parrot bill. Kauai, Hawaii.

PALILA p. 270
Yellow head, gray back, thick stubby bill. Hawaii.

LAYSAN FINCH p. 270
Yellowish, olive back; thick stubby bill. Male has yellowish head,
lacks streaks. Laysan, Nihoa.

MILLERBIRD p. 267
Brown back, buffy-white breast; warbler-like. Nihoa.

OMAO (HAWAIIAN THRUSH) p. 267
Dark brown above, gray below; dark legs. Kauai, Hawaii.

PUAIOHI (SMALL KAUAI THRUSH) (not illustrated) p. 271
Smaller than Omao; pink legs. Very rare, Kauai.

OOAA (KAUAI OO) p. 271
Blackish; yellow thighs, white patch. Very rare, Kauai.

ELEPAIO p. 267
Cocks tail, quivers wings. Note white rump (lacking in immature).
Races vary in color, throat pattern. Kauai, Oahu, Hawaii.

Imm.

Adult

APAPANE

IIWI

Imm.

Adult

Hawaii ♀

Hawaii

♂

Kauai
(Sexes similar)

AKEPA

NIANIAU

Kauai

Hawaii

AMAKIHI

NUKUPUU

Oahu
♂

Kauai
♂

♂

Hawaii

CREEPER

MAUI PARROTBILL

AKIAPOLAAU

KAUAI
AKIALOA

CRESTED
HONEYCREEPER

OU ♂

PALILA

♀

LAYSAN
FINCH

MILLERBIRD

OMAO (HAWAIIAN THRUSH)

OOAA
(KAUAI OO)

Kauai
♂

Imm.

Hawaii
♂

Oahu
♂

ELEPAIO

Plate 60

HAWAIIAN LAND BIRDS (INTRODUCED)

Scores of exotics have been liberated in the Islands. The majority have failed; these have succeeded. (The Cardinal, Mockingbird, Western Meadowlark, etc., are illustrated elsewhere in this book.)

BUSH WARBLER (UGUISU) p. 274
  Olive-brown above, light eye-stripe, warbler bill. Oahu.

VARIED TIT (YAMAGARA) p. 273
  Chickadee pattern, buffy cheek, rusty sides. Kauai, Oahu.

JAPANESE WHITE-EYE (MEJIRO) p. 275
  Greenish; conspicuous white eye-ring, yellow throat.
  All main islands.

RED-BILLED LEIOTHRIX (HILL ROBIN) p. 274
  Orange-red bill, orange-yellow breast, red in wing.
  Oahu, Molokai, Maui, Hawaii.

HOUSE FINCH (LINNET) p. 276
  See Plate 55. Males in some areas tend to be orange.
  All main islands.

RED-CRESTED (BRAZILIAN) CARDINAL p. 276
  Adult: Red face and crest, gray back. *Immature:* Chestnut-brown face and crest. Kauai, Oahu, Maui.

STRAWBERRY FINCH p. 275
  Male: Tiny; crimson. *Female:* Red bill, red rump. Oahu.

HOUSE SPARROW pp. 212, 276
  Male: Black bib, gray crown. *Female:* Plain dingy breast, dull eye-stripe. All main islands.

INDIAN MYNA (PIHA' E-KELO) p. 275
  Sooty brown, large white patches in wings and tail.
  All main islands.

RICEBIRD p. 275
  Very small; brown head, scaled underparts.
  All main islands.

SHAMA p. 274
  White rump, bright chestnut belly. Kauai, Oahu.

DYAL p. 274
  Known from Shama by white belly, white wing patch.
  Local, Oahu.

HWA-MEI (CHINESE THRUSH) p. 273
  Rusty brown; white "spectacles."
  Kauai, Oahu, Molokai, Maui, Hawaii.

CANARY p. 276
  All-yellow or yellow and white. Midway (Sand I.).

SKYLARK pp. 158, 273
  Streaked; white outer tail feathers, slight crest.
  All main islands (very local on some).

BARRED DOVE p. 273
  A small dove, heavily scaled and barred.
  All main islands.

COTURNIX (JAPANESE QUAIL) p. 272
  A small quail; sandy, streaked, striped head.
  Kauai, Molokai, Lanai, Maui, Hawaii.

BUSH WARBLER

VARIED TIT

JAPANESE WHITE-EYE

RED-BILLED LEIOTHRIX

HOUSE FINCH ♂

Imm.

Adult
RED-CRESTED (BRAZILIAN) CARDINAL

STRAW-BERRY FINCH ♀ ♂

HOUSE SPARROW ♀ ♂

INDIAN MYNA

RICEBIRD

CANARY

SHAMA

DYAL

HWA-MEI (CHINESE THRUSH)

SKYLARK

BARRED DOVE

COTURNIX

BLACK-BACKED THREE-TOED WOODPECKER   Pl. 40
Picoides arcticus   9–10
(Arctic Three-toed Woodpecker)

    Field marks: Note the combination of *solid black back, barred sides.* The 2 three-toed woodpeckers inhabit fir forests of the mts. and the North; their presence can be detected by large patches of bark scaled from dead conifers. Their sides are heavily barred and males have *yellow* caps.

    Similar species: (1) Northern Three-toed Woodpecker has barred or white back. (2) See also Williamson's Sapsucker.

    Voice: A short sharp *kik* or *chik.* Also in series.

    Where found: Boreal forests of N. America. **West:** *Resident* from c. Alaska, s. Mackenzie south (east of Cascade summits) to high Sierra in c. California; south in Rockies, Black Hills to n. Wyoming, w. S. Dakota; east across boreal woods of Canada.

    Habitat: Boreal forests; fir, lodgepole pine. **Nest:** Excavated hole in stub, tree, pole. Eggs (4–5) white.

NORTHERN THREE-TOED WOODPECKER   Pl. 40
Picoides tridactylus   8–9½

    Field marks: The males of the 2 three-toed woodpeckers are our only woodpeckers normally with *yellow* caps. The *"ladder-back"* or *white back* will further distinguish this species. Both species have barred sides. The female lacks the yellow cap and resembles the Hairy Woodpecker, but note the *barred sides.* In most birds the white of the back is broken by bars.

    Similar species: (1) Black-backed Three-toed Woodpecker has a solid *black* back. (2) Rarely, aberrant immature Hairy Woodpeckers have yellowish or orange caps, but they lack the barrings on the flanks and have more white on the face. (3) See female Williamson's Sapsucker (barred back, sides).

    Voice: Similar to Black-backed Three-toed Woodpecker's.

    Where found: Boreal forests of N. Hemisphere. **West:** *Resident* from n. Alaska, n. Yukon, n. Mackenzie south to high mts. of s. Oregon, e. Nevada, c. Arizona, c. New Mexico; also east across boreal woods of Canada and in Black Hills. **Habitat:** Conifer forests. **Nest:** In hole in dead conifer. Eggs (4) white.

Cotingas: Cotingidae

A TROPICAL group, very varied in color, pattern, behavior, and nesting; includes umbrella-birds, bell-birds, and cocks-of-the-rock. **Food:** Insects, berries. **Range:** Tropical America. **No. of species:** World, 90; West, 1.

ROSE-THROATED BECARD *Platypsaris aglaiae* 6½ **Pl. 42**
(Xantus' Becard)

    Field marks: A big-headed, thick-billed bird, somewhat resembling a flycatcher. *Male:* Dark gray above, pale to dusky below, with *blackish cap and cheeks* and a lovely *rose-colored throat.* *Female:* Brown above, *dark cap,* and *light buffy collar* around nape. Underparts washed with buff.

Voice: A thin slurred whistle, *seeoo;* sometimes preceded by a weak chatter (I. Davis).

Where found: Mexican border to Costa Rica. Rare local *summer resident* in se. Arizona, extreme sw. New Mexico (?), lower Rio Grande Valley, Texas. **Habitat:** Wooded canyons, river groves, sycamores. **Nest:** A woven football-shaped mass suspended from forest tree. Eggs (4–6) spotted.

Tyrant Flycatchers: Tyrannidae

FLYCATCHERS usually perch quietly upright on exposed branches and sally forth to snap up passing insects. Bill rather flattened, with bristles at base in most species. Song not well developed, but many species have characteristic "dawn songs," seldom given at other times of day. **Food:** Mainly flying insects. Some eat fruit, reptiles, etc. **Range:** New World; majority in tropics. **No. of species:** World, 365; West, 29 (+3 accidentals).

EASTERN KINGBIRD *Tyrannus tyrannus* 8–9 **Pl. 41**
　　Field marks: When this large black and white flycatcher flies, the *white band* at the *tip* of its fanlike tail leaves no doubt as to its identity. Its concealed red crown mark is rarely seen. Often seems to fly quiveringly on "tips of wings." Harasses hawks, Crows (a habit shared by certain other birds).
　　Voice: A rapid sputter of high bickering notes: *dzee-dzee-dzee,* etc., and *kit-kit-kitter-kitter,* etc. Also a nasal *dzeeb.*
　　Where found: C. Canada to Gulf of Mexico. Winters Peru to Bolivia. **West:** *Breeds* from ne. B.C., s. Mackenzie, c. Saskatchewan south to Puget Sound, and east of Cascades to ne. California, n. Nevada, n. Utah, Colorado, ne. New Mexico, Texas panhandle. *Casual,* s. California, Arizona. *Accidental,* n. Alaska. **Habitat:** Wood edges, parklands, river groves, farms, shelter belts, orchards, roadsides. **Nest:** A twiggy, well-lined saucer in tree, bush, or on post. Eggs (3–5) spotted.

THICK-BILLED KINGBIRD *Tyrannus crassirostris* 9 **Pl. 41**
　　Field marks: Differs from similar kingbirds (Cassin's, Western, Tropical) by its largely whitish underparts. Throat white, breast grayish white, belly pale yellow (sometimes almost white). Tail, gray-brown.
　　Similar species: Large bill, bull-headed appearance suggests Gray Kingbird of Florida.
　　Voice: A quick, shrill, slightly nasal *j'eerrr* or *wicha-weerrr* (I. Davis). *Brrr-zee* or *purr-eet* (D. Zimmerman).

Where found: Mainly w. Mexico and w. Guatemala. **West:** Recently discovered breeding along Guadalupe Canyon in extreme se. Arizona, sw. New Mexico. **Habitat:** Semiarid canyons, sycamores. **Nest:** A thin, frail cup of twigs, grass, in sycamore.

TROPICAL KINGBIRD   Pl. 41
Tyrannus melancholicus   8–9½
(Couch's Kingbird, "Olive-backed Kingbird")

Field marks: Very similar to Western and Cassin's Kingbirds, but tail slightly *forked, dusky brown,* not black, *without white edgings.* Back olive, or olive-gray, head gray with dark mask through eye, belly *bright yellow.* Little or no gray across breast. The common kingbird of the lower Rio Grande.

Similar species: (1) Cassin's Kingbird, (2) also some Western Kingbirds in worn plumage lack white tail sides; their tails are *blackish* without strong notch.

Voice: A high nasal *queer* or *chi-queer,* resembling notes of Cassin's Kingbird but higher. From Texas, E. Kincaid describes a long-drawn *bereeeeeeer* (suggesting a distant Pauraque).

Where found: S. Arizona, s. Texas to Argentina. **West:** *Breeds* irregularly in se. Arizona. Variable *resident* in s. Texas (south of a line from Falcon Dam to Raymondville). *Casual* along Rio Grande to El Paso; also w. Arizona, coastal s. California (fall). *Accidental,* B.C., Washington. **Habitat:** River groves, scattered trees. **Nest:** A saucer of twigs, often with Spanish moss, on horizontal limb. Eggs (3–5) pink or buff, spotted.

WESTERN KINGBIRD *Tyrannus verticalis* 8–9½   **Pl. 41**
Field marks: Smaller than Robin, with pale gray head and back, pale yellow belly. The best index to the 3 yellow-bellied kingbirds is their tails. In this species the *black* tail has a *narrow white edging* on each side. Immature and worn birds do not always have these margins but the grayish upper parts, pale gray head and chest, and yellowish belly identify them.

Similar species: (1) Ash-throated and (2) Wied's Crested Flycatchers have wing-bars, *rufous* tails. See (3) Cassin's Kingbird and (4) Tropical Kingbird.

Voice: Shrill bickering calls; a sharp *whit* or *whit-ker-whit.*

Where found: Sw. Canada, upper Mississippi Valley to n. Mexico. Winters mainly from nw. Mexico to Nicaragua. **West:** *Breeds* from s. B.C., s. Alberta, s. Saskatchewan south throughout most of w. U.S. **Habitat:** Open country with scattered trees, farms, roadsides. **Nest:** A saucer of twigs, grass, wool, on horizontal branch, pole, building. Eggs (3–5; 7) boldly spotted.

CASSIN'S KINGBIRD *Tyrannus vociferans* 8–9   **Pl. 41**
Field marks: Like Western Kingbird but darker, with a dark *olive-gray* rather than a gray back, and *no distinct white sides* on

black tail. (Tail is sometimes lightly *tipped* with whitish.)
Cassin's appears to have *whiter chin* than the 2 similar kingbirds,
owing to *darker chest.*
Similar species: Some Western Kingbirds may lack white sides
of tail, but grayer back, paler breast identify them. Cassin's
prefers somewhat higher altitudes. Calls very different.
Voice: A low nasal *queer* or *chi-queer* or *ki-dear;* also an excited
ki-ki-ki-dear, ki-dear, ki-dear, etc.
Where found: West: *Breeds* from Utah, se. Montana south
through Rocky Mt. states to s. Mexico, Guatemala. Also s. California west of San Joaquin Valley and the deserts. *Casual,*
Oregon, Nevada, w. S. Dakota, nw. Nebraska. *Winters* in
Mexico, Guatemala; some in s. California. **Habitat:** Semiopen
high country, scattered trees, pine-oak mts., ranch groves.
Nest: A cup of twigs, grass, wool, on limb of tree, pole, post.
Eggs (3–5) spotted.

SCISSOR-TAILED FLYCATCHER   Pl. 42
Muscivora forficata   11–15
Field marks: A beautiful bird, pale pearly gray, with an ex-
tremely long scissorlike tail. Usually the "scissors" are folded.
The sides and wing-linings are salmon-pink.
Similar species: Young bird with short tail may suggest Western
Kingbird. Note touch of pinkish on belly (instead of extensive
pale yellow). Breast whiter, more white in tail.
Voice: A harsh *keck* or *kew;* a repeated *ka-leep;* also shrill,
excited kingbird-like bickerings and stutterings.
Where found: *Breeds* from se. Colorado (?), s. Nebraska south
to e. New Mexico, w. and s. Texas. *Winters* chiefly s. Mexico
to Panama. *Casual,* California, Arizona. *Accidental,* Alberta,
Idaho, Utah, Wyoming. **Habitat:** Roadsides, ranches, farms,
mesquite, semiopen country. **Nest:** A shallow cup of twigs,
grass in tree, bush, on telegraph pole, etc. Eggs (4–6) spotted.

KISKADEE FLYCATCHER   *Pitangus sulphuratus*   9–10½
(Derby Flycatcher)   **Pl. 41**
Field marks: A very large bull-headed flycatcher, near size of a
small Belted Kingfisher (like that bird, it may even catch small
fish). It has much rufous in wings and tail. In Texas, the bright
yellow underparts and crown patch and *strikingly patterned
black and white face* identify it at once.
Voice: A loud *git-a-hear!* (*kis-ka-deer!*); *ki-deer!* or *weer!* Song,
dewey, tittit-a-dewey, tittit-a-dewey, etc. (I. Davis).
Where found: S. Texas to Argentina. *Resident* of lower Rio
Grande Valley. Occasional north to Laredo, Beeville. *Accidental,*
California (escape?). **Habitat:** Streamside thickets, groves,
orchards, towns. **Nest:** Football-shaped, with entrance in side;
in acacia, mesquite, palm, thorny tree. Eggs (2–5) dotted.

SULPHUR-BELLIED FLYCATCHER   Pl. 41
Myiodynastes luteiventris   7½–8½

Field marks: A large flycatcher with a bright *rufous tail,* black stripe through eye; underparts *yellowish with black streakings.* No other U.S. flycatcher is streaked *above and below.*

Voice: "A high penetrating *kee-zee' ick! kee-zee' ick!* given by both male and female, often in duet" (G. M. Sutton).

Where found: *Breeds* from se. Arizona (Santa Rita, Huachuca, Graham, Chiricahua Mts.) to Costa Rica. Winters in w. S. America. **Habitat:** In Arizona, sycamores in canyons. **Nest:** A cup of leaf stems in hole in sycamore. Eggs (3–4) red-blotched.

GREAT CRESTED FLYCATCHER   *Myiarchus crinitus*   8–9
(Crested Flycatcher)

Field marks: A large eastern flycatcher with *cinnamon wings and tail,* gray throat and breast, and yellow belly. Raises a slight bushy crest when excited.

Similar species: See the other similar cinnamon-tailed flycatchers: (1) Wied's Crested Flycatcher and (2) Ash-throated Flycatcher. (3) Kingbirds have black or dusky tails.

Voice: Note, a loud whistled *wheeep!* with rising inflection; also a throaty, rolling *prrrrrreet!*

Where found: S. Canada, e. and c. U.S. Winters e. Mexico to Colombia. **West:** Sparse *summer visitor* to se. and c. Saskatchewan (102°–106° W). Also *breeds* in vicinity of 100° in Texas (Edwards Plateau, ne. Panhandle). *Casual* migrant in w. parts of Great Plains. *Accidental,* Arizona. **Habitat:** Woodlands, river groves. **Nest:** In cavity in tree, often with snakeskin. Eggs (5–6; 8) streaked with reddish.

WIED'S CRESTED FLYCATCHER   Pl. 41
Myiarchus tyrannulus   8½–9½
(Mexican Crested Flycatcher, "Mexican Flycatcher")

Field marks: Similar to Ash-throated Flycatcher, but averages longer, with a proportionately larger bill. Throat grayer, breast more yellow, back more olive. These are subtle differences. To tell the two apart one must also have a keen ear.

Similar species: (1) See Ash-throated Flycatcher. (2) Great Crested Flycatcher, which occurs in range of Wied's Crested in s. Texas (mainly as a migrant), has a *brown* (not blackish) lower mandible, *brighter* underparts (more abrupt separation of gray and yellow below), and different call notes (typical note, a loud whistled *wheeeep!* with rising inflection).

Voice: A sharp *whit* and a rolling throaty *purreeer.* Voice much more vigorous and raucous than Ash-throated Flycatcher's. "Dawn song made up of 2 phrases repeated alternately: *whit-will-do* and *three-for-you*" (I. Davis).

Where found: *Breeds* from s.-c. Arizona, sw. New Mexico, s.

Texas (north to Beeville) south to n. Argentina. *Casual,* se. California, s. Nevada. Winters mostly south of U.S. **Habitat:** In Arizona, saguaros, sycamore canyons; in Texas, woodlands, river groves. **Nest:** In cavity in tree or post, or woodpecker hole in saguaro. Eggs (3–6) spotted, streaked.

ASH-THROATED FLYCATCHER   Pl. 41
Myiarchus cinerascens   7½–8½

Field marks: A medium-sized flycatcher, smaller than a king-bird, with 2 white wing-bars, *whitish* throat, *very pale yellowish belly,* and *rufous tail.* Head slightly bushy. Except in s. Arizona, sw. New Mexico, and Texas this is the only flycatcher breeding in w. U.S. that has a rufous tail.

Similar species: (1) Some kingbirds have yellow bellies, but their tails are *blackish.* In Southwest see (2) Wied's Crested Flycatcher, (3) Olivaceous Flycatcher. (4) East of Rockies see Great-crested Flycatcher.

Voice: *Pwit;* also a rolling *chi-beer* or *prit-wherr.*

Where found: *Breeds* from s. Oregon, e.-c. Washington, s. Idaho, sw. Wyoming south through California, Arizona, New Mexico, w. and c. Texas to s. Mexico. *Winters* from s. California, sw. Arizona south. *Casual,* B.C., Montana, sw. Kansas, w. Oklahoma. **Habitat:** Semiarid country, deserts, brush, mesquite, piñon-juniper, open woods. **Nest:** In hole in tree, post, mesquite, yucca. Eggs (4–5; 7) streaked.

OLIVACEOUS FLYCATCHER   Pl. 41
Myiarchus tuberculifer   6½–7

Field marks: Of the same type as the Ash-throated Flycatcher, rufous-tailed and pale yellow-bellied, but considerably smaller, with a grayish instead of white throat.

Voice: A mournful drawling whistle, slurring down, *peeur.*

Where found: *Breeds* from mts. of se. Arizona, extreme sw. New Mexico to nw. Argentina. Winters from s. Sonora south. *Casual,* w. Texas, Colorado. **Habitat:** Oak slopes, pine-oak canyons, junipers. **Nest:** In tree cavity. Eggs (3–5) streaked.

EASTERN PHOEBE   *Sayornis phoebe*   6¼–7¼   Pl. 42

Field marks: Note the *tail-wagging.* A sparrow-sized flycatcher, gray-brown above, whitish below; has neither conspicuous wing-bars nor an eye-ring. This lack of conspicuous wing-bars and the persistent tail-wagging are key points. The bill is *all-black.* Young birds may have dull brownish wing-bars.

Similar species: Wood pewees and other small flycatchers have conspicuous wing-bars. Their bills are yellowish or whitish on the lower mandible. They do not wag their tails.

Voice: Song, a well-enunciated *phoe-be,* or *fi-bree* (2nd note alternately higher or lower). Note, a sharp *chip.*

Where found: East of Rockies; c. Canada to s. U.S. Winters se. U.S. to s. Mexico. **West:** *Breeds* west to c. Mackenzie, ne. B.C., Alberta, sw. S. Dakota (Black Hills); locally e. Colorado, e. New Mexico. *Casual,* Wyoming, California, Arizona. **Habitat:** Streamsides, farms, roadsides, towns. **Nest:** A thick cup of mud, moss, grass, on ledge, bridge, building. Eggs (4–5; 8) white.

BLACK PHOEBE *Sayornis nigricans* 6¼–7   **Pl. 42**
Field marks: The only *black-breasted* flycatcher in U.S. Upper parts, head, and breast *black;* belly *white,* in sharp contrast to black of sides and breast. Has phoebe tail-wagging habit.
Voice: Song, a thin, strident *fi-bee, fi-bee,* the first 2 notes rising, the last 2 dropping; note, a sharp *tsip.*
Where found: *Resident* from n. California, s. Nevada, sw. Utah, nw. Arizona, c. New Mexico, w. Texas to n. Argentina. *Casual,* w. Oregon. **Habitat:** Shady streams, walled canyons, farmyards, towns; near water. **Nest:** A cup of mud, grass, on ledge, bridge, or building near water. Eggs (3–6) white or dotted.

SAY'S PHOEBE *Sayornis saya* 7–8   **Pl. 42**
Field marks: A large, pale phoebe with a pale *rusty* belly and under tail coverts. *Black tail* and rusty underparts give it the look of a small Robin, but it has flycatcher habits.
Similar species: (1) See kingbirds. (2) Female Vermilion Flycatcher may suggest Say's Phoebe. It has breast streaks.
Voice: A plaintive *pee-ur* or *pee-ee;* also a trilling note.
Where found: W. N. America (east on Plains roughly to 100°). *Breeds* from n.-c. Alaska, Yukon, w. Mackenzie, c. Alberta, s. Saskatchewan south to c. Mexico; absent west of Cascade-Sierra divide except locally in c. and s. California, w. Oregon. *Winters* from n. California, n. Arizona, c. New Mexico south. **Habitat:** Open arid country, deserts, brushy plains, prairie farms, canyon mouths, buttes. **Nest:** A bracket of grass, wool, on ledge, rock wall, bridge, building. Eggs (4–5; 7) white.

THE EMPIDONAX COMPLEX *Empidonax*   **Pl. 42**
Eight small flycatchers in w. N. America share in common the characters of dark back, light underparts, *light eye-ring,* and *2 white wing-bars.* One, the Buff-breasted Flycatcher (Arizona, New Mexico), has a buffy breast and is distinctive. Two have a yellowish wash on the underparts; one is widespread (Western Flycatcher) and the other (Yellow-bellied Flycatcher) is confined to Canada, mainly east of the Rockies. The other 5 (Traill's, Hammond's, Dusky, Gray, and Least) are whiter below and so similar as to confound the experts. They are more readily identified by nesting habits, habitat, and voice than by subtle color differences. Unfortunately, in migration they may depart from typical habitat and they seldom sing their names. Col-

lecting has proven that it is nearly impossible to name many individuals in the field, even in the spring, so the wise field man usually lets most of them go as just Empidonaxes.

YELLOW-BELLIED FLYCATCHER   Pl. 42
Empidonax flaviventris 5-5¾
Field marks: The decidedly *yellowish* underparts (including throat) separate this Canadian flycatcher from any other small flycatcher in Canada except the Western, which has a different range (mainly west of mts. in B.C., local in sw. Alberta).
Voice: A simple, spiritless *per-wee* or *chu-wee*, rising on 2nd syllable. Also *killic*.
Where found: Canada, ne. U.S. Migrates through e. and c. U.S. Winters Mexico to Panama. **West:** *Breeds* in s. Mackenzie, ne. B.C., n. and c. Alberta, c. Saskatchewan, n. N. Dakota (Turtle Mtn.). **Habitat:** In Canada, boreal forests, muskegs, alders. **Nest:** A deep cup hidden in sphagnum. Eggs (3-5) dotted.

TRAILL'S FLYCATCHER   *Empidonax traillii* 5¼-6¾ **Pl. 42**
(Alder Flycatcher)
Field marks: This widespread species is the brownest of the genus and averages a bit larger than the others. See *Voice*.
Voice: Song, a burry *way-be' o*, or *weep-a-dee' ar;* in parts of range a sneezy *fitz-bew*. Note, a low *pep* or *wit*. A burry *weep* (like 1st note of song) is probably diagnostic in migration.
Where found: Alaska, Canada to sw. and e.-c. U.S. Winters Mexico to Argentina. **West:** *Breeds* from c. Alaska, c. Yukon, c. Mackenzie, n. Saskatchewan south to sw. California (San Diego), s. Nevada, s. Arizona, sw. New Mexico, w. Texas. **Habitat:** Breeds in willow and alder thickets in low valleys, swamps, canyons, or in high mt. meadows; brushy bogs, muskegs. **Nest:** A loose cup in fork of shrub. Eggs (3-4) spotted.

LEAST FLYCATCHER   *Empidonax minimus* 5-5¾   **Pl. 42**
Field marks: An e. *Empidonax* that gets into Wyoming, Montana, and w. Canada mainly in those sections that lie east of the Rockies. Grayer above and whiter below than the other small flycatchers of this group. Its voice and the open groves of trees which it inhabits identify it.
Voice: A sharply snapped dry *che-bek';* very emphatic. The *k* sound is distinctive.
Where found: Canada, east of Rockies; n.-c. and ne. U.S. Winters Mexico to Panama. **West:** *Breeds* from sw. Yukon, c. Mackenzie south through ne. and s.-c. B.C., Alberta, Saskatchewan to Montana, c. Wyoming, sw. S. Dakota (Black Hills). *Migrant* through Great Plains. **Habitat:** Breeds in open woodlands, poplar and aspen groves, orchards. **Nest:** A neatly woven cup in crotch of small tree. Eggs (3-6) white.

HAMMOND'S FLYCATCHER   Pl. 42
Empidonax hammondii   5–5½

Field marks: It is a standing joke among western ornithologists that *no one seems to have an infallible way* of telling Hammond's and Dusky Flycatchers apart in the field. Both breed in the Transition and Canadian zones of the mts., extending higher up than does the Western Flycatcher. The habitats of the two hardly overlap, the Hammond's, on the whole, occurs higher up in the taller firs, while the Dusky prefers chaparral or a mixture of chaparral and conifers. As a rule, this species is more olive, not so gray; the underparts are more yellowish, contrasting with a grayer chest. These points are so tricky as to be of almost no use. "In hand" characters for *hammondii* are: (1) bill narrower, shorter (11.5 mm.); (2) wing formula — 10th primary (outer) longer than 5th.

Voice: Voice descriptions vary. The author can hear no great difference in the songs of Dusky and Hammond's. Birds that he was assured were *hammondii* sang a thin colorless song as follows: *se-lip, twur, treeip.* R. Hoffmann wrote that the low *twur* or *tsurp* note is always typical of *hammondii.* H. Cogswell says that Dusky may sometimes give this note. Dr. D. E. Davis interprets the song of the Dusky as *clip, whee, zee,* the *zee* note highest. Notes, *whit* (male); *tweep* (female).

Where found: *Breeds* from se. Alaska, s. Yukon, B.C., sw. Alberta south in high mts. to nw. and c.-e. California (Sierra), nw. New Mexico. Through lowlands in migration. *Winters* from se. Arizona to Nicaragua. **Habitat:** High coniferous forest; in migration, other trees, thickets. **Nest:** A neat cup saddled on limb (15–50 ft.). Eggs (3–4) white, rarely dotted.

DUSKY FLYCATCHER   *Empidonax oberholseri*   5¼–6
(Wright's Flycatcher)   Pl. 42

Field marks and Voice: See Hammond's Flycatcher.
Where found: *Breeds* from s. Yukon, nw. B.C., sw. Alberta, sw. Saskatchewan (Cypress Hills), w. S. Dakota (Black Hills) south in mts. to s. California, s. Nevada, c. Arizona, n. New Mexico. *Winters* in Mexico. *Migrant* east to w. Texas. **Habitat:** Breeds in mt. chaparral (Canadian-zone brush) with scattering of trees; in s. California mts., also open conifer forest. **Nest:** A neat cup in crotch of bush or low sapling usually lower than Hammond's (maximum 15–18 ft.). Eggs (3–5) white.

GRAY FLYCATCHER   *Empidonax wrightii*   5½   Pl. 42
Field marks: Similar to Dusky or Hammond's Flycatchers. This species may be identified even in migration or winter if the lower mandible is more abruptly flesh-colored and if the back is *gray* with scarcely a hint of olive or brown, and if the underparts have *no,* or scarcely any, tinge of yellow. It can be safely

identified on the breeding grounds by habitat. This is usually sagebrush. In Utah it may be piñon and juniper.

Voice: R. Hoffmann stated that the song is less varied than Dusky's or Hammond's, with only 2 elements, a vigorous *chiwip* and a fainter *cheep* on a higher pitch. In ne. California, H. Cogswell notes it as *hesick — pitick*.

Where found: *Breeds* in Great Basin from c. Oregon, s. Idaho, sw. Wyoming, c. Colorado south to e. California (Inyo Mts.), s. Nevada, c. Arizona, w. New Mexico. *Winters* from s. California (sparse), c. Arizona to s. Mexico. *Migrant* in w. Texas. *Accidental,* Yukon. **Habitat:** Breeds in sagebrush, piñon, junipers. In winter, willow thickets, brush. **Nest:** A woven cup of grass in sagebrush or small tree. Eggs (3–4) white.

WESTERN FLYCATCHER *Empidonax difficilis* 5½–6 **Pl. 42**
Field marks: This most frequently encountered *Empidonax* in most parts of w. U.S. Upper parts olive-brown, underparts washed with *yellowish,* wing-bars whitish, eye-ring white. Very similar to the other small flycatchers of this group, but underparts usually more yellowish, *including the throat.* Most individuals of Traill's, Hammond's, and Dusky have a faint wash of yellow on the underparts, but their throats are whitish.
Similar species: See Yellow-bellied Flycatcher (Canada).
Voice: A sharp lisping *pseet?* or *seest?* with rising inflection (male). Dawn song (sometimes heard all day), 3 thin notes: *pseet-trip-seet!* (*seet* highest); arrangement varies.
Where found: *Breeds* from se. Alaska, w. B.C., sw. Alberta (local), w. Montana, Black Hills south to Honduras. *Migrant* on w. edge of Great Plains. *Winters* Mexico to Honduras. **Habitat:** Moist woods, mixed or conifer forest, canyons, groves; must have water, shade. **Nest:** A cup of moss, rootlets, on ledge, cabin, log, cutbank, tree trunk. Eggs (3–4) spotted.

BUFF-BREASTED FLYCATCHER
Empidonax fulvifrons 4½–5
Field marks: A very small flycatcher of the *Empidonax* group with a white eye-ring and white wing-bars. Distinguished from its confusing relatives by its *rich buffy breast.*
Voice: *Chicky-whew* (Lusk). *Chee-lick* (H. Brandt).
Where found: Breeds from mts. of c. and se. Arizona, c.-w. New Mexico to Honduras. *Winters* from Sonora south. **Habitat:** Canyon groves, oak-pine forest. **Nest:** A lichen-disguised cup on branch of tree. Eggs (3–4) creamy white.

COUES' FLYCATCHER *Contopus pertinax* 7–7¾ **Pl. 42**
Field marks: In some of the high mts. near the Mexican border a large gray flycatcher may be seen which looks like a large wood pewee but has a larger head, slight bushy crest, and less

conspicuous wing-barring. Lower mandible more conspicuously yellow. Resembles closely the Olive-sided Flycatcher, but underparts more uniformly gray, throat *grayer; no white strip* through center of breast separating dusky sides.
Voice: A thin plaintive whistle, *ho-say, re-ah,* or *ho-say, ma-re-ah* (nickname is "Jose Maria"). Note, *pip-pip* or *pil-pil.*
Where found: *Breeds* from c. and se. Arizona, sw. New Mexico south to n. Nicaragua. Winters mainly south of U.S. *Accidental,* se. California, se. Colorado, w. Texas. **Habitat:** Pine and pine-oak forests of mts., wooded canyons. **Nest:** A woven cup saddled to branch of large tree. Eggs (3–4) spotted.

EASTERN WOOD PEWEE *Contopus virens* 6–6¾ **Pl. 42**
Field marks: Very similar to Western Wood Pewee but not as strongly olive-gray on breast and sides.
Voice: A sweet plaintive whistle: *pee-a-wee,* slurring down, then up. Also *pee-ur,* slurring down. Very unlike nasal song of Western Wood Pewee.
Where found: S. Canada, e. U.S. Winters Costa Rica to Peru.
West: *Breeds* west of 100° only in Edwards Plateau, Texas (to San Angelo). Sparse *migrant* west to Colorado, Texas panhandle. *Casual,* Montana. *Accidental,* e. Oregon, se. Arizona. **Habitat:** Woodlands, groves. **Nest:** Similar to Western Wood Pewee's.

WESTERN WOOD PEWEE **Pl. 42**
Contopus sordidulus 6–6½
Field marks: A sparrow-sized flycatcher, dusky gray-brown above, olive-gray on breast and sides. It has 2 narrow white wing-bars but *no* white eye-ring. The slightly larger size, much darker back, darker underparts, and lack of an eye-ring distinguish it from any of the smaller flycatchers, as do the much longer wings, which extend halfway down the tail.
Similar species: See Eastern Wood Pewee.
Voice: A nasal *peeyee* or *peeeer.*
Where found: *Breeds* from c. Alaska, s. Yukon, s. Mackenzie, c. Saskatchewan south to Cent. America; east to c. Manitoba, w. N. Dakota, w. S. Dakota, w. Texas (probably w. parts of Edwards Plateau). Winters Panama to Peru. **Habitat:** Woodlands, pine-oak forest, open conifers, river groves. **Nest:** A lichen-covered cup on horizontal branch. Eggs (3–4) spotted.

OLIVE-SIDED FLYCATCHER **Pl. 42**
Nuttallornis borealis 7–8
Field marks: A rather large, stout, bull-headed flycatcher, usually seen perched at the tip of a dead tree or branch, from which it makes wide sallies after passing insects. Resembles the smaller wood pewee. Note the large bill and *dark chest patches* separated or nearly separated by a narrow strip of white (suggests

a "dark unbuttoned jacket"). *Two cottony tufts* sometimes poke out from behind wings.
Similar species: (1) Wood pewees are smaller, have light wing-bars. (2) In Arizona, New Mexico, see Coues' Flycatcher.
Voice: Note, a trebled *pip-pip-pip.* Song, a spirited whistle: *quick-three-beer!,* middle note highest, last sliding.
Where found: Alaska, Canada, w. and ne. U.S. Winters in n. S. America. **West:** *Breeds* from c. Alaska, c. Yukon, c. Mackenzie south to mts. of n. Baja California, c. Nevada, ne. Arizona, New Mexico, w. Texas (Guadalupe Mts.); east in boreal forest across Canada. **Habitat:** Conifer forests, burns; eucalyptus groves (San Francisco Bay). In migration, varied places; usually seen on tip of dead tree or branch. **Nest:** A twiggy saucer out on branch of conifer. Eggs (3) buff, spotted.

VERMILION FLYCATCHER   Pl. 42
Pyrocephalus rubinus   5½–6½
   Field marks: *Male: Crown, throat, and underparts, flaming vermilion;* upper parts and tail dusky brown to blackish. Crown often raised in bushy crest. *Female and immature:* Upper parts brownish gray; breast white, narrowly streaked; lower belly and under tail coverts washed with pinkish or yellow.
   Similar species: Say's Phoebe might be confused with female.
   Voice: A slightly phoebe-like *p-p-pit-zeee* or *pit-a-zee;* elaborated during male's butterfly-like hovering display flight.
   Where found: Mainly *resident* from s. California (San Diego and deserts), s. Nevada, sw. Utah, c. Arizona, s. New Mexico, w. and s. Texas to s. Argentina. In winter, coast of s. California. *Casual,* Colorado. **Habitat:** Near water in desert country; mesquite, willows, cottonwoods. **Nest:** A flat twiggy saucer on horizontal fork of limb. Eggs (2–3) blotched.

BEARDLESS FLYCATCHER   Pl. 42
Camptostoma imberbe   4¼
   Field marks: A very small, nondescript flycatcher whose general appearance and behavior suggest a kinglet, a vireo, or an immature Verdin. Upper parts olive-gray; underparts dingy white; indistinct wing-bars and eye-ring. Distinguished from *Empidonax* flycatchers by its smaller size, smaller head, different behavior, and very small bill.
   Similar species: (1) Bell's Vireo (different voice) is a bit larger; slightly more yellowish on sides; wing-bars whitish or grayish (in many individuals of Beardless, wing-bars are buffy or brownish). (2) Immature Verdin (very similar) tends to be more pure gray above; no wing-bars. Has distinctive voice.
   Voice: Call note a thin *peeee-yuk* or *squee-ut.* Also a series of fine gentle notes, *ee, ee, ee, ee, ee,* increasing in volume toward the middle of the series (G. M. Sutton).

Where found: *Resident* from s. Arizona, s. Texas (Rio Grande Delta) to Costa Rica. Habitat: Low woods, mesquite, stream thickets, lower canyons. Nest: Globular (entrance on side); in tree tangle, palmetto, mistletoe. Eggs (2–3) speckled.

Larks: Alaudidae

MOST LARKS are streaked, brown, terrestrial birds. Hind claw elongated, almost straight. Voices musical; often sing high in display flight. Often gregarious. Sexes usually similar. Food: Mainly seeds, insects. Range: Old World except for our Horned Lark and introduced Skylark. No. of species: World, 75; West, 2.

SKYLARK *Alauda arvensis* 7–7½ Pl. 60
Field marks: Slightly larger than a sparrow, brown, strongly streaked; underparts buff-white; breast streaked. Tail with conspicuous white on outer feathers. Short, rounded *crest*.
Similar species: See Water Pipit (p. 188), Vesper Sparrow (p. 236), longspurs (pp. 248–49).
Voice: Note, a clear, liquid *chir-r-up*. Song, in hovering flight, a high-pitched, tireless torrent of runs and trills; *very long sustained*.
Where found: Eurasia, n. Africa. West: *Resident* on Vancouver I. (Saanich Peninsula) and in Hawaiian Is. Introduced. Habitat: Farm fields, cultivated land. Nest: A grass-lined hollow on ground. Eggs (3–4; 7) usually spotted.

HORNED LARK *Eremophila alpestris* 7–8 Pl. 54
Field marks: Note the head pattern. A brown ground bird, larger than House Sparrow, with black "whiskers," 2 small black *horns* (not always noticeable), and a black shield below the light throat. *Walks,* does not hop; overhead, light-bellied with a *black* tail; folds wings tightly after each beat. Females and immatures duller, but show Horned Lark pattern.
Similar species: See pipits (pp. 188–89), longspurs (pp. 248–49).
Voice: Song, tinkling, irregular, high-pitched, often long sustained; given from ground or very high in air in manner of pipits or Skylark. Note, a clear *tsee-ee* or *tsee-titi*.
Where found: Breeds widely in N. Hemisphere (south locally to n. Africa, n. S. America); some migration in n. races. West: *Breeds* from n. Alaska, arctic Canada south locally throughout w. N. America. *Winters* from s. Canada south. Habitat: Plains, deserts, prairies, fields, sparse sage flats, golf courses, airports, dirt roads, shores, alpine meadows, tundra. Nest: A grass-lined depression on ground. Eggs (3–5) gray, spotted.

Swallows: Hirundinidae

SLIM, streamlined form and graceful flight characterize these sparrow-sized birds. Tiny feet, long pointed wings, and short bills with very wide gapes. **Food:** Flying insects caught in flight, rarely berries. **Range:** Nearly cosmopolitan, except polar regions and some islands. **No. of species:** World, 75; West, 8 (+1 accidental).

VIOLET-GREEN SWALLOW   Pl. 43
Tachycineta thalassina 5 5½
> **Field marks:** Note the *white patches that almost meet* over base of tail. Dark above, adults glossed with green and purple; clear white below. Separated from Tree Swallow by greener back, white rump patches. White of face *partially encircles eye.*
> **Similar species:** (1) Tree Swallow and (2) White-throated Swift (p. 130).
> **Voice:** A twitter; a thin *chip* or *chit chit.* A rapid *chit-chit-chit wheet, wheet.*
> **Where found:** *Breeds* from c. Alaska (Yukon River), sw. Yukon, B.C., sw. Alberta, nw. Montana, sw. S. Dakota (Black Hills) south locally to mts. of s. Mexico. Widespread in migration; east to w. edge of Great Plains. Winters mainly in Mexico, Cent. America; a few in s. California. **Habitat:** Widespread when foraging; when nesting, open forests, foothill woods, mts., canyons, cliffs, towns. **Nest:** In hole in tree, cliff, building, bird box. Eggs (4–5; 7) white.

TREE SWALLOW *Iridoprocne bicolor* 5–6¼   Pl. 43
> **Field marks:** Steely blue-black or green-black above, *clear white* below. Immature is dusky brown above; has incomplete dusky collar on breast. The Tree Swallow glides in circles, ending each glide with 3 or 4 quick flaps and a short climb.
> **Similar species:** (1) Violet-green Swallow shows conspicuous white rump patches; has white partly encircling eye. Immature Tree might be confused with (2) Rough-winged Swallow (dingy throat), (3) Bank Swallow (complete breastband).
> **Voice:** Note, *cheet* or *chi-veet.* A liquid twitter. Song, *weet, trit, weet,* repeated with variations.
> **Where found:** Alaska, Canada, to California, c.-e. U.S. Winters s. U.S. to Cent. America. **West:** *Breeds* from n.-c. Alaska, sw. Yukon, c. Mackenzie, n. Saskatchewan south through Pacific states to s. California; in interior to c. Nevada, Utah, c. New Mexico. *Winters* from c. California, s. Arizona south. **Habitat:** Open country near water; marshes, mt. meadows, streams, lakes, wires; when nesting, requires dead trees, snags, preferably near water. **Nest:** A feather-lined cup in hole in tree, building, nest box. Eggs (4–6; 10) white.

BANK SWALLOW　*Riparia riparia*　4¾–5½　　**Pl. 43**
　　Field marks: A small brown-backed swallow. Note the *distinct dark breastband.* Flight irregular, more fluttery than other swallows'; glides short, unstable (C. H. Blake).
　　Similar species: (1) Rough-winged Swallow lacks breastband, has a *dingy throat.* Bank Swallow is a colonial nester, Rough-wing rather solitary. (2) See young Tree Swallow.
　　Voice: A dry trilled chitter or rattle, *brrt* or *tri-tri-tri.*
　　Where found: Breeds widely in N. Hemisphere. Winters in S. America, Africa, s. Asia. **West:** *Breeds* from n.-c. Alaska, s. Yukon, nw. Mackenzie, c. Saskatchewan south locally to s. California, w. Nevada, n. Utah, s.-c. New Mexico, w. Texas. *Migrant* through sw. U.S. **Habitat:** Usually near water; over fields, marshes, streams, lakes. **Nest:** Of grass, in hole in sand or clay bank; in colony. Eggs (4–5; 8) white.

ROUGH-WINGED SWALLOW　　　　　　　　**Pl. 43**
Stelgidopteryx ruficollis　5–5¾
　　Field marks: A *brown-backed* swallow, lighter brown than Bank Swallow; *no breastband;* note the *dusky throat.* Flight unlike Bank Swallow's, more like Barn Swallow's; direct, with wings folded back at end of stroke.
　　Similar species: (1) Bank Swallow has dark breastband; nests colonially. (2) See young Tree Swallow (late summer).
　　Voice: A harsh *trrit,* rougher than Bank Swallow's.
　　Where found: S. Canada to Argentina. Winters mostly south of U.S. **West:** *Breeds* from s. B.C., s. Alberta, s. Saskatchewan throughout w. U.S. A few winter in s. California. **Habitat:** Near streams, lakes, washes. **Nest:** In hole in bank, crevice in rocks, masonry, roadcut. Not colonial. Eggs (4–8) white.

BARN SWALLOW　*Hirundo rustica*　5¾–7¾　　**Pl. 43**
　　Field marks: The only U.S. swallow that is truly *swallow-tailed;* the only one with *white tail spots.* Blue-black above, cinnamon-buff below with darker throat. Flight direct, close to ground; wing-tips pulled back at end of stroke; not much gliding.
　　Voice: A soft *vit* or *kvik-kvik, vit-vit.* About nest, a harsh irritated *ee-tee* or *keet.* Song, a long musical twitter interspersed with gutturals.
　　Where found: Breeds widely in N. Hemisphere. Winters in S. America, Africa, s. Asia. **West:** *Breeds* from n.-c. Alaska, s. Yukon, w. Mackenzie, nw. Saskatchewan south through w. U.S. **Habitat:** Open or semiwooded country, farms, ranches, fields, marshes, lakes; usually near habitation. **Nest:** An open mud cup lined with feathers; under bridge, on beam of barn or in building; rarely in cliff ledge. Eggs (4–6; 9) speckled.

CLIFF SWALLOW *Petrochelidon pyrrhonota* 5-6 **Pl. 43**
  Field marks: Note the *rusty* or *buffy* rump. Overhead, the bird appears *square-tailed* with a *dark* throat patch. Glides in a long ellipse, ending each glide with a much steeper climb than other swallows ("like a roller coaster" — C. H. Blake).
  Similar species: (1) In Edwards Plateau, and near Carlsbad Caverns, New Mexico, see Cave Swallow. (2) Barn Swallow builds open nest *usually,* but not always, *inside* barn; when nesting on barns, Cliff Swallow (colonial) builds mud jug under eaves.
  Voice: A low *chur.* Alarm note, *keer.* Song, creaking notes and guttural gratings; harsher than Barn Swallow's song.
  Where found: Alaska, Canada to c. Mexico. Winters in Brazil, Chile, Argentina. **West:** *Breeds* from c. Alaska, c. Yukon, c. Mackenzie, c. Saskatchewan south through w. U.S. **Habitat:** Open to semiwooded country, farms, cliffs, canyons, rivers, lakes. **Nest:** A gourdlike jug of mud under bridge, eaves of building or on cliff face; in colony. Eggs (4-6) spotted.

CAVE SWALLOW *Petrochelidon fulva* 5-6 **Pl. 43**
(Coahuila Cliff Swallow)
  Field marks: Similar to Cliff Swallow (rusty rump) but throat and cheeks *pale* or *buffy,* forehead *dark chestnut.*
  Similar species: Cliff Swallow has face colors reversed; forehead patch pale, throat and cheeks dark chestnut. Very locally in w. Texas (Big Bend) and se. Arizona, a race of the Cliff Swallow, *P. pyrrhonata minima* (Mexican Cliff Swallow), occurs in which the forehead is often dark on young birds. Such birds would be dark on *both* forehead and throat.
  Voice: A clear *weet* or *cheweet;* a loud accented *chu, chu.* Song, "a series of squeaks blending into a complex melodic warble; ending in double-toned notes" (Selander and Baker).
  Where found: Se. New Mexico, s.-c. Texas, ne. and s. Mexico, Yucatan, W. Indies. Winter range unknown. **West:** Known to nest in 5 limestone caves in se. New Mexico (near Carlsbad Caverns) and about 16 caves in s. edge of Edwards Plateau, Texas (w. Kerr, Edwards, n. Uvalde, n. Kinney, e. Valverde Cos.). Colonial. **Nest:** An open cup of mud, straw, in cave or sinkhole. Eggs (2-5) speckled.

PURPLE MARTIN *Progne subis* 7¼-8½ **Pl. 43**
  Field marks: The largest N. American swallow. The male is uniformly blue-black *above and below.* No other N. American swallow is black-bellied. Female light-bellied; throat and breast grayish, often a faint collar around neck. Glides in circles, alternating quick flaps and glides; spreads tail often.
  Similar species: (1) Tree Swallow is much smaller than female Martin; immaculate white, not gray on underparts. (2) Starling in flight (triangular wings) may suggest Martin.

Voice: Throaty and rich *tchew-wew,* etc., or *pew, pew.* Song, gurgling, running to a succession of low rich gutturals.
Where found: S. Canada to n. Mexico, Gulf states. Winters in S. America. **West:** *Breeds* from sw. B.C. south (mainly w. of Cascade-Sierra divide) to s. California. Also locally in Rockies, Great Plains from ne. B.C., c. Alberta, c. Saskatchewan south to s. Arizona, s. New Mexico, Texas panhandle. Absent from most of Great Basin. *Accidental,* Alaska. **Habitat:** Open or lumbered forests, towns, farms, saguaro deserts. Wide-ranging in migration. **Nest:** In tree hollow, building, martin house, woodpecker hole in saguaro. Eggs (3–5; 8) white.

Jays, Magpies, and Crows: Corvidae

LARGE passerine birds — longish, powerful bills with nostrils usually covered by forward-pointing bristles. Crows and ravens are very large, black. Magpies have long tails. Jays are usually colorful (blue, green). Sexes look alike. **Food:** Omnivorous. **Range:** Nearly cosmopolitan except some islands, polar regions. **No. of species:** World, 100; West, 14 (+1 accidental; +1 in Hawaii).

GRAY JAY *Perisoreus canadensis* 10–13　　　　**Pl. 44**
(including Canada Jay, Oregon Jay)
　　Field marks: The only *gray* jay in N. America. A large, fluffy, gray bird of the cool conifer forests; larger than a Robin, with a *black* patch across back of head, and a *white forehead* (or crown); suggests a huge, overgrown chickadee. Juvenal birds (1st summer) are *dark slate-colored,* almost blackish (the only mark is a faint white "whisker").
　　Voice: A soft *whee-ah;* also many other notes, some harsh.
　　Where found: Boreal forests of N. America. **West:** *Resident* from tree limit in Alaska, n. Canada south through boreal forests of w. Canada; through Pacific states to n. California (not Sierra); in Rocky Mt. region to Arizona, n. New Mexico; also Black Hills. **Habitat:** Coniferous forests. **Nest:** A twiggy, feather-lined bowl; usually in conifer. Eggs (3–5) greenish gray, spotted.

BLUE JAY *Cyanocitta cristata* 11–12½　　　　**Pl. 44**
　　Field marks: A large *bright blue* bird with a *crest;* white spots in wings and tail; pale gray underparts; black "necklace."
　　Similar species: (1) Steller's Jay, only other U.S. jay with a crest, lacks white spots. (2) Scrub and (3) Mexican Jays lack crests and white spots. (4) See Belted Kingfisher (p. 137).
　　Voice: A harsh slurring *jeeah;* other notes, some musical.

Where found: S. Canada, east of Rockies to Gulf states. **West:** Partially *resident* across c. Alberta, c. Saskatchewan; also on Great Plains west to edge of Rockies in c. Wyoming, c. Colorado, Texas panhandle. *Casual,* e. Washington, Idaho, New Mexico. **Habitat:** Woodlands, groves, towns. **Nest:** A bowl of twigs in tree. Eggs (3–5; 7) variable, spotted.

STELLER'S JAY *Cyanocitta stelleri* 12–13½   **Pl. 44**
    Field marks: Between Rockies and Pacific, the only jay with a crest. A *large dark black and blue bird with a long crest.* Foreparts blackish; rear parts (wings, tail, belly) deep blue.
    Similar species: (1) Blue Jay (east of Rockies) has white spots in wings and tail. (2) Scrub and (3) Mexican Jays are paler, lack crests, prefer oaks, scrub (Steller's prefers conifers).
    Voice: A loud *shook-shook-shook* or *shack-shack-shack* or *wheck — wek — wek — wek — wek* or *kwesh kwesh kwesh;* many other notes. Frequently mimics Red-tailed Hawk, Golden Eagle.
    Where found: *Resident* from s. Alaska, w. and s. B.C., sw. Alberta south through conifer regions of Pacific states and through mts. of w. U.S. to Nicaragua. *Accidental,* Saskatchewan. **Habitat:** Conifer and pine-oak forests. **Nest:** A twiggy, rootlet-lined bowl in conifer. Eggs (3–5) greenish, spotted.

SCRUB JAY *Aphelocoma coerulescens* 11–13   **Pl. 44**
(California Jay; including Santa Cruz Jay)
    Field marks: Look for this *crestless* jay in the oaks. Head, wings, and tail *blue;* back pale brownish. Underparts pale gray; dark band of short streaks across breast (variable). In flight, often pitches down slopes in long shallow curves.
    Similar species: (1) Steller's Jay has crest, black foreparts; prefers conifers. (2) On mts. near border see Mexican Jay.
    Voice: Rough rasping notes: *kwesh . . . kwesh.* Also a harsh *check-check-check-check* and a rasping *shreek* or *shrink.*
    Where found: W. U.S. to s. Mexico. Also c. Florida. **West:** *Resident* from sw. Washington, w. and s. Oregon, extreme s. Idaho, s. Wyoming south locally throughout w. U.S., west of Plains. **Habitat:** Foothills, oaks, oak-chaparral, brush, river woods, piñon, junipers. **Nest:** A twiggy bowl in bush or low tree. Eggs (3–6) reddish or green, spotted.

MEXICAN JAY *Aphelocoma ultramarina* 11½–13   **Pl. 44**
(Arizona Jay)
    Field marks: A blue jay without a crest. Resembles Scrub Jay but fluffier; both upper parts and underparts more *uniform;* back grayer. Lacks the dusky "necklace" across the breast which usually gives the Scrub Jay its whiter-throated look. Also lacks the narrow whitish line over eye. Voice very different.

Voice: A rough, querulous *wink? wink?* or *zhenk?*
Where found: *Resident* from mts. of c. and se. Arizona, sw. New Mexico, w. Texas (Chisos Mts.) to c. Mexico. **Habitat:** Open oak forests (Arizona); oak-pine (w. Texas). **Nest:** A twiggy bowl in oak, sometimes pine. Eggs (4–5; 7) green, spotted (w. Texas) or unspotted (Arizona).

GREEN JAY   *Cyanocorax yncas*   10–12   **Pl. 44**
    Field marks: The only *green* jay in U.S. Throat patch *black;* top of head bright blue, sides of tail yellow.
    Voice: A rapid *cheh cheh cheh cheh;* also a slower *cleep, cleep, cleep,* etc.; a dry throaty rattle; also other calls.
    Where found: S. Texas to n. Honduras; also Venezuela to n. Bolivia. In U.S., *resident* only in s. tip of Texas north to Norias and upriver to Laredo. A small colony at San Antonio. **Habitat:** Brush, woodlands. **Nest:** A twiggy bowl in thicket or small tree. Eggs (3–5) spotted.

BLACK-BILLED MAGPIE   *Pica pica*   17½–22; tail 9½–12
(American Magpie)   **Pl. 44**
    Field marks: Magpies are the only large *black and white* land birds in N. America with long *wedge-shaped* tails. In flight, the iridescent greenish-black tail streams behind; large white patches flash in the wings. Bill black in this species.
    Similar species: Yellow-billed Magpie has yellow bill.
    Voice: A rapid harsh *queg queg queg queg.* Also a nasal querulous *maag?* or *aag-aag?*
    Where found: Eurasia, w. N. America. **West:** *Resident* from sw. and c. coastal Alaska, s. Yukon, c. Alberta, Saskatchewan south (east of Cascade-Sierra divide) to e.-c. California, s.-c. Nevada, se. Utah, n. New Mexico, w. Kansas. *Casual,* w. of Cascade-Sierra, s. California, n. Arizona, w. Texas. **Habitat:** Foothills, ranches, sagebrush, river thickets, shelter belts, prairie brush; in Alaska, coastal country. **Nest:** A very large domed mass of sticks with entrance on each side; in tree or bush; often in scattered colony. Eggs (6–9; 13) greenish, blotched.

YELLOW-BILLED MAGPIE   **Pl. 44**
Pica nuttalli   16–18; tail 9½–10¼
    Field marks: Similar to Black-billed Magpie, but bill *yellow.* Has a touch of bare yellow skin behind eye.
    Voice: Similar to Black-billed Magpie's *maag?* etc.
    Where found: *Resident* in California, chiefly in Sacramento and San Joaquin Valleys and adjacent low foothills; also valleys of Coast Ranges from San Francisco Bay to Santa Barbara Co. **Habitat:** Stream groves, scattered oaks, ranches, farms. **Nest:** Like Black-bill's; in loose colony. Eggs (5–8) olive, spotted.

COMMON RAVEN *Corvus corax* 21½–27 **below**
Field marks: Note the wedge-shaped tail. Much larger than Common Crow. Hawklike, it alternates flapping with soaring. It soars on flat wings; the Crow with wings "bent upward." When it is perched, not too distant, note the "goiter" (shaggy throat feathers) and heavier "Roman nose" effect of bill.
Similar species: See White-necked Raven (size of Crow).
Voice: A croaking *cr-r-ruck* or *prruk;* a metallic *tok.*
Where found: Widespread in N. America (Arctic to Nicaragua); Eurasia, Africa. **West:** *Resident* from Aleutians, n. Alaska, arctic Canada south throughout w. N. America; in Canada, east across boreal forests; in w. U.S. east to e. foothills of Rockies.
Habitat: Mts., deserts, canyons, coastal cliffs, boreal forests.
Nest: A large mass of sticks, bones, wool on cliff, sometimes in tree. Eggs (4–7) greenish, spotted.

SILHOUETTES OF CROW AND RAVEN

WHITE-NECKED RAVEN *Corvus cryptoleucus* 19–21
Field marks: A small raven near size of Common Crow. Within the range of the White-neck, the larger Common Raven is most often seen in mts. and canyons; the White-neck prefers mesquite flats, yucca deserts. This species flies with the typical flat-winged glide of the raven; has a somewhat wedge-shaped tail. The white feather bases on neck and breast show only when the feathers are ruffled. Often gregarious.
Similar species: (1) See Common Raven. (2) Common Crow

overlaps range of White-neck locally (Texas panhandle, adjacent areas), but favors less arid situations, rivers, etc.
Voice: A hoarse *kraak,* flatter and higher than Common Raven's.
Where found: *Resident* in sw. U.S. from se. Arizona, s. New Mexico, se. Colorado south to c. Mexico; east to s.-c. Nebraska, w. Kansas, w. Texas (Panhandle, Edwards Plateau). **Habitat:** Mainly arid country, rangeland, plains, deserts. **Nest:** A loose bowl of sticks (even wire!) in tree, mesquite, yucca, telegraph pole, etc. Eggs (4–7) greenish, blotched and lined.

COMMON CROW *Corvus brachyrhynchos* 17–21   **p. 165**
Field marks: This large chunky, ebony-hued bird needs little description. No other large birds save the ravens are so *completely* black. Glossed with purplish in strong sunlight. Bill and feet strong and black. Often gregarious.
Similar species: See (1) White-necked Raven, which is often called "crow," (2) Common Raven, (3) Northwestern Crow.
Voice: A loud *caw* or *cah* or *kahr,* easily imitated.
Where found: Canada to s. U.S. **West:** *Breeds* from c. B.C., sw. Mackenzie, n. Saskatchewan south to n. Baja California, c. Arizona, c. New Mexico, nw. and c. Texas (Panhandle and Edwards Plateau). *Winters* mainly south of Canada. **Habitat:** Woodlands, farmlands, river groves, shores. **Nest:** A well-made bowl of sticks in tree. Eggs (4–6; 9) greenish, spotted.

NORTHWESTERN CROW *Corvus caurinus* 16–17
Field marks: This small beachcombing crow of the Northwest reminds one of the Fish Crow of the Atlantic Coast. Smaller than the Common Crow, it has a quicker wingbeat, different voice. Replaces Common Crow on narrow nw. coast strip.
Voice: Usually more resonant than Common Crow's; *khaaa* or *khaaw.* Also, *cowp-cowp-cowp.*
Where found: *Resident* from s. Alaska (Kodiak, Sitka) south along coasts of B.C., Vancouver I., Puget Sound, w. Washington; occasionally up Columbia River to Portland. **Habitat:** Near tidewater, shores. **Nest:** Similar to Common Crow's.

PIÑON JAY *Gymnorhinus cyanocephala* 9–11¾   **Pl. 44**
Field marks: In appearance and actions like a small *dull blue* crow, hardly larger than a Robin, with a long sharp bill. Easily told from Scrub Jay by its short tail, uniform blue coloration, and crowlike flight; from Steller's Jay by lack of crest (Steller's Jay depresses crest when flying). Often in large noisy flocks; walks about on ground like crows.
Voice: A high nasal cawing, *kaa-eh, karn-eh* (descending inflection); has mewing effect. Jaylike notes; chattering.
Where found: *Resident* from c. Oregon, s. Idaho, e.-c. Montana,

Black Hills south through e. California (east of Sierra) to n. Baja
California, s. Nevada, c. Arizona, c. New Mexico, w. Oklahoma.
Wanders widely, reaching s.-c. Washington, Idaho, Montana,
s. California, n. Chihuahua and w. edge of Great Plains. Gregarious. **Habitat:** Piñon pines, junipers ("cedars"); ranges into
sage. **Nest:** A bowl of twigs in piñon, juniper, scrub oak; in
colony. Eggs (3–4; 5) speckled.

CLARK'S NUTCRACKER   **Pl. 11**
Nucifraga columbiana   12–13
    Field marks: Built like a small crow, with a *light gray* body and
    large *white patches* in black wings and tail. Should be confused
    with no other bird of high mts. if patches are seen.
    Similar species: Gray Jay does not have white patches.
    Voice: A flat grating caw, *khaaa* or *khraa.*
    Where found: *Resident* from c. B.C., sw. Alberta south through
    high Cascades, Sierra to mts. of n. Baja California; in Great
    Basin ranges, Rockies, Black Hills to e. Arizona, w. New Mexico.
    Wanders to Puget Sound, c. Alaska, s. Yukon, w. parts of Great
    Plains, w. California, s. Arizona, w. Texas, n. Nuevo León.
    Habitat: High mts.; conifers near tree line. **Nest:** A deep bowl
    of twigs in conifer. Eggs (2–4; 6) green, spotted.

Titmice, Verdins, and Bushtits:
Paridae

SMALL, plump, small-billed birds, very acrobatic when feeding.
Sexes usually alike. Often roam in little bands. **Food:** Insects;
also seeds, acorn mast, berries. **Range:** Widespread in N. America,
Eurasia, Africa. **No. of species:** World, 64; West, 12 (+1 marginal;
+1 introduced in Hawaii).

BLACK-CAPPED CHICKADEE   **Pl. 45**
Parus atricapillus   4¾–5¾
    Field marks: The various chickadees are distinctively patterned
    with dark caps, black bibs, white cheeks. These tame acrobats
    are smaller than most sparrows. This species can be separated
    from other widespread w. chickadees by the *solid black cap* in
    conjunction with the *gray back.* Sides buffy.
    Similar species: (1) Mountain Chickadee has white eyebrow-
    stripe. (2) Chestnut-backed Chickadee has rusty back. (3)
    Carolina Chickadee (very similar) approaches 100° in Texas.
    See Texas *Field Guide.* (4) See also other Chickadees.
    Voice: A clearly enunciated *chick-a-dee-dee-dee* or *dee-dee-dee.*
    In spring a clear whistle: *fee-bee,* 1st note higher.
    Where found: Alaska, Canada, n. half of U.S. **West:** *Resident*

from c. Alaska, s. Mackenzie to nw. California, e. Oregon, ne. Nevada, c. Utah, n. New Mexico, w. Kansas. **Habitat:** Mixed and deciduous woods, willow thickets, groves. **Nest:** A fur-lined hole in rotting stub or tree. Eggs (4–9; 13) speckled.

MEXICAN CHICKADEE   *Parus sclateri* 5   **Pl. 45**
   Field marks: Similar to Black-capped Chickadee, but *black of throat more extensive,* spreading across upper breast. Note the *dark gray sides.* The only Chickadee in its U.S. range.
   Voice: Nasal and husky for a chickadee. A low *dzay-dzeee.*
   Where found: *Resident* from se. Arizona (Chiricahua Mts.), sw. New Mexico (Animas Mts.) to Oaxaca. **Habitat:** Conifers, pine-oak forest. **Nest:** In hole in tree. Eggs (6) dotted.

MOUNTAIN CHICKADEE   *Parus gambeli* 5–5¾   **Pl. 45**
   Field marks: Similar to Black-capped Chickadee but black of cap interrupted by *white line over each eye.* Sides lack buff.
   Voice: Song, 3 high clear whistled notes, *fee-bee-bee,* 1st note highest, next 2 on same pitch; or 3–4 notes going down the scale in halftones. "Chickadee" notes huskier than Black-cap's: *tsick-a-zee-zee-zee.*
   Similar species: Other chickadees have solid caps.
   Where found: *Resident* from nw. B.C., sw. Alberta to n. Baja California, se. Arizona, s. New Mexico, w. Texas (Guadalupe Mts.). **Habitat:** Mt. forests, conifers; in winter to lower levels. **Nest:** In tree cavity. Eggs (7–9; 12) white or dotted.

GRAY-HEADED CHICKADEE   *Parus cinctus* 5½   **Pl. 45**
   Field marks: This subarctic chickadee can be separated from the Boreal Chickadee by its dark gray cap, whiter cheeks. It also lacks the rich brown flanks; has a "dusty" appearance.
   Similar species: Boreal Chickadee is much browner, smaller.
   Voice: A peevish *dee-deer* or *chee-ee* (O. Murie).
   Where found: Tree limit; n. Eurasia, nw. N. America. **West:** *Resident* at tree limit in Alaska (south to Yukon River), n. Yukon, nw. Mackenzie. **Habitat:** Spruce, birch, willow thickets. **Nest:** In hole in tree, stub. Eggs (7–9) spotted.

BOREAL CHICKADEE   *Parus hudsonicus* 5–5½   **Pl. 45**
(Brown-capped Chickadee, Columbian Chickadee)
   Field marks: Note the *dull brown* cap, rich brown flanks. The small size, black bib, whitish cheeks, and tiny bill mark it as a chickadee, but the general color is *brown* rather than gray.
   Similar species: (1) Black-capped Chickadee is grayer, has a *black* cap. (2) In far North see Gray-headed Chickadee.
   Voice: Notes slower, more drawling than lively *chick-a-dee-dee-dee* of Black-cap; instead, a wheezy *chick-che-day-day.*
   Where found: Boreal forests of Alaska, Canada, n. New England.

West: *Resident* from tree limit south to extreme n.-c. and ne. Washington, nw. Montana and s. edge of boreal forests in Alberta, Saskatchewan. **Habitat:** Coniferous forest. **Nest:** In hole in tree or stub. Eggs (5–9) dotted.

CHESTNUT-BACKED CHICKADEE   Pl. 45
Parus rufescens   4½–5
Field marks: The cap, bib, and white cheeks indicate it as a chickadee; the *chestnut back* as this species. Sides chestnut.
Voice: Hoarser than Black-cap's: *tsick-i-see-see* or *zhee-che-che*. Also a harsh *zee* or *zze-zze*. No whistled song.
Where found: *Resident* in coast belt from s. Alaska to c. California (San Luis Obispo Co.); locally in mts. of se. B.C., n. Idaho, nw. Montana, e. Washington, e. Oregon, n. and c.-c. California. **Habitat:** Moist conifer forests; adjacent oaks, shade trees. **Nest:** In hole in tree, stub. Eggs (5–7; 9) dotted.

BLACK-CRESTED TITMOUSE   Pl. 45
Parus atricristatus   5–6
Field marks: A small gray bird with a *slender black crest;* underparts white, sides rusty. Light spot above bill. Females may have some gray in crest. Young may be gray-crested.
Similar species: (1) Young birds almost indistinguishable from Plain Titmouse. (2) East of our area in Texas (Ft. Worth, Austin, Victoria) hybridizes with Tufted Titmouse (black spot above bill). See Texas or Eastern *Field Guide.*
Voice: Chickadee-like notes. Song, a whistled *peter peter peter peter* or *hear hear hear hear.* Varied.
Where found: Texas (east at least to Graham, Ranger, Killeen, Austin, Rockport); ne. Mexico. **West:** *Resident* from Texas panhandle (canyons) to Rio Grande; west locally to Trans-Pecos. **Habitat:** Oak woods, cedars, groves, towns. **Nest:** In hole in tree, post, bird box. Eggs (4–7; 12) spotted.

PLAIN TITMOUSE   *Parus inornatus* 5–5½   Pl. 45
Field marks: The birds bearing the name "titmouse" are our only *small* gray-backed birds with pointed crests (female Phainopepla is larger). This, the sole titmouse in most of the West, is the only one without distinctive markings.
Similar species: "Plain Titmice" seen in w. Texas (Big Bend, Edwards Plateau) may be young Black-crested Titmice, which have short gray crests and are virtually indistinguishable.
Voice: *Tchick-a-dee-dee,* similar to notes of chickadee. Song, a whistled *weety weety weety* or *tee-wit tee-wit tee-wit.*
Where found: *Resident* from s. Oregon, s. Idaho, sw. Wyoming, s.-c. Colorado south to n. Baja California, c. and se. Arizona, s. New Mexico; in winter to extreme w. Texas. **Habitat:** Oak woods, piñon, juniper; locally river woods, shade trees. **Nest:** In hole in tree. Eggs (6–9; 12) white or lightly dotted.

BRIDLED TITMOUSE *Parus wollweberi* 4½–5   **Pl. 45**
Field marks: The crest and black and white *"bridled"* face
identify this small gray bird of the desert mts.
Voice: Notes similar to those of other titmice and chickadees
but higher. Song, a repeated 2-syllabled phrase.
Where found: *Resident* from mts. of se. Arizona, sw. New Mexico
to s. Mexico. **Habitat:** Oak and sycamore canyons, pine-oak
woods. **Nest:** In hole in oak. Eggs (5–7) white.

VERDIN *Auriparus flaviceps* 4–4½   **Pl. 45**
Field marks: A very small gray bird with a *yellowish head;* bend
of wing *rufous* (not always visible). Immature lacks the yellow
and rusty; might be mistaken for Bushtit (see below).
Similar species: (1) Common Bushtit is longer-tailed than immature Verdin; does not usually live in desert valleys; prefers oak
slopes. (2) See Beardless Flycatcher (p. 157).
Voice: An insistent *see-lip.* A rapid chipping. Song, *tsee, seesee.*
Where found: *Resident* from se. California, s. Nevada, sw. Utah,
w. and s. Arizona, c. New Mexico, w. and s. Texas to n. and w.
Mexico. **Habitat:** Brushy desert valleys, mesquite, semiarid
savannahs. **Nest:** A ball or thorny twigs (hole on side) in bush
or low tree. Eggs (3–5) greenish, dotted.

COMMON BUSHTIT *Psaltriparus minimus* 3¾–4¼ **Pl. 45**
Field marks: Very small plain birds that move from bush to
tree in straggling flocks, constantly conversing in light gentle
notes. The nondescript look, gray back, pale underparts,
brownish cheeks, stubby bill, and longish tail identify them.
Females are said to have light eyes, males dark. The race known
as the Lead-colored Bushtit, *P. m. plumbeus* (Rocky Mts., Great
Basin), differs from other bushtits in having a gray crown.
Similar species: (1) Males of Black-eared Bushtit (mts. of sw.
New Mexico, w. Texas) have black or black-flecked cheeks. A
light-cheeked bird with dark eyes would most likely be a male
Common Bushtit. Females of the two are usually indistinguish-
able. (2) See also Blue-gray Gnatcatcher (p. 186).
Voice: Insistent light *tsit's, lisp's,* and *clenk's.*
Where found: *Resident* from sw. B.C. south along coast to s.
Baja California; in interior from s.-c. Washington, s. Idaho,
n.-c. Utah, c. Colorado, Texas panhandle to n. Mexico. Wanders
a bit in winter. *Casual,* Wyoming. **Habitat:** Oak scrub, chaparral, broad-leaved and mixed woods, piñons, junipers. **Nest:** A
long woven pouch in bush, tree. Eggs (5–7; 15) white.

BLACK-EARED BUSHTIT *Psaltriparus melanotis* 4–4½
(Lloyd's Bushtit)   **Pl. 45**
Field marks: Similar to Common Bushtit but male has *black or
black-flecked* cheeks. Female, similar to female Common Bushtit

but face may be grayer, occasionally with flecks of black; ordinarily not distinguishable. More restricted to higher altitudes of mts. than Common Bushtit.
Voice: Similar to Common Bushtit's.
Where found: *Resident* from sw. New Mexico (San Luis Mts.), w. Texas (Davis, Chisos Mts.) to Guatemala. **Habitat:** Oaks, junipers, pines. **Nest:** Similar to Common Bushtit's; shorter.

Nuthatches: Sittidae

SMALL, stout, tree-climbers with strong woodpecker-like bills, powerful feet. Stubby tails not braced woodpecker-like in climbing. The only tree-climbers that habitually go down tree trunks headfirst. Sexes similar. **Food:** Bark insects; seeds, nuts; attracted by suet. **Range:** Mostly N. Hemisphere. **No. of species:** World, 29 (Mayr-Amadon), 17 (Van Tyne-Berger); West, 3.

WHITE-BREASTED NUTHATCH   Pl. 45
Sitta carolinensis 5–6
   Field marks: Nuthatches climb down trees headfirst. This species is known by its black cap and beady black eye on a white face. Chestnut under tail coverts.
   Similar species: (1) Red-breasted Nuthatch (black eye-stripe). (2) Pygmy Nuthatch (brown cap). (3) Chickadees (black bibs).
   Voice: Song, a series of low, nasal, whistled notes on same pitch: *whi, whi, whi, whi, whi, whi, whi* or *who, who, who,* etc. Note, a nasal *yank;* also a nasal *tootoo.*
   Where found: S. Canada to s. Mexico. **West:** *Resident* from s. B.C., Montana, se. Saskatchewan south to mts. of Mexico. Wanders in winter. Absent in treeless parts of Great Plains, deserts. *Casual,* Alberta. **Habitat:** Mixed forests, groves, river woods. **Nest:** In hole in tree. Eggs (5–9) spotted.

RED-BREASTED NUTHATCH   Pl. 45
Sitta canadensis 4½–4¾
   Field marks: Our only nuthatch with a *broad black* line through the eye and a white line over it. Small; rusty below.
   Similar species: White-breast has no bold eye-stripes.
   Voice: Call higher, more nasal than that of White-breast: *ank* or *enk,* like a "baby" nuthatch or a "tiny tin horn."
   Where found: Se. Alaska, Canada, w. U.S., ne. U.S. Winters to s. U.S. **West:** *Breeds* from se. Alaska, s. Yukon east across forests of Canada; south on coast to c. California; in mts. to s. California, se. Arizona, Colorado, Black Hills. *Winters* irregularly to s. Arizona, s. New Mexico, Texas. **Habitat:** Conifer forests; in winter, also other trees. **Nest:** In hole in dead conifer, stub; entrance smeared with pitch. Eggs (4–7) spotted.

PYGMY NUTHATCH *Sitta pygmaea* 3¾–4½ **Pl. 45**
Field marks: A very small pine-loving nuthatch with a *gray-brown cap coming down to the eye*. A whitish spot on nape.
Voice: A piping *kit-kit — kit* or *pip-pip* and a high *ki — dee;* incessant, sometimes becoming an excited chatter.
Where found: *Resident* from s. B.C., n. Idaho, Montana, Black Hills south through w. U.S. mainly in yellow-pine belt of mts. to c. Mexico. Also coastal pines in c. California. Habitat: Yellow pines, other pines, douglasfir. Nest: In hole in stub, conifer. Eggs (6–9) spotted.

Creepers: Certhiidae

SMALL, slender stiff-tailed birds with slender, slightly curved bills with which they probe the bark of trees. **Food:** Bark insects. **Range:** Widespread in cooler parts of N. Hemisphere. **No. of species:** World, 6; West, 1.

BROWN CREEPER *Certhia familiaris* 5–5¾ **Pl. 45**
Field marks: A slim, well-camouflaged, brown-backed tree-climber. Much smaller than a House Sparrow, with a slender decurved bill and a stiff tail, braced when climbing. It ascends a tree spirally, then flies to the base of the next tree.
Voice: Note, a single high thin *seee,* similar to quick trebled note (*see-see-see*) of Golden-crowned Kinglet. Song, a thin sibilant *see-ti-wee-tu-wee* or *see-see-see-sisi-see.*
Where found: Eurasia; s. Alaska, Canada to Nicaragua. In East to s. mts.; winters to Gulf states. West: Mainly *resident* from s.-c. Alaska, B.C., c. Alberta, c. Saskatchewan south on coast to c. California (Monterey Co.); in mts. to s. California, se. Arizona, sw. New Mexico, w. Texas (Guadalupe Mts.). *Irregular migrant* to lowlands. Habitat: Mature forest, groves. Nest: Behind strip of loose bark. Eggs (4–8) dotted.

Wrentits: Chamaeidae

THE WRENTIT is usually placed in a family of its own, but some authorities regard it as merely an isolated offshoot of the large Old World family of babblers (Timaliidae; 282 species). **Food:** Insects, berries. **Range:** Oregon to nw. Baja California. **No. of species:** World, 1; West, 1.

WRENTIT *Chamaea fasciata* 6–6½ **Pl. 45**
Field marks: Far more often heard than seen. The long, rounded, slightly cocked tail and *streaked brownish* breast are

good marks if this dark sparrow-sized bird can be seen as it slips through the brush. Eye *white*. Behavior wrenlike.

Similar species: Common Bushtit is smaller and grayer; usually travels in flocks; does not hide so persistently.

Voice: Song (heard throughout year), staccato ringing notes on one pitch; starting deliberately, running into a trill. *Yip — yip — yip-yip-yip-yip-ytr-tr-tr-tr-tr-tr-r-r-r-r-r* (H. Cogswell). Also a slower double-noted version. Note, a soft *prr*.

Where found: *Resident* of coastal Oregon, California (west of Sierra and sw. deserts), n. Baja California. **Habitat:** Chaparral, brush, parks, garden shrubs. **Nest:** A compact cup in low bush. Eggs (3–5) pale blue.

DIPPER

Dippers: Cinclidae

PLUMP, stub-tailed birds; resemble large wrens. Solitary. Dive, swim under water; walk on bottom. **Food:** Insects, aquatic invertebrates, small fishes. **Range:** Eurasia, w. N. America, w. S. America (Andes). **No. of species:** World, 5; West, 1.

DIPPER (WATER OUZEL) *Cinclus mexicanus* 7–8½ **above**
Field marks: A chunky *slate-colored* bird of rushing mt. streams. Shaped like a large wren (size of a large thrush) with a stubby tail. Legs pale, eyelids *white*. Note the bobbing motions, slaty color, flashing eyelid. Dives, submerges.
Voice: Note, a sharp *zeet* given singly, or repeated. Song clear

and ringing, Mockingbird-like in form (much repetition of notes), but higher, more wrenlike. Sings throughout year.
Where found:_Resident_ from Aleutians, n.-c. Alaska, c. Yukon, sw. Alberta, Black Hills south mainly in mts. to s. California, s. Nevada, se. Arizona, s. New Mexico. Also mts. of Mexico to w. Panama. **Habitat:** Fast-flowing streams in or near mts. Lower levels in winter. **Nest:** A bulky ball of moss (opening on side) on rock wall of stream. Eggs (3–6) white.

Wrens: Troglodytidae

SMALL, mainly brown birds, stumpy, with slender, slightly decurved bills; tails often cocked. Most are energetic; some are gifted songsters. **Food:** Insects, spiders. **Range:** New World; especially Middle and S. America; only 1 species (Winter Wren) in Eurasia. **No. of species:** World, 63; West, 10.

HOUSE WREN *Troglodytes aedon* 4½–5¼   **Pl. 46**
   Field marks: Recognized as a wren by its small stubby shape, energetic actions, tail-cocking habit; as this species by its gray-brown color and *lack of any very evident eye-stripe.*
   Similar species: See (1) Bewick's Wren and (2) Winter Wren.
   Voice: A rapid churring note; a harsh scold. Song, stuttering and gurgling; rising in a burst, falling at the end.
   Where found: S. Canada to Baja California, sw. U.S. and c. parts of e. U.S. Winters in s. U.S., Mexico. *West: Breeds* from s. B.C., n. Alberta, c. Saskatchewan to s. California, se. Arizona, s. New Mexico, w. Texas (Trans-Pecos). *Winters* from San Francisco Bay (a few), sw. U.S. south. **Habitat:** Thickets, open woods, brush, gardens, towns. **Nest:** In hole in tree, stub, bird box. Eggs (5–8; 12) pinkish, dotted.

BROWN-THROATED WREN *Troglodytes brunneicollis* 4¼–5
   Field marks: Although this bird was given full specific status in the 5th edition of the A.O.U. *Check-list,* some authorities now regard it as conspecific with the House Wren. It differs mainly in having a distinct buff eye-stripe, rustier back, buffier underparts, small spots on sides of breast.
   Voice: Basically like House Wren's; differs recognizably.
   Where found: *Resident* of mts. of se. Arizona (Rincon, Santa Rita, Huachuca, Chiricahua Mts.) to s. Mexico. **Habitat and Nest:** Similar to House Wren's. Eggs have redder dots.

WINTER WREN *Troglodytes troglodytes* 4–4½   **Pl. 46**
   Field marks: A very small round *dark* wren, smaller than House Wren; has a *much stubbier* tail, light line over the eye, and *brownish, heavily barred flanks;* often bobs and bows.

Similar species: House Wren is grayer; has longer tail.
Voice: Song, a rapid succession of high tinkling warbles, trills, long sustained; often ends on a *very high* light trill. Note, a hard *kip* or *kip kip;* suggests Song Sparrow's *chip.*
Where found: Northern parts of N. Hemisphere. In N. America winters to s. U.S. **West:** *Breeds* from Pribilofs, Aleutians, s. Alaska east across forests of Canada; south through Pacific states to c. California (coast and Sierra); in n. Rockies to nw. Wyoming. *Winters* from Alaska south through Pacific states and in interior from e. Washington, Idaho, Colorado to Arizona, New Mexico, w. Texas. **Habitat:** Coniferous forests, woodland underbrush; sea cliffs (Alaska). **Nest:** Of moss and twigs in exposed roots, crevice, rocks. Eggs (5–7) dotted.

BEWICK'S WREN *Thryomanes bewickii* 5–5½   **Pl. 46**
Field marks: Note the white eyebrow line and whitish tips of outer tail feathers (not always easy to see). The Bewick's Wren (pronounced *Buick's*) is dark brown above and has whitish underparts, whiter than in other U.S. wrens. It wobbles its rather long tail from side to side.
Similar species: (1) House Wren lacks white eye-stripe and white tail spots. Bewick's Wren sometimes nests in bird boxes, and to some people it is their "house" wren. (2) Rock Wren is grayer, with buffy tail-tips, finely streaked breast.
Voice: Song variable; high opening notes, followed by lower burry notes, ending on a thin trill; sometimes suggests Song Sparrow. Another rendering is *swee, swee, cheeeeeeee* (1st 2 notes high, last trilled). A rasping scold note.
Where found: Sw. B.C., s. Ontario through middle and w. U.S. to s.-c. Mexico. **West:** Mainly *resident* from Puget Sound, Nevada, Utah, sw. Wyoming, c. Colorado south. **Habitat:** Thickets, underbrush, piñon, juniper, chaparral, gardens. **Nest:** In hole, crevice, cranny, bird box. Eggs (4–7; 11) spotted.

CAROLINA WREN *Thryothorus ludovicianus* 5¼–6 **Pl. 46**
Field marks: A large, rusty wren, *rufous* above and buffy below, with a conspicuous *white stripe* over the eye.
Similar species: Bewick's Wren lacks the rusty look, has white tail corners (tail is longer).
Voice: A clear chanting whistle, *chirpity, chirpity, chirpity, chirpity, chirp* or *tea-kettle, tea-kettle, tea-kettle, tea.* Variable. Usually 3-syllabled (sometimes 2-syllabled).
Where found: S. Ontario, s. New England south through e. U.S. to ne. Mexico, Gulf states. **West:** *Resident* in c. Texas, barely west of 100° (Edwards Plateau, Del Rio). Rare visitor to Panhandle, s. Staked Plain. *Casual,* Colorado, New Mexico. **Habitat:** Thickets, streamside undergrowth. **Nest:** In hole, bird box, brushpile, cranny. Eggs (4–6; 8) spotted.

CACTUS WREN
Pl. 46
Campylorhynchus brunneicapillum   7–8¾

Field marks: A very large wren of arid country. Distinguished from other U.S. wrens by its much larger size and heavy spotting, which in adults gathers into a cluster on the upper breast. White stripe over the eye and white spots in outer tail.

Similar species: Sage Thrasher is more thrasher-like in appearance, grayer, *without* white stripings on back.

Voice: A monotonous *chuh-chuh-chuh-chuh,* etc., or *chug-chug-chug-chug-chug,* on one pitch, gaining rapidity; unbirdlike.

Where found: Sw. U.S. to c. Mexico. *Resident* in s. California, s. Nevada, sw. Utah, c. and s. Arizona, s. New Mexico, w. Texas.

Habitat: Cactus or yucca, mesquite, arid brush, deserts. **Nest:** Football-shaped, of straw (entrance in side); in cactus or thorny bush. Eggs (4–5; 7) dotted.

LONG-BILLED MARSH WREN
Pl. 46
Telmatodytes palustris   4¼–5½

Field marks: The wren of the marsh; brown, with a conspicuous white line over the eye; known from other *small* wrens with white eye-stripes by the white *stripes on back.*

Similar species: See Short-billed Marsh Wren (rare in West).

Voice: Song, reedy, gurgling, ending in a guttural rattle: *cut-cut-turrrrrrrrr-ur,* often at night. Note, a low *tsuck.*

Where found: S. Canada to n. Baja California, Gulf Coast. Winters to c. Mexico. **West:** *Breeds* from c. B.C., n. Alberta, c. Saskatchewan south locally to s. California, sw. Arizona, c. New Mexico, w. Texas. *Winters* in Pacific states and from n. Utah, Colorado south. **Habitat:** Marshes (tule, cattail, bulrush, brackish). **Nest:** Coconut-shaped (hole in side); lashed to stems in marsh. Eggs (3–7; 10) brown, dotted.

SHORT-BILLED MARSH WREN
Pl. 46
Cistothorus platensis   4–4½

Field marks: A stubby wren of wet meadows, *grassy* and sedgy marshes. Underparts very *buffy;* crown *streaked* with black.

Similar species: Long-bill has more contrastingly striped upper parts, conspicuous white line over eye, solid unstreaked crown, and, when tail is cocked, whitish under tail coverts.

Voice: Song, dry staccato chattering: *chap chap chap chap chap chap chap chapper-rrrrr.* Call note, *chap.*

Where found: S. Canada to c. U.S.; winters to Gulf states. Also local from Mexico to Tierra del Fuego. **West:** *Breeds* in c. and se. Saskatchewan. Rare or casual *migrant* in w. parts of Great Plains from Alberta to Texas panhandle. **Habitat:** Grassy marshes, sedge. **Nest:** A ball of grass in tussock; hole in side. Eggs (4–7; 10) white.

CAÑON WREN   *Catherpes mexicanus*   5½–5¾   **Pl. 46**
Field marks: Note the white bib. A rusty wren, with *dark reddish-brown belly*, contrasting with a *white breast and throat*.
Similar species: Rock Wren is gray, with lightly streaked breast, light belly.
Voice: A gushing cadence of clear curved notes tripping down the scale; sometimes picking up at the end: *te-you, te-you te-you tew tew tew tew* or *tee tee tee tee tew tew tew tew*.
Where found: *Resident* from c.-s. B.C., n. Idaho, s. Montana, sw. S. Dakota south through mts. of w. U.S. to s. Mexico. Absent in humid nw. coast belt north of San Francisco. Habitat: Cliffs, canyons, rockslides; stone buildings. Nest: A cup in crevice in rocks, building. Eggs (4–6) dotted.

ROCK WREN   *Salpinctes obsoletus*   5–6¼   **Pl. 46**
Field marks: A rather *gray* wren with *finely streaked* breast (streaks visible at close range). Shows conspicuous *light or buffy patches* in corners of ample tail.
Similar species: (1) Cañon Wren (only U.S. wren that shares same habitat) has dark belly, white throat. (2) Bewick's Wren (brushy places) has much darker back, unstreaked breast.
Voice: Song, a varied chant, *tew, tew, tew, tew* or *chr-wee, chr-wee, chr-wee* or *che-poo, che-poo, che-poo,* etc. Call, a loud dry trill on one pitch; also a clear *ti-keer*.
Where found: *Breeds* from c.-s. B.C., s. Alberta, sw. Saskatchewan, w. N. Dakota through w. U.S. (east roughly to 100°); south to Costa Rica. Very local in nw. coast belt. *Winters* from sw. U.S. south. Habitat: Plains to high mts.; rocky slopes, talus, rock dams, walls. Nest: In crevice in rocks, walls; often with path of rock chips. Eggs (5–8; 10) dotted.

Mockingbirds and Thrashers: Mimidae

"MIMIC-THRUSHES" are noted for their apparent powers of mimicry. Excellent songsters. Strong-legged; usually longer-tailed than true thrushes; bill usually more decurved. Food: Insects, fruits. Range: New World; most numerous in tropics. No. of species: World, 30; West, 10.

MOCKINGBIRD   *Mimus polyglottos*   9–11   **Pl. 47**
Field marks: Note the *large white patches* on wings and tail, conspicuous in flight. More slender than Robin, with long mobile tail. On ground, sometimes periodically raises wings above body, displaying patches.
Similar species: (1) Shrikes have black facial masks; show less white in wings, tail. (2) See Townsend's Solitaire (p. 185).

Voice: Song, a long continued succession of notes and phrases of great variety. The Mockingbird rapidly repeats each phrase, often a half-dozen times or more, before going on to the next. (Some thrashers repeat once; Catbird does not repeat.) Many e. Mockingbirds are excellent mimics; in the West, Mockingbirds are less versatile, mimicking relatively few species. Often sing at night in spring. Note, a loud *tchack;* also *tchair.*
Where found: S. Canada to s. Mexico, W. Indies. **West:** *Breeds* from California (c. coast and head of Sacramento Valley), n. Utah, se. Wyoming, sw. S. Dakota. Partially migratory in n. interior. *Casual* north to s. Canada. *Introduced* in Hawaii. **Habitat:** Towns, farms, ranches, roadsides, mesquite, brush, desert streamsides. **Nest:** A rootlet-lined cup in bush or dense tree. Eggs (3–6) blue-green, spotted.

CATBIRD   *Dumetella carolinensis*   8–9¼   **Pl. 47**
Field marks: Smaller and slimmer than Robin; dark *slaty-gray* with a *black* cap, blackish tail. *Chestnut* under tail coverts (seldom noticed). Flips tail jauntily. Skulks in undergrowth.
Similar species: The other dark all-gray songbirds — Dipper, young Starling, females of Cowbird, Rusty and Brewer's Black-birds — are shorter-tailed, lack black cap, chestnut crissum. *Note:* Brown Towhee in w. Texas is often called "catbird."
Voice: Catlike mewing note, distinctive. Song, a disjointed succession of notes and phrases, some musical. Notes not re-peated as in songs of Mockingbird and some thrashers.
Where found: S. Canada to Gulf states. Winters se. U.S. to Panama, W. Indies. **West:** *Breeds* from s. B.C. (west to Puget Sound), c. Alberta, c. Saskatchewan south to e. Oregon, e. Arizona, n. New Mexico, w. Oklahoma. *Casual,* California, Nevada, w. Texas. **Habitat:** Undergrowth, brush. **Nest:** A twiggy, rootlet-lined cup in bush or tangle. Eggs (3–5; 6) blue-green.

BROWN THRASHER   *Toxostoma rufum*   10½–12   **Pl. 47**
Field marks: A slim rufous bird. Slightly longer than Robin; bright *rufous* above, *heavily striped* below. Has *wing-bars,* a slightly curved bill, a long tail, yellow eyes.
Similar species: (1) See Long-billed Thrasher (s. Texas). (2) Thrushes are shorter-tailed; spotted, rather than striped, and lack wing-bars. Their eyes are brown.
Voice: Song, a succession of deliberate notes and short phrases, resembling Catbird's song, but more musical, each phrase usually in *pairs.* Note, a harsh *chack.*
Where found: East of Rockies; s. Canada to Gulf states. Winters in se. U.S. **West:** *Breeds* from se. Alberta, s.-c. Saskatchewan south through c. Montana, Wyoming, e. Colorado to Texas panhandle. A few *winter* at edge of our area in e. Colorado, c.

Texas. *Casual or accidental,* Oregon, Utah, California, Arizona, New Mexico. **Habitat:** Brushy places, thorny thickets. **Nest:** A twiggy cup in bush or tangle. Eggs (3–5) dotted.

LONG-BILLED THRASHER *Toxostoma longirostre* 10–12
(Sennett's Thrasher)   **Pl. 47**
   Field marks: Similar to Brown Thrasher but less rufous; breast streaks blackish rather than brown. Cheeks *grayer.* Bill noticeably longer, more decurved, all-black.
   Similar species: The other resident thrasher in the lower Rio Grande, the Curve-billed, is grayish, lacks black stripes.
   Voice: Notes and phrases of song similar to other thrashers'; some pairing as in Brown Thrasher. Call note, *too-ree.*
   Where found: S. Texas, e. and s.-c. Mexico. *Resident* in s. Texas north to Del Rio, San Antonio, Beeville, Corpus Christi; *casual* west to Big Springs. *Accidental,* Colorado. **Habitat:** Woodland undergrowth, mesquite. **Nest:** A twiggy cup in thorny bush, cactus, undergrowth. Eggs (2–5) dotted.

BENDIRE'S THRASHER *Toxostoma bendirei* 9–11 **Pl. 47**
   Field marks: Of the various drab desert thrashers this one may usually be known by its *shorter, more Robin-like bill* (lower mandible is quite straight). Breast faintly spotted (may not show in worn birds). Eye clear yellow.
   Similar species: Curve-billed Thrasher usually has a longer, more curved bill, more blurry spotting, more orange eye. *Caution:* Young Curve-bill may have bill like Bendire's.
   Voice: Song, a *continuous* clear, double-noted warble, not broken into phrases. Note, a soft *tirup.*
   Where found: *Breeds* locally from deserts of se. California, s. Nevada, s. Utah, n. Arizona, nw. New Mexico to Sinaloa. *Winters* from s. Arizona south. *Casual,* sw. California, Nevada, Colorado. **Habitat:** Desert, farmland, cholla, thorny bushes. **Nest:** In thorny bush. Eggs (3–4) pale greenish, spotted.

CURVE-BILLED THRASHER   **Pl. 47**
Toxostoma curvirostre 9½–11½
   Field marks: In the deserts there are several very similar thrashers, slim Robin-sized birds with decurved bills, long tails, gray-brown backs. This, the commonest species, can be told from the other 3 species that have *well-curved* bills by the *faintly spotted breast.* Some individuals have narrow white wing-bars. Eye, pale orange or reddish.
   Similar species: See Bendire's Thrasher (lighter breast spots).
   Voice: Note, a sharp liquid *whit-wheet!* like a human whistle of attention. Song, a musical series of notes and phrases, almost grosbeak-like in quality but faster. Not much repetition.
   Where found: *Resident* from s. Arizona, s. New Mexico, w. half

of Texas to s. Mexico. *Casual,* se. California, Nevada, w. Oklahoma. **Habitat:** Deserts, arid brush. **Nest:** A twiggy cup in cholla, bush. Eggs (2–4) pale blue-green, dotted.

CALIFORNIA THRASHER   Pl. 47
Toxostoma redivivum   11–13

Field marks: A large dull gray-brown thrasher, with *pale cinnamon* belly and under tail coverts; tail long, bill *sickle-*shaped. The eye is dark brown.

Similar species: This is the only thrasher of this type in California west of the desert divides (except very locally where Le Conte's and Crissal overlap). See Brown Towhee (p. 233).

Voice: Note, a dry *chak,* a sharp *g-leek.* Song, a long sustained series of notes and phrases, some musical, some harsh. Phrases may be *repeated* once or twice but not several times as in Mockingbird; more leisurely.

Where found: *Resident* in California (west of Sierra, deserts) from head of Sacramento Valley to n. Baja California. **Habitat:** Chaparral, foothills, valley thickets, parks, gardens. **Nest:** A twiggy cup in bush. Eggs (2–4) pale blue, speckled.

LE CONTE'S THRASHER *Toxostoma lecontei* 10–11 **Pl. 47**

Field marks: A *very pale* thrasher of the desert with a *dark tail,* dark eyes.

Similar species: Crissal and California Thrashers are much darker; Curve-billed Thrasher has lightly spotted breast.

Voice: Song infrequent; more disjointed, less repetitious than songs of most other thrashers. Note, *ti-rup.*

Where found: Sparse *resident* from s. California (se. deserts, w. and s. sides of San Joaquin Valley), s. Nevada, sw. Utah, w. and c. Arizona to nw. Mexico. **Habitat:** Desert flats with sparse bushes, *Atriplex.* **Nest:** A bulky bowl of twigs in cholla, thorny bush. Eggs (2–4) pale blue-green, speckled.

CRISSAL THRASHER *Toxostoma dorsale* 10½–12½ **Pl. 47**

Field marks: A rather dark desert thrasher with a *deeply curved bill.* Note the dark *chestnut under tail patch* (or crissum) darker than in other thrashers. No breast spots. Yellowish eyes.

Similar species: (1) Curve-billed Thrasher is grayer, has faint spotting, lacks rufous crissum. (2) Le Conte's is extremely pale. (3) California Thrasher has paler crissum.

Voice: Song sweeter, less spasmodic than in other thrashers. Note, *pichoory* or *chideary,* often repeated 2–3 times.

Where found: *Resident* from se. California, s. Nevada, sw. Utah, n. Arizona, s. New Mexico, w. Texas (Trans-Pecos) south to c. Mexico. **Habitat:** Dense brush along desert streams, mesquite thickets. **Nest:** A twiggy cup in bush, mesquite. Eggs (2–4) pale blue-green, unmarked.

SAGE THRASHER *Oreoscoptes montanus* 8–9 **Pl. 47**
Field marks: A bit smaller than Robin; similar in shape, some
actions. Gray-backed with a Robin-like bill, heavily streaked
breast, white spots at tip of tail, pale yellow eye. Small size,
shorter tail, shorter bill, striped breast distinguish it from other
typically w. thrashers.
Similar species: (1) See Cactus Wren (p. 176). (2) Young
Mockingbird (spotted) has large white patches in wing and tail.
Voice: Song, clear ecstatic warbled phrases, sometimes repeated
in thrasher fashion; more often continuous, suggestive of Black-
headed Grosbeak. Note, a blackbird-like *chuck*.
Where found: *Breeds* from c.-s. B.C., c. Idaho, s. Montana, sw.
Saskatchewan (isolated colony) south (east of Cascades, Sierra)
to s. California, s. Nevada, n. Arizona, n. New Mexico, Texas
panhandle, w. Oklahoma. *Winters* from c. California, s. Arizona,
s. New Mexico, w. Texas to n. Mexico. *Casual,* w. Washington,
w. Oregon, s. Alberta. **Habitat:** Sagebrush, brushy slopes, mesas;
in winter, also deserts. **Nest:** A twiggy cup in bush. Eggs
(4–5; 7) blue, spotted.

Thrushes, Bluebirds, Solitaires: Turdidae

LARGE-EYED, slender-billed, usually stout-legged songbirds. Our
species that bear the name "thrush" (with exception of Varied
Thrush) are brown-backed with *spotted* breasts. Robins, bluebirds,
solitaires, etc., suggest relationship through their spotted young.
Among the finest singers. **Food:** Insects, worms, snails, berries,
fruits. **Range:** Nearly worldwide. **No. of species:** World, 304;
West, 12 (+4 accidentals; +2 natives, 2 introduced in Hawaii).

ROBIN *Turdus migratorius* 9–11 **Pl. 48**
Field marks: A very familiar bird; recognized by its gray back
and *brick-red* breast. In male, the head and tail are blackish;
in the female, grayer. Bill *yellow.* Young Robin has speckled
breast, but gray back and rusty underparts identify it. Robins
walk on lawns with erect stance.
Voice: Song, a clear caroling; short phrases, rising and falling,
often long continued. Notes, *tyeep* and *tut-tut-tut.*
Where found: Alaska, Canada to s. Mexico. Winters mainly
south of Canada; some to Guatemala. **West:** *Breeds* from limit
of trees to s. California, se. Arizona (mts.), s. New Mexico, w.
and c. Texas. *Winters* in Pacific and sw. states; a few north to
s. Canada. **Habitat:** Towns, lawns, farmland, open forest,
streamsides; in winter, berry-bearing trees. **Nest:** A mud-walled,
grass-lined bowl, usually in tree. Eggs (3–4; 6) blue.

VARIED THRUSH *Ixoreus naevius* 9–10   **Pl. 48**
  Field marks: Similar to Robin but with an *orange eye-stripe,*
  orange wing-bars, and a *black band* across the rusty breast.
  Female: Breastband gray. *Young:* Breastband imperfect or
  speckled with orange; underparts speckled with dusky. Rusty
  wing-bars and eye-stripe distinguish it from young Robin.
  Voice: A long, eerie, quavering whistled note, followed, after a
  pause, by one on a lower or higher pitch.
  Where found: *Breeds* from c. Alaska, c. Yukon, nw. Mackenzie
  south to nw. California, mts. of ne. Oregon, n. Idaho, nw.
  Montana. *Winters* mainly from s. B.C., through Pacific states.
  Irregular, w. Nevada. *Accidental,* Saskatchewan, Wyoming,
  Colorado, Arizona, New Mexico, w. Texas. **Habitat:** Thick, wet
  forest, conifers; in winter, woods, ravines, thickets. **Nest:** A
  cup of twigs, moss, in small tree. Eggs (3–5) blue, dotted.

HERMIT THRUSH *Hylocichla guttata* 6½–7¾   **Pl. 48**
  Field marks: A spotted brown thrush with a reddish tail. When
  perched has a habit of cocking its tail and dropping it slowly.
  Similar species: (1) The other w. thrushes are uniformly colored
  above. (2) Fox Sparrow (reddish-tailed) has a conical bill; tends
  to be streaked, not spotted.
  Voice: Note, a low *chuck;* also a scolding *tuk-tuk-tuk* and a harsh
  pay. Song, clear, ethereal and flutelike; 3 or 4 phrases on *different
  pitch levels,* each preceded by a *long introductory note;* a deliberate pause between each phrase.
  Where found: Alaska, Canada to n. Baja California, e. W.
  Virginia. Winters mainly s. U.S. to Guatemala. **West:** *Breeds*
  from c. Alaska east across boreal woods of Canada; south in w.
  U.S. to high mts. of s. California, se. Arizona, s. New Mexico,
  w. Texas. *Winters* mainly in Oregon, California, sw. border
  states. **Habitat:** Conifer or mixed woods, forest floor; in winter,
  woods, thickets, parks. **Nest:** A cup of moss, grass, rootlets in
  small tree or on ground. Eggs (3–5) blue.

SWAINSON'S THRUSH *Hylocichla ustulata* 6½–7¾ **Pl. 48**
(Russet-backed Thrush, Olive-backed Thrush)
  Field marks: A spotted thrush that is uniformly brown above
  is one of 3 species. If it also has a conspicuous *buffy eye-ring,*
  buffy cheeks, it is Swainson's Thrush.
  Similar species: (1) Veery lacks broad buff eye-ring, is more
  tawny above (Swainson's is olive-brown). (2) Hermit Thrush
  has a reddish tail. (3) In far North see Gray-cheeked Thrush.
  Voice: Song, melodious, breezy flutelike phrases, distinguished
  by tendency of each phrase to climb *upward.* Note, *whit.* Migrants at night, a short *heep.*
  Where found: Alaska, Canada, w. and ne. U.S. Winters Mexico
  to Peru. **West:** *Breeds* from c. Alaska east across boreal woods

of Canada; south through lowlands of Pacific states to sw. California; in mts. of w. U.S. to c.-e. California, c. Nevada, n. Arizona, n. New Mexico. *Migrates* through sw. U.S. **Habitat:** Willow thickets, river woods, aspens, forest undergrowth; conifers in North. **Nest:** A cup of twigs, dead leaves, rootlets in bush, small tree. Eggs (3–5) blue, spotted.

GRAY-CHEEKED THRUSH *Hylocichla minima* 7–8 **Pl. 48**
Field marks: A dull gray-brown thrush, identified, when seen well, by *grayish cheeks* and lack of a conspicuous eye-ring.
Similar species: (1) Swainson's Thrush is also uniformly gray-brown above but has *buffy cheeks* and a conspicuous *buffy eye-ring;* its breast is suffused with buff. (2) Veery is somewhat tawnier above, has tawny wash on breast.
Voice: Note, *vee-a* or *quee-a,* higher and more nasal than Veery's note. Song, thin and nasal; suggests Veery's, but often rises abruptly at close (Veery's goes down); *whee-wheeoo-titi-whee.*
Where found: Ne. Siberia, Alaska, Canada, ne. U.S. Winters in W. Indies, S. America. **West:** *Breeds* from tree limit to sw. Alaska, n. B.C., n. Saskatchewan. *Migrates* east of Rockies; rarely west to w. edge of Plains. *Accidental,* Idaho, Arizona. **Habitat:** Boreal forest, tundra scrub. **Nest:** A cup of grass, leaves in low conifer, alder. Eggs (3–6) blue, spotted.

VEERY *Hylocichla fuscescens* 6½–7¾ **Pl. 48**
(Willow Thrush)
Field marks: Note the *uniformly* warm brown cast. No strong eye-ring (may have a dull whitish ring). Of all our brown thrushes the least spotted; the spots are often indistinct.
Similar species: (1) Swainson's Thrush has broad buffy eye-ring, buffy chest. (2) Hermit Thrush has reddish tail. (3) Gray-cheeked Thrush is grayer brown, lacks buff wash on breast.
Voice: Song, liquid, breezy, ethereal; wheeling downward: *vee-ur, vee-ur, veer, veer.* Note, a low *phew* or *view.*
Where found: S. Canada, n. and c. U.S. Winters in n. S. America. **West:** *Breeds* from s.-c. B.C., c. Alberta, c. Saskatchewan south through n. Great Basin, Rockies to e. Oregon, n. Nevada, ne. Arizona, s. Colorado. Very sparse migrant in Southwest. **Habitat:** Damp deciduous woods, willows. **Nest:** A cup of leaves, grasses, on or near ground. Eggs (3–5) blue.

EASTERN BLUEBIRD *Sialia sialis* 6½–7½ **Pl. 48**
Field marks: Similar to Western Bluebird, but throat *rusty,* not blue, and back *solid blue,* without a rusty patch (some Western Bluebirds lack this patch).
Voice: Note, a musical *chur-wi* or *tru-ly.* Song, 3 or 4 soft gurgling notes. More musical than Western Bluebird.
Where found: East of Rockies, s. Canada to Gulf states; also

se. Arizona to Nicaragua. Migrant in North. **West:** *Breeds* from
s. Saskatchewan south through Great Plains to Edwards Plateau,
Texas. A few west to foothills of Rockies in Montana, Wyoming,
Colorado. Also mts. of se. Arizona. **Habitat:** Open country with
scattered trees; farms. **Nest:** In hole in tree, post, bird box.
Eggs (3–7) pale blue.

WESTERN BLUEBIRD   *Sialia mexicana*   6½–7   **Pl. 48**
Field marks: A little larger than a House Sparrow; head, wings,
and tail *blue;* breast and back *rusty-red.* (In some birds the back
is partially or wholly blue.) Appears dumpy, round-shouldered
when perched. Females are paler, duller. Young birds are
speckle-breasted, grayish, devoid of red (there is always some
telltale blue in wings and tail).
Similar species: (1) See Eastern Bluebird. (2) Male Lazuli
Bunting has white *wing-bars.* (3) Mountain Bluebird has *blue*
breast (see female Mountain Bluebird).
Voice: A short *pew* or *mew.* Also a hard chattering note.
Where found: *Breeds* from s. B.C., w. Montana to mts. of s.
California, se. Arizona, New Mexico, w. Texas (Trans-Pecos);
and into high mts. of c. Mexico. *Winters* from Puget Sound, s.
Utah, sw. Colorado south. **Habitat:** Scattered trees, open conifer
forests, farms; in winter, semiopen terrain, brush, deserts. **Nest:**
In hole in tree, stub, bird box. Eggs (4–6; 8) pale blue.

MOUNTAIN BLUEBIRD   *Sialia currucoides*   6½–7¾   **Pl. 48**
Field marks: *Male:* Turquoise blue, paler below; belly whitish.
Female: Dull brownish with a touch of blue on rump, tail, and
wings. Has a straighter posture than female Western Bluebird
and lacks rusty wash on gray-brown breast.
Similar species: (1) Other bluebirds have red breasts. (2) Male
Blue Grosbeak has a thick bill, brown wing-bars. (3) Male
Indigo Bunting is smaller, very much darker. (4) Female
Mountain Bluebird suggests Townsend's Solitaire.
Voice: A low *chur* or *phew.* Song, a short, subdued warble.
Where found: *Breeds* from c. Alaska, s. Yukon, s. Mackenzie,
s.-c. Saskatchewan south (mainly east of Cascade-Sierra divide)
to high mts. of s. California, se. Nevada, n. Arizona, s. New
Mexico; east on Great Plains to ne. N. Dakota, Black Hills, w.
Nebraska, w. Oklahoma. *Winters* mainly from Oregon, Colorado
south. **Habitat:** Open terrain with scattered trees; in winter,
also treeless terrain. **Nest:** In hole in tree, stub, cliff, bird box.
Eggs (4–6; 8) pale blue.

WHEATEAR   *Oenanthe oenanthe*   5½–6   **p. 250**
Field marks: Note the conspicuous *white rump* and sides of tail,
contrasting with black on tail (like a broad inverted T). Breeding
male has blue-gray back, black wings, black ear patch, white

stripe over eye, buffish underparts. Male in autumn is buffier, with brownish back. Female like autumn male. Restless, flitting from rock to rock, "bobbing" and fanning tail.
Voice: A hard *chak-chak* or *chack-weet, weet-chack.* Song, snatches of warbling, chattering discords; often in flight.
Where found: Eurasia, Alaska, nw. and ne. Canada, Greenland. In winter to Africa, India. **West:** *Breeds* from n. Alaska, n. Yukon south to Mt. McKinley National Park, sw. Yukon. **Habitat:** High rocky barrens, slopes. **Nest:** Of grass, feathers in rock crevice. Eggs (5-6) pale blue.

BLUETHROAT *Luscinia svecica* 5½ **p. 250**
Field marks: A small sprightly bird, tail spread and flirted frequently, showing *conspicuous chestnut base.* Male in summer has *bright blue throat patch* with *chestnut spot* in center. Chestnut band between throat patch and white lower breast. Female has whitish throat, partially outlined in black.
Voice: A sharp *tac* and a soft *wheet.* Song, repetitious notes, musical and varied; often a cricket-like note.
Where found: Eurasia, Alaska, winters to India, n. Africa. **West:** *Breeds* near coast of n. Alaska from Wales to Colville River. **Habitat:** Dwarf willow, thick brush. **Nest:** A well-lined cup on ground. Eggs (4-6) greenish, dotted.

TOWNSEND'S SOLITAIRE **Pl. 48**
Myadestes townsendi 8-9½
Field marks: A slim gray bird, with a white *eye-ring,* white *sides* of tail, and a *buffy wing patch.* The beginner is likely to be confused, imagining it to be some sort of a thrasher, flycatcher, or almost anything but a solitaire.
Similar species: The white in the tail and the light wing patches give it a not too remote resemblance to a Mockingbird. Note the eye-ring and the darker breast.
Voice: Song, long and warbled, suggesting Black-headed Grosbeak's, but more rapid. Note, a sharp *eek.*
Where found: *Breeds* from c.-e. Alaska, s. Yukon, sw. Mackenzie south through high mts. to s. California (San Jacinto Mts.), ne. Arizona, n. New Mexico. Also n. Mexico (Durango). *Winters* from Canadian border to n. Mexico, c. Texas. **Habitat:** Mt. forests; in winter, canyons, brushy slopes, junipers. **Nest:** On ground, in bank, cliff, rocks, stump. Eggs (3-5) spotted.

Gnatcatchers, Kinglets, Old World Warblers: Sylviidae

TINY, active birds with small slender bills. Gnatcatchers have long mobile tails. Kinglets have bright crowns. This family includes the numerous Old World warblers. **Food:** Mainly insects, insect eggs, larvae. **Range:** Most large forested areas of world except lower S. America. **No. of species:** World, 313 (Mayr-Amadon), 398 (Van Tyne-Berger); West, 5 (+1 accidental; +2 in Hawaii).

ARCTIC WARBLER *Phylloscopus borealis* 4¾   **Pl. 51**
(Kennicott's Willow Warbler)
  Field marks: A small, plain Old World warbler, dull greenish brown above, whitish below; light stripe over eye, a trace of a narrow whitish wing-bar, pale legs. Sexes similar.
  Similar species: Tennessee Warbler (fall) is greener above, yellower below; eyeline yellowish, legs dark.
  Voice: Song, a repeated *tchick* followed by a short trill.
  Where found: Near tree limit across n. Eurasia, Alaska. Winters in tropical Asia. **West:** *Breeds* in w. Alaska from w. Brooks Range, Colville River south to Katmai, Mt. McKinley. **Habitat:** Willow scrub. **Nest:** A domed cup on ground at base of shrub. Eggs (5–7) speckled.

BLUE-GRAY GNATCATCHER *Polioptila caerulea* 4–5
(Western Gnatcatcher)   **Pl. 46**
  Field marks: Looks like a miniature Mockingbird. A tiny, slender mite, even smaller than a chickadee, blue-gray above and whitish below, with a narrow white eye-ring and a *long, contrastingly colored tail* (black in center, white on sides; often cocked like a wren's tail, flipped about).
  Similar species: See Black-tailed Gnatcatcher.
  Voice: Note, a thin peevish *zpee* or *chee.* Song, a thin, squeaky, wheezy series of notes, easily overlooked.
  Where found: S. Utah, s. Ontario to Guatemala, Bahamas. Winters from s. U.S. to Honduras. **West:** *Breeds* from n. California, c. Nevada, s. Idaho, sw. Wyoming, Colorado south. *Winters* from c. California, s. Nevada, c. Arizona, w. Texas south. **Habitat:** Open mixed woods, oaks, chaparral, piñon, junipers; in winter to river woods and thickets. **Nest:** A small lichen-covered cup on limb. Eggs (4–5) pale blue, spotted.

BLACK-TAILED GNATCATCHER *Polioptila melanura* 4½
(Plumbeous Gnatcatcher)   **Pl. 46**
  Field marks: Similar to Blue-gray Gnatcatcher but breeding male has a black cap and much less white on sides of tail (outer

web only). Winter male (without cap) and female are duller than Blue-gray Gnatcatcher. From underside, tail is largely *black;* in Blue-gray, largely *white.* The race in sw. California, *P. m. californica,* has dull gray underparts.
Voice: Note, a thin harsh *chee,* repeated 2–3 times (Blue-gray Gnatcatcher usually gives single note); or *pee-ee-ee.*
Where found: *Resident* from s. California, s. Nevada, c. Arizona, s. New Mexico, w. Texas (Trans-Pecos) south to n. Mexico.
Habitat: Desert brush, ravines, dry washes, mesquite, sage.
Nest: A small felted cup in crotch of low brush. Eggs (3–4) pale blue, spotted.

GOLDEN-CROWNED KINGLET   Pl. 49
Regulus satrapa 3¼–4
   Field marks: Note the crown patch: *yellow* in the female, *orange-red* in the male. Kinglets are tiny olive-gray birds, smaller than most warblers; often difficult to spot among the evergreens. An upward flip of the wings is distinctive. This species (except for summer young) always shows a conspicuous bright crown patch *bordered by black,* and a *white stripe* over the eye.
   Similar species: See Ruby-crowned Kinglet.
   Voice: Call note, a high wiry *see-see-see.* Song, a series of high thin notes (similar to call notes) ascending in pitch then dropping into a little chatter.
   Where found: S. Alaska, c. Canada, south in w. mts. to Guatemala. In East, to w. N. Carolina; winters to Gulf states. **West:** *Breeds* from s. Alaska, c. Yukon, Lake Athabaska south to high mts. of s. California (very local), se. Arizona, n. New Mexico. *Winters* widely from s. Canada south. **Habitat:** Conifers. In winter, also other trees. **Nest:** A ball of moss (open at top) tucked under tip of conifer branch. Eggs (5–9; 11) spotted.

RUBY-CROWNED KINGLET   Pl. 49
Regulus calendula 3¾–4½
   Field marks: Note the conspicuous *broken white eye-ring,* which gives the bird a big-eyed appearance. A tiny birdlet; olive-gray above, with 2 pale wing-bars; male with a *scarlet* crown patch (usually concealed; erected when excited). Occasional males have yellow crowns. Any kinglet not having a conspicuous crown patch and eye-stripe is of this species. The stubbier tail distinguishes it from any of our warblers, as does the dark bar bordering the rear wing-bar. Kinglets nervously twitch their wings; seem always in motion.
   Similar species: (1) See Golden-crowned Kinglet. (2) See also Hutton's Vireo (p. 194).
   Voice: Note, a husky *ji-dit.* Song, quite loud; 3–4 high notes, several low notes, and a chant, *tee tee tee, tew tew tew tew, ti-dadee, ti-dadee, ti-dadee.* Variable.

Where found: Canada, Alaska, w. U.S. Winters to Guatemala, Gulf states. **West:** *Breeds* from c. Alaska east across forests of Canada; and south to high mts. of s. California, s. Arizona, c. New Mexico. *Winters* from s. B.C., s. Utah, Colorado south. **Habitat:** Conifer forests; in winter other woodlands, thickets. **Nest:** Similar to Golden-crown's. Eggs (6–9; 11) spotted.

Pipits, Wagtails: Motacillidae

TERRESTRIAL birds, with long hind claws, thin bills. Wag tails almost constantly. Pipits are brown streaked birds with white outer tail feathers. Wagtails are more slender, strongly patterned, with long tails, slender legs. **Food:** Insects, spiders, seeds. **Range:** Nearly cosmopolitan (most species in Old World). **No. of species:** World, 48; West, 3 (+3 accidentals).

YELLOW WAGTAIL   *Motacilla flava*   6½   **p. 250**
   Field marks: Note the long, *constantly wagging tail* (black with white sides). A *very slender,* long-legged bird with *yellow underparts.* Olive-gray above, with dark cheek patch and white line above eye. Juvenal bird is whiter below, has white throat outlined with black. Flight undulating.
   Voice: A loud musical *tsoueep.* Song, *tsip-tsip-tsipsi.*
   Where found: Eurasia, w. Alaska. In winter, S. Africa, India. **West:** *Breeds* across n. Alaska to n. Yukon; south in w. Alaska to Nunivak. **Habitat:** Willow scrub on tundra. **Nest:** On ground, in tussock, bank. Eggs (4–7) olive-buff, mottled.

WATER PIPIT   *Anthus spinoletta*   6–7   **Pl. 54**
(American Pipit)
   Field marks: A slender, brown, tail-wagging ground bird. Near size of a sparrow, but with a *slender* bill; underparts *buffy* with streaks; *outer tail feathers white.* On ground, walks; almost *constantly bobs tail.* In flight, dips up and down. Learn the note — most Pipits are detected flying over.
   Similar species: (1) Vesper Sparrow and (2) longspurs, have conical finch bills; do not wag tails. (3) On Great Plains see also Sprague's Pipit.
   Voice: Note, a thin *jeet* or *jee-eet.* In aerial flapping song flight, *chwee chwee chwee chwee chwee chwee chwee.*
   Where found: Colder parts of N. Hemisphere. Winters to El Salvador, n. Africa, s. Asia. **West:** *Breeds* from tundra in Aleutians, n. Alaska, n. Canada south on mt. tops to n. Oregon, n. Arizona, n.-c. New Mexico. Widespread in migration. *Winters* from Puget Sound, s. Utah, Colorado south. **Habitat:** Tundra, alpine zone; in migration and winter, plains, bare fields, shores. **Nest:** Of grass, on ground. Eggs (4–7) spotted.

SPRAGUE'S PIPIT *Anthus spragueii* 6¼–7   **Pl. 54**
Field marks: Note the *pale legs* (flesh or yellowish). A buffy
sparrow-like bird with a striped back and white outer tail
feathers (suggests a Vesper Sparrow or longspur with a *thin* bill).
Back *streaked* conspicuously with *buff and black.* More solitary
than Water Pipit; when flushed often "towers" high in air in
aimless flight, then drops.
Similar species: (1) Water Pipit wags tail more, has a darker
(not strongly striped) back, a deeper buff breast. Legs *darker,*
light brown to black (Sprague's, *pale flesh* or *straw-colored*).
(2) Longspurs and (3) Vesper Sparrow have conical finch bills.
Vesper Sparrow usually hops (pipits walk).
Voice: Sings high in air, a sweet thin jingling series, descending
in pitch: *ching-a-ring-a-ring-a-ring-a* (W. Salt and A. Wilk).
Flight note not as sharp as Water Pipit's.
Where found: *Breeds* from c. parts of prairie provinces south to
n. Wyoming, N. Dakota. *Winters* from s. Arizona, Texas to s.
Mexico. **Habitat:** Plains, short-grass prairies. **Nest:** Of grass
(partly domed) on ground. Eggs (4–5; 6) spotted.

Waxwings: Bombycillidae

SLEEK crested birds often with red waxy tips on secondary wing
feathers. Gregarious. **Food:** Berries, insects. **Range:** N. Hemisphere. **No. of species:** World, 3; West, 2.

BOHEMIAN WAXWING *Bombycilla garrula* 7½–8¾ **p. 190**
Field marks: Note the *deep rusty* under tail coverts (white in
Cedar Waxwing). Similar to Cedar Waxwing; larger, grayer (no
yellow on belly); wings with strong *white and yellow* markings.
Voice: *Zreee,* rougher than note of Cedar Waxwing.
Where found: N. Eurasia, nw. N. America. Winters to s.
Eurasia, ne. and sw. U.S. **West:** *Breeds* from c. Alaska, n.
Mackenzie south sparsely to n. Washington, n. Idaho, nw.
Montana, sw. Alberta. *Winters* irregularly to nw. states (esp.
Rocky Mt. area); sparsely to s. California, Arizona, n. New
Mexico, Texas panhandle. **Habitat:** Boreal forest, muskeg; in
winter, widespread in search of berries. **Nest:** Of twigs, moss;
in conifer. Eggs (4–6) pale blue, dotted.

CEDAR WAXWING *Bombycilla cedrorum* 6½–8 **p. 190**
Field marks: Note the *yellow band* at the tip of the tail. A
sleek, *crested,* brown bird, larger than a House Sparrow. Most
adults have waxy red "droplets" on tips of secondary wing
feathers, rarely on tail feathers. Young (late summer) are gray,
softly streaked below. Gregarious; fly in compact flocks. Often
exhibit fly-catching habits.

Similar species: Bohemian Waxwing has rusty crissum.
Voice: A high thin lisp or *zeee;* sometimes slightly trilled.
Where found: Se. Alaska, Canada, to s.-c. U.S. Winters s.
Canada to Panama, W. Indies. **West:** *Breeds* from se. Alaska,
n.-c. B.C., n. Alberta, nw. Saskatchewan south to nw. California,
n. Utah, n. Colorado. *Winters* from s. B.C., s. Montana south.
Habitat: Open woodlands, fruiting trees, orchards; in winter,
widespread, irregular. **Nest:** A cup of twigs, grass, moss on
horizontal branch. Eggs (3–6) blue-gray, dotted.

PHAINOPEPLA   BOHEMIAN   CEDAR
                  WAXWING   WAXWING

Silky Flycatchers: Ptilogonatidae

SLIM, typically crested, waxwing-like birds. **Range:** Sw. U.S. to
Panama. **Food:** Berries, mistletoe; insects. **No. of species:**
World, 4; West, 1.

PHAINOPEPLA *Phainopepla nitens* 7–7¾ **above**
    Field marks: *Male:* A slim, *glossy black* bird with a *slender crest.*
White wing patches are conspicuous in flight. *Female: Dark gray*
with slender crest; wing patches light gray, not conspicuous.
Has fly-catching habits.
Similar species: (1) Cedar Waxwing is much browner than

female Phainopepla, has yellow tailband. (2) Mockingbird (white wing patches) has also much white in tail.
Voice: Note, a soft low *wurp*. Song, a weak, casual warble, wheezy and disconnected.
Where found: *Breeds* from n. California (n. Sacramento Valley), s Nevada, s. Utah, sw. New Mexico, w. Texas (Trans-Pecos) to s. Mexico. *Winters* in deserts of Southwest. **Habitat:** Desert scrub, mesquite, oak foothills, mistletoe, pepper trees. **Nest:** A shallow cup on fork of limb. Eggs (2–3; 4) speckled.

Shrikes: Laniidae

SONGBIRDS with hawklike behavior and hook-tipped bills. Perch watchfully on conspicuous vantage points. Prey sometimes impaled on thorns or barbed wire (often called "butcher birds"). **Food:** Insects, lizards, mice, small birds. **Range:** Widespread in Old World; 2 in N. America, none in S. America. **No. of species:** World, 67 (Mayr-Amadon), 72 (Van Tyne-Berger); West, 2.

NORTHERN SHRIKE *Lanius excubitor* 9–10¾   **Pl. 47**
(Northwestern Shrike)
   Field marks: In winter, in n. U.S. or s. Canada, a Robin-sized bird in the *tip* of a tree in open country may be a Northern Shrike. A closer look shows it to be light gray above, white below, with a *black mask*. Very similar to Loggerhead Shrike; *faintly barred* breast, *pale* base on lower mandible (except in spring). Young birds are brown with fine breast-barrings. Perhaps the most definitive mark is the *longer, heavier, and more strongly hooked bill.*
   Similar species: Adult Loggerhead Shrike is a bit smaller, lacks breast-barrings, has a solid black bill. The black mask meets over base of bill. The young Loggerhead is faintly barred below in late summer, but is *gray* (not brown). In general, winter shrikes in the colder sections are Northerns.
   Voice: Song, a disjointed thrasher-like succession of harsh notes, musical notes. Note, *shek-shek;* a grating *jaaeg.*
   Where found: Alaska, Canada, Eurasia, n. Africa. Winters to c. U.S. **West:** *Breeds* from n. Alaska, c. Yukon, n. Mackenzie south to s. Alaska, nw. B.C., Lake Athabaska. *Winters* c. Alaska, s. Canada south irregularly to n. California, c. Nevada, c. Arizona, n. New Mexico, Texas panhandle. **Habitat:** Semiopen or open country with lookout posts. **Nest:** Bulky; of twigs, feathers, in bush, conifer. Eggs (4–6; 9) spotted.

LOGGERHEAD SHRIKE *Lanius ludovicianus* 8–10 **Pl. 47**
   Field marks: Note the *black mask*. Big-headed, slim-tailed, slightly smaller than a Robin; gray above, white below. Shrikes

sit quietly on a wire or bush top; taking flight, they drop low and progress on a beeline course, rising to their next lookout, showing a small white patch on the black wings.

Similar species: (1) Mockingbird is slimmer, longer-tailed, has larger white wing patches and lacks the black mask. Perched, the shrike scans the ground; looks short-legged, big-headed (Mocker is longer-legged, alert-looking). The Shrike's flight is more flickering. (2) See Northern Shrike.

Voice: Song, halfhearted notes and phrases; repeated Mockingbird-like, but deliberate, with long pauses (*queedle, queedle,* over and over, or *tsurp-see, tsurp-see*). Note, *shack, shack.*

Where found: S. Canada to s. Mexico. Partial migrant. **West:** *Breeds* from s. B.C., c. Alberta, c. Saskatchewan south through w. U.S.; absent from nw. coast belt. *Winters* mainly in sw. states. **Habitat:** Open country with lookout posts, wires, scattered trees, low scrub, deserts. **Nest:** A well-lined cup in bush, tree. Eggs (4–7) spotted.

Starlings: Sturnidae

A VARIED family; many are blackbird-like in appearance. Usually short-tailed, sharp-billed; mainly gregarious. **Food:** Omnivorous; insects, berries, seeds. **Range:** Widespread in Old World. Two species (Starling and Crested Myna) introduced in N. America. **No. of species:** World, 103; West, 2 (+1 introduced in Hawaii).

STARLING *Sturnus vulgaris* 7½–8½   **Pl. 52**
    Field marks: A very gregarious, garrulous, short-tailed "blackbird," with somewhat the shape of a meadowlark. In flight, has a triangular look, and flies swiftly and directly, not rising and falling like most blackbirds. In spring, glossed with purple and green (visible at close range); bill *yellow*. In winter, more heavily speckled with light dots; bill dark, changing to yellow as spring approaches. Young Starlings are dusky gray, a little like the female Cowbird, but the tail is shorter, and the bill longer and more spikelike.
    Similar species: The Starling is the *short-tailed* "blackbird"; (1) grackles are long-tailed; (2) Red-winged, Rusty, and Brewer's Blackbirds and Cowbird are medium-tailed. (3) See Meadowlark for comparison of flight (p. 213).
    Voice: A harsh *tseeeer;* a whistled *whoo-ee.* Also clear whistles, clicks, bill rattles, chuckles, woven into a rambling "song." Sometimes mimics.
    Where found: Eurasia, n. Africa. Partially migratory. Introduced in N. America and elsewhere. **West:** The Starling, spreading westward, has now reached the coast from Vancouver

I. to s. California. Largely migratory in n. sections. **Habitat:** Farms, ranches, open country, open groves, fields. **Nest:** In hole in tree, building. Eggs (4–6; 8) pale bluish.

CRESTED MYNA

(In Hawaiian Islands see Indian Myna,
Plate 60)

CRESTED MYNA *Acridotheres cristatellus* 10½ **above**
Field marks: A large, chunky, short-tailed black bird with large *white wing patches;* bill *yellow,* legs yellow. Has a curious short *bushy crest* on forehead.
Voice: Starling-like; repeated phrases. Said to be a mimic.
Where found: Se. Asia. Introduced in Philippines and B.C.
West: *Resident* in and near Vancouver City, B.C.; local s. Vancouver I. *Casual,* w. Washington, nw. Oregon. **Habitat:** Agricultural land. **Nest:** In hole in tree, building, bird box. Eggs (4–5; 7) light blue-green.

Vireos: Vireonidae

SMALL olive or gray-backed birds; much like wood warblers, but with somewhat heavier bills (with a more curved ridge and slight hook) than in most warblers. Usually less active, searching for insects under leaves instead of flitting about. They may be divided into those species with wing-bars and those without. Those without wing-bars generally have eye-stripes. Those possessing bars usually have eye-rings. Some of the latter might be confused with the *Empidonax* flycatchers, but they do not sit in the upright flycatcher posture, and the light loral spot between eye-ring and bill is more

evident, giving the appearance of spectacles. **Food:** Mostly insects.
Range: Canada to Argentina. **No. of species:** World, 41 (Mayr-
Amadon), 37 (Van Tyne-Berger); West, 8 (+3 marginals).

BLACK-CAPPED VIREO *Vireo atricapilla* 4¼-4¾ **Pl. 49**
  Field marks: A small, sprightly vireo with *top and sides of head
  usually glossy black* in adult male, slaty gray in female. It has
  conspicuous white "spectacles" formed by the eye-ring and loral
  patch and 2 conspicuous wing-bars.
  Voice: Song hurried, harsh; phrases remarkable for variety and
  restless, almost angry quality. Alarm note, a harsh *chit-ah,* not
  unlike Ruby-crowned Kinglet's (G. M. Sutton).
  Where found: *Breeds* from c. Oklahoma (local), w. and c. Texas
  (mainly Edwards Plateau) south to Coahuila. *Winters* in w.
  Mexico. **Habitat:** Oak scrub, brushy hillsides. **Nest:** A neat
  cup hung in thick bush, low tree. Eggs (3-5) white.

HUTTON'S VIREO *Vireo huttoni* 4¼-4¾ **Pl. 49**
  Field marks: Note the *incomplete eye-ring;* broken by a dark
  spot *above* the eye. A small olive-brown vireo with 2 broad
  white wing-bars, *partial* eye-ring, large light loral spot.
  Similar species: (1) Ruby-crowned Kinglet closely resembles it,
  but Hutton's Vireo has a heavier bill (with slight hook), is
  slightly larger, lacks dark wing-bar. It is more deliberate; does
  not twitch its wings. (2) The small *Empidonax* flycatchers, sit
  upright and have more complete eye-rings.
  Voice: A double-noted *zu-weep* with rising inflection, sometimes
  continuously repeated; vireo quality. Frequently a hoarse deliberate *day dee dee,* very different from the *ji-dit* of Ruby-
  crowned Kinglet (Laidlaw Williams).
  Where found: *Breeds* from sw. B.C. through Pacific states (west
  of Cascades, Sierra) and from c. Arizona, sw. New Mexico, w.
  Texas (Chisos Mts.) to Guatemala. *Resident* in most of range
  but some migration. **Habitat:** Woods and adjacent brush;
  prefers oaks. **Nest:** A cup of down, moss hung from twig of
  tree, shrub. Eggs (3-4) dotted.

BELL'S VIREO *Vireo bellii* 4¼-5 **Pl. 49**
  Field marks: A small grayish vireo with 1 or 2 light wing-bars
  and pale yellowish-washed sides; nondescript. Distinguished
  from Warbling Vireo by the wing-bar(s) and narrow eye-ring.
  Most "wing-barred" vireos have more conspicuous eye-rings.
  Similar species: In desert mts. see Gray Vireo. In c. Texas
  (close to 100°) dark-eyed young White-eyed Vireos have been
  called Bell's Vireos. See Texas *Field Guide.*
  Voice: Sings "as if through clenched teeth"; husky, unmusical
  phrases at short intervals: *cheedle cheedle chee? — cheedle cheedle
  chew!* First phrase ends in rising inflection; 2nd phrase, given

more frequently, has downward inflection and sounds as if bird were answering its own question.
Where found: Middle and sw. U.S., n. Mexico. Winters Mexico to Nicaragua. **West:** *Breeds* from n. California (head of Sacramento Valley), s. Nevada, sw. Utah, c. Arizona, sw. New Mexico, w. Texas south; east of mts. from e. Colorado, Nebraska south. **Habitat:** Willow thickets along lowland streams, mesquite. **Nest:** A pensile cup in low tree. Eggs (3–5) dotted.

GRAY VIREO   *Vireo vicinior*   5–5¾   Pl. 49
Field marks: A plain, gray-backed vireo of arid mts.; has a *narrow white eye-ring* but differs from other vireos with eye-rings by having *no wing-bars* or 1 faint bar. Though drab, it has character, flopping its tail like a gnatcatcher.
Similar species: Bell's Vireo usually has 2 wing-bars (sometimes 1); often has a faint wash of yellow on sides. Its habitat is different (low stream edges).
Voice: Song similar to Solitary Vireo's; more rapid, "patchy."
Where found: *Breeds* from s. California (nw. to Cajon Pass, Liebre Mt., Walker Pass), s. Nevada, sw. Utah, sw. Colorado (Mesa Verde) south locally to c. Mexico. Also locally in w. Oklahoma, w. Texas. *Winters* in n. Mexico; rarely sw. Arizona. **Habitat:** Brushy mt. slopes, mesas, open chaparral, scrub oak, junipers. **Nest:** A pensile cup in bush. Eggs (3–4) dotted.

SOLITARY VIREO   *Vireo solitarius*   5–6   Pl. 49
(Blue-headed Vireo)
Field marks: A vireo with white wing-bars. Note the gray head, *conspicuous white eye-ring,* and *snowy white throat.* The breeding races of the Pacific states (*V. s. cassinii*) and Canada (*V. s. solitarius*) are handsome with their yellow-olive sides and contrast of gray head, olive back. The race in the Rockies, *V. s. plumbeus* (Utah, Wyoming south), is gray, lacking the olive tones. The main field marks, mentioned above, hold.
Similar species: (1) Hutton's Vireo has dull throat; eye-ring broken at top. (2) Bell's Vireo has inconspicuous wing-bars and eye-ring.
Voice: Song, short whistled phrases, with rising and falling inflection, rendered with a short wait between phrases.
Where found: Canada to El Salvador. Winters from s. U.S. to Nicaragua, Cuba. **West:** *Breeds* from c. B.C., sw. Mackenzie east across Canadian forest and south through w. U.S. (mt. regions southerly). *Winters* from se. Arizona, sw. New Mexico south. **Habitat:** Mixed forests, pine-oak woods. **Nest:** A neat basket hung from low branch of tree. Eggs (3–5) dotted.

YELLOW-GREEN VIREO   *Vireo flavoviridis*   6¼–6¾   Pl. 49
Field marks: Note the yellow tones. A rare inhabitant of the Rio Grande Delta. Very similar to Red-eyed Vireo, in behavior

and voice, but head-stripes less distinct. Sides washed with yellowish, under tail coverts *yellow* (Red-eyed, white).
Similar species: See Red-eyed and Philadelphia Vireos.
Voice: Song similar to Red-eyed's; longer pauses.
Where found: Southern tip of Texas (rare *summer resident*) to Panama. Winters in upper Amazon Basin. *Accidental,* California. **Habitat:** Resaca woodlands, shade trees. **Nest:** A small cup hung from forked twig of tree. Eggs (2–3) spotted.

RED-EYED VIREO *Vireo olivaceus* 5½–6½   **Pl. 49**
Field marks: Olive-green above, white below, *no wing-bars;* characterized by the *gray cap* and the *black-bordered white eyebrow-stripe* over the eye. Red eye is of little aid.
Similar species: Warbling Vireo is paler, more uniform above, without black borders on eyebrow stripe. Songs unlike.
Voice: Song, short abrupt phrases of Robin-like character, separated by deliberate pauses, repeated as often as 40 times in a minute. Monotonous. Note, a nasal whining *chway.*
Where found: Canada to Gulf states. Winters in Amazon Basin. *West: Breeds* from Puget Sound, ne. B.C., sw. Mackenzie, c. Saskatchewan south to n. Oregon, n. Idaho, Montana, and through Wyoming, e. Colorado to c. Texas (Edwards Plateau). *Casual,* California, Utah, Arizona, w. Texas. **Habitat:** Woodlands, shade trees, groves. **Nest:** A small basket-like cup hung from forked twig of bush, tree. Eggs (3–4) dotted.

PHILADELPHIA VIREO *Vireo philadelphicus* 4½–5 **Pl. 49**
Field marks: A small vireo with the combination of *unbarred* wings and *yellow-tinged* underparts (especially on breast). Has a light eye-stripe (not an eye-ring).
Similar species: (1) Warbling Vireo is paler and usually lacks the yellow (some have a tinge on sides). At close range there is a *dark spot* between eye and bill (lores) in the Philadelphia. (2) Orange-crowned Warbler (finer bill) is more active, dingier, more uniform in color. (3) Fall Tennessee Warbler has a more needlelike bill, usually clear-white under tail coverts.
Voice: Song similar to Red-eyed Vireo's; higher, slower.
Where found: S. Canada, ne. edge of U.S. Winters in Cent. America. *West: Breeds* from ne. B.C. east across cool forests of Alberta, Saskatchewan. *Casual migrant,* Montana, Colorado, w. Texas. *Accidental,* Arizona. **Habitat:** Second-growth; poplar, willow, alder. **Nest:** A neat cup of birch bark, usnea, suspended in forked twig of tree, bush. Eggs (3–5) spotted.

WARBLING VIREO *Vireo gilvus* 4½–5½   **Pl. 49**
Field marks: Of those w. vireos that have *no* distinct wing-bars or eye-rings, this is the most widespread. A pale-backed vireo; whitish below; head *inconspicuously* striped.
Similar species: (1) Red-eyed Vireo has a more contrastingly

striped head and shows contrast between gray cap and olive back. (2) Philadelphia Vireo (Canada) has yellowish underparts. (3) Gray and (4) Bell's Vireos tend to have eye-rings.
Voice: Song, a languid warble unlike broken phraseology of other vireos; suggests Purple Finch's song but less spirited, with burry undertone. Note, a wheezy querulous *twee.*
Where found: Canada to s. U.S., n. and w. Mexico. Winters Mexico to Guatemala. **West:** *Breeds* from n. B.C., s. Mackenzie, c. Saskatchewan south throughout most of w. U.S. *Casual,* se. Alaska. **Habitat:** Deciduous and mixed woods, aspen groves, poplars, shade trees. **Nest:** A basket-like cup hung from forked twig of tree. Eggs (3–5) spotted.

Wood Warblers: Parulidae

THESE are "butterflies" of the bird world — bright-colored birdlets, usually smaller than sparrows (except the Chat), usually with thin bills. The majority have some yellow on them. Vireos are similar, but their colors generally are duller and their bills heavier, less needle-pointed. The movements of most species are rather sluggish, unlike the active flittings of most warblers.

A number of e. warblers have been recorded occasionally or accidentally in the West, especially along the w. edge of the Plains in the Rocky Mt. states. A number have even turned up on the coast. Descriptions of these waifs will be found in the Eastern *Field Guide.* **Food:** Mainly insects. **Range:** Alaska and Canada to Argentina. **No. of species:** World, 109 (Mayr-Amadon), 119 (Van Tyne-Berger); West, 36 (+16 accidentals and marginals).

BLACK-AND-WHITE WARBLER   **Pl. 50**
Mniotilta varia 4½–5½
   Field marks: *Striped lengthwise with black and white;* creeps along trunks and branches of trees. Has a *striped crown,* white stripes on back. Female has whiter underparts.
   Similar species: (1) Black-throated Gray and (2) Blackpoll Warblers (males in spring) have *solid black caps.*
   Voice: Song, a thin *weesee weesee weesee weesee weesee weesee weesee;* suggests one of Redstart's songs but higher-pitched and longer (*weesee* repeated at least 7 times). A 2nd, more rambling song drops in pitch in middle of series.
   Where found: Canada to Gulf states. Winters mainly from Mexico, W. Indies to n. S. America. **West:** *Breeds* from ne. B.C., sw. Mackenzie, c. Saskatchewan south to e. Montana and Black Hills. Also c. Texas (Edwards Plateau). *Migrates* mainly east of Rockies; stragglers west to Pacific states. **Habitat:** Woodlands, trunks and limbs of trees. **Nest:** A hair-lined cup on ground, stump. Eggs (4–5) spotted.

TENNESSEE WARBLER *Vermivora peregrina* 4½-5 **Pl. 51**
  Field marks: Quite plain. *Male in spring:* A *conspicuous white
  stripe over the eye;* head gray, contrasting with greenish back;
  underparts whitish. *Female in spring:* Similar, head less gray,
  underparts slightly yellowish. Light eyebrow line is best mark.
  Adults and immature in autumn: Greenish above, pale dingy
  yellow below; known by combined characters of *unstreaked*
  yellowish breast and *conspicuous* yellowish line over eye.
  Similar species: (1) Red-eyed and (2) Warbling Vireos are
  larger, with somewhat thicker bills, slower actions. (3) Autumn
  birds resemble Orange-crowned Warbler but differ as follows:
  (a) under tail coverts are *white* in typical Tennessees (some immatures show a tinge of yellow); (b) Tennessee has more conspicuous eye-stripe; (c) is *greener,* has paler underparts, with
  no suggestion of faint streaking; (d) almost invariably shows
  trace of a light wing-bar. (4) See also Philadelphia Vireo (p. 196).
  Voice: Song, staccato, 2- or 3-parted: *tizip-tizip-tizip-tizip-tizip-
  tizip-zitzitzitzitzizizizizi* (ending like an emphatic Chipping
  Sparrow's). Suggests Nashville Warbler's song but louder; more
  tirelessly repeated. W. W. H. Gunn's rendition is *ticka ticka
  ticka ticka swit swit chew-chew-chew-chew-chew.*
  Where found: Canada, ne. edge of U.S. Winters Mexico to
  Venezuela. **West:** *Breeds* from s. Yukon, c. Mackenzie to s.-c.
  B.C., nw. Montana, sw. and c. Alberta, c. Saskatchewan.
  Migrant on Plains; casually in fall to Pacific states. **Habitat:**
  Deciduous and mixed forests; in migration, groves, brush.
  Nest: On ground, in woods, bog, muskeg. Eggs (4-7) spotted.

ORANGE-CROWNED WARBLER   **Pl. 51**
Vermivora celata 4½-5½
  Field marks: A dull-colored warbler *without wing-bars or other
  distinctive marks;* olive-green above, *greenish-yellow below;* sexes
  similar. "Orange crown" seldom noticeable. The points to
  remember are: greenish-yellow underparts, faint blurry streaks
  on breast, lack of wing-bars. The race *V. c. sordida* (Channel
  Is. and coast of s. California) is dull-colored, greenish drab
  throughout, not much paler below (dull autumn immatures of
  other races may be similar to it).
  Similar species: (1) Nashville Warbler (which also has a rusty
  crown patch) has brighter yellow underparts and a white eye-
  ring. (2) Hutton's Vireo and (3) Ruby-crowned Kinglet both
  have light wing-bars. In Canada (especially) see also (4) Tennessee Warbler and (5) Philadelphia Vireo (p. 196).
  Voice: Song, a weak, colorless trill, dropping in energy at the end.
  Often changes pitch, rising then dropping.
  Where found: Alaska, Canada, w. U.S. Winters s. U.S. to
  Guatemala. **West:** *Breeds* from n.-c. Alaska, Yukon, nw.
  Mackenzie east across forests of Canada; south through B.C.,

Pacific states to Baja California; through mt. states to se. Arizona, n. New Mexico. *Winters* in lowlands of w. Oregon, California, s. Nevada, s. Arizona, w. Texas. **Habitat:** Brushy woodland clearings, hillsides, aspens, undergrowth, chaparral. **Nest:** Hidden on ground or in low shrub. Eggs (4–6) spotted.

NASHVILLE WARBLER *Vermivora ruficapilla* 4–5 **Pl. 51**
(Calaveras Warbler)
Field marks: Note the *white eye-ring* in conjunction with the *yellow* throat. Underparts yellow; *head gray,* contrasting with olive-green back; males may show a dull chestnut crown patch.
Similar species: MacGillivray's and Connecticut Warblers have white eye-rings but their throats are grayish. In females and autumn birds the grayish or brownish suggestion of a hood is a clue, as is their larger size and more sluggish ways.
Voice: Song, 2-parted: *seebit, seebit, seebit seebit, titititititi* (ends like Chipping Sparrow's).
Where found: S. Canada, w. and n. U.S. *Winters,* s. Texas, s. Florida to Guatemala. **West:** *Breeds* from s. B.C., nw. Montana south in Pacific states to se.-c. California (Sierra); in interior to w. Nevada (Lake Tahoe), n. Utah. Also c. Saskatchewan. *Migrates* through Pacific states; in lesser numbers elsewhere in w. U.S. **Habitat:** Open mixed woods with undergrowth, forest edges. **Nest:** On or near ground. Eggs (3–5) spotted.

VIRGINIA'S WARBLER *Vermivora virginiae* 4–4½ **Pl. 51**
Field marks: A small *gray-looking* warbler with a pale breast and *yellowish rump and under tail coverts.* At close range a narrow white eye-ring, a rufous spot on the crown, and a touch of yellow on the breast can be seen. Has tail-flicking habit. Immatures lack the colors on crown and breast; are gray with a touch of yellow at base of tail.
Similar species: (1) Lucy's Warbler has chestnut rump. (2) In Chisos Mts. (Texas) and Mexico see Colima Warbler.
Voice: Song, loose, colorless notes on nearly the same pitch; rises slightly at end: *chlip-chlip-chlip-chlip-chlip-wick-wick.* Resembles song of Audubon's Warbler in quality.
Where found: Great Basin ranges, s. Rockies. *Breeds* from ne. Nevada, se. Idaho, n. Colorado to se. California, se. Arizona, sw. New Mexico. *Migrant* in Trans-Pecos. Winters in w. Mexico. **Habitat:** Oak canyons, brushy slopes, piñons. **Nest:** On ground under grass or bush. Eggs (3–5) speckled.

COLIMA WARBLER *Vermivora crissalis* 5¼ **Pl. 51**
Field marks. In the high Chisos Mts. (between 6000 and 7000 ft.) in Texas, a deliberate-acting, gray-looking warbler with a yellow rump and under tail coverts is most likely this little-

known species (but it could be a migrant Virginia's Warbler).
It differs from Virginia's chiefly in lacking the yellowish wash
on the breast (but if present it is more green and diffuse).
Crissum darker, more aniline yellow. The bird is darker on the
back and distinctly larger.

Similar species: Young Virginia's (lacking yellow on breast) is
smaller, with a smaller bill; paler above; more ocher rump.

Voice: Note, a sharp *psit.* Song, "a simple trill, much like that
of Chipping Sparrow but rather shorter and more musical and
ending in 2 lower notes" (J. Van Tyne).

Where found: *Breeds* in w. Texas (Chisos Mts.), n.-c. Mexico.
Winters in Mexico to Colima, Michoacan. **Habitat:** Small oaks,
maples, madroñas, pines in canyons. **Nest:** A well-lined cup on
ground among dead leaves. Eggs (4) spotted.

LUCY'S WARBLER *Vermivora luciae* 4   Pl. 51

Field marks: A small desert warbler; known by its *chestnut rump
patch.* Gray above, white below; small patch of chestnut on
crown, white eye-ring. Immature lacks the chestnut patches.

Similar species: Virginia's Warbler has *yellowish* rump patch.

Voice: Song, a high, rapid *weeta weeta weeta che che che che che,*
on 2 pitches. Suggests Nashville Warbler if ending on lower
pitch; or Yellow Warbler if ending higher.

Where found: *Breeds* in deserts adjacent to Colorado River in
se. Nevada, sw. Utah, se. California; and from w. and c. Arizona,
s.-c. New Mexico south to nw. Mexico; casually east to El Paso.
Winters in w. Mexico. **Habitat:** Mesquite along desert streams;
willows, cottonwoods. **Nest:** A well-lined cup in tree cavity or
under loose bark. Eggs (4–5) speckled.

OLIVE-BACKED WARBLER *Parula pitiayumi* 4–4¾
(Sennett's Warbler, "Pitiayumi Warbler")   Pl. 51

Field marks: A small *bluish* warbler with a yellow throat and
breast, 2 white wing-bars and a greenish patch on the back.
Male: A suffusion of tawny orange across breast. *Black face*
sharply separates yellow throat from blue crown. *Female:* Similar; face pattern not so contrasting; orange on breast lacking.

Similar species: Parula Warbler (migrant, lower Rio Grande) is
very similar but male has a dark *band* below throat. Both sexes
have a *white eye-ring,* longer lower wing-bar.

Voice: Song, a buzzy trill which climbs the scale, *zzzzzzzzee-up;*
also *bz-bz-bz-bz-zeeeeee-up,* ascending the scale by short steps.
Both songs almost identical with Parula Warbler's.

Where found: *Resident* from lower Rio Grande Valley, Texas
(upriver to Rio Grande City), south to n. Argentina. **Habitat:**
Woodlands with Spanish moss. **Nest:** A purselike cup in clump
of Spanish moss. Eggs (3–4) spotted.

OLIVE WARBLER *Peucedramus taeniatus* 4½–5 **Pl. 51**
Field marks: *Male: Orange-brown head and upper breast* set
off by a *black cheek patch.* Back dark gray, belly white; broad
white wing-bars. *Female:* Less distinctive; crown and nape
olive, breast and sides of throat yellowish, back gray, wing-bars
white. Has a dusky ear patch.
Similar species: Female might be confused with: (1) female
Townsend's Warbler, but lacks breast-streakings; (2) female
Hermit Warbler, but more yellow on breast, less on face; cheek
patch darker, bill longer.
Voice: Song, a ringing chant; several variations: *tiddle tiddle
tiddle ter* or *peter peter peter peter* (titmouse-like).
Where found: *Breeds* from mts. of c. Arizona, sw. New Mexico
to Nicaragua. *Winters* north to sc. Arizona, sw. New Mexico.
Habitat: Pine and fir forests of high mts. **Nest:** A thick cup
high in conifer. Eggs (3–4) grayish, speckled.

YELLOW WARBLER *Dendroica petechia* 4½–5¼ **Pl. 50**
Field marks: This small bird appears to be *all yellow.* Many
other N. American warblers are yellow below, but none is so
yellow on the back, wings, and tail. Many have white spots in
the tail; this is the only one with *yellow* spots (with exception
of dissimilar female Redstart). Male shows chestnut-red breast-
streakings (in female, faint or lacking).
Similar species: (1) Female Wilson's Warbler has no tail spots.
(2) Some dull autumn Yellow Warblers (females and young) and
especially examples of the dark race of s. Alaska and w. B.C.,
D. p. rubiginosa, look almost as greenish as Orange-crowns
(which lack tail spots). *Look for the yellow tail spots.* There is
also at least a trace of *yellow feather-edging in the wings.* (3)
American Goldfinch has black wings, *black* tail.
Voice: Song, a cheerful, bright *tsee-tsee-tsee-tsee-titi-wee* or *weet
weet weet weet tsee tsee,* given rapidly. Variable.
Where found: Alaska, Canada to c. Peru. Winters from Mexico,
Bahamas south. **West:** *Breeds* from c. Alaska, n. Yukon, nw.
Mackenzie throughout West. **Habitat:** Willows, poplars, stream-
side trees and shrubs, town shade trees. **Nest:** A deep felted
cup in upright crotch of shrub, tree. Eggs (4–5) spotted.

MAGNOLIA WARBLER *Dendroica magnolia* 4½–5 **Pl. 50**
Field marks: The "Black and Yellow Warbler." Upper parts
blackish, with large white patches on wings and tail; underparts
yellow, with heavy black stripings. In any plumage, the best
mark is the black tail, crossed midway by a *broad white band*
(from below, tail looks white with a broad black band at tip).
In fall, Magnolias are olive above, yellow below, with stripings
reduced to a few sparse marks on flanks.
Similar species: Other Canadian species with black stripes on

yellow underparts are (1) Townsend's, (2) Cape May, and (3) Canada Warblers, but none of these has the bold black and white upper plumage with its distinctive tail pattern.

Voice: Song suggests Yellow Warbler's; shorter: *weeta weeta weetsee* (last note rising) or *weeta weeta wit-chew.*

Where found: Canada, ne. U.S. to mts. of w. Virginia. Winters from Mexico, W. Indies to Panama. **West:** *Breeds* from ne. B.C. east across boreal forests of Canada. *Rare migrant* east of mts. *Casual,* Alaska, California, Nevada, Arizona. **Habitat:** Low conifers; in migration, other trees. **Nest:** A loose shallow, rootlet-lined cup in small evergreen. Eggs (3–5) spotted.

CAPE MAY WARBLER *Dendroica tigrina* 5–5½ **Pl. 50**

Field marks: *Male, breeding: The only N. American warbler with chestnut cheeks.* Underparts yellow, narrowly striped with black; rump yellow, crown black. *Female, immature, and autumn birds* lack chestnut cheeks and are duller; breast often almost white, lined with dusky streaks. A good point is a dim, *suffused patch of yellow behind the ear.*

Similar species: Obscure autumn birds are nondescript, heavily streaked below, but with an unstriped back. Similar birds are: (1) female Myrtle Warbler and (2) female Audubon's Warbler, which have striped backs, more *conspicuous* yellow rumps; (3) Palm Warbler (browner; yellow under tail coverts; *wags tail*).

Voice: Song, a very high thin *seet seet seet seet,* repeated 4 or more times. Easily confused with song of Bay-breast.

Where found: Canada, ne. edge of U.S. Winters in Caribbean area. **West:** *Breeds* in s. Mackenzie, ne. B.C., n. Alberta, n. Saskatchewan. *Accidental,* California, Colorado, Arizona. **Habitat:** Spruce forests; in migration, other trees. **Nest:** A cup of grass, moss, high in conifer. Eggs (5–7) spotted.

MYRTLE WARBLER *Dendroica coronata* 5–6 **Pl. 50**

Field marks: Very similar to Audubon's Warbler, but throat *white* instead of yellow. Adult males have 2 narrow white wing-bars instead of a broader white patch.

Voice: Song, very similar to Audubon's Warbler, a junco-like trill, that either *rises* or *falls* in pitch at the end. Call note, *check,* different in timbre from Audubon's.

Where found: Alaska, Canada, ne. U.S. Winters from n. Ohio, Nova Scotia to Panama. **West:** *Breeds* from n.-c. Alaska, n. Yukon, nw. Mackenzie south to s. Alaska, n. B.C., c. Alberta, c. Saskatchewan. *Winters* from nw. Oregon south to s. California, s. Arizona; on Great Plains from se. Colorado south.

Habitat: Coniferous and mixed forests. In winter varied; woods, river thickets, brush, gardens, etc. **Nest:** A cup lined with hair, feathers, in conifer. Eggs (4–5) spotted.

AUDUBON'S WARBLER *Dendroica auduboni* 5–5½ **Pl. 50**
Field marks: Note the bright *yellow rump* and the note (a loud *tchip*). *Male in spring:* Blue-gray above; heavy black breast patch (like an inverted U); throat, crown, side patches yellow. Differs from Myrtle Warbler in having a *yellow throat,* large white wing patches. *Female in spring:* Brown, not gray; pattern similar except for wing patch (has 2 white bars). *Winter adults and young:* Brownish above; whitish below, streaked; throat yellowish (sometimes dim), rump yellow.
Similar species: See Myrtle Warbler (white throat).
Voice: Song, junco-like but 2-parted, either rising or dropping in pitch, *seet-seet-seet-seet-seet, trrrrrrrr*. Note, a loud *tchip*.
Where found: *Breeds* from c. B.C., sw. Alberta, sw. Saskatchewan (Cypress Hills) south throughout conifer-clad mts. of w. U.S. to s. Durango, Mexico. *Winters* from sw. B.C., n. Idaho, sw. Utah, Colorado to Guatemala. *Casual* in se. Alaska. **Habitat:** Conifer forests. In winter, varied; open woods, treetops, brush, thickets, gardens, beaches. **Nest:** A feather-lined cup in conifer. Eggs (3–5) spotted.

BLACK-THROATED GRAY WARBLER **Pl. 50**
Dendroica nigrescens 4½–5
Field marks: *Male:* Gray above and white below with *black throat, cheek, and crown.* A small yellow spot before eye (often difficult to see). Females lack the black throat but retain the black cheek and crown patches.
Similar species: (1) Townsend's Warbler has *yellow* on face and underparts instead of white. (2) Black-throated Sparrow (a desert finch) has similar black and white head pattern, but has conical bill, lacks side-stripes. (3) Chickadees also have black caps and black bibs but have *white* cheeks. In Canada (mainly) see (4) Black-and-White and (5) Blackpoll Warblers.
Voice: Song, a buzzy chant, *zeedle zeedle zeedle zeet' che* (next to last note higher). Song variable, sometimes ending on higher note; recognizable by its quality, "full of *z*'s."
Where found: *Breeds* from sw. B.C. (mainland), Washington, s. Idaho, c. Wyoming to n. Baja California, ne. Sonora, se. Arizona, n. New Mexico. *Winters* in s. California (sparse), s. Arizona, Mexico. **Habitat:** Dry oak slopes, piñons, junipers, open mixed woods. In migration, varied trees, brush. **Nest:** A compact cup in bush, tree (often oak). Eggs (3–5) spotted.

TOWNSEND'S WARBLER **Pl. 50**
Dendroica townsendi 4¼–5
Field marks: *Male:* Easily distinguished by the *black and yellow patterned head, yellow underparts,* and striped sides. *Female:* Throat largely yellow, not black; may be known by *well-defined dark cheek patch on yellow face.*

Similar species: Hermit Warbler lacks black cheek, crown.
Voice: Song, similar to Black-throated Gray's: *dzeer dzeer dzeer tseetsee* or *weazy, weazy, seesee.* "The first 3 or 4 notes similar in pitch, with a wheezy, buzzy quality, followed by 2 or more high-pitched sibilant notes" (H. H. Axtell).
Where found: *Breeds* from s. Alaska, s. Yukon to Washington, n. Idaho, w. Wyoming. *Migrant* east to w. edge of Plains. *Winters* from Oregon, California to Nicaragua. **Habitat:** Tall conifers, cool fir forests; in winter, also oaks, madroñas, laurels. **Nest:** A shallow cup in conifer. Eggs (3–5) spotted.

BLACK-THROATED GREEN WARBLER   Pl. 50
Dendroica virens 4½–5¼

Field marks: *Adult male:* Bright *yellow cheeks* framed by *black throat* and olive-green crown and back; belly whitish (often with yellowish wash). *Female:* Much less black on throat; particularly in young birds; yellow cheeks are the main clue.
Similar species: (1) Hermit Warbler (Pacific states) has yellow crown (male), gray back, no black on sides. On female Hermit note the gray back. See also (2) Golden-cheeked Warbler (Edwards Plateau and Mexico) and (3) Townsend's Warbler.
Voice: A high lisping *zoo, zee, zoo-zoo, zee* or a more rapid *zee-zee-zee-zoo-zee* (*zee* notes same pitch; *zoo* notes lower).
Where found: Canada, ne. U.S.; in mts. to n. Georgia. Winters e. Mexico to Colombia. **West:** *Breeds* east of Rockies in boreal forests of s. Mackenzie, Alberta, Saskatchewan. A few *migrate* through Plains, west sparsely to Rocky Mt. states. *Casual,* California, Arizona, New Mexico, w. Texas. **Habitat:** Conifer forests. **Nest:** A neat cup in conifer. Eggs (4–5) spotted.

GOLDEN-CHEEKED WARBLER   Pl. 50
Dendroica chrysoparia 4½–5

Field marks: Breeds in the "cedar" hills of the Edwards Plateau, Texas; the warbler with yellow cheeks, black throat usually found there. *Male:* Similar to Black-throated Green Warbler but with *black back* and black line through eye. *Female:* Similar to male but back olive-green.
Similar species: Migrant Black-throated Greens when in c. Texas prefer the lowlands to the cedar ridges. Females are very similar, but Golden-cheek may have flecks of black on back; belly *snowy white* (lacking tinge of yellow).
Voice: Song, a hurried *tweeah, tweeah, tweesy* (H. P. Attwater) or *bzzzz, layzeee, dayzeee* (E. Kincaid).
Where found: *Breeds* only in Texas; mainly in Edwards Plateau; west to San Angelo, Rocksprings; east locally to Austin, San Antonio. An offshoot colony near Dallas. Winters s. Mexico to Nicaragua. **Habitat:** Junipers, oaks; also streamside trees. **Nest:** A small cup in juniper. Eggs (3–5) spotted.

HERMIT WARBLER *Dendroica occidentalis* 4½–4¾ **Pl. 50**
Field marks: Note the bright *yellow head* set off by the *black throat* and dark gray back. In the female the black of the throat is much reduced or wanting but the yellow face, gray back, and whitish underparts identify it.
Similar species: (1) Male Townsend's Warbler has black cheek and crown patches. Female has olive back, *yellow* breast. (2) In Canada (east of Rockies) see Black-throated Green Warbler.
Voice: Song, 3 high lisping notes followed by 2 abrupt lower ones: *sweety, sweety, sweety, chup' chup'* or *seedle, seedle, seedle, chup' chup'*. Abrupt end notes distinctive.
Where found: *Breeds* from Washington through Coast Ranges and Sierra to nw. and se.-c. California, w. Nevada (Lake Tahoe). *Migrates* through California, Arizona. *Casual,* New Mexico, w. Texas. *Winters* Mexico to Nicaragua; rarely coastal California. **Habitat:** Conifer forests; in migration, other trees. **Nest:** A small cup well up in conifer. Eggs (3–5) spotted.

BLACKBURNIAN WARBLER **Pl. 50**
Dendroica fusca 4½–5½
    Field marks: A "fire-throat." *Male in spring:* Black and white with *flaming orange* about head and throat. *Female:* Paler; orange enough on throat to be recognized. *Autumn:* Pattern similar, but paler, orange more yellowish. Note the clean-cut yellow head-stripings and pale back-stripes.
    Similar species: The differently patterned male Redstart is the only other small N. American bird with similar colors.
    Voice: Song begins with repeated *zip*'s and ends on a very high up-slurred note: *zip zip zip zip titi tseeeeee*. Wiry end note is diagnostic if audible. Also a 2-parted song, more like Nashville's: *teetsa teetsa teetsa teetsa zizizizizi.*
    Where found: Canada, ne. U.S.; south in mts. to n. Georgia. Winters Guatemala to Peru. **West:** *Breeds* locally in c. Saskatchewan; c. Alberta (?). *Casual migrant* west through Plains to Rocky Mt. states. **Habitat:** Conifer forests (summer). **Nest:** A small cup high in conifer. Eggs (4–5) spotted.

GRACE'S WARBLER *Dendroica graciae* 4½–5 **Pl. 50**
    Field marks: A *gray-backed warbler with a yellow throat.* Belly white; 2 white wing-bars, *yellowish line* over the eye, and strong black stripes on the sides.
    Similar species: (1) See Audubon's Warbler (yellow rump). (2) Yellow-throated Warbler (e. and c. U.S., mainly east of 100°) has *white* eyebrow-stripe, white spot behind ear.
    Voice: *Cheedle cheedle che che che che,* etc. (ends in trill).
    Where found: *Breeds* from s. Utah, s. Colorado south locally through mts. of Arizona, New Mexico, w. Texas to n. Nicaragua. *Winters* south of U.S. **Habitat:** Pine-oak forests of mts. **Nest:** A small cup high in conifer. Eggs (3–4) spotted.

CHESTNUT-SIDED WARBLER   Pl. 50
Dendroica pensylvanica   4½–5¼
   Field marks: *Adults in spring:* Note the combination of *yellow crown, chestnut sides. Autumn:* Greenish above, white below, with white eye-ring, 2 pale yellow wing-bars. Adults usually retain some chestnut. The lemon-colored shade of green, in connection with white underparts, is determinative.
   Similar species: Bay-breasted Warbler appears dark-headed (has chestnut throat, *dark chestnut crown*).
   Voice: Territorial song, similar to Yellow Warbler's: *see see see see see Miss Beech' er* or *please please pleased ta meet' cha,* last note dropping. Nesting song, longer, formless.
   Where found: S. Canada, ne. U.S.; in mts. to n. Georgia. Winters Nicaragua through Panama. **West:** *Breeds* in c. Saskatchewan, n. N. Dakota (Turtle Mts.). *Casual* west to Alberta (has bred), Wyoming, Colorado, w. Oklahoma, w. Texas. *Accidental,* California, Arizona. **Habitat:** Shrubs, brushy slashings. **Nest:** A grass cup in low bush, briars. Eggs (3–5) speckled.

BAY-BREASTED WARBLER   Pl. 51
Dendroica castanea   5–6
   Field marks: *Male in spring:* Dark-looking, with *chestnut* throat, crown, upper breast and sides. Note the *spot of pale* buff on neck. *Female in spring:* Paler; more washed out. *Autumn birds:* Olive-green above; 2 white wing-bars; dull buff-white below. Some birds have traces of bay.
   Similar species: (1) Adult Chestnut-sided Warbler has *yellow* crown (Bay-breast, dark). (2) Fall Blackpoll is *very* similar to fall Bay-breast. It is: (a) tinged with greenish below and streaked (Bay-breast is buffier, streaks indistinct or wanting); (b) Blackpoll has *white* under tail coverts (Bay-breast *buff*); (c) Blackpoll usually has *pale yellowish legs* (Bay-breast, blackish; but this character varies).
   Voice: A high sibilant *teesi teesi teesi;* resembles song of Black-and-White; thinner, shorter, more on one pitch.
   Where found: Canada, ne. edge of U.S. Winters Panama to Venezuela. **West:** *Breeds* sparsely in n. Alberta, c. Saskatchewan. *Casual migrant* on Plains west to mt. states. *Accidental,* California, New Mexico. **Habitat:** Coniferous forests. **Nest:** A loose cup in conifer. Eggs (4–6; 7) spotted.

BLACKPOLL WARBLER   *Dendroica striata*   5–5¾   Pl. 50
   Field marks: *Male in spring:* A striped gray warbler with a *solid black cap and white cheeks. Female in spring:* Less heavily streaked, lacking the black cap; a plain, black-streaked warbler, greenish gray above, white below. *Autumn birds:* Streaked, greenish-looking warblers, olive-green above; dingy yellow below, faintly streaked; 2 white wing-bars.
   Similar species: (1) Black-throated Gray Warbler has black

cheeks. (2) Black-and-White Warbler has white *stripe* through crown. (3) See fall Bay-breasted Warbler (*Similar species*). **Voice:** Song, a thin, deliberate *zi-zi-zi-zi-zi-zi-zi-zi* on one pitch, becoming slightly louder, then fading (crescendo, diminuendo). A more rapid version on nesting grounds. **Where found:** Alaska, Canada, ne. U.S. Winters in tropical S. America. **West:** *Breeds* from tree limit south in boreal forests to s. Alaska, n. B.C., c. Alberta, n.-c. Saskatchewan. *Spring migrant* on w. Plains from e. Colorado to s. Alberta. *Casual,* New Mexico, Texas panhandle. *Accidental,* California. **Habitat:** Low conifers; in migration, various trees. **Nest:** A feather-lined cup in small spruce. Eggs (3–5) spotted.

PALM WARBLER *Dendroica palmarum* 4½–5½ **Pl. 50**
Field marks: Note the constant *bobbing* of the tail. Brown above; yellowish or whitish below, narrowly streaked; *yellow under tail coverts,* white spots in tail corners. In spring, *chestnut cap* (obscure in fall, winter). Sexes similar.
Voice: Song, a repetitious series of weak notes, *thi-thi-thi-thi-thi-thi* or *zhe-zhe-zhe-zhe-zhe-zhe-zhe.*
Where found: Canada, ne. edge of U.S. Winters in s. U.S., Caribbean area. **West:** *Breeds* from ne. B.C., sw. Mackenzie across n. half of Alberta, Saskatchewan. *Casual* or sparse migrant through Plains west to mt. states. Casual or accidental in Pacific states, Arizona, New Mexico. **Habitat:** Wooded borders of muskegs. In migration, low trees, bushes, ground. **Nest:** Of moss, grass, in moss of dry muskeg. Eggs (4–5) spotted.

OVENBIRD *Seiurus aurocapillus* 5½–6½ **Pl. 50**
Field marks: Heard much more often than seen. A sparrow-sized ground warbler; *walks* on pale *pinkish* legs over the forest floor. Suggests a small thrush — olive-brown above, but striped rather than spotted beneath. A *light orange* patch on crown.
Voice: Song, an accented *teach'er,* TEACH'ER, TEACH'ER, etc., repeated rapidly in a crescendo, till the air rings. At night, a complicated flight song with 2 or 3 revealing *teach* notes.
Where found: S. Canada to e. Colorado, n. Georgia. Winters from se. U.S. to n. S. America. **West:** *Breeds* from ne. B.C., s. Mackenzie, c. Saskatchewan south locally on lower e. slopes of Rockies and adjacent plains to Colorado, c. Nebraska. *Sparse migrant* on w. Great Plains. *Accidental* in Alaska. Recorded in all states except Oregon. **Habitat:** Near ground in deciduous woods; in migration, thickets. **Nest:** A leaf-domed cup on ground in woods. Eggs (3–5; 6) spotted.

NORTHERN WATERTHRUSH **Pl. 50**
Seiurus noveboracensis 5½–6½
(Grinnell's Waterthrush)
Field marks: Though a warbler, it often walks along the water's

edge and teeters in the manner of a Spotted Sandpiper. A brown-backed bird about the size of a sparrow, with a *conspicuous* whitish or *buffy eyebrow-stripe and heavily striped underparts*. Underparts whitish or tinged with yellowish or buffy.

Voice: Note, a sharp *chip*. Song, a vigorous, rapid *twit twit twit sweet sweet sweet chew chew chew,* dropping in pitch at end. Variable, but the *chew chew chew* is often diagnostic.

Where found: Alaska, Canada, n. edge of U.S. *Winters* mainly in American tropics. **West:** *Breeds* from n.-c. Alaska, Mackenzie south to s. B.C., n. Idaho, w. Montana, n. N. Dakota. *Migrant* mainly east of Rockies; rarely west to Pacific states. **Habitat:** Swampy or wet woods, streamsides, lakeshores; in migration, also thickets. **Nest:** A mossy cup in streambank or foot of stump. Eggs (4–5) spotted.

CONNECTICUT WARBLER *Oporornis agilis* 5¼–6 Pl. 51

Field marks: This species, like the Mourning and MacGillivray's Warblers, possesses a *gray hood* set off against the yellow and olive of its body. It has a *complete white eye-ring*. It always lacks the black on throat of spring males of the other 2 species. *Fall females and young* are duller, with no gray, but there is a suggestion of a hood (a *brownish* stain across the upper breast). Eye-ring always present.

Similar species: (1) Breeding Mourning Warbler (Canada, east of Rockies) is smaller, *lacks* eye-ring (in fall often has a broken one). Breeding male has *black throat*. The yellow under tail coverts reach half the length of the tail; in Connecticut, nearly to end. (2) Breeding MacGillivray's Warbler (Rockies, west), has an *incomplete* white eye-ring but otherwise shares field marks of Mourning, including flecks of black on throat of male. (3) Nashville Warbler (white eye-ring) is much smaller, with bright *yellow throat*.

Voice: A repetitious *chip chup-ee, chip chup-ee, chip chup-ee, chip* or *sugar-tweet, sugar-tweet, sugar-tweet* (W. W. H. Gunn).

Where found: C.-s. Canada to n. Minnesota, n. Wisconsin, n. Michigan. Winters in n. S. America. **West:** *Breeds* from e. B.C. across c. Alberta, c. Saskatchewan. *Casual migrant* west to Montana, Colorado, Texas panhandle. *Accidental,* Utah. **Habitat:** Poplar bluffs, muskeg, mixed woods near water. In migration, undergrowth. **Nest:** A frail grass cup in moss or grass. Eggs (4–5) spotted.

MOURNING WARBLER   Pl. 51
Oporornis philadelphia 5–5¾

Field marks: The e. counterpart of MacGillivray's Warbler. Breeding birds (both sexes) have *no eye-ring*. Male is blacker on throat than male MacGillivray's. Autumn birds (with broken eye-ring) not separable in the field.

Similar species: See (1) MacGillivray's Warbler (Rockies, west), (2) Connecticut Warbler (Canada, east of Rockies).
Voice: Song, *chirry, chirry, chorry chorry* (*chorry* lower).
Where found: Canada, ne. U.S.; in mts. to Virginia. Migrant east of 100° en route to tropical America. **West:** *Breeds* east of Rockies in c. Alberta, c. Saskatchewan. **Habitat:** Woodland clearings, slashings, thickets. **Nest:** A bulky cup of leaves, grass in briars, ferns, grass. Eggs (3–5) spotted.

MacGILLIVRAY'S WARBLER
Pl. 51
Oporornis tolmiei 4¾–5½
Field marks: *Male:* Olive above, yellow below, with a *slate-gray hood* (blackish on throat), completely encircling the head and neck. Has a white *eye-ring*, broken fore and aft. *Female:* Similar but hood much paler, washed out on throat.
Similar species: (1) See Nashville Warbler (bright yellow throat). In Canada, east of Rockies, and in c. Texas see also (2) Mourning Warbler and (3) Connecticut Warbler.
Voice: Song, a rolling *chiddle-chiddle-chiddle, turtle-turtle,* voice dropping on last notes; or *sweeter-sweeter-sweeter, sugar-sugar.* Also *chiddle-chiddle-chiddle, wick-wick.*
Where found: *Breeds* from se. Alaska, sw. Yukon, n. B.C., s. Alberta, sw. Saskatchewan south to c. California (coast and mts.), and in mts. to s. Nevada, c. Arizona, c. New Mexico. In migration cast to w. edge of Plains and Edwards Plateau (Texas). *Winters* Mexico to Colombia; rarely California. **Habitat:** Low dense undergrowth; shady, damp thickets. **Nest:** A grass cup in low bush or weeds. Eggs (3–5) spotted.

YELLOWTHROAT *Geothlypis trichas* 4½–5¾ Pl. 51
Field marks: A wrenlike warbler, *male* with a *black mask,* or "domino." Throat yellow. *Females and immatures* are olive-brown with a rich yellow throat, buffy-yellow breast, and *whitish belly;* no black mask. Distinguished from similar warblers by *whitish belly,* brownish sides, and by habitat.
Voice: Song, a rapid, well-enunciated *witchity-witchity-witchity-witch;* sometimes shortened to *witchy-witchy-witchy-witch.* Note, a husky *tchep;* distinctive.
Where found: Canada, U.S. to s. Mexico. Winters s. U.S. to W. Indies, Canal Zone. **West:** *Breeds* from se. Alaska, c. B.C., n. Alberta, c. Saskatchewan south. *Winters* from n. California, w. and s. Arizona, w. Texas south. **Habitat:** Swamps, marshes (fresh and salt), wet thickets, streamsides. **Nest:** A loose grass cup on or near ground. Eggs (3–5) spotted.

YELLOW-BREASTED CHAT *Icteria virens* 6½–7½ Pl. 51
(Long-tailed Chat)
Field marks: Note the *white* "spectacles," *bright yellow* throat

and breast. Olive-green above; white belly. Sexes similar. Except for its color, the Chat seems more like a Catbird or a Mockingbird than a warbler. Its very large size (for a warbler), *rather long tail,* bill contour, eccentric song and actions, and brushy habitat all suggest those larger birds.

Voice: Song, clear repeated whistles, alternated with harsh notes and soft crowlike *caw*'s. Occasionally mimics. Suggests Mockingbird, but repertoire more limited; much longer pauses between phrases. Single notes, such as *whoit* or *kook,* are distinctive. Often sings on the wing, with dangling legs, and like Mockingbird frequently sings at night.

Where found: S. Canada to c. Mexico, Gulf Coast. Winters Mexico to Panama. **West:** *Breeds* from s. interior B.C., s. Alberta, s. Saskatchewan throughout w. U.S. **Habitat:** Stream tangles, briars, willow thickets, moist canyons. **Nest:** A cup of leaves, grass in bush, briars. Eggs (3–5) spotted.

RED-FACED WARBLER   Pl. 51
Cardellina rubrifrons 5–5¼

Field marks: A gray-backed warbler with a bright-red face and breast; black patch on head, white nape, white belly. The only other U.S. warbler with the same shade of red, the Painted Redstart, has no red on the face. Adults similar.

Voice: A clear sweet song similar to that of Yellow Warbler (Painted Redstart has a more repetitious quality).

Where found: *Breeds* from c. Arizona, sw. New Mexico to Durango, Mexico. *Casual,* w. Texas. Winters Mexico, Guatemala. **Habitat:** Open forests in high mts. **Nest:** On ground, under tree or grass clump. Eggs (3–4) dotted.

WILSON'S WARBLER *Wilsonia pusilla* 4¼–5   Pl. 51
(Pileolated Warbler)

Field marks: *Male:* A yellow warbler with a *round black cap. Females* sometimes do, and *immatures* do not, show traces of the cap. They appear as small, very active warblers, olive above, bright yellow below, with no streaks or wing-bars; golden-looking, with a yellow stripe above the beady black eye.

Similar species: Yellow Warbler has yellow spots in tail (Wilson's has no tail spots).

Voice: Song, a thin rapid little chatter dropping in pitch at the end: *chichichichichichetchet.*

Where found: Alaska, Canada, w. and ne. U.S. Winters Mexico to Panama. **West:** *Breeds* from n. Alaska, Yukon, nw. Mackenzie southeast across boreal forests of Canada; south through B.C. and Pacific states to s. California; through Rockies to c. Nevada, n. New Mexico. **Habitat:** Thickets along woodland streams, moist tangles, low shrubs, willows, alders. **Nest:** A loose grass cup on or near ground. Eggs (3–6) dotted.

CANADA WARBLER *Wilsonia canadensis* 5–5¾ **Pl. 50**
Field marks: The "necklaced warbler." Solid gray above, bright
yellow below; white under tail coverts. Male has a *necklace of
short black stripes* across breast. *Females and immatures* similar,
but necklace fainter, sometimes nearly wanting. All have *yellow
"spectacles."* Note the combination of gray upper parts, *lack of
white in wings and tail.*
Voice: Song, a staccato burst, irregularly arranged. *Chip,
chupety swee-ditchety* (W. W. H. Gunn). Note, *tchip.*
Where found: Canada, ne. U.S. to mts. of n. Georgia. Winters
Honduras to n. S. America. **West:** *Breeds* in n.-c. Alberta, c.
Saskatchewan. *Casual* on w. Great Plains. *Accidental,* California. **Habitat:** Forest undergrowth. **Nest:** Of leaves, rootlets,
in bank, weeds, stump. Eggs (3–5) spotted.

AMERICAN REDSTART *Setophaga ruticilla* 4½–5¾ **Pl. 51**
Field marks: A butterfly-like bird, constantly flitting, drooping
wings and spreading its tail. Has fly-catching habits. *Male:*
Black with *bright orange patches on wings and tail;* belly white.
Female: Olive-brown above, white below; yellow flash-patches on
wings and tail. *Immature male:* Variable; much like female;
yellow often tinged with orange.
Voice: Three commonest songs: *zee zee zee zee zwee* (last note
higher), *tsee tsee tsee tsee tsee-o* (drop on last syllable), and *teetsa
teetsa teetsa teetsa teet* (double-noted). Songs often alternated.
Note, a clear *tseet.*
Where found: Canada to ne. Texas, n. Georgia. Winters from
Mexico, W. Indies to n. S. America. **West:** *Breeds* from n. B.C.,
s. Mackenzie east across wooded Canada; south (east of Cascades) to e. Oregon, n. Utah, n. Colorado. *Migrant* through
Plains; rarely but regularly through sw. states. **Habitat:** Second-
growth deciduous woods, alders. **Nest:** A neat cup in upright
crotch in sapling. Eggs (3–5) spotted.

PAINTED REDSTART *Setophaga picta* 5–5¼ **Pl. 51**
Field marks: A beautiful bird; postures with half-spread wings
and tail in redstart fashion. Black head and upper parts; *large
white patches* in wings and on sides of tail; *large bright red patch*
on lower breast. Sexes similar.
Similar species: Red-faced Warbler is our only other warbler
with similar red (Painted Redstart has no red on face).
Voice: Song, a repetitious *weeta weeta weeta wee* or *weeta weeta
chilp chilp chilp.* Note, an unwarblerlike *clee-ip.*
Where found: *Breeds* in mts. from n. Arizona, sw. New Mexico,
w. Texas (Chisos Mts.) to n. Nicaragua. Winters mainly south
of U.S. Strays visit s. California (many records). **Habitat:** Oak
canyons, pine-oak forest in mts. **Nest:** A grassy cup on ground,
usually on steep bank. Eggs (3–4) speckled.

Weaver Finches, etc.: Ploceidae

A WIDESPREAD, varied group of which the introduced House Sparrow (not related to our native sparrows) is the best-known example. **Food:** Mainly insects, seeds. **Range:** Widespread in Old World; most species in Africa. **No. of species:** World, 263 (of which sparrow-weavers are 35); West, 1 (+2 in Hawaii). Some recent authorities put the subfamily Carduelinae (goldfinches, crossbills, etc.) here instead of in the Fringillidae. (Based on their classification, not followed here, the breakdown would be: World, 313; West, 19; +2 in Hawaii.)

HOUSE SPARROW *Passer domesticus* 5¾-6¼
("English Sparrow") **below, Pl. 60**
  Field marks: A species with which everyone is familiar. Sooty birds often bear a poor resemblance to clean country males with the black throat, white cheeks, chestnut nape. Females and young lack the black throat, are dull brown above and dingy whitish below; dull eye-stripe.
  Voice: Garrulous and varied. A loud *cheep;* also *chissis* and various grating, twittering, and chirping notes.
  Where found: Native to Eurasia, n. Africa. Introduced in N. America, S. America, s. Africa, Australia, Hawaii, etc. **West:** *Resident* in most settled sections from c. B.C., s. Mackenzie south. **Habitat:** Cities, towns, farms. **Nest:** A bulky mass, usually in cavity or in building; sometimes in branches of tree. Eggs (5-6) speckled.

HOUSE SPARROW
(See also Plate 60)

Meadowlarks, Blackbirds, and Orioles: Icteridae

A VARIED group possessing conical, sharp-pointed bills and rather flat profiles. Sexes usually unlike. **Food:** Insects, small fruits, seeds, waste grain, small aquatic life. **Range:** New World; most species in tropics. **No. of species:** World, 88; West, 17 (+2 marginals, 1 accidental).

BOBOLINK *Dolichonyx oryzivorus* 6–8   **Pl. 54**
   Field marks: *Male in spring:* Our only songbird that is *solid black below and largely white* on black; like a dress suit reversed. *Female and autumn male:* A bit larger than House Sparrow; rich buff with dark stripings on crown and back.
   Similar species: (1) Male Lark Bunting is black with white *confined to wings.* (2) Female Red-winged Blackbird is duskier than female Bobolink, has longer bill, heavy stripes on breast.
   Voice: Song, in hovering flight and quivering descent, ecstatic and bubbling, starting with low reedy notes and rollicking upward. Flight note, a clear *pink.*
   Where found: S. Canada, n. U.S. Migrates through e. U.S. Winters in s. S. America. **West:** *Breeds* from s. B.C., c. Alberta, s.-c. Saskatchewan south (east of Cascades) very locally to ne. California, n. Utah, c. Colorado. *Casual,* New Mexico (has bred), Texas panhandle. *Accidental,* California, Arizona. **Habitat:** Hay meadows, open fields; in migration, also marshes. **Nest:** A grass-lined cup in grass. Eggs (4–7) blotched.

EASTERN MEADOWLARK *Sturnella magna* 8½–11
(including Rio Grande Meadowlark)
   Similar species: Nearly identical with Western Meadowlark, but not as pale; yellow of throat not so extensive (does not touch cheeks). Safely recognized only by song.
   Voice: Song, clear slurred whistles, *tee-you, tee-yair,* very unlike bubbly flutelike song of Western Meadowlark.
   Where found: Se. Canada, e. U.S., Cuba; also sw. U.S. to Brazil. Partial migrant. **West:** Colonies west of 100° in sw. S. Dakota, w. Nebraska, Texas panhandle. *Breeds* also in Arizona, s. and c. New Mexico, w. Texas (Rio Grande). **Habitat and Nest:** Similar to Western Meadowlark's.

WESTERN MEADOWLARK   **Pl. 54**
Sturnella neglecta 8½–11
   Field marks: In the grass country a chunky brown bird flushes, showing a conspicuous patch of *white* on each side of its short, wide tail. Several short, rapid wingbeats alternate with short

periods of sailing. Should it perch on a fence post, the glass reveals a bright yellow breast crossed by a black V. When walking, it nervously flicks its tail open and shut.

Similar species: See Eastern Meadowlark. Other ground birds that show white outer tail feathers (pipits, longspurs, Vesper Sparrow, juncos) are very much smaller, slimmer.

Voice: A variable song of 7–10 notes, flutelike, gurgling, and double-noted. Notes, *tchuck* and a guttural chatter.

Where found: Sw. Canada, upper Mississippi Valley to c. Mexico. Partial migrant. **West:** *Breeds* from c. B.C., c. Alberta, c. Saskatchewan south. *Winters* from Canadian border (rarely) south. *Accidental,* Alaska. *Introduced* in Hawaii (Kauai).

Habitat: Open fields, meadows, plains, prairies. **Nest:** A grassy saucer, partially domed, among grass. Eggs (3–7) spotted.

YELLOW-HEADED BLACKBIRD   Pl. 52
Xanthocephalus xanthocephalus   8–11

Field marks: *Male:* A Robin-sized marsh blackbird with an *orange-yellow* head and breast; shows a white wing patch in flight. Females smaller and browner; most of yellow confined to throat and chest; lower breast streaked with white. Gregarious.

Voice: Song, low hoarse rasping notes produced with much effort; "like very rusty hinges." Note, a low *kruck* or *kack*.

Where found: S. Canada, w. U.S., upper Mississippi Valley, nw. Mexico. Winters sw. U.S., Mexico. **West:** *Breeds* from c. B.C., Alberta, n.-c. Saskatchewan south to s. California, Arizona, n. New Mexico, very local in nw. coast belt. *Winters* mainly from se. Oregon, c. Arizona, s. New Mexico, w. Texas (Rio Grande) south. **Habitat:** Fresh marshes, tules; forages in fields, open country. **Nest:** A woven cup fastened to tules or reeds above water; in loose colony. Eggs (3–5) blotched.

RED-WINGED BLACKBIRD   *Agelaius phoeniceus*   7–9½
(Red-wing)   Pl. 52

Field marks: *Male:* Black, with red *epaulets.* Often the scarlet is concealed, only the yellowish margin is then visible. One race, *A. p. californica* ("Bicolored" Red-winged Blackbird) of the Central Valley of California, has solid red epaulets without yellow edges. *Immature male:* Sooty-brown, mottled, but with red shoulder patches. *Female and young:* Brownish; identified by the sharp-pointed bill, blackbird appearance, and *well-defined black stripings* below. Gregarious.

Similar species: In California see Tricolored Blackbird.

Voice: A loud *check* and a high, slurred *tee-err.* Song, a liquid gurgling *o-ka-lay* or *o-ka-lee-onk.*

Where found: Canada to W. Indies, Costa Rica. **West:** *Breeds* from c. B.C., c. Mackenzie throughout West. *Winters* from s. B.C., n. Idaho, Wyoming south. *Casual,* Alaska. **Habitat:**

Breeds in marshes, swamps, hayfields; forages also in cultivated land, edges of water. **Nest:** A woven cup fastened to reeds, tules, deep grass, bush. Eggs (3–5) bluish, spotted, scrawled.

TRICOLORED BLACKBIRD   *Agelaius tricolor*   7½–9
(Tricolored Red-wing)
    Field marks: *Male:* Similar to Red-wing but has a darker red patch (visible mainly in flight) with a conspicuous white margin. *Female:* Darker than most races of Red-wing, especially below; bill thicker at base, more sharply pointed. Nests in dense colonies often numbering many thousands (Red-wing is territorial). Highly gregarious at all times.
    Voice: Song more nasal than Red-wing's: *on-ke-kaaangh.* Notes include a nasal *kemp* (II. Cogswell).
    Where found: *Breeds* from s. Oregon (Tule, Klamath Lakes) south through California; mainly in Sacramento, San Joaquin Valleys and near coast from Sonoma Co. to nw. Baja California. *Winters* mainly in California range. **Habitat:** Cattail or tule marshes; forages in fields, irrigated lands. **Nest:** A deep woven cup attached to reeds, cattails, tules, or bush in marsh; in colony. Eggs (3–4; 6) greenish, scrawled.

ORCHARD ORIOLE   *Icterus spurius*   6–7¼   **Pl. 53**
    Field marks: Smaller than Robin. *Adult male:* The only all-*dark* oriole in U.S.; rump and underparts *deep chestnut.* Head, neck, back, wings, and tail black. *Immature male:* Greenish above, yellow below; black throat. *Female and young:* Olive-green above, yellow below, with 2 white wing-bars.
    Similar species: (1) Males of other orioles are orange, or yellow and black. (2) Female and young male Hooded Orioles are larger than similar Orchards, have longer bills, and are a bit warmer in color below (less greenish). (3) See these plumages of Scott's Oriole. (4) See also female tanagers (pp. 220–22).
    Voice: Song, a fast-moving outburst interspersed with piping whistles, guttural notes; unlike abrupt piping of most orioles. A strident slurred *what-cheer* or *wheer,* at or near end.
    Where found: Se. Canada, e. and c. U.S. to c. Mexico. Winters Mexico to n. S. America. *West: Breeds* locally west of 100° from e. Montana, N. Dakota through Plains to se. New Mexico, w. Texas (Panhandle, Trans-Pecos). *Casual,* California, s. Arizona. **Habitat:** Orchards, farms, towns. **Nest:** A basket-like pouch hung from branch. Eggs (4–5; 7) scrawled.

BLACK-HEADED ORIOLE   *Icterus graduacauda*   8–9¼
(Audubon's Oriole)   **Pl. 53**
    Field marks: A *yellow* oriole with black head, wings, and tail. No other resident U.S. oriole has a *yellowish* back (other male U.S. orioles have black backs). Sexes similar.

Similar species: Our only other black-headed, *yellow* oriole, Scott's, is not found in the s. Texas range of this species.
Voice: Song, low whistled notes of human quality, disjointed, with halftones; suggests a boy learning to whistle.
Where found: S. Texas to Guatemala. *Resident* in lower Rio Grande Valley. Occasional north to Beeville and upriver to Eagle Pass. **Habitat:** Woodlands, thickets. **Nest:** A pouch of grass hung in tree. Eggs (3–5) blotched, streaked.

HOODED ORIOLE *Icterus cucullatus* 7–7¾   **Pl. 53**
Field marks: *Male:* Orange and black with a black throat and *orange crown,* or "hood." The only *common* U.S. oriole with an orange crown. *Female:* Back, olive-gray, head and tail more yellowish, underparts yellowish, wings with 2 white bars. Similar to female Bullock's Oriole, but underparts entirely yellowish. *Immature male:* Resembles female but *throat black.*
Similar species: (1) Female and immature Bullock's have whitish belly; bill shorter, less curved. (2) Immature male Orchard Oriole is a bit more greenish; has a shorter bill. (3) In Rio Grande Delta and Mexico see Lichtenstein's Oriole.
Voice: Song, throaty notes and piping whistles: *chut chut chut whew whew,* opening notes throaty. Note, a sharp *eek.*
Where found: *Breeds* from c. California, s. Nevada, sw. Utah, c. Arizona, sw. New Mexico, w. and s. Texas (near Rio Grande) to s. Mexico. *Winters* in Mexico; rarely in s. Texas. **Habitat:** Open woodlands, thickets, palms, shade trees. **Nest:** A pouch tucked under old palm fronds, yucca, or Spanish moss. Eggs (3–5) spotted.

LICHTENSTEIN'S ORIOLE *Icterus gularis* 8¼–10 **Pl. 53**
(Alta Mira Oriole)
Field marks: Very similar to Hooded Oriole, but considerably larger, and usually more intensely orange. The points to look for are the bill (much thicker at base) and the upper wing-bar, which is *yellow* or *orange,* not white. Sexes similar.
Voice: A harsh rasping "fuss" note, *ike-ike-ike* (E. Kincaid). Song, disjointed whistled notes.
Where found: Southern tip of Texas to Nicaragua. Rare resident in Rio Grande Delta. Has bred in Cameron and Hidalgo Cos. **Habitat:** Woodlands. **Nest:** A well-woven stocking, 2 ft. long, swinging from high branch. Eggs (3–4) spotted, scrawled.

SCOTT'S ORIOLE *Icterus parisorum* 7¼–8¼   **Pl. 53**
Field marks: *Male:* A lemon-yellow oriole with *black back,* head, wings, and tail. The *solid black head* and pale *yellow* pattern distinguish it from other orioles in its U.S. range. *Female:* More greenish yellow beneath than most other female orioles. *Immature male:* Has a black throat similar to that of young male

Hooded and Orchard Orioles. Dingier underparts, grayer back, more extensive black on face help identify it.

Similar species: (1) Female Orchard Oriole is also greenish, but is smaller; bill shorter. (2) Female Hooded has warmer yellow underparts. (3) Female Bullock's, whitish belly.

Voice: Song, rich whistles; suggests Western Meadowlark.

Where found: Sw. U.S., n. Mexico. *Breeds* in se. California, s. Nevada, Utah, Arizona, s. New Mexico, w. Texas (Trans-Pecos, s. Staked Plain). Winters in Mexico. *Casual,* sw. California. **Habitat:** Dry woods and scrub in desert mts., yucca "forests," Joshua trees, oak slopes, piñons. **Nest:** A grassy pouch in yucca, piñon, small tree. Eggs (2–4) blotched, streaked.

BALTIMORE ORIOLE *Icterus galbula* 7–8   **Pl. 53**
Field marks: Smaller than Robin. *Male: Fiery orange and black,* with *solid black head. Female and young:* Olive-brown above, burnt yellow-orange below; 2 white wing-bars. Some females have black on head, suggesting male's hood. Hybridizes with Bullock's Oriole on Great Plains.

Similar species: (1) Male Bullock's Oriole has orange face, large white wing patch. Female Bullock's has grayer back, whitish belly. (2) Female Orchard Oriole is greener.

Voice: Song, a series of rich, piping whistled notes. Note, a low whistled *hew-li.*

Where found: Canada, e. and c. U.S. Winters Mexico to n. S. America. **West:** *Breeds* east of Rockies in c. Alberta, c. Saskatchewan and south on Great Plains; west sparsely to e. Montana; w. Nebraska, extreme c. Colorado, w. Oklahoma, w. Texas (e. Panhandle; casually Trans-Pecos). *Casual,* Wyoming, New Mexico. *Accidental,* B.C., California, Arizona. **Habitat:** Open woods, elms, shade trees. **Nest:** A deep silvery pouch hung from tip of tree branch. Eggs (4–6) scrawled.

BULLOCK'S ORIOLE *Icterus bullockii* 7–8½   **Pl. 53**
Field marks: The most widespread oriole in the West. *Male:* Fiery *orange and black,* with large *white wing patches.* Note the black crown, *orange cheeks. Female and young:* Olive-gray above, more yellowish on tail; yellow throat and breast; 2 white wing-bars. Less extensively yellow below than other female orioles; usually *whitish on belly;* back decidedly grayer. Immature male resembles female but has a *black throat.*

Similar species: (1) Male Hooded Oriole (sw. U.S.) has orange crown. (2) On Plains see Baltimore Oriole. (3) Female and immature Hooded and Baltimore Orioles have completely yellow bellies. (4) Female tanagers resemble female orioles, but are darker above and on sides of head, have curved ridge on bill.

Voice: A series of accented double notes with 1 or 2 piping notes. Note, a sharp *skip;* also a chatter.

Where found: *Breeds* from s. B.C., se. Alberta, sw. Saskatchewan south through w. U.S. (sparse in nw. coast belt) to n. Mexico; east onto Great Plains. Winters w. Mexico to Costa Rica. **Habitat:** River groves, open oak woods, towns, farms. **Nest:** A pouch hung from branch of tree. Eggs (3-6) scrawled.

RUSTY BLACKBIRD *Euphagus carolinus* 8½-9¾   **Pl. 52**
Field marks: *Male:* Very similar to male Brewer's Blackbird, but at close range shows *dull greenish* head reflections. The iridescence is not noticeable as in Brewer's Blackbird or Common Grackle. *Female in spring:* Slate-colored; resembles female Brewer's Blackbird, but eyes *yellow* (not dark). *Winter adults and young:* Washed with rusty; closely *barred* beneath.
Similar species: (1) See Brewer's Blackbird. (2) Grackles also have whitish eyes, but the larger size, long rounded or keeled tail, and brighter iridescence identify them. (3) Cowbirds are smaller, *dark-eyed, short-billed.*
Voice: Note, a loud *chack.* "Song," a split creak like a rusty hinge: *kush-a-lee* alternating with *ksh-lay.*
Where found: Alaska, Canada, ne. edge of U.S. Winters to Gulf Coast. **West:** *Breeds* from n. Alaska, nw. Mackenzie to c. B.C., c. Alberta, c. Saskatchewan. *Winters* east of Rockies from Canadian border (a few) to Texas. *Casual,* Idaho, Utah, California, Arizona, New Mexico. **Habitat:** River groves, wooded swamps; muskegs (summer). **Nest:** A bulky cup in bush or tree near water. Eggs (3-6) light blue-green, blotched.

BREWER'S BLACKBIRD   **Pl. 52**
Euphagus cyanocephalus 8-10
Field marks: *Male:* A blackbird with pale yellow eyes; *purplish* reflections on head and greenish on body in strong light. Usually looks quite black. In winter, Brewer's may have some rusty barring, but note the dark-eyed females (female Rusty has light eyes). *Female:* Grayish, with *brown* eyes.
Similar species: (1) See Rusty Blackbird (east of Rockies). Where both species occur they tend to separate out: Brewer's preferring fields and farms; Rusty, river groves and swamps. (2) Female Cowbird has a short bill.
Voice: Note, a harsh *check.* Song, a harsh wheezy *que-ee* or *ksh-eee,* like the creaking of a rusty hinge.
Where found: Sw. Canada, w. and n.-c. U.S. Winters w. and s. U.S. to s. Mexico. **West:** *Breeds* from c. B.C., c. Alberta, c. Saskatchewan south to s. California, s. Nevada, c. Arizona, n. New Mexico, w. Texas (local). *Winters* from Washington, Idaho, Montana south. *Accidental,* Alaska. **Habitat:** Varied open country, lakeshores, fields, farms, parks, cities. **Nest:** A twiggy grass-lined cup, on ground, in bush or tree, in loose colony. Eggs (4-6; 8) heavily spotted.

BOAT-TAILED GRACKLE   *Cassidix mexicanus*   **Pl. 52**
(Great-tailed Grackle)   ♂16–17, ♀12–13
   Field marks: A very large iridescent blackbird, *well over a foot long,* with a long, wide *keel-shaped* tail. Females are brown, not black, and are *much* smaller than males.
   Similar species: Common Grackle is much smaller, and would be the one found north of Texas. Female Boat-tail is much browner than female Common Grackle and has a pale breast.
   Voice: A harsh *check check check;* a loud *may-ree, may ree!* Also a variety of harsh whistles and clucks.
   Where found: New Jersey coast to Texas; sw. U.S. to n. Peru. Two species may be involved (Selander). **West:** *Breeds* locally in s. Arizona, New Mexico, w. Texas; spreading. Some withdrawal in winter. **Habitat:** Riversides, groves, thickets, towns. **Nest:** A bulky grass-lined cup in reeds, bush, or tree; in colony. Eggs (3–5) bluish, scrawled.

COMMON GRACKLE   *Quiscalus quiscula*   11–13½   **Pl. 52**
(Bronzed Grackle)
   Field marks: A large shiny blackbird, larger than a Robin, with a long wedge-shaped tail. A crease in the center often gives the tail a keel-shaped appearance, particularly in spring. The flight is more even, not rising and falling as much as other blackbirds'. Male is glossed with iridescent purple on head, deep bronze on back. Female is smaller, less iridescent.
   Similar species: (1) Brewer's Blackbird and (2) Rusty Blackbird are smaller (size of Red-wing), with less heavy bills, shorter tails. (3) Boat-tailed Grackle (sw. border) is much larger, with longer tail, less iridescence; female is brown.
   Voice: Note, *chuck* or *chack;* "song," a split rasping note that is both husky and squeaky.
   Where found: Canada to Gulf states. Migratory in North. **West:** *Breeds* east of Rockies from s. Mackenzie south to ne. New Mexico, sw. Kansas. *Winters* from Colorado (rarely) to Texas. *Accidental,* Alaska, Washington, Idaho, Utah, Nevada. **Habitat:** Croplands, towns, streamsides. **Nest:** A bulky cup in tree, tree cavity, bush, reeds; often in colony. Eggs (4–6; 7) greenish, blotched, scrawled.

BROWN-HEADED COWBIRD   *Molothrus ater*   6–8   **Pl. 52**
(Common Cowbird)
   Field marks: A rather small blackbird with a short, *sparrow-like bill. Male:* A blackbird with a *brown head. Female:* All gray; the finchlike bill is a good mark. *Juvenal:* Paler than female, buffy gray with soft breast-streakings; often seen fed by smaller birds. When with other blackbirds, cowbirds are smaller and feed with tails lifted high.
   Similar species: Gray female Cowbird can be told from (1)

female Rusty and (2) female Brewer's Blackbirds by *shorter bill,* smaller size. Some other all-gray birds are (3) young Starling (shorter-tailed, longer-billed) and (4) Catbird (darker, *chestnut* crissum). (5) Near sw. border see Bronzed Cowbird.

Voice: Flight call, *weee-titi* (high whistle, 2 lower notes). Song, bubbly and creaky, *glug-glug-gleeee.* Note, *chuck.*

Where found: S. Canada to n. Mexico. Migrant in North. **West:** *Breeds* from sw. and ne. B.C., s. Mackenzie throughout most of w. U.S. *Winters* mainly from California, s. Arizona south. **Habitat:** Farms, fields, barnyards, wood edges, river groves. **Parasitic:** Lays speckled eggs in nests of other species.

BRONZED COWBIRD *Tangavius aeneus* 6½–8¾ **Pl. 52**
(Red-eyed Cowbird)

Field marks: *Male:* Larger than Brown-headed Cowbird (does not have brown head). Bill longer. Red eye can be seen only at close range. In breeding season, a conspicuous *ruff* on nape. *Female:* Smaller, with smaller ruff; dull blackish, much like male, not gray like female of other cowbird.

Voice: High-pitched mechanical creakings (E. Kincaid).

Where found: U.S.–Mexican border to w. Panama. *Summers* in c. and s. Arizona, sw. New Mexico, s. Texas (north to Eagle Pass). *Winters* in s. Arizona (rarely), s. Texas. *Casual,* se. California. **Habitat:** Croplands, brush, semiopen country. **Parasitic:** Lays pale blue-green eggs in nests of orioles, other species.

Tanagers: Thraupidae

MALE tanagers are brilliantly colored, our species exhibiting bright red. Females are greenish above and yellow below, suggesting large warblers or vireos. They may be confused with female orioles, but are less active, have darker cheeks and (except for Western Tanager) lack wing-bars. The shorter, thicker bills are usually notched or "toothed." **Food:** Insects, small fruits. **Range:** New World; most species in tropics. **No. of species:** World, 196 (Mayr-Amadon), 222 (Van Tyne-Berger); West, 3 (+1 marginal).

WESTERN TANAGER *Piranga ludoviciana* 6¼–7½ **Pl. 53**

Field marks: Our only tanager with wing-bars. *Male:* Yellow, with black back, wings, and tail; wing-bars, *red face.* Males in autumn lose most of red. *Female:* Dull greenish above, yellowish below; *white or yellowish wing-bars.*

Similar species: (1) Female resembles female oriole but tail and sides of face darker; bill more swollen, less sharply pointed. (2) Females of our other tanagers lack wing-bars.

Voice: Note, a dry *pi-tic* or *pit-i-tic.* Song, short phrases; similar

to those of Black-headed Grosbeak or Robin in form, but less sustained, hoarser.
Where found: *Breeds* from n. B.C., s. Mackenzie east to c. Saskatchewan; south through w. U.S. to mts. of n. Baja California, se. Arizona, s. New Mexico, w. Texas. *Migrant* east to Plains. *Winters* Mexico to Costa Rica; rarely s. California. *Accidental,* Alaska. **Habitat:** Open conifer or mixed forests; widespread in migration. **Nest:** A shallow saucer on horizontal branch of pine, oak, fir. Eggs (3–5) blue, spotted.

SCARLET TANAGER *Piranga olivacea* 6½–7½ **Pl. 53**
Field marks: *Male: Bright scarlet* with *black* wings and tail. *Female, immature,* and *winter male:* Dull green above, yellowish below, with brownish or blackish wings.
Similar species: (1) Male Summer Tanager and (2) Cardinal (crested) are all-red, lack black wings and tail. (3) Female Summer Tanager is deeper yellow; wings not as dusky. (4) Female Western Tanager has wing-bars.
Voice: Note, a low *chip-burr.* Song, 4 or 5 short phrases, Robin-like but hoarse (like Robin with sore throat).
Where found: Se. Canada to Oklahoma, n. Georgia. Winters in S. America. **West:** *Breeds* west of 100° in w.-c. Nebraska. Occasional migrant on Great Plains; recorded from Saskatchewan to Texas panhandle. *Accidental,* n. Alaska, B.C., California, Arizona. **Habitat:** Forest and shade trees, especially oaks.

HEPATIC TANAGER *Piranga flava* 7–7¾ **Pl. 53**
Field marks: *Male:* Darker than Summer Tanager; dull orange-red; *dark ear patch, blackish bill. Female:* Dusky above, yellowish below; known from female orioles by shorter bill, lack of wing-bars; from female Summer Tanager by more orange-yellow throat, gray ear patch, and *blackish* bill.
Similar species: Male Summer Tanager is rosier, has *pale yellowish* bill. Females, see above. Hepatic Tanager prefers mt. woodlands; the Summer, low stream woods.
Voice: Song, very similar to Black-headed Grosbeak's (Summer Tanager sounds more like Robin). Call note, a single *chuck.*
Where found: *Breeds* from nw. Arizona, n. New Mexico, w. Texas (Trans-Pecos) to Argentina. *Winters* mainly from n. Mexico south. *Casual,* Colorado. **Habitat:** Open mt. forests, oaks, pines. **Nest:** A shallow saucer on branch of large tree. Eggs (3–5) bluish, spotted.

SUMMER TANAGER *Piranga rubra* 7–7¾ **Pl. 53**
(Cooper's Tanager)
Field marks: *Male: Rose-red all over,* with yellowish bill; no crest. *Female:* Olive above, deep yellow below. Young male acquiring adult plumage may be patched with red and green.

Similar species: (1) Cardinal has a *crest,* black face. (2) Hepatic Tanager is darker, has blackish bill. (3) Female Western Tanager has wing-bars.
Voice: Note, a staccato *pi-tuck* or *pik-i-tuck-i-tuck;* song, Robin-like phrases, less nasal and resonant than that of Western Tanager's; quality similar to Robin's.
Where found: C. and s. U.S. to c. Mexico. Winters Mexico to Brazil. **West:** *Breeds* from se. California (Colorado River), s. tip of Nevada, c. Arizona, c. New Mexico, w. Texas south. *Casual,* sw. California, Colorado. **Habitat:** River woods, cottonwoods, willow groves. **Nest:** A shallow cup on horizontal branch. Eggs (3-4) bluish-green, spotted.

Grosbeaks, Finches, Sparrows, and Buntings: Fringillidae

THE obvious feature of this family is the bill, short and stout, adapted for seed-cracking. There are 3 main types of bills: that of the grosbeaks, extremely large, thick at base, and a bit rounded in outline; the more Canary-like bill of the finches, sparrows, and buntings; and that of the crossbills, the mandibles of which are crossed at the tips. Many species are highly colored; the sparrows are brown and streaked. **Food:** Seeds, insects, small fruits. **Range:** Worldwide. **No. of species:** World, 425; West, 69 (+2 marginals, +5 accidentals; +2 in Hawaii). Some recent authorities put the subfamily Carduelinae (goldfinches, crossbills, etc.) in the Ploceidae (weaver finches) instead of in the Fringillidae. (Based on their classification, not followed here, the breakdown would be: World, 375; West, 56 +1 marginal, +3 accidentals; +2 in Hawaii.)

CARDINAL　*Richmondena cardinalis*　7½-9　　**Pl. 55**
　Field marks: *Male:* Our only all-red bird with a pointed crest; black patch at base of heavy red bill. *Female:* Buff-brown, with a touch of red; has a crest and heavy red bill.
　Similar species: (1) Male Summer Tanager has no crest. (2) Female Pyrrhuloxia has gray back, stubby yellow bill.
　Voice: Song, clear slurred whistles, diminishing in pitch. Several variations: *what-cheer cheer cheer,* etc.; *whoit whoit whoit; birdy, birdy, birdy,* etc. Note, a short thin *chip.*
　Where found: S. Ontario to Gulf states; sw. U.S. to B. Honduras. **West:** *Resident* from se. California (Parker Dam), s. Arizona, sw. and se. New Mexico, w. Texas south. Also north on Great Plains to ne. Colorado, Nebraska. *Casual,* Saskatchewan. *Introduced* in Hawaii, s. California (San Gabriel River). **Habitat:** Woodland edges, river thickets, towns. **Nest:** A loose cup in bush or thicket. Eggs (3-4) spotted.

PYRRHULOXIA *Pyrrhuloxia sinuata* 7½–8¼ **Pl. 55**
Field marks: *Male:* A slender *gray and red bird with a crest* and a small, stubby, almost parrot-like bill. The rose-colored breast and crest suggest the Cardinal, but the gray back and *yellow* bill set it apart. *Female:* Note the *yellow* bill. Gray back, buff breast; a touch of red in wings and crest.
Similar species: Female Cardinal (browner) has reddish bill.
Voice: Song, a clear *quink quink quink quink quink,* on one pitch; also a slurred, whistled *what-cheer, what-cheer,* etc., thinner and shorter than Cardinal's song.
Where found: *Resident* from s. Arizona, s. New Mexico, w. and s. Texas to c. Mexico. Habitat: Mesquite, thorn scrub, deserts. Nest: A compact cup in thorny bush. Eggs (3–4) dotted.

ROSE-BREASTED GROSBEAK **Pl. 56**
Pheucticus ludovicianus 7–8½
Field marks: *Male:* Black and white, with a large triangle of *rose-red* on breast, large pale bill. In flight, a ring of white flashes across black upper plumage. *Female:* Streaked, like a large sparrow; recognized by large grosbeak bill, broad white wing-bars, conspicuous white line over eye.
Similar species: Female Black-headed Grosbeak has browner breast, with light streaks on sides only.
Voice: Very similar to Black-headed Grosbeak's (see below).
Where found: Canada to e. Kansas, Missouri, n. Georgia (mts.). Winters from Mexico to nw. S. America. West: *Breeds* east of Rockies from ne. B.C. across forests of Alberta, Saskatchewan. *Migrant* on Great Plains; west casually to mt. states (has bred n. Colorado). *Accidental,* California, Nevada, Arizona. Habitat: Light deciduous woods, aspens. Nest: A frail flat saucer in tree, bush. Eggs (3–5) pale blue, spotted.

BLACK-HEADED GROSBEAK **Pl. 56**
Pheucticus melanocephalus 6½–7¾
Field marks: *Male:* Rusty breast, *black* head, boldly marked black and white wings, and large pale bill make it a striking bird. In flight shows black and white wing and tail pattern, cinnamon rump. *Female:* Largely brown; streaked. Breast washed with *light* brown (usually) and lightly streaked on sides.
Similar species: Female Rose-breasted Grosbeak (East) usually has a whiter, more streaked breast.
Voice: Song, rising and falling passages; resembles Robin's song but more fluent and mellow. Note, a sharp *ik* or *eek.*
Where found: *Breeds* from s. B.C., s. Alberta, sw. Saskatchewan south through w. U.S. to s. Mexico. *Winters* mainly in Mexico. Habitat: Pine-oak woods, mixed forest, tall chaparral, piñon, streamside groves, orchards, parks. Nest: A loose saucer in tree or bush. Eggs (3–4) bluish, spotted.

BLUE GROSBEAK *Guiraca caerulea* 6–7½ **Pl. 56**
Field marks: *Male:* Deep dull blue, with a thick bill and 2 *tan*
wing-bars. *Female:* About size of Cowbird; warm brown, lighter
below, with 2 *buffy* wing-bars; rump tinged with blue. Immature
males are a mixture of brown and blue.
Similar species: (1) The male may appear black at a distance,
suggesting a Cowbird. (2) See Indigo Bunting (much smaller)
and (3) female Lazuli Bunting.
Voice: Song, a rapid warble; short phrases rising and falling;
suggests song of Purple or House Finch or Orchard Oriole, but
slower and more guttural. Note, a sharp *chink.*
Where found: California across U.S. to s. New Jersey; south to
Costa Rica. Winters Mexico to Panama. **West:** *Breeds* from
n.-c. California (n. Sacramento Valley), w.-c. Nevada, e. Utah,
Colorado, w. S. Dakota south. *Casual,* Montana. **Habitat:**
Brushy, weedy places; willows, river thickets. **Nest:** A loose cup
in bush or low tree. Eggs (3–4) pale bluish.

INDIGO BUNTING *Passerina cyanea* 5¼–5¾ **Pl. 56**
Field marks: *Male:* A small finch that is deep rich blue *all over.*
In autumn the male becomes more like the brown female, but
there is usually some blue in wings and tail. *Female:* Brown;
breast paler, with indistinct streakings; a small plain finch
devoid of *obvious* stripings, wing-bars, or other marks. Hybrid-
izes with Lazuli Bunting where ranges overlap.
Similar species: Blue Grosbeak is much larger, with heavy
bill, tan wing-bars.
Voice: Very similar to Lazuli Bunting's (see below).
Where found: Se. Canada to Gulf states. Winters Mexico,
W. Indies to Panama. **West:** *Breeds* west on Plains to Black
Hills, w. Kansas, w. Oklahoma, Texas panhandle; has bred
casually in Colorado, Utah, Arizona, even California (with
Lazuli). Stray birds reported in Alberta, Saskatchewan, and
all w. states except Washington, Idaho. **Habitat:** Brush, sprout-
lands. **Nest:** A cup in crotch of bush. Eggs (3–4) pale blue.

LAZULI BUNTING *Passerina amoena* 5–5½ **Pl. 56**
Field marks: *Male:* A small bright blue finch. Head and upper
parts *turquoise* blue; band across breast and sides *cinnamon;*
belly and wing-bars white. *Female:* Nondescript; *brownish,*
whitening on throat and belly; whitish wing-bars. A trace of
gray-blue in wings and tail. Lack of streakings on back or
breast distinguishes it from the sparrows.
Similar species: (1) Western Bluebird is larger, has a more
slender bill, *lacks wing-bars.* (2) Female Blue Grosbeak is
larger, darker, has larger bill, *tan wing-bars.* (3) Female Indigo
Bunting lacks strong wing-bars.
Voice: Song, high and strident, with well-measured phrases at

different pitches, introductory notes usually paired: *sweet-sweet, chew-chew,* etc. Note, a sharp *tsip.*
Where found: *Breeds* from s. B.C., s. Alberta, s. Saskatchewan south to nw. Baja California, s. Nevada, c. Arizona, n. New Mexico; east to c. N. Dakota, ne. S. Dakota, c. Nebraska, w. Kansas. *Winters* s. Arizona, Mexico. **Habitat:** Sage, broken brushy slopes, briars, burns, streamsides. **Nest:** A loose cup in bush. Eggs (3–4) pale blue.

VARIED BUNTING *Passerina versicolor*   4½–5½   **Pl. 56**
Field marks: *Male:* A small dark finch with a plum-purple body (looks black at a distance). Crown blue, with a *bright red patch on the nape;* "colored like an Easter egg." *Female:* A small plain *gray-brown* finch with lighter underparts. *No wing-bars, stripes, or distinctive marks of any kind.*
Similar species: (1) Male Painted Bunting has a bright red breast. (2) Female Seedeater is smaller and browner than female Varied Bunting; has wing-bars. (3) Female Indigo Bunting is browner, with a hint of wing-bars and faint breast streaks.
Voice: Song, a thin bright finch song, more distinctly phrased and less warbled than Painted Bunting's; notes not so distinctly paired as in songs of Lazuli or Indigo Buntings.
Where found: *Breeds* very locally from s. Arizona, sw. New Mexico (?), w. and s. Texas (along Rio Grande) to Guatemala. *Accidental,* se. California. Winters from n. Mexico south. **Habitat:** Streamside thickets, brush. **Nest:** A grassy cup in bush. Eggs (3–4) bluish white.

PAINTED BUNTING *Passerina ciris*   5–5½   **Pl. 56**
Field marks: Perhaps the most gaudily colored N. American bird. *Male:* A little Chipping-Sparrow-sized finch, a patchwork of *bright red, green, and indigo.* Red on rump and underparts, green on back, blue-violet on head. *Female:* Greenish above, paling to lemon-green below; no wing-bars or streaks.
Similar species: Our only other small strongly greenish finch, the female Lesser Goldfinch, has blackish wings, white bars.
Voice: Song, a bright pleasing warble; resembles song of Warbling Vireo, but more wiry. Note, a sharp *chip.*
Where found: S. U.S., ne. Mexico. **West:** *Breeds* in s. New Mexico, most of Texas, w. Oklahoma. *Casual,* s. Colorado, se. Arizona. Winters from Mexico, Florida to Panama, Cuba. **Habitat:** Woodland edges, roadsides, brush, streamside growth. **Nest:** A woven cup in crotch of bush. Eggs (3–5) spotted.

DICKCISSEL *Spiza americana*   6–7   **Pl. 54**
Field marks: Near size of House Sparrow. *Male:* Suggestive of a tiny meadowlark, with *yellow breast, black bib.* In the fall the black bib is obscured or lacking. *Female:* Very much like female House Sparrow; paler, with much whiter stripe over eye, touch

of yellow on breast, *bluish bill.* Chestnut bend of wing is also an aid. Often travels in large flocks.

Similar species: (1) Female looks much like House Sparrow (see above). (2) Might also be confused with female Bobolink.

Voice: Song, a staccato rendition of its name: *dick-ciss-ciss-ciss* or *chup-chup-klip-klip-klip.* Also a short electric-buzzer or "raspberry" call; often heard at night in migration.

Where found: Montana, Ontario to Texas, Louisiana. Winters Mexico to n. S. America. **West:** *Breeds* on Plains west to e. Montana, e. Wyoming, c. Colorado, w. Oklahoma, Texas panhandle. Straggler to Canadian prairies, California, Nevada, Arizona, New Mexico. **Habitat:** Fields, alfalfa, prairies, roadsides. **Nest:** Of grass in weeds, low bush. Eggs (3–5) pale blue.

EVENING GROSBEAK   **Pl. 55**
Hesperiphona vespertina   7–8½

Field marks: A chunky, short-tailed finch, size of Starling; has a very large, conical, whitish bill. The undulating flight indicates a finch, and its stocky shape, large white wing patches mark it as this species. *Male:* Dull yellow, with dark head, yellow eye-stripe and black and white wings; suggests an overgrown American Goldfinch. *Female:* Silvery gray, with just enough yellow, black, and white to be recognizable.

Similar species: (1) Snow Bunting is our other winter finch with large white patches. (2) Female Pine Grosbeak (stubby black bill) is longer, has less white in wing, none in tail.

Voice: A ringing *cleer* or *clee-ip.* Song, a short warble.

Where found: Canada, w. and ne. U.S., Mexico. Winters to se. U.S., Mexico. **West:** *Breeds* from n.-c. B.C. east across boreal forests of Canada; south in mts. to c.-e. California, se. Arizona, s. New Mexico. *Winters* irregularly to coast, lowlands, Great Plains. **Habitat:** Conifer forests; in winter, box elders, maples, fruiting shrubs. **Nest:** A frail saucer in conifer. Eggs (3–4) bluish, speckled.

PURPLE FINCH   *Carpodacus purpureus*   5½–6¼   **Pl. 55**
(including California Purple Finch)

Field marks: Size of House Sparrow. *Male:* Dull rose-red, brightest on head and rump ("like a sparrow dipped in raspberry juice"). *Female and immature:* Heavily striped, brown, sparrowlike. *Broad whitish line* behind eye; *heavy dark jaw-stripe.* The larger bill distinguishes them from sparrows.

Similar species: (1) Male House Finch has dark streaks on flanks. Female House Finch is paler, streaks lighter, lacks strong face pattern; bill stubby. (2) See Cassin's Finch. See also (3) Common Redpoll and (4) Pine Grosbeak.

Voice: Song, a fast, lively warble; resembles song of House Finch, but lower in pitch, shorter, less disjointed. Note, a dull metallic *tick,* unlike any note of House Finch.

Where found: Canada, ne. U.S.; Pacific states. Winters to s. U.S. **West:** *Resident* from sw. B.C. through Pacific states (west of Cascade-Sierra divide) to s. California (wintering east to Arizona). *Breeds* also from nw. B.C. east across wooded Canada, wintering in U.S. east of Plains. *Casual,* Colorado, nw. Texas. **Habitat:** Woodlands (mixed and conifer). **Nest:** A compact cup in conifer. Eggs (4–5) blue-green, spotted.

CASSIN'S FINCH *Carpodacus cassinii* 6–6½ **Pl. 55**
(Cassin's Purple Finch)
  Field marks: *Male:* Similar to Purple Finch and House Finch. Red of breast paler; *squarish red crown patch contrasts abruptly* with brown of neck. In addition, the *lack* of sharp dark flank- and belly-streakings distinguishes it from House Finch. *Female:* Sparrow-like; underparts narrowly streaked. Sharper stripings, strong face pattern, larger bill distinguish it from female House Finch; whiter underparts, sharper breast-stripings from female Purple Finch.
  Similar species: See above. See also Common Redpoll.
  Voice: Song, a lively warble, similar to Purple Finch's; not so closely knit (between songs of House and Purple Finches).
  Where found: *Breeds* from s. B.C., sw. Alberta south in mts. to s. California, s. Nevada, n. Arizona, n. New Mexico. *Winters* to adjacent lower levels and south to mts. of Mexico; rare toward coast; east to w. Texas. **Habitat:** Open conifer forests of high mts. **Nest:** A grass cup in pine. Eggs (4–5) bluish, spotted.

HOUSE FINCH *Carpodacus mexicanus* 5–5¾ **Pl. 55**
("Linnet")
  Field marks: *Male:* Near size of House Sparrow, brownish with bright *red breast,* forehead, stripe over eye, and rump. Resembles males of Purple and Cassin's Finches (which do not nest about buildings); is brighter red. Some are almost orange. *Narrow dark stripes* on flanks and belly are best distinction. *Female:* Sparrow-like; gray-brown above; underparts streaked with dusky; face without strong stripings, bill stubby.
  Similar species: See (1) Purple Finch and (2) Cassin's Finch.
  Voice: A bright lengthy song, loose and disjointed; frequently ends in a harsh nasal *wheer* or *che-urr.* Notes, finchlike, musical; some suggest chirping of House Sparrow.
  Where found: *Resident* from s. B.C., n. Idaho, Wyoming, w. Nebraska south throughout most of w. U.S. to s. Mexico. *Introduced,* Hawaii. **Habitat:** Varied; towns, ranches, open woods, coastal scrub, canyons, deserts. **Nest:** Compact; in bush, tree, cactus, building. Eggs (4–5) blue-green, spotted.

WHITE-COLLARED SEEDEATER **Pl. 55**
Sporophila torqueola 4–4½
(Sharpe's or "Morrelet" Seedeater)
  Field marks: *Male:* A tiny finch with whitish or buffy underparts

and blackish cap and upper parts. Much white in wing; bill stubby and swollen; a narrow, incomplete breastband and a *light collar* around nape. *Female:* The small size, buffy underparts, and very stubby bill are good marks; light wing-bars.
Similar species: American Goldfinch in winter plumage resembles female somewhat but has blacker wings, white rump.
Voice: A sweet loud song; begins on several high repeated notes and drops to several notes on a lower pitch: *sweet sweet sweet sweet, cheer cheer cheer cheer* (often only 2 *cheer*'s).
Where found: S. Texas to Costa Rica. *Resident* in Rio Grande Delta. **Habitat:** Weedy places, tall grass, brush. **Nest:** A compact cup in bush. Eggs (4–5) blue-green, spotted.

PINE GROSBEAK *Pinicola enucleator* 8–10   **Pl. 55**
Field marks: Nearly size of Robin; a winter finch with a moderately long tail; our largest finch. Often very tame. Undulates very deeply in flight. *Male:* Dull rose-red; dark wings with 2 white bars. *Female:* Gray with 2 white wing-bars; head and rump tinged with dull yellow. *Immature male:* Similar to female but with touch of reddish on head and rump.
Similar species: (1) White-winged Crossbill (size of House Sparrow) has cross-tipped bill. (2) Evening Grosbeak is short-tailed, stocky. See also (3) Purple Finch and (4) Cassin's Finch.
Voice: Call, a whistled *tee-tee-tew,* suggesting Greater Yellowlegs but finchlike. Alarm, a musical *chee-vli.* Song, whistling notes interspersed with a twanging note.
Where found: Boreal forests of N. Hemisphere. **West:** *Resident* from n. Alaska, nw. Mackenzie east across boreal forests of Canada; south locally in high mts. to c.-e. California, e. Arizona, n. New Mexico. *Winters* irregularly to Great Basin, Great Plains (casually to Texas panhandle). **Habitat:** Conifer forests; in winter, mixed woods, fruiting trees. **Nest:** A loose cup in low conifer. Eggs (3–4) pale blue, spotted.

GRAY-CROWNED ROSY FINCH   **Pl. 55**
Leucosticte tephrocotis 5¾–6¾
Field marks: Rosy finches are sparrow-sized birds of the high snowfields; walk, do not hop. *Dark brown,* with a *pinkish wash* on wings and rump; *light gray patch* on back of head. Females are duller; the gray patch reduced or almost wanting. In the race *L. t. littoralis,* Hepburn's Rosy Finch (Alaska to n. California), the gray extends across the cheeks. The 3 "species" are lumped by some authorities.
Similar species: See Black and Brown-capped Rosy Finches.
Voice: High chirping notes, suggestive of House Sparrow.
Where found: *Breeds* from islands in Bering Sea, Aleutians, n.-c. Alaska, w. Mackenzie south through high mts. in B.C., Pacific states to Sierra in c. California; in Rockies to n. Idaho,

nw. Montana, n. Wyoming (Bighorns). *Winters* to Nevada, n. Arizona, n. New Mexico. *Casual* on Canadian prairies. **Habitat:** Rocky summits, alpine cirques and snowfields; islands (Alaska); winters in open country at lower levels (east of Sierra, Cascades). **Nest:** A grass cup in rock crevice. Eggs (3–5) white.

BLACK ROSY FINCH   *Leucosticte atrata*   6   **Pl. 55**
   Field marks: Similar to Gray-crowned Rosy Finch, but body blackish instead of chestnut-brown.
   Voice: Similar to preceding species'. "A rather high-pitched plaintive *cheew* repeated continuously" (C. W. Lockerbie).
   Where found: *Breeds* in high mts. of sw. Montana, c. Idaho, w. Wyoming, ne. Nevada, n. Utah. *Winters* at lower levels and south to sw. Utah, n. Arizona, n. New Mexico. *Casual, ne.* California. **Habitat and Nest:** Similar to Gray-crown's.

BROWN-CAPPED ROSY FINCH   **Pl. 55**
Leucosticte australis   5¾–6¼
   Field marks: Similar to Gray-crowned Rosy Finch, but with brown of body *lighter* and head without pale patch; crown dusky. Female Gray-crowns often have little evidence of a light crown patch but are duskier, not so light a brown.
   Voice: Similar to other rosy finches'.
   Where found: *Breeds* in high mts. of s. Wyoming, Colorado, n. New Mexico. *Winters* at adjacent lower levels. **Habitat and Nest:** Similar to other rosy finches'.

HOARY REDPOLL   *Acanthis hornemanni*   5¼–5½   **Pl. 55**
   Field marks: Among the Common Redpolls look for a "frostier" bird. If it has an immaculate *unstreaked whitish rump,* it is this species. Rump may be tinged with pink in male; breast paler pink than in Common Redpoll, sides unstreaked (usually). Female lacks pink; both sexes have crimson foreheads.
   Voice: Similar to Common Redpoll's.
   Where found: Arctic; circumpolar. **West:** *Breeds* along Arctic slope and south along Bering Sea to Hooper Bay, Alaska. *Winters* south irregularly to s. B.C., Montana, sw. S. Dakota. **Habitat and Nest:** Similar to Common Redpoll's.

COMMON REDPOLL   *Acanthis flammea*   5–5½   **Pl. 55**
   Field marks: Note the *bright red cap* on the forehead. A little, streaked, gray-brown bird with a *black chin* and dark streaks on flanks. *Male* is pink-breasted. In size, shape, and actions redpolls resemble goldfinches and siskins.
   Similar species: (1) Purple, Cassin's, and House Finches are larger, redder, have red rumps, lack black chin. (2) Siskin is darker, more heavily striped. (3) See Hoary Redpoll.
   Voice: In flight, a rattling *chet-chet-chet-chet.* Song, a trill, followed by the rattling *chet-chet-chet-chet.*

Where found: Circumboreal. *Breeds* from n.-c. Alaska, n. Mackenzie south to s. Alaska, n. B.C., Great Slave Lake. *Winters* irregularly from s. edge of breeding range to ne. California, ne. Nevada, n. Utah, n. Colorado. **Habitat:** Birches, tundra scrub. In winter, weedy, brushy country. **Nest:** On ground or in low bush. Eggs (3–6) pale green, spotted.

PINE SISKIN *Spinus pinus* 4½–5¼   **Pl. 55**
Field marks: A small dark, *heavily* streaked finch with a deeply notched tail. A *touch of yellow* in wings and at tail base (not always evident). In size and actions resembles American Goldfinch. Learn the calls; most Siskins are heard flying.
Similar species: (1) Winter goldfinches are unstreaked; (2) female Purple Finch is larger (size of House Sparrow) with a larger bill; (3) redpolls are paler, without heavy streakings across breast. None of these show yellow in wings or tail, nor have they the Siskin's more pointed profile.
Voice: Call, a loud *clee-ip* or *chlee-ip,* also a light *tit-i-tit.* A long buzzy *shreeeee* is unique. Song, similar to American Goldfinch's; more coarse and wheezy.
Where found: S. Alaska, Canada to Guatemala. Partially migratory. **West:** *Breeds* from s. Alaska, s. Yukon, s. Mackenzie east through forests of Canada; south along coast to c. California; in mts. to s. California, se. Arizona, s. New Mexico, w. Texas (Guadalupe Mts.). *Winters* widely at lower levels from s. Alaska, s. Canada south. **Habitat:** Conifer forests, mixed woods, alders, treetops, nearby weedy areas. **Nest:** A neat cup in conifer. Eggs (3–6) pale blue, speckled.

AMERICAN GOLDFINCH *Spinus tristis* 4½–5½   **Pl. 55**
(Common Goldfinch)
Field marks: *Male in summer:* A *small yellow bird with black wings;* forehead and tail black. *Female in summer:* Dull yellow-olive, darker above, with blackish wings and conspicuous wing-bars; distinguished from other small olive-yellow birds (warblers, etc.) by its conical bill. *Winter birds:* Much like summer females; grayer. Flight deeply undulating.
Similar species: (1) Yellow Warbler is yellowish all over, including wings and tail. (2) Female Lesser Goldfinch differs from female American by greener back; lacks whitish rump.
Voice: Song, sustained, clear, light, Canary-like. In flight, each dip is often punctuated by *ti-dee-di-di.*
Where found: S. Canada to s. U.S., n. Baja California. Winters s. Canada to n. Mexico. **West:** *Breeds* from s. B.C., c. Alberta, c. Saskatchewan to s. California, c. Nevada, c. Utah, s. Colorado. *Winters* from s. B.C., Montana south. **Habitat:** River groves, willows, poplars, orchards, roadsides. **Nest:** A compact, felted cup in bush, tree. Eggs (3–6) pale blue.

LESSER GOLDFINCH *Spinus psaltria* 3¾–4¼   **Pl. 55**
(Arkansas, Green-backed, or "Dark-backed" Goldfinch)
> **Field marks:** *Male:* A very small finch with a black cap, *black or greenish back,* and *bright yellow* underparts; bold white marks on wings. The black cap is retained in winter (male Americans become brownish and lose caps). Males of the race *S. p. psaltria,* Arkansas Goldfinch (s. Rocky Mt. region), have black backs; males of the race *S. p. hesperophilus,* Green-backed Goldfinch, have greenish backs. *Female:* Very similar to female American Goldfinch, but smaller, more greenish; *has dark rump.*
> **Similar species:** American Goldfinch always shows *white* near rump. Summer male has yellow back.
> **Voice:** Sweet plaintive notes *tee-yee* (rising inflection) and *tee-yer* (dropping). Song, musical; more phrased than American Goldfinch's; notes often paired.
> **Where found:** *Breeds* from w. Oregon, n. Nevada, n. Utah, n. Colorado, nw. Oklahoma through sw. U.S. to Peru. Mainly migratory in Rocky Mt. region. *Casual,* Wyoming. **Habitat:** open brushy country, open woods, wooded streams, gardens.
> **Nest:** A small cup in bush or low tree. Eggs (4–5) pale bluish.

LAWRENCE'S GOLDFINCH *Spinus lawrencei* 4 4½   **Pl. 55**
> **Field marks:** Note the *yellow wing-bars. Male:* Gray-headed, with a *black face* (only U.S. goldfinch with a *black chin*); some yellow on breast and rump; broad yellow wing-bars. No seasonal change. *Female:* Lacks black face. Gray color, 2 *yellow* wing-bars distinguish it from our other goldfinches.
> **Voices:** Song similar to that of American Goldfinch. Call note, distinctive: *tink-oo,* syllables emphasized equally.
> **Where found:** *Breeds* from n. California (w. of Sierra) to n. Baja California. *Winters* from c. California, s. tip of Nevada, c. Arizona, sw. New Mexico, w. Texas (El Paso) into n. Mexico. **Habitat:** Open oak or oak-pine woods, dry chaparral, edges.
> **Nest:** A neat cup in bush, tree. Eggs (4–5) white.

RED CROSSBILL *Loxia curvirostra* 5¼–6½   **Pl. 55**
> **Field marks:** Note the crossed mandibles. Size of House Sparrow; heavy head, short tail. Acts like a small parrot as it dangles around evergreen cones, the cracking of which often betrays its presence. *Male: Brick-red,* brighter on rump; wings and tail dusky. Young males are more orange. *Female:* Dull olive-gray; yellowish on rump and underparts. Juvenal birds striped above and below, suggest large Pine Siskins.
> **Similar species:** (1) White-winged Crossbill has white wing-bars. (2) In mts. of Southwest see Hepatic Tanager (p. 221).
> **Voice:** Note, a hard *jip-jip* or *jip-jip-jip.* Song *jip-jip-jip-jeeaa-jeeaa,* or warbled passages and chips.
> **Where found:** Conifer forests of N. Hemisphere. In N. America

south in mts. to n. Nicaragua (in East to N. Carolina). **West:**
Breeds from se. Alaska, s. Yukon, n. Alberta south along coast
to c. California; in mts. locally throughout West. Wanders
irregularly. **Habitat:** Conifer forests and groves. **Nest:** A
feather-lined saucer in conifer. Eggs (3–5) spotted.

WHITE-WINGED CROSSBILL   Pl. 55
Loxia leucoptera   6–6¾
    Field marks: Note the wing-bars, crossed mandibles. *Male:* Dull
rose-pink, with black wings and tail and 2 *broad white wing-bars.*
Female: Olive-gray with yellowish rump; like Red Crossbill,
but with 2 white wing-bars (evident in flight).
    Similar species: See (1) Pine Grosbeak and (2) Red Crossbill.
    Voice: Notes, a liquid *peet* and a dry *chif-chif.* Song, a succession
of loud trills on different pitches.
    Where found: Boreal forests of N. Hemisphere. **West:** *Breeds*
from tree limit to s. Alaska, c. B.C., c. Alberta, c. Saskatchewan.
Wanders irregularly; south to Washington, Colorado. *Casual,*
Oregon, New Mexico. **Habitat:** Spruce forests. **Nest:** A feather-
lined cup in conifer. Eggs (3–4) pale blue, spotted.

OLIVE SPARROW   *Arremonops rufivirgata*   5½–6   Pl. 56
(Texas Sparrow)
    Field marks: Note the *2 broad dull brown stripes on crown.* A
plain olive-backed finch with no wing-bars. Underparts lighter;
a dingy wash across breast and along sides.
    Similar species: Green-tailed Towhee is larger, with a grayer
breast, clear-cut white throat, and solid rufous crown.
    Voice: Song, a series of dry notes on one pitch, starting deliber-
ately and trailing into a rattle.
    Where found: S. Texas to s. Mexico; w. Costa Rica. *Resident*
in s. tip of Texas; noted north to Del Rio, Sabinal, Beeville,
Rockport. **Habitat:** Undergrowth, weedy thickets. **Nest:**
Round, domed; in bush, cactus. Eggs (3–4) white.

GREEN-TAILED TOWHEE   *Chlorura chlorura*   6¼–7   Pl. 56
    Field marks: Note the *rufous cap* and *conspicuous white throat.*
A bit larger than House Sparrow; a finch with a plain olive-green
back, gray breast.
    Similar species: Brown Towhee is browner, has buff throat.
    Voice: A mewing note, and a *chink* like Brown Towhee. Song,
variable; opening with sweet notes, ending in long burry notes:
weet-chur-cheeeeeee — churrr. Often confused with Fox Sparrow's song but less brilliant; has a dry burr.
    Where found: *Breeds* mainly from c. Oregon, s. Idaho, w.
Montana south in mts. (along or east of Cascade-Sierra divide)
to s. California, Arizona, se. New Mexico. *Winters* from s.
Arizona, sw. New Mexico, w. Texas to c. Mexico. In migration,
east to Plains; a few west to s. California coast. **Habitat:** Dry

brushy mt. slopes, low chaparral, open pines, sage, manzanita. **Nest:** On ground or in low bush. Eggs (4) spotted.

RUFOUS-SIDED TOWHEE *Pipilo erythrophthalmus* 7–8½
(Spotted Towhee) **Pl. 56**
   Field marks: Note the *rufous sides.* Smaller and more slender than Robin; rummages noisily among dead leaves. *Male:* Head and upper parts black; rows of *white spots on back and wings; sides robin-red;* belly white. Flashes large white spots in tail corners. *Female:* Similar, but dusky brown where male is black. Young in summer are streaked below like large slender sparrows but have the tail pattern of this towhee.
   Voice: Note, *chwee* or *shrenk.* Song, a drawn-out, buzzy *chweeeeeee.* Sometimes *chup chup chup zeeeeeeeeee;* variable.
   Where found: S. Canada to Guatemala, Florida. **West:** *Breeds* from s. B.C., se. Alberta, s. Saskatchewan to sw. California, s. Arizona, s. New Mexico, w. Texas (mts.). *Winters* mainly from s. B.C., Utah, Colorado south. **Habitat:** Brush, chaparral, undergrowth, forest edges, city shrubs. **Nest:** A loose cup on ground or in low bush. Eggs (3–6) spotted.

BROWN TOWHEE *Pipilo fuscus* 8¼–10 **Pl. 56**
   Field marks: Note the pale *rusty under tail coverts* and the streaked buffy throat. A dull gray-brown bird with a moderately long dark tail; suggests a very plain overgrown sparrow. The grayer forms, sometimes known as the Cañon Towhee (Arizona to Colorado, w. Texas), differ from the Brown Towhees of Oregon and California by their rufous crown and pale color.
   Similar species: (1) Most thrashers are larger, with slim curved bills. See (2) Abert's Towhee, (3) Green-tailed Towhee.
   Voice: Note, a metallic *chink.* Song, a rapid *chink-chink-ink-ink-ink-ink-ink,* on one pitch. Often ends in a trill. Sometimes *chilp-chilp-chilp-chilp-chilp-chilp.*
   Where found: *Resident* from sw. Oregon through California (west of Sierra) and from w. and c. Arizona, c. Colorado, w. Oklahoma, w. and c. Texas to s. Mexico. **Habitat:** Brushy, stony areas, open chaparral, open woods, canyons, piñon-juniper, gardens. **Nest:** A cup in bush or low tree. Eggs (3–4) spotted.

ABERT'S TOWHEE *Pipilo aberti* 8–9 **Pl. 56**
   Field marks: Note the *black patch* at the base of the bill. A desert species, similar to the Brown Towhee, but browner, the entire underparts buffy brown.
   Voice: A sharp single *peek* (J. T. Marshall, Jr.).
   Where found: *Resident* from se. California (Colorado Desert), se. Nevada, sw. Utah, c. Arizona, sw. New Mexico (Gila River) south to ne. Baja California, nw. Sonora. **Habitat:** Desert streams, brush, mesquite. **Nest:** A grass cup in bush, low tree. Eggs (3–4) pale blue-green, scrawled.

LARK BUNTING   *Calamospiza melanocorys*   6–7½   **Pl. 54**
Field marks: *Male in spring:* A bit larger than House Sparrow;
black-bodied, *with large white wing patch. Females, young, and
winter males* are brown, streaked on breast; usually some of the
flock show whitish wing patches. Gregarious.
Similar species: (1) Male Bobolink has white patches above,
but not on wings. (2) Striped brown Lark Buntings suggest
female Purple Finches except for whitish wing patch.
Voice: Song, "Cardinal-like slurs, chat-like (unmusical) *chug*'s,
clear piping notes and trills; each note repeated 3–11 times"
(Norma Stillwell). Note, a soft *hoo-ee.*
Where found: *Breeds* from prairies of s. Canada south through
Plains to e. New Mexico; Texas panhandle, w. Oklahoma; locally
west of Plains in Idaho, Utah, Wyoming, w. Colorado. *Winters*
from s. California, s. Nevada, c. Arizona, s. New Mexico, w. and
c. Texas to c. Mexico. *Casual,* B.C. **Habitat:** Plains, prairies;
in winter, also arid brush, desert scrub. **Nest:** A loose cup on
ground. Eggs (4–5) pale blue.

SAVANNAH SPARROW   *Passerculus sandwichensis*   4½–5¾
(including Belding's and Large-billed Sparrows)   **Pl. 57**
Field marks: This streaked open-country sparrow suggests a
Song Sparrow but usually has a *yellowish stripe* over the eye,
a whitish stripe through the crown, a short notched tail, pinker
legs. The tail notch is an aid when flushing sparrows. Some
birds lack the yellowish in the eye-stripe. A small dark race,
P. s. beldingi (Belding's Sparrow), resident in salt marshes of
s. California, was until recently regarded as a distinct species.
Its breast streaks are heavier, median stripe indistinct, legs
browner. A Mexican race, *P. s. rostratus* (Large-billed Sparrow),
which winters in the same area, is pale, without well-defined
markings on back and crown; breast streaks more diffuse. It
too was regarded as a distinct species.
Similar species: (1) Song Sparrow's tail is rounded (not
notched). (2) On Great Plains see Baird's Sparrow.
Voice: Song, a dreamy lisping *tsit-tsit-tsit, tseeee-tsaaay* (last
note lower). Note, a light *tsip.*
Where found: Alaska, Canada, to Guatemala. Winters to El
Salvador, W. Indies. **West:** *Breeds* from Arctic slope south
along coast to San Diego; in interior to e. California (Sierra),
s. Arizona, New Mexico, w. Nebraska. *Winters* from s. B.C.,
s. Utah, c. New Mexico, n. Texas south. **Habitat:** Prairies, fields,
meadows, salt marshes, open country, shores. **Nest:** A grass-
lined hollow on ground. Eggs (4–5) spotted.   ·

GRASSHOPPER SPARROW   **Pl. 57**
Ammodramus savannarum   4½–5¼
Field marks: A *short-tailed* flat-headed little sparrow with a
feeble flight. Crown with a pale median stripe; back striped

with chestnut and black. Differs from other sparrows of open meadows in having an *unstreaked* buffy breast. The conspicuously striped back, and short, sharp tail are also good marks. Young birds in late summer have streaked breasts.

Similar species: Savannah has streaked breast, notched tail.
Voice: Two songs: (1) a long, sizzling insect-like tumble of notes; (2) 2 low introductory notes and a thin dry buzz, *pi-tup zeeeeeeeeeeee* (introductory notes often inaudible).
Where found: S. Canada to s. U.S., W. Indies; also s. Mexico to Ecuador. Winters from s. U.S. south. **West:** *Breeds* from s. B.C. (casual), s. Alberta (casual), s. Saskatchewan south very locally to s. California, se. Arizona, Colorado, n. Texas. *Winters* from c. California, s. Arizona, s. New Mexico south. **Habitat:** Grassland, hay meadows, prairies. **Nest:** A grassy cup in grass. Eggs (4–5) spotted.

BAIRD'S SPARROW   *Ammodramus bairdii*   5–5½   **Pl. 57**
Field marks: A prairie sparrow. Note the light breast crossed by a *narrow band of fine black streaks*. Head yellow-brown, streaked with black. The best mark is the broad *center stripe on the crown,* which is conspicuously *ocher*.
Similar species: Savannah Sparrow has more extensive streakings on underparts, tail is strongly notched, and the light stripe through crown is narrower (whitish, not yellow-brown).
Voice: Song begins with 2 or 3 high musical *zip*'s and ends with a trill on a lower pitch; more musical than Savannah's.
Where found: N. Great Plains. Winters sw. U.S., n. Mexico. **West:** *Breeds* from s. Alberta, s. Saskatchewan south to Montana, nw. S. Dakota. *Migrant* on Great Plains. *Winters* from s. New Mexico, w. Texas south. **Habitat:** Prairies (long grass). **Nest:** Of grass, hidden in grass. Eggs (4–5) blotched.

LE CONTE'S SPARROW   **Pl. 57**
Passerherbulus caudacutus   4½–5¼
Field marks: A sharp-tailed sparrow of weedy marshes. Note the *bright buffy-ocher* eyeline and breast (with streaks *confined to sides*). Other points are the pinkish-brown nape, *white stripe through crown,* very strongly striped back.
Similar species: (1) Sharp-tailed Sparrow has solid crown. (2) Grasshopper Sparrow lacks streaks on sides.
Voice: Song, 2 extremely thin grasshopper-like hisses, 1st note barely audible.
Where found: S.-c. Canada to n. prairie states. Migrant mostly east of 100° to Gulf states. **West:** *Breeds* east of Rockies from ne. B.C., s. Mackenzie south to n. Montana, n. N. Dakota. *Casual,* Utah, Colorado, New Mexico, Texas panhandle. **Habitat:** Tall grass, weedy meadows, marshes. **Nest:** A grass cup in grass. Eggs (4–5) spotted.

SHARP-TAILED SPARROW   Pl. 57
Ammospiza caudacuta 5–6
Field marks: A marsh sparrow. Note the deep *ocher-yellow of the face,* which completely surrounds the gray ear patch. Breast very buffy, almost devoid of streaking or with faint blurry streaks. Back sharply striped.
Similar species: Le Conte's Sparrow has sharp stripes on sides of breast, white median stripe through crown.
Voice: Song, a gasping buzz, *tuptup-sheeeeeeeee.*
Where found: Prairies of Canada; Atlantic Coast from e. Canada to N. Carolina. Winters along coast from New York to Texas.
West: *Breeds* from ne. B.C., Great Slave Lake to c. Alberta, e. Montana, N. Dakota. *Casual,* California, Colorado. **Habitat:** Marshes, muskegs, reedy margins. **Nest:** A coarse grass cup in marsh. Eggs (4–5) spotted.

VESPER SPARROW *Pooecetes gramineus* 5–6½   Pl. 57
Field marks: Note the *white outer tail feathers,* conspicuous when the bird flies. Otherwise suggests a grayish Song Sparrow, but has a *whitish eye-ring, chestnut* bend of wing.
Similar species: Some other open-country birds with white tail feathers are: (1) meadowlarks (much larger, chunkier); (2) juncos (largely slate-gray); (3) longspurs (which see); (4) pipits (thin-billed, *walk* instead of hop, *bob tails*); (5) Lark Sparrow (large white spots in *corners of tail*).
Voice: Song, throatier than that of Song Sparrow; begins with 2 low clear minor notes, followed by 2 higher ones.
Where found: Canada, to s.-c. U.S. Winters to Mexico, Gulf states. **West:** *Breeds* from c. B.C., sw. Mackenzie, c. Saskatchewan south to Oregon, c.-e. California, c. Arizona, c. New Mexico, w. Nebraska. *Winters* from c. California, c. Arizona, s. New Mexico, w. Texas south. **Habitat:** Fields (sparse brush), open country, sagebrush, roadsides. **Nest:** A grass cup in grass. Eggs (4–6) spotted.

LARK SPARROW *Chondestes grammacus* 5½–6¾   Pl. 58
Field marks: Note the *black tail with much white in the corners* (as in Rufous-sided Towhee — not as in Vesper Sparrow). Note also the *chestnut ear patches,* striped crown, and *single central breast spot.* Young birds are finely streaked below and lack the central button; otherwise recognizable.
Similar species: See Vesper Sparrow.
Voice: A broken song; clear notes and trills with pauses in between; best characterized by buzzing and churring passages.
Where found: S. Canada south (west of Appalachians) to n. Mexico. Winters s. U.S. to El Salvador. **West:** *Breeds* from s. edge of Canada through w. U.S. (absent w. Washington). *Winters* from c. California, s. Arizona, w. Texas south. **Habitat:**

Open country with bushes, trees; open brush, farms. **Nest:** A cup on ground or in low bush. Eggs (3–5) spotted.

RUFOUS-WINGED SPARROW   Pl. 57
Aimophila carpalis 5–5½

Field marks: Very local within the U.S. Suggests a Chipping Sparrow but grayer above, with a light median stripe through the crown; more pronounced "whiskers." Plumper; tail not notched. The most certain mark is the *rufous shoulder* (not easily seen). In flight, a slight dip (unlike Chipping).
Similar species: (1) Rufous-crowned Sparrow is much browner, with a solid rufous cap; has brown (not black) streaks on back; inhabits rocky slopes. (2) Brewer's Sparrow lacks median crown-stripe. (3) Botteri's Sparrow is darker, has a buffier (less gray) breast, lacks median crown line; whiskers fainter.
Voice: Song, 1 or 2 sweet introductory notes and a rapid series of musical chips on one pitch.
Where found: *Resident* from c.-s. Arizona (local; Coyote Mts., Tucson Mts., e. Tucson, Oracle), Sonora to Sinaloa. **Habitat:** Tall desert grass (tubosa), desert thorn brush. **Nest:** Woven of slender grass stems in bush. Eggs (4) pale blue.

RUFOUS-CROWNED SPARROW   Pl. 58
Aimophila ruficeps 5–6

Field marks: Note the black "whisker" bordering the throat. A dark sparrow with an unstreaked breast and *rufous cap.*
Similar species: (1) Chipping Sparrow has stronger eye-stripe, notched tail, black back stripes (Rufous-crown has *rounded* tail, brown stripes, whiskers). (2) See Swamp Sparrow.
Voice: Song, stuttering and gurgling, 1st part ascending slightly, last notes descending; suggests House Wren. Note, a nasal *chur, chur, chur* or *dear, dear, dear.*
Where found: *Breeds* from n.-c. California, n. Arizona, s. New Mexico, se. Colorado (rarely), w. Oklahoma south locally to s. Mexico. Largely resident except in n. Arizona, Colorado, Oklahoma. **Habitat:** Grassy or rocky slopes with sparse low bushes; open pine-oak woods. **Nest:** A grass-lined cup on ground. Eggs (3–4) white.

BOTTERI'S SPARROW *Aimophila botterii* 5¼–6¼ Pl. 57
Field marks: A very local, nondescript sparrow with a plain buff-gray breast. Cassin's, the only other sparrow breeding in the same habitat, is almost identical, but grayer above. Botteri's has a much browner tail. Best told by voice (below).
Similar species: (1) See Cassin's Sparrow. (2) In winter, Grasshopper Sparrow may invade the same area. It is browner, has conspicuous light stripes on the back, and a stripe through the crown. Botteri's is apparently not present in winter.

Voice: Song, a constant tinkling and "pitting," sometimes running into a dry rattle. Very unlike song of Cassin's.
Where found: Se. Arizona (local), s. tip of Texas (Cameron, Willacy Cos.) to s. Mexico. Winters south of U.S. **Habitat:** In Arizona, coarse desert grass (sacaton); in s. Texas, brushy coastal prairie. **Nest:** On ground. Eggs (3–5) white.

CASSIN'S SPARROW *Aimophila cassinii* 5¼–5¾ Pl. 57

Field marks: Note the "skylarking" song. A plain grayish sparrow of open country; underparts dingy white or buffy white without markings, or with a touch of streaking on the lower sides. Its dull grayish upper parts obscurely marked with brown and the unmarked breast are the best clues.
Similar species: Other obscure, clear-breasted sparrows of open country: (1) Grasshopper is browner, more contrastingly striped on back; has buffier breast, median crown-stripe. (2) Brewer's is Chippy-like (notched tail); striped buff and black above. (3) Botteri's (very local) does not "skylark."
Voice: Song, quite sweet, 1 or 2 short opening notes, a high sweet trill, and 2 lower notes: *ti ti tseeeeeee tay tay;* vaguely suggestive of Savannah Sparrow. Often "skylarks" or flutters into the air, giving the trill at the climax.
Where found: *Breeds* from se. Arizona, nw. New Mexico, w. Kansas to ne. Mexico. *Winters* from se. Arizona, w. and s. Texas south. *Casual,* Nevada, Colorado. **Habitat:** Arid grassy country with bushes. **Nest:** A deep cup on ground. Eggs (3–4) white.

BLACK-THROATED SPARROW Pl. 58
Amphispiza bilineata 4¾–5¼
(Desert Sparrow)

Field marks: Note the face pattern. A pretty, gray desert sparrow with white underparts, *white face-stripes,* and *jet-black throat.* Sexes similar. Young birds lack black throat but have cheek pattern; breast finely streaked.
Similar species: (1) Black-throated Gray Warbler (similar face pattern) has wing-bars, warbler bill. (2) Young birds somewhat resemble Sage Sparrow.
Voice: Song, a sweet *cheet cheet cheeeeeeee* (2 short, clear opening notes and a fine trill on a lower or higher pitch).
Where found: *Breeds* east of Sierra from se. Oregon (?), n. Nevada, s. Idaho, sw. Wyoming, nw. Oklahoma through deserts to n. Mexico. Migrant in n. parts of range. **Habitat:** Arid brush, creosote-bush deserts, "cholla gardens." **Nest:** A loose cup in bush or cactus. Eggs (3–4) white.

SAGE SPARROW *Amphispiza belli* 5–6 Pl. 58

Field marks: A gray sparrow of arid brush; note the combination of *single breast spot* and *dark "whiskers" on sides of throat.*

Dark cheek, white eye-ring, and whitish line over eye. A race resident west of the Sierra in California, *A. b. belli* (Bell's Sparrow), was until recently regarded as a distinct species. It is much darker, with heavier black whiskers.

Voice: Song, a simple set pattern, *tsit-tsoo-tseee-tsay,* 3rd note highest. Song of *belli* race, "4 to 7 notes forming a jerky but somewhat melodic phrase; higher notes with a squeaky, sibilant tone, lower notes tinkling" (H. H. Axtell).

Where found: *Breeds* from e. Washington, s. Idaho, w. Wyoming south to Baja California, s. Nevada, n. Arizona, nw. New Mexico. *Winters* from c. California, c. Nevada, sw. Utah, c. New Mexico south to n. Mexico. *Casual* in nw. coast belt and east of Rockies. **Habitat:** Dry brushy foothills, open chaparral, sagebrush plains; in winter, also deserts. **Nest:** A loose cup in bush. Eggs (3–4) speckled.

THE JUNCO COMPLEX   Pl. 56

Juncos are unstriped, gray, sparrow-shaped birds with *conspicuous white outer tail feathers,* gray or black heads, pale bills. Some species show areas of rusty on back or sides. In identifying juncos, the 3 major points are the *head* (whether black or gray), *sides* ("pinkish" or gray), and *back* (rusty or gray). Females are duller. There is frequent hybridization or intergradation; therefore it is impossible to name all individuals.

> *Species with gray sides:*
> White-winged Junco (white wing-bars)
> Slate-colored Junco (fairly uniform gray)
> Gray-headed Junco (rusty back, dark eye)
> Mexican Junco (rusty back, yellow eye)

> *Species with rusty or "pinkish" sides:*
> Oregon Junco (rusty or brown back)

WHITE-WINGED JUNCO *Junco aikeni* 6–6¾   Pl. 56

Field marks: Note the wing-bars. A gray junco with a *gray back.* Resembles Slate-colored Junco; larger, paler, usually with 2 *white wing-bars.* Has considerably more white in tail.

Similar species: All specimens outside the range outlined below should be carefully examined, since occasional Slate-colored Juncos may show a touch of white in wing. In White-winged Junco the 4 outer tail feathers on each side are white.

Voice: Song, a loose musical trill, similar to other juncos'.

Where found: Mainly in Black Hills area. *Breeds* in se. Montana, w. S. Dakota, ne. Wyoming, nw. Nebraska. *Winters* from breeding area south to Colorado, n. New Mexico, w. Oklahoma. *Casual,* n. Arizona. **Habitat:** Open pine forests. **Nest:** Similar to that of other juncos.

SLATE-COLORED JUNCO　*Junco hyemalis*　5½–6¼　**Pl. 56**
Field marks: A gray junco with a *gray back*. The *uniform coloration* above, without rusty or brown areas, is distinctive. Some females and young may have a trace of buff on the sides, but the sides blend into the hood and are not sharply separated, as in the Oregon Junco. The back also blends into the hood.
Similar species: See Oregon Junco.
Voice: Song, a loose musical trill on one pitch. Very similar to Oregon Junco's. Note, a light smack; twittering notes.
Where found: Alaska, Canada; in e. mts. to n. Georgia. Winters to s. U.S., n. Mexico. *West: Breeds* from tree limit south to n. B.C., c. Alberta, c. Saskatchewan. *Winters* from s. Canada south (mainly east of Rockies; sparingly west). **Habitat:** Coniferous and mixed woods. In winter, undergrowth, roadsides, brush.
Nest: A hair-lined cup on ground in woods. Eggs (3–5) spotted.

OREGON JUNCO　*Junco oreganus*　5–6　　　　**Pl. 56**
(including Pink-sided Junco)
Field marks: Note the buffy or rusty sides. *Male:* A *rusty-backed* junco with a *black head*. Bill pink. *Female:* Head grayer, rusty of back not so sharply defined, but "pink" or brownish sides sharply separated from gray of hood. Juvenal birds are streaked below but are grayer than sparrows and exhibit white outer tail feathers. This is the only junco common in the Pacific states (Slate-colored is seen sparsely; Gray-headed is casual. To search for them, look for juncos with *gray* sides). There are a number of races of the Oregon Junco, but only one is readily separable, *J. o. mearnsi* (Pink-sided Junco), which breeds in the n. Rockies (south to s. Idaho, n. Wyoming). Males have a *paler gray* head and a *dull brown* back. The combination of clear-gray hood and bright "pink" sides denotes this race (until recently, regarded as a different species).
Similar species: (1) Gray-headed Junco has *gray* sides. Hybrids (Gray-headed × Pink-sided) occur where ranges meet. (2) Oregon × Slate-color hybrids also occur where ranges meet.
Voice: Song, a loose musical trill on same pitch. Note, a light smack; twittering notes.
Where found: *Breeds* from se. coastal Alaska, c. B.C., s. Alberta, sw. Saskatchewan south on coast to c. California (Monterey Co.); through Cascades, Sierra to mts. of s. and Baja California; in Rockies to s. Idaho, n. Wyoming. *Winters* from s. B.C., sw. Alberta to Mexico. **Habitat:** Conifer and mixed forests; in winter, also roadsides, brush, parks, gardens. **Nest:** A well-lined cup on ground in woods. Eggs (4–5) spotted.

GRAY-HEADED JUNCO　*Junco caniceps*　5½–6　**Pl. 56**
(including Red-backed Junco)
Field marks: The combination of *ash-gray* sides and wings and *bright rufous* back distinguishes this species from all other U.S.

juncos except the Mexican Junco. The head is also ashy gray, even in males. Two races are separable: (1) *J. c. caniceps* (c. Rockies) has the entire bill pale. (2) *J. c. dorsalis* (New Mexico, Arizona, w. Texas) has a *dark upper mandible* and paler hood. (Until recently, regarded as a dark-eyed race of the Mexican Junco, *J. phaeonotus*.)

Similar species: (1) Oregon Junco has rusty or pink-buff sides, rusty wings; male has blackish hood. (2) Mexican Junco has *yellow eye*. (3) Hybrids occur (Gray-headed × Oregon).

Voice: A loose light trill on one pitch.

Where found: *Resident* in mt. regions east of Sierra from extreme e. California, n. Nevada, se. Idaho, s. Wyoming south to c. Arizona, s. New Mexico, w. Texas (Guadalupe Mts.). *Winters* to n. Mexico. *Casual*, s. California. **Habitat:** Mt. forests; in winter associates with other juncos. **Nest:** A grassy cup on ground. Eggs (4–5) speckled.

MEXICAN JUNCO *Junco phaeonotus* 5½–6½   **Pl. 56**
(Arizona Junco)

   Field marks: The only U.S. junco with a *yellow eye*. The combination of grayish sides and *bright rufous* back distinguishes this pale-breasted species from all other juncos except the Gray-headed, which has a dark eye. It also lacks the hooded effect and is whitish-throated. Walks rather than hops.

Similar species: Gray-headed Junco has dark eye.

Voice: Song, musical, unjuncolike, more complicated; 3-parted, often thus: *chip chip chip, wheedle wheedle, che che che che che.*

Where found: *Resident* in high mts. of se. Arizona, extreme sw. New Mexico; south to s. Mexico. **Habitat:** Conifer forests, tall pine-oak woods. **Nest:** A well-lined cup on ground under log, stump. Eggs (3) bluish-white, unmarked.

TREE SPARROW *Spizella arborea* 5½–6½   **Pl. 58**

   Field marks: To identify the "Winter Chippy" note the single *dark spot* or "stickpin" on the breast, and the solid *red-brown cap*. Bill dark above, yellow below; 2 white wing-bars.

Similar species: See Chipping Sparrow.

Voice: Song, sweet, variable; opening on 1 or 2 high, clear notes. Note, *tseet;* feeding note, a musical *teelwit.*

Where found: Alaska, n. Canada. Winters s. Canada to c. U.S.

West: *Breeds* from Arctic slope to n. B.C., s. Mackenzie, n. Saskatchewan. *Winters* from s. Canada south (mainly east of Cascades, Sierra) to s. Nevada, n. Arizona, c. New Mexico, w. Texas. **Habitat:** Arctic scrub, willow thickets; in winter, brush, roadsides, weedy edges. **Nest:** A feathered-lined cup on ground or in bush. Eggs (4–5) pale blue, speckled.

CHIPPING SPARROW *Spizella passerina* 5–5¾   **Pl. 58**

   Field marks: *Spring:* A small gray-breasted sparrow with a bright *rufous cap,* a *black line* through the eye, and a *white line* over it. *Winter adults* are browner, not so gray-breasted; cap and eyebrow line duller. Immatures are buffier, with a light stripe through crown.

Similar species: See (1) Rufous-crowned, (2) Clay-colored, and (3) Brewer's Sparrows.

Voice: Song, a dry rattle on one pitch. Note, a short *chip.*

Where found: Canada to Nicaragua. Winters s. U.S. south. **West:** *Breeds* from n. B.C., c. Yukon, s. Mackenzie south through w. U.S. *Casual,* Alaska. *Winters* from c. California (rarely), s. Nevada, c. Arizona, s. New Mexico, w. Texas south. **Habitat:** Open woodland, conifers, farms, orchards, towns. **Nest:** A hair-lined cup in bush, tree. Eggs (3–5) light blue, speckled.

CLAY-COLORED SPARROW   Pl. 58
Spizella pallida 5–5½

Field marks: A small pale sparrow of the Great Plains; clear-breasted, Chipping-Sparrow-like, but not so gray. *Light stripe* through crown; *sharply outlined brown ear patch.*

Similar species: (1) Chipping Sparrows with brown ear patches are often miscalled Clay-colored Sparrows. Both birds possess them in fall and winter. The patch in the Clay-colored adult is *outlined* above and below by black lines; the fall Chipping lacks them. The only sure point in most autumn birds is the rump; *buffy* in the Clay-colored, gray in the Chipping. (2) See also Brewer's Sparrow. (3) Immature White-crowned (larger) has a superficial resemblance.

Voice: Song, unbirdlike; 3 or 4 low flat buzzes, *bzzzz, bzzzz, bzzzz* (slow tempo).

Where found: W. Canada, n.-c. U.S. Winters mainly in Mexico. **West:** *Breeds* from ne. B.C., s. Mackenzie south (east of Rockies), to se. Colorado, Nebraska. *Migrates* through Great Plains. *Winters* from Rio Grande Valley, Texas to s. Mexico. *Casual,* Idaho, nw. Montana, Utah, Arizona. **Habitat:** Open brush, "parklands," brushy prairies. **Nest:** A hair-lined cup in grass or bush. Eggs (3–5) blue, spotted.

BREWER'S SPARROW   *Spizella breweri* 5–5¼   Pl. 58

Field marks: A small pale sparrow of the sagebrush. Clear-breasted; resembles Chipping Sparrow but sandier, *crown finely streaked,* no hint of rufous or median line.

Similar species: Young Chipping and Clay-colored Sparrows in fall or winter might be confused with it, but their crowns are usually browner with a pale median line.

Voice: Song, long musical buzzy trills on different pitches; suggests trilling and chopping of Canary, but weaker; sounds like a Chipping Sparrow trying to sing like a Canary.

Where found: *Breeds* from sw. Yukon, s. Alberta, sw. Saskatchewan south (east of Cascades, Sierra) to s. California, c. Arizona, n. New Mexico. *Winters* in s. parts of border states,

n. Mexico. **Habitat:** Sagebrush, brushy plains; also near tree line in n. Rockies; in winter also weedy fields. **Nest:** On ground, in sagebrush or low conifer (high mts.). Eggs (3–4) pale blue, speckled.

FIELD SPARROW *Spizella pusilla* 5¼–6 Pl. 58

Field marks: Note the *pink bill* of this rusty-capped sparrow. It has rather rusty upper parts and a clear breast; less noticeable facial striping than the other red-capped sparrows; a narrow *eye-ring* sometimes gives it a big-eyed expression.
Similar species: (1) Chipping Sparrow has well-defined eye-stripings, dark bill. (2) See Rufous-crowned Sparrow.
Voice: Song, opening on deliberate, sweet, slurring notes and speeding into a trill (which ascends, descends, or stays on same pitch). Note, *tsee;* has querulous quality.
Where found: Se. Canada, U.S. (east of Rockies) to Gulf states. Winters in e. and c. U.S., ne. Mexico. **West:** *Breeds* west to Montana, ne. Colorado, w. Oklahoma, Texas panhandle, Edwards Plateau (resident). **Habitat:** Brushy pastures, bushes.
Nest: A hair-lined cup in grass, low bush. Eggs (4–5) spotted.

BLACK-CHINNED SPARROW Pl. 58
Spizella atrogularis 5–5½

Field marks: A very different, somewhat junco-like sparrow; has a streaked brown back, but *head and underparts gray.* In the male the *flesh-colored bill* is set off conspicuously by a black chin patch that encircles it. Females lack the patch; can be told by the *unmarked gray head and breast,* brown back.
Voice: Song, a series of notes on about same pitch, or descending slightly; starts with several high, thin, clear notes and ends in a rough trill, *sweet, sweet, sweet, weet-trrrrrrr.*
Where found: *Breeds* from c. California, s. Nevada (local), s. Utah, s. New Mexico, w. Texas (Trans-Pecos) to s. Mexico. *Winters* mainly from s. Arizona, w. Texas south. **Habitat:** Brushy mt. slopes, open chaparral, sagebrush. **Nest:** A compact cup in low bush. Eggs (3–4) pale blue or spotted.

HARRIS' SPARROW *Zonotrichia querula* 7–7¾ Pl. 58

Field marks: A large sparrow, longer than Fox Sparrow. Sexes alike. In breeding plumage recognizable by *black crown, face, and bib encircling pink bill.* In winter adults, black crown is veiled with gray. Young birds in 1st winter are *white on throat,* less black on crown, buffy brown on rest of head, and blotched and streaked on breast. Birds in 2nd winter plumage are black *on the chin* (G. M. Sutton).
Similar species: In full plumage, has remote resemblance to male House Sparrow. In behavior, like White-crowned Sparrow, but when disturbed flies into trees rather than into brush.

Voice: Song has quavering quality of White-throated Sparrow's; clear whistles, all on same pitch, or 1st one or two at one pitch, rest at a slightly higher or lower pitch, *general effect being minor.* Winter songs interspersed with chuckling sounds. Alarm note, a loud *weenk* or *wink* (G. M. Sutton).
Where found: N.-c. Canada. Winters mainly in s.-c. U.S. **West:** *Breeds* in Mackenzie. *Migrates* through Alberta, Saskatchewan, and Great Plains. *Winters* from s. B.C., n. Idaho, n. Colorado, n. Nebraska south sparsely to s. California, c. Arizona; more commonly east of mts. to s.-c. Texas. **Habitat:** Stunted boreal forest; in winter, brushy edges, open woodlands. **Nest:** A grass cup on ground. Eggs (4) pale bluish, spotted.

WHITE-CROWNED SPARROW   p. 245, Pl. 58
Zonotrichia leucophrys 5½–7

Field marks: *Adult:* A grayish breast and a puffy crown *striped with black and white* make this abundant bird a very handsome sparrow. *Immature:* Browner, with head-stripings of dark brown and light buff; *bill bright pinkish or yellowish* (often with dusky tip). In the Rocky Mt. region, 2 races, Gambel's and Mountain White-crown, can be readily separated (see below). In c. California 4 races occur. Of these, the Mountain White-crown is seldom noted away from the Sierra. Around San Francisco students often try to separate the various races by appearance and song, but this is risky because even the resident race, *nuttalli,* varies in song from place to place and the several races tend to intergrade morphologically.

Z. l. oriantha (Mountain White-crown) differs in having the white eyebrow-stripe start *from the eye.* It breeds in high mts. from the Canadian border to the Sierra of s.-c. California and in Rockies to n. New Mexico. Winters in sw. U.S.

Z. l. gambelii (Gambel's White-crown). White eye-stripe *starts from bill.* Cleaner, grayer-appearing on neck, lighter backstriping (light gray, red-brown) than the 2 coastal races. Bill *pinkish* or *flesh-colored* (not yellowish). Song, more wheezy and drawling throughout. Breeds from n.-c. Alaska, nw. Canada throughout much of w. Canada; migrant in w. U.S. except in nw. coast belt; winters from California, Utah south.

Z. l. nuttalli (Nuttall's White-crown). Browner on neck and breast than Gambel's; bill *yellowish* with dusky tip (Gambel's, flesh-colored or orange-brown). Head-stripes wider, back-stripes darker (blackish on tan). Resident along coast of California from Mendocino Co. to Santa Barbara Co.

Z. l. pugetensis (Puget Sound White-crown). A dark race, similar to Nuttall's but somewhat less dingy, less yellow on bill. Breeds in humid coast belt from sw. B.C. to nw. California; winters along coast to s. California.

Similar species: White-throated Sparrow has: (1) a conspicuous white throat, (2) yellow spot before eye, (3) black bill. It is considerably browner. Young White-throats, though duller, always look like White-throats, have dark bills.

Voice: Song, 1 or more plaintive or wheezy whistles on different pitches, followed by a husky trill or series of trills and *chillip*'s. Arrangement varies. Note, a loud *pink*.

Where found: Alaska, Canada, w. U.S.; winters in w. and s. U.S., Mexico, Cuba. **West:** *Breeds* along edge of tundra in Arctic and south along coast and in high mts. to s.-c. California, c. Arizona, n. New Mexico. *Winters* from s. B.C., n. Idaho, Wyoming, to c. Mexico. **Habitat:** Scattered cover; low brush, mt. thickets, boreal scrub; in winter, gardens, towns, roadsides, open scrub. **Nest:** A well-lined cup on ground or in bush. Eggs (3–5) pale blue-green, spotted.

HEADS OF WHITE-CROWNED SPARROWS

A. *Gambelli* race: White stripe starts from bill (*nuttalli* and *pugetensis* races similar). B. *Oriantha* race: White stripe starts from eye.

GOLDEN-CROWNED SPARROW   Pl. 58
Zonotrichia atricapilla   6–7

Field marks: *Adult:* Similar to White-crowned Sparrow, with no white head-stripes; instead, a dull golden-yellow central crown-stripe, heavily bordered with black (not fully developed in some adults). Immatures (and many winter adults) look like large female House Sparrows, but are longer-tailed, darker, grayer on sides of neck and breast, and usually have a dull yellowish suffusion on the forecrown. They may lack the yellow and have little to distinguish them unless it be the fine streaking on the otherwise unpatterned crown.

Similar species: Immature White-crown (buffy median crown-stripe but not yellow) has a broad buffy line over each eye, and a pink or yellowish (not dark) bill.

Voice: Song, 3 high whistled notes of plaintive minor quality, coming down scale; sometimes a final faint trill.

Where found: *Breeds* from nw. Alaska (Wales) south on coast to se. Alaska; inland from s. Yukon to mts. of s. B.C., w. Alberta. *Winters* from s. B.C., through Pacific states to n. Mexico; rarely east to Utah, Colorado, New Mexico. *Casual,* Saskatchewan,

w. Texas. **Habitat:** Boreal scrub, spruce; in winter, partly as White-crown, favors denser shrubs. **Nest:** Rootlet-lined; under bush. Eggs (4–5) pale blue, speckled.

WHITE-THROATED SPARROW   Pl. 58
Zonotrichia albicollis   6–7

Field marks: *Adult:* Gray-breasted with *white throat patch, striped black and white crown,* and *yellow* spot between bill and eye. Bill blackish. *Immature:* Duller; head-stripes brown and buffy, but same essential pattern; bill dark.

Similar species: Adult White-crowned Sparrow lacks clean-cut white throat, yellow loral spot; has a pink or yellow bill.

Voice: Song, several clear, pensive whistles easily imitated; 1 or 2 clear notes, followed with 3 quavering notes on a different pitch. Note, a hard *chink;* also a slurred *tseet.*

Where found: Canada, ne. U.S. Winters from New England to s. U.S., n. Mexico. **West:** *Breeds* from s. Yukon, c. Mackenzie to ne. B.C., c. Alberta, se. Saskatchewan. *Winters* in very small numbers in Pacific states and from Nevada, Utah, Colorado south. Sparse migrant through Plains. **Habitat:** Woodland undergrowth, thickets, brush. **Nest:** A rootlet-lined cup on ground or in bush. Eggs (4–5) speckled.

FOX SPARROW   *Passerella iliaca*   6¼–7¼   Pl. 57

Field marks: Note the *rusty tail.* Larger than House Sparrow; dark brown, gray, or rusty with heavily streaked underparts. The spots, shaped like inverted V's, often cluster in a large spot on the upper breast. The many races can be roughly divided into 3 types: (1) bright rusty Fox Sparrows; (2) dark brown-headed Fox Sparrows with darker bills; (3) gray-headed Fox Sparrows with large yellowish bills. It is hopeless to separate them further; in winter several races might be in the same flock. The only race identified readily is the Yukon Fox Sparrow, *P. i. zaboria* (w. Canada, east of mts.; most of Alaska), which winters mainly in the East but may rarely be seen west to the Pacific Coast. No other w. Fox Sparrow shows such bright rusty, especially on tail and on breast-stripes.

Similar species: Hermit Thrush has a similar reddish tail, but is *thin-billed* and spotted rather than striped.

Voice: A brilliant musical song; usually begins with 1 or 2 clear notes, followed by a sliding note: *sweet sweet cheer chillip chillip,* etc. Arrangement varies. (See Green-tailed Towhee.) Notes, a loud dry *chek,* a thin lisp.

Where found: Alaska, Canada; w. U.S. In winter to s. U.S. **West:** *Breeds* from tree limit south on outer coast to nw. Washington; in high mts. to s. California, c. Nevada, c. Utah, c. Colorado; also east across Canadian forest. *Winters* from s. B.C. through Pacific states; and from s. Utah, Colorado to s. Arizona,

New Mexico, w. Texas. **Habitat:** Stunted boreal woodlands, mt. chaparral, forest undergrowth. In winter, woodland undergrowth, chaparral, parks, gardens. **Nest:** A feather-lined cup on ground or in bush. Eggs (4–5) pale greenish, speckled.

LINCOLN'S SPARROW *Melospiza lincolnii* 5–6 **Pl. 57**
Field marks: Lincoln's Sparrow is a skulker. It resembles a Song Sparrow, but is trimmer; side of face grayer, breast-streakings *much finer,* often not aggregated into a central spot; best identified by a wash of *creamy buff* across upper breast. It has a narrow white eye-ring.
Similar species: The buffy breast and fine streakings distinguish it from most sparrows except young Song Sparrow. Lincoln's has a more contrastingly striped crown (rusty brown on light gray) and a narrow eye-ring
Voice: Song, sweet and gurgling; suggests both House Wren and Purple Finch; starts with low passages, rises abruptly, drops. **Where found:** Alaska, Canada, w. and ne. U.S. In winter, s. U.S. to Guatemala. **West:** *Breeds* from n.-c. Alaska, c. Yukon, east across Canadian forest; south in high mts. to s. California, c. Arizona, n. New Mexico. *Migrates* in lowlands. *Winters* from w. Oregon, c. Arizona, w. Texas south. **Habitat:** Willow and alder thickets, muskegs, brushy bogs. In winter, lowland thickets, tall weeds, bushes. **Nest:** A grass cup on ground in bog or muskeg. Eggs (4–5) blotched.

SWAMP SPARROW *Melospiza georgiana* 5 5¾ **Pl. 58**
Field marks: A rather stout, dark rusty sparrow, with gray breast, outlined *white throat, reddish cap. Immature* birds are dimly streaked and have no red on the striped crown.
Similar species: (1) Chipping Sparrow is less robust and shows a white or buffy stripe over the eye. (2) Field and (3) Tree Sparrows both show prominent wing-bars. (4) Rufous-crowned Sparrow has different habitat.
Voice: Song, a trill, similar to Chipping Sparrow's but slower, sweeter, stronger (sometimes on two pitches simultaneously). Note, a hard *chink,* similar to White-throat's.
Where found: Canada, ne. U.S. Winters to Gulf states. **West:** *Breeds* east of Rockies from ne. B.C., s. Mackenzie to c. Alberta, c. Saskatchewan. *Winters* Colorado to Texas. Recorded casually in all w. states. **Habitat:** Bushy marshes, muskegs. **Nest:** A grass cup in marsh tussock. Eggs (4–5) spotted.

SONG SPARROW *Melospiza melodia* 5–7 **Pl. 57**
Field marks: Note the heavy breast streaks confluent into a *large central spot.* The bird pumps its tail as it flies. Young birds are more finely streaked, often without the central spot. Many subspecies vary in size and color; those of arid sections are paler;

those in humid regions darker. Aleutian birds (nonmigratory) are especially large and dark. Do not attempt to untangle various migrants in the field.

Similar species: (1) Savannah Sparrow often shows yellow over eye, has pinker legs, shorter *notched* tail. (2) Fox Sparrow is larger, more heavily marked. (3) See Lincoln's Sparrow.

Voice: Song, a variable series of notes, some musical, some buzzy; usually starts with 3–4 bright repetitious notes, *sweet sweet sweet,* etc. Note, a low nasal *tchep.*

Where found: Alaska, Canada; to c. Mexico. Winters to Gulf Coast, Mexico. **West:** *Breeds* from Aleutians, coast of s. Alaska, s. Yukon, s. Mackenzie to s. California, s. Arizona, n. New Mexico, n. Nebraska. *Winters* from Aleutians through Pacific states and from Idaho, Montana south. **Habitat:** Thickets, brush, marshes, roadsides, gardens, sea beaches (Alaska). **Nest:** A grass cup on ground or in bush. Eggs (3–5) spotted.

McCOWN'S LONGSPUR   Pl. 54
Rhynchophanes mccownii 5¾–6

Field marks: *Spring male:* Crown and patch on breast black; tail largely white. Hind neck *gray* (brown or chestnut in other longspurs). *Female and winter male:* Note tail pattern (opp. Plate 54). Black is like an inverted T.

Similar species: (1) Male Chestnut-collared Longspur in spring has chestnut collar, black belly. (2) Horned Lark (similar breast splotch) has thin bill, black face patch.

Voice: Song, in display flight, clear sweet warbles, suggesting Lark Bunting (R. J. Niedrach). Note, a dry rattle.

Where found: *Breeds* from s. Alberta, s. Saskatchewan, sw. Manitoba to ne. Colorado, nw. Nebraska. *Winters* from Arizona, Colorado, Kansas to n. Mexico. **Habitat:** Plains, prairies. **Nest:** A grass-lined hollow on ground. Eggs (3–4) streaked.

LAPLAND LONGSPUR *Calcarius lapponicus* 6–7   Pl. 54
(Alaska Longspur)

Field marks: Longspurs are birds of open country; like Horned Larks and pipits, they usually walk, seldom hop. In flight they appear to have *shorter tails.* In winter, sparse black streaks on the sides, reddish on the nape, and a smudge across the upper breast help identify males. Winter females are more nondescript (see tail pattern, opp. Plate 54). In spring, males acquire a black face, outlined with white; females are rather like winter males.

Similar species: (1) Other longspurs have much more white on outer tail feathers (see tail pattern, opp. Plate 54). (2) Pipits and (3) Horned Larks have thin bills, longer tails.

Voice: A musical *teew* or a rattle and a whistle, *ticky-tick-tew.* Song (in display flight), vigorous, musical.

Where found: Arctic; circumpolar. Winters s. Canada to s. U.S.; c. Eurasia. **West:** Breeds mainly in Aleutians, Pribilofs, Alaska, and along Arctic coasts. Winters from s. B.C., Montana, S. Dakota south to ne. California, ne. Arizona, Texas panhandle. Casual, s. California, sw. Arizona. **Habitat:** Tundra; in winter, fields, prairies. **Nest:** A feather-lined depression on tundra. Eggs (4–7) pale olive, spotted.

SMITH'S LONGSPUR *Calcarius pictus* 5¾–6½ **Pl. 54**
Field marks: A *buffy* longspur; warm buff on entire underparts. Tail with white sides as in Vesper Sparrow (no dark end band). Male in spring, deeper buff; cheek with *white spot strikingly* outlined with triangle of black. White stripe over eye. Females and winter birds nondescript; breast lightly streaked; some males may show white patch near shoulder.
Similar species: (1) See Vesper Sparrow, (2) Sprague's Pipit (p. 189), and (3) other longspurs (study tail diagram, opp. Plate 54).
Voice: Rattling or clicking notes in flight (suggests winding of cheap watch). Song, sweet and warbler-like; ends like a Chestnut-sided Warbler's (*we' chew*).
Where found: N. Alaska to Hudson Bay. Winters east of 100° in s.-c. U.S. **West:** Breeds in n. Alaska (Brooks Range), n. Mackenzie. Migrates through Alberta, Saskatchewan. **Habitat:** Tundra; in migration, prairies, airports. **Nest:** A grass-lined hollow on tundra. Eggs (3–5) spotted.

CHESTNUT-COLLARED LONGSPUR **Pl. 54**
Calcarius ornatus 5½–6½
Field marks: *Male, breeding: Solid black below* except on throat; nape chestnut. *Female and winter birds:* Sparrow-like, nondescript; the best field mark is the tail pattern (a dark triangle on white tail).
Similar species: Lapland and Smith's Longspurs (also Vesper Sparrow and pipits) have straight white sides on tail. In McCown's Longspur the black forms an inverted T.
Voice: Song, short, feeble, but musical, "suggestive of Western Meadowlark" (R. J. Niedrach). Note, a finchlike *ji-jiv*.
Where found: Breeds from s. Canadian prairies to ne. Colorado, n. Nebraska, sw. Minnesota. Winters from n. Arizona, ne. Colorado, Kansas to n. Mexico. Casual, B.C., Utah, California. **Habitat:** Plains, prairies. **Nest:** A grass-lined depression on ground. Eggs (3–5) speckled.

SNOW BUNTING *Plectrophenax nivalis* 6–7¼ **p. 250**
Field marks: Note the great amount of white. In winter, some individuals look quite brown, but when they fly large white wing patches flash forth. Overhead, they look almost entirely

WHITE WAGTAIL

Black-backed
race (lugens)

BLUETHROAT

♂

♂

Note: A gray-
backed race of
White Wagtail
(*ocularis*) has
also occurred
in Alaska.

♂

♂

Breeding

YELLOW WAGTAIL

♂

WHEATEAR

Winter

♂

Immature, winter

SNOW BUNTING

♂

Breeding

McKAY'S BUNTING
(Hall and St. Matthew Is.)

SNOW BUNTING AND ALASKAN SPECIALTIES

white (pipits and Horned Larks are black-tailed). They often travel in large flocks. In arctic dress the male has a black back, pure white head and underparts.

Voice: Note, a sharp whistled *teer* or *tew;* also a rough purring *brrt.* Song, a musical larklike *ti-ti-chu-ree,* repeated.

Where found: Arctic; circumpolar. In winter to c. Eurasia, c. U.S. **West:** *Breeds* from Arctic coast south to Aleutians, Kodiak *Winters* from s. Alaska, B.C., Canadian prairies to n. California, e. Oregon, n. Utah, ne. Colorado, Kansas. *Casual,* ne. New Mexico. **Habitat:** Tundra (summer); prairies, fields, shores. **Nest:** A feather-lined hollow on tundra. Eggs (4–6) spotted.

McKAY'S BUNTING *Plectrophenax hyperboreus* 7 **p. 250**
(McKay's Snow Bunting)

Field marks: The male in breeding plumage is almost pure white except for tips of primaries and tips of central tail feathers. Females show some dark on back. In winter, light touches of brown, but much less than in Snow Bunting.

Similar species: Breeding male Snow Bunting has *black* back. Females and winter birds are much browner.

Voice: Song of male is said to suggest American Goldfinch.

Where found: *Breeds* only on Hall I. and St. Matthew I., Bering Sea, Alaska. *Winters* to coast of w. Alaska, Nunivak. **Habitat:** Tundra, barrens, shores. **Nest:** On ground, in rock crevice or in drift log. Eggs (3–4) spotted.

Part II

The Hawaiian Islands

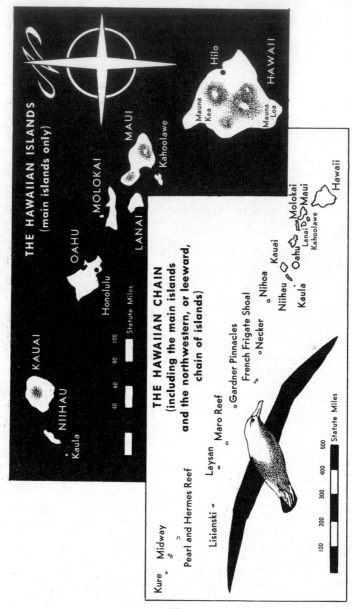

THE HAWAIIAN ISLANDS
(main islands only)

KAUAI

NIIHAU

Kaula

OAHU

Honolulu

MOLOKAI

LANAI

MAUI

Kahoolawe

Mauna Kea

Mauna Loa

Hilo

HAWAII

Statute Miles

40 60 80 100

THE HAWAIIAN CHAIN
(including the main islands and the northwestern, or leeward, chain of islands)

Kure

Midway

Pearl and Hermes Reef

Lisianski

Laysan

Maro Reef

Gardner Pinnacles

French Frigate Shoal

Necker

Nihoa

Niihau

Kauai

Kaula

Oahu

Molokai

Lanai

Maui

Kahoolawe

Hawaii

Statute Miles

100 200 300 400 500

Water Birds

(Including Sea Birds, Freshwater Waterfowl, Shorebirds)

IN THE Hawaiian Islands birds of cold seas — gulls and cormo-rants — occur only as lost waifs (see "Casual and Accidental Species," p. 285). Terns, tropicbirds, boobies, shearwaters, and petrels, on the other hand, abound. The major islands have their specialties, such as the White-tailed Tropicbird and the rare Manx (Newell's) Shearwater and Dark-rumped Petrel, which seek the crater walls for their nesting. Islets off the main islands offer sanctuary, but in the northwest chain of islands exist the principal seafowl nurseries.

Good ponds for migrant ducks are few in the islands. Progress has decreed their drainage and we might well see the complete disappearance of the Stilt and other island endemics.

BLACK-FOOTED ALBATROSS *Diomedea nigripes*   **p. 14**
See page 8. *Breeds* (Oct.–July) on nw. chain of islands. Some-times seen following ships off main islands.

LAYSAN ALBATROSS *Diomedea immutabilis*   **p. 14**
See page 8. *Breeds* (Nov. Aug.) on nw. chain of islands. Sometimes seen near main islands.

WEDGE-TAILED SHEARWATER (UAU KANI)   **p. 257**
Puffinus pacificus   16–18
  Field marks: See family discussion of shearwaters (p. 9). Note the strongly wedge-shaped tail, *flesh-colored feet*. Most indi-viduals in the Hawaiian Islands are dark brown above, whitish below. A small minority have brownish underparts.
  Similar species: (1) Bonin Petrel is smaller, has shorter tail, whitish forehead, gray back. (2) Dark Wedge-tail is known from other dark Hawaiian shearwaters and petrels by *flesh* feet.
  Voice: At night, in colony, a moaning *ooooóo-how* (rising and dropping); also *huh-ooooooo*. Called "moaning bird."
  Where found: Warmer parts of Pacific and Indian Oceans.
  Hawaiian Is.: *Breeds* abundantly on nw. chain, Niihau (Lehua), Kauai (Kilauea Lighthouse), and on islets off Oahu, Maui (Molokini), and Hawaii. **Habitat:** Ocean. **Nest:** In burrow or on ground under vegetation, in colony. Eggs (1) white.

SOOTY SHEARWATER *Puffinus griseus*   **Pl. 2**
See page 10. Differs from dark phase of Wedge-tail by whitish underwing, blackish feet, and stubbier tail. Christmas Island Shearwater is smaller and blacker, with blackish underwing. The Sooty is said to be transient at sea off main islands.

CHRISTMAS ISLAND SHEARWATER p. 257
Puffinus nativitatus 14–15
  Field marks: An all-blackish shearwater. Feet blackish.
  Similar species: (1) Bulwer's Petrel is smaller (10–11), has a longer, wedge-shaped tail, light brown band on wing coverts and different flight (lacks rigid scaling of shearwater). (2) Sooty Storm Petrel (11) has forked tail and light brown band on wing coverts. (3) Wedge-tailed Shearwater (dark phase) is larger (16–18), has flesh-colored feet. (4) Sooty Shearwater (16–18) has whitish underwing.
  Voice: At night in colony, moaning, similar to Wedge-tail's.
  Where found: Tropical Pacific. **Hawaiian Is.:** *Breeds* (Apr.–Oct.) on nw. chain, Niihau (Lehua) and off Oahu (Moku Manu).
  Nest: Under bushes or in rocks or burrows. Eggs (1) white.

MANX SHEARWATER (AO) *Puffinus puffinus* 12½–15
(Newell's Shearwater) **Pl. 2**
  See page 13. The contrasting glossy-black upper parts (including forehead) separate it from other white-breasted Hawaiian shearwaters and petrels. The Hawaiian race, once considered possibly extinct, has been reported recently from Niihau, Kauai, Oahu, Hawaii. Formerly more widespread. *Breeds* (Apr.–Nov.) probably in burrows about cliffs (500–1000 ft.) near the sea, where its night cry, *ao,* suggests its native name.

DARK-RUMPED PETREL (UAU) p. 257
Pterodroma phaeopygia 15½–17
  Field marks: Large; dark above, clear white below. Note the *white forehead,* which is said to give the bird a white-headed look. Upper half of webbed foot flesh, end blackish.
  Similar species: (1) Bonin Petrel has light gray back and rump; breeds on nw. chain only. (2) Wedge-tailed Shearwater has dark forehead, completely pink feet. (3) Manx (Newell's) Shearwater has black forehead, black feet.
  Voice: At night, a repeated *ă-ōō;* also a nasal drawn-out *ē;* a croak; a high-pitched *witch* (F. Richardson, D. H. Woodside).
  Where found: Tropical e. Pacific (Hawaiian and Galápagos Is.). *Breeds* locally near volcanoes on Maui (Haleakala) and Hawaii; formerly all main islands. **Nest:** In burrow in wall of crater, cliff, volcanic slope. Eggs (1) white.

BONIN PETREL *Pterodroma hypoleuca* 13 p. 257
  Field marks: Size of a small shearwater; identified by its pale *gray back* and rump contrasting with black on nape, wings, and tail. Forehead and underparts white.
  Similar species: See (1) Wedge-tailed Shearwater and (2) Dark-rumped Petrel (main islands).
  Voice: At night, in colony, squeals, growls, snarls. Called "little moaning bird."

HAWAIIAN SHEARWATERS AND PETRELS

Light (normal) phase

WEDGE-TAILED SHEARWATER

CHRISTMAS ISLAND SHEARWATER

DARK-RUMPED PETREL

BONIN PETREL

SOOTY STORM PETREL

HARCOURT'S STORM PETREL

BULWER'S PETREL

Where found: W. and c. Pacific. **Hawaiian Is.:** *Breeds* (Aug.–June) abundantly on nw. chain of islands. **Habitat:** Ocean. **Nest:** In burrow; in colony. Eggs (1) white.

BULWER'S PETREL (OU) *Bulweria bulwerii* 10–11 **p. 257**
Field marks: A blackish petrel with a long *wedge-shaped tail.* Feet slaty; tarsus straw-brown. Brownish band on wing coverts. *Note:* Ou is also the name of a rare drepanidid (p. 270).
Similar species: (1) Sooty Storm Petrel has forked tail. (2) Christmas Island Shearwater (14–15) lacks pale band on wing coverts; has a shorter tail, stiff scaling flight.
Voice: At night, in colony, a barking *cow-ow* (or *o-u*). Also a rapid series *ow-ow-ow-ow,* etc., "like a motorboat" (W. V. Ward).
Where found: W. and c. Pacific; e. Atlantic. **Hawaiian Is.:** *Breeds* (Apr.–Oct.) locally on nw. chain and on islets off main islands. **Habitat:** Ocean. **Nest:** Under coral rocks or in shore cave or burrow. Eggs (1) white.

HARCOURT'S STORM PETREL (OEOE) **p. 257**
Oceanodroma castro 7–8
(Hawaiian Storm Petrel)
Field marks: A small blackish petrel; the only Hawaiian petrel with a *white rump.* The white extends to under tail coverts.
Where found: C. and e. Pacific; e. Atlantic. **Hawaiian Is.:** *Ranges* from Gardner Pinnacle to main islands. **Habitat:** Ocean.
Nest: Believed to breed on inland cliffs of main islands.

SOOTY STORM PETREL **p. 257**
Oceanodroma markhami 11
Field marks: Subspecies *tristrami.* Sooty brown with light brown band on wing coverts. Note *forked tail.* No white on rump.
Similar species: (1) Harcourt's Storm Petrel (7–8) has white rump. (2) Christmas Island Shearwater and (3) Bulwer's Petrel have rounded or wedge-shaped tails.
Where found: Pacific; Japan to S. America. **Hawaiian Is.:** *Breeds* locally on nw. chain. *Casual* near main islands. **Nest:** In burrow. Eggs (1) white, faintly spotted.

WHITE-TAILED TROPICBIRD (KOAE) **p. 259**
Phaethon lepturus 32 (incl. 16 in. tail streamers)
Field marks: See family discussion of tropicbirds (p. 13). This species is distinguished by *large black wing patches* above and 2 very long *white* tail streamers. Bill yellow to orange-red. Young lack streamers; barred with black above; bill yellow.
Similar species: (1) Red-tailed Tropicbird lacks large black wing patches above; has red bill, red streamers. Young has *black bill.* (2) In California, see Red-billed Tropicbird (p. 13; barred back, red bill). (3) *Caution:* White birds around cliffs might also be feral pigeons (Rock Dove).

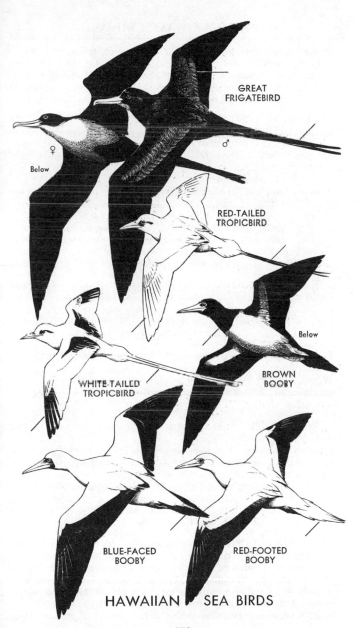

GREAT
FRIGATEBIRD

♀

Below

♂

RED-TAILED
TROPICBIRD

WHITE-TAILED
TROPICBIRD

Below

BROWN
BOOBY

BLUE-FACED
BOOBY

RED-FOOTED
BOOBY

HAWAIIAN SEA BIRDS

Voice: A harsh ternlike scream. Also *tik-et, tik-et.*
Where found: Pan-tropical oceans. **Hawaiian Is.:** *Resident* about all main islands. *Occasional,* Midway. **Habitat:** Ocean, sea cliffs; frequent inland on main islands. **Nest:** Usually in sea cliff, palis, or wall of crater. Eggs (1) reddish, blotched.

RED-TAILED TROPICBIRD (KOAE ULA)   p. 259

Phaethon rubricauda   34 (incl. 16 in. tail streamers)
Field marks: Whiter than the preceding; lacks large black wing patches above. Bill red. Quill-like central tail feathers red; may be invisible in distance, giving stub-tailed look. Young bird has barred back, *black* bill.
Similar species: (1) See preceding species. (2) In California see Red-billed Tropicbird (p. 13; barred back, white streamers).
Voice: A hoarse *wow.* A raucous *ratchet, ratchet.*
Where found: Pacific and Indian Oceans. **Hawaiian Is.:** *Breeds* on nw. chain and Niihau. *Occasional* off Oahu and Hawaii. **Nest:** Under bushes; sometimes in open near trees; occasionally cliff (Niihau). Eggs (1) reddish, spotted.

BLUE-FACED BOOBY   *Sula dactylatra*   32–36   p. 259

Field marks: See family discussion of boobies (p. 15). A robust white booby with much black in the wings and a *dark face* ("Masked Booby"), yellow bill. Feet olive-green. Note the *black tail. Immature:* Known from other dark Hawaiian boobies by light patch on upper back.
Similar species: Red-footed Booby has white tail, red feet.
Voice: Near nest, a loud honk (C. Robbins).
Where found: Tropical oceans. **Hawaiian Is.:** *Breeds* locally on nw. chain. **Nest:** On ground (sand or coral rock). Eggs (2) pale blue, chalky.

BROWN BOOBY   *Sula leucogaster*   28–32   p. 259

(White-bellied Booby)
Field marks: A dark brown, almost blackish booby with a *white belly,* in *clean-cut contrast* to a dark breast. Bill and feet yellow. Immature is chocolate above and below; *yellowish feet.*
Voice: On nesting grounds, coarse quacks, grunts, wheezes.
Where found: Tropical oceans. **Hawaiian Is.:** *Resident* on nw. chain and Oahu (Ulupau Head, Moku Manu). **Nest:** On ground near bush. Eggs (2) blue-white, chalky.

RED-FOOTED BOOBY (A)   *Sula sula*   26–30   p. 259

Field marks: Note the *bright red feet* in adults. Bill pale blue. *White phase:* White with much black in wings; *white tail. Brown phase:* Much less frequent in Hawaiian Is.; light brown mantle; usually white tail and underparts. A gray phase may sometimes occur. *Immature:* Gray-brown throughout.
Similar species: Blue-faced Booby has black tail, masked face.

Voice: In colony, *kek, kek, kek;* a piglike *oink, oink;* a long growl (W. V. Ward, H. Johnson).
Where found: Tropical oceans. **Hawaiian Is.:** *Breeds* on nw. chain, Kauai (Kilauea Lighthouse, Lehua), Oahu (Ulupau Head, Moku Manu). **Nest:** Of twigs, usually in tree or shrub, in colony. Eggs (1) chalky blue.

GREAT FRIGATEBIRD (IWA) *Fregata minor* 39–40 p. 259

Field marks: Spread 7 ft. A slim dark sea bird with angled wings, deeply forked tail. Similar to Magnificent Frigatebird of coastal continental America (illus., p. 14), but male retains light brown wing coverts to adulthood. Female has whitish throat, red eye-ring. Immature has rufous tinge on white head and breast. Forked tail usually folded in long point.
Voice: Silent at sea. At colony, grunts, trills, gurgles.
Where found: E. and c. Pacific to w. Indian Ocean; locally s. Atlantic. **Hawaiian Is.:** *Ranges* throughout islands; *breeds* in nw. chain. **Habitat:** Oceanic coasts. **Nest:** Stick platform on bushes or rocks. Eggs (1) white.

BLACK-CROWNED NIGHT HERON (AUKUU) Pl. 4
Nycticorax nycticorax
See page 22. *Resident* on main islands.

NENE *Branta sandvicencis* 22½–28 p. 262
(Hawaiian Goose)
Field marks: (Pronounced *Nay-nay.*) The only wild goose resident in Hawaii. A heavily barred, gray-brown goose with *black face.* Buff neck with dark furrows. Feet (semiwebbed) and bill black.
Voice: A high-pitched *chuck, chuck, chuck — ah-yaw, ah-yaw, chuck, chuck,* etc. (W. V. Ward, H. Johnson).
Where found: Endemic on Hawaii (now very rare but being augmented by birds reared at Pohakuloa game-bird farm on Mauna Kea). Formerly Maui. **Habitat:** Old lava flows of Mauna Loa (5000–7500 ft.); also Hualalai. **Nest:** A down-lined hollow in kipuka (sparsely vegetated area) on lava flow. Eggs (2–8) cream-white.

HAWAIIAN DUCK (KOLOA) *Anas wyvilliana* 20 p. 262
Field marks: Regarded by some recent authorities as a small race of the Mallard. *Male:* Intermediate in plumage between female and male (in eclipse) of typical Mallard. Often has dusky greenish head, dark chestnut breast but lacks neck ring. *Female:* Similar to female Mallard, ruddier; wing-mirror green.
Where found: *Resident* mainly on Kauai (especially mt. streams) scarce on Oahu. *Casual* on other main islands. Recently transplanted on Hawaii. **Nest:** Similar to Mallard's. Eggs (6–12).

LAYSAN
DUCK

♂

NENE
(Hawaiian Goose)

KOLOA
(Hawaiian Duck)

♂

LAYSAN DUCK *Anas laysanensis* 16   **above**
(Laysan Teal)
   Field marks: Regarded by some authorities as an isolated race
   of Mallard. Teal-sized. *Male:* Dusky with blackish face, *white
   patch around eye. Female:* Similar, browner.
   Similar species: Hawaiian Duck lacks white eye patch.
   Where found: *Resident* on Laysan I. (a recent increase). **Nest:**
   A shallow bowl under bush. Eggs (6) pale greenish.

PINTAIL (KOLOA MAPU) *Anas acuta*   **Pls. 7, 9, 14**
   See page 32. *Winters* on suitable ponds, lagoons throughout
   islands. The most common migrant duck.

AMERICAN WIDGEON *Mareca americana*   **Pls. 7, 9, 14**
   See page 35. *Winters* in small numbers on ponds of main islands.

SHOVELER (KOLOA MOHA) *Spatula clypeata* **Pls. 7, 9, 14**
   See page 35. Common *winter* visitor to ponds, lagoons on main
   islands. Rarely observed on nw. chain.

COMMON GALLINULE (ALAE ULA)   **Pl. 24**
Gallinula chloropus
   See page 73. A race is *resident* locally on ponds and marshes of
   Kauai, Oahu, Molokai. Recently introduced on Maui.

AMERICAN COOT (ALAE KEOKEO) *Fulica americana*
(Hawaiian Coot)   **Pl. 24**
   See page 74. *Resident* on ponds and lagoons of main islands.

AMERICAN GOLDEN PLOVER (LOLEA)   **Pls. 25, 28**
Pluvialis dominica
See page 77. Common, nearly year-round visitor to all islands.
Occurs both on shores and inland (pastures, lawns, airports).

BLACK-BELLIED PLOVER   **Pls. 25, 28**
Squatarola squatarola
See page 78. Sparse visitor to all Hawaiian Is.

RUDDY TURNSTONE (AKEKEKE)   **Pls. 25, 28**
Arenaria interpres
See page 78. Common, nearly year-round visitor throughout
Hawaiian Is., frequenting sand shores, rocky islets, even uplands.

BRISTLE-THIGHED CURLEW (KIOEA)   **Pl. 26**
Numenius tahitiensis
See page 80. Scarce on main islands; common *migrant* and
winter visitor on sandy islands of nw. chain. *Note:* Kioea is also
the name of an extinct Meliphagid (Honeyeater), *Chaetoptila
angustipluma,* formerly resident on island of Hawaii.

WANDERING TATTLER (ULILI)   **Pls. 29, 31**
Heteroscelus incanum
See page 82. *Winters* throughout islands (especially windward
shores).

SANDERLING (HUNAKAI) *Crocethia alba*   **Pls. 29, 32**
See page 90. *Winters* throughout islands (especially leeward
shores).

BLACK-NECKED STILT (AEO) *Himantopus mexicanus*
(Hawaiian Stilt)   **Pls. 26, 27**
See page 91. Very similar to the North American bird and
certainly conspecific (although usually listed as *H. himantopus*).
Resident on ponds, lagoons, on Niihau, Kauai, Oahu, Maui.
This resident form will not survive unless some ponds are saved.

RED PHALAROPE *Phalaropus fulicarius*   **Pls. 25, 29, 32**
See page 92. Undoubtedly a regular *transient* in vicinity of the
islands. Recorded Laysan, Kauai, Oahu, Maui, Hawaii.

POMARINE JAEGER *Stercorarius pomarinus*   **Pl. 3**
See page 93. Small numbers occur on ocean near main islands.

SOOTY TERN (EWAEWA) *Sterna fuscata* 15–17   **p. 265**
Field marks: *Blackish above and white below.* Patch on fore-
head white; bill and feet black. *Immature:* Dusky throughout;
upper parts flecked with white. Skims and dips for food.
Similar species: See Gray-backed Tern.
Voice: A nasal *ker-wack-wack* or *wide-a-wake.* Also *whee-you.*
Where found: Tropical oceans. **Hawaiian Is.:** *Breeds* (Mar.–
Sept.) on nw. chain; also Oahu (Ulupau, Moku Manu, Manana).
Nest: On bare ground in colony. Eggs (1; rarely 2) spotted.

GRAY-BACKED TERN *Sterna lunata* 14–15 **p. 265**
Field marks: Note the combination of *dark gray back, black cap.*
White stripe on forehead above eye. Bill and feet black.
Where found: Tropical Pacific. **Hawaiian Is.:** *Breeds* (Feb.–
June) on islands of nw. chain and off Oahu (Moku Manu).
Nest: On bare sand or gravel. Eggs (1) spotted.

BLUE-GRAY NODDY *Procelsterna cerulea* 9½–10 **p. 265**
Field marks: Suggests a gray Fairy Tern; *entirely blue-gray*
except for slaty primaries and white line on rear edge of wing.
No cap. Bill black. Feet black with pale webs. *Immature:*
Brownish gray or slaty above, whitish below.
Where found: Tropical Pacific. **Hawaiian Is.:** *Breeds* locally
on French Frigate Shoal, Necker, Nihoa, Kaula. **Nest:** On
sand; locally in ledges or cavities in rock. Eggs (1) spotted.

BROWN NODDY (NOIO KOHA) **p. 265**
Anous stolidus 15–16
Field marks: A dark *brown* tern with a *grayish-white cap* and
blackish *rounded* tail. Immature lacks full whitish crown, has
whitish forehead.
Similar species: See White-capped (Hawaiian) Noddy.
Voice: A ripping *karrrk* or *arrrrowk.* A harsh *eye-ak.*
Where found: Tropical oceans. **Hawaiian Is.:** *Breeds* on nw.
chain; also Oahu (islets off e. coast and Ulupau Head). **Nest:**
On coral sand, usually under bush. Less commonly a bulky
nest of twigs in low bush. Eggs (1) buff, spotted.

WHITE-CAPPED NODDY (NOIO) *Anous minutus* 13½
(Hawaiian Noddy, Hawaiian Tern) **p. 265**
Field marks: Similar to Brown Noddy but smaller, darker, and
cap whiter; tail *gray,* paler than back; voice different.
Voice: A nasal churring, *chrrrrrr* or *krrrrrr.* Also a shrill, slightly
rising whistle, *wheeee* or *hooeeew* (Eugene Eisenmann).
Where found: Tropical Atlantic and Pacific. **Hawaiian Is.:**
Resident throughout. **Habitat:** Ocean; unlike Brown Noddy,
often over ponds, lagoons. **Nest:** In crevice of sea cliff (main
islands) or of sticks or weeds in tree or bush (islets and nw.
chain). Eggs (1) buff, spotted.

WHITE (FAIRY) TERN *Gygis alba* 12–13 **p. 265**
Field marks: This most ethereal of sea birds is *snow-white.* A
black ring about its dark eye imparts a huge-eyed look. Bill
black, blue at base; feet black or bluish with yellow webs.
Voice: A low nasal grunting, *unk-unk-unk-unk.* When excited
rises to *eenk-eenk-eenk* (Eugene Eisenmann).
Where found: Tropical oceans. **Hawaiian Is.:** *Breeds* on islands
of nw. chain. Sometimes seen off main islands. **Nest:** Spotted
egg (1) balanced on rock, tree limb or crotch.

SOOTY TERN
(Immature — speckled back)

SOOTY TERN
(Adult — black back)

GRAY-BACKED TERN
(Gray back)

WHITE (FAIRY) TERN
(All white)

BLUE-GRAY NODDY
(All gray)

BROWN NODDY
(Black tail)

WHITE-CAPPED NODDY
(Gray tail)

HAWAIIAN TERNS

265

Native Land Birds

LAND BIRDS of 8 families have populated Hawaii without known help by man. The hawk, owl, crow, and Old World warbler families, each represented by one living native species, and the thrushes, represented by 2 living native species, are summarized elsewhere in this book. The Elepaio is an Old World flycatcher (Muscicapidae). The extinct Kioea and 4 species of Oo (3 extinct), belong to the Honeyeaters (Meliphagidae) of the Australian region. The one endemic family, the Hawaiian Honeycreepers or Drepanididae (Apapane through Palila), is perhaps the world's best example of "adaptive radiation." Probably of American origin, this family has suffered the tragic extinction of 8 of its 22± species. The outlook for the surviving species is hopeful only where there are large wilderness areas such as Hawaii National Park on Maui and Hawaii and the untouched virgin forests on Kauai.

Light phase   Dark phase

HAWAIIAN HAWK

HAWAIIAN HAWK (IO)   *Buteo solitarius*   15½–18   **above**
Field marks: The *only* hawk resident in Hawaii. A small chunky *Buteo* (see family discussion, p. 50). Two phases — (1) *dark phase:* very dark above and below; (2) *light phase:* upper parts dark; underparts light buff; often streaked.
Voice: A thin high-pitched scream, *kee-oh!* (or *i-o!*).
Where found: *Resident* only on Hawaii I. Needs protection; beneficial. **Habitat:** Widespread; open forest, agricultural land, grassland. **Nest:** A platform of sticks in tree.

SHORT-EARED OWL (PUEO) *Asio flammeus* **p. 120**
See page 125. *Resident* on all main islands (sea level to 6000+ ft.). *Casual,* Midway. Prefers grassland; also occurs locally about towns, canyons, lava flows, open forest and mt. ridges (filling niches because of lack of other owls). See Barn Owl (p. 118; recently introduced on Hawaii, Oahu).

HAWAIIAN CROW (ALALA) *Corvus tropicus* 18–20
Field marks: Similar to N. American crows but duller, tinged with *brownish,* especially on wings. The dark phase of the Hawk is the only other large dusky land bird on island of Hawaii.
Voice: Corvid notes; a high crack-voiced *caw* or *car.*
Where found: *Resident* only on Hawaii where confined locally to slopes of Kona side (especially near Puuwaawaa). **Habitat:** Dry woods, adjacent country. **Nest:** A bowl of sticks in tree.

OMAO (HAWAIIAN THRUSH) **Pl. 59**
Phaeornis obscurus 7–8
Field marks: Plump; dark brown above, unspotted *gray underparts.* Has habit of quivering wings like a young bird.
Similar species: (1) The Hwa-mei (more widely distributed) is larger (9), rustier; has white "spectacles." (2) The Small Kauai Thrush (very rare) has flesh legs.
Voice: Note, a hoarse *chee-ow* or *mao* (slurring down); also a rolling *prrcet.* Song, an emphatic, accented *chup-wechew-chup.*
Where found: Local on Hawaii; scarce, Kauai. Extinct, Oahu, Molokai, Lanai. **Habitat:** Mt. forests, alpine scrub (Mauna Loa).

MILLERBIRD *Acrocephalus familiaris* 5½ **Pl. 59**
Field marks: A small, plain Old World warbler, gray-brown above, buffy white below; thin warbler-type bill.
Where found: Nihoa (the only other passerine on Nihoa, the Laysan or Nihoa Finch, has a thick bill). The Laysan race of the Millerbird is now extinct. **Habitat:** Low scrub, grass.

ELEPAIO *Chasiempis sandwichensis* 5½ **Pl. 59**
Field marks: Note the wrenlike *cocked tail.* Often quivers wings. A small, tame, brown- or gray-backed Old World flycatcher with a rather long blackish tail, white rump, 2 white wing-bars. The subspecies on the 3 islands differ in the black and white on the throat (absent in gray-backed Kauai race) and in the amount of rufous. Immatures are tawny-breasted; lack white rump.
Voice: An explosive "wolf-whistle," *whee-you, whee-you!* (or *el-e-pai-o!*). Also a sharp *wit* and *wick-wick-wick-wick-wick.* Female, a catlike mew. A scold like treefrog's call.
Where found: Common on Kauai, Oahu, Hawaii. **Habitat:** Mt. forests, ranging lower than other endemic forest birds. **Nest:** A small cup made of scales of tree fern or lichens held together by cobwebs; low in tree, shrub. Eggs (2–3) dotted.

APAPANE *Himatione sanguinea* 5¼   **Pl. 59**
    Field marks: Deep *crimson,* with black wings and tail. Note the slightly curved *blackish bill.* Legs black. The *white* lower belly and under tail coverts mark it from the Iiwi in flight or overhead. Often cocks tail. *Immature:* Gray-brown above, buff below, red coming in irregularly. Note the black bill.
    Similar species: Iiwi has salmon bill, lacks white abdomen.
    Voice: Mellow minor whistles, *eep* and *erp.* Song, varied: *eep, eep-erp* or repetitious phrases, *tchee, tchee, tchee* or *ticka, ticka, ticka, ticka,* etc. (W. V. Ward).
    Where found: Abundant on Hawaii; common on Kauai, Oahu, Maui; local, Molokai; scarce, Lanai. A pale race on Laysan (*H. s. freethi,* Laysan Honeycreeper) is now extinct. **Habitat:** Mt. forests, subalpine scrub, flowering trees, *especially ohia.* **Nest:** A grass-lined cup in tree. Eggs (3) spotted.

CRESTED HONEYCREEPER *Palmeria dolei* 7   **Pl. 59**
    Field marks: Note the *orange-red nape* and bushy *white crest* on forehead. The color plate explains the unique appearance.
    Voice: A loud clear whistle; a loud grating *churr* (Paul H. Baldwin). Song has notes resembling some of Iiwi and Apapane.
    Where found: Persists only on ne. slope of Haleakala (5800–6700 ft.) on Maui. Very scarce. Extinct on Molokai. **Habitat:** Mt. rain forests, flowering trees, especially ohia.

IIWI *Vestiaria coccinea* 5¾   **Pl. 59**
    Field marks: (Pronounced *Ee-vee* or *Ee-ee-vee.*) Note the *deeply curved salmon bill.* A *vermilion* bird with black wings (with small white patch), black tail. Legs orange. Young birds are ocheryellow with black wings and tail, pale curved bill.
    Similar species: The more numerous Apapane is deeper red, has a nearly straight *black bill, white* lower belly and crissum.
    Voice: Harsh metallic notes; rusty creaks. A creaky finchlike *ii-wi* or *ee-vee* (rising inflection). Also *eek* or *coo-eek.*
    Where found: Fairly common locally on Kauai, Hawaii; very scarce on Oahu, Maui. Near extinction on Molokai; extinct, Lanai. **Habitat:** Mt. forests, where trees are flowering (especially ohia and mamane). **Nest:** A shallow cup in ohia or koa.

AMAKIHI *Loxops virens* 4½   **Pl. 59**
    Field marks: It is virtually safe to call any small greenish bird with no white eye-ring an Amakihi unless proven otherwise (except on Kauai). This and Apapane are probably the most common native land birds in Hawaiian Is. The Amakihi is a small plump Drepanidid, mainly olive-green above, yellowish, or creamy gray below. A *dark loral mark* joins the eye and the *curved* dark bill. The races on the various islands differ in the amount of yellow. Feeds characteristically among twigs and

small branches (Kauai race often acts like Creeper).
Similar species: (1) See Creeper (much rarer and difficult to differentiate). (2) On Kauai, see also Anianiau (Lesser Amakihi). (3) Japanese White-eye has conspicuous white eye-ring.
Voice: A mewing note, rough querulous *dzee*. Male gives a loose Chippy-like trill *on one pitch: ti-ti-ti-ti-ti-ti,* etc. "often incorporated into a more complicated song" (Paul H. Baldwin). Female, a brief twittering medley.
Where found: Common on Kauai, Oahu, Maui, Hawaii; local, Molokai; scarce, Lanai. **Habitat:** Brush to dense mt. forests. **Nest:** A cup of grass, twigs in tree fern, ohia. Eggs spotted.

ANIANIAU (LESSER AMAKIHI) *Loxops parva* 4¼ **Pl. 59**
Field marks: A small yellowish bird. A bit smaller than Amakihi; brighter yellow throughout, including upper parts. *No dark lores* before eye; bill shorter, straighter, paler.
Similar species: (1) Amakihi has darker back, dark eyeline, longer, more curved bill, different voice. (2) Kauai form of Creeper is olive-gray or gray-brown above, *whitish* below.
Voice: Note, *ps-seet* (upslurred); suggests Western Flycatcher.
Where found: Kauai; locally common. **Habitat:** High forests.

CREEPER (ALAUWAHIO) *Loxops maculata* 4½–5 **Pl. 59**
Field marks: Usually rare and difficult to identify. *Very similar* to the numerous Amakihi but usually duller; *bill straighter.* Creeps on trunks and big limbs (Amakihi *usually* forages among twigs, small branches). Voice different. Females duller than males on Oahu, Maui. *Kauai form* (Akikiki): More easily recognized; brownish gray above, cream whitish below; perhaps a distinct species. Travels in flocks. *Note:* Kauai form of Amakihi often acts like Creeper but is much yellower than Kauai form of Creeper; has a strongly curved bill.
Voice: A single whistle or *cheep*. Song, soft and twittering, with a rapid *descending* trill, unlike Amakihi's (Paul H. Baldwin).
Where found: Locally common in high mt. forests on Kauai; rare on Oahu, Maui, Hawaii. Extinct on Molokai (red male), Lanai.

AKEPA *Loxops coccinea* 4½–5 **Pl. 59**
Field marks: *Hawaii race:* Male, bright *red-orange* with brownish wings and tail. Short pale siskin-like bill. Female, green above, yellow below; tail longer, more notched, bill shorter than in similar yellow-green species. Lower mandible slightly twisted to side (evident only in hand). *Kauai race:* Greenish above, yellow below. Note the *black lores, yellow crown.* Sexes similar. *Maui race:* Males vary from dull yellow to brownish orange.
Similar species: (1) Iiwi and (2) Apapane are larger, redder, and longer-billed than male Hawaii Akepa and have *black* wings

and tail. (3) See House Finch (p. 227; orange males often invade Akepa habitat). (4) Amakihi has more slender, curved bill, shorter tail than yellowish Akepas.
Voice: A high whistle, *tsee-eu* or *tiddy-weet.* Song, soft and twittering, including a careless *uneven* trill (Paul H. Baldwin).
Where found: Local and rare in koa forests of Kauai and Hawaii. Near extinction on Maui; extinct on Oahu.

AKIAPOLAAU *Hemignathus wilsoni* 5½   **Pl. 59**
Field marks: Larger and stubbier than Amakihi. Note the long slender *sickle-like upper mandible.* The much shorter, *straight lower mandible* is said to be used woodpecker-like for pounding, the thin hook for probing. Listen for tapping?
Voice: A rich whistle. Song, varied, including a brilliant warbling suggestive of an elaborate trill (Paul H. Baldwin).
Where found: Endemic on Hawaii; rare and local. **Habitat:** Upper mt. forests; branches and trunks of tall koa, mamane.

OU *Psittirostra psittacea* 6–6½   **Pl. 59**
Field marks: Note the bright *yellow head* (male) and the pale rather parrot-like bill. The yellow head is cleanly separated from the *olive-green body.* Female lacks yellow head.
Similar species: Palila has gray (not green) back and lacks strong hook on its black bill; yellow extends onto breast. *Note:* The Hawaiian name of Bulwer's Petrel is Ou.
Voice: Song, clearly whistled. A plaintive call (G. C. Munro).
Where found: Local and very scarce on Hawaii. Still exists on Kauai. Extinct on other main islands. **Habitat:** Dense mt. rain forest with fern understory.

LAYSAN FINCH *Psittirostra cantans* 6–7   **Pl. 59**
Field marks: A large finchlike bird (a Drepanidid, not a finch) with a thick, heavy bill. *Male:* Yellow head and breast (suggesting Palila); brownish back, wings, and tail. *Female:* Duller, with streakings on head, back, and underparts.
Similar species: There is no other living songbird on Laysan; only one other on Nihoa (Millerbird).
Voice: A fine song. Said to mimic local sea birds.
Where found: Endemic to Laysan and Nihoa. Introduced but extirpated on Midway. **Habitat:** Low shrubs, grass. **Nest:** A grass cup in bush, grass, or rocks. Eggs (2–3) dotted.

PALILA *Psittirostra bailleui* 6–6½   **Pl. 59**
Field marks: Note the *stubby thick bill.* Husky, finchlike. Yellow head and breast, *gray* back, whitish belly. Sexes similar.
Similar species: Ou has *green* back and a more hooked pale bill.
Voice: A plaintive finchlike *whee-whee-o* or "wolf whistle."
Where found: Locally common on slopes of Mauna Kea, Hawaii. **Habitat:** Open mamane-naio woods.

Near Extinct and Extinct Birds

THE **Crested Honeycreeper** and **Ou** perhaps should be placed in this critical category. The existence of 5 other birds, once thought possibly extinct, has recently been substantiated:

PUAIOHI (SMALL KAUAI THRUSH) *Phaeornis palmeri* 7
Differs from Omao by size, *flesh* (not dark) legs; white over eye. Taken by F. Richardson on Kauai in 1960.

OOAA (KAUAI OO) *Moho braccatus* 7¾ **Pl. 59**
A slender, sooty bird. Note the slender black bill, *yellow thighs,* white wing patch, *pointed tail.* **Voice:** Mellow whistles, *oh-oh.* Also a fast *whip-poor-will,* the *will* double, descending (F. Richardson). Alakai Swamp, Kauai (1960, F. Richardson).

KAUAI AKIALOA *Hemignathus procerus* 7½ **Pl. 59**
A bright greenish-yellow bird with Creeper habits but with an extremely long sickle-like bill, 2⅛ in. long. Still exists in upper rain forest of Kauai (F. Richardson).

NUKUPUU *Hemignathus lucidus* 5⅝ **Pl. 59**
Similar to Akiapolaau but short lower mandible *decurved.* Observed by Richardson on Kauai, 1960. Extinct, Oahu, Hawaii.

MAUI PARROTBILL *Pseudonestor xanthophrys* 5½ **Pl. 59**
A stub-tailed olive bird with a very large hooked *parrot-like bill,* and broad *yellow stripe* over eye. Note, a *kee-wit* (G. C. Munro). Still exists on n. slope of Haleakala, Maui.

The species listed below are believed to be extinct. In addition, a number of subspecies have disappeared on certain islands. For illustrations of these tragic birds consult *Birds of Hawaii* by George C. Munro or the works of Baron Rothschild.

HAWAII RAIL   *Pennula sandwichensis,* Hawaii
LAYSAN RAIL   *Porzanula palmeri,* Laysan
BISHOP'S OO   *Moho bishopi,* Molokai
HAWAII OO   *Moho nobilis,* Hawaii
OAHU OO   *Moho apicalis,* Oahu
KIOEA   *Chaetoptila angustipluma,* Hawaii
GREEN SOLITAIRE   *Loxops sagittirostris,* Hawaii
AKIALOA   *Hemignathus obscurus,* Oahu, Lanai, Hawaii
GREATER KOA FINCH   *Psittirostra palmeri,* Hawaii
LESSER KOA FINCH   *Psittirostra flaviceps,* Hawaii
GROSBEAK FINCH (Kona Finch)   *Psittirostra kona,* Hawaii
ULA-AI-HAWANE   *Ciridops anna,* Hawaii
MAMO   *Drepanis pacifica,* Hawaii
BLACK MAMO   *Drepanis funerea,* Molokai.

Introduced Birds

THE HAWAIIAN ISLANDS have lost more endemic birds than any other area their size except the Mascarene Islands in the Indian Ocean, and have gained more exotics; there may be a sinister connection, because of the transmission of avian diseases to native birds that had no immunity. More than 100 species have been liberated. Most have not taken hold. Only the successful ones, some desirable, some questionable, are discussed in the following pages. A few others, Cattle Egret, Lesser Prairie Chicken, Gambel's Quail, Bobwhite, Erckel's Francolin, Guinea-fowl, Barn Owl, Dyal, Blue Flycatcher, Collared Laughing-thrush, Mongolian Lark, Orange-breasted Bunting, and Black-headed Mannikin, are still of uncertain status and may or may not succeed.

CALIFORNIA QUAIL   *Lophortyx californicus*   **Pl. 22**
See page 67. *Established* locally on all major islands; most common on leeward sides of Molokai, Hawaii; scarce on Oahu. Gambel's Quail, *L. gambelii* (p. 67) is said to be established on Kahoolawe; has been released on Hawaii.

CHUKAR   *Alectoris graeca*   **Pl. 22**
See page 68. Well *established* on Lanai, Hawaii; locally on Kauai, Oahu (very scarce), Molokai, Maui.

COTURNIX (JAPANESE QUAIL)   **Pl. 60**
Coturnix coturnix   7
   Field marks: A tiny stub-tailed quail; general color sandy, strongly streaked; face striped.
   Voice: Liquid *quic, quic-ic* (male); *queep — queep* (female).
   Where found: Eurasia. **Hawaiian Is.:** *Established* locally on Kauai, Molokai, Lanai, Maui, Hawaii. **Habitat:** Grass country, farmland. **Nest:** Among grass. *Note:* The **Pectoral Quail,** *C. pectoralis,* is said to be the form of Coturnix on Niihau.

JUNGLE FOWL   *Gallus gallus*   ♂ 32½, ♀ 20
The ancestor of the domestic chicken; cock usually rufous, with green-black tail. (Like Bantam gamecock.) Probably first introduced by early Polynesians. Inhabits forests on Kauai (abundant at Kokee); local, Niihau. Formerly all major islands.

RING-NECKED PHEASANT   *Phasianus colchicus*   **Pl. 22**
See page 68. *Established* locally on all major islands.

GREEN PHEASANT   *Phasianus versicolor*
This pheasant, a resident of Japan, differs from Ring-neck in being dark green with purple neck; *no neck-ring.* Has a distinctly

higher voice. *Established* locally on Kauai, Molokai, Lanai, Maui, and Hawaii. Often hybridizes with Ring-neck. More of a bird of open forest than Ring-neck. Pure form most numerous on moist windward slopes of Mauna Kea and Mauna Loa.

PEAFOWL *Pavo cristatus*
Identical to the well-known ornamental Peacock. White individuals are frequent. A native of India and Ceylon. *Established* in small areas on Niihau, Kauai, Oahu, Molokai, Maui, and Hawaii. Inhabits open woods, forest edges, brushland.

TURKEY *Meleagris gallopavo* **p. 69**
See page 70. *Established* on Niihau. Very local on ranch areas on leeward side of Hawaii.

ROCK DOVE *Columba livia* **Pl. 23**
See page 114. Sustains self in wild about towns, farms, cliffs; local on Midway, Lanai, Oahu, Molokai, Hawaii.

SPOTTED DOVE *Streptopelia chinensis* **Pl. 23**
(Chinese Spotted Dove, Lace-necked Dove)
See page 115. Widespread (except high mts.) on main islands.

BARRED DOVE *Geopelia striata* 8 **Pl. 60**
Field marks: A very small tame dove; *thickly barred or scaled;* head gray, breast tawny. White outer feathers on slender tail.
Similar species: (1) Spotted Dove (larger) lacks scaling, has spotted collar. (2) Rock Dove (large) usually has white rump.
Voice: A rattling *cow-ca-how* or *cow-ca-cowcowcowcowcow;* higher-pitched than call of Spotted Dove.
Where found: Malaysia. **Hawaiian Is.:** Widespread on main islands. **Habitat:** Sea level to 4000 ft.; cities, farms, pastureland.
Nest: A twig saucer in bush, tree. Eggs (2) white.

SKYLARK *Alauda arvensis* **Pl. 60**
See page 158. *Established* widely on Niihau, Maui, Hawaii; locally on Oahu, Molokai, Lanai; very scarce on Kauai.

VARIED TIT (YAMAGARA) *Parus varius* 5 **Pl. 60**
Field marks: Chickadee-like appearance. *Black bib.* Crown *black* with buff patch on nape; cheeks cream-buff. Sides and patch on back rusty.
Voice: *Tee-tee-tee* or *tee-tee-tay.* Also *titititititi.*
Where found: Japan, Korea. **Hawaiian Is.:** *Established* very locally on Kauai; local on trails of Oahu. **Habitat:** Forests.

HWA-MEI *Garrulax canorus* 9 **Pl. 60**
(Chinese Thrush)
Field marks: A large reddish-brown thrushlike bird. Note the

white "spectacles." A babbler (Timaliidae), not a true thrush.
Similar species: (1) See Omao (Hawaiian Thrush). (2) *G. albogularis,* the Collared or White-throated Laughing-thrush, is occasionally seen on Kauai. About 11 in.; olive-brown, with white throat, rufous belly, rufous, white-tipped tail. A *Garrulax* is also reported from Poamoho Trail, Oahu, where its human-sounding whistles may be heard.
Voice: A rich variety of phrases, each repeated 2 or 3 times; suggests Mockingbird. Call, *wheeree.*
Where found: China. **Hawaiian Is.:** Common on Kauai, local on Oahu, Hawaii; scarce, Molokai, Maui. **Habitat:** Forest undergrowth, brush. **Nest:** A cup in bush. Eggs (3–4) blue.

RED-BILLED LEIOTHRIX *Leiothrix lutea* 5–6 **Pl. 60**
(Hill Robin, Pekin Robin)
Field marks: A small olive-green babbler (Timaliidae) with a bright *orange-red bill.* Throat bright yellow shading into orangish breast; red patch in wing. Tail well-forked. Large light patch around eye. Sexes similar. *Immature:* Dark gray above, lighter below. Bill and feet black.
Voice: Notes, a nasal *bzzzt;* a *chuck;* a *chip.* Song, short melodious phrases (suggests Robin or Black-headed Grosbeak).
Where found: Se. Asia. **Hawaiian Is.:** Abundant on Oahu, Maui, Hawaii; local on Molokai. **Habitat:** Underbrush, low growth at all elevations, from towns to lava flows. **Nest:** A grass cup in bush or low tree. Eggs (3–4) pale blue, spotted.

MOCKINGBIRD *Mimus polyglottos* **Pl. 47**
See page 177. *Established* on Maui; locally on Oahu, Molokai, Lanai, Hawaii.

SHAMA *Copsychus malabaricus* 9 **Pl. 60**
Field marks: A slim long-tailed thrush; black with *white rump* and tail sides. Belly *bright chestnut.* Sexes similar.
Similar species: The Dyal, *C. saularis* (se. Asia), also occurs in upper Manoa and Tantalus areas, Oahu. Differs in having a white wing patch, white belly; lacks white rump (suggests small magpie). See illustration, Plate 60.
Voice: Song, melodic flute-notes, glissandos; often at dusk. Suggestive of Western Meadowlark.
Where found: Se. Asia. **Hawaiian Is.:** *Established* locally on Kauai and Oahu (Tantalus, upper Manoa and Nuuanu Valleys). **Habitat:** Forest undergrowth, hau thickets.

BUSH WARBLER (UGUISU) *Cettia diphone* 5–5½ **Pl. 60**
Field marks: A very plain Old World warbler with a *whitish line over the eye.* Dull olive-brown above, dull gray-white below; legs pale flesh. Sexes similar.

Similar species: Millerbird of Nihoa is similar.
Voice: Song, a long low whistle ending with an emphatic twist, *prrrrrrr-p'we-chew!* Also a stuttered trill followed by a decelerating *pe-chew, pe-chew, pe-chew . . . pe-chew . . . pe-chew.*
Where found: Japan, e. Asia. **Hawaiian Is.:** *Established* locally in forest undergrowth on Oahu.

INDIAN MYNA (PIHA' E-KELO) Pl. 60
Acridotheres tristis 9
  Field marks: A stocky brown bird with a *black head,* large *white patch* on each wing and white tip on its rather short black tail. Bill, legs, and bare patch near eye, yellow. Sexes similar. Gregarious; usually walks, but can hop.
  Similar species: The Crested Myna (or Mynah) of Vancouver, B.C., is a black and white bird of Chinese origin.
  Voice: Loud clear repeated notes, harsh whistles, gurglings, liquid sounds. Occasionally mimics.
  Where found: India. **Hawaiian Is.:** *Established* abundantly on all main islands. **Habitat:** Widespread in towns, agricultural land, few in forests. **Nest:** Untidy; in tree cavity, cliff, under eaves, crevice in building. Eggs (3–4) blue.

JAPANESE WHITE-EYE (MEJIRO) Pl. 60
Zosterops japonica 4½
  Field marks: A small greenish bird with a *conspicuous white eye-ring.* Back dull olive-green, throat lemon-yellow; upper breast and sides brownish. Sexes similar. Abundant.
  Similar species: See Amakihi.
  Voice: Note, *tsee,* a thin nasal *tyee* or *tee-yee.* A scolding twitter. Song, a rather thin warble, rambling but musical.
  Where found: Japan. **Hawaiian Is.:** *Established* on all main islands. **Habitat:** Wherever there are trees or brush. **Nest:** A vireo-like cup in bush, tree. Eggs (3–4) white or bluish.

STRAWBERRY FINCH *Estrilda amandava* 4 **Pl. 60**
  Field marks: *Male:* A tiny crimson finch dotted with small white spots ("strawberry seeds"). In winter, resembles female. *Female:* Brown, paler below; bill and rump red.
  Where found: Se. Asia. **Hawaiian Is.:** *Established* about Pearl Harbor, Oahu. Scarce. **Habitat:** Fields, croplands.

RICEBIRD *Lonchura punctulata* 4 **Pl. 60**
  Field marks: Brown color, thick black bill, deep brown throat, daintily scalloped breast identify this tiny bird. Flocks.
  Voice: A plaintive wheezy *chee;* also *ba-hee.*
  Where found: Malaysia. **Hawaiian Is.:** All main islands. **Habitat:** Weedy country, farms, ricefields, forest edges. **Nest:** A ball of grass, in tree, shrub. Eggs (3–4) white.

HOUSE SPARROW *Passer domesticus* **p. 212, Pl. 60**
See page 212. *Established* on all main islands (except Niihau?).

WESTERN MEADOWLARK *Sturnella neglecta* **Pl. 54**
See page 213. *Established* on Kauai.

CARDINAL *Richmondena cardinalis* **Pl. 55**
See page 222. *Established* on all main islands.

RED-CRESTED (BRAZILIAN) CARDINAL **Pl. 60**
Paroaria cristata 7½
  Field marks: Gray above, white below. *Face and crest red.*
  Red runs onto upper breast, forming a V-shaped wedge. Sexes
  similar. *Immature:* Face and crest chestnut-brown.
  Voice: Song, phrased, more Robin-like than Cardinal's.
  Where found: Brazil, Argentina. **Hawaiian Is.:** Widespread on
  Oahu; local on Kauai, Maui. **Habitat:** Lowlands, towns,
  thickets, dry brush. **Nest:** In bush, low tree. Eggs (3–4) spotted.

HOUSE FINCH *Carpodacus mexicanus* **Pl. 60**
("Linnet")
  See page 227. Male House Finches in Hawaii, unlike the typical
  red males of w. N. America, run the gamut from yellow to red,
  orange predominating locally. *Established* on all main islands.

CANARY *Serinus canaria* **Pl. 60**
  Similar to the familiar caged Canary, but much whiter than
  most. *Established* in casuarina trees on Sand Island, Midway.
  Note: Laysan Finch, often called "Laysan Canary," was introduced on Midway but disappeared about 1944.

Note: This completes Part II, covering the
birds regularly found in the Hawaiian Islands.
A list of additional species that have occurred
casually or accidentally in the islands will be
found in Appendix II, page 285.

Appendix I: Accidental and Marginal Species in Western North America

Accidentals are the rarest of the rarities. They turn up but few times in the lifetime of most birders. Accidentals are here roughly defined as species that have been recorded less than 20 times west of the 100th meridian in North America (including the Aleutians, but not Hawaii). I have been somewhat flexible in also treating in the main text a species such as the Blue-footed Booby (14–15 records), because its local occurrence seems more than accidental. On the other hand, records of certain eastern warblers listed here may already have passed the arbitrary figure of 20.

Marginal species as included in this list are those that flirt with the 100th meridian — eastern birds normally approaching this invisible line and crossing it occasionally. Several species from Mexico that have occurred accidentally in the lower Rio Grande Valley are also included in this listing.

Of the 104 species listed here, a rough breakdown of their primary origins may be of interest: 39 Asia; 32 e. N. America; 17 Mexico, 11 Pacific; 5 c. Canadian Arctic.

For illustrations and details of the following stragglers consult either *A Field Guide to the Birds* (Eastern), *A Field Guide to the Birds of Texas,* or *A Field Guide to the Birds of Britain and Europe.* A Field Guide to Mexican Birds is in preparation. Many of the western accidentals are excellently illustrated by Don Eckelberry in Richard Pough's *Audubon Western Bird Guide.*

SHORT-TAILED ALBATROSS *Diomedea albatrus* 33–37. Spread 7½ ft. Illustration, page 14. Note the *white back,* pink bill. A white albatross, with black wings and tip of tail. Immature is very dark brown and resembles Black-footed Albatross, but bill and feet are *pink or flesh-colored* (not black); no white face patch. (Bonin Is. in w. Pacific. Near extinction; about 14 pairs on Torishima in 1956.) Formerly ranged from Bering Sea to Baja California. Last sight records, 70 mi. off San Francisco (Feb. 1946) and Gulf of Alaska (Nov. 1947). Other sight records of white albatrosses off Alaska and California may refer to Laysan Albatross, page 8.

WHITE-CAPPED ALBATROSS *Diomedea cauta* 35–39. Spread 7½–8 ft. Similar to Laysan Albatross (white body, dark back) but head pale gray, with lighter crown. Feet gray. Underwing whiter. (Vicinity of Australia, New Zealand.) Accidental off coast of Washington.

CAPE PETREL *Daption capensis* 14. Boldly spotted above; *2 large roundish white patches on each wing;* tail white, with black band at tip. (Breeds in Antarctic.) One old record for California (Monterey).

BLACK-TAILED SHEARWATER *Adamastor cinereus* 18–19½. Differs from our other white-bellied shearwaters by dark feet and dark underwing. (S. Hemisphere.) One old record off Monterey, California.

SCALED PETREL *Pterodroma inexpectata* 14. Identified by the sharply separated white chest, dark belly. Black stripe on fore edge of white underwing. (New Zealand.) Straggler to Alaska (Kiska, Alaskan Peninsula, Kodiak, Sitka). Reported 400 mi. off San Francisco.

COOK'S PETREL *Pterodroma cookii* 13–14. Similar to Scaled Petrel but lacks dark belly. Gray above, white below; black eye mark; whitish webs in primaries. (S. Pacific.) Accidental in Aleutians (near Adak).

WHITE-WINGED PETREL *Pterodroma leucoptera* 12. Similar to Cook's Petrel; blacker cap, grayer, more wedge-shaped tail. (Japan, e. Australia, to Chile.) Recorded 600 mi. off San Francisco.

WILSON'S PETREL *Oceanites oceanicus*. See under Leach's Petrel, page 12. See also Eastern *Field Guide*. (Antarctic; ranges to N. Hemisphere.) Accidental off California (Pt. Loma, Monterey Bay, Farallon Is.).

BLUE-FOOTED BOOBY *Sula nebouxii* 32–34. Illustration, page 14. See page 16. (W. Mexico to Ecuador.) Occasional visitor to se. California (Salton Sea) and w. Arizona (Lower Colorado River). 14–15 records. Accidental, Washington.

BROWN (WHITE-BELLIED) BOOBY *Sula leucogaster*. Illustration, page 259. See section on Hawaii, page 260. (Tropical oceans.) Accidental in se. California (Imperial Dam), w. Arizona (Havasu Lake).

OLIVACEOUS (MEXICAN) CORMORANT *Phalacrocorax olivaceus*. See Texas *Field Guide*. A difficult identification problem. *It is said* that the Olivaceous differs from the Double-crest as follows: (1) it is smaller (24–28); Double-crest is 30–36; (2) has a paler (less orange-yellow) throat pouch; (3) when breeding has a narrow white border behind throat pouch. But these points are not too reliable in the field. At *very close range* a sure point is the feathers of the back and scapulars: more *pointed* in Olivaceous, more rounded in Double-crested. (Caribbean, Gulf of Mexico.) Recorded on Rio Grande at Eagle Pass, Texas, and may visit water impoundments elsewhere west of 100°. Casual, New Mexico, Colorado.

ANHINGA (WATER-TURKEY) *Anhinga anhinga*. See Eastern or Texas *Field Guide*. (Se. U.S. to Argentina.) Recorded in se. California, s. Arizona, New Mexico, Colorado, nw. and c. Texas.

REDDISH EGRET *Dichromanassa rufescens*. See Eastern or Texas *Field Guide*. Recorded in s. California (San Diego), sw. Arizona, Colorado.

YELLOW-CROWNED NIGHT HERON *Nyctanassa violacea*. See Eastern or Texas *Field Guide*. (Se. U.S. to Brazil.) Straggler west of 100° to e. Colorado, nw. Texas. Accidental in s. California, New Mexico.

WHITE IBIS *Eudocimus albus*. See Eastern or Texas *Field Guide*. Albino of White-faced Ibis has been recorded (therefore, note red face and bill). (Se. U.S. to S. America.) Accidental in s. California, Colorado.

ROSEATE SPOONBILL *Ajaia ajaja.* See Eastern or Texas *Field Guide.* (S. U.S. to Argentina.) Casual in se. California (Lower Colorado River, Imperial Valley). Accidental in Utah, Colorado, Texas panhandle.

WHOOPER SWAN *Olor cygnus.* See European *Field Guide.* (Eurasia.) Accidental, St. Paul I., Alaska.

BEAN GOOSE *Anser fabalis.* See European *Field Guide.* (Eurasia.) Accidental in Alaska (St. Paul, St. Lawrence Is.).

MOTTLED DUCK *Anas fulvigula.* See Eastern or Texas *Field Guide.* (Coastal Texas to Florida.) Accidental in Colorado.

FALCATED TEAL *Anas falcata* 19. Male, a chunky gray teal with a dark crested head and a black stripe bordering its white throat. (Asia.) Accidental, Alaska (Pribilofs, Aleutians), B.C., California.

BAIKAL TEAL *Anas formosa* 16. *Male:* Head with striking harlequin pattern (buffy spot before eye, crescent on cheek, eyebrow-stripe and neck-line). (Asia.) Casual in Alaska (Wainwright, King I., Wales, St. Lawrence I.). Accidental, Imperial Valley, California.

COMMON POCHARD *Aythya ferina.* See European *Field Guide.* Male very similar to male Redhead but bill *black,* with pale blue band; eye red, not yellow. (Eurasia.) Accidental, Pribilofs, Alaska.

BAER'S POCHARD *Aythya baeri.* A Redhead with reverse pattern — male with black head, ruddy-chestnut breast. (Asia.) Accidental about 1841 in "northwestern America" (A.O.U. *Check-list*).

TUFTED DUCK *Aythya fuligula.* See European *Field Guide.* Male like Ring-necked Duck but back of head with thin crest, sides pure white; wing-stripe *white.* (Eurasia.) Accidental in Alaska (St. Paul, Attu Is.), California.

SWALLOW-TAILED KITE *Elanoides forficatus.* See Eastern or Texas *Field Guide.* (Se. U.S. to Argentina.) Accidental in New Mexico, Colorado.

GRAY SEA EAGLE *Haliaeetus albicilla.* See European *Field Guide.* Adult like a pale Bald Eagle with only the tail white. A bird like a Bald Eagle with a *light brown head* and yellow bill would be this straggler (a *light brown* head and *black bill* would most likely be an aberrant immature Bald Eagle). (N. Eurasia.) Casual in Alaska: Unalaska, Kodiak, Dutch Harbor (sight records).

STELLER'S SEA EAGLE *Haliaeetus pelagicus* 34–36. Adult differs from Bald Eagle by large *white shoulder patches,* white thighs, dark head (yellow bill), *wedge-shaped* white tail. Immature may be told by wedge-shaped tail; told from Gray Sea Eagle (casual in Alaska) by dark, not buffy head. (Sea of Okhotsk, Sea of Japan.) Casual in Alaska (Unalaska, Pribilofs, Kodiak).

EUROPEAN CRANE *Grus grus.* See European *Field Guide.* (Eurasia.) Accidental in Alaska, Alberta.

KING RAIL *Rallus elegans.* See Eastern or Texas *Field Guide.* (E. and c. U.S.) Casual migrant west to Texas panhandle.

PURPLE GALLINULE   *Porphyrula martinica.* See Eastern or Texas *Field Guide.* (Se. U.S. to Argentina.) Casual, Arizona, New Mexico, Texas panhandle. Accidental, Utah, Colorado.

AMERICAN OYSTERCATCHER   *Haematopus palliatus.* See Eastern or Texas *Field Guide.* (Coasts; Baja California to Chile; New Jersey to Argentina.) No record since 1910 in s. California.

MONGOLIAN PLOVER   *Charadrius mongolus*   7½. Near size of Semipalmated Plover, with *broad chestnut breastband.* In winter, has a narrower dusky band (then black legs, larger bill separate it from Semipalmated). (Asia.) Casual w. Alaska. Recorded Choris Peninsula, Nunivak, St. Lawrence Is., Wales, Goodnews Bay (said to have bred).

WILSON'S PLOVER   *Charadrius wilsonia.* See Eastern or Texas *Field Guide.* (Se. U.S., Baja California to Peru.) Accidental, s. California.

DOTTEREL   *Eudromias morinellus.* See European *Field Guide.* (N. Eurasia.) Casual in w. Alaska (St. Lawrence, King, Sledge Is., Wales, Pt. Barrow). May occasionally breed. Accidental in w. Washington.

AMERICAN WOODCOCK   *Philohela minor.* See Eastern or Texas *Field Guide.* (Se. Canada to Gulf states.) Recorded Montana, Wyoming, Colorado.

EUROPEAN JACKSNIPE   *Lymnocryptes minimus.* See European *Field Guide.* (Eurasia.) Accidental in Alaska (Pribilofs), California (Butte Co.).

ESKIMO CURLEW   *Numenius borealis.* See Eastern or Texas *Field Guide.* (Nearly extinct. There have been recent sight records in coastal Texas: Apr. 20, 1945; Apr. 5–26, 1959.) Bred formerly in n. Mackenzie. Casual formerly in Colorado, Montana. Accidental, Pribilofs.

WOOD SANDPIPER   *Tringa glareola.* See European *Field Guide.* (Eurasia.) Accidental in Alaska (St. George, Sanak Is.), Hawaii.

POLYNESIAN TATTLER   *Heteroscelus brevipes.* Similar to Wandering Tattler but paler, shorter-legged; *rump barred* (not solid dark). (Ne. Asia.) Accidental on Pribilofs and St. Lawrence I.

GREAT KNOT   *Calidris tenuirostris*   11½. Breast heavily blotched; lacks red of breeding Knot. In winter, similar to Knot; rump whiter, bill longer, legs blackish. (Ne. Siberia.) Accidental in Alaska (Wales).

PURPLE SANDPIPER   *Erolia maritima.* See Eastern *Field Guide.* (N. coasts of N. Atlantic; Arctic coasts of e. N. America and n. Eurasia.) Recorded in summer in Arctic west to Banks I., N.W.T.

LONG-TOED STINT   *Erolia subminuta*   5¾. May be a race of the Least Sandpiper (very similar). (Ne. Asia.) Accidental in Pribilofs.

CURLEW SANDPIPER   *Erolia ferruginea.* See Eastern or European *Field Guide.* (Eurasia.) Accidental in n. Alaska (Pt. Barrow), B.C.

RUFF   *Philomachus pugnax.* See Eastern or European *Field Guide.* (Eurasia.) Accidental in Alaska (St. Paul, St. Lawrence Is.).

SPOON-BILL SANDPIPER   *Eurynorhynchus pygmeum*   6½. A "peep"-sized sandpiper with a curious spoonlike bill-tip. In spring, has a bright rusty head and breast similar to that of its Asiatic associate, the Rufous-necked Sandpiper. (Ne. Siberia.) Accidental in Alaska (Wainwright Inlet).

ICELAND GULL *Larus glaucoides.* See Eastern *Field Guide.* (Breeds Ellesmere, Baffin Is., Greenland.) Accidental, Washington.

GREAT BLACK-BACKED GULL *Larus marinus.* See Eastern *Field Guide.* (N. Atlantic.) Sight record for Melville I. in Canadian Arctic.

BLACK-TAILED GULL *Larus crassirostris* 19. Size of Ring-billed Gull. *Adult:* White, with slaty mantle, *yellow* legs, *black tail.* Black ring on bill; red tip. (Japan, China.) Accidental, San Diego, California.

BLACK-HEADED GULL *Larus ridibundus.* See Eastern *Field Guide.* (Eurasia; regular in small numbers on e. coast of N. America.) Recorded in Aleutians (Kiska), California (sight record, San Francisco Bay).

LITTLE GULL *Larus minutus.* See Eastern *Field Guide.* (Eurasia.) Rare but regular visitor to ne. N. America. Accidental, Saskatchewan.

DOVEKIE *Plautus alle.* See Eastern *Field Guide.* In summer differs from smaller Least Auklet in having entire head and throat black. (N. Atlantic and adjacent Arctic Ocean.) Recorded at Pt. Barrow, Alaska.

CRAVERI'S MURRELET *Endomychura craveri* 10. See Xantus' Murrelet (p. 110), under *Similar species.* (Gulf of California.) Formerly straggled north along California coast to Monterey. No record since 1914.

COMMON PUFFIN *Fratercula arctica.* See Eastern *Field Guide.* (n. N. Atlantic.) Recorded west in Arctic to Mackenzie Bay, Yukon.

RUDDY GROUND DOVE *Columbigallina talpacoti* 6–7. A tiny cinnamon-backed dove. (Mexico to Argentina.) No U.S. specimen. Careful sight record, Rio Grande Delta, Texas, Dec. 1950, Jan. 1951 (I. Davis, L. Goldman).

THICK-BILLED PARROT *Rhynchopsitta pachyrhyncha* 15–16½. A stocky green parrot with a longish tail, heavy black bill, red forehead. In flight, a yellow patch under wing. (N. and c. Mexico.) Formerly a sporadic visitor to mts. of se. Arizona, sw. New Mexico. Unrecorded since 1922.

ORIENTAL CUCKOO *Cuculus saturatus* 13. Very similar to European Cuckoo. See European *Field Guide.* (Asia.) Accidental in Alaska (St. Lawrence I., Seward Peninsula, St. Paul, Rat Is.).

CHUCK-WILL'S-WIDOW *Caprimulgus carolinensis.* See Eastern or Texas *Field Guide.* (Se. U.S.) Barely reaches 100° W. in Edwards Plateau, Texas.

WHITE-RUMPED SWIFT *Apus pacificus* 7. Size of Black Swift; tail more deeply forked; *white rump.* (Asia.) Accidental in Pribilofs.

COMMON SWIFT *Apus apus.* See European *Field Guide.* Smaller than Black Swift, tail more forked; chin white. (Eurasia.) Accidental in Pribilofs.

HELOISE'S HUMMINGBIRD *Atthis heloisa* 2¾. Male resembles male Lucifer Hummingbird (purple throat); smaller; bill *short, straight;* tail *rounded,* rufous base, *white tips.* (Mexico.) Accidental, se. Arizona.

RIEFFER'S HUMMINGBIRD *Amazilia tzacatl.* Similar to Buff-bellied Hummingbird but belly *grayish.* (Mexico.) Accidental s. Texas (Ft. Brown); 1876.

RINGED KINGFISHER *Megaceryle torquata* 15–16. See illustration in Texas *Field Guide.* Much larger than Belted Kingfisher; entire belly *chestnut.* (Mexico to Tierra del Fuego.) Casual in s. Texas (7+ records).

WRYNECK *Jynx torquilla.* See European *Field Guide.* (Eurasia.) Accidental in Alaska (Wales).

GRAY KINGBIRD *Tyrannus dominicensis.* See Eastern *Field Guide.* (Florida, W. Indies, Venezuela.) Accidental in B.C. (Cape Beale).

NUTTING'S FLYCATCHER *Myiarchus nuttingi* 7. Similar to Ash-throated Flycatcher; smaller, browner above. Probably not separable in field. (Sonora to Costa Rica.) Accidental, Arizona (Roosevelt).

ACADIAN FLYCATCHER *Empidonax virescens.* See Eastern or Texas *Field Guide.* (E. and c. U.S.) Accidental in B.C., w. N. Dakota.

GRAY-BREASTED MARTIN *Progne chalybea.* Both sexes resemble female Purple Martin, but are smaller (6½ in.) and have a *darker forehead.* (Mexico to Argentina.) Accidental in Rio Grande Delta, Texas.

SAN BLAS JAY *Cissilopha san-blasiana* 12–13½. Head and under-parts *solid black,* back *bright blue.* (W. Mexico.) Accidental Arizona (Tucson).

CAROLINA CHICKADEE *Parus carolinensis.* See Eastern or Texas *Field Guide.* (Se. and c. U.S.) Barely reaches 100° W. in n. and c. Texas.

EYE-BROWED THRUSH *Turdus obscurus.* See European *Field Guide.* (Siberia.) Accidental in Aleutians (Amchitka).

CLAY-COLORED ROBIN (Tamaulipas Thrush, Gray's Robin) *Turdus grayi* 9–9½. Resembles Robin but gray-brown above; pale buff below. (Ne. Mexico to n. Colombia.) Sight records in s. Texas: Brownsville, Mar. 10–17, 1940 (I. Davis); Mission, May 14–19, 1959 (11 observers).

WOOD THRUSH *Hylocichla mustelina.* Illustration, Pl. 48. See Eastern or Texas *Field Guide.* (Se. Canada, e. U.S.) Casual in Wyoming, Colorado, New Mexico, w. Texas.

RUBYTHROAT *Luscinia calliope* 6. A small grayish thrush; male has *scarlet throat patch;* white "whiskers," white line over eye. (Ne. Asia.) Accidental in w. Aleutians (Kiska).

MIDDENDORFF'S GRASSHOPPER WARBLER *Locustella ocho-tensis* 5¼. A brown, streak-backed Old World warbler with plain whitish underparts, white line over eye; tail *deeply rounded* with *black sub-terminal band, whitish tips.* (Ne. Asia.) Accidental in Alaska (Nunivak).

GRAY-SPOTTED FLYCATCHER *Hemichelidon griseisticta* 4½. A small Old World flycatcher; gray-brown above, white below; breast and flanks heavily streaked. (E. Asia.) Accidental in Aleutians (Amchitka).

MOUNTAIN ACCENTOR *Prunella montanella* 6. Streaked brown above, *pale buff* below; sides streaked with rusty. *Dark cheek patch, buff stripe* over eye. (Asia.) Accidental in Alaska (Nunivak, St. Lawrence Is.).

WHITE WAGTAIL *Motacilla alba.* Illustration, page 250. See European *Field Guide.* (Eurasia.) Accidental in Alaska (Attu I., mouth of Yukon, Wales).

PECHORA PIPIT *Anthus gustavi* 5¾. A pale pipit with *buff* outer tail feathers. (Siberia.) Accidental in Alaska (St. Lawrence I.).

RED-THROATED PIPIT *Anthus cervinus.* See European *Field Guide.* (N. Eurasia.) Accidental in Alaska (St. Lawrence I., St. Michael; bred at Wales).

WHITE-EYED VIREO *Vireo griseus.* See Eastern or Texas *Field Guide.* (E. and c. U.S., ne. Mexico.) Breeds to and across 100th meridian in Texas (near Rio Grande and probably in Edwards Plateau). Recorded in Panhandle in migration. Accidental, Utah.

YELLOW-THROATED VIREO *Vireo flavifrons.* See Eastern or Texas *Field Guide.* (Se. Canada, e. and c. U.S.) Breeds on Edwards Plateau, Texas, roughly to 100° W. Casual migrant on plains west to Saskatchewan, Wyoming, e. Colorado, w. Texas.

PROTHONOTARY WARBLER *Protonotaria citrea.* See Eastern or Texas *Field Guide.* (E. U.S.) Accidental Wyoming, Colorado, California, Arizona, New Mexico.

SWAINSON'S WARBLER *Limnothlypis swainsonii.* See Eastern or Texas *Field Guide.* (Se. U.S.) Accidental, Colorado.

WORM-EATING WARBLER *Helmitheros vermivorus.* See Eastern or Texas *Field Guide.* (E. U.S.) Recorded w. Texas, n. Colorado.

GOLDEN-WINGED WARBLER *Vermivora chrysoptera.* See Eastern or Texas *Field Guide.* (E. U.S.) Accidental, ne. Colorado.

BLUE-WINGED WARBLER *Vermivora pinus.* See Eastern or Texas *Field Guide.* (E. U.S.) Accidental, California, Arizona.

PARULA WARBLER *Parula americana.* See Eastern or Texas *Field Guide,* or see under Olive-backed Warbler, page 200. (Se. Canada to Gulf states.) In c. Texas, *breeds* close to 100° at Kerrville. Bred at Pt. Lobos, California. Casual migrant on w. Great Plains (recorded Alberta, Saskatchewan to w. Texas); also Oregon, Arizona, New Mexico.

BLACK-THROATED BLUE WARBLER *Dendroica caerulescens.* See Eastern or Texas *Field Guide.* (Se. Canada, mts. of e. U.S.) Casual migrant along w. edge of Plains from Alberta to Texas panhandle. Recorded in Oregon, Idaho, Utah, California, Arizona, New Mexico.

CERULEAN WARBLER *Dendroica cerulea.* See Eastern or Texas *Field Guide.* (E. U.S.) Accidental, California, Nevada, Colorado.

YELLOW-THROATED WARBLER *Dendroica dominica.* See Eastern or Texas *Field Guide.* Similar to Grace's Warbler but has white patch on neck, *white* eye-stripe. (Se. U.S.) Accidental, Colorado.

PINE WARBLER *Dendroica pinus.* See Eastern or Texas *Field Guide.* (E. N. America.) Recorded in Alberta, w. N. Dakota, w. S. Dakota, w. Texas.

PRAIRIE WARBLER *Dendroica discolor.* See Eastern or Texas *Field Guide.* (Ontario to Gulf states.) Accidental, Arizona.

LOUISIANA WATERTHRUSH *Seiurus motacilla.* See Eastern or Texas *Field Guide.* (E. U.S.) Recorded Texas panhandle, s. California.

KENTUCKY WARBLER *Oporornis formosus.* See Eastern or Texas *Field Guide.* (E. U.S.) Breeds nearly to 100° W. in Edwards Plateau, Texas (Kerrville). Casual in Texas panhandle. Accidental, Arizona, New Mexico.

GROUND-CHAT (Rio Grande Yellowthroat) *Chamaethlypis poliocephala.* See illustration in Texas *Field Guide.* (Mexico to Panama.) Formerly occasional in summer in Rio Grande Delta. No recent records.

GOLDEN-CROWNED WARBLER (Brasher's Warbler) *Basileuterus culicivorus.* See illustration in Texas *Field Guide.* (Mexico to Argentina.) Careful sight record near Harlingen, Texas, Sept. 5, 1943 (I. Davis).

HOODED WARBLER *Wilsonia citrina.* See Eastern or Texas *Field Guide.* (E. U.S.) Casual west to w. N. Dakota, Wyoming, w. Nebraska, Colorado, w. Oklahoma, New Mexico, w. Texas. Accidental, California.

SCARLET-HEADED ORIOLE *Icterus pustulatus* 7½–8. Male, orangish (orange head, black throat); known by *black stripings* on back. (W. Mexico.) Accidental in s. California (La Mesa), Arizona (Tucson).

BRAMBLING *Fringilla montifringilla.* See European *Field Guide.* (N. Eurasia.) Accidental in Alaska (St. Paul I.).

HAWFINCH *Coccothraustes coccothraustes.* See European *Field Guide.* (Eurasia.) Accidental in Alaska (St. Paul I.).

BULLFINCH *Pyrrhula pyrrhula.* See European *Field Guide.* (Eurasia.) Accidental in Alaska (St. Lawrence, Nunivak Is., Nulato).

FIVE-STRIPED SPARROW *Aimophila quinquestriata* 5¾. Above, brown; below, gray; white line over eye, 5 stripes on throat (3 white, 2 black); black spot on breast. (W. Mexico.) Accidental, s. Arizona (Madera Canyon).

WORTHEN'S SPARROW *Spizella wortheni* 5½. Resembles Field Sparrow; grayer, rusty of crown less extensive, eye-ring more conspicuous. (E. Mexico.) Once taken in New Mexico (Silver City).

RUSTIC BUNTING *Emberiza rustica.* See European *Field Guide.* (N. Eurasia.) Casual in Aleutians (Kiska, Amchitka, Adak).

Appendix II: Casual and Accidental Species in the Hawaiian Islands

THE FOLLOWING, all on the North American list save 5 (Wandering Albatross, *Diomedea exulans*, Reef Heron, *Demigretta sacra*, Garganey, *Anas querquedula*, Silver Gull, *Larus novaehollandiae*, and Black-naped Tern, *Sterna sumatrana*), have found their way once or more, across 2400 statute miles or more of ocean, to the Hawaiian Is. Most can be regarded as accidental. A few are casual (more than 5 records). The Canada Goose, Mallard, Osprey, and some gulls and shorebirds may prove to be regular.

SHORT-TAILED ALBATROSS
WANDERING ALBATROSS
FULMAR
PELAGIC CORMORANT
REEF HERON
COMMON EGRET
WHITE-FACED IBIS
CANADA GOOSE
   (incl. CACKLING GOOSE)
BLACK BRANT
EMPEROR GOOSE
WHITE-FRONTED GOOSE
SNOW GOOSE
MALLARD
GADWALL
GREEN-WINGED TEAL
BLUE-WINGED TEAL
GARGANEY
EUROPEAN WIDGEON
REDHEAD
CANVASBACK
GREATER SCAUP
LESSER SCAUP
BUFFLEHEAD
OLDSQUAW
HARLEQUIN DUCK
RUDDY DUCK
RED-BR. MERGANSER
MARSH HAWK
OSPREY

PEREGRINE
SEMIPALMATED PLOVER
SNOWY PLOVER
KILLDEER
COMMON SNIPE
WHIMBREL
GREATER YELLOWLEGS
LESSER YELLOWLEGS
SHARP-TAILED SANDPIPER
PECTORAL SANDPIPER
WESTERN SANDPIPER
DUNLIN
DOWITCHER
BAR-TAILED GODWIT
NORTHERN PHALAROPE
GLAUCOUS GULL
GLAUCOUS-WINGED GULL
WESTERN GULL
HERRING GULL
CALIFORNIA GULL
RING-BILLED GULL
FRANKLIN'S GULL
BONAPARTE'S GULL
BLACK-LEGGED
   KITTIWAKE
SILVER GULL
ARCTIC TERN
BLACK-NAPED TERN
LEAST TERN
BELTED KINGFISHER

Learning Bird Songs

IN LEARNING bird voices (and some birders do 90 percent of their field work by ear), there is no substitute for the actual sounds. Authors often attempt to fit songs into syllables, words, and phrases. Musical notations, comparative descriptions, and even ingenious systems of symbols have been employed. But since the advent of sound recording, these older techniques have been eclipsed.

Use the *Field Guide to Western Bird Songs* in conjunction with this book. This album (published in 1962) contains the most comprehensive collection of sound recordings yet attempted. It includes the calls and songs of more than 500 land and water birds — a large percentage of all species found in the continental United States west of the Rockies, in Hawaii, and in Alaska. Three 12-inch LP records prepared by Peter Paul Kellogg, Arthur A. Allen, William W. H. Gunn, and others of the Laboratory of Ornithology, Cornell University, have been arranged to accompany this *Field Guide to Western Birds,* 2nd edition.

The song descriptions in this book are merely reminders, for handy use in the field. To prepare yourself for your field trips, play the records. Read each description in the *Field Guide* for an analysis. Play the records repeatedly and compare similar songs. Repetition is the key to learning bird voices. Remember, however, that there are "song dialects": birds in your locality may not always sing precisely as the ones on the record do. Nevertheless, the quality will be the same and the general effect will be recognizable.

CONSERVATION NOTE

BIRDS and all wildlife are necessary to healthy land and contribute to our happiness and standard of living.

Help support the cause of wildlife conservation by taking an active part in the work of the National Audubon Society (950 Third Ave., New York City 10022), your local Audubon Society, and the National Wildlife Federation (1412 16th St., N.W., Washington, D.C. 20036). These and other conservation organizations deserve your support.

Index

NUMBERS in boldface type refer to the illustrations. They are placed only after the common English names of species and after certain Hawaiian names that are main entries in the text or have no English equivalent. They are not used after the scientific names.

The names of all birds are those officially designated in the 5th edition of the A.O.U. *Check-list* (1957). Common names that were in use in the 4th edition of the *Check-list* (1931) and have been changed are also listed. If a common name appears in quotes the name has never been officially sanctioned, but has attained wide popular use. Obsolete or little-used vernacular names are not listed.

289